CRIMINOLOGY

This book is dedicated to my wife, Grace; my parents, Lawrence and Winifred; my sons, Robert and Michael; and my grandchildren, Robbie, Ryan, Mikey, Randy, Christopher, and Stevie.

—Anthony Walsh

To family and friends who have given me the support I've needed to pursue and develop my academic interests over the years.

—Lee Ellis

CRIMINOLOGY
An Interdisciplinary Approach

Anthony Walsh
Boise State University
Lee Ellis
Minot State University

SAGE Publications
Thousand Oaks ▪ London ▪ New Delhi

For information:

Sage Publications, Inc.
2455 Teller Road
Thousand Oaks, California 91320
E-mail: order@sagepub.com

Sage Publications Ltd.
1 Oliver's Yard
55 City Road
London EC1Y 1SP
United Kingdom

Sage Publications India Pvt. Ltd.
B-42, Panchsheel Enclave
Post Box 4109
New Delhi 110 017 India

Printed in the United States of America on acid-free paper

Library of Congress Cataloging-in-Publication Data

Walsh, Anthony, 1941-
Criminology : an interdisciplinary approach / Anthony Walsh, Lee Ellis.
    p. cm.
Includes bibliographical references and index.
ISBN 1-4129-3840-6 or 978-1-4129-3840-2 (pbk.)
    1. Criminology. 2. Criminal behavior. 3. Sociobiology. I. Ellis, Lee, 1942- II. Title.
HV6025.W3653 2007
364—dc22

                                    2006022332

10   11   10   9   8   7   6   5   4   3   2

Acquiring Editor:	Jerry Westby
Editorial Assistant:	Kim Suarez
Production Editor:	Sanford Robinson
Copy Editor:	Gillian Dickens
Typesetter:	C&M Digitals (P) Ltd.
Indexer:	Molly Hall
Cover Designer:	Michelle Kenny

Contents

Foreword

It is a great pleasure for me to welcome this well-researched and wide-ranging textbook on criminology. Both established scholars and beginning students will learn a great deal from it, as I did. Crime is a pressing social problem, and criminology is a fast-expanding area, so books of this nature are greatly needed.

The authors, Anthony Walsh and Lee Ellis, are especially famous for their biosocial contributions to criminology, and in this book they make heroic efforts to integrate knowledge from biology, psychology, sociology, and other disciplines. They show clearly that the days when criminology was dominated by one discipline are long gone.

Many criminologists, including myself, would agree that a comprehensive theory of offending and antisocial behavior must include biological, individual, family, peer, school, situational, and community influences. Eight wide-ranging integrated theories are described in a book that I recently edited (Farrington, 2005). Anthony Walsh and Lee Ellis provide extremely valuable expositions of criminological theories in this textbook, including structural and process theories, critical theories, psychosocial theories, biosocial theories, and developmental theories. These chapters will be very useful to scholars who wish to develop wide-ranging theories and to students who wish to understand why some people become persistent offenders.

This book also contains up-to-date and informative chapters on violence, serial and mass murder, property crime, public order crime, white collar crime, and organized crime. Commendably, it tackles crucial modern problems such as cybercrime and terrorism. It addresses important issues of definition and measurement, Victimology, drugs, alcohol, and mental illness. All chapters contain useful exercises, questions, and glossaries of terms at the end.

This book is written in a scholarly but accessible style and should capture and hold the interest of readers. Hopefully, it will encourage some readers to go on to more advanced studies in criminology and to pursue some of these topics in greater depth. Students should finish the book with a greatly increased knowledge and understanding of criminological theories and types of crimes in particular. The book's greatest strength is to foster the biopsychosocial perspective on crime, and I hope that readers will be inspired by this perspective for many years to come.

David P. Farrington
Professor of Psychological Criminology
Cambridge University

 Reference

Farrington, D. P. (Ed.). (2005). Integrated developmental and life-course theories of offending. In D. P. Farrington, (Series Ed.), *Advances in Criminological Theory*, Vol. 14. New Brunswick, NJ: Transaction.

Preface

This text has been written to provide a contemporary survey of the ever-growing field of criminology. It will acquaint readers with how the discipline has developed over the past two centuries and with its major theories, both historic and current. We view crime and the criminal offender in this text as phenomena embedded in, and continually influenced by, multiple social, psychological, and biological systems. Because most criminologists received their training within the sociological tradition of criminology, our major theoretical thrust is sociological. All crime takes place in a social context, and many crimes get defined in and out of existence depending on the normative standards of society at the time.

The most unique feature of this text is the expanded coverage it gives to theories that combine both biological and social environmental variables as contributing to criminal behavior (so-called biosocial theories). The biobehavioral sciences such as behavior genetics, evolutionary psychology, and the various hormonal and neurological sciences have enjoyed explosive growth over the past two decades and have provided us with a wealth of information relevant to explaining criminal behavior. In fact, sociologist Matthew Robinson has gone so far as to say that "the biological sciences have made more progress in advancing our understanding about behavior in the past 10 years than sociology has made in the past 50 years."[1]

Perhaps in recognizing the spirit of Robinson's point themselves, many presidents of the American Society of Criminology (ASC) have used their presidential addresses to the ASC to plead for the integration of biosocial concepts into criminological research and theorizing. This is what we have attempted to do in this text by giving attention to the close links between involvement in criminal behavior and a number of psychological/psychiatric conditions such as childhood conduct disorder, attention deficit hyperactivity disorder, and antisocial personality disorder. The genetic, neurohormonal, and evolutionary mechanisms behind these and other similar conditions are also briefly touched upon in layperson's terms.

We have found in our teaching that students who are hostile to obtuse and abstract theories relating to conditions in society they perceive as no longer existing become far more engaged when discussing "real" mechanisms. They are often able to relate what they learned about the brain in Psych. 101, or about genes or hormones in Bio. 101, to criminal behavior rather than experiencing a disconnection between what the various disciplines have to say vis-à-vis criminal behavior. This text attempts to put all of the relevant concepts from biology, psychology, and sociology together to explain criminal behavior. Because we are perceiving, thinking, processing beings (the stuff of psychology) who have genes, brain, hormones, and an evolutionary history (the stuff of biology), it is folly to ignore these disciplines. However, it does not mean that we are disregarding the primary importance of culture and experience.

Culture and our experiences within it regulate and direct our perceptions and thoughts and, to a great extent, how our brains are "wired" and how and when our genes are expressed.

Another difference between this test and others is the ordering of the chapters. Because biological theories were proposed quite early in the history of criminology, most texts cover so-called "biological theories" first. In the present text, theories with major biological elements are confronted last. This is primarily because contemporary biosocial theories build on strict environmental theories, and they tend to be somewhat more complicated. In other words, science typically begins with descriptions of what it seeks to understand by looking at what is readily observable. It then continues to ask questions that demand that we look below the surface to try to uncover why we observe what we do. For example, we might look at slum neighborhoods and find that crime is rampant there. Then we have to find out why this is so by examining how residents of those areas adapt to such conditions, what their experiences have been, and how those experiences have molded present behavior. But not everyone experiencing the same thing responds in the same way, so we must now ask about individual differences and keep on asking "why" questions until all possibilities have been apparently exhausted.

Our hope is that through reading this text, students will come to understand and appreciate the rich history and the numerous contemporary perspectives represented in the discipline of criminology. Through this understanding, future generations of criminologists will be in the best position to better deal with the many problems that societies face with regard to criminal behavior.

☒ Reference

1. Robinson, M. (2004). *Why crime? An integrated systems theory of antisocial behavior.* Upper Saddle River, NJ: Prentice Hall. (Quote on p. x)

Acknowledgments

W e would first of all like to thank executive editor Jerry Westby, a man who recognizes excellence when he sees it. That shameless plug aside, Jerry's faith in and commitment to the project is greatly appreciated, as are those of his very able assistants Denise Simon and Kim Suarez. These tireless three kept up a most useful three-way dialog between authors, publisher, and a parade of excellent reviewers, making this text the best that it could possibly be. Our copy editor, Gillian Dickens, spotted every errant comma, dangling participle, and missing reference in the manuscript, for which we are truly thankful, and production editor Sanford Robinson made sure everything went quickly and smoothly thereafter.

We are also most grateful for the many reviewers who spent considerable time providing us with the benefit of their expertise during the writing/rewriting phase of the text's production. Trying to please so many individuals is a trying task, but one that is ultimately satisfying and one that undoubtedly made the book better than it would otherwise have been. These expert criminologists were

Kelly Asmussen
Peru State College

David Baker
The University of Toledo

Dennis Brewster
Oklahoma State University

Keith Clement
University of West Florida

Addrain Conyers
Southern Illinois University

Sue Cote
California State University Sacramento

Virginia Fink
University of Colorado Denver

Julia Hall
Drexel University

Denise Huggins
Central State University, Ohio

Cathryn Lavery
Iona College

Daniel R. Lee
Indiana University of Pennsylvania

Bin Liang
Oklahoma State University, Tulsa

Danielle Liautaud-Watkins
William Paterson University

Heather Melton
University of Utah

Kristine Miller
University of Texas Dallas

Ellyn Ness
Mesa Community College

Allison Payne
The College of New Jersey

Robert Peetz
Midland College

Lois Presser
University of Tennessee

Keith Price
West Texas A&M University

Phillip Quinn
University of Tampa

Craig T. Robertson
University of North Alabama

Robert Schug
California State University Los Angeles
University of Southern California

Tracey Steele
Wright State University

Staci Strobl
John Jay College of Criminal Justice

Tom Stucky
Indiana University—Purdue
University at Indianapolis

Brent Teasdale
University of Akron

Jim Thomas
Northern Illinois University

K.B. Turner
University of Memphis

John Wang
California State University Long Beach

The authors would also like to express their grateful appreciation to Cecil Greek of Florida State University for the use of his wonderful photographs throughout the book. Cecil additionally helped with photo research and wrote many of the captions that accompany the photos. Without his able assistance, the unique photo program in the book would not complement the text as successfully as it does.

We also thank graduate students Peter Collins, Cody Stoddard, and Brian Iannnaccione for helping with the test bank; Professor Erin Conley for putting together the excellent instructor's manual CD that accompanies this text; and Professor Huei-Hsia Wu for the equally excellent PowerPoint presentation that also accompanies it.

Finally, Anthony Walsh would like to acknowledge the love and support of his most wonderful wife, Grace Jean, for her love and support during this and numerous other projects. She is a real treasure and the center of my universe.

CRIMINOLOGY, CRIME, AND CRIMINAL LAW

The joint 1996 wedding ceremony in Lincoln, Nebraska, of Majed Al-Timimy, 28, and Latif Al-Husani, 34, both Iraqi refugees who arrived after the first Gulf War, was to be a strictly traditional affair with a Muslim cleric specially flown in from Ohio to perform the ceremony. A fellow Iraqi refugee had arranged for the two men to marry two of his daughters, aged 13 and 14. The marriage took place and everything seemed to be going according to plan until one of the girls ran away, and the concerned father and her husband reported it to the police. It was at this point that American and Iraqi norms of legality and morality clashed head-on. Under Nebraska law, people under 17 years old cannot marry, so both grooms and the father and mother of the girls were arrested and charged with a variety of crimes from child endangeriment to rape.

According to an Iraqi woman interviewed by the police (herself married at 12 in Iraq), both girls were excited and happy about the wedding. The Iraqi community was shocked that these men faced up to 50 years in prison for their actions, especially since earlier generations of Americans had been legally permitted to marry girls of this age. The men were sentenced to 4 to 6 years in prison and paroled in 2000 with conditions that they have no contact with their "wives." Thus, something that is legally and morally permissible in one culture can be severely punished in another. Were the actions of these men child sex abuse or simply normal, unremarkable marital sex? Which culture is right? Can we really ask such a question? Is Iraqi culture "more right" than American culture, given that marrying girls of that age was permissible here too at one time? Most important, how can criminologists hope to study crime scientifically if what constitutes a crime is relative to time and place?

▨ What Is Criminology?

If the content of the news and popular television shows is any indication, most of us are wildly interested in the subject matter of criminology. In the past few years, we have sat transfixed as Kobe Bryant, Martha Stewart, and the BTK killer flashed across our television screens, and shows such as *Law & Order, NYPD, Cops,* and *CSI: Miami* have sent many a student on a search for a course in criminology. There is something about the dark side of human nature that fascinates us all, and crime and criminal behavior are certainly on the dark side. **Criminology** is an interdisciplinary science that gathers and analyzes data on crime and criminal behavior. As with all scientific disciplines, its goal is to understand the phenomena that it studies and to use that understanding for the benefit of humankind. In pursuit of this understanding, criminology asks questions such as the following:

- ◆ Why do crime rates vary from time to time and from culture to culture?
- ◆ Why are some individuals more prone to committing crime than others?
- ◆ Why do crime rates vary across different ages, genders, and racial/ethnic groups?
- ◆ Why are some harmful acts criminalized and not others?
- ◆ What can we do to prevent crime?

When we say that criminology is the *scientific* study of crime and criminal behavior, we mean that criminologists use the scientific method to try to answer the questions they ask rather than simply speculate about them from their armchairs. The scientific method is a tool for winnowing truth from error by demanding evidence for one's conclusions. Evidence is obtained by formulating hypotheses derived from theory that are rigorously tested with the data at hand.

Although most contemporary criminologists have been trained primarily in sociology and criminal justice, there is a growing realization (perhaps even a consensus) that criminology is an inherently *interdisciplinary* field.[1,2] Scientists from many disciplines other than sociology, such as anthropology, biology, economics, and psychology/psychiatry, have contributed greatly to criminology, but there has been reluctance among some criminologists to accept and integrate findings from them into their understanding of crime.

According to a growing number of prominent criminologists, there is something of a crisis in criminology.[3,4] A subset of them considers the crisis to be a function of the failure to recognize the contributions of the more fundamental sciences such as genetics, physiology, neurophysiology, endocrinology, and evolutionary biology. Some have even called for such recognition in the context of their presidential addresses to the American Criminological Society[5-8] and the Academy of Criminal Justice Sciences.[9]

The failure to incorporate these sciences is unfortunate because philosophers of science have long maintained that the only route to progress in any science is to integrate insights from the more advanced adjacent sciences.[10,11] Chemistry advanced when it dropped its opposition to the intrusion of physics and its "newfangled" ideas about something called atoms in the late 19th century. Biology took enormous strides when it dropped its opposition to the intrusion of chemistry in the mid-20th century after the discovery of the structure of DNA, and psychology has come a long way since more fully embracing biology. In fact, the core concepts of these disciplines (ions in chemistry and genes in biology) came from disciplines previously discounted as irrelevant. A very interesting history surrounds the initial opposition of these sciences to their "antidisciplines" and their eventual acceptance of them,[12] but we can't get into that here.

A prominent inscription on a prominent wall at the Massachusetts Institute of Technology (MIT) reads, in part, as follows: "Many of the most important discoveries of the future will come from those wise enough to explore the unknown territories between different disciplines."[13] We believe that the time has come to present approaches that do this more fully in an introductory textbook. This text is still primarily sociological in orientation because sociologists have conducted the vast majority of theorizing and research in criminology. It is also primarily sociological in orientation because no matter what insights other sciences may provide criminologists, criminal behavior always takes place in a social context, and the perspective from which most criminologists work is sociological.

✕ What Is Crime?

What sort of person comes to mind when you hear the word *criminal?* The term can be applied to many types of behavior, some of which nearly all of us have been guilty of at some time in our lives. However, very few people ever commit murder, robbery, or major theft. Those who do, especially those who do so repeatedly, are what most people think of as "real criminals." Even so, it is important to recognize that the dividing line between "real criminals" and most of the rest of us is fuzzy and difficult to specify with precision. Nearly all of us can think of acts that we feel *ought* to be criminal but are not, or acts that should not be criminal but are. As you can imagine, the roster of possible wrongs that someone or another considers crimes is enormous, with only a select few being defined as criminal by the law. Furthermore, ask yourself how many crimes would people have to commit before they are considered *real* criminals—three, four, or maybe five? Or would the answer depend on how serious each crime was? The main purpose of exploring topics such as these is to acquaint you with how criminologists conceptualize their discipline and what they include and exclude from study.

Despite the difficulties attending the definition of crime, we need one to proceed. Perhaps the most often quoted definition comes from Paul Tappan, who defined **crime** as "an intentional act in violation of the criminal law committed without defense or excuse, and penalized by the state."[14] Thus, a crime is an *act* in violation of a *criminal law* for which a *punishment* is prescribed; the person committing it must have *intended* to do so and must have done so without legally acceptable *defense* or *justification*.

A fundamental point on which all criminologists agree is that crime is a legal concept defined by the political state and its subdivisions. The fact that crime is a legal rather than a scientific concept has implications for the scientific study of crime. Hypothetically, a society could eradicate crime tomorrow simply by rescinding all of its criminal statutes. Of course, this would not eliminate the behavior specified by the laws; in fact, the behavior would doubtless increase since the behavior could no longer be officially punished. While it is absurd to think that any society would try to solve its crime problem by eliminating its criminal statutes, legislative bodies are continually revising, adding to, and deleting from their criminal statutes.

✕ Crime as a Moving Target

Every vice is somewhere and at sometimes a virtue. Numerous examples of acts defined as crimes in one country are tolerated and even expected behavior in another, such as the example given at the beginning of this chapter of adult males marrying and being sexually active with girls as young as 12. Female circumcision (*clitorectomy*) involving the surgical removal of the clitoris is found in many parts of Africa and the Middle East. It is performed on prepubertal girls without anesthetic and has been known to cause death due to infection.[15] Anyone performing such a procedure in the United States would be charged with child abuse and malicious wounding. Likewise, while many countries have historically regarded abortion as a crime, most democratic countries permit it today. Ironically, many of these same countries have laws making it a crime for mothers to drink excessively or take various drugs during pregnancy because they might harm their unborn infants.[16] In several cultures, infanticide (the killing of infants by a parent) is not defined as a criminal act,[17] while in other societies, parents can be held criminally liable for failing to take their children for proper medical treatment, even if doing so violates the parent's religious beliefs.[18]

Laws vary within the same culture from time to time as well as across different cultures. Until the Harrison Narcotics Act of 1914, there were few legal restrictions in the United States on the sale, possession, or use of most drugs such as heroin and cocaine. Following the Harrison Act, many drugs became controlled substances, their possession became a crime, and a brand new class of criminals was created overnight. Stalking is hardly novel behavior, but certain high-profile cases moved the state of California to recognize the dangers inherent in the practice and to pass the nation's first antistalking law as recently as 1990.[19]

Crimes pass out of existence also—even acts that had been considered crimes for centuries by some groups. The private hoarding of gold was a crime in the United States from 1934 to 1974, but today it is something of a virtue. Until the U.S. Supreme Court invalidated sodomy statutes in *Lawrence v. Texas* (2003),[20] sodomy was legally punishable in many states. Most states targeted only homosexual sodomy, but a few extended the reach to include heterosexual sodomy, even between consenting spouses. Likewise, burning the American flag had serious legal consequences until 1989, when the Supreme Court invalidated anti–flag burning statutes as unconstitutional in *Texas v. Johnson* (1989).[21] What constitutes a crime, then, can be defined in and out of existence by the courts or by legislators. As long as human societies remain diverse and dynamic, there will always be a moving target of activities with the potential for nomination as crimes, as well as illegal activities nominated for decriminalization.

If what constitutes crime differs across time and place, how can criminologists hope to agree on a scientific explanation for crime and criminal behavior if the target keeps moving? Science is about making a universal statement about stable or homogeneous phenomena. Atoms, genes, the gas laws, the laws of thermodynamics, photosynthesis, and so on are not defined or evaluated differently by scientists around the globe according to local customs or ideological preferences. The phenomenon we call "crime," however, keeps moving around, and because it does, some criminologists have declared it impossible to generalize about what is and is not "real" crime. For example, Darnell Hawkins has written that "we cannot discover what *real* crime is, or who the *real* criminals are."[22]

What criminologists such as Hawkins are saying is that crime is a socially constructed phenomenon that lacks any "real" objective essence because crimes are defined into existence rather than discovered, although they obviously do not deny the harm underlying the criminal act. At one level, of course, everything is socially constructed; nature does not reveal herself to us, sorted into ready-labeled packages; humans must do it for her. *Social construction* means nothing more than that humans have perceived a phenomenon, named it, and categorized it according to some classificatory rule (also socially constructed) that makes note of the similarities and differences among the things being classified. Most classification schemes are not arbitrary; if they were, we would not be able to make sense of anything. Categories have empirically meaningful referents and are used to impose order on the diversity of phenomena that humans experience, although arguments exist about just how coherent that order is. But then, few concepts (or constructs) outside of mathematics are defined and understood in such a way as to make every application of them unproblematic.

⬚ Crime as a Subcategory of Social Harms

So, what *can* we say about crime? How *can* we conceive of it in ways that at least most people would agree are coherent and correspond with their view of reality? Criminologist John Hagan[23] has provided a useful way of looking at the definition problem by viewing crime as a continuous variable and as a subcategory of all harmful acts. Hagan's definition has three measures of harmful acts, ranging from low to high and weak to strong. His first measure is the degree of *consensus* or agreement existing in the population about right and wrong acts.

Research has consistently shown that there is substantial agreement among average citizens both within and across modern societies regarding the average seriousness ratings given to a variety of criminal offenses. Studies comparing average seriousness ratings of deviant acts in the United States beginning in the 1920s have concluded that rankings have changed only slightly. Among the trends that have been noted both in the United States and other industrial countries is an increase in seriousness ratings of white-collar crimes compared to ratings of nonviolent street crimes, as well as a decrease in seriousness ratings given to most offenses associated with "abnormal" sexual behavior.[24] A survey of 3,334 households found remarkably high consensus across age, gender, race, and socioeconomic status (SES) on the seriousness of 17 different offenses.[25] On average, this study found about a 96% agreement between citizens of diverse backgrounds about the wrongfulness and seriousness of different crimes. Thus, people everywhere seem to share at least a rough sense of what is acceptable behavior under most circumstances. In all societies, nearly everyone condemns behavior that intentionally victimizes others, especially if the victims are members of the social group to which those making the judgment belong.

The second dimension is the *severity* of the law's response to a given crime. The more serious the legal penalty, says Hagan, "the more serious the societal evaluation of the act."[26] The first two dimensions are highly correlated, as you would expect. There would be almost unanimous agreement that the bombing of the Murrah Federal Building in Oklahoma City in 1995, which took the lives of 169 people and injured more than 500 others, was wrong. The social response to the perpetrator, Timothy McVeigh, was extremely severe—the death penalty. On the other hand, there would be little consensus that smoking marijuana is all that wrong, and the legal penalties for doing so are weak.

The third dimension is the amount of *harm* caused, a dimension that obviously underlies both consensus about wrongfulness and severity of legal response—Timothy McVeigh caused a tremendous amount of harm; pot smokers perhaps harm only themselves. Thus, one thing about crime that is not disputed is that it is a subcategory of harmful acts, most of which are not regulated by the law.

Harmful acts, such as smoking tobacco and drinking to excess, are not considered anyone's business other than the actor's if they take place in private or even in public if the person creates no annoyance. *Socially harmful* acts are acts in a category that some political body has decided in nonarbitrary ways are in need of regulation (health standards, air pollution, etc.) but not by the criminal law, except under exceptional circumstance. Radical theorists aver that arbitrariness is more likely to enter the picture when authorities decide *not* to regulate socially harmful behavior, such as racism, sexism, colonialism, harmful business practices, and any number of other acts they feel are more harmful than acts that are criminalized. Private wrongs (such as someone reneging on a contract) are socially harmful but not sufficiently so to require the heavy hand of the criminal law. Such wrongs are regulated by the civil law in which the wronged party (the plaintiff), rather than the state, initiates legal action and the defendant does not risk deprivation of his or her liberty if the plaintiff prevails.

Finally, a small subcategory of harmful acts is considered so socially harmful that they come under the purview and coercive power of the criminal justice system. Even though we have narrowed down the concept of crime, we are still confronted with the problem of human judgment in determining what goes into this subcategory. But this is true all along the line; smoking was once actually considered rather healthy, and air pollution and unhealthy conditions were simply facts of life about which nothing could be done. Categorization always requires a series of human judgments, but that does not render the categorizations arbitrary.

⊠ Beyond Social Construction: The Stationary Core Crimes

We have defined crimes as serious socially harmful acts, but how can we rescue this from accusation that even "seriously harmful" is a judgment that moves around across time and space? We suggest that few people would argue that an act is not seriously harmful if it is universally condemned—that is, if a stationary core of offenses is defined as wrong at almost all times and in almost all cultures. Some of the strongest evidence in support of the stationary core perspective comes from the International Criminal Police Organization (Interpol),[27] headquartered in Lyon, France. Besides assisting member nations with investigations of international terrorism and organized crime, Interpol serves as a repository for crime statistics from each of its 125 member nations. Interpol's data show that such acts as murder, assault, rape, and theft are considered serious crimes in every single country. While there are variations in exactly what constitutes each of these offenses, most of them are extremely minor.

Criminologists call these universally condemned crimes **mala in se** ("inherently bad"). Crimes that are time and culture bound are described as **mala prohibita** ("bad because they are prohibited"). But how can we be sure that an act is inherently bad? We would say that the litmus test for determining a mala in se crime is that no one, except under the most bizarre of circumstances (see Focus On . . .), would want to be victimized by one. While millions of people seek to be "victimized" by prostitutes, drug dealers, bookies, or any of a number of other providers of illegal goods and services, no one wants to be murdered, raped, robbed, or have their property stolen. Being victimized by such actions evokes physiological reactions (anger, helplessness, sadness, depression, a desire for revenge) in all cultures, and would do so even if the acts were not punishable by law or custom. Mala in se acts engage these emotions not because some legislative body has identified and defined them as wrong; they do so because they hammer at our deepest primordial instincts. Evolutionary psychologists propose that these built-in emotional mechanisms exist because mala in se crimes threatened the survival and reproductive success of our distant ancestors, and they function to strongly motivate people to try to prevent such acts from occurring and punish offenders if they do.[28–30] In this sense, then, mala in se crimes are very real.

Mala in Se or Mala Prohibita?
The Cannibal and His Willing Victim

We have said that the litmus test for a mala in se crime is that no one would want to be a victim of such a crime. You would think that killing, butchering, and eating another human being would certainly pass such a test. But what if the cannibal's dinner was a willing victim and the country in which the cannibal and his victim lived had no law forbidding cannibalism? This strange state of affairs existed in Rotenburg in central Germany in 2001. Germany's own Hannibal Lecter, one Armin Meiwes, had advertised online seeking volunteers for "slaughter and consumption." Among the over 200 replies Meiwes received was an e-mail from Bernd-Jurgen Brandes stating, "I am your meat." Meiwes and Brandes (a successful software engineer) videotaped their agreement, and Meiwes taped the subsequent killing and butchering of Brandes. Brandes stated on the tape that being eaten would be the "fulfillment of my dream."

The prosecution in this case argued for a conviction of murder and "disturbing the peace of the dead," which would have gotten Meiwes a life sentence. The defense argued that what Meiwes had done was simply to assist Brandes in his suicide, which carried a 5-year sentence. The panel of judges hearing the case agreed that Meiwes could not be convicted of murder, split the difference, and handed Meiwes an 8½-year prison sentence in January 2004. Which argument would you have followed if you were one of the judges?

In common-law countries such as the United States, Meiwes would have been convicted of murder because one person cannot give another the consent to kill him or her—you can give your consent to many things, but not this. What Meiwes committed was clearly a mal in se crime, and Brandes's consent doesn't change that at all. The behavior of both men was obviously bizarre, and just because we find instances in which people do want to be victimized by acts that 99.9% of their fellow humans would find repugnant does not change the inherent badness of those acts.

Source: Schofield, M. (2004, January 31). German sentenced to 8 and a half years for killing, eating man. *Idaho Statesman*, p. 3.

⊠ Victimful and Victimless Crimes

Crimes can also be viewed as arrayed along a victimization continuum and divided into three crime categories: (1) crimes for which there is an obvious intended victim (e.g., murder and rape), (2) crimes in which victimization is the result of carelessness (e.g., negligent manslaughter), and (3) crimes in which participation in the crime is voluntary (e.g., prostitution, drug offenses). The distinction between victimless and victimful crimes has to do with harm to an unwilling victim. (There is no standard antonym for *victimless* to succinctly describe a crime having a victim. The term *victimful*[31] has been coined to show that it has the same relationship to *victimless* as the term *harmful* does to *harmless*.) A victimless crime is consensual and nonpredatory; a victimful crime is nonconsensual and predatory, and it is mala in se almost by definition.

▲ **Photo 1.1**   In some cities, efforts are made to zone "adult" establishments such as this Tampa strip club into a specific area. This club features a second floor designed to look like a UFO, where customers are enticed to "blast off" by lap dancing with the strippers. Critics argue that bunching such establishments in the same neighborhood adds to the crime problem in the immediately surrounding area.

⬚ The Felony-Misdemeanor Distinction

The legal concepts of *felony* and *misdemeanor* are used in criminological research to separate the more serious from the less serious offenses. Historically, the term *felony* was used as a synonym for violent and property offense, while **misdemeanors** covered all other crimes. The word **felony** has the same roots as the word *treachery*, whereas *misdemeanor* comes from a French root meaning "bad motivation" or "bad intention." The legal distinction between felonies and misdemeanors is that felonies carry a maximum penalty of greater than 1 year of imprisonment, and misdemeanors carry a maximum penalty of less than 1 year in jail. Most felonies are victimful crimes, although they can include some "victimless" crimes such as selling drugs. Some victimful crimes may be charged as misdemeanors depending on the seriousness of the act, such as a minor assault or the theft of property or money below a certain value.

Figure 1.1 illustrates the relationship of "real" core crimes to acts that have been arbitrarily defined as crimes and all harmful acts that may potentially be criminalized. The figure is inspired by John Hagan's efforts to separate "real" crimes (mala in se) from those that are merely "socially constructed" (mala prohibita).

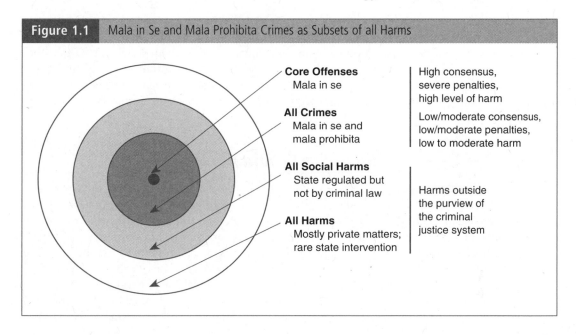

Figure 1.1 | Mala in Se and Mala Prohibita Crimes as Subsets of all Harms

Core Offenses
Mala in se

All Crimes
Mala in se and
mala prohibita

All Social Harms
State regulated but
not by criminal law

All Harms
Mostly private matters;
rare state intervention

High consensus,
severe penalties,
high level of harm

Low/moderate consensus,
low/moderate penalties,
low to moderate harm

Harms outside
the purview of
the criminal
justice system

◪ Criminality

A long time ago, a famous criminologist suggested that one way to avoid the crime definition problem was to study individuals who committed *deviant* acts (violations of conduct norms), regardless of the legal status of those acts.[32] We suggest, however, that deviant acts present us with a far greater definitional problem than criminal acts since what is and what is not deviant changes far more rapidly than what is and what is not a crime. Perhaps studying individuals who commit predatory *harmful* acts, regardless of the legal status of the acts, is a better strategy. Criminologists do this when they study criminality.

Criminality is a clinical or scientific term rather than a legal one, and it can be defined independently of legal definitions of criminal acts. Crime is an intentional act of commission or omission contrary to the law; **criminality** is a property of individuals that signals the willingness to commit those crimes and other harmful acts.[33] Criminality is a continuously distributed trait that is a combination of other continuously distributed traits that signals the willingness to use force, fraud, or guile to deprive others of their lives, limbs, or property for personal gain. People can use and abuse others for personal gain regardless of whether the means used have been defined as criminal; it is the propensity to do this that defines criminality independent of the labeling of an act as a crime or of the person being legally defined as a criminal.

Defining criminality as a continuous trait acknowledges that there is no sharp line separating individuals with respect to this trait—it is not a condition that one has or has not. Just about everyone at some point in life has committed an act or two in violation of the law. But that doesn't make us all criminals; if it did, the term would become virtually synonymous with the word *human!* The point is, we are all situated somewhere on the criminality continuum, which ranges from saint to sociopath, just as our heights range from the truly short to the truly tall. Some are so extreme in height that any reasonable person would call them "tall." Likewise, a small number of individuals have violated so many criminal statutes over such a long period of time that few would question the appropriateness of calling them "criminals." Thus, both height and criminality can be thought of as existing along a continuum, even though the words we use often imply that people's heights and criminal tendencies come in more or less discrete categories (tall/short, criminal/noncriminal). In other words, just as height varies in fine gradations, so too does involvement in crime.

☒ The Legal Making of a Criminal

There is a simple legal answer to the question "What is a criminal?" A criminal is someone who has committed a crime and has been judged guilty of having done so. Whatever factors criminologists might decide lead to criminal behavior, a person is not "officially" a criminal until he or she has been defined as such by the law. Before the law can properly call a person a criminal, it must go through a series of actions governed at all junctures by well-defined legal rules collectively called *criminal procedure.* These procedural rules vary greatly from culture to culture, but almost all modern cultures have a set of rational (i.e., logical and predictable) rules guiding the serious business of officially labeling a person a criminal. In this section, we introduce you to the U.S. criminal justice system by following the processing of felony cases from arrest to trial and beyond.

Basic Principles of U.S. Criminal Law

U.S. criminal law has its origins in English common law, which was brought to these shores by the early British colonists. No system is imported whole, however, and there have been many changes over the years, but both systems remain faithful to the general principles of common law as it existed in the 18th century. Any differences between the two systems are mainly differences in specifics rather than basic underlying legal philosophy. This section is thus applicable to both legal systems and to all other systems sharing the common-law tradition (e.g., Canada, Australia, New Zealand), although there may be slight differences of interpretation from country to country.

What Constitutes a Crime?

Corpus delicti is a Latin term meaning "body of the crime" and refers to the elements of a given act that must be present to legally define it as a crime. All crimes have their own specific *elements,* which are the essential constituent parts that define the act as criminal. In addition to their specific elements, all crimes share a set of general elements or principles underlying and supporting the specific elements. Five principles have to be satisfied before a person is "officially" labeled a criminal, but in actuality, it is only necessary for the state to prove two to satisfy corpus delicti: *actus reus* and *mens rea.* The other principles, while just as important to the legal definition of a criminal, are either abstract principles of no concern to the particular case at hand or are proven in the course of proving actus reus and mens rea. Taken together, each of the five elements forms the basis of the general principle of criminal liability.[34]

Actus reus means *guilty act* and refers to the principle that a person must commit some forbidden act or neglect some mandatory act before he or she can be subjected to criminal sanctions. In effect, this principle of law means that people cannot be criminally prosecuted for thinking something or being something, only for *doing* something. This prevents governments from passing laws criminalizing statuses and systems of thought they don't like. For instance, although drunken *behavior* may be punishable crime, *being* an alcoholic cannot be punished because "being" something is a status, not an act. Attempted criminal acts, although not accomplished for one reason or another, are crimes, as is conspiracy to commit a crime the moment the conspirators take some action to put their plan into motion.

Mens rea means *guilty mind* and refers to whether or not the act was intentional—that is, whether the suspect had a wrongful purpose in mind when carrying out the actus reus. For instance, although receiving stolen property is a criminal offense, if you were to buy a stolen television set from an acquaintance without knowing it had been stolen, you would have lacked mens rea and would not be subject to prosecution. If you were to be prosecuted, the state would have to prove that you knew the television was stolen. Negligence, recklessness, and carelessness that result in some harmful consequences, even though not intended, *do not* excuse such behavior from criminal prosecution under mens rea. Conditions that may preclude prosecution under this principle are self-defense, defense of others, youthfulness (a person younger than age 7 years cannot be held responsible), insanity (although being found insane does not preclude long-term confinement), and extreme duress or coercion.

Concurrence means that the act (actus reus) and the mental state (mens rea) concur in the sense that the criminal intention actuates the criminal act. For instance, if John sets out with his tools to burglarize Mary's apartment and takes her VCR, he has fused the guilty mind with the wrongful act and has therefore committed burglary. However, assume John and Mary are friends who habitually visit each other's apartment unannounced. One day, John decides to visit Mary, finds her not at home, but walks in and sits down as he has done with her blessing many times before. While sitting there, John suddenly decides that he could sell Mary's VCR for drug money and takes her VCR. Has John committed burglary in this scenario? Although the loss to Mary is the same in both scenarios, in the latter instance, John cannot be charged with burglary because he did not enter her apartment "by force or fraud," the crucial element needed to satisfy such a charge. In this case, the concurrence of guilty mind and wrongful act occurred after lawful entry, so he is only charged with theft, a less serious crime.

Causation refers to the necessity to establish a causal link between the criminal act and the harm suffered. This causal link must be proximate, not ultimate. For instance, suppose Tony wounds Frank in a knife fight. Because Frank has no medical insurance, rather than seeking professional medical treatment, he pours alcohol on his wound and bandages it himself. Three weeks later, Frank's self-treated wound has become severely infected and results in his death. What crime could the prosecutor charge Tony with? Certainly the wounding led to Frank's death (the ultimate cause), but Frank's disregard for the seriousness of his injury, not the fight, was the most proximate cause of his death. The question the law asks in cases like this is, "What would any reasonable person do?" We think most people would agree that the reasonable person would have sought medical treatment. This being the case, Tony cannot be charged with any form of homicide; the most he could be charged with is aggravated assault.

Harm refers to the negative impact a crime has either to the victim or to the general values of the community. Although the harm caused by the criminal act is often obvious, the harm caused by many so-called "victimless" crimes is often less obvious. Yet some victimless crimes can cause more social harm in the long run than many crimes with obvious victims.

An Excursion Through the U.S. Criminal Justice System

Now that you are aware of the principles behind the process of officially labeling someone a criminal, we will discuss the process itself. The best way to explain the process within limited space is to follow the processing of felony cases from arrest to trial and beyond. There are many points at which the arrested person may be shunted off the criminal justice conveyor belt via the discretionary decisions of a variety of criminal justice officials. This process will vary in some specifics from state to state, but the principles underlying the specifics are uniform. Presented here are the stages and procedures that are most common among our 50 state court systems.

Arrest A felony suspect first enters the criminal justice system by **arrest.** When a person has been legally detained to answer criminal charges, he or she has been arrested. Some arrests are made on the basis of an *arrest warrant,* which is an official document signed by (usually) a judge on the basis of evidence presented by law enforcement officials indicating that the person named in the warrant has probably committed a crime. The warrant formally authorizes the police to execute the arrest, although most arrests are initiated by the police without a warrant. A police officer making a warrantless arrest is held to the same legal constraints involved in making application for a warrant. To make a legal felony arrest, the officer must have **probable cause.** Probable cause means that the officer must possess a set of facts that would lead a reasonable person to conclude that the arrested person had committed a specific felony crime. Although a person can be stopped on the basis of an officer's suspicion and frisked for a weapon, he or she cannot be arrested on the basis of suspicion alone, even if illegal items such as drug paraphernalia are discovered (the discovery of a weapon, however, would constitute probable cause for arrest). It is only after a formal arrest that the Fifth Amendment rights (Miranda Rule) against self-incrimination come into play.

Preliminary Arraignment After arrest and booking into the county jail, the felony suspect must be presented in court for the **preliminary arraignment** before a magistrate or municipal judge. The preliminary arraignment must take place at the earliest opportunity. The preliminary arraignment has two purposes: (1) to advise suspects of their constitutional rights (right to counsel and right to remain silent) and of the tentative charges against them and (2) to set bail. Bail can be either granted or denied at this point. The suspect may be released on monetary bail on "own recognizance." If bail is denied, it is usually because of the gravity of the crime, the risk the suspect poses to the community, or the risk that the suspect might flee the court's jurisdiction. There is no constitutional right to bail. The Eighth Amendment only states that "excessive bail shall not be required." The traditional assumption has been that bail is only designed to ensure the suspect's appearance at the next court hearing, and *excessive* means that the amount set should be within the suspect's means. Under these assumptions, many dangerous offenders were released on bail in the past. Although this still happens, it does so less than in the past. The 1984 Bail Reform Act, which has passed constitutional muster, established the principle that individuals deemed dangerous to the community could be detained pending disposition of the case.[35]

Preliminary Hearing The **preliminary hearing,** which usually takes place about 10 days after the preliminary arraignment, is a proceeding before a magistrate or municipal judge in which three major matters must be decided: (1) whether or not a crime has actually been committed,

(2) whether or not there are reasonable grounds to believe that the person before the bench committed it, and (3) whether or not the crime was committed in the jurisdiction of the court. These matters determine if the suspect's arrest and detention is legal. The onus of proving the legality of the suspect's arrest and detention is on the prosecutor, who must establish probable cause and present the court with evidence pertinent to the suspect's probable guilt. This is usually a relatively easy matter for the prosecutor since defense attorneys rarely cross-examine witnesses or introduce their own evidence at this point—their primary use of the preliminary hearing is only to discover the strength of the prosecutor's case.

The Grand Jury If the prosecutor is successful, the suspect is *bound over* to a higher court for further processing. Prior to the suspect's next court appearance, prosecutors in some states must seek an indictment (a document formally charging the suspect with a specific crime or crimes) from a **grand jury**. The grand jury, so called to distinguish it from the "petit" or trial jury, is nominally an investigatory body and a buffer between the awesome power of the state and its citizens, but some see it as a historical anachronism that serves only prosecutorial purposes.[36] The grand jury is composed of citizens chosen from voter or automobile registration lists and numbers anywhere from 7 to 23 members.

Arraignment Armed with an indictment (or an *information* filed on the basis of the preliminary hearing outcome in states not requiring grand jury proceedings), the prosecutor files the case against the accused in felony court (variably called a district, supreme, superior, or common pleas court), which sets a date for **arraignment**. The arraignment proceeding is the first time defendants (their status has changed from suspect to defendant on the basis of the indictment or information) have the opportunity to respond to the charges against them. After the charges are read to the defendant, he or she must then enter a formal response to them, known as a plea.

The plea alternatives are guilty, not guilty, or no contest (*nolo contendere*). A guilty plea is usually the result of a plea bargain agreement concluded before the arraignment. About 90% of all felony cases in the United States are settled by plea bargains in which the state extends some benefit to the defendant (e.g., reduced charges, a lighter sentence) in exchange for his or her cooperation. By pleading guilty, defendants give up their right to be proven guilty "beyond a reasonable doubt," their right against self-incrimination, and their right to appeal.

A "no-contest" plea is the equivalent of a "guilty" plea in terms of criminal processing and is treated as such. Defendants usually plead no contest rather than guilty to protect themselves from civil litigation arising from the same set of circumstances involved in the criminal case. A guilty plea is a direct admission of guilt and can thus be used in civil proceedings. A no-contest plea, however, admits nothing, and thus the conviction based on it cannot be used in civil court. A "not guilty" plea results in a date being set for trial; a "guilty" or "no-contest" plea results in a date being set for sentencing.

The Trial A **trial** by a jury of one's peers is a right going back as far as the Magna Carta in 1215 and is enshrined in the Sixth Amendment to the Constitution. A trial is an examination of the law and the facts of a case by a judge or a jury for the purpose of reaching a judgment. If a defendant wishes, and state statutes allow for it, he or she can forgo the constitutional right to a jury trial and submit to a bench trial (trial by a judge). The trial is an adversarial process pitting the prosecutor against the defense attorney, with each side trying to "vanquish" the other. There is no sense that each side is interested in seeking truth or justice in this totally partisan process. It is the task of the judge to ensure that both sides play by the rules. The prosecution's job is a little more difficult than the defense's since it must "prove beyond a reasonable doubt" that the accused is indeed guilty. Except in states that allow for nonunanimous jury decisions, the defense need only plant the seed of reasonable doubt in the mind of one stubborn juror to upset the prosecution's case.

Having heard the facts of the case, and having been instructed by the judge on the principles of law pertaining to it, the jury is charged with reaching a verdict. The jury's verdict may be guilty or not guilty; if it cannot reach a verdict (a "hung" jury), the judge may declare a mistrial. A hung jury results in either dismissal of the charges by the prosecutor or in a retrial. If the verdict is guilty, in most cases, the judge will delay sentencing (usually for a period of about 30 days) to allow time for a presentence investigation report to be prepared. It is at the point of conviction that the person officially becomes a criminal.

Probation Presentence investigation reports (PSIs) are prepared by **probation** officers and contain a variety of information about the crime and the offender's background (criminal record, education and work history, marital status, substance abuse, and attitude). On the basis of this information, the probation officer offers a sentencing recommendation. The most important factors influencing these recommendations are crime seriousness and the defendant's criminal history. Other factors, such as the officer's assessment of the rehabilitative potential of the defendant, are important but less so. A variety of studies have found that these recommendations are followed by judges around 90% of the time.[37]

One of the sentencing options open to the judge is to place the offender on probation, the most common sentence for felonies in the United States today. A probation sentence is actually a suspended commitment to prison that is conditional on the offender's good behavior. If at any time during their probationary period, offenders do not abide by the imposed probation conditions (consisting of a variety of general and offender-specific conditions), they may face revocation of probation and the imposition of the original prison sentence. Probation officers supervise and monitor offenders' behavior and ensure that all conditions of probation (e.g., substance abuse counseling, fines and restitution paid, restraining orders followed) are adhered to. Probation officers thus function as both social workers and law enforcement officers—sometimes conflicting roles that officers may find difficult to reconcile.

Incarceration If the sentence imposed for a felony conviction is some form of incarceration, the judge has the option of sentencing the offender to a state penitentiary, a county jail, or a county work release program. The latter two options are almost invariably imposed as supplements to probation orders.

Parole Parole is a conditional release from prison granted to inmates some time prior to the completion of their sentences. An inmate is granted **parole** by an administrative body called a parole board, which decides for or against parole based on such factors as inmate behavior while incarcerated and the urgency of the need for cell space. Once released on parole, parole officers, whose job is almost identical to that of probation officers, supervise parolees. In many states, probation and parole officers are one and the same. The primary difference between probation and parole is that probationers are under the supervision of the courts and parolees are under the supervision of the state Department of Corrections. Revocation of probation is a judicial function; revocation of parole is an executive administrative function.

▲ **Photo 1.2**   This "new generation" jail is only one of half a dozen facilities located at Riker's Island, NYC. There are traditional-looking jail buildings, a boot camp, a women's facility, and even a floating hulk at Riker's. New-generation jails feature pod-style architecture rather than cellblocks while corrections officers spend their entire shift in the day rooms with inmates (direct supervision).

⌧ The Role of Theory in Criminology

When an FBI agent asked the notorious Depression-era bank robber Willie Sutton why he robbed banks, Sutton is reported to have replied, "Because that's where the money is." In his own simple way, Sutton was offering a theory explaining the behavior of bank robbers. Behind his witty answer is a model of a kind of person who has learned how to take advantage of opportunities provided by convenient targets flush with a valued commodity. Thus, if we put a certain kind of personality and learning together with opportunity and coveted resources, we get bank robbery. This is what theory making is all about: trying to grasp how all the known correlates of a phenomenon are linked together in noncoincidental ways to produce an effect.

Just as medical scientists want to find out what causes disease, criminologists are interested in finding out factors that cause crime and criminality. As is the case with disease, there are a variety of risk factors to be considered when searching for causes of criminal behavior. The very first step in detected causes is to discover **correlates,** which are factors that are linked or related to the phenomenon a scientist is interested in. To discover if two factors "go together"—are correlated—we must see if they vary together; that is, if one variable goes up or down, the other goes up or down as well.

Establishing causality requires much more sophisticated procedures than simply establishing a correlation. Take gender, the most thoroughly documented correlate of criminal behavior ever identified. Literally thousands of studies throughout the world, with some European studies going back five or six centuries, have consistently reported strong gender differences in all sorts of antisocial behavior, including crime—and the more serious the crime, the stronger that difference is. All studies are unanimous in indicating that males are more criminal and antisocial than females. Establishing *why* gender is such a strong correlate of crime is the real challenge, as it is with any other correlate. Trying to establish causes is the business of theory.

Theories are devised to explain how a number of different correlates may actually be *causally related* to crime and criminality rather than simply associated with them. We emphasize that when criminologists talk of causes, they do not mean that when *X* is present, *Y will* occur in a completely prescribed way. They mean that when *X* is present, *Y* has a certain *probability* of occurring, and perhaps only if *X* is present along with factors *A, B,* and *C.* In many ways, crime is like illness because there may be as many routes to becoming criminal as there are to becoming ill. In other words, criminologists have never uncovered a **necessary cause** (a factor that *must* be present for criminal behavior to occur and in the absence of which criminal behavior has never occurred) or a **sufficient cause** (a factor that is able to produce criminal behavior without being augmented by some other factor).

There is a lot of confusion about the term *theory* among laypersons. We often hear statements such as, "That's just theory" or "They teach evolution as if it was a fact when it's just a theory." Theory is also often negatively contrasted with practice: "That's all right in theory, but it won't work in the real world." Such statements imply that a theory is a poor relative of a fact, something impractical we grasp at in the absence of solid, practical evidence. Nothing could be further from the truth. Theories help us to make sense of a diversity of seemingly unrelated facts and propositions, and they even tell us where to look for more facts, which make theories very practical things indeed.

We all use theory every day to fit facts together. A detective, for instance, is confronted with a number of facts about a mysterious murder, but their meaning and relatedness to one another is ambiguous, and some may even appear contradictory. Using years of experience, training, and good common sense, the detective constructs a theory linking those facts together so that they begin to make some sense, to begin to tell their story. The vision of reality derived from the available facts then guides the detective in the search for additional facts in a series of "*if* this is true, *then* this should be true" statements. There may be many false starts as our detective misinterprets some facts, fails to uncover others, and considers some to be relevant when they are not. Good detectives, like good scientists, will adjust their theory as new facts warrant; poor detectives and poor scientists will stand by their favored theory by not looking for more facts or by ignoring, downplaying, or hiding contrary facts that come to their attention. When detectives do this, innocent people suffer and guilty people remain unknown; when scientists do this, the progress of science suffers.

What Is Theory?

We define a **theory** as a set of logically interconnected propositions explaining how phenomena are related and from which a number of hypotheses can be derived and tested. Theories should provide coherent explanations of the phenomena they address, correspond with the relevant empirical facts, and provide practical guidance for researchers looking for further facts. This guidance takes the form of a series of statements that can be logically deduced from the assertions of the theory. We call these statements **hypotheses**, which are statements about relationships between and among factors we expect to find based on the logic of our theories. Hypotheses and theories support one another in the sense that theories provide the raw material (the ideas) for generating hypotheses, and hypotheses support or fail to support theories by exposing them to empirical testing.

The physical and natural sciences enjoy a great deal of agreement about what constitutes the core body of knowledge within their disciplines and thus have few competing theories, especially at the most general levels. Within criminology and the social/behavioral sciences in general, there is little agreement about the nature of the phenomena we study, and so we suffer an embarrassment of theoretical riches. Given the number of criminological theories, students may be forgiven for asking which one is true. Scientists never use the term *truth* in scientific discourse; rather, they tend to ask which theory is most useful. Criteria for judging the merits of a theory are summarized as follows:

1. *Predictive Accuracy:* A theory has merit and is useful to the extent that it accurately predicts what is observed. That is, the theory has generated a large number of research hypotheses that have supported it. This is the most important criterion.

2. *Predictive Scope:* Refers to the scope or range of the theory and thus the scope or range of the hypotheses that can be derived from it. That is, how much of the empirical world falls under the explanatory umbrella of Theory A compared to how much falls under Theory B.

3. *Simplicity:* If two competing theories are essentially equal in terms of the first two criteria, then the less complicated one is considered more "elegant."

4. *Falsifiability:* A theory is never proven true, but it must have the quality of being falsifiable or disprovable. If a theory is formulated in such a way that no amount of evidence could possibly falsify it, then the theory is of little use.[38]

How to Think About Theories

You will be a lot less confused and cynical about the numerous theories in criminology if you keep certain things in mind when thinking about them. First, there are theories that deal with different **levels of analysis.** A level of analysis is that segment of the phenomenon of interest that is measured and analyzed. For instance, we can ask about the causes of crime by concentrating our inquiries at levels of analysis such as whole societies, subcultures and neighborhoods, families, or individuals. Answers to the question of crime causation at one level do not generally answer the same question at another level. For instance, suppose that at the individual level, strong evidence supports the notion that crime is linked to impulsiveness and low IQ. Do you think that this evidence would help us to understand why the crime rate in Society A is 2.5 times that of Society B or why the crime rate in Society C last year was only 75% as high as it was 20 years ago? It would do so only in the extremely unlikely event that Society A has 2.5 times as many impulsive, low-IQ people as Society B or that Society C has lost 25% of its people with those characteristics in the past 20 years. If the question posed asks about crime rates in whole societies, the answers must address sociocultural differences among different societies or in the same society at different times.

Conversely, if crime rates are found to be quite strongly related to the degree of industrialization or racial/ethnic diversity in societies, this tells us nothing about why some people in an industrialized, heterogeneous society commit crimes and others in the same society do not. To answer questions about individuals, we need theories about individuals. Generally speaking, questions of cause and effect must be answered at the same level of analysis at which they were posed, and thus different theories are required at different levels. However, a firm grasp of crime causation will eventually require theories that integrate propositions from every level of analysis. These propositions must be mutually consistent across levels of analysis in ways that theoretical propositions in the more advanced sciences are. No such theory exists in criminology at the present time.

The second reason we have so many theories is that causal explanations are also offered at different temporal levels: *ultimate* (distant in time) and *proximate* (close in time) explanations. Figure 1.2 illustrates this continuum. We can offer different temporal explanations regardless of the level of analysis. If we define a criminal act as something that occurs when a person who is psychologically prepared to commit such an act is presented with a situation conducive to its commission (such as Willie Sutton and banks), the possible levels of explanation range from the ultimate (the evolutionary history of the species) to the most proximate level (the immediate precipitating situation). Between these extreme levels are explanations such as genetic, temperamental, developmental, personality, familial, experiential, and social environmental. We will be discussing theories and offering explanations for crime at all levels, but you should realize that in reality, these levels describe an integrated whole. This text views human behavior in a way described by Christopher Peterson: "Most contemporary psychologists prefer to regard people as biopsychosocial beings, believing that people and their behavior are best explained in terms of relevant biological mechanisms, psychological processes, and social influences."[39]

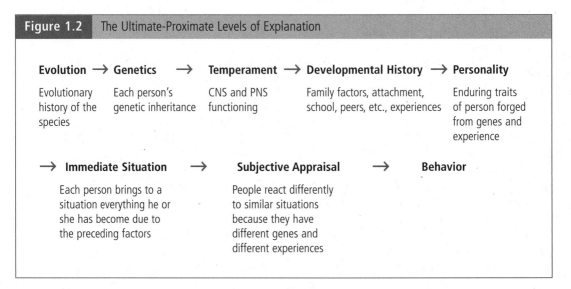

Figure 1.2	The Ultimate-Proximate Levels of Explanation

Evolution → **Genetics** → **Temperament** → **Developmental History** → **Personality**

Evolutionary history of the species | Each person's genetic inheritance | CNS and PNS functioning | Family factors, attachment, school, peers, etc., experiences | Enduring traits of person forged from genes and experience

→ **Immediate Situation** → **Subjective Appraisal** → **Behavior**

Each person brings to a situation everything he or she has become due to the preceding factors | People react differently to similar situations because they have different genes and different experiences

NOTE: Evolutionary forces lead to species-specific genomes. Each person has a unique genotype. These genotypes lead to differential central and peripheral nervous system (CNS and PNS) functioning. This functioning is modified by the person's developmental history. Working together, the person's temperament and developmental history form his or her personality. This personality may often lead the person to different situations and lead him or her to appraise those situations differently from other persons. The behavior elicited from that appraisal is thus the result of everything that preceded it, plus pure chance.

Let us look at a simple diagrammatic illustration of what is meant by the above statement. Crime rates in a population change, sometimes drastically, from time to time without any corresponding change in the gene pool or personalities of the people in the population. Because causes are sought only among factors that vary, changing sociocultural environments must be the only causes of changing crime rates. What environmental changes do, however, is raise or lower individual thresholds for engaging in crime, and some people have lower thresholds than others. People with weak criminal propensities (or high prosocial propensities) require high levels of environmental instigation to commit crimes, but some individuals would engage in criminal behavior in the most benign of environments. When or if individuals cross the threshold to commit criminal acts depends on the interaction between where their personal thresholds are set and where environmental thresholds are set. Figure 1.3 illustrates this point.

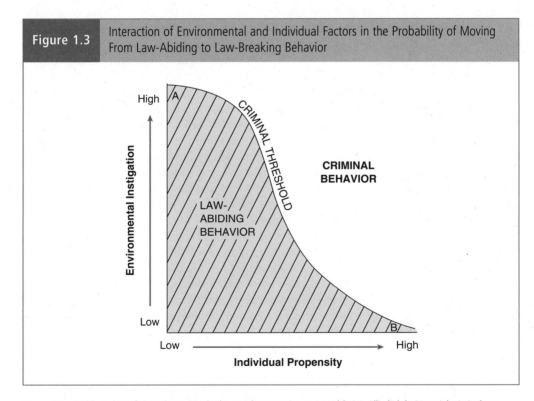

| Figure 1.3 | Interaction of Environmental and Individual Factors in the Probability of Moving From Law-Abiding to Law-Breaking Behavior |

SOURCE: From Walsh, A. (2003). Introduction to the biosocial perspective. In A. Walsh & L. Ellis (Eds.), *Biosocial criminology: Challenging environmentalism's supremacy* (pp. 3–12). Huntington, NY: Nova Science Publishers. Reprinted with permission from Nova Science.

NOTE: Angled lines each represent a hypothetical individual. Person A has a low underlying criminal disposition and thus requires strong environmental instigation to cross the threshold from law-abiding to law-breaking behavior. Person B has a strong underlying criminal disposition and will cross the threshold even under extremely low environmental instigation.

Before we discuss the various theories, you should be aware of a number of pitfalls to avoid when interpreting the overall meaning of a body of research literature. Interpreting the meaning of empirical tests of theory is not nearly so straightforward as interpreting studies concerned only with documenting correlates of crime. There is little room for error when contrasting rates of antisocial behavior between and among the various demographic variables such as age, gender, and race/ethnicity. Nor is there much difficulty (unless one wants to split fine hairs) in defining and classifying people into those categories. But theory testing looks for causal explanations rather than simple descriptions, and that's where our problems begin. For example, when we consistently find positive correlations between criminal behavior and some other factor, it is tempting to assume that something causal is going on, but as we have said previously, correlations merely *suggest* causes—they do not demonstrate them. Resisting the tendency to jump to causal conclusions from correlations is the first lesson of statistics.

Ideology in Criminological Theory

It is essential that we understand the role of ideology in criminology, although we rarely see a discussion of it in textbooks, leading students to believe that criminological arguments are settled with data in the same manner that natural science arguments are. Unfortunately, this is not always the case. **Ideology** is a way of looking at the world, a general emotional picture of "how things should be." By definition, it implies a selective interpretation and understanding of evidence that come to our senses rather than an objective and rational evaluation of the evidence.[40] Ideology forms, shapes, and colors our concepts of crime and its causes in ways that lead to a tendency to accept or reject new evidence according to how well or poorly it fits our ideology.

According to Thomas Sowell,[41] two contrasting visions have shaped thoughts about human nature throughout history, and these visions are in constant conflict with each other. The first of these visions is the **constrained vision,** so called because believers in this vision view human activities as constrained by an innate human nature that is self-centered and largely unalterable. The **unconstrained vision** denies an innate human nature, viewing it as formed anew in each different culture. The unconstrained vision also believes that human nature is perfectible, a view scoffed at by those who profess the constrained vision. A major difference between the two visions is that the constrained vision says, "this is how the world *is*"; the unconstrained vision says, "this is how the world *should be.*" These visions are what sociologists call *ideal types,* which are conceptual tools that accentuate differences between competing positions for purposes of guiding the exploration of them. Many "visions" are hybrids of the two extremes; Sowell lists Marxism, for instance, as a prominent hybrid of the two visions.

The two contrasting ways of approaching a social problem such as crime are aptly summed up by Sowell: "While believers in the unconstrained vision seek the special causes of war, poverty, and crime, believers in the constrained vision seek the special causes of peace, wealth, or a law-abiding society."[42] Note that this implies that unconstrained visionaries (mostly liberals) believe that war, poverty, and crime are aberrations to be explained, while constrained visionaries (mostly conservatives) see these things as historically normal and inevitable, although regrettable, and believe that what has to be understood are the conditions that prevent them. We will see the tension between visions constantly as we discuss the various theories in this book.

Given this, it should be no surprise to discover that criminological theories differ on how they approach the "crime problem." A theory of criminal behavior is at least partly shaped by the ideological vision of the person who formulated it, and that, in turn, is partly due to the ideological atmosphere prevailing in society. Sowell avers that a vision "is what we sense or feel *before* we have constructed any systematic reasoning that could be called a theory, much less deduced any specific consequences as hypotheses to be tested against evidence."[43] Those who feel drawn to a particular theory likewise owe a great deal of their attraction to it since they share the same vision as its formulator. In other words, "visions," more so than hard evidence, all too often lead criminologists to favor more strongly one theory over another than most of them care to acknowledge.[44]

Orlando Patterson[45] views ideology as a major barrier to advancement in the human sciences. He states that conservatives believe that only "the proximate internal cultural and behavioral factors are important ('So stop whining and pull up your socks, man!')," and "liberals and mechanistic radicals" believe that "only the proximate and external factors are worth considering ('Stop blaming the victim, racist'!)." Patterson's observation reminds us of the ancient Indian parable of the nine blind men feeling different parts of an elephant. Each man described the elephant according to the part of its anatomy he had felt, but each failed to appreciate the descriptions of the others who felt different parts. The men fell into dispute and departed in anger, each convinced of the utter stupidity, and perhaps the malevolence, of the others. The point is that ideology often leads criminologists to "feel" only part of the criminological elephant and then to confuse the parts with the whole. As with the blind men, criminologists sometimes question the intelligence and motives (e.g., having some kind of political agenda) of other criminologists who have examined different parts of the criminological elephant. Needless to say, such criticisms have no place in scientific criminology.

There is abundant evidence that political ideology is linked to favored theories among contemporary criminologists. One study asked 137 criminologists which theory they considered to be "most viable with respect to explaining variations in serious and persistent criminal behavior."[46] Twenty-three different theories were represented in their responses, but obviously they cannot all be the "most viable," so something other than hard evidence was instrumental in making their choices. The researchers found that the best predictor of a favored theory was the criminologists' stated ideology (divided into conservative, moderate, liberal, and radical categories), and the second best predictor was the discipline in which criminologists received the bulk of their training. Ideology and the lack of interdisciplinary training will no doubt continue to plague the development of a theory of crime and criminality that is acceptable to all criminologists. When reading this text, try to understand where the originators, supporters, and detractors of any particular theory being discussed are "coming from" ideologically as well as theoretically.

SUMMARY

Criminology is the scientific study of crime and criminals. It is an interdisciplinary/multidisciplinary study, although criminology has yet to integrate these disciplines in any comprehensive way.

The definition of crime is problematic, largely because acts defined as criminal vary across time and culture and even within cultures. Many criminologists feel that because crimes are social constructions, we cannot define what real crimes are and who the real criminals are. We tried to counter this argument by pointing out that there is a stationary core of crimes that are universally condemned and always have been. These crimes are victimful predatory crimes that cause serious harm. These crimes are defined as mala in se, or "inherently bad," as opposed to mala prohibita—"bad because they are forbidden" crimes.

A person is not "officially" a criminal until he or she has been found guilty beyond a reasonable doubt of having committed a crime. To prove that he or she did, the state has to prove corpus delicti ("the body of the crime"), which essentially means that he or she committed a criminal act (actus reus) with full awareness that the act was wrong (mens rea— guilty mind). Other basic principles—concurrence, harm, and causation—are proven in the process of proving corpus delicti.

Theory is the "bread and butter" of any science, including the science of criminology. We will see that there are many contending theories seeking to explain crime and criminality. Although we do not observe such theoretical disagreement in the more established sciences, the social/behavioral sciences are very young, and human behavior is extremely difficult to study. When judging among the various theories, we have to keep certain things in mind, including the predictive accuracy, scope, simplicity, and falsifiability. We must also remember that crime and criminality can be discussed at many levels (society-wide, subcultural, family, or individual) and that one theory that may do a good job of predicting crime at one level may do a poor job at another level.

Theories can also be offered at different temporal levels. They may focus on the evolutionary history of the species (the most ultimate level), the individual's subjective appraisal of a situation (the most proximate level), or any other temporal level in between. A full account of an individual's behavior may have to take all these levels into consideration because any behavior, including criminal behavior, arises from an individual's propensities interacting with the current environmental situation as that individual perceives it. This is why we approach the study of crime and criminality from social, psychosocial, and biosocial perspectives.

Criminologists have not traditionally done this, preferring instead to examine only aspects of criminal behavior that they find congenial to their ideology and, unfortunately, often maligning those who focus on other aspects. The main dividing line in criminology has separated conservatives (who tend to favor explanations of behavior that focus on the individual) and liberals (who tend to favor structural or cultural explanations). We noted that criminologists' favored theories of crime were strongly correlated with their sociopolitical ideology.

On Your Own

Log on to the web-based student study site at http://www.sagepub.com/criminologystudy for more information about the vignettes and materials presented in this chapter, suggestions for activities, study aids such as review quizzes, and research recommendations including journal article links and questions related to this chapter.

EXERCISES AND DISCUSSION QUESTIONS

1. Describe a recent change, or proposed change, in some criminal statute that you have learned about in the mass media. Offer your views on why some people want to make these changes and why others might resist them. Also offer your opinion on how much impact such changes might make on the level of crime in your area.

2. Which of the following 10 acts do you consider mala in se crimes, mala prohibita crimes, or no crime at all? Defend your choices.

A. Drug possession
B. Vandalism
C. Drunk driving
D. Collaborating with the enemy
E. Sale of alcohol to minors
F. Fraud
G. Spouse abuse
H. Adult male having consensual sex with underage person
I. Prostitution
J. Cannibalism in a culture in which it is normative (i.e., accepted as normal behavior)

3. Describe the difference between crime and criminality.

4. Why is it important to consider ideology when evaluating criminologists' work? Is it possible for them to divorce their ideology from their work?

5. What does the term *theory* mean to you?

6. The table below presents in no particular order a list of 7 acts that are often considered criminal offenses. Add 3 more offenses that interest you to this list. Then, rate each of the 10 acts on a scale from 1 to 10 in terms of your perception of each one's seriousness (with 10 being the most serious). Without letting anyone see your ratings, give your list to a member of the opposite gender and ask him or her to rate the offenses on the same 10-point scale. After he or she is finished, compare the two ratings with the other person present and discuss each inconsistency of 2 or more ranking points. Write a one- to two-page double-spaced report on what you learned from this exercise about how you and the other person differ and resemble one another in your thoughts about the seriousness of crime. Is there a gender difference?

Offense	Ranking by Someone Else	Your Ranking
Alcohol consumption by a minor		
Assassinating an unpopular political leader		
Killing a repeatedly abusive spouse		
Raping a stranger with threats from a deadly weapon		
Committing rape on a date by threatening bodily harm		
Driving while extremely drunk		
Molesting a young child		
Total of all rankings		

7. Go to http://www.Isus.edu/la/journals/ideology/ for the online journal *Quarterly Journal of Ideology.* Click on *archive* and find and read "Ideology: Criminology's Achilles' Heel." What does this article say about the "conflict of visions" in criminology?

KEY WORDS

Actus reus	Felony	Parole
Arraignment	Grand jury	Preliminary arraignment
Arrest	Harm	Preliminary hearing
Causation	Hypotheses	Probable cause
Concurrence	Ideology	Probation
Constrained vision	Level of analysis	Sufficient cause
Corpus delicti	Mala in se	Theory
Correlates	Mala prohibita	Trial
Crime	Mens rea	Unconstrained vision
Criminality	Misdemeanor	
Criminology	Necessary cause	

REFERENCES

1. Cote, S. (2002). *Criminological theories: Bridging the past to the future.* Thousand Oaks, CA: Sage.

2. Guarino-Ghezzi, S., & Trevino, J. (Eds.). (2005). *Understanding crime: A multidisciplinary approach.* Cincinnati, OH: Anderson.

3. Bernard, T. (2002). Twenty years of testing theories: What have we learned and why? In S. Cote (Ed.), *Criminological theories: Bridging the past to the future* (pp. 5–13). Thousand Oaks, CA: Sage.

4. Cote (2002).

5. Farrington, D. (2000). Explaining and preventing crime: The globalization of knowledge—the American Society of Criminology 1999 presidential address. *Criminology, 38,* 1–24.

6. Short, J. (1998). The level of explanation problem revisited: The American Society of Criminology 1997 presidential address. *Criminology, 36,* 3–36.

7. Wellford, C. (1997). Controlling crime and achieving justice: The American Society of Criminology 1996 presidential address. *Criminology, 35,* 1–11.

8. Zahn, M. (1999). Thoughts on the future of criminology: The American Society of Criminology presidential address. *Criminology, 37,* 1–15.

9. Fishbein, D. (1998). Building bridges. *Academy of Criminal Justice Sciences ACJS Today, 17,* 1–5.

10. Lubinski, D., & Humphreys, L. (1997). Incorporating intelligence into epidemiology and the social sciences. *Intelligence, 24,* 159–201.

11. Wilson, E. O. (1998). *Consilience: The unity of knowledge.* New York: Knopf.

12. Walsh, A. (2002). *Biosocial criminology: Introduction and integration.* Cincinnati, OH: Anderson.

13. Guarino-Ghezzi and Trevino (2005).

14. Tappan, P. (1947). Who is the criminal? *American Sociological Review, 12,* 96–112. (Quote on p. 100)

15. Gallard, C. (1995). Female genital mutilation in France. *British Journal of Medicine, 310,* 1592–1593.

16. Ellis, L., & Walsh, A. (2000). *Criminology: A global perspective.* Boston: Allyn & Bacon.

17. Bonnet, C. (1993). Adoption at birth: Prevention against abandonment or neonaticide. *Child Abuse & Neglect, 17,* 501–513.

18. Toubia, N. (1994). Female circumcision as a public health issue. *New England Journal of Medicine, 331,* 712–740.

19. Violence Against Women Grants Office. (1998). *Stalking and domestic violence: The third annual report to Congress under the Violence Against Women Act.* Washington, DC: Author.

20. Lawrence v. Texas, 539 US 558 (2003).

21. Texas v. Johnson, 491 US 397 (1989).

22. Hawkins, D. (1995). Ethnicity, race, and crime: A review of selected studies. In D. Hawkins (Ed.), *Ethnicity, race, and crime: Perspectives across time and space* (pp. 11–45). Albany: State University of New York Press. (Quote on p. 41)

23. Hagan, H. (1985). *Modern criminology: Crime, criminal behavior and its control.* New York: McGraw-Hill.

24. Borg, J. (1985). Judged seriousness of crimes and offenses: 1927, 1967, and 1984. *Archives of Psychology, 137,* 115–122.

25. Thomas, C. (1976). Public opinion on criminal law and legal sanctions: An examination of two conceptual models. *Journal of Criminal Law and Criminology, 67,* 100–116.

26. Hagan (1985, p. 49).

27. Interpol. (1992). *International crime statistics.* Lyons, France: Author.

28. Daly, M., & Wilson, M. (1988). *Homicide.* New York: Aldine De Gruyter.

29. O'Manique, J. (2003). *The origins of justice: The evolution of morality, human rights, and law.* Philadelphia: University of Philadelphia Press.

30. Walsh, A. (2003). Introduction to the biosocial perspective. In A. Walsh & L. Ellis (Eds.), *Biosocial criminology: Challenging environmentalism's supremacy* (pp. 3–12). Huntington, NY: Nova Science Publishers.

31. Ellis, L. (1988). The victimful-victimless crime distinction, and several universal demographic correlates of victimful criminal behavior. *Personality and Individual Differences, 9,* 535–548.

32. Sellin, T. (1938). *Culture conflict and crime.* New York: Social Science Research Council.

33. Gottfredson, M., & Hirschi, T. (1990). *A general theory of crime.* Stanford, CA: Stanford University Press.

34. Walsh, A., & Hemmens, C. (2000). *From law to order: The theory and practice of law and justice.* Lanham, MD: American Correctional Association.

35. United States v. Salerno, 481 US 739 (1987).

36. Abadinsky, H. (2003). *Law and justice: Introduction to the American legal system.* Upper Saddle River, NJ: Prentice Hall.

37. Champion, D. (1999). *Probation, parole, and community corrections.* Upper Saddle River, NJ: Prentice Hall.

38. Ellis, L. (1994). *Research methods in the social sciences.* New York: McGraw-Hill & Benchmark.

39. Peterson, C. (1997). *Psychology: A biopsychosocial approach.* New York: Longman. (Quote on p. 20)

40. Barak, G. (1998). *Integrating criminologies.* Boston: Allyn & Bacon.

41. Sowell, T. (1987). *A conflict of visions: Ideological origins of political struggles.* New York: William Morrow.

42. Sowell (1987, p. 31).

43. Sowell (1987, p. 14).

44. Cullen, F. (2005). Challenging individualistic theories of crime. In S. Guarino-Ghezzi & J. Trevino (Eds.), *Understanding crime: A multidisciplinary approach* (pp. 55–60). Cincinnati, OH: Anderson.

45. Patterson, O. (1998). *Rituals of blood: Consequences of slavery in two American centuries.* Washington, DC: Civitas Counterpoint. (Quote on p. ix)

46. Walsh, A., & Ellis, L. (2004). Ideology: Criminology's Achilles' heel? *Quarterly Journal of Ideology, 27,* 1–25.

MEASURING CRIME AND CRIMINAL BEHAVIOR

A weary English bobby (a popular nickname for British police officers) patrolling his foot beat on a chilly November night hears the unmistakable sounds of grunting urgency from the pitch-dark entranceway of a closed greengrocer's shop. He smiles to himself and tiptoes toward the sound. When he reaches the entranceway, he switches on his flashlight and booms out the favorite line of the stereotypical bobby: "What's goin' on 'ere then?" The squeaking couple immediately come to attention and adjust their dress before the young man—obviously still in a state of arousal—stammers, "Why, nothing, constable." The officer recognizes the woman as a local "slapper" (prostitute), and he vaguely recognizes the man (more of a boy of around 17 really) as a local supermarket worker. The constable reasons that he should arrest both parties for public indecency but that would entail about an hour of paperwork (an hour in the warm police station with a nice cup of tea sounds good though) and lead to the profound embarrassment of the poor boy. He finally decides to give the boy some sound advice about sexually transmitted diseases and a stern warning to the woman and sends them both on their way.

This short story illustrates that official statistics are measuring police behavior as much as they are measuring crime. Sir Josiah Stamp, director of the Bank of England in the 1920s, cynically stated this criticism: "The government are very keen on amassing statistics. They collect them, raise them to the nth power, take the cube root and prepare wonderful diagrams. But you must never forget that every one of these figures comes in the first instance from the village watchman, who just puts down what he damn pleases."[1] We don't recommend this kind of cynicism, but we do counsel that you keep a healthy skepticism about statistics as you read this chapter.

✎ Categorizing and Measuring Crime and Criminal Behavior

When attempting to understand, predict, and control any social problem, including the crime problem, the first step is to determine its extent. Gauging the extent of the problem means discovering how much of it there is, where and when it occurs most often, and among what social categories it occurs most frequently. It also helps our endeavors if we have knowledge of the patterns and trends of the problem over time. Note that we did not address "why" questions (why does crime occur, why is it increasing/decreasing, who commits it and why, and so on); such questions can only be adequately addressed after we have reliable data about the extent of the problem. However, it is fair to warn you that all social statistics are suspect to some extent, and crime statistics are perhaps the most suspect of all. They have been collected from many different sources in many different ways and have passed through many sieves of judgment before being recorded. With this caveat in mind, let us examine the major sources of crime data in the United States.

There is a wide variety of data provided by government and private sources to help us come to grips with America's crime problem, all with their particular strengths and weaknesses. The major data sources that we have can be grouped into three categories: *official statistics, victimization survey data,* and *self-reported data.* Official statistics are those derived from the routine functioning of the criminal justice system. The most basic category of official statistics comes from the calls made to police by victims or witnesses and by crimes that the police discover on patrol. Other major categories of official crime data consist of information about arrests, convictions, and correctional (prison, probation/parole) populations.

The *Uniform Crime Reports:* Counting Crime Officially

The primary source of official crime statistics in the United States is the annual *Uniform Crime Reports* (*UCR*) compiled by the Federal Bureau of Investigation (FBI). The *UCR* reports crimes known to the nation's police and sheriff's departments and the number of arrests made by these agencies; federal crimes are not included. Offenses known to the police are recorded whether or not an arrest is made or if an arrested person is subsequently prosecuted and convicted. Participation in the *UCR* reporting program is voluntary, and thus not all agencies participate. This is unfortunate for anyone hoping for comprehensive crime data. In 2004, law enforcement agencies participating in the program represented approximately 278 million U.S. residents, or about 94.2% of the population.[2] This means that crimes committed by about 6% of the U.S. population (about 17 million people) were not included in the *UCR* data.

The *UCR* separates crimes into two categories: **Part I offenses** (or **Index Crimes**) and **Part II offenses.** Part I offenses includes four violent (homicide, assault, forcible rape, and robbery) and four property offenses (larceny/theft, burglary, motor vehicle theft, and arson). Notice that these are all universally condemned mala in se offenses. Part I offenses correspond with what most people think of as "serious" crime. The FBI's definitions of all Part I offenses are given below and will be elaborated on in subsequent chapters.

▲ **Photo 2.1**   The first step in the collection of crime statistics is in the hands of beat officers who respond to citizen calls. Here these NYPD officers write down whether the crime report is founded or unfounded (no real crime has taken place) into their daily report logs. It is very easy for agencies to affect their local crime rates simply by "instructing" officers to either list more cases as founded or unfounded.

Murder is "the willful (non-negligent) killing of one human being by another."

Forcible rape is "the carnal knowledge of a female forcibly and against her will."

Robbery is "the taking or attempted taking of anything of value from the care, custody, or control of a person or persons by force or threat of force or violence and/or putting the victim in fear."

Aggravated assault is "an unlawful attack by one person upon another for the purpose of inflicting severe or aggravated bodily injury."

Burglary is "the unlawful entry of a structure to commit a felony or theft."

Larceny-theft is "the unlawful taking, leading, or riding away from the possession or constructive possession of another."

Motor vehicle theft is "the theft or attempted theft of a motor vehicle."

Arson is "any willful or malicious burning or attempting to burn, with or without intent to defraud, a dwelling house, public building, motor vehicle or aircraft, personal property of another, etc."

Determining Crime Rates

The *UCR* reports the number of instances of each crime reported to the police as well as their rate of occurrence. The rate of a given crime is the actual number of reported crimes standardized by some unit of the population. We expect the raw number of crimes to increase as the population increases, so comparing the number of crimes reported today with the number reported 30 years ago, or the number of crimes reported in New York with the number reported in Wyoming, tells us little without considering population differences. For instance, California reported 2,407 murders to the FBI in 2003, and Louisiana reported 586. These figures don't provide an accurate image of the comparative murder picture in these states unless we take their respective populations into consideration. To obtain a **crime rate,** we divide the number of reported crimes in a state by its population and multiply the quotient by 100,000, as in the following comparison of California and Louisiana rates.

$$\text{Rate} = \frac{\text{CA murders} = 2,407}{\text{CA population} = 35,484,453} = .000086 \times 100,000 = 6.8.$$

$$\text{Rate} = \frac{\text{LA murders} = 586}{\text{LA population} = 4,490,334} = .000130 \times 100,000 = 13.0.$$

Thus, a person in Louisiana is almost at twice the risk of being murdered as he or she is in California. This statement is based on statewide averages; the actual risk will vary widely from person to person, based on factors such as age, race, sex, socioeconomic status (SES), and place of residence.

Figure 2.1 presents the FBI's famous "crime clock," which provides estimates of the relative frequency with which each Part I Index Crime (arson is omitted) was committed in the United States in 2004. Students should pay attention to the FBI's caveat about interpreting the clock printed beneath it. To put these figures in perspective: A fatal traffic accident occurs every 14 minutes, a nonfatal injury traffic accident every 15 seconds, and one with only damage to the vehicle every 6.6 seconds.[3]

Part II Offenses

Part II offenses are treated as less serious offenses and are recorded based on arrests made rather than cases reported to the police. Part II offense figures understate the extent of criminal offending far more than is the case with Part I figures because only a very small proportion of these crimes results in arrest. Part II offenses may not be "true" criminal offenses (e.g., runaway) or, if they are, may not be particularly serious (e.g., gambling and other "victimless" crimes). However, *sex offenses* covers all offenses of a sexual nature except forcible rape, prostitution, and commercial vice. Such offenses cover everything from exhibitionism to incest. The former may be relatively harmless, but the latter can have devastating effects. This is not to say that the states will not charge incestuous or other types of child molestation offenders with serious felony crimes such as lewd and lascivious conduct or sexual battery. Table 2.1 lists the estimated number of all Part I and Part II offenses for which arrests were made in 2000 compared with 2004 and broken down by sex and age. The *UCR* provides numerous tables such as this.

Figure 2.1	The FBI's Crime Clock for 2004

Every 23.1 seconds: One Violent Crime
Every 32.6 minutes: One Murder
Every 5.6 minutes: One Forcible Rape
Every 1.3 minutes: One Robbery
Every 36.9 seconds: One Aggravated Assault
Every 3.1 seconds: One Property Crime
Every 14.7 seconds: One Burglary
Every 4.5 seconds: One Larceny-theft
Every 25.5 seconds: One Motor Vehicle Theft

SOURCE: Federal Bureau of Investigation. (2005). *Crime in the United States, 2004.* Washington, DC: Government Printing Office.

NOTE: The crime clock should be viewed with care. The most aggregate representation of *UCR* data, it conveys the annual reported crime experience by showing a relative frequency of occurrence of Part I offenses. It should not be taken to imply a regularity in the commission of crime. The crime clock represents the annual ratio of crime to fixed time intervals.

Cleared Offenses

If a person is arrested and charged for a Part I offense, the *UCR* records the crime as **cleared by arrest.** A crime is also recorded as cleared if it is cleared by *exceptional means.* A crime is cleared by exceptional means if the police have identified a suspect and have enough evidence to support arrest but he or she could not be taken into custody immediately or at all. Such circumstances exist when the suspect dies or is in a location where the police cannot presently gain custody—for instance, if the suspect is in custody on other charges in another jurisdiction or is residing in a country with no extradition treaty with the United States. Figure 2.2 shows that surprisingly few crimes are cleared in the United States. Violent crimes are more likely to be cleared than property crimes because the authorities pursue violent crime investigations more vigorously and because victims of such crimes may be able to identify the perpetrator(s).

Problems With the UCR

The *UCR* is useful to researchers and law enforcement agencies because it provides them with tallies of serious crimes known to the police. Rates can be compared across geographic locations

▲ **Photo 2.2**   The annual *Uniform Crime Reports* are produced by the FBI. To the J. Edgar Hoover Building in Washington, D.C., local, county, and state criminal justice agencies send their annual crime data. *UCR* data are, by their nature, incomplete, as many crimes are never reported to the police at all. This "dark figure of crime" might be as high as 50% of all crime incidents.

(states, counties, and cities) and over time going back to 1930, thus providing data about crime trends and fluctuations. It also provides data to law enforcement agencies to assist them in the administration, operation, and management of their agencies. However, *UCR* data have serious limitations that restrict their usefulness for criminological research, particularly research seeking to uncover causes of crime. Some of the more serious of these limitations are outlined as follows.

◆ The *UCR* data significantly underrepresent the actual number of criminal events in the United States each year. According to a nationwide victim survey, only 49.9% of victims of violent crime and 39% of victims of property crime indicated that they reported their victimization to the police.[4] Victims are more likely to report violent crimes if injuries are serious and are more likely to report property crimes when losses are high. Reasons most often given for not reporting include the opinion that the police could not or would not do anything about it, that the offense was a private matter, and that it "was no big deal," as well as fear of reprisal. An important exception to the underreporting complaint is criminal homicide, for which the *UCR* provides the most reliable and timely data available.

Table 2.1 Estimated Number of Arrests for Part I and Part II Crimes by Sex and Age in 2000 and 2004

Offense charged	Males Total 2000	2004	Percent change	Males Under 18 2000	2004	Percent change	Females Total 2000	2004	Percent change	Females Under 18 2000	2004	Percent change
TOTAL[1]	6,345,009	6,185,599	-2.5	1,011,721	893,547	-11.7	1,822,827	1,935,212	+6.2	386,462	377,182	-2.4
Murder and nonnegligent manslaughter	6,655	6,568	-1.3	572	546	-4.5	842	860	+2.1	79	51	-35.4
Forcible rape	16,256	15,264	-6.1	2,687	2,402	-10.6	194	214	+10.3	26	43	+65.4
Robbery	54,937	55,713	+1.4	13,789	13,185	-4.4	6,164	6,894	+11.8	1,438	1,353	-5.9
Aggravated assault	221,440	209,180	-5.5	29,998	28,162	-6.1	54,852	54,004	-1.5	8,992	8,677	-3.5
Burglary	149,363	152,527	+2.1	51,288	43,509	-15.2	22,843	26,343	+15.3	6,650	5,902	-11.2
Larceny-theft	453,659	432,974	-4.6	142,354	113,048	-20.6	256,556	269,413	+5.0	83,723	81,004	-3.2
Motor vehicle theft	68,766	69,452	+1.0	23,211	18,352	-20.9	12,964	14,290	+10.2	4,760	3,777	-20.7
Arson	8,440	7,811	-7.5	4,680	4,123	-11.0	1,449	1,442	-0.5	605	622	+2.8
Violent crime[2]	299,288	286,725	-4.2	47,046	44,295	-5.8	62,052	61,972	-0.1	10,535	10,124	-3.9
Property crime[2]	680,228	662,764	-2.6	221,533	179,032	-19.2	293,812	311,488	+6.0	95,738	91,305	-4.6
Other assaults	596,709	575,276	-3.6	97,400	100,699	+3.4	180,093	190,397	+5.7	43,021	49,988	+16.2
Forgery and counterfeiting	39,848	41,893	+5.1	2,624	1,774	-32.4	25,687	27,883	+8.5	1,335	949	-28.9
Fraud	115,825	102,342	-11.6	4,197	2,803	-33.2	98,865	87,840	-11.2	2,015	1,610	-20.1
Embezzlement	6,173	5,786	-6.3	660	429	-35.0	6,177	5,897	-4.5	617	257	-58.3
Stolen property; buying, receiving possessing	59,328	62,201	+4.8	14,251	11,556	-18.9	12,508	14,600	+16.7	2,641	2,258	-14.5
Vandalism	140,960	132,323	-6.1	60,138	52,484	-12.7	25,651	26,867	+4.7	8,488	8,720	+2.7
Weapons; carrying, possessing, etc.	85,855	94,323	+9.9	19,383	21,156	+9.1	7,434	8,299	+11.6	2,150	2,721	+26.6
Prostitution and commercialized vice	17,448	13,197	-24.4	294	281	-4.4	28,561	31,586	+10.6	323	610	+88.9
Sex offenses (except forcible rape and prostitution)	48,738	47,721	-2.1	9,418	9,153	-2.8	3,522	3,444	-2.2	668	662	-0.9
Drug abuse violations	754,883	811,879	+7.6	101,885	92,553	-9.2	161,597	190,667	+18.0	17,909	19,710	+10.1
Gambling	5,320	5,745	+8.0	820	1,046	+27.6	657	611	-7.0	31	35	+12.9
Offenses against the family and children	65,253	56,050	-14.1	3,193	2,161	-32.3	18,717	17,500	-6.5	1,823	1,329	-27.1
Driving under the influence	704,473	655,849	-6.9	10,380	8,866	-14.6	138,345	150,005	+8.4	2,115	2,417	+14.3
Liquor laws	308,870	260,310	-15.7	65,951	48,720	-26.1	93,917	89,966	-4.2	30,254	26,410	-12.7
Drunkenness	356,057	302,896	-14.9	11,128	8,227	-26.1	54,762	53,548	-2.2	2,700	2,469	-8.6
Disorderly conduct	298,583	266,694	-10.7	72,806	73,238	+0.6	88,404	91,876	+3.9	28,558	35,112	+22.9
Vagrancy	11,984	13,636	+13.8	1,189	2,204	+85.4	3,364	3,426	+1.8	338	924	+173.4
All other offenses (except traffic)	1,658,025	1,709,488	+3.1	176,264	154,369	-12.4	444,471	505,447	+13.7	60,972	57,679	-5.4
Suspicion	1,952	1,080	-44.7	529	254	-52.0	463	302	-34.8	167	91	-45.5
Curfew and loitering law violations	56,414	50,151	-11.1	56,414	50,151	-11.1	24,806	21,346	-13.9	24,806	21,346	-13.9
Runaways	34,747	28,350	-18.4	34,747	28,350	-18.4	49,425	40,547	-18.0	49,425	40,547	-18.0

1 Does not include suspicion.

2 Violent crimes are offenses of murder, forcible rape, robbery, and aggravated assault. Property crimes are offenses of burglary, larceny-theft, motor vehicle theft, and arson.

Source: Federal Bureau of Investigation. (2005). *Crime in the United States, 2004.* Washington, DC: Government Printing Office.

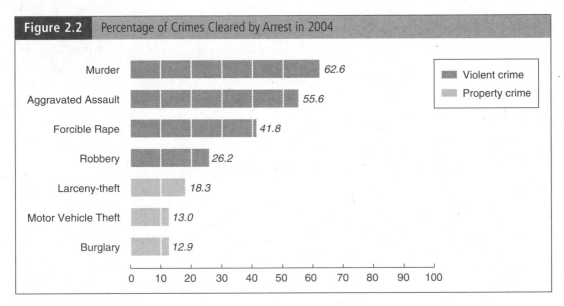

Figure 2.2 Percentage of Crimes Cleared by Arrest in 2004

Murder — 62.6
Aggravated Assault — 55.6
Forcible Rape — 41.8
Robbery — 26.2
Larceny-theft — 18.3
Motor Vehicle Theft — 13.0
Burglary — 12.9

Violent crime
Property crime

0 10 20 30 40 50 60 70 80 90 100

Sᴏᴜʀᴄᴇ: Federal Bureau of Investigation. (2005). *Crime in the United States, 2004*. Washington, DC: Government Printing Office.

- ◆ Drug offenses, the offenses many criminologists believe are fueling America's prison boom,[5] are not included. Nor are federal crimes, thus missing many highly costly white-collar crimes such as stock market fraud, hazardous waste dumping, tax evasion, and false claims for professional services. These crimes are addressed in Chapter 15.

- ◆ The voluntary nature of the *UCR* program means that the crimes committed in the jurisdictions of nonparticipating law enforcement agencies are not included in the data. Even with full voluntary compliance, all departments would not be equally efficient and thorough (or honest) in their record keeping.

- ◆ Crime data may be falsified by police departments for political reasons. The National Center for Policy Analysis[6] reports that police departments in Philadelphia, New York, Atlanta, and Boca Raton, Florida, had underreported and/or downgraded crimes in their localities (and these are just the departments we know about). With promotions, pay raises, and even continued employment based on performance, pressure is generated to "prove" such performance by presenting improved crime statistics.

- ◆ The *UCR* even underreports crimes that are known to the police because of the FBI's hierarchy rule. The **hierarchy rule** requires police to report only the highest (most serious) offense committed in a multiple offense–single incident to the FBI and to ignore the others. For instance, if a man robs five patrons in a bar, pistol whips one patron who tried to resist, locks the victims in the beer cooler, and then rapes the female bartender, only the rape is reported to the FBI. The rule, of course, does not prevent the state from charging the perpetrator with five counts of robbery, one count of aggravated assault, and one count of rape. Parenthetically, the hierarchy rule prevents criminologists from comparing cross-national data because countries such as England and Australia would record all seven crimes in their official statistics.

Given these sorts of difficulties, why should official crime statistics be trusted at all? Many criminologists have expressed serious reservations about official crime statistics over the years.[7] The most frequent criticism has been that these data are too easily affected by discretionary police policies to be considered reliable, as was illustrated in the opening vignette of this chapter. Efforts to improve the reliability and validity of official statistics are occurring all the time, with the most ambitious being the National Incident-Based Reporting System (NIBRS) described below.

NIBRS: The "New and Improved" *UCR*

The **National Incident-Based Reporting System** (NIBRS) began in 1982 and is designed for the collection of more detailed and more comprehensive crime statistics than are presently collected by the *UCR*. The NIBRS is currently a component of the *UCR* program and is eventually expected to replace it entirely. As opposed to the current *UCR*, which monitors only relatively few crimes and gathers few details associated with them, NIBRS collects data on 46 "Group A" offenses and 11 "Group B" offenses. There is no hierarchy rule under the NIBRS system; it reports multiple victims, multiple offenders, and multiple crimes that may be part of the same incident. It also provides information about the circumstances of the offense and about victim and offender characteristics, such as offender-victim relationship and age, sex, and race of victims and perpetrators (if known). The *UCR* only reports such characteristics for homicide in its *Supplementary Homicide Reports*.

Despite the promise of the NIBRS, it has yet to come anywhere near to realizing its full potential. Only 19 states and three cities with populations greater than 500,000 (Austin, Memphis, and Nashville) were reporting crime incidents to the NIBRS as of 2004.[8] This is because the promise of the NIBRS for research purposes is its weakness in terms of agency participation. Many departments lack the manpower and technical expertise to collect and process the wide and detailed range of information that is part of each crime incident their officers deal with, and administrators see little benefit to their department to justify the effort.[9] If the NIBRS does eventually replace the *UCR* as planned, we should see an improvement in the reliability and validity of crime data across law enforcement jurisdictions as well as enjoy a greater richness of information. Nevertheless, there will still be a lot of concern over what criminologists have come to call the **dark figure of crime.** The dark (or hidden) figure refers to all of the crimes committed that never come to official attention.[10]

Crime Victimization Survey Data

One way of illuminating the dark figure of crime (albeit, not very brightly) is through crime victimization surveys. Crime victimization surveys involve asking a large number of people if they have been criminally victimized within some specified time frame, regardless of whether they reported the incident to police. The first two known victimization surveys were conducted in Scandinavia, with the first one dating back to Denmark in 1720.[11] At that time, a concerned citizen of the city of Aarhus went door-to-door asking city residents if they had been the victim of any crime in recent years and to provide details if they had. The second known survey was carried out more than two centuries later in Norway in the late 1940s.[12] Although these early surveys lacked scientific rigor, they provided the template for numerous victimization surveys beginning in the 1970s.

The first such survey was completed in the United States in 1967 based on interviews of adults from 10,000 households.[13] Currently, twice a year, Census Bureau personnel interview a national representative sample of people age 12 or older on behalf of the Bureau of Justice Statistics (BJS). This biannual survey is known as the **National Crime Victimization Survey** (NCVS), and in 2004, 149,000 people from 84,360 households were interviewed.[14] The NCVS requests information on crimes committed against individuals and households (whether reported to the police or not) and for circumstances of the offense (time and place it occurred, perpetrator's use of a weapon, any injuries incurred, and financial loss). In addition, interviewers request personal information about victims (age, sex, race, income, and education level) and offenders (approximate age, sex, race, and victim-offender relationship).

Having collected and analyzed all this information, the data derived from the sample are extrapolated to the entire population of the United States. If the sample reveals an aggravated assault rate of 5 per 1,000 individuals older than age 12, for instance, the NCVS will report a rate of 5 per 1,000 (or 500 per 100,000) for the United States. It is perfectly scientifically acceptable to make inferences from samples to populations like this, assuming that samples are truly representative of the populations from which they are taken, which the NCVS samples are. Figure 2.3 is the front sheet of an NCVS interview schedule, and Figure 2.4 provides graphs of violent and property crime trends from 1993 to 2004 and selected highlights from the 2004 survey.

Problems With the NCVS

Over the years, NCVS surveys have revealed that many more crimes occur than are reported to the police, thus providing a valuable service (indeed, they may have been the impetus for the FBI's gradual shift to the NIBRS incident-based system). Nevertheless, victimization surveys have their own dark figures as well as other problems that make them almost as suspect as the *UCR*. Some of these problems include the following:

- Crimes such as drug dealing and all "victimless" crimes such as prostitution and gambling are not revealed in such surveys for obvious reasons. And because murder victims cannot be interviewed, this most serious of crimes is not included.
- Because NCVS only surveys households, crimes committed against commercial establishments such as stores, bars, and factories are not included. This exclusion results in a huge underestimate of crimes such as burglaries, robberies, theft, and vandalism.
- Victimization data do not have to meet any stringent legal or evidentiary standards in order to be reported as an offense; if the respondent says he or she was robbed, a robbery will be recorded. *UCR* data, on the other hand, pass through the legal sieve to determine whether the reported incident was indeed a robbery. Between 5% and 20% of all crimes reported to the police are not officially recorded because the police have determined that they were *unfounded* (unsubstantiated).[15]
- Other problems associated with face-to-face interviewing involve memory lapses; an open door combined with the apparent loss of some object may be called a burglary when the only thing really lost is the "victim's" memory, and a stolen kiss may be reported as an attempted rape. Other problems involve providing answers the respondent thinks the interviewer wants to hear, forgetting an incident, embellishing an incident, and any number of other misunderstandings, ambiguities, and even downright lies that occur when one person is asking another about his or her life experiences.

Figure 2.3	Page 1 of the NCVS Interview Schedule

NOTICE - We are conducting this survey under the authority of Title 13, United States Code, Section 8, Section 9 of this law requires us to keep all information about you and your household strictly confidential. We may use this information only for statistical purposes. Also, Title 42, Section 3732, United States Code, authorizes the Bureau of Justice Statistics, Department of Justice, to collect information using this survey. Title 42, Sections 3789g and 3735, United States Code, also requires us to keep all information about you and your household strictly confidential. According to the paperwork Reduction Act of 1996, no persons are required to respond to a collection of information unless such collection displays a valid CMB number.

NCVS-2

Form
[9-16-2004]
U.S. DEPARTMENT OF COMMERCE
Economics and Statistics Administration
U.S. CENSUS BUREAU
ACTING AS COLLECTING AGENT FOR THE
BUREAU OF JUSTICE STATISTICS
U.S. DEPARTMENT OF JUSTICE

CRIME INCIDENT REPORT
NATIONAL CRIME VICTIMIZATION SURVEY

Control number

PSU	Segment/ Suffix	Sample designation/ Suffix	Serial/ Suffix	HH No.	Spinoff indicator

Notes

1a. LINE NUMBER OF RESPONDENT ⟶ 601 ☐☐ Line number *(ex., 01)*

1b. SCREEN QUESTION NUMBER ⟶ 602 ☐☐ Screen question number *(ex, 39)*

1c. INCIDENT NUMBER ⟶ 603 ☐☐ Incident number *(ex., 01)*

CHECK ITEM A Has the respondent lived at this address for more than 6 months? *(If not sure, refer to 33a on the NCVS-1 or ASK.)*
☐ Yes (more than 6 months) – **SKIP** *to 3*
☐ No (6 months or less) – *ASK 2*

2. You said that during the last 6 months – *(Refer to appropriate screen question for description of crime.)* **Did (this/the first) incident happen while you were living here or before you moved to this address?**
605
1 ☐ While living at this address
2 ☐ Before moving to this address

3. You said that during the last 6 months – *(Refer to appropriate screen question for description of Xv*
606 ☐☐ ☐☐☐☐
Month   Year

607 _____ Number of incidents

CHECK ITEM B
608
1 ☐ 1–5 incidents (not a "series") – **SKIP** *to 6*
2 ☐ 6 or more incidents – *Fill Check Item C*

CHECK ITEM C
609
1 ☐ Similar – *Fill Check Item D*
2 ☐ Different (not a "series") – **SKIP** *to 6*

CHECK ITEM D
610
1 ☐ Yes (not a "series") – **SKIP** *to 6*
2 ☐ No (is a "series") – *Reduce entry in screen question if necessary – Read 5*

612
During day
1 ☐ After 6 a.m. – 12 noon
2 ☐ After 12 noon – 3 p.m.
3 ☐ After 3 p.m. – 6 p.m.
4 ☐ Don't know what time of day

At night
5 ☐ After 6 p.m. – 9 p.m.
6 ☐ After 9 p.m. – 12 midnight
7 ☐ After 12 midnight – 6 a.m.
8 ☐ Don't know what time of night

OR
9 ☐ Don't know whether day or night

N C V S 2 I N C I D E N T R E P O R T

| **Figure 2.4** | Highlights From the 2004 NCVS Survey Data |

Highlights

The National Crime Victimization Survey reveals that violent and property crime rates in 2004 did not change from the previous year

Violent victimizations per
1,000 population age 12 or over

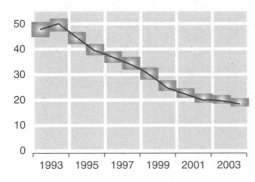

Property victimizations per
1,000 households

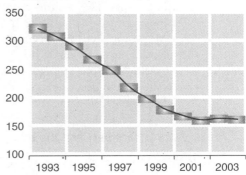

The best estimate and range of estimates

Each vertical bar shows the range within which the true victimization rate was likely to fall. For discussion of displaying estimates, see <http:/www.ojp.usdoj.gov/bjs/pub./pdf./dvctue.pdf>.

- Though the downward trend in crime rates has stabilized, violent and property crime rates in 2004 remain at the lowest levels recorded since the survey's inception in 1973.

- Rates for all major categories of nonlethal crime remained stable from 2003 to 2004.

- The rate of violent crime dropped 9% from the period 2001-02 to the period 2003-04.

- From 1993 to 2004 the rate for crimes of violence was down 57%, from 50 to 21 victimizations per 1,000 persons age 12 or older.

- Reporting of crime to the police increased significantly from 1993 to 2004. Reporting rose from 42% to 50% of violent crimes and from 34% to 39% of property crimes.

- During 2004, 22% of all violent crime incidents were committed by an armed offender; 6%, by an offender with a firearm.

- During 2004 males were about as vulnerable to violence by strangers (50% of the violence against males) as by nonstrangers (48%), while females were most often victimized by nonstrangers (64%).

- Between 2001-02 and 2003-04 violent crime decreased 17% in the West, from 3l to 26 victimizations per 1,000 persons age 12 or older.

- Violent victimizations in urban areas fell 14% from 2001-02 to 2003-04.

- Based on preliminary 2004 data from the FBI, the number of persons murdered in the United States decreased 3.6% between 2003 and 2004.

SOURCE: Catalano, S. (2005). *Criminal victimization, 2004.* Washington, DC: Bureau of Justice Statistics.

◆ Consistent with the above, there are suggestions that just as underreporting plagues *UCR* data, overreporting may plague NCVS data.[16] Whatever the case may be, we find many anomalies when comparing the two sources of data. For instance, the 2005 *UCR* reports 94,635 cases of rape versus the 2005 NCVS's report of 209,880. This presents no problem at first blush—after all, there are many reasons why more than half of all rape victims would not report their victimization. The problem is that only 35.8% (75,137) of the NCVS rape victims said they reported it to the police, and that number is 19,498 *fewer* victims than were "known to the police" that year. The same situation exists for other crimes; that is, substantially more crimes appear in police records than NCVS victims claim to have reported to the police. The discrepancy is easily explained for burglary and motor vehicle theft because the NCVS does not include commercial establishments in their reports. It is more difficult to explain the violent crime discrepancy, however. One explanation for this is that the NCVS does not include victims younger than 12 years of age whereas the *UCR* does, although it is difficult to believe that children younger than 12 account for 15% to 20% of all violent crimes known to the police.

Areas of Agreement Between the UCR and NCVS

Despite these and other problems, it would be surprising if official and survey data did not converge to agreement on at least some significant points. While we will never obtain a firm grip on just how much crime is committed every year, both the *UCR* and NCVS agree on the demographics of crime. They inform us that males, the young, the poor, and African Americans are more likely to be perpetrators and victims of crime than are females, older persons, wealthier persons, and persons of other racial or ethnic categories. Both sources also agree as to the geographic areas and times of the year and month when various crimes are more likely to occur, although in the case of aggravated assault, cities with high rates according to the NCVS tend to have low rates according to the *UCR*.[17]

Comparing arrest rates for violent crimes by gender and race reported in the *UCR* with victims' reports of the gender and race of their assailants in the NCVS, we find a high degree of agreement. Examining the data over a 3-year period, O'Brien[18] found that NCVS victims reported that 91.5% of those who robbed them and 87.7% of their aggravated assault assailants were male, as were 91.2% and 84.3%, respectively, of those arrested for those offenses. Likewise, NCVS victims reported that 64.1% of those who robbed them and 40% of their aggravated assault assailants were African American. These percentages fit the *UCR* arrest statistics for race almost exactly; 62.2% arrested for robbery were African American, as were 40% of those arrested for aggravated assault. Rape figures were less consistent, but O'Brien cautions that because fewer than 100 rapes are reported to NCVS interviewers each year, rape victimization rates are unreliable.

Another area of broad agreement is recent crime trends. The 2005 NCVS[19] reports that victimization rates for violent crimes declined 57% from 1993 to 2004 and that property crime victimization fell 49%. The *UCR* violent crime rate fell from 746 per 100,000 in 1993[20] to 465.5 per 100,000 in 2004[21] for a decrease of 37.6%, and the *UCR* property crime rate fell from 4,737 to 3,517, a decrease of 25.75%. While the decreases reported by the *UCR* and the NCVS differ (as we would expect), they both report very large and very welcome changes in the U.S. crime picture over the period.

Self-Reported Crime Surveys

Self-report surveys of criminal offending are a way criminologists are able to collect data for themselves without having to rely on government sources. These surveys involve asking people to disclose their delinquent and criminal involvement on anonymous questionnaires or face-to-face interviews. Questionnaires used in these surveys typically provide a list of offenses and request respondents to check each offense they recall having committed and how often. Sometimes, they also ask respondents if they have ever been arrested and, if so, how many times.

The first two studies of criminal behavior using self-reports were conducted in the United States in the 1940s.[22,23] With several refinements in methodology, a major study was conducted in the 1950s[24] around which most modern studies have been modeled. Self-reported surveys have relied primarily on college and high school students for participants, although prison inmates and probationers/parolees have also been surveyed.

Several studies have addressed the issue of the accuracy and honesty of self-reported offenses in various ways, and the results have generally been encouraging, at least for uncovering the extent of minor offenses. In one study, respondents were asked to report offenses they had committed; 2 weeks later, they were given back their questionnaires and told that they could amend their answers, knowing they would subsequently undergo a polygraph ("lie detector") test.[25] Very little dishonesty was detected (only 20% of the participants elicited a polygraph response), but it should be noted that few serious offenses were included and that the study involved only 45 students.

Another study compared self-reported crimes by nondelinquent high school students with crimes reported by officially adjudicated delinquents.[26] Half of the respondents in each group were randomly assigned to receive one of two slightly different questionnaires. One required respondents to disclose their name (with assurance that they would not be prosecuted for any of their disclosures), while the other assured respondents that their answers would be completely anonymous. Regardless of which questionnaire they completed, on average, the delinquent group disclosed almost four times as many offenses as the nondelinquents. Other studies have also shown that officially identified delinquents and criminals self-report substantially more offenses on anonymous questionnaires than do members of their nondelinquent peers.[27,28] Had these differences not be found, the validity of the self-report procedure would have been in doubt.

A large number of other studies have been conducted to assess the reliability and validity of self-report data. For example, one study found a high level of agreement between self-reports of the same teenage individuals completed at one time and then 1 month later. Their responses coincided fairly well with reports of overall behavior problems given by their parents and with police and court records.[29] It is noteworthy that this particular study was not completed anonymously. A similar study, which compared self-reported delinquency with ratings of delinquent tendencies of the same adolescents by parents and teachers, found substantial (although far from perfect) agreement among all three measures.[30]

Perhaps the greatest strength of self-report research is that researchers can correlate a variety of characteristics of respondents with their admitted offenses that go beyond the demographics of age, race, and gender. For instance, they can attempt to measure various constructs thought to be associated with offending, such as impulsiveness, empathy, and sensation seeking, as well as their peer associations and their attitudes. Exceptionally ambitious studies carried out over decades in concert with medical and biological scientists, such as the Dunedin study[31] that we shall be referring to often in this book, are able to gather a wealth of health, genetic, neurological, and physiological data as well.

The evidence reviewed indicates that self-report crime measures provide largely accurate information about some forms of antisocial offending and reveal that almost everyone has committed some sort of illegal act sometime in their lives. However, there are a number of reasons why self-report crime surveys also provide a distorted picture of criminal involvement, some of which are listed below.

Problems With Self-Reported Crime Surveys

◆ Most self-reported studies survey "convenience" samples of high school and college students, populations in which we don't expect to find many seriously criminally involved individuals. Most self-report studies thus eliminate the very people we are most interested in gathering information about. One strength of the self-report method, however, is that it appears to capture the extent of illegal drug usage among high school and college students, something that neither the UCR nor the NCVS attempts to do.

◆ Self-report studies typically uncover only fairly trivial antisocial acts such as fighting, stealing items worth less than $5, smoking, and truancy. Almost everyone has committed one or more of these acts. These are hardly acts that help us to understand the nature of serious crime. A connected problem is that some researchers lump respondents who report one delinquent act together with adjudicated delinquents who break the law in many different ways many different times. This practice has been used to conclude that there is no relationship, for instance, between social class and delinquency,[32] a conclusion that has been called "extraordinarily senseless."[33]

◆ Even though most people are forthright in revealing their peccadilloes, most people do not have a serious criminal history, and those who do have a distinct tendency to underreport their crimes.[34] As the number of crimes people commit increases, so does the proportion of offenses they withhold reporting.[35,36] For instance, researchers have asked respondents with known arrest histories whether they have ever been arrested and found that 20% to 40% replied negatively,[37,38] with those arrested for the most serious offenses having the greatest probability of denial.[39]

◆ There is also evidence that reporting honestly varies across race/ethnicity and gender. Specifically, males tend to report their antisocial activities less honestly than females and African Americans less honestly than other racial/ethnic groups.[40] For instance, Cernkovich, Giordano, and Rudolph[41] state that "Black males underreport involvement in every level of delinquency, especially at the high level of the continuum." This evidence renders any statements about gender or racial differences regarding antisocial behavior that are based on self-report data highly suspect. When it comes to relying on self-report data to assess the nature and extent of serious crime, it is well to remember the gambler's dictum: "Never trust an animal that talks."

⊠ The Dark Figure of Crime Revisited

Recall that we defined the dark figure of crime as that portion of the total crimes committed each year that never comes to light. Figure 2.5 presents three diagrams that show the different dark

Figure 2.5	Differing Proportions of Reported/Unreported Crimes for the Three Major Measures of Victimful Crimes

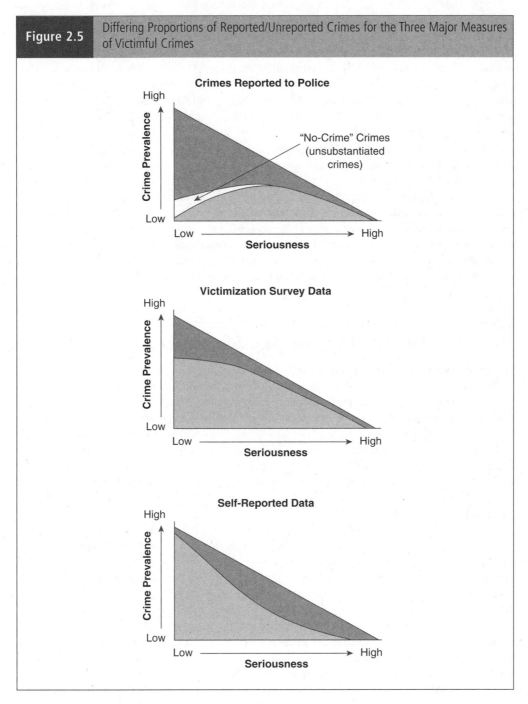

NOTE: Light shading = proportion of crimes reported. Dark shading = proportion not reported.

figures for the three major measures of criminal behavior. (The dark figures are represented by the dark shading in each diagram.)

Each diagram shows the degree to which crimes of varying degrees of seriousness are most likely to be detected by each measure ("victimless" crimes excluded). In the top diagram displaying *UCR* data, you can see that very few trivial offenses are reported in official statistics, and most of those that are will be dismissed as unfounded by the police. For official statistics, then, the dark figures are highly concentrated at the nonserious end of the crime seriousness spectrum.

The middle diagram reveals that the dark figures for victimization data are primarily concentrated in the nonserious end of the spectrum also, although to a lesser degree than in the case of official data. The failure of victimization data to pick up these minor offenses is largely due to survey participants not remembering all incidents of victimization.

In the bottom diagram, we see that most of the dark figures in the case of self-reports are concentrated in the upper end of the seriousness continuum rather than the lower end. This is partly due to (a) nearly all self-report surveys excluding most persistent serious offenders from their subject pools, and (b) many of the most serious offenders who remain in self-report subject pools do not reveal the full extent of their criminal histories.

What Can We Conclude About the Three Main Measures of Crime in the United States?

All three main measures of crime in the United States are imperfect measures, as Figure 2.5 demonstrates, but they are all that we have. Which one of them is "best" depends on what we want to know. Despite numerous criticisms lodged against official *UCR* data, they are still probably the best single source of data for studying serious crimes—indeed, they are the only source for studying murder rates and circumstances. For studying less serious (and yet much more common) types of crimes, either victimization or self-report survey data are best. If the interest is in drug offenses, self-reports are the preferable data source. All three measures offer a narrow window through which we may view the extent of crime in the United States, but if we stand back a bit and take in the view from all three windows simultaneously, we will get a much better picture.

Because all three data sources converge on some very important points about crime, they enable us to proceed with at least some confidence in our endeavors to understand the whys of crime. The basic demographics of crime constitute the raw social facts that are the building blocks of our criminological theories. If street crime is concentrated among the lower socioeconomic classes and in the poorest neighborhoods, we can begin to ask such things as whether poverty "causes" crime or if some other variable causes both. Is social disorganization in a neighborhood independent of the people living in it or completely dependent on the people living in it? Why do females always and everywhere commit far less crime (particularly the most serious crimes) than males? If African Americans commit so much more crime than other racial or ethnic groups, what is unique about the history and culture of Black Americans that might explain why? If people "age in" and "age out" of crime, what is going on socially, psychologically, and biologically during those periods that explain this onset and desistance of offending? These and many dozens of other "why" questions can be asked once we have a firm grip on the raw facts.

The Crime Problem or the Criminality Problem?

We have taken note of the fact that both the *UCR* and the NCVS report that the crime rate in the United States has taken a significant plunge since about 1993. Criminologist Elliot Currie notes that this decline has led to a haughty "triumphalism" about crime—that we in the United States have the crime problem under control. Currie punctures this smug attitude by pointing out that the decline that began in the early 1990s represented not "a sudden fall from a plateau" but rather "a falling-off from an extraordinary peak," and what the drop really means is that "we have hidden our crime problem, not beaten it."[42]

Currie contends that we should be more concerned with our criminality problem than with our crime problem. By *criminality problem,* Currie means the problem of the nation's production of persons willing to commit crimes both inside and outside our prisons, whereas the *crime problem* represents criminal activity by those outside prison walls. We had about 2 million individuals behind prison walls in 2003,[43] and so what we have really done is shift the total pool of criminals from one place (the streets) to another (jail or prison) and claimed that we have "fixed" the crime problem. Currie likens this claim to public health people measuring the extent of illness in society while excluding from the count all those people in hospital. We would not claim to have won the war on disease simply because we shunt more and more people into hospital, would we? Quite the contrary, says Currie: What we need is "a measure of the amount of criminality by the offenders currently on the streets combined with the amount of latent criminality represented by offenders currently incarcerated."[44]

Currie uses the crime of robbery to illustrate his point. He says that in 1995, there were 135,000 inmates in state and federal institutions whose most serious crime was robbery, with each robber committing, on average, 5 robberies per year. If this is the case, had these robbers been on the street, they would have been responsible for an additional 135,000 × 5 or 675,000 robberies on top of the 580,000 actual robberies reported to the police in 1995. Thus, Currie's criminality index for robbery in 1995 was 1,250,000. Computing the criminality index rather than the crime index presents us with a "robbery rate" more than twice as large. We could compute the criminality index to get the actual rate + latent rate for each of the other Part I crimes.

Currie concludes by reiterating that we haven't beaten the crime problem; we have merely shifted it out of sight and mostly out of mind. In other words, our society still produces an unacceptably high number of criminals, and the fact that we have more of them behind bars than we did 20 years ago doesn't change anything. Yes, we have taken more of them off the streets, and thus the streets are safer, but we still have an unacceptably high criminality problem. Our society should concentrate, says Currie, on doing something about the criminality problem, and the crime problem would take care of itself.

⌧ The Financial Cost of Crime

Criminal activity exacts a huge financial and emotional price in the United States. The emotional pain and suffering borne by crime victims is obviously impossible to quantify, but a number of efforts have been made to estimate the annual financial costs. Estimates will vary according to what is included or excluded in the study. Most estimates focus on the costs of running the criminal justice system, which includes the salaries and benefits of personnel, and the maintenance costs of buildings (offices, jails, prisons, stations) and equipment (vehicles, weapons, uniforms, etc.). Researchers will add to this the costs associated with each crime by multiplying the average cost per incident by the number of incidents, as reported in the *UCR*. All of these costs combined are considered the *direct* costs of crime. To the extent that the *UCR* underreports crimes, the cost estimate will be low unless researchers figure underreporting into their estimates.

The *indirect* costs of crime must also be considered as part of the burden of crime. Cataloging the various components of indirect cost is an enormous undertaking. These include all manner of surveillance and security devices, protective devices (guns, alarms, security guards) and insurance costs, medical services, and the productivity and taxes lost of incarcerated individuals. Economist David Anderson[45] lists a cascade of direct and indirect costs of crime and concludes that the aggregate burden of crime in the United States (in 1997 dollars) is about $1,102 *billion*, or a per capita burden of $4,118. Crime thus places a huge financial burden on everyone's shoulders, as well as a deep psychological burden on its specific victims.

▧ Interpreting Crime Trends

It is much easier to note that crime increased or decreased by *x*% over a specified time period than it is to explain why it did so. Despite the accumulation of tons of factual data, it is difficult to arrive at a sturdy conclusion that fits them together to everyone's satisfaction. Facts only describe events; they do not explain them. Any explanation for major fluctuations in crime rates requires that we have an understanding of macro-level processes—that is, the historical, social, political, economic, and demographic processes unfolding around the same time that increases or decreases in crime are recorded and how they interact. The effects of any particular process on crime may be immediate, such as a series of riots and general mayhem following some perceived injustice, or it may only be felt a decade or so down the road. Whatever process or alleged cause we examine, you should keep in the forefront of your mind that just as there is no single cause of crime or criminality, there is no single cause that explains crime trends.

Examine the total *UCR* violent and property crime rates per 100,000 for 1963, 1993, and 2003 and ask yourself whether crime has gone up or down.

Year	Violent	Property
1963	168.2	2,021.1
1993	746.8	4,737.7
2003	475.0	3,588.4

If we compare 1993 with 2003, we conclude that crime dropped significantly, but if we take 1963 as our beginning year and compare it with 2003, we would conclude that crime has gone up significantly. Whether crime has "gone up" or "gone down" thus depends on where we choose to look. Interpretations of crime trends should be read with caution because the author may have chosen a beginning and ending year to support his or her favored explanation. With that caveat in mind, we briefly examine possible reasons for crime rate fluctuations since the 1960s.

Poverty President Lyndon Johnson's "War on Poverty" beginning in the 1960s was conceived as something that would remove, or at least greatly reduce, what many considered to be a major cause of crime. The reasoning was that since crime is perceived as an activity engaged in mostly by the poor, fewer poor people would mean fewer crimes. The poverty rate for families in low crime year 1963 was 15.9; in high crime year 1993, it was 12.3,[46] but the expected bonus of crime reduction did not materialize during the interim. As billions of tax dollars were spent on antipoverty programs during those three decades, violent and property crime rates soared. Specifically, as the poverty rate in the United States *decreased* by about 29%, we saw an overall *increase* in the crime rate of approximately 350%. On the other hand, the family poverty rate decreased 23% from 1993 to 2003,[47] a decrease that was accompanied by an approximate 60% decrease in overall crime rates. We thus have evidence that changes in the poverty rate can be accompanied by either an increase or decrease in the crime rate, depending on what years we begin and end with and what other processes are operating at the same time. For instance, much of the reduction in poverty achieved from 1963 to 1993 was the result of government welfare, but after the Welfare Reform Act of 1996, the decline in poverty was more a function of a robust economy.

Affluence Perhaps affluence (or at least, relative affluence) is more a "cause" of increasing crime rates than poverty. But how can affluence "cause" crime? The effects of affluence vary with social context and can have both good and bad consequences. It's not that the average affluent person commits more crimes than the average poor person; rather, a more general level of affluence makes more things available to steal, rob, loot, and kill for. In addition, convenience stores and ATM machines competing for their share of the general affluence stay open all hours of the day and night, thus making them convenient for robbers and thieves as well as for shoppers. Affluence may also "cause" crime by flaunting itself in the faces of the poor, who naturally would like their share. Some "have-nots" want their share now, and by means fair or foul. An affluent society offers many targets for such people to aim at. International data show that affluent societies have the highest property crime rates and that poor countries usually report the highest rates of violent crime.[48] Increased property crime may be the price we have to pay for increased affluence, especially if affluence is not evenly distributed.

What about the large decrease in property crimes from 1993 to 2003, which was a period of increasing affluence? One of the benefits of affluence is that that many of the high-price items previously worth stealing, such as computers, cell phones, VCR and DVD players, and digital cameras, become so cheap and commonplace that few people resort to stealing them (not worth the bother). Also, being aware of the crime problem, affluent people are able to buy security devices for their homes and vehicles that deter would-be thieves. Thus, a factor that may contribute to high crime rates in one period may contribute to their decline in another.

Moral Breakdown and Societal Well-Being Many people believe that a breakdown in the general moral order (the moral consensus) that occurred in the tumultuous 1960s may be the explanation for the rise in crime through the early 1990s. The Vietnam War protests, the civil rights movement, the gay rights movement, and the rise of feminism all challenged traditional notions of right and wrong. Riding the coattails of these movements came the youth counterculture complete with hippies, drugs, free sex, and what Fox and Levin[49] have called the "War Against Guilt."

These occurrences produced a crisis in political legitimacy, which tended to spill over to a general disrespect for all kinds of moral values, including those that say we should not steal, kill, and otherwise act badly toward one another.[50] We will see in Chapter 4 that many criminologists have noted that high crime rates almost inevitably accompany rapid social changes such as those experienced during the latter half of the 1960s and early 1970s. The essence of this argument is that when norms and values break down in response to the stresses and confusion of rapid social change, social bonds (ties to families, schools, work, religion, and so on) that serve to constrain antisocial behavior are fractured, and people are freed to satisfy their avaricious appetites by any means, fair or foul.

The Family As the basic institution of any society, problems with the family can be expected to affect other areas of society. The divorce rate in the United States increased by approximately 101% from 1960 to 1993.[51] Divorce typically means a lower standard of living for women and children and a lower level of supervision of children's behavior, so it is possible that the increasing divorce rate (perhaps itself a consequence of the breakdown of the moral consensus) had a lot to do with the increasing crime rate during that period. During the period of rapid decline in the crime rate from 1993 to 2002, the divorce rate declined by 21%.[52]

One of the most contentious reasons offered for the decline in the crime rate beginning in the early 1990s is the legalization of abortion. Economists John Donohue and Steven Levitt[53] published a statistically elegant paper in which they claim that legalized abortion accounts for as much as 50% of the decline in crime from the early 1990s to the early 2000s. The essence of their argument is that were it not for abortion, hundreds of thousands of unwanted children would have been born, and that this unwantedness is a major predictor of criminality. Such children are likely to grow up in poor single-parent homes and to be at significant risk for abuse and neglect. Abortion also reduces the size of the cohort, so that there would be fewer young males in the high-crime ages to mug you when they grow up.

This argument has intuitive appeal (fewer children born into criminogenic environments obviously means less crime down the road), but it is also possible that legalized abortion may have actually increased the number of unwanted children because as abortion rates were going up, so was the rate of births to unmarried mothers.[54] This may have occurred because the availability of abortion granted females license to be freer to engage in unprotected sex. We cannot know this, of course, but we mention it to warn you that just because two trends (crime, abortion, and illegitimacy rates) vary together, it does not mean that one is the cause of the other. This is equally true for all the other possible explanations for fluctuating crime trends.

Deindustrialization Perhaps the deindustrialization of the United States has something to do with increasing crime rates. From 1979 to 1993, the United States lost more than 4.5 million well-paying manufacturing jobs to overseas competition, to company downsizing, or to automation.[55] In their place have been created a large number of dead-end service jobs offering low salaries and few benefits or career prospects. The workplace transition has affected minorities and Whites of low socioeconomic backgrounds most severely, resulting in a lot of frustration and the hardening of poverty. Such a scenario combines both the "poverty" and "moral breakdown" explanations by pointing to a very important socioeconomic transition (deindustrialization) that could lead to both.

Deindustrialization certainly has intuitive appeal as an explanation for increasing crime rates, but the biggest jump in crime (from 1965 to 1975) occurred *before* this process had barely begun. The specter of deindustrialization was hardly a whisper until after the OPEC oil embargo of 1973 and probably not a part of the awareness of most Americans until the Reagan era. Oddly enough, crime rates were dropping slightly as the effects of deindustrialization were beginning to make themselves known among working-class Americans. From the peak in 1980, each year through 1985 showed slight decreases from the previous year in some index offenses. The industrial sector of the United States is still hemorrhaging jobs at a remarkable rate, thus depriving less educated Americans of well-paying jobs, but the crime rate has been declining steadily even as the bleeding continues.

The Prison Boom Advocates of "get tough" policies credit the increased numbers of offenders being imprisoned for the decrease in crime.[56] The United States has the highest incarceration rate in the world and it is now about five times what it was in 1972.[57] The "get tough" explanation has intuitive appeal: An incarcerated felon is no longer free to commit crimes, and the more criminals we catch and incapacitate, the fewer crimes we will have. In addition, other offenders and potential offenders will perceive that the probability of going to prison is getting much greater than it used to be and be deterred from criminal activity. It would be a great surprise if increased incarceration rates did not reduce crime (see "Focus On . . ." next page). Two studies came to the separate conclusion that the rise in incarceration accounts for about 25% of the decline in violent crime over the period in question.[58,59]

On the other hand, there are those who believe that the increasing rate of incarceration may have provided only a temporary reprieve and that it may actually lead to increased crime rates in the future when angry and unemployable prisoners are released. There are also those who feel that increasing incarceration may increase crime because imprisoning men supposedly weakens families and communities and reduces supervision of children.[60] However, a Bureau of Justice Statistics report[61] indicated that 48% of imprisoned parents were never married and 28% of those who were ever married were divorced or separated, and very few lived with their children prior to imprisonment. Moreover, most parents had been convicted of violent or drug crimes, and 85% had drug problems. This makes it difficult to see how families and communities would suffer by the absence of such people.[62,63]

The "Baby Boomer Bubble" The explanation for fluctuations in crime rates may be something as simple as the changing age composition of the population. Beginning with the return of the troops at the end of World War II and continuing for about two decades afterwards, an unusually high number of children were born in the United States, creating what sociologists have called the "baby boom." We know that young persons commit a disproportionate share of crime, so it may have been inevitable when the first cohort of baby boomers became teenagers (in the early 1960s) that we would have a rather dramatic increase in crime. This explanation also has flaws, the most serious being the fact that the crime bust of the 1990s was accompanied by an increase rather than a decrease in age cohorts in the teens and early 20s, although it was very minimal.[64]

Drug Market Stability Just as the prohibition of the manufacture and sale of alcohol in the 1920s and 1930s spawned large increases in violent crime as various gangs vied for control of the alcohol market, the illicit drug market, especially the market for crack cocaine, spawned huge increases in violent crime in the 1980s. As the strong drove out the weak, gang battles over territory more or less ceased and the drug market stabilized. We have also witnessed a large-scale reduction in the crack cocaine market as law enforcement made this market a special target and as younger individuals noted the ravages of the drug and declined to use it. We will discuss this at greater length in Chapter 12.

FOCUS ON . . .

Is the United States Hard or Soft on Crime?

We have seen that some criminologists have attributed the drop in crime in the United States to the increasing use of incarceration. Despite this, we still hear from conservatives and from the public in general that the U.S. criminal justice system is soft on crime. Look at the incarceration rates per 100,000 for selected countries in 2004 shown in Figure 2.6 (facing page) and see if you agree.[65] Only Russia comes close to the U.S. rate, and the closest any modern Western nation comes to the U.S. rate is England and Wales, with a rate five times lower. These rates are calculated based on 100,000 *citizens,* which is not the same as the rate per 100,000 *criminals,* so we cannot assess the question on these figures alone. The U.S. homicide rate is about five times that of England and Wales, which matches our five times greater incarceration rate, but when it comes to property crimes, Americans are about in the middle of the pack of nations when it comes to the probability of being victimized (less than in England and Wales). On the other hand, burglars serve an average of 16.2 months in prison in the United States, compared with 6.8 months in Britain and 5.3 months in Canada.[66] So, is the United States softer or harder on criminals? Does it depend on which countries we compare ourselves with?

SUMMARY

Crime and criminal behavior are measured in several ways in the United States. The oldest measure is the FBI's *Uniform Crime Reports* (*UCR*), which is a tabulation of all crimes reported to the police in most of the jurisdictions in the United States in the previous year. The *UCR* is divided into two parts: Part I records the eight Index Crimes (murder, rape, robbery, aggravated assault, burglary, larceny-theft, motor vehicle theft, and arson), and Part II records arrests made for all other crimes. *UCR* data seriously underestimate the extent of crime because they only record reported crimes, ignore drug offenses, and only report the most serious crime in a multiple-crime event. The problems with the *UCR* led to the implementation of the National Incident-Based Reporting System (NIBRS), although the system hasn't lived up to its promise.

The second major source of crime statistics is the National Crime Victimization Survey (NCVS). This survey consists of many thousands of interviews of householders throughout the United States asking them about their crime victimization (if any) during the previous 6 months. The NCVS also has problems because it leaves out crimes against commercial establishments and relies exclusively on the memory and the word of interviewees.

The third source of crime data is self-report data collected by criminologists themselves. The advantage of self-report data is that they are derived "from the horse's mouth," and

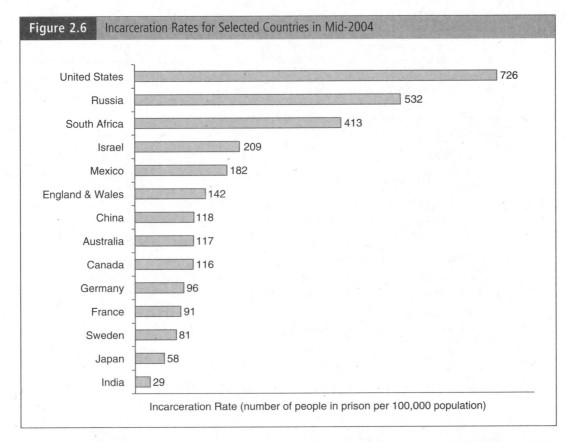

Figure 2.6 Incarceration Rates for Selected Countries in Mid-2004

Incarceration Rate (number of people in prison per 100,000 population)

SOURCE: Mauer, M. (2005). *Comparative international rates of incarceration: An examination of causes and trends.* Washington, DC: The Sentencing Project. Reproduced with permission.

typically the questionnaires used ask about "victimless" offenses not covered in either the *UCR* or NCVS. The major problems with self-report data are that they do not capture serious criminal behavior and are subject to dishonesty in the form of underreporting, especially underreporting by those most seriously involved in criminal activity.

The *UCR*, NCVS, and self-report data come to different conclusions on a variety of points, but they agree about where, when, and among whom crime is most prevalent, as well as the fact that crime has fallen dramatically in the United States over the past decade. Taken together, then, we have a fairly reliable picture of the correlates of crime from which to develop our theories about explanatory mechanisms.

Interpreting crime trends is a messy business fraught with danger. A number of possible reasons for why crime rates climbed precipitously from 1963 to 1993 and then dropped almost as dramatically from 1993 to 2003 were offered. Each seemed plausible until an alternative explanation was offered. We can only interpret trends when we have complete information about everything relevant that was happening in society during the period in question, and then only with extreme caution.

On Your Own

Log on to the web-based student study site at http://www.sagepub.com/criminologystudy for more information about the vignettes and materials presented in this chapter, suggestions for activities, study aids such as review quizzes, and research recommendations including journal article links and questions related to this chapter.

EXERCISES AND DISCUSSION QUESTIONS

1. Consult your college library and browse one or more government documents (such as the *Sourcebook of Criminal Justice Statistics*, published annually by the U.S. Department of Justice) for information on some crime-related topic that interests you. Examples might be "United States crime trends" or "How age is related to crime rates." Then write a one- to two-page summary of what the document indicates about the topic.

2. Do you think it is wise to make "authoritative" statements or formulate theories of criminal behavior, especially serious criminal behavior, based on self-report data?

3. Can you think of other problems possibly associated with asking people about their delinquent or criminal behavior or their victimization other than discussed in the chapter?

4. If you were the American "crime czar," what would you do to get the various law enforcement agencies to fully implement NIBRS—and no, you just can't order them to do so.

5. What does Elliot Currie mean when he talks about criminality rather that the crime problem? What can we do about the criminality problem?

6. Defend you favored reason for why the crime rate went up so precipitously from 1963 to 1993 against an alternative reason.

KEY WORDS

Aggravated assault	Hierarchy rule	Part I offenses (or Index
Arson	Larceny-theft	Crimes)
Burglary	Motor vehicle theft	Part II offenses
Cleared offenses	Murder	Robbery
Crime rate	National Crime	Self-report surveys
Dark figure of crime	Victimization Survey	*Uniform Crime Reports*
Forcible rape	National Incident-Based	
	Reporting System	

REFERENCES

1. Nettler, G. (1984). *Explaining crime* (3rd ed.). New York: McGraw-Hill. (Quote on p. 39)
2. Federal Bureau of Investigation. (2005). *Crime in the United States, 2004: Uniform Crime Reports.* Washington, DC: Government Printing Office.
3. Kappeler, V., & Potter, G. (2005). *The mythology of crime and criminal justice* (4th ed.). Long Grove, IL: Waveland.
4. Catalano, S. (2005). *Criminal victimization, 2004.* Washington, DC: Bureau of Justice Statistics.
5. Robinson, M. (2005). *Justice blind: Ideals and realities of American criminal justice.* Upper Saddle River, NJ: Prentice Hall.
6. National Center for Policy Analysis. (1998, August 17). *Does punishment deter?* (NCPA Policy Backgrounder 148). Washington, DC: Author.

7. Robinson (2005).

8. Finkelhor, D., & Ormrod, R. (2004, June). Prostitution of juveniles: Patterns from NIBRS. *Juvenile Justice Bulletin.*

9. Dunworth, T. (2001). Criminal justice and the IT revolution. *Federal Probation.* Retrieved from http://search.epnet.com/citation.asp?tb=1

10. Blumstein, A., Cohen, J., & Rosenfeld, R. (1991). Trend and deviation in crime rates: A comparison of UCR and NCS data for burglary and robbery. *Criminology, 29,* 237–263.

11. Clinard, M. (1978). Comparative crime victimization surveys: Some problems and results. *International Journal of Criminology and Penology, 6,* 221–231.

12. Wolfgang, M., Figlio, R., & Sellin, T. (1972). *Delinquency in a birth cohort.* Chicago: University of Chicago Press.

13. Ennis, P. (1967). *Criminal victimization in the United States: A report of a national survey.* Washington, DC: Government Printing Office.

14. Catalano (2005).

15. Lonsway, K., & Fitzgerald, L. (1994). Rape myths. *Psychology of Women Quarterly, 18,* 133–164.

16. O'Brien, R. (2001). Crime facts: Victim and offender data. In J. Sheley (Ed.), *Criminology: A contemporary handbook* (pp. 59–83). Belmont: CA, Wadsworth.

17. O'Brien (2001).

18. O'Brien (2001).

19. Catalano (2005).

20. Federal Bureau of Investigation (FBI). (1994). *Crime in the United States, 1993: Uniform Crime Reports.* Washington, DC: Government Printing Office.

21. FBI (2005).

22. Porterfield, A. (1946). *Youth in trouble.* Fort Worth, TX: Leo Potishman Foundation.

23. Wallerstein, J., & Wyle, C. (1947). Our law-abiding lawbreakers. *Federal Probation, 25,* 107–112.

24. Short, J., & Nye, F. (1957). Reported behavior as a criterion of deviant behavior. *Social Problems, 5,* 207–213.

25. Clark, J., & Tifft, L. (1966). Polygraph and interview validations of self-reported deviant behavior. *American Sociological Review, 31,* 516–523.

26. Kulik, J., Stein, K., & Sarbin, T. (1968). Disclosure of delinquent behavior under conditions of anonymity and nonanonymity. *Journal of Consulting and Clinical Psychology, 32,* 506–509.

27. Cernkovich, S., Giordano, P., & Pugh, M. (1985). Chronic offenders: The missing cases in self-report delinquency research. *Journal of Criminal Law and Criminology, 76,* 705–732.

28. Mak, A. (1993). Self-report delinquency scale for Australian adolescents. *Australian Journal of Psychology, 45,* 75–79.

29. Williams, S., & McGee, R. (1994). Reading attainment and juvenile delinquency. *Journal of Child Psychology and Psychiatry, 35,* 441–459.

30. Caspi, A., Moffitt, T., Silva, P., Stouthamer-Loeber, M., Krueger, R., & Schmutte, P. (1994). Are some people crime-prone? Replications of the personality-crime relationship across countries, genders, races, and methods. *Criminology, 32,* 163–194.

31. Moffitt, T. (1993). Adolescent-limited and life-course-persistent antisocial behavior: A developmental taxonomy. *Psychological Review, 100,* 674–701.

32. Tittle, C., Villemez, W., & Smith, D. (1978). The myth of social class and criminality: Evidence of the relationship between social class and criminal behavior. *American Sociological Review, 49,* 398–411.

33. Harris, A., & Shaw, J. (2001). Looking for patterns: Race, class, and crime. In J. Sheley (Ed.), *Criminology: A contemporary handbook* (pp. 129–163). Belmont, CA: Wadsworth.

34. Hindelang, M., Hirschi, T., & Weis, J. (1981). *Measuring delinquency.* Beverly Hills, CA: Sage.

35. Hirschi, T., Hindelang, M., & Weis, J. (1980). The status of self-report measures. In M. Klien & K. Teilman (Eds.), *Handbook of criminal justice evaluation* (pp. 473–488). Beverly Hills, CA: Sage.

36. Cernkovich et al. (1985).

37. Hindelang et al. (1981).

38. Petersilia, J. (1980). Criminal career research: A review of recent evidence. In N. Morris & M. Tonry (Eds.), *Crime and research* (Vol. 2, pp. 321–379). Chicago: University of Chicago Press.

39. Farrington, D. (1982). Longitudinal analyses of criminal violence. In M. Wolfgang & N. Weiner (Eds.), *Criminal violence.* Beverly Hills, CA: Sage.

40. Kim, J., Fendrich, M., & Wislar, J. (2000). The validity of juvenile arrestees' drug use reporting: A gender comparison. *Journal of Research in Crime and Delinquency, 37,* 429–432.

41. Cernkovich, S., Giordano, P., & Rudolph, J. (2000). Race, crime, and the American dream. *Journal of Research in Crime and Delinquency, 37,* 131–170. (Quote on p. 143)

42. Currie, E. (1999). Reflections on crime and criminology at the millennium. *Western Criminology Review, 2.* Retrieved from http://wcr.somoma.edu/v2n1/currie.html. (Quote on pp. 5–6)

43. Harrison, P., & Beck, A. (2005, April). Prison and jail inmates at midyear 2004. *Bureau of Justice Statistics Bulletin.*

44. Currie (1999, p. 7).

45. Anderson, D. (1999). The aggregate burden of crime. *Journal of Law and Economics, 42,* 611–642.

46. U.S. Census Bureau. (2004). *Statistical abstracts of the United States.* Retrieved from http://:www.census.gov/prod/2004pubs/03statab/vitstat.pdf

47. U.S. Census Bureau. (2005). *Housing and household economic statistics division.* Retrieved from http//:www.census.gov/hhes/www/poverty/hispov/hispov13.html

48. LaFree, G., & Drass, K. (2002). Counting crime booms among nations: Evidence for homicide victimization rates, 1956 to 1998. *Criminology, 40,* 769–799.

49. Fox, J., & Levin, J. (2005). *Extreme killing: Understanding serial and mass murder.* Thousand Oaks, CA: Sage.

50. LaFree, G. (1999). Declining violent crime rate in the 1990s: Predicting crime booms and busts. *Annual Review of Sociology, 25,* 145–168.

51. U.S. Census Bureau (2004).

52. U.S. Census Bureau (2004).

53. Donohue, J., & Levitt, S. (2001). The impact of legalized abortion on crime. *Quarterly of Economics, 116,* 379–420.

54. Lykken, D. (1995). *The antisocial personalities.* Hillsdale, NJ: Lawrence Erlbaum.

55. Barnet, R. (1994). The end of jobs. In K. Finsterbusch (Ed.), *Sociology 94/95* (pp. 161–166). Guilford, CT: Dushkin.

56. Methvin, E. (1995). Imprisoning more criminals will prevent crime. In D. Bender & B. Leone (Eds.), *Crime and criminals: Opposing viewpoints* (pp. 121–128). San Diego: Greenhaven.

57. Mauer, M. (2005). *Comparative international rates of incarceration: An examination of causes and trends.* Washington, DC: The Sentencing Project.

58. Spelman, W. (2000). The limited importance of prison expansion. In A. Blumstein & J. Wallman (Eds.), *The crime drop in America* (pp. 97–129). Cambridge, UK: Cambridge University Press.

59. Rosenfeld, R. (2000). Patterns in adult homicide. In A. Blumstein & J. Wallman (Eds.), *The crime drop in America* (pp. 130–163). Cambridge, UK: Cambridge University Press.

60. DeFina, R., & Arvanites, T. (2002). The weak effect of imprisonment on crime: 1971–1998. *Social Science Quarterly, 83,* 635–653.

61. Mumola, C. (2000). *Incarcerated parents and their children.* Washington, DC: Bureau of Justice Statistics.

62. Jafee, S., Moffitt, T., Caspi, A., & Taylor, A. (2003). Life with (or without) father: The benefits of living with two biological parents depend on the father's antisocial behavior. *Child Development, 74,* 109–126.

63. Rodney, E., & Mupier, R. (1999). Behavioral differences between African American male adolescents with biological fathers and those without biological fathers in the home. *Journal of Black Studies, 30,* 45–61.

64. LaFree (1999).

65. Mauer (2005).

66. Mauer (2005).

THE EARLY SCHOOLS OF CRIMINOLOGY AND MODERN COUNTERPARTS

"L isa" is a 30-year-old mother of three children ages 8, 6, and 4. Her husband left her a year ago for another woman, and his present whereabouts are unknown. Because Lisa only has a 10th-grade education and cannot afford child care costs, she was forced onto the welfare rolls. As Christmas approached, she realized that she had no money to buy her children any presents, so she took a temporary Christmas job at the local Wal-Mart store, where she earned $1,200 over a 2-month period. Lisa did not report this income to the welfare authorities as required by law; a welfare audit uncovered her crime. The terrified and deeply ashamed Lisa pled guilty to grand theft, which carries a possible sentence of 2 years in prison, and was referred to the probation department for a presentence investigation report (PSI) and sentencing recommendation.

"Chris" is a 30-something male with a record of thefts and other crimes committed since he was 10 years old. Chris also pled guilty before the same judge on the same day and was likewise referred for a PSI. Chris had stolen money and parts totaling $1,200 from an auto parts store during one of his very brief periods of employment.

These two cases point to a perennial debate among criminal justice scholars, with one side favoring the so-called classical school position and the other favoring the positivist position. Both positions are ultimately about the role of punishment in deterring crime, but the classical position maintains that punishment should fit the crime and nothing else—that is, all people convicted of similar crimes should receive the same punishment regardless of any differences they may have. Both Lisa and Chris freely chose to commit the crime, and the fact that Chris has a record and Lisa does not is irrelevant. The positivist position is that punishment should fit the offender and be *appropriate to rehabilitation. Lisa and Chris's crimes were motivated by very different considerations, they are very different people morally, and blindly applying similar punishments to similar crimes without considering the possible consequences is pure folly.*

Think about these two cases as you read about classical and positivist thought about human nature, punishment, and deterrence in this chapter.

⊠ The Classical Scholars

Modern criminology is the product of two main schools of thought: the classical school originating in the 18th century and the positivist school originating in the 19th century. The early contributors to criminology were amateur dabblers—a mixed bag of philosophers, physicians, lawyers, judges, theologians, and anthropologists whose primary interests lay in penology (prison management and the treatment of offenders) rather than criminology per se. The study of crime and criminal behavior arose as a secondary consequence of the interest shown by these pioneers in penal reform.

You may ask yourselves why a discussion of the "old masters" is necessary; after all, you don't see such discussions in physics, chemistry, or biology texts. The reason for this is that unlike those disciplines, modern criminology is still confronted by the same problems that confronted its pioneers, particularly the problem of explaining crime and criminality. Thus, their works are of more than passing interest to us.

Preclassical Notions of Crime and Criminals

Prior to the 18th century, explanations of a wide variety of phenomena tended to be of a religious or spiritual nature. Good fortune and disaster alike were frequently attributed to benevolent or malevolent supernatural forces. A simple extension of this worldview was to define crime as the result of demonic possession or the evil abuse of free will. Because of the legacy of Original Sin, all human beings were considered born sinners, and so it made no sense to ask questions like, "What causes crime?" The gift of the grace of God kept men and women on the straight and narrow, and if they deviated from this line, it was because God was no longer their compass.

Demonological explanations of crime began to wane in the 18th century with the beginning of a period that cultural historians call the **Enlightenment,** which was essentially a major shift in the way people began to view the world and their place in it. This new worldview questioned traditional religious and political values, such as absolute monarchy and demonic possession. In their place they substituted humanism, rationalism, and a belief in the primacy of the natural over the supernatural world. Enlightenment thinkers believed in the dignity and worth of the individual, a view that would eventually find expression in the law and in the treatment of criminal offenders.

The Classical School

Cesare Beccaria and Reform

The father of classical criminology is generally considered to be the Italian nobleman and professor of law, Cesare Bonesana, Marchese di Beccaria. In 1764, Beccaria published what was to become the manifesto for the reform of judicial and penal systems throughout Europe—*Dei Delitti e della Pene* (*On Crimes and Punishment*).[1] The widespread acclaim of this book among intellectuals eventually led to its acceptance by the legal and political authorities. The book is an impassioned plea to humanize and rationalize the law and to make punishment more just and reasonable.

Beccaria's humanist philosophy stood in sharp contrast to the treatment of criminals at the time, which included torture for all manner of offenses, for the extraction of statements from suspects, and even at times from witnesses. Judges of the period often levied vicious and arbitrary penalties against convicted criminals, with the harshness of punishment often based on the respective social positions of offenders and victims and on a judge's penchant for mercy or cruelty. Public punishment was viewed both as social vengeance and as a means of instilling a deterrent fear into the population; the crueler the punishment, the greater its deterrent effect was assumed to be.

Beccaria did not question the need for punishment, but he believed that laws should be designed to preserve public safety and order, not to avenge crime. He also took issue with the common practice of secret accusations, arguing that such practices led to general deceit and alienation in society. He argued that accused persons should

▲ **Photo 3.1**   Cesare Beccaria (1738–1794)

be able to confront their accusers, know the charges brought against them, and enjoy the benefit of a public trial before an impartial judge as soon as possible after arrest and indictment.

If offenders are found guilty, punishment should fit the crime (i.e., be proportionate to the harm done to society), be identical for identical crimes, and be applied without reference to the social status of either the offender or the victim. Beccaria championed not only the abolition of the death penalty but also the cause of merciful punishments, which he believed should only minimally exceed the level of damage done to society. Punishment, however, must be certain and swift to make a lasting impression on the criminal. To ensure a rational and fair penal structure, punishments for specific crimes must be decreed by written criminal codes and the discretionary powers of judges severely curtailed. The judge's task was to determine guilt or innocence and then to impose the legislatively prescribed punishment if the accused is found guilty.

Jeremy Bentham and Human Nature

Perhaps an even more prominent figure of the classical school was British lawyer and philosopher Jeremy Bentham, a contemporary and an admirer of Beccaria. In the English-speaking world, Bentham's legacy extended beyond the reformation of the criminal law to embrace police and correctional reforms.[2] His major work, *A Fragment on Government and an Introduction to the Principles of Morals and Legislation,*[3] is essentially a philosophy of social control based on the

▲ **Photo 3.2** Jeremy Bentham, often credited as the founder of University College London, insisted that his body be put upon display there after his death. You can visit a replica of it today.

principle of utility, which prescribed "the greatest happiness for the greatest number." The principle posits that any human action at all should be judged moral or immoral by its effect on the happiness of the community. Thus, the proper function of the legislature is to promulgate laws aimed at maximizing the pleasure and minimizing the pain of the largest number in society—"the greatest good for the greatest number."[4] Having its basis in the natural human need for happiness, the principle of utility can be seen as a principle of natural law.

If legislators are to legislate according to the principle of utility, they must understand human motivation, which for Bentham was easily summed up as follows: "Nature has placed mankind under the governance of two sovereign masters, pain and pleasure. It is for them alone to point out what we ought to do, as well as to determine what we shall do."[5] This was essentially the Enlightenment concept of human nature, which was seen as hedonistic, rational, and endowed with free will. The classical explanation of criminal behavior—and even how to prevent it—can be derived from these three assumptions about human nature.

Hedonism is a doctrine with the central tenet that the achievement of pleasure or happiness is the main goal of life. We don't have to learn to be hedonistic; pleasure is intrinsically desirable, and pain is intrinsically undesirable. All other life goals are seen only as instrumentally desirable; that is, they are only desirable as means to the end of achieving pleasure or avoiding pain. Thus, hedonism is the greatest single motivator of human action.

Rational behavior is behavior that is consistent with logic. People are said to behave rationally when we observe a logical "fit" between the goals they strive for and the means they use to achieve them. Rationality is not to be confused with morality. Crime is rational (at least in the short run) if the criminal employs reason and acts purposely to gain desired ends. The goal of human rationality is self-interest, and self-interest governs our behavior whether in conforming or deviant directions.

Hedonism and rationality are combined in the concept of **hedonistic calculus,** a method by which individuals are assumed to logically weigh the anticipated benefits of a given course of action against its possible costs. If the balance of consequences of a contemplated action is thought to enhance pleasure and/or minimize pain, then individuals will pursue it; if not, they will not. If people miscalculate, as they frequently do, it is because they are ignorant of the full range of consequences of a given course of action, not because they are irrational.

Free will enables human beings to purposely and deliberately choose to follow a calculated course of action. If people seek to increase their pleasures illegally, they do so freely and with full knowledge of the wrongness of their acts. Given this knowledge, society has a perfectly legitimate right to punish those who harm it.

It follows from the classical assumptions about human nature that if crime is to be deterred, punishment (pain) must exceed the pleasures gained from the fruits of crime. Hedonistic and rational criminals will weigh the costs against the benefits of crime and desist if, on balance, the costs exceed the benefits. Estimations of the value of various pleasures and pains are to be considered with reference to four circumstances: intensity (severity), duration, certainty, and propinquity (how soon after the crime that pleasure or pain is forthcoming).[6]

The Legacy of the Classical School

The **classical school** of criminology, so called because its mode of inquiry was the armchair philosophy practiced by the ancient "classical" Greek philosophers,[7] was a school of philosophical jurisprudence bent on establishing a set of reformist moral values in criminal justice, not a school of empirical data collection and analysis attempting to build a theory of criminality. Regardless of their influence on criminological theory, the influence of the classical theorists on the legal and penal systems of Europe and North America is immeasurable. Many European monarchs (the "Enlightened Despots") of the 18th century were moved to adopt their principles, and the American Constitution and the 1789 French *Declaration of the Rights of Man* were very much influenced by them.[8] All modern criminal justice systems in the world assume the classical position that persons are free agents who deserve to be punished when they transgress the law. We may also recognize many of the ideas championed by Beccaria in such rights as freedom from cruel and unusual punishment, the right to a speedy trial, the prohibition of ex post facto laws, the right to confront one's accusers, and equality under law, contained in the U.S. Bill of Rights and other documents at the heart of Western legal systems today. The emphasis on rationality, on free will, and on personal responsibility within the modern legal system reflects the once radical image of human beings posited by the great Enlightenment thinkers.

⊠ The Rise of Positivism

What Is Positivism?

Classicists tended to define criminal acts as natural consequences of the unrestrained human tendency to seek pleasure—as simply hedonistic abuses of free will. The problem with such an explanation, if accepted without qualification, is that it provides little possibility of further investigation. In the 19th century, criminologists began to move away from the classical assumptions, especially the assumption of free will as it is commonly understood, and toward a more scientific view of human behavior. This is not to say that hedonism, rationality, and free will are mythical human attributes. They may, in fact, define the "essence" of human nature, but to accept these constructs in pure form poses great difficulties for science, a method of inquiry that seeks measurable "causes" of the phenomena it explores. The increasingly popular view among criminologists of this period was that crime resulted from internal and/or external forces impinging on individuals, biasing or even completely determining their behavioral choices. This position became known as *determinism,* and its adherents were known as *positivists.*

Just as the spirit of rationalism in the 18th century ushered in the classical school, the spirit of science in the second half of the 19th century ushered in the positivist school. The term **positivism** is used to designate the extension of the scientific method—from which more *positive* knowledge can be obtained—to social life. Positivists in the human sciences insisted on divorcing science from metaphysics and morals and looking only at what is, not what ought to be. The writings of natural scientists, particularly those of Charles Darwin on evolution, generated a major new way of thinking about human nature among intellectuals just as revolutionary as the writings of the Enlightenment philosophers a century earlier. The flattering image of human beings that emerged from the Enlightenment gave way to the evolutionary view that we are different only in degree from other animal forms and that science could explain human behavior just as it could explain events in the nonhuman world. Positivist criminologists were more concerned with discovering biological, psychological, or social determinants of criminal behavior than with the classical concerns of legal and penal reforms.

Enrico Ferri, one of the early positivists, gives us perhaps the best short description of the differences between classical and positivist criminologists. Note that even back then, criminologists from different schools of thought were taking jabs at one another: "We are empirical *scientists;* you lot are just armchair speculators":

> For [the classicists] the facts should give place to syllogisms [reasoning from a taken-for-granted premise to a logical conclusion]; for us [positivists] the facts govern and no reasoning can occur without starting from the facts. For them science only needs paper, pen, and ink and the rest comes from a brain stuffed with . . . abundant reading of books. . . . For us science requires spending a long time in examining the facts one by one, evaluating them, reducing them to a common denominator, [and] extracting the central idea from them. For them a syllogism or an anecdote suffices to demolish a myriad of facts gathered by years of observation and analysis; for us, the reverse is true.[9]

A Bridge Between the Classical and Positivist Schools

There is not always the sharp discontinuity between the classical and positivist schools that we are sometimes led to believe. For instance, although traditionally placed firmly in the classical camp, the work of Jeremy Bentham may be considered a bridge between the two schools. Despite Bentham's classical view of human nature, he never lost sight of its intricacies. While always maintaining the freedom of the will, he argued that it was moved by "motives" arising from the "bodily senses," which were differentially felt by people according to certain internal and external factors. He devoted an entire chapter of *A Fragment on Government* to 32 biological, psychological, and social factors (e.g., intelligence, temperament, personality, gender, age, education, occupation) that he thought of as "circumstances influencing sensibility."[10] Although he only devoted a single paragraph to each one, the fact that he recognized internal and external constraints on free will and rationality leads us to believe that Bentham may have been both the last of the old classical criminologists and the first of the positivist criminologists.

Cartographic Criminology

Some of the earliest positivist attempts to leave the armchair and collect facts about crime to understand it came from cartographers. Cartographers are scholars who employ maps and other geographic information in their research, and those who employ these methods to study crime are called **cartographic criminologists.** Rather than exploring why individuals commit crimes, cartographic criminologists are more interested in where and when criminal behavior is most prevalent.

The first publication of detailed statistics relating to criminal activity for an entire country occurred in France in 1827, more than 100 years before the publication of the first edition of the *Uniform Crime Reports* (*UCR*) in the United States. This work was used by two scholars to make statements about crime and its causes that anticipated by about a century those of two theories we will explore in the next chapter. Two scholars used this work to make statements about crime and its causes. They were prescient in that they made statements relevant to crime causation that would be made 100 years later. The first was a Frenchman named Andre-Michel Guerry, and the other was a Belgian named Lambert-Adolphe-Jacques Quetelet. Quetelet compared crime rates in France across ages, sexes, and seasons. He saw the same reflections in his data that we see today in the American *UCR*—that is, young males living in poor neighborhoods commit the most crime. He thought sociologically about crime before the discipline officially existed, writing that "society prepares the crime and the guilty is only the instrument by which it is accomplished."[11]

Both Quetelet and Guerry discounted the idea that crime is caused by poverty, noting that the wealthiest regions of France had the greatest level of property crimes. However, Guerry noted that the level of wealth in a region does not necessarily correspond to the level of wealth among all its citizens and that being poor amid riches (as in urban France), not being poor per se (as in rural France), is the condition that produces the most "misery" (today we call this *relative deprivation*). He also noted that among the factors affecting crime are areas "where a frequent mixture of people takes place, and where the inequality of fortune is most felt."[12]

Guerry produced many fine-shaded ecological maps to represent crime rates in different areas. This method of presenting data crossed the English Channel to influence British researchers Henry Mayhew and Joseph Fletcher. Using British crime data from the 1830s to 1840s, both men independently mapped out the concentration of various kinds of criminal activity across England and Wales, as well as other factors such as population density and rates of illegitimacy. They came to many of the same conclusions that U.S. researchers would later come to (i.e., crime and delinquency are concentrated in poor neighborhoods undergoing population changes). Many British cities were experiencing the same demographic changes in the early 1800s that American cities were to experience in the early 1900s. Rural people flocked to the big cities to obtain work in the new factory system, and in the obscurity of these cities of strangers, social bonds weakened, morals declined, and crime flourished.[13]

Given the many conclusions of the cartographic school that are consistent with many modern criminological positions, it is surprising that more attention is not paid to it. The influence of the school declined in the latter part of the 19th century as interest started to focus more on the individual criminal and less on his or her environment. It would reemerge in the Chicago in the early 20th century as human ecology.

Biological Positivism: Cesare Lombroso and the Born Criminal

Five years after Charles Darwin shocked the world with the publication of his theory of evolution, an Italian army psychiatrist named Cesare Lombroso published *Criminal Man,*[14] which is considered the first book devoted solely to the causes of criminality ever written. Lombroso is

▲ **Photo 3.3**   Cesare Lombroso (1836–1909)

widely acclaimed as the father of modern criminology, although he is often criticized for the views put forth in his book. His basic idea was that many (not all, as is commonly assumed) criminals are born criminal and that they are evolutionary "throwbacks" to an earlier form of life. The term used to describe the appearance of organisms resembling ancestral (prehuman) forms of life is **atavism.** Lombroso was influenced by Ernst Haeckel's famous **biogenetic law,** which stated that ontogeny (individual development) recapitulates phylogeny (evolutionary development of the species).[15] Criminals were thus "throwbacks" to a more primitive stage of evolution and could be identified by a number of measurable physical stigmata. These stigmata included protruding jaws, drooping eyes, large ears, twisted and flatish noses, long arms relative to the lower limbs, sloping shoulders, and a coccyx that resembled "the stump of a tail."[16]

The concept of atavism highlights an important point of difference between the classical and positivist schools: While the classicists viewed criminals and noncriminals as essentially similar beings who simply chose different pathways, positivists viewed them as being quite different beings. Lombroso was just one of many who sought to understand behavioral phenomena with reference to the principles of evolution as they were understood at the time. If humankind was just at one end of the continuum of animal life, it made sense to many people that criminals—who acted "beastly" and lacked reasoned conscience—were biologically inferior beings.

In addition to the atavistic-*born criminal,* Lombroso identified two other types: the **insane criminal** and the **criminaloid.** Although insane criminals bore some stigmata, they were not born criminals; rather, they become criminals as a result "of an alteration of the brain, which completely upsets their moral nature."[17] Among the ranks of Lombroso's insane criminals were alcoholics, kleptomaniacs, nymphomaniacs, and child molesters. Criminaloids had none of the physical peculiarities of the born or insane criminal and were considered less dangerous. Criminaloids were further categorized as *habitual criminals,* who become so by contact with other criminals, the abuse of alcohol, or other "distressing circumstances"; *juridical criminals,* who fall afoul of the law by accident; and the *criminal by passion,* hot-headed and impulsive persons who commit violent acts when provoked.

Although Lombroso is best remembered for his concept of the atavistic-born criminal, his later work, *Crime: Its Causes and Remedies,*[18] listed a bewildering variety of possible "causes," including unlikely candidates such as tobacco, hair color, and "goitrous districts." Notwithstanding Lombroso's recognition that crime has multiple causes, he still argued that "organic causes" accounted for 35% to 40% of the "fatal influence" on crime.[19]

Perhaps it is because of this latter point that Lombroso has been reviled and ridiculed as a biological determinist. Some criminologists, while acknowledging Lombroso's many errors

▶ **Photo 3.4**   This porcelain head for sale in a New Orleans antique store shows the sections of the brain, as detailed by 19th-century phrenologists. They believed that each section was responsible for a particular human personality trait. If a section were enlarged or shrunken, the personality would be likewise abnormal. Doctors, particularly those doing entry examinations at American prisons, would examine the new inmate's head for bumps or cavities to develop a criminal profile. For example, if the section of brain responsible for "acquisitiveness" was enlarged, the offender probably was a thief. Lombroso and his school combined phrenology with other models that included external physical appearance traits that could single out criminals from the general population.

in logic, research design, measurement, and elitist and sexist ideas, insist that his contributions are both misunderstood and undervalued. His methodology, although very badly flawed by modern standards, was an improvement over previous attempts at positivistic criminology.[20] From Lombroso on, there has been an enduring commitment to sort, sift, and measure all sorts of physical, psychological, economic, and social phenomena in an attempt to get to the bottom of crime and criminality.

FOCUS ON . . .

Lombrosoism Before and After Lombroso

There have always been those for whom human character and personality are transparent in physical appearance. In Shakespeare's play, Julius Caesar distrusts Cassius because he "has a lean and hungry look." Such folk wisdom was systematized almost 300 years before the publication of Cesare Lombroso's *Criminal Man* by another Italian physician, Giambattista della Porta, who developed a theory of human personality called *Physiognomy.* Porta claimed that the study of physical appearance, particularly of the face, could reveal much about a person's personality and character. Thieves, for instance, were said to have large lips and sharp vision.

(Continued)

(Continued)

Almost 200 years later, Johann Kasper Lavater published his three-volume *Essays on Physiognomy,* which was highly acclaimed in medical and scientific circles. Lavater went further than Porta in claiming that the "higher" character of the English aristocrat and the "lower" character of the London thief could be discerned simply from a detailed study of their faces. In a similar vein, Hubert Lauvergne's 1844 study of French convicts concluded that they had faces that easily reveal their "brutal and impassible (incapable of feeling) instincts." Lauvergne's descriptions of the facial features of convicts (massive jaws and receding foreheads) conjured up the same ape-like image that Lombroso's descriptions would 32 years later.

Lauvergne was a student of Franz Josef Gall, the founder, along with John Spurzheim, of another exotic system of assessing character from physical features called *phrenology.* Phrenologists claimed that the contours of an individual's skull revealed his or her psychic makeup. The basic idea was that various cognitive functions are localized in the cerebral cortex (the thinking part of the brain). Parts of the cortex regulating the most dominant functions were thought to be bigger than parts regulating the less dominant ones. Thus, the relative sizes of a person's cranial bumps pointed to the relative strengths of his or her personality and character. Criminals were said to have cranial maps showing large protuberances in parts of the cortex thought to regulate craftiness, brutishness, moral insensibility, and so on, as well as small bumps in such "localities" as intelligence, honor, piety, and so forth. Thus the measure (or is it the "mismeasure"?) of humanity had a rather long history predating Lombroso. Lombroso occupies his place in criminology because his work was solely criminological; the works discussed here are more general works having little influence on criminology.

Some late-20th-century criminologists have renewed interest in possible connections between physical appearance and criminal behavior. A survey of inmates in New York found that about half of them had at least a moderate degree of disfigurement other than tattoos,[21] and a review of the literature on the subject concluded that prisons house a disproportionate number of disfigured males.[22]

A 1993 article examined what are called *minor physical anomalies* (MPAs) and their relationship to crime.[23] These MPAs are not the obvious stigmata of Lombroso's atavists; they are rather minor defects, some of which require expert observation. MPAs include webbed toes, extra toes, widely spaced eyes, and minor disfigurements of fingers and ears. The researchers hypothesize that genetic factors responsible for MPAs also affect aspects of the central nervous system (such as producing hyperactivity or impulsiveness) in such a way as to put the individual at risk for antisocial behavior. Evidence for this hypothesis is mixed. It was found that MPAs were related to violent crimes, but only if offenders came from unstable or broken homes.[24] Other studies find support for the MPA-crime relationship, while others do not. One major review of the literature concluded that with all the problems attending such studies, the relationship must be considered inconsistent at best.[25]

Advocates of rehabilitation have recognized for some time that unattractive physical features have a negative effect on rehabilitation efforts, probably because they may lead to low self-esteem and to rejection by others. Because of this, plastic surgery has been used in some U.S. prisons as a rehabilitative tool. A review of nine studies of prison plastic surgery outcomes found that six reported a reduction in the likelihood of recidivism, two reported no difference, and one found a higher recidivism rate among the surgery group.[26] Thus, the first scientifically researched correlate of crime has not entirely disappeared as a focus of interest for some criminologists, although none of them think of "disfigured" criminals as genetic "throwbacks" to an earlier evolutionary period.

Raffael Garofalo: Natural Crime and Offender Peculiarities

Lombroso and two of his Italian contemporaries, Raffael Garofalo and Enrico Ferri, founded what became known as the **Italian school of criminology**. Both Garofalo and Ferri were lawyers who accepted as given the positivist notion that behavior has discoverable causes, but, like the classicists, they were more interested in criminal procedure and penology than in crime causation.

Garofalo[27] is perhaps best known for his efforts to formulate a "natural" definition of crime. Classical thinkers accepted the legal definition of crime uncritically: crime is what the law says it is. This appeared to be rather arbitrary and "unscientific" (like the Anglo-American system of linear measurement) to Garofalo, who wanted to anchor the definition of crime in something natural (like tying linear measurement to the circumference of the Earth, as in the metric system). Garofalo felt that definitions of crime should be anchored in human nature, by which he meant that a given act would be considered a crime if it was universally condemned, and it would be universally condemned if it offended the natural altruistic sentiments of probity (integrity, honesty) and pity (compassion, sympathy). Natural crimes are evil in themselves (*mala in se*), whereas other kinds of crimes (*mala prohibita*) are wrong only because they have been made wrong by the law.

Garofalo rejected the classical principle that punishment should fit the crime, arguing instead that it should fit the criminal. As a good positivist, he believed that criminals have little control over their actions. This repudiation of moral responsibility and fitting the punishment to the offender would eventually lead to sentencing aimed at the humane and liberal goals of treatment and rehabilitation. For Garofalo, however, the only question to be considered at sentencing was the danger the offender posed to society, which was to be judged by an offender's *peculiarities*.

By "peculiarities," Garofalo was not referring to Lombrosian stigmata but rather to particular characteristics that place offenders at risk for criminal behavior. He developed four categories of criminals, each meriting different forms of punishment: *extreme, impulsive, professional,* and *endemic.* Society could only be defended from extreme criminals by swiftly executing them, regardless of the crime for which they are being punished. Impulsive criminals, a category that included alcoholics and the insane, were to be imprisoned. Professional criminals are psychologically normal individuals who use the hedonistic calculus before committing their crimes and thus require "elimination," either by life imprisonment or transportation to a penal colony overseas. Endemic crimes, by which Garofalo meant crimes peculiar to a given region, and mala prohibita crimes could best be controlled by changes in the law.

Enrico Ferri and Social Defense

Ferri, like Garofalo, dismissed the notion of free will as myth, and he derived the same policy implications from its dismissal. Prepositivistic notions of culpability, moral responsibility, and intent were to be subordinate to an assessment of the offender's strength of resistance to the criminal impulse, with the express purpose of averting future danger to society. He believed that moral insensibility and lack of foresight, underscored by low intelligence, were the criminal's most marked characteristics: The criminal has "defective resistance to criminal tendencies and temptations, due to that ill-balanced impulsiveness which characterizes children and savages."[28]

Ferri's primary concern was social preservation, not the nature of criminal behavior. With Lombroso and Garofalo, Ferri was instrumental in formulating the concept of **social defense** as the rationale for punishment. This theory of punishment asserts that its purpose is not to deter or to rehabilitate but to defend society from criminal predation. Ferri reasoned that the characteristics of criminals prevented them from basing their behavior on rational calculus principles, so how could such behavior be deterred, and how could born criminals be rehabilitated? Given the assumptions of biological positivism, the only reasonable rationale for punishing offenders is to incapacitate them for as long as possible so that they no longer pose a threat to the peace and security of society. This theory of punishment provides us with an excellent example of how our assumptions about human nature drive our policies for dealing with crime and criminals.

Charles Goring's Assault on Lombroso

The most famous of Lombroso's critics was a British physician named Charles Goring, who in 1913 published a book titled *The English Convict: A Statistical Study.*[29] This book contained the results of his study of more than 3,000 English convicts whose physical characteristics were compared to those of male university students and soldiers. The only significant differences he found were that the average criminal was shorter and lighter than the average noncriminal, a fact easily explained by the lower socioeconomic origins of the convicts. Goring's exhaustive comparisons found no other significant differences between criminals and noncriminals, leading him to the "inevitable conclusion" that "*there is no such thing as a physical criminal type.*"[30]

Goring's work has been considered the first to adopt the modern view that criminality is probably the result of the interaction of a variety of hereditary and environmental factors at a time when most theorists thought in terms of either/or,[31] and as a link between early biological positivism and the less deterministic psychological and psychiatric schools.[32] For instance, Goring found strong associations between the criminality of parents and children, between siblings, and between spouses. Although family behavioral resemblances necessarily include genetic and environmental influences, Goring attributed these correlations predominantly to a characteristic he called "criminal diathesis," which he saw as a form of "defective intelligence" preventing the development of proper social and moral instincts.[33] Thus, much thought about the problem of criminal behavior was beginning to shift away from biological to psychological positivism.

The Legacy of Positivism

The great legacy of the positivist school, as Enrico Ferri reminded us, was the shift from armchair philosophizing about human behavior to using the concepts and methods of science. An essential tenet of positivism is that human actions have causes and that these causes are to be sought in the uniformities that preceded those actions. Although early positivism produced ideas that many today consider false and even dangerous, even these provided valuable contributions by stimulating opposition. The whole business of science is a never-ending exchange of thesis, antithesis, and synthesis, molding and sharpening ideas on the wheel of criticism and countercriticism. Few new ideas, especially in science, have been accepted uncritically, and even the most revered of ideas of one period may not survive the long haul as new ideas emerge and new methods and techniques of measurement are developed to test them.

There are no sharp discontinuities and clear-cut distinctions between classicism and positivism on all matters. The classical affirmation of human abilities and freedom of expression did much to push science into the forefront as a method of gathering knowledge, as did its abandonment of supernaturalism and its embrace of the natural. Positivism did not disprove or destroy classical principles; it simply shifted emphasis from crime and penology to the individual offender. Positivism enabled criminologists to escape the excesses of a simplistic free-will interpretation of criminality, but its own deterministic excesses have moved some criminologists to return to modified classical notions of human nature. This is not to say that these criminologists have abandoned positivistic empirical science; positivism is a *method*, a way of exploring things, not a theory about those things. It is unfortunate that for some people, positivism has come to connote absolute determinism—and only biological and psychological determinism at that[34]—such that "if X, then Y *will* follow," but our reading of the literature reveals no hard determinism of this sort. To the extent that they use the scientific method to detect patterns predicting criminal behavior in a *probabilistic* way, almost all contemporary criminological theories are positivistic.

⊠ Neoclassicism: Rational Choice Theory

The 1970s saw the beginnings of a swing away from the ideals of the positivist school, which implied that factors beyond the control of the offender were responsible for crime, and toward a return to the classical notion that offenders are free actors responsible for their own actions. Rational choice theorists believe that factors such as poverty, low IQ, impulsiveness, or broken homes are not required to explain crime. Although such factors may influence a person's choice to engage or not to engage in crime, the choice is made like any other choice to benefit the chooser. As opposed to the "hard" determinism of the positivists, neoclassicist criminologists are "soft" determinists because while criminal behavior is ultimately a choice, the choice is made in the context of personal and situational constraints and the availability of opportunities.

Rational choice theorists view criminal acts as specific examples of the general principle that all human behavior reflects the rational pursuit of *maximizing utility* (*utility* refers to benefits and advantages), which is the modern economists' version of Bentham's principle of maximizing pleasure and minimizing pain. People are conscious social actors free to choose crime, and they will do so if they perceive that its utility exceeds the pains they might conceivably expect if discovered.

Criminologists have long been aware that even their most sophisticated and comprehensive models of criminal behavior have failed to account for anywhere near half of the variation in offending, which leaves ample room for idiosyncratic reasons for engaging in it, such as "choice" or "free will." **Rational choice theory** is not committed to a free-will position but strongly implies it.[35] The theory does not assume that we are all equally at risk to commit criminal acts or that we do or do not commit crimes simply because we do or do not "want to." It recognizes that personal factors such as temperament, intelligence, and cognitive style, as well as background factors such as family structure, class, and neighborhood, affect our choices,[36] but it largely ignores these factors in favor of concentrating on the conscious thought processes involved in making decisions to offend.

According to rational choice theory, rationality is the quality of thinking and behaving in accordance with logic and reason such that one's reality is an ordered and intelligible system. Rationality means that there is a logical correspondence between the goals we have and the means we use to obtain them. This does not mean that the theory contains an image of people as walking calculating machines or that the theory is even concerned about just how people actually go about their subjective calculations.

Rationality is both subjective and bounded, and unwanted outcomes can be produced by rational strategies.[37] We do not all make the same calculations or arrive at the same game plan when pursuing the same goals, for we contemplate our anticipated actions with less than perfect knowledge, with different mind-sets, and with different reasoning abilities. Our emotions (guilt, shame, anxiety, etc.) also function to keep our temptations in check by "overriding" purely rational calculations of immediate gain.[38] We do the best we can to order our decisions relating to our self-interest with the knowledge and understanding we have about the possible outcomes of a particular course of action. All people have mental models of the world and behave rationally with respect to them, even if others might consider our behavior to be irrational. Criminals behave rationally from their private models of reality, but their rationality is constrained, as is everyone's, by ability, knowledge, emotional input, and time.[39]

As previously noted, however, rather than focusing on these things, rational choice theory focuses on *criminal events* and not on offenders and how they came to be. Rational choice theory simply assumes a criminally motivated offender and focuses on the process of the choice to offend. Cornish and Clarke refer to this process as **choice structuring** and define it as "the constellation of opportunities, costs, and benefits attaching to particular kinds of crime."[40] Thus, a criminal event requires motivated offenders meeting situations that they perceive as an opportunity to acquire something they want. Each event is the result of a series of choice structuring decisions to initiate the event, continue, or desist, and each particular kind of crime is the result of a series of different decisions that can only be explained on their own terms: The decision to rape is arrived at quite differently than the decision to burglarize.

Explanations of criminal *events* must be crime specific because offenses have properties of their own (expected payoff, risk and skills involved, whether or not a partner is needed, etc.). Certain offenses are differentially attractive to different offenders because of these properties, which interact with the characteristics of the offender (degree of risk willing to take, "professional pride," loner or team player). Thus, offenders make their decisions by appraising how potential offense properties "fit" with their personal characteristics. Properties of offenses provide potential offenders with a basis for selecting among alternative courses of action, thus *structuring* their choices.[41]

Cohen and Felson's Routine Activities Theory and Victimization

Lawrence Cohen and Marcus Felson[42] have devised a neoclassical theory in the tradition of rational choice theory that may explain high crime rates in different societies and neighborhoods without invoking individual differences—it simply points to the routine activities in that society or neighborhood. Routine activities are defined as "recurrent and prevalent activities which provide for basic population and individual needs."[43] In other words, they are the day-to-day activities characterizing a particular community. In disorganized communities, the routine activities are such that they practically invite crime.

According to Cohen and Felson, crime is the result of (a) *motivated offenders* meeting (b) *suitable targets* that lack (c) *capable guardians.* Cohen and Felson take motivated offenders for granted and do not attempt to explain their existence. The theory is thus very much like rational choice theory in that it describes situations in which criminal victimization is likely to occur. In poor disorganized communities, there is never a shortage of motivated offenders, and although the pickings are generally slim in such areas, victimization is more prevalent in them than in more affluent areas.[44] One of the obvious reasons for high victimization rates in poor disorganized areas (besides the abundance of motivated offenders) is that they tend to lack capable guardians for either persons or property.

Routine activities theory looks at crime from the points of view of both the offender and crime prevention. A crime will only be committed when a motivated offender believes that he or she has found something worth stealing or someone to victimize who lacks a capable guardian. A capable guardian is a person or thing that discourages the motivated offender from committing the act. It can be the presence of a person, police patrols, strong security protection, neighborhood vigilance, or whatever. Because of disrupted families, transient neighbors, poverty, and all the other negative aspects of disorganized neighborhoods, except for police patrols, capable guardians are in short supply. Crime is a "situation," and crime rates can go up or down depending on how these situations change without any changes at all in offender motivation. Recurring situations conducive to acquiring resources with minimal effort may also tempt more individuals to take advantage of them. In other words, in terms of Figure 1.3 (see Chapter 1), higher levels of environmental instigation lower the threshold for more individuals to become motivated offenders.

Deterrence and Choice: Pain Versus Gain

The principle that people respond to incentives and that they are deterred by the threat of punishment is the philosophical foundation behind all systems of criminal law. Rational choice theory evolved out of deterrence theory and the economic principle of expected utility, both of which can be encapsulated by the principle of behaviorist psychology that states that *behavior is governed by its consequences.* A positive consequence of crime for criminals is that it affords them something they want for little effort; a negative consequence is the punishment attached to their crimes if they are caught. The hedonistic calculus predicts that punishment (pain) will deter crime only if it exceeds the pleasure (gain) it offers. These pleasures may be material (money, property, sex, drugs), psychological (self-esteem, feelings of power and control, excitement, reputation, revenge), or a combination of both.

Deterrence, the prevention of criminal acts by the use or threat of punishment, has long been considered the primary function of punishment. Deterrence may be either *specific* or *general.* **Specific deterrence** refers to the effect of punishment on the future behavior of the person who experiences the punishment. Punishment is said to have worked if the person desists from future criminal activity; if he or she continues to engage in criminal activity, it did not. For specific deterrence to work, a previously punished person must make a mental connection between an intended criminal act and the punitive consequences suffered as a result of similar acts committed in the past. Unfortunately, such connections, if made, rarely have

▲ **Photo 3.5** Cohen and Felson's routine activities theory argued that "target hardening" was a major deterrent to crime. While the number of surveillance cameras outside New Scotland Yard in London may seem to be excessive, there are thousands of these cameras all over the city. Using tapes from such cameras, local criminal justice officials were able to follow the paths taken by the suicide bombers who blew up mass transit vehicles in July 2005. However, the cameras had no deterrent effect as the criminals were highly "motivated offenders."

the socially desired effect, either because memories of the previous consequences were insufficiently emotionally strong or the offender discounted them.

Committing another crime after previously being punished for one is called **recidivism** ("falling back" into criminal behavior). Recidivism is a lot more common among ex-convicts than repentance and rehabilitation. Nationwide, about 33% of released inmates recidivate within the first 6 months, 44% within the first year, 54% by the second year, and 67.5% by the third year.[45] These are just the ones who are caught, so we can safely say that there is very little specific deterrent effect.

As Jeremy Bentham informed us long ago, the influence of punishment on future behavior depends on its certainty, celerity (swiftness), and severity. In other words, there must be a relatively high degree of certainty that punishment will follow a criminal act, will be administered very soon after the act, and will be quite harsh. As we saw in Chapter 2 when discussing clearance rates, the probability of getting caught is very low, especially for property crimes. If a person is actually caught, the wheels of criminal justice grind excruciatingly slowly, with many months passing between the act and the imposition of punishment. So much for certainty and celerity, which leaves us with severity as the only element of punishment we can realistically manipulate. It is unfortunate that the only element over which the criminal justice system has a great deal of control (it can increase or decrease statutory penalties almost at will) is the least effective element.[46]

Studies using official data from the United States and the United Kingdom find substantial negative correlations between the likelihood of conviction (a measure of certainty) and crime rates for a variety of crimes but a much weaker negative correlation for the severity of punishment.[47] A negative correlation means that as one variable goes up (in this case, the likelihood of conviction), the other one (crime rate) goes down. As we saw in the previous chapter, it has been claimed that increased incarceration rates have accounted for about 25% of the decline in violent crime over the past decade or so.[48,49] Unfortunately, we cannot determine from raw incarceration rates if we are witnessing a *deterrent* effect (has violent crime declined because more people have perceived a greater punitive effect?) or an *incapacitation* effect (has violent crime declined because more violent people are behind bars and thus not at liberty to commit violent crimes on the outside?).

The effect of punishment on future behavior also depends on the **contrast effect,** which is the distinction between the circumstances of punishment and the usual life experience of the person being punished. The prospect of incarceration is a nightmarish contrast for those who enjoy a loving family and the security of a valued career. The mere prospect of experiencing the embarrassment of public disgrace that threatens the families and careers of those who have invested time, effort, and emotional energy in acquiring and nurturing them is a strong deterrent. For those lacking strong family ties and a commitment to a legitimate career, punishment has little effect because the contrast between the punishment and their normal lives is minimal. For people with little or nothing to lose, arrest may be perceived as little more than an inconvenience, an opportunity for a little rest and recreation and a chance to renew old friendships. Specific deterrence thus works least for those who need deterring the most.

General deterrence refers to the preventive effect of the threat of punishment on the general population; it is thus aimed at *potential* offenders. The punishment of offenders serves as examples to the rest of us of what may happen if we violate the law. As Radzinowicz and King put it, "People are not sent to prison primarily for their own good, or even in the hope that they will be cured of crime. Confinement is used as a measure of retribution, a symbol of condemnation, a vindication of the law. It is used as a warning and deterrent to others."[50] Put another way, the existence of a system of punishment for law violators deters a large but unknown number of individuals who might commit crimes if no such system existed.

Deterrence theorists tend to assume a more rational human being than do rational choice theorists, with their models being full of complicated mathematical models defining cost/benefit ratios. They are aware that criminals rarely have accurate information about the probabilities of punishment, but they assume that rough perceptions exist among criminals regarding these probabilities and that they act accordingly. For instance, deterrence theorists have explained the huge increase in crime between 1960 and the early 1990s as largely a function of criminal perceptions that punishment probabilities had been greatly reduced since the 1960s.[51]

Deterrence theorists will calculate the probability of imprisonment for a given crime, and they assume that the perception among criminals roughly matches their calculations. Reynolds[52] gives us an example based on the probability of imprisonment for the crime of burglary. The probability of an event (imprisonment) is the product of all preceding events (reporting, arrest, prosecution, indictment, conviction, and prison vs. probation). The resulting probability, multiplied by the median prison sentence for burglary (17 months), is equal to only 7.1 days. This probability was averaged over thousands of burglary events and will obviously vary from incident to incident and from person to person. A burglar could have committed many burglaries prior to arrest that may have netted him or her many thousands of dollars for a few hours of relatively effortless activity. Factoring out morality, burglary is a very rational career option for capable individuals. Although the probabilities of a burglary being reported and the burglar being arrested still remain about the same as Reynolds reported (see the 2004 clearance rate in Chapter 2), the subsequent probabilities assuming arrest (prosecution, conviction, imprisonment, and length of sentence) have considerably increased.

Reviews of deterrence research indicate that legal sanctions do have a "substantial deterrent effect."[53] Punishment has a greater deterrent effect for instrumental crimes (crimes that bring material rewards) than for expressive crimes (crimes that bring psychological rewards). The more certain it is, and the more swiftly it is applied, but as we have seen, there is little evidence that increasing the severity of sanction (in the form of sentence length) has any effect.[54] These findings underscore the classical notions that individuals do (subconsciously at least) calculate the ratio of expected pleasures to possible pains when contemplating a course of action.

Evaluation of Neoclassical Theories

Critics complain that neoclassical theories overemphasize the rationality of human beings and ignore the social conditions that may make it rational for some to engage in crime.[55] However, emphasizing rationality (albeit, bounded rationality) dignifies criminals as active participants in determining their own futures, not as passive recipients (or "victims") of malignant social forces. Nevertheless, we do need to understand these forces, as well as psychological differences, that turn some people into "motivated offenders." In economists' terms, what makes some of us willing to expend one resource (our potential loss of freedom) to attain another (the fruits of crime)? Many of us don't spend our resources all that wisely because of a tendency to favor immediate gain over long-term consequences, and we would like to know why some of us more strongly favor immediate gain than others. In short, it is claimed that these theories implicitly assume that everyone perceives the same reality similarly and ignore irrational and impulsive crimes that are preceded by little thought.[56]

In defense of neoclassical theories, advocates insist that they do not assume a model of "pure" rationality; rather, they assume a limited rationality constrained by ability, knowledge, and time.[57] These theories also do not claim to be theories exploring the role of social or psychological forces in producing crime or criminals; instead, they explore criminal events with the purpose of trying to prevent them. They seek to deny the motivated offender the opportunity to commit a crime by target hardening, which is a very practical thing. In addition, the notion that individuals are responsible for their own actions meshes well with American values. If this assumption grants society "permission" to punish criminals who make purposeful decisions to flout the law,[58] then so be it, for the act of punishment presupposes free human beings and thus dignifies them.

Figure 3.1	Summary and Comparisons of the Classical and Positivist Schools Pertaining to Certain Issues	

	Classical	Positivist
Historical Period	18th-century Enlightenment, early period of Industrial Revolution.	19th-century Age of Reason, mid–Industrial Revolution.
Leading Figures	Cesare Becarria, Jeremy Bentham.	Cesare Lombroso, Raffael Garofalo, Enrico Ferri.
Purpose of School	To reform and humanize the legal and penal systems.	To apply the scientific method to the study of crime and criminality.
Image of Human Nature	Humans are hedonistic, rational, and have free will. Our behavior is motivated by maximizing pleasure and minimizing pain.	Human behavior is determined by psychological, biological, or social forces that constrain our rationality and free will.
Image of Criminals	Criminals are essentially the same as noncriminals. They commit crimes after calculating costs and benefits.	Criminals are different from noncriminals. They commit crimes because they are inferior in some way.
Definition of Crime	Strictly legal; crime is whatever the law says that it is.	Based on universal human abhorrence; crime should be limited to inherently evil (mala in se) acts.
Purpose of Punishment	To deter. Punishment is to be applied equally to all offenders committing the same crime. Judicial discretion to be limited.	Social defense. Punishment to be applied differently to different offenders based on relevant differences and should be rehabilitative.

⧉ Connecting Criminological Theory and Social Policy

Theories of crime causation imply that changing the conditions that the theory holds responsible for causing crime can reduce and even prevent it. We say "imply" because few theorists are explicit about the public policy implications of their work. Scientists are primarily concerned with gaining knowledge for its own sake; they are only secondarily concerned with how useful that knowledge may be to practitioners and policy makers. Conversely, policy makers are less concerned with hypothesized "causes" of a problem and more concerned with what can be done about the problem that is both politically and financially feasible.

Policy is simply a course of action designed to solve some problem that has been selected from among alternative courses of action. Solving a social problem means attempting to reduce the level of the problem currently being experienced or to enact strategies that try to prevent it from occurring in the first place. Social science findings can and have been used to help policy makers determine which course of action to follow to "do something" about the crime problem, but policy makers must consider many other concerns that go beyond maintaining consistency with social science theory and data. The question of "what to do about crime" involves political and financial considerations, the urgency of other problems competing for scarce financial resources (schools, highways, environmental protection, public housing, national defense), and a host of other major and minor considerations.

Policy choices are, at bottom, value choices. As such, only those policy recommendations that are ideologically palatable are likely to be implemented. Given all of these extra-theoretical considerations, it would be unfair to base our judgment of a theory's power solely, or even primarily, by its impact on public policy. Even if some aspects of policy are theory based, unless all recommendations of the theory are fully implemented, the success or failure of the policy cannot be considered evidence of theoretical failure anymore than a baker can blame a recipe for a lousy cake if he or she neglects to include all the ingredients it calls for.

Connecting problems with solutions is a tricky business in all areas of government policy making, but nowhere is it more difficult than in the area of criminal justice. No single strategy can be expected to produce significant results and may sometimes make matters worse. For example, we have seen that President Johnson's "War on Poverty" was supposed to have a significant impact on the crime problem by attacking what informed opinion of the time considered its "root cause." We also saw that programs and policies developed to reduce poverty did so, but that reducing poverty had no effect on reducing crime; in fact, crime rose as poverty was falling. Another high-profile example of failed policy is the Volstead Act of 1919, which prohibited the manufacture and sale of alcohol in the United States. Although based on a true premise (alcohol is a major factor in facilitating violent crime), it failed because it ushered in a wild period of crime as gangs fought over control of the illegal alcohol market. Policies often have effects that are unanticipated by policy makers, and these effects can be positive or negative.

Nevertheless, every theory has policy implications deducible from its primary assumptions and propositions. The deep and lasting effects of the classical theories of Beccaria and Bentham on legal systems around the world have already been noted, but the broad generalities about human nature contained in those theories offer little specific advice on ways to change criminals or to reduce their numbers. Although we caution against using the performance of a theory's public policy recommendations as a major criterion to evaluate its power, the fact remains that a good theory *should* offer useful practical recommendations, and we will discuss a theory's policy implications when appropriate.

Policy and Prevention: Implications of Neoclassical Theories

If you were the kind of motivated rational criminal assumed by neoclassical theorists, what sort of questions would you ask yourself at the potential crime site before you made your decision to commit the crime or not? We bet that among them would be the following: "Is there a quick and direct route out of the area after the job is done?" "How vulnerable are the targets (is the car unlocked, is the door open, is the girl walking down a dark alley alone)?" "What are my chances of being seen by people in the area?" "If people in this area do see me, do they look likely to do something about it?" The policy implications of rational choice and routine activities theories boil down to trying to arrange things such that criminals will dissuade themselves from committing crimes by the answers they arrive at to questions such as these—that is, making their choice structuring decisions as difficult as possible.

Rational choice and routine activities theories thus shift the policy focus from large and costly social programs, such as antipoverty, recreational, and educational programs, to target hardening and environmental designs that might dissuade a motivated offender from offending. In other words, they shift attention away from policies designed to change offenders' attitudes and behavior by trying to provide them with legitimate opportunities and better living conditions, as well as make it more difficult and more costly for them to offend. Examples of target hardening include antitheft devices on automobiles, the use of vandal-resistant materials on public property, improved city lighting, surveillance cameras in stores and at public gathering places, check guarantee cards, banning the sale of alcohol at sporting events, neighborhood watches, and curfews for teenagers.

Environmental designs (more associated with *routine activities* theory) primarily include the concept of *defensible space,* defined as "a model for residential environments which inhibit crime by creating the physical expression of a social fabric that defends itself."[59] It endeavors to bring people together into a tribe-like sense of community, not by manipulating attitudes and values but by designing the physical environment so as to awaken the human sense of territoriality. The best possible physical environment for the growth of crime is the large barracks-like blocks of apartments with few entrances, few private spaces, and few demarcation barriers that say, "This space is mine." Families must be given back a sense of ownership, for if everything is "owned" in common (elevators, walkways and staircases, balconies, grass and shrubberies), then no one takes care of it, and it deteriorates rapidly. Streets must be blocked off, both to generate a sense of belonging to "my special little neighborhood" and so that criminals cannot easily access or escape them.

City government can help to foster this sense of pride by removing abandoned cars and other trash from vacant lots and perhaps building miniature parks on those lots. It could also engage in concerted programs to raze deteriorating vacant houses, repave and weed sidewalks, and generally spruce up older neighborhoods. This could all be done cheaply with neighborhood associations, volunteers, jail inmates, and probationers providing the labor, along with private corporations and city agencies providing funds.[60] Dirty, deteriorating, graffiti-marred neighborhoods not only demoralize law-abiding inhabitants but also foster a sense among the criminal elements that nobody cares and therefore anything goes.

The policy recommendations of deterrence theory are straightforward and obvious: Increase the costs of committing crime, and there will be less of it. Nobel Prize–winning economist Gary Becker[61] is a major adherent of the position. Comparing crime rates in Great Britain and the United States, Becker showed how crime rates rose in the former as its penal philosophy became more and more lenient, but they fell in the United States as its penal philosophy became more and more punitive. He dismisses the idea that criminals lack the knowledge and the foresight to take the punitive probabilities into consideration when deciding whether to continue committing crimes. He says that "interviews of young people in high crime areas who do engage in crime show an amazing understanding of what punishments are, what young people can get away with, how to behave when going before a judge."[62]

"Get tough" messages are the kinds of simple, easily implemented solutions that policy makers love—build prisons and fill 'em up. But getting tough is expensive, as many legislative bodies have found out. Many states started putting more and more offenders behind bars for longer periods and implemented mandatory sentencing laws in the 1980s but soon found their prisons so overcrowded that the courts intervened. This resulted in the repeal of some states' mandatory sentencing laws and the institution of early release programs. Thus, releasing offenders to the streets became the solution to a current problem, but that solution *was* the problem a few years earlier.[63] This goes to show how remarkably complicated and even perverse policy decisions can be and why we should not judge a criminological theory based on its impact (or lack of) on public policy.

In contrast to the classical notion that punishment should fit the crime and nothing else, Lombroso (who described himself as a humanist socialist) believed that punishment should be designed to fit the offender rather than the crime.[64] Lombroso felt that prisons were schools of vice and preferred fines, suspended sentences, and/or community service for minor offenders. Punishment should only be determined after a thorough assessment of offenders and their needs, and it should be aimed at rehabilitation. This requires wide judicial discretion and indeterminate sentences (both of which Beccaria disdained). These liberal treatment policy recommendations for offenders stand in stark contrast to Lombroso's recommendations for "congenital" offenders. For these individuals, he recommended either the death penalty (which he came to reluctantly support in his later years) or life imprisonment. He justified these penalties not in terms of just deserts but rather in terms of social defense.

SUMMARY

Prior to the beginning of the classical school of criminology, criminal behavior was thought of as either demonic possession or the evil abuse of free will. Because of the doctrine of Original Sin, all human beings were considered born sinners but behaved in socially acceptable ways by the grace of God. This kind of thinking started to wane with the coming of the period that historians call the Enlightenment. It was out of this period that the classical school of criminology was born. The leading light of this school was Cesare Beccaria, an Italian nobleman whose aim was to reform an arbitrary and cruel system of criminal justice. Jeremy Bentham, best known for his concept of the "hedonistic calculus," was another leading figure. Classical thinking has had a tremendous impact on the great majority of legal systems in the world.

The next step in the evolution of criminology came with cartographic criminologists such as Guerry, Quetelet, Mayhew, and Fletcher. These scholars studied maps and statistics to pinpoint where and when crime was most likely to occur. Many of the conclusions derived from this method remain consistent with those arrived at from modern scholars employing the same methods. These included relative deprivation (poverty in the midst of wealth is worse than poverty per se), social disorganization (caused by the frequent mixing and movement of different groups in and out of neighborhoods), and the weakening of social and moral bonds.

With the advance of science in the 19th century came a new way of thinking about human nature and crime, much of it being greatly influenced by Darwin's work on evolution. Cesare Lombroso is widely considered the father of criminology, but he is much criticized for his ideas. Unlike classical thinkers, Lombroso saw criminals as being different from noncriminals in that they are atavistic "throwbacks" to an earlier evolutionary period and could be identified by a number of bodily stigmata. Although he never said that all criminals are born criminals, he is widely thought to have done so and is thus often condemned as a biological determinist.

Other early positivists included Lombroso's fellow Italians, Raffael Garofalo and Enrico Ferri. Both men were more interested in penal philosophy than in criminology per se. Garofalo was interested in developing a "natural" definition of crime and in generating categories of criminals for the purpose of determining what should be done with them. Ferri was instrumental in formulating the concept of social defense as the only justification for punishment. This theory of punishment avers that criminals cannot be deterred (they lack the ability to understand moral behavior or deterrent consequences) or rehabilitated (how do you change born criminals?), so they must be incapacitated as long as possible.

Classical (or neoclassical) theories reemerged in the form of rational choice, routine activities, and deterrence theories in the 1970s. Rational choice, routine activities, and deterrence theories assume that humans are rational and self-seeking, although rationality is bounded by knowledge levels and thinking abilities. These theories downplay personal and background factors that influence choices in favor of analyzing the processes leading to offenders' choices to offend. These processes involve the properties of offenses interacting with properties of offenders to produce criminal events in a process known as choice structuring. Offenders make choices based on how they see their characteristics "fitting" the characteristics of criminal opportunities, all the time thinking about the ratio of expected rewards to possible punishments.

Routine activities theory looks at a criminal event as a motivated offender meeting a suitable target lacking a capable guardian. These ideas show how crime rates can go up or down without a change in the prevalence of motivated offenders by increasing or decreasing suitable targets and capable guardians.

Deterrence theory strongly emphasizes the hedonistic calculus and the utility of punishment to deter crime. If the pain of punishment is to deter crime, it must outweigh crime's pleasures. Punishment must be certain, swift, and sure, and it is most effective when it contrasts negatively with the person's everyday life. Punishment as applied today is ineffective because it is not swift, certain, or severe. Certainty of punishment has been shown to deter, but increasing the severity of punishment has not.

All theories have explicit or implicit recommendation for policy since they posit causes of crime or criminality. Removing those alleged causes should reduce crime if the theory is correct. However, the complex nature of crime and criminality makes policy decisions based on them very risky indeed. Policy makers must consider many other issues demanding scarce resources, so the policy content of a theory should never be used to pass judgment on the usefulness of theory for criminologists.

On Your Own

Log on to the web-based student study site at http://www.sagepub.com/criminologystudy for more information about the vignettes and materials presented in this chapter, suggestions for activities, study aids such as review quizzes, and research recommendations including journal article links and questions related to this chapter.

EXERCISES AND DISCUSSION QUESTIONS

1. What were the major changes brought about by the classical thinkers?

2. Is there any aspect of the early positivists that you think might still be useful and applicable to modern criminology?

3. If humans are primarily motivated by the hedonistic calculus, is simple deterrence the answer to the crime problem?

4. What advantages (or disadvantages) does positivism offer us over classicism?

5. Is Ferri's social defense rationale for punishment preferable to one emphasizing rehabilitation of offenders?

6. If a theory cannot inform public policy, is it any good? Why or why not?

7. Go to http://www.la.utexas.edu/research/poltheory/beccaria/delitti/delitti .c41.html and click on the section entitled *Of the Means of Preventing Crime*. How do Beccaria's ideas compare with those of the positivists on preventing crime? What is Beccaria's idea of "real crime," and how does it compare with the discussion in Chapter 1?

KEY WORDS

Atavism	Enlightenment	Positivism
Biogenetic law	Free will	Principle of utility
Cartographic criminologists	General deterrence	Rational
Choice structuring	Hedonism	Rational choice theory
Classical school	Hedonistic calculus	Recidivism
Contrast effect	Insane criminal	Routine activities theory
Criminaloid	Italian school of criminology	Social defense
Deterrence	Policy	Specific deterrence

REFERENCES

1. Beccaria, C. (1963). *On crimes and punishment* (H. Paulucci, Trans.). Indianapolis: Bobbs-Merrill. (Original work published 1764)
2. Jones, D. (1986). *History of criminology: A philosophical perspective.* Westport, CT: Greenwood.
3. Bentham, J. (1948). *A fragment on government and an introduction to the principles of morals and legislation* (W. Harrison, Ed.). Oxford, UK: Basil Blackwell. (Original work published 1789)
4. Bentham (1789/1948, p. 151).
5. Bentham (1789/1948, p. 125).
6. Bentham (1789/1948, p. 151).
7. Jacoby, J. (1979). *Classics of criminology.* Oak Park, IL: Moore.
8. Jones (1986, pp. 43–47).
9. Curran, D., & Renzetti, C. (2001). *Theories of crime* (2nd ed.). Boston: Allyn & Bacon. (Quote on p. 16)
10. Bentham (1789/1948).
11. Vold, G., & Bernard, T. (1986). *Theoretical criminology.* New York: Oxford University Press. (Quote on p. 132)

12. Rennie, Y. (1978). *The search for criminal man.* Lexington, MA: Lexington Books. (Quote on p. 36)

13. Levin, Y., & Lindesmith, A. (1971). English ecology and criminology of the past century. In H. Voss & D. Petersen (Eds.), *Ecology, crime, and delinquency* (pp. 47–64). New York: Appleton-Century-Crofts.

14. Lombroso, C. (1876). *Criminal man.* Milan: Hoepli.

15. Gibson, M. (2002). *Born to crime: Cesare Lombroso and the origins of biological criminology.* Westport, CT: Praeger.

16. Lombroso-Ferrero, G. (1972). *Criminal man according to the classification of Cesare Lombroso.* Montclair, NJ: Patterson Smith. (Original work published 1911)

17. Lombroso-Ferrero (1911/1972, p. 74).

18. Lombroso, C. (1911/1968). *Crime: Its causes and remedies* (H. Horton, Trans.). Montclair, NJ: Patterson Smith.

19. Lombroso (1911/1968).

20. Gibson (2002).

21. Kurtzberg, R., Safer, H., & Mandell, W. (1969). Plastic surgery in correction. *Federal Probation, 33,* 45.

22. Thompson, K. (1990). Refacing inmates: A critical appraisal of plastic surgery programs in prison. *Criminal Justice and Behavior, 17,* 448–460.

23. Brennan, P., Mednick, S., & Kandel, E. (1993). Congenital determinants of violent and property offending. In D. Pepler & K. Rubin (Eds.), *The development and treatment of childhood aggression* (pp. 81–92). Hillsdale, NJ: Lawrence Erlbaum.

24. Raine, A. (1993). *The psychopatholgy of crime: Criminal behavior as a clinical disorder.* San Diego: Academic Press.

25. Krouse, J., & Kauffman, J. (1982). Minor physical anomalies in exceptional children: A review and critique of research. *Journal of Abnormal Child Psychology, 10,* 247–264.

26. Thompson (1990).

27. Garofalo, R. (1968). *Criminology.* Montclair, NJ: Patterson Smith. (Original work published 1885)

28. Ferri, E. (1917). *Criminal sociology.* Boston: Little, Brown. (Original work published 1897. Quote on p. 11)

29. Goring, C. (1972). *The English convict: A statistical study 1913.* Montclair, NJ: Patterson Smith. (Original work published 1913)

30. Goring (1913/1972, p. 173).

31. Vold and Bernard (1986, p. 87).

32. Gilsinan, J. (1990). *Criminology and public policy: An introduction.* Englewood Cliffs, NJ: Prentice Hall.

33. Goring (1913/1972, p. 26).

34. Cordella, P., & Siegel, L. (Eds.). (1996). *Readings in contemporary criminological theory.* Boston: Northeastern University Press.

35. Cornish, D., & Clarke, R. (Eds.). (1986). *The reasoning criminal.* New York: Springer-Verlag.

36. Clark, R., & Cornish, D. (1985). Modeling offenders' decisions: A framework for research and policy. In M. Tonry & N. Morris (Eds.), *Crime and justice annual review of research* (pp. 147–185). Chicago: University of Chicago Press.

37. Bentham (1789/1948).

38. Mealey, L. (1995). The sociobiology of sociopathy: An integrated evolutionary model. *Behavioral and Brain Sciences, 18,* 523–541.

39. Cornish and Clarke (1986).

40. Cornish, D., & Clarke, R. (1987). Understanding crime displacement: An application of rational choice theory. *Criminology, 25,* 933–947. (Quote on p. 933)

41. Cornish and Clarke (1987, p. 935).

42. Cohen, L., & Felson, M. (1979). Social change and crime rate trends: A routine activities approach. *American Sociological Review, 44,* 588–608.

43. Cohen and Felson (1979, p. 593).

44. Catalano, S. (2005). *Criminal victimization, 2004.* Washington, DC: Bureau of Justice Statistics.

45. Robinson, M. (2005). *Justice blind: Ideals and realities of American criminal justice.* Upper Saddle River, NJ: Prentice Hall.

46. National Center for Policy Analysis. (1998, August 17). *Does punishment deter?* (NCPA Policy Backgrounder 148). Washington, DC: Author.

47. Langan, P., & Farrington, D. (1998). *Crime and justice in the United States and England and Wales, 1981–1996.* Washington, DC: Bureau of Justice Statistics.

48. Spelman, W. (2000). The limited importance of prison expansion. In A. Blumstein & J. Wallman (Eds.), *The crime drop in America* (pp. 97–129). Cambridge, UK: Cambridge University Press.

49. Rosenfeld, R. (2000). Patterns in adult homicide. In A. Blumstein & J. Wallman (Eds.), *The crime drop in America* (pp. 130–163). Cambridge, UK: Cambridge University Press.

50. Radzinowicz, L., & King, J. (1979). *The growth of crime: The international experience.* Middlesex, UK: Penguin. (Quote on p. 296)

51. Reynolds, M. (1990). Crime pays, but so does imprisonment. *Journal of Social, Political and Economic Studies, 15,* 259–300.

52. Reynolds (1990).

53. Nagin, D. (1998). Criminal deterrence research at the onset of the twenty-first century. In M. Tony (Ed.), *Crime and justice: A review of research* (Vol. 23, pp. 1–42). Chicago: University of Chicago Press.

54. McCarthy, B. (2002). New economics of sociological criminology. *Annual Review of Sociology, 28,* 417–442.

55. Curran and Renzetti (2001, p. 21).

56. Lanier, M., & Henry, S. (1998). *Essential criminology.* Boulder, CO: Westview.

57. Cornish and Clarke (1986, p. 1).

58. Williams, F., & McShane, M. (1994). *Criminological theory.* Englewood Cliffs, NJ: Prentice Hall.

59. Newman, O. (1972). *Defensible space.* New York: Macmillan. (Quote on p. 3)

60. Taylor, R., & Harrell, A. (1996). *Physical environment and crime.* Washington, DC: U.S. Department of Justice.

61. Becker, G. (1997). The economics of crime. In M. Fisch (Ed.), *Criminology 97/98* (pp. 15–20). Guilford, CT: Dusskin.

62. Becker (1997, p. 20).

63. Gilsinian, J. (1990). *Criminology and public policy: An introduction.* Englewood Cliffs, NJ: Prentice Hall.

64. Gibson (2002).

SOCIAL STRUCTURAL THEORIES

On June 15, 1975, 12-year-old Kody Scott graduated from elementary school in Los Angeles. During the ceremony, his thoughts were on "the hood" and his one ambition in life, which was to join the Eight Tray Crips, become a "ghetto star," and major in murder, robbery, and general mayhem. He went straight from the graduation to his initiation into the gang, which involved taking part in the gunning down of 15 members of a rival faction of L.A.'s other notorious gang, the Bloods. Two years later, during a robbery in which the victim tried to run, Kody beat and stomped the man into a coma. A police officer at the scene said that "whoever did this is a monster," a name Kody proudly took as his street moniker. Monster did time in juvenile detention and then served several prison terms. During one of these terms, he converted to Afrocentric Islam and changed his name to Sanyika Shakur. He also wrote Monster: The Autobiography of an L.A. Gang Member while in prison, which provides a frightening portrayal of the poverty, violence, and alienation of ghetto life. Shakur was paroled in 1995; returned to prison on parole violations in 1996, 1997, and 1998; and again was incarcerated for a shooting in 2000. Paroled again sometime later, he was rearrested in 2004 for "battery with great bodily harm" and again sent to prison.

Shakur was allegedly the illegitimate son of an ex-football player named Dick Bass. His mother subsequently married another man and had four more children. She divorced their father when Shakur was 6 years old and had to raise the children alone. Shakur was mistreated by his stepfather and never included in family outings. He spent almost all his childhood in the wild and chaotic streets, which he says was the only thing that really interested him. As you read this chapter about disorganized neighborhoods, blocked opportunities to legitimate success, and lower-class values, try to imagine Shakur at the center of it all and how these things may have shaped his life.

◧ The Social Structural Tradition

All criminological theories contain a view of human nature that is sometimes explicit, but most often implicit. Sociologists tend to formulate their theories and make their arguments consistent with the assumption that human nature is socially constructed; that is, the human mind is basically a "blank slate" at birth and formed by cultural experiences. Given this assumption, the task of sociological criminology is to discover why social animals commit antisocial acts. If human nature is socially constructed, the presence of antisocial characters among us reflects defective social construction, not defective human materials. We must therefore search for flaws and defects in the "blueprints" of society and not in the individual products of those faulty blueprints. Among the many destructive social forces structural theorists analyze are discriminatory class structures, poverty, racism, discrimination, cultural conflicts, and capitalism.

Almost all sociological theories of crime emphasize social structure to various degrees. By **social structure**, we mean how society is organized by social institutions—the family, as well as educational, religious, economic, and political institutions—and stratified on the basis of various roles and statuses. Social structure is society's framework, structuring the patterns of relationships that its members have with one another, and can do so with varying degrees of success depending on how organized or disorganized the structure is (how the various institutions that comprise the structure "mesh" with one another). Structural theorists favor external "out-there" reality as being of primary importance in determining human social behavior; that is, they tend to work from assumptions made from general models of society and to deduce everyday experiences of individuals from those models. Structural theorists are more interested in seeking the causes of group crime rates rather than why particular individuals commit crimes since they believe that society prepares crime and individuals are only the instruments that give it life, and if we wish to reduce crime, we must change society, not the individual.

Theories that examine whole societies and their structures are called *macro* ("large") theories. In contrast to macro theories, *micro* ("small") theories work in the opposite direction. Micro theories examine the everyday experiences of individuals within intimate social groups and emphasize the subjective inner social reality of individuals rather than the "objective" world "out there." The adjectives *macro* and *micro* refer to the units of analysis (whole societies or individuals in groups), not the expansiveness or scope of the theories themselves.

For the purpose of locating structural criminological theories within a more general sociological framework, we have to understand the assumptions of two separate models of society: the consensus and conflict models. Although we are talking about modern sociological models of society, the essential elements of these two models have dominated political thought for at least as far back as Plato and Aristotle.

The **consensus** or **functionalist perspective** is one that views society as a system consisting of mutually sustaining parts and characterized by broad normative consensus. All the various social institutions have their own particular specialized social functions to perform to keep society running smoothly. Functionalists often draw analogies with the physical body, comprising specialized parts (heart, lungs, brains, kidneys, and so on) that function in unison to keep the whole body healthy. When any one of these parts malfunctions, all the other parts, and thus the whole body, are negatively affected. Likewise, because social institutions are also integrated parts of a larger whole (the social body), a change in any part affects the proper functioning of the entire social system. Because we never know how institutional change will ultimately affect the larger social whole, many functionalists tend to distrust large-scale social change. Anything that threatens that normative consensus is dysfunctional and therefore undesirable.

This chapter explores criminological theories that may be broadly construed as consensus theories; theories that assume that conflict rather than consensus characterizes society are explored in Chapter 6. Consensus theorists are aware that conflicts between individuals and groups with different interests occur. However, they believe that these conflicts can be patched up by a neutral legal system that all parties are said to respect. The legal system functions as society's "immune system," protecting the other social institutions from harm. Law is said to reflect society's deeply held values and is deemed legitimate by all segments of society. As we shall see, conflict theorists have a different view of the law.

◼ Sociological Positivism

Perhaps in response to the almost total emphasis on individual differences by scientists in other disciplines, early sociological positivism tended to ignore them in their explanations of crime in favor of examining group structures and processes. Most sociologists took seriously the proposition that wholes (societies, institutions, groups) are greater than the sums of their parts (individuals), that these social groupings are real, and that they enjoy an existence of their own separate from their individual members. Although by definition, these groups cannot exist apart from the individuals who comprise them, once formed, they take on an existence independent of any one individual. Causes of crime favored by sociologists in this tradition are compounds of a variety of social phenomena that are summarized by terms such as *social disorganization, anomie,* or *group conflict.* The appreciation of the social context of criminal behavior is sociology's greatest contribution to our understanding of crime.

Durkheim, Modernization, and Anomie

French sociologist Émile Durkheim, although not a criminologist, provided criminology with one of its most revered and enduring concepts: **anomie.** Anomie (*a* = "without"; *nomos* = norms) is a term meaning "lacking in rules" or "normlessness," which Durkheim used to describe a condition of normative deregulation in society. Durkheim's anomie refers to a property of social structures, not a state of mind; it is a condition that sometimes *leads* to a deviant state of mind bereft of moral guidance, but it is not a term describing that state of mind.

Durkheim was much concerned with social solidarity and the threat posed to it by rapid social change. He distinguished between two forms of social solidarity: *mechanical* and *organic.* **Mechanical solidarity** exists in small, isolated, and self-sufficient prestate societies in which individuals, because they share common experiences and circumstances (there is only minimal division of labor), share common values and develop strong emotional ties to the collectivity. Under these circumstances, informal social controls are extremely strong, and antisocial behavior is generally minimal.

Organic solidarity is characteristic of modern societies in which there is a high degree of occupational specialization. This division of labor generates greater diversity of experiences and circumstances and, eventually, weaker common values and social bonds. These weak bonds tend to be instrumental rather than emotional and are generated by transitory contractual relationships entered into to fulfill needs that individuals in mechanical societies supply for themselves. As societies become more complex, the problem of maintaining social cohesion becomes more problematic because of ambiguities and contradictions regarding the rules and standards of moral behavior generated by the division of labor and rapid social change. Crime and other forms of deviance grow in proportion to the degree of social deregulation in society.

▲ Photo 4.1   Émile Durkheim (1858–1917)

Although Durkheim felt that crime is to be abhorred, he did not view it as abnormal. He argued that because crime is found at all times and in all societies, it is a normal and inevitable social phenomenon. Not only that, criminals and other deviants are socially useful (functional) in that they serve to identify the limits of acceptable behavior. If society could successfully repress all those it currently identifies as criminals and deviants, it would become sensitive to less odious forms of nonconformity, which then may be elevated to criminal status. This could go on almost indefinitely with successive rounds of repression, more redefinition, and more repression until eventually a pathological conformity would stifle creativity, progress, and personal freedom. For Durkheim, crime is one of the prices we pay for personal freedom and for social progress. He even asserted that when crime drops significantly below average levels (such as in wartime), it is sign that something is wrong in society.[1]

Durkheim was interested in the origins of fluctuating crime rates, not why people are differentially susceptible to the deviance-generating conditions of social deregulation. Hence Durkheim's famous dictum that the causes of social facts (such as crime rates) "should be sought among the social facts preceding it."[2] Durkheim also wrote, "From the fact that crime is a normal phenomenon of normal sociology, it does not follow that the criminal is an individual normally constituted from the biological and psychological points of view."[3] He did not mean that criminals *are* abnormal from the biological and/or psychological points of view; he only asserted that the sociological normality of *crime* does not necessarily imply the biological and psychological normality of the *criminal*. Durkheim also asserted that in any society, there are always individuals who "diverge to some extent from the collective type," and among them is the "criminal character."[4]

Durkheim viewed all human beings as similar in their "essential qualities" but added that "one sort of heredity will always exist, that of natural talent."[5] This is the crux of the crime problem at the individual level because for Durkheim, human wants and needs are insatiable: "Human activity naturally aspires beyond assignable limits and sets itself unattainable goals."[6] Durkheim insisted that individuals cannot be happy unless their wants are sufficiently proportional to their means.[7] When a person gets less than he or she expects, the individual is ripe for criminal behavior. Remember, all people are said to aspire to maximize their pleasures (here Durkheim is true to the classical spirit), but deficiencies in "natural talent" will thwart some from attaining their goals legitimately. These people must then either lower their expectations or goals or else attempt to attain them illegitimately.

Early sociological positivism was more balanced than early biological or psychological positivism because it arose partly in response to them. Early sociological theories were more likely to accord biology and psychology their fair share of causal influence than were later ones, and their emphasis on social factors forced biological and psychological theorists to rethink many of their positions. Durkheim's writings contributed greatly to the recognition of sociology as an autonomous science, a science that was to capture criminology for itself in the early 20th century.

The Chicago School of Ecology

The first criminological theory to be developed in the United States was the Chicago school of human ecology. This school, developed at the University of Chicago in the 1920s and 1930s primarily through the works of Clifford Shaw and Henry McKay,[8] is the intellectual heir of the European cartographic school of criminology. *Ecology* is a term used in biology to describe the interrelations of living organisms and their environment—how each affects and is affected by the other. Sociologists use the term **social ecology** to describe the interrelations of human beings and the communities in which they live. Early social ecologists viewed the city as a kind of superorganism with "natural areas" differentially adaptive for different ethnic groups (hence the formation of little Italys, Chinatowns, etc.). In these areas, there was a symbiotic (mutually beneficial) relationship between individuals and between individuals and their cultural and physical environments. Social ecologists saw this symbiosis erode as successive waves of different ethnic groups in certain city neighborhoods displace the former inhabitants. They likened this social process to the biological ecological concepts of

▲ **Photo 4.2** The Chicago school of ecology predicted that immigrant ethnic groups would migrate from one neighborhood to another as both the city grew in size (expanding zones) and group members achieved financial success in America. However, ethnic enclaves such as Ukraine Village in Chicago remain for several reasons, even when surrounded by low-income, high-crime ghetto communities. The largest Ukrainian church in America is located in this neighborhood, along with the Ukrainian Museum and Ukrainian Cultural Center.

invasion, dominance, and succession, which describe the process of occupation of ecological niches by species of plant and animal life previously alien to those niches.

In their analysis of Cook County Juvenile Court records spanning the years from 1900 to 1933, Shaw and McKay noted that the majority of delinquents always came from the same neighborhoods regardless of the ethnic composition of those neighborhoods. This suggested the existence of "natural areas" that may facilitate crime and delinquency independent of other factors. Their findings also increased confidence among sociologists in their assertion that the environment was more important than ethnic group or individual differences in explaining criminal behavior. Shaw and McKay did not claim that residential areas were necessary and sufficient causes of antisocial behavior; they only sought to demonstrate that crime and delinquency were heavily concentrated in certain neighborhoods regardless of the racial or ethnic identities of their residents.

Previous research in social ecology characterized the spatial patterns of U.S. cities as radiating outwards from central business and industrial areas in a series of concentric circles, or *ecological zones*. As shown in Figure 4.1, Zone I is the Loop area of Chicago, and Zone II was the factory zone, around which earlier Chicago residents had built their homes. Zone II was inhabited by the poorest residents of the city and was further characterized by business and industrial expansion into it. In response to this expansion, Zone II residents invaded Zone III, the zone of working-class homes, making this zone less desirable, and those who could afford to do so moved out. Successive waves of poor foreign and native immigrants invaded and occupied these old inner-city neighborhoods, just as they had in the British cities studied by Mayhew and Fletcher in the 1800s, discussed in Chapter 3. This process had a ripple effect, like a stone dropped in a river. Successive waves of newcomers to the poorest neighborhoods precipitate constant movement from zone to zone as more established groups seek to escape the intrusion of the newcomers. Urban decay and crime are consequences of this population movement. Note that the delinquency rates decreased linearly from 9.8 in the poorest zone to 1.8 in the most affluent suburban zone.

Social Disorganization

The decline in crime and delinquency that occurred from the inner city outwards had long been known and was not in itself theoretically significant or useful. What Shaw and McKay needed was a mechanism that explained it. They found such a mechanism in the concept of **social disorganization,** which essentially means the breakdown, or serious dilution, of the power of informal community rules to regulate conduct. Almost a century earlier, cartographic criminologists had pointed out that social disorganization is created by the continuous redistribution of neighborhood populations, and Durkheim pointed out that rapid social change weakens social controls. The mix of peoples with limited resources, bringing with them a wide variety of cultural traditions sometimes at odds with traditional American middle-class norms of behavior, is not conducive to developing and/or maintaining a sense of community.

A neighborhood in the process of losing its sense of community (of becoming disorganized) was called a **transition zone.** A zone in transition was one that was being "invaded" by members of "alien" racial or ethnic groups, bringing with them values and practices that conflicted with those already established by the "natural" inhabitants of the area. The conflict over values and conduct norms arising when culturally heterogeneous groups are thrown together generates social disorganization (the "consensus" dear to the hearts of functionalists had broken down). Crime and delinquency thus arise as a consequence of social disorganization and the loss of a traditional sense of a "natural" community, and these are themselves the result of racial/ethnic diversity in an area.

Social disorganization is really the loss of neighborhood collective efficacy. Personal efficacy refers to the ability or power to achieve some outcome deemed personally desirable. **Collective efficacy** refers to the shared power of a group of connected and engaged individuals to influence an outcome that the collective deems desirable, such as the maintenance of public order. According to Robert Sampson, "The key causal mechanism in collective efficacy theory is social control enacted under certain conditions of social trust."[9] The loss of this control, cohesion, and trust in the collective ability to direct the affairs of the neighborhood

| Figure 4.1 | Zone Map of Male Delinquents in Chicago 1925–1933 |

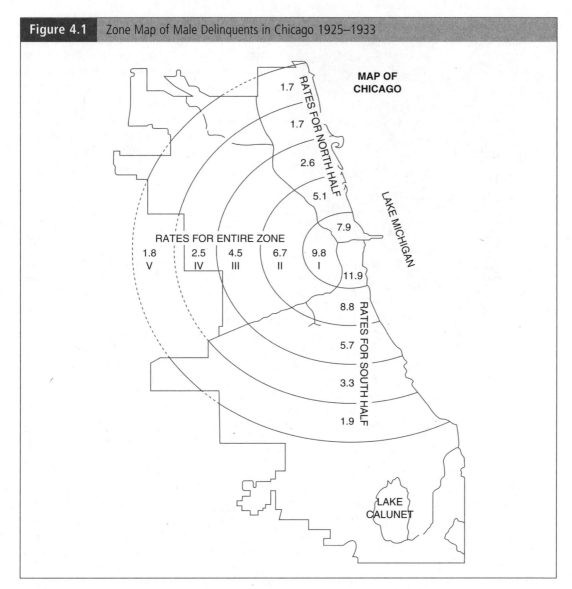

in positive directions is what the concept of social disorganization is all about. In other words, the same things that predict the loss of collective efficacy—concentrated poverty, lack of home ownership, rundown buildings, family disruptions, and so on—are the same things that predict social disorganization.

Social disorganization affects crime and delinquency in two ways. First, the lack of social controls in disorganized neighborhoods facilitates crime by failing to inhibit it. The social control exercised by any community is a function of its ability to bring people together to

▲ **Photo 4.3** A variation of the social disorganization model suggests that "broken windows" and other signs of neighborhood decay tell teens and adult neighborhood residents that it's OK to commit crimes.

organize strategies to combat community problems. Because a community in flux is culturally fractured, conventional institutions of control such as the family, church, school, informal neighborhood clubs, and voluntary organizations are unable to exert appropriate supervision over restless youths. Without the kinds of informal social controls operative in more established communities, slum youths are freed to follow their natural impulses and inclinations.

The second way that social disorganization contributes to crime and delinquency is the provision of positive incentives to engage in it. In the absence of prosocial values, a set of values supporting antisocial behavior is likely to develop to fill the vacuum. Thus, slum youths have both negative and positive inducements to crime and delinquency, represented by the absence of social controls and the presence of delinquent values, respectively. These conditions are transmitted across generations until they become intrinsic properties of the neighborhood.

The breakdown of the social regulatory structure leading to the elevation of antisocial behavior by freeing "natural inclinations" was a proposition made by Durkheim in his anomie theory. The major differences between Durkheim and Shaw and MacKay is that (a) the former concentrated on whole societies while the latter looked at social deregulation at the neighborhood level, and (b) in addition to the effects of social disorganization in promoting crime by failing to inhibit it, Shaw and MacKay also posited the crime-promoting effects of a set of deviant values that filled the vacuum left by the dissolution of prosocial values.

Shaw and McKay's findings have been replicated in many urban areas, but what are the effects in rural areas, generally thought to be more traditional and communitarian by their very nature? A study of 264 rural counties in four states by D. Wayne Osgood and Jeff Chambers found that "the principles of social disorganization theory hold up quite well in rural settings."[10] In common with Shaw and McKay, the researchers traced social disorganization to high rates of population turnover and high rates of ethnic diversity, but they found that the most important factor was high rates of female-headed households. Single-parent households are highly related to the kinds of problems Shaw and McKay identified as being related to social disorganization some 75 years previously (i.e., low economic status, dilapidated living accommodations, and poor supervision of children). The most notable finding of the study was that "a 10 percent increase in female-headed households was associated with 73- to 100-percent higher rates of arrest for all offenses except homicide [it was associated with a 33% increase in homicide]."[11] Ecological theory is illustrated in Figure 4.2.

Figure 4.2	Diagrammatic Presentation of Ecological Theory

Influx of native and foreign immigrants into cities looking for work and congregating in poorest areas → Value conflict and decrease in formal and informal social controls lead to SOCIAL DISORGANIZATION → Deterioration of neighborhood and development of delinquent values → **Delinquency and crime**

After a period of prominence lasting into the 1960s, the popularity of ecological theory declined rapidly.[12] One of the criticisms that helped to hasten its demise was W. S. Robinson's concept[13] of **ecological fallacy,** which states that we cannot make inferences about individuals and groups on the basis of information derived from a larger population of which they are a part. Even in the heyday of ecological theory, it was often shown that Asians and Jews living in high crime areas had very low crime rates.[14] To find high crime rates in a neighborhood with a large Asian population living there and then to assume that Asians commit crimes at a rate matching the neighborhood rate is an example of the ecological fallacy. Low Asian crime rates in high-crime neighborhoods also suggested that the rejection of group and individual differences as explanations for crime and delinquency was premature.[15]

Closely allied to this issue is Ruth Kornhauser's question: "How do we know that area differences in delinquency rates result from the aggregated characteristics of communities rather than the characteristics of individuals selectively aggregated into communities?"[16] This pointed question implies that some people remain in slum areas while others leave as soon as they are able, and the decision to stay or leave may depend as much on individual factors (e.g., ability, ambition) as on situational factors (e.g., poverty, unemployment). Some theorists argue that ecological factors have no independent effect on crime once the human composition of areas (what kinds of people live there) is taken into consideration. Others argue the opposite, while still others argue that people and places are equally important in explaining crime.

Strain Theory: Robert Merton's Extension of Anomie Theory

American sociologist Robert Merton[21] expanded Emile Durkheim's anomie theory to develop a popular explanation of crime that has come to be known as strain theory. The central feature of Merton's theory is that American culture defines monetary success (the "American Dream") as the predominant goal for which all its citizens should aspire, the attainment of which symbolizes a person's character and self-worth. In addition to espousing valued goals, cultures prescribe procedures for legitimately attaining them. At the bottom of America's crime problem, says Merton, is that while American culture places disproportionate emphasis on success goals, American social structure restricts access to legitimate means of attaining them to certain segments of the population. It is this disjunction between cultural goals and the structural impediments to achieving them that is anomic, and it is in this gap where crime is bred.

Unlike Durkheim, Merton viewed anomie as a permanent condition of society caused by this disjunction rather than as an occasional condition arising in periods of rapid social change and declining during periods of social stability. Strain theory views crime as a normal

People Versus Places: Do Neighborhoods Matter?

An interesting study of serious juvenile offending supports the middle ground in the people versus place debate—that is, there are neighborhood effects, but they are mediated by individual differences. Wikstrom and Loeber[17] studied the characteristics of the 90 neighborhoods in Pittsburgh, Pennsylvania, in conjunction with selected individual differences of 1,530 male juveniles residing in them. Neighborhoods were divided into *advantaged, middle-range, disadvantaged-nonpublic,* and *disadvantaged-public* according to a variety of demographic indicators. The percentage of families living in poverty ranged from zero in the most advantaged neighborhood to 86 in the most disadvantaged neighborhoods, which were 99% African American and had 72% of its families on welfare. In the most advantaged neighborhoods, there were no African Americans and no families on welfare.

The percentage of youths self-reporting serious offending in each of the four neighborhood types ranged from 30.9% in the most affluent neighborhood to 63.7% in the least affluent, which may be interpreted as neighborhood effects. Neighborhood effects were less clear, however, when the researchers controlled for individual risk factors (impulsiveness, guilt proneness, and parental supervision). Based on measures of these characteristics, boys were placed into *high-risk, balanced,* and *high-protective* categories. The percentage of boys scoring high on the *risk index* in those same neighborhoods was 13.3%, 19.9%, 28.8%, and 34.9%, respectively. Thus, boys at low risk for antisocial behavior were mostly concentrated in the advantaged environments, and boys at high risk were mostly concentrated in disadvantaged neighborhoods.

There were no neighborhood effects among boys at high risk for antisocial behavior, with about 70% of high-risk boys committing antisocial acts in all neighborhoods. Among boys in the *high-protective* category, the percentage of youths reporting that they committed serious offenses ranged from 11.1% in the most advantaged neighborhood category to 37.5% in the most disadvantaged neighborhood category. Mindful of the pitfalls of self-report data relevant to over- and underreporting, these data do suggest neighborhood effects for boys at low to medium risk for antisocial behavior but none for boys at high risk.

Other recent ecological studies have come to similar conclusions—that is, neighborhood effects are mediated by the characteristics of people living in them, but neighborhoods per se also appear to have independent effects on crime.[18,19] A particularly useful experimental study randomly assigned families from low-income neighborhoods into three conditions: (1) families given housing vouchers and special assistance to move into low-poverty neighborhoods, (2) families given housing vouchers but no assistance to move into neighborhoods of their choice, and (3) families who remained in the low-income neighborhood.[20] Official records showed that families moving into better neighborhoods reduced violent offending among their juveniles by 30% to 50%, although property offenses increased slightly (more and better things to steal, perhaps?). Studies such as this underline the fact that whatever individual risk factors are related to crime, they are always expressed in a social context, and some contexts make the expression more likely than others.

response to conditions that limit the opportunities for some individuals to obtain the economic success for which we are all supposed to strive.

It has been argued that Merton presented two theories in 1938: an anomie theory and a strain theory.[22] Anomie is the structural-cultural disjunction described above, and strain theory is the way people adapt to life in the context of anomie. Although the theory examines the responses of individuals to anomic conditions, the cause of crime is not found within individuals, who must be constrained by normative controls, as ecological theorists and Durkheim contend; rather, it is found in sociocultural contradictions. According to Merton, being unable to attain one's culturally defined wants legitimately invites frustration (strain) and may result in efforts to obtain them illegitimately. Merton disagreed with Durkheim's assessment that acquisitiveness is an intrinsic property of human nature (a perspective from the constrained vision), viewing it instead as a culturally generated characteristic (an unconstrained vision).

Modes of Adaptation

Note that Merton is claiming that culture and social structure actually exert pressure on some people to engage in *nonconforming* (criminal) behavior rather than conforming behavior. Thus, society is the cause of anomie, not the victim of it. Merton identified five **modes of adaptation** that various people adopt in response to this societal pressure. These modes refer to role adjustments to the alleged disjunction between goals and means, not to the personalities of individuals adopting them. Modes of adaptation are defined in terms of acceptance or rejection of cultural goals and the approved institutional means of attaining them. The modes are briefly described as follows:

Conformity Cultural **conformity** is by far the most common mode of adaptation because most people have the means of legally attaining cultural goals at their disposal. Conformists accept the success goals of American society and the prescribed means of attaining them (hard work, education, persistence, dedication). If most members of a culture were not conformists, society would cease to exist in its present form. Merton considered all adaptations other than conformity to be "deviant."

Ritualism The ritualist is the nine-to-five slugger who has long given up on ever achieving material success but who nevertheless continues to work within legitimate boundaries because he or she accepts the legitimacy of the opportunity structure. These are the "decent" people of the world, behaving morally (at least with respect to staying within legal boundaries) despite that lack of material rewards for doing so. The ritualist is deviant because of the rejection of cultural goals, but it is not a criminal adaptation.

Innovation The innovator accepts the validity of the cultural goals of monetary success but rejects legitimate means of attaining them. Innovation is the mode of adaptation most associated with crime. Since lower-class and minority individuals are those least likely to have legitimate opportunities available to them, and since they have been only weakly socialized to accept the legitimacy of the opportunity structure, it should not surprise us that crime occurs disproportionately among them. However, strain theorists emphasize that innovative adaptations may occur in any social class to the extent that there is an overweening stress on goals coupled with obstructions in the way of their attainment. Crime is an innovative avenue to success—a method by which deprived people (the not-so-deprived also) get what they have been taught by their culture to want.

Retreatism Retreatists reject both the cultural goals and the institutionalized means of attaining them; they are in society but not of it. People adopting this mode drop out of society and often take refuge in drugs, alcohol, and transience. These people drop out of society for a number of reasons. They may find society's goals not worth striving for, or if they do, they may lack the characteristics necessary to grasp opportunities for attaining them, or they simply may have been denied opportunities. Retreatists are frequently in trouble with the law because of crimes committed to support a drug and/or alcohol habit.

Rebellion Rebels are in a unique position in Merton's scheme in that they reject both the goals and the means of capitalist American society, but unlike retreatists, rebels wish to substitute alternative legitimate goals and alternative legitimate means. They may be committed to some form of sociopolitical ideal, such as socialism, or perhaps to various race/hate groups such as the Aryan Nations or the Nation of Islam. Rebellion is a noncriminal adaptation as long as rebels confine their rebellion to the written and spoken word and do not engage in illegal *behavior*.

To sum up, Merton's theory stresses the power of culture to generate conformity. Although Merton was concerned with conformity to American success goals, they are essentially the same goals of any capitalist culture. Complete value consensus within the United States is not implied in the theory, but it does stress that materialistic success is a particularly prominent goal among all segments of American society. Although strain is disproportionately felt among the lower classes, Merton's theory is not a simple "poverty" explanation of crime. It is a theory about the pressure on individuals to conform to cultural goals even after they are faced with the realization (or at least the perception) that social structure cannot deliver the success that culture had promised them.

The strain Merton speaks of presumably only occurs in open-class societies in which people believe that they can achieve whatever level of success their talents will allow. Societies characterized by rigid status hierarchies in which the accident of birth determines people's place in society do not generate strain because people do not expect to achieve above their "station." Poverty in an affluent, open-class, and achievement-oriented society, even if that "poverty" may be abundance in another society, may be more psychologically difficult to bear than grinding poverty in a rigidly stratified poor country. In other words, *relative deprivation,* the economic gap between haves and have-nots, is more important than absolute deprivation in generating strain. Individuals who must bear the pain of relative deprivation may adapt to the situation by discounting or abandoning ineffective legitimate means of striving and adopt illegitimate ones. Thus, strain theory views crime as both adaptive and reactive. It is adaptive because it is instrumental in attaining valued goals, and it is reactive because it is prompted by frustration, envy, and resentment. Figure 4.3 outlines the theory.

Institutional Anomie Theory

Institutional anomie theory (IAT) is the brainchild of Steven Messner and Richard Rosenfeld.[23] Although they situate their theory within the anomie tradition, they are far more explicitly critical of U.S. capitalism than are more traditional anomie/strain theorists, and they are even more critical than some of the so-called critical theories presented in Chapter 6. IAT places the blame for the high rate of crime in the United States unequivocally on the doorstep

Figure 4.3	Diagrammatic Presentation of Anomie/Strain Theory

Cultural and Structural Context

Middle-class success goals shared by all members of society → Limited access to legitimate means (education, jobs) for some → Disjunction between goals and means (the ideal and the reality) → ANOMIE

Social-psychological response

Individuals adapt to anomie by accepting or rejecting goals & means

GOALS	MEANS		MODE OF ADAPTATION TO ANOMIE	
Accepts	Accepts	————>	CONFORMITY	(nondeviant)
Rejects	Accepts	————>	RITUALISM	(deviant, noncriminal)
Rejects	Rejects	————>	RETREATISM	(deviant, social dropout, could be criminal)
Accepts	Rejects	————>	INNOVATION	(deviant, criminal)
Rejects	Rejects	————>	REBELLION	(deviant, wants to substitute new goals and means)

of the much-vaunted American Dream and its capitalist underpinnings: "High crime rates are intrinsic to the basic cultural commitments and institutional arrangements of American society. In short, at all social levels, *America is organized for crime.*"[24] Messner and Rosenfeld show that the income and wealth gaps in the United States between the richest and poorest are greater than in any other Western industrialized nation and that this is not an aberration of the American Dream but an expression of it. They maintain that the American Dream entails "a competitive allocation of monetary rewards [that] requires both winners and losers, and winning and losing have meaning only when rewards are distributed unequally."[25]

Messner and Rosenfeld's theory is not a simplistic denunciation of capitalism because all the countries they compare American violent crime rates with have capitalist economies. The difference between the United States and those other countries, they maintain, is the subjugation of all other social institutions to the economy in the United States. They refer to the subjugation of other institutions to the economy as the **institutional balance of power.**[26] What this essentially means is that American culture tends to *devalue* the noneconomic function and roles of other social institutions; it obliges them to *accommodate* themselves to economic requirements, and these economic norms have *penetrated* into other institutional domains and upset the natural balance between them.[27] In short, the American economy exerts a strong constraining influence on individuals to structure and organize their lives in a certain way.

How does this institutional imbalance work? To begin with, a great deal of the focus of the family, religion, education, law, and government is brought to bear on instilling in

Americans the beliefs and values of the marketplace to the detriment of the institution-specific beliefs and values they are supposed to inculcate—nurturance, spirituality, love of learning, justice, and democratic principles, respectively. The dominance of the economy thus disrupts the prosocial functioning of the other institutions and substitutes an overweening concern for the pursuit of monetary rewards, which IAT sees as profoundly criminogenic.

Messner and Rosenfeld provide a number of examples of devaluation, accommodation, and penetration in their work. They show how family schedules have to accommodate themselves to the schedules, rewards, and penalties of the workplace. (How often do you hear people complaining about finding time for their families as opposed to finding time for their jobs?) American workers have little time for family vacations compared to workers in other major capitalist nations, and they have few family support mechanisms such as paid maternity leave, supplemental income allowances, child care facilities, and family allowances (money paid to all families with dependent children without regard to need) enjoyed by workers in other advanced capitalist countries.

Education, too, is dominated by economic concerns since it is largely seen as a means to occupational attainment. Few students attend college because of their love of learning but are rather seeking "practical" knowledge they can take into the marketplace, and some universities are beginning to view students as "customers" rather than students. Elementary and secondary school teachers are not given the status or rewards that similarly educated individuals who make a more direct contribution to the economy receive, and universities are often dependent on business for financial support.

Messner and Rosenfeld likewise find the political realm to be highly dependent on economic interests. If a candidate for high political office is not independently wealthy, he or she must seek funds from business interests and thus become beholden to them. Local governments must court business by maintaining an atmosphere hospitable to business investment. Everywhere in the United States, it seems, Messner and Rosenfeld find everything to be dominated by "bottom-line" thinking. As U.S. President Calvin Coolidge said about 70 years before them, "The business of America is business."

For Messner and Rosenfeld, the answer to the high rate of crime (particularly violent crime) in the United States is **decommodification**. Before we define this ungainly word, we should define its opposite—*commodification,* which means the transformation of social relationships formerly untainted by economic considerations into saleable commodities. Thus, decommodification refers to social policies intended to free social relationships from economic considerations by freeing the operation of the other social institutions from the domination of the economy, or to at least gain a certain degree of balance. In Messner and Rosenfeld's conception, "Decommodified social policies permit actions and choices by citizens—to get married, have children, seek higher education, engage in political activity—that are, in principle, unconstrained by market principles."[28]

There have been a number of studies designed to test IAT, especially Messner and Rosenfeld's claim that countries high on their "decommodification index" have lower rates of homicide than the United States. Messner and Rosenfeld's own study[29] supported the notion, although the effects are quite weak and may be accounted for by any number of other variables not examined, such as the greater availability of guns in the United States compared to those other countries.[30] This is true for other studies that have found weak associations with homicide and decommodification within the United States by examining homicide rates across different counties[31] or across historical periods from 1900 to 1997.[32]

Robert Agnew's General Strain Theory

Robert Agnew[33] has made several attempts to fine-tune and reformulate strain theory, culminating in laying a foundation for a **general strain theory.** Agnew identifies several other sources of strain besides the disjunction between expectations and actual achievements. Strain can also result from the removal of positively valued stimuli, such as the loss of a boyfriend/girlfriend and having to move to a new neighborhood. These problems may induce delinquency or crime via efforts to prevent or regain the loss via illegal means or to gain revenge on those deemed responsible for the loss. Strain also arises from the presentation of negative stimuli such as child abuse/neglect and negative school experiences. These can lead to delinquency and crime via efforts to escape the stimuli by running away from home and truancy.

We all experience multiple strains throughout our lives, but the impact of strain differs according to its *magnitude, recency, duration,* and *clustering* (miseries that cluster together produce a whole greater than the sum of its parts and may overwhelm coping resources). Agnew tells us that strain can result in crime and delinquency through the development of a generally negative attitude about other people: "Repeated or chronic strain may lead to a hostile attitude—a general dislike and suspicion of others and an associated tendency to respond in an aggressive manner."[34]

Strain is thus primarily the result of *negative emotions* that arise from negative relationships with others and not necessarily from blocked opportunities to financial success, as Merton argued. Although Agnew added much to the understanding of strain, his greatest contribution is to remind us that the most important factor is not strain per se but how one copes with it. Although none of us is happy when we are strained and may curse and throw things, few of us cope with it by committing crimes. How we cope with strain depends on many things, including the level of social support we enjoy; the number, frequency, duration, and intensity of the strain-inducing circumstances we face; and what kind of persons we are. According to Agnew, the individual traits that differentiate between people who cope poorly with strain and others who cope well include "temperament, intelligence, creativity, problem-solving skills, interpersonal skills, self-efficacy, and self-esteem." He goes on to say that "these traits affect the selection of coping strategies by influencing the individual's sensitivity to objective strains and the ability to engage in cognitive, emotional, and behavioral coping."[35]

Agnew points out a potentially fatal flaw in Merton's version of anomie/strain theory. A strict interpretation of it should lead us to predict a sharp increase in criminal behavior in late adolescence/early adulthood, when many such individuals begin to seriously enter the job market.[36] If there is a disjunction between cultural goals and structural impediments to achieving them, a number of young adults entering the job market will feel its bite for the first time and respond with one of Merton's deviant adaptations. However, just when the alleged cause of criminal behavior becomes most salient for young people, we observe a significant decrease in criminal behavior among them rather than an increase. But to be fair to Merton, he was writing at a time when Jim Crow laws denied full participation in American life to African Americans.

Agnew sees the way out of this criticism (falling crime and delinquency rates just when the theory predicts they should increase) by appealing to theories that posit two general pathways to offending—one that begins before puberty and continues long into adulthood and one that is limited to adolescence—and by integrating his theory with them.[37] The reaction to strain will differ according to which of these two pathways offenders follow. Persons most likely to react negatively to strain have traits such as hyperactivity, attention deficit disorder, impulsiveness, and insensitivity. Such persons are "less likely to form close attachments to prosocial

▲ **Photo 4.4** Strain theories presume that lower-class citizens envy the rich but, lacking the means to become productive, often turn to crime as an alternative pathway. These brand-new condos were built by tearing down some of the neighboring high-rise slum buildings in Cabrini Green. Police patrol the streets that separate the new housing, unaffordable to the ghetto residents, making sure that the new condos are safe from burglaries or robberies.

others . . . do well in school . . . and obtain rewarding jobs."[38] By adding psychological variables into the mix, Agnew has moved anomie strain theory away from its "pure" sociological origins toward a more eclectic vision.[39]

Subcultural Theories

Albert Cohen and Status Frustration

Both Durkheim's and Merton's versions of anomie theory focus on the larger society and the general culture. Neither focuses on the actual process by which individuals adopt a particular mode of adaptation other than stating that criminal behavior results from either normatively unrestrained "insatiable appetites" or "strain" resulting from the inability to achieve a middle-class lifestyle when exhorted by culture to do so. The modes of adaptation, however, suggest that distinct criminal subcultures might develop, particularly among lower-class individuals because these are the people expected to feel the bite of blocked opportunity more sharply. New subcultures develop when a significant number of people who feel alienated from the larger host culture (although they obviously share significant elements of it) forge a lifestyle that is sufficiently distinctive from the mainstream culture.

In his book *Delinquent Boys,* Albert Cohen[40] proposed a mechanism by which lower-class youths adapt to the limited avenues of success open to them. Cohen took issue with the notion that criminal behavior is a rational method of meeting desired goals because it does not describe much of the criminal behavior occurring in lower-class neighborhoods. Rationality implies that criminal activity is engaged in because it is a means of getting what one wants, not an end in itself. But much delinquent behavior is characterized by what Cohen called **short-run hedonism**. Short-run hedonism means that the actor is seeking immediate gratification of his or her desires without regard for any long-term consequences. Much delinquent behavior is also *nonutilitarian,* engaged in "just for the hell of it." It is frequently *malicious,* netting offenders no tangible benefit, and it is generally *negative* in the sense that it turns positive middle-class norms of behavior upside down (e.g., destroying rather than creating). All of this points to the conclusion that much lower-class crime and delinquency is expressive rather than instrumental, meaning that it may fulfill psychological needs more than material needs.

According to Cohen, the conditions experienced by boys growing up in lower-class environments limit their ability to take advantage of educational opportunities and thus the occupational opportunities necessary for success in the mainstream culture. Through no fault of their own, these young people lack access to middle-class avenues of approval and self-worth. Because they cannot adjust to what Cohen calls **middle-class measuring rods,** they experience status frustration. The frustration is so pervasive among the lower classes that an oppositional culture is spawned with behavioral norms that are consciously contrary to those of the middle class. Cohen saw criminal culture as a kind of mass reaction formation, or collective solution, to the problem of perceived blocked opportunities.

The real problem for Cohen is **status frustration,** not blocked opportunity. Lower-class youths desire approval and status, but because they cannot meet middle-class criteria, they become frustrated. It is seeking status via alternate means that explains the nonutilitarian, malicious, and negative nature of much of lower-class antisocial behavior. To gain approval and respect, members of criminal subcultures establish "new norms, new criteria of status which defines as meritorious the characteristics they *do* possess, the kinds of conduct of which they *are* capable."[41] These status criteria are most often physical in nature, such as being ready and able to respond violently to challenges to one's manhood or gaining a reputation as a "stud."

More recently, David Rowe has also denied that young males compare themselves with "distant middle-class standards" and asserts that the "main source of strain is an attempt by males to win in male-male encounters a high level of social prestige in local peer groups."[42] Jack Katz[43] draws the same conclusion: Chronic criminals are seduced by a life of action and value their "bad ass" reputations, as well as the status such a reputation brings with it, more than the middle-class American Dream. Katz argues that the primary appeal of criminal behavior is the intrinsic rewards—the thrills, the euphoria, and the rush of taking risks and getting away with it, not the frequently negligible material rewards of such behavior.

Even when criminals garner significant material rewards from their crimes, there is still a large element of excitement involved for them as well. Recall from Chapter 1 bank robber Willie Sutton's droll answer when asked why he robbed banks ("Because that's where the money is"). Sutton elaborated on that answer in his biography by telling us such things as, "Because I enjoyed it. I was more alive when I was inside a bank, robbing it, than at any other time in my life."[44] Sampson and Laub propose that crime is analogous to addiction and state that "the action entailed in committing it is seductive, alluring, and hard to give up despite its clear costs."[45] There is little doubt that many criminals are attracted to the "highs" they achieve through their criminal activities. Walter Gove and Charles Wilmoth[46] even identify the specific brain areas and chemicals associated with these highs and also propose that a life of crime can be addictive for people like Willie (see Chapter 8).

Cloward and Ohlin's Opportunity Structure Theory

One of the most influential extensions of strain theory has been Richard Cloward and Lloyd Ohlin's **opportunity structure theory,** outlined in their book, *Delinquency and Opportunity.*[47] As was the case with Cohen, Cloward and Ohlin's work brought together elements of the ecological and strain traditions and added elements of their own. Consistent with earlier strain theories, Cloward and Ohlin accepted the proposition that delinquents and criminals want to conform to mainstream means of attaining success but cannot. On the other hand, most lower-class youths have little interest in the usual indicators of middle-class economic success, preferring "big cars," "flashy clothes," and "swell dames."[48]

Cloward and Ohlin take issue with Merton's implicit assumption that all those denied legitimate opportunities have equal access to illegitimate opportunities. Access to illegitimate means of goal attainment is no more equally open to all than is access to legitimate means—it takes more than talent and motivation to make it within either the legitimate or illegitimate opportunity structures. To obtain and take advantage of the most rewarding illegitimate opportunities, aspiring delinquents often need an "in," a friend, relative, or acquaintance who can show them "the ropes." Youths born into an established and organized delinquent subculture—the illegitimate "opportunity structure"—have a definite career advantage over "wannabe" outsiders.

According to Cloward and Ohlin, individuals within the delinquent opportunity structure join *criminal gangs*. Although differential opportunity structure theory is concerned with lower-class "street-corner"-style gangs, the best illustrative example of this type of gang is organized crime gangs. The Mafia, for instance, has a pool of aspiring "sponsored" recruits, an apprenticeship period and a status hierarchy, and its heroes and its own code of "ethics" (see Chapter 15).

Cloward and Ohlin identified two other gang types that develop from the frustration generated by blocked opportunities in lower-class culture: *conflict gangs* and *retreatist gangs*. Both gang types arise in disorganized lower-class neighborhoods in response to the lack of access to both legitimate *and* illegitimate opportunities. Conflict gangs are generated in slum areas with a high degree of transience and instability as opposed to stable areas with an established illegitimate opportunity structure. The malintegration of individuals living in these areas precludes the development of organized methods of dealing with frustration, the generation of values supportive of a successful criminal lifestyle (e.g., gang loyalty), or the formation of a network of supportive others. The members of these loose-knit gangs commit senseless acts of violence and vandalism, and their efforts to make a living from criminal activity tend to be "individualistic, unorganized, petty, poorly paid and unprotected."[49]

Other individuals in lower-class areas form retreatist gangs. One difference between conflict and retreatist gang members is that retreatists are "double failures" while conflict gang members tend to have failed only within the criminal subculture. Retreatists are also more "escapist" in their response in that almost all of them abuse drugs and/or alcohol and are more likely to blame their failure on personal shortcomings. In both conflict and retreatist gangs, the concern is not with remote goals but rather with the immediate gratification of present wants.

Walter Miller's Theory of Focal Concerns

Walter Miller[50] was an anthropologist who closely studied the cultural life of the lower classes. His observations led him to take issue with Cohen's thesis that gangs are formed as a *reaction* to status deprivation. Criminals and delinquents may resent the middle class, but resentment is born out of envy for what middle-class people have, not for what they are. It is not a matter of "If you can't join 'em, lick 'em" but rather that the components of a middle-class lifestyle such as hard work, stable habits, study, and responsibility are not appealing to them, although the rewards of such a lifestyle are. Miller asserted that lower-class behavior and values must be viewed on their own terms and not as simple negations of, or reaction to, those of the middle class. He also identified six **focal concerns** that are part of a value system and a lifestyle that has emerged from the realities of life on the bottom rung of society. Miller emphasized that these concerns may be applicable to males outside of lower-class subcultures and that it is only the "hard-core" lower class for which they are constant guiding principles. These interrelated focal concerns are the following:

1. *Trouble* is something to stay out of most of the time, but life is trouble, and it is something that confers status if it is the right kind (being able to handle oneself).

2. *Toughness* is very important to the status of lower-class males. Being strong, brave, macho, sexually aggressive, unsentimental, and "not taking any shit" is part of the reason that trouble is so prevalent in lower-class areas.

3. *Smartness* refers to street smarts and is the ability to survive on the streets using one's wits—to con others, to outfox the law, to dupe suckers and squares.

4. *Excitement* is the search for fun, often defined in terms of fighting, sexual adventurism, gambling, and getting drunk or stoned. Being smart and tough is advantageous to this search and often leads to trouble.

5. *Fate* is a belief in that the locus of control is external to oneself and that "lady luck" is more reliable as a guide to decision making than is forethought.

6. *Autonomy* means personal freedom, being outside the control of authority figures such as teachers, employers, and the police, and thus being able to "do my own thing."

The hard-core lower-class lifestyle typified by these focal concerns catches those engaged in it in a web of situations that virtually guarantee delinquent and criminal activities. The search for *excitement* leads to sexual adventures in which little preventative care is taken (*fate*), and the desire for personal freedom (*autonomy*) is likely to preclude marriage if pregnancy results. Miller was concerned about the fact that many lower-class males thus grow up in homes lacking a father or any other significant male role model. This leaves them with little supervision and leads them to seek their male identities in what Miller called "one-sex peer units."[51] Same-sex peer groups (gangs) are the heart and soul of lower-class social life because they provide the two things otherwise missing but that are central to all humans: a sense of belonging and status. Once in the gang, the focal concerns that led to their formation are practiced and recycled. Nevertheless, young males are able to get their status needs met among the only other people who will accept them and the only other people who they themselves are inclined to accept. Miller thus agrees with those who view delinquency more in terms of efforts to seek status (a "rep") within lower-class culture than in terms of rational alternative ways of achieving material success. The major difference between Miller and Cohen is that Cohen sees gang-related behavior as a frustrated reaction to the inability to measure up to middle-class standards, while Miller sees it as a product of a distinctive lower-class culture with its own integrity.

FOCUS ON . . .

Does Poverty Cause Crime, or Does Crime Cause Poverty?

According to Frank Schmalleger, the basic underlying assumption of all structural theories is that the "root causes" of crime are poverty and various social injustices. There is no doubt that poverty and crime are strongly related, but which is the cause and which is the effect? It has long been considered almost an article of faith by many criminologists that poverty causes crime, but as Schmalleger notes, "Some now argue the inverse of the 'root causes' argument, saying that poverty and what appear to be social injustices are produced by crime, rather than the other way around."[52]

In terms of social disorganization theory, crime "causes" poverty by stripping communities of their businesses and the jobs they provide, thus affecting average community income. In areas where robberies, thefts, break-ins, vandalism, and muggings are an everyday occurrence, the cost of doing business is sharply increased (increased insurance premiums, additional expenses for security guards and alarm systems, etc.). After building costs and space constraints, crime is the most important reason for companies either not moving into inner-city areas or for moving out of them if they are already there.[53] Democratic Congressman John Lewis summed up the crime-poverty relationship this way: "In a very real sense it is crime that has caused poverty, and is the most powerful cause of poverty today."[54]

Anomie/strain theory assumes that not being able to achieve occupational success leads to poverty, which leads to crime. However, individuals who do poorly in school and drop out, do time in juvenile detention, and acquire a criminal record severely compromise their future opportunities to gain meaningful employment, form prosocial networks, and become attractive as marriage partners to prosocial females. Economists find that incarceration reduces employment opportunities by about 40%, wages by about 15%, and wage growth by about 33%.[55] So, did the "system" deny these folks opportunities for monetary success and so forced them into crime, or did they deny themselves by committing the crimes they did?

This is not to deny that most individuals who do poorly in school, acquire a juvenile record, and so forth, are from lower-class backgrounds, or that growing up in poverty increases exposure to criminogenic forces. However, it does not necessarily follow that the poverty these individuals found themselves in caused their criminal behavior. Crime rates were lower during the Great Depression than they are currently, the majority of poor people do not become criminals, and many poor children of all racial/ethnic groups possessing good cognitive skills and a modicum of ambition and persistence achieve middle-class status.[56] A male of any race (fewer than 3% of White or Black males) in the United States is virtually assured of avoiding poverty if he finishes high school and finds and maintains a steady job; avoiding unwed motherhood is an added proviso for females.[57] Being born in poverty does not doom individuals to perpetuate it in their own adult lives, nor does it doom them to a life of crime. Perhaps we should be asking questions such as what factors differentiate those born into poverty who escape it from those who do not. Whatever these factors are, they may be more plausible candidates as causes of crime than the poverty that both groups initially shared.

✉ Youth Gangs

Malcolm Klein defines a youth gang as "any denotable adolescent group who (a) are generally perceived as a distinct aggregation by others in the neighborhood, (b) recognize themselves as a denotable group (almost invariably with a group name), and (c) have been involved in a sufficient number of delinquent incidents to call forth a consistent negative response from neighborhoods' residents and/or law enforcement agencies."[58] There have been youth gangs as long as there have been youths whose energy and talents their communities did not put to constructive use. In London in the 1600s, there were a variety of youth gangs with names like "Dead Boys, Mims, and Bugles . . . who found amusement in breaking windows, demolishing taverns, assaulting the watch [early forms of police]" and who "fought pitched battles among themselves dressed with colored ribbons to distinguish the different factions."[59] New York City has been plagued with gangs almost since its beginning, with the Forty Thieves, an Irish gang of the 1820s, supposedly being the first recorded youth gang in the United States.[60]

The Increasing Prevalence of Youth Gangs

Gangs are more prevalent in the United States today than ever before. When gang theorists wrote in the 1950s and 1960s, they did so in relatively crime-free times in which the number of cities reporting a gang problem was 58. The latest figures from the 2002 National Youth Gang Survey estimated that there were 21,500 gangs and 731,500 gang members in 2002, and approximately half of all homicides in Chicago and Los Angeles in that year were gang related.[61] This increase over the past four decades has been attributed to the loss of millions of manufacturing jobs in the United States as companies move overseas in search of cheap labor and robots perform many of the routine jobs that remain.[62] These transitions have hit our most vulnerable citizens, the young and the uneducated, the hardest and have also led to negative demographic transitions. Factories leaving neighborhoods cause more social disorganization than factories moving in because it changes the community composition without the compensatory benefit of providing work.

Marching in lock step with the economic changes have been large demographic changes. Many African American communities have lost the stabilizing influences of middle-class professionals as affirmative action programs have allowed them to achieve financial success and to move to better neighborhoods. Males who were left behind had little to offer females in terms of the security and stability of marriage, and as a result, there has been a steady increase of unwed motherhood in these neighborhoods, which has further decreased the level of social control in them. Deindustrialization thus set in motion a chain of events that has created a large segment of the population that has become economically marginalized and socially isolated from mainstream culture.

These marginalized and isolated people (mainly African Americans and Hispanics) have become known as the "underclass" and the "truly disadvantaged."[63] It is in the neighborhoods where these people live that the most fertile soil for the growth of gangs exists. A survey of the ethnic composition of gangs found that 47% were Hispanic, 31% African American, 13% White, and 7% Asian.[64] It is estimated that over 25% of Black males between the ages of 15 and 24 in Los Angeles County are members of the nation's two most notorious youth gangs, the Crips and the Bloods.[65]

◀ **Photo 4.5** For youth in gangs, a number of alternatives to prison may be available. Here a teen has been sent to a drug treatment program. Notice that he is permitted to personalize his dorm area and wear his own clothes.

Why Do Young People Join Gangs?

Irving Spergel writes that "youths join gangs for many reasons: status, security, money, power, excitement, and/or new experiences."[66] Some older and more established gangs may provide housing, food, and clothes for its most needy members.[67] Illegal activities such as drug selling and extortion provide gang members with funds to buy other material wants and needs, and gangs are well known for providing members access to sexual partners.[68] Joining a gang has become almost a survival imperative in some areas where unaffiliated youths are likely to be victimized. Having "homies" to watch your back can make you feel safe and secure. Gang membership also provides a means of satisfying belongingness needs—having a place in the world among people who care. Gang members often display their belonging through initiation rites, secret gang signals, special clothing, "colors," and tattoos, all of which shout out loud, "I belong!" "I'm valued!" A youth camp counselor describes this function of gangs well: "The gang serves emotional needs. You feel wanted. You feel welcome. You feel important. And there is discipline and there are rules."[69]

This sense of belonging and being valued is integral to developing self-esteem, but the kind of self-esteem gained in a gang context is not the healthy kind. The gang affords its members opportunities to exercise hypermasculine behavior (machismo), which many theorists view as a function of the absence of fathers in boys' lives.[70,71] Similar effects of father absence are found in many cultures. Surveying the anthropological literature, Ember and Ember state that "societies in which children are reared in mother-child households or the father spends little time in child care tend to have more physical violence by males than do societies in which fathers are mostly around."[72]

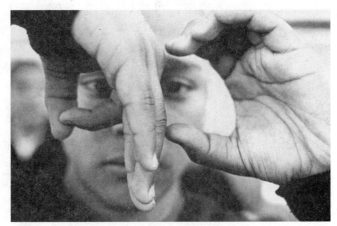

▶ **Photo 4.6** Young member of the Cypress gang in Los Angeles flashing a gang sign. Gangs claim to replace the family cohesiveness the youth may not have at home, while symbols such as colors and signs clearly demarcate members from outsiders or rival gangs.

Social institutions (especially the family and the economy) satisfy most of the needs we have discussed for most of us, but in the virtual absence of the influence of these institutions in the lives of those most affected by the economic and demographic transitions of the past few decades, the gang offers an attractive substitute means of achieving their needs. Thus, the gang functions for many of its members as (1) family, (2) friendship group, (3) play group, (4) a protective agency, (5) educational institution, and (6) employer.

Girls in Gangs

Females are a minor (but growing) part of the modern gang scene. About 11% of all gang members are females according to police sources, although the proportion of self-identified gang members who are female from a survey of a number of cities ranged from 8% to 38%.[73]

Girls join gangs for many of the same reasons that boys do; that is, gangs function as a surrogate family and as a source of friendship, camaraderie, and self-affirmation. They also offer excitement and are a source of potential marriage mates. Most female gang members marry gang members, although only about 20% of gang males marry female gang members.[74] Most female gang members are from single-parent homes, a high proportion of them have experienced sexual abuse at home, and most have their first child at an early age and out of wedlock.[75,76]

There are three basic types of female gang involvement: all-female gangs, mixed-gender gangs, and female auxiliaries of male gangs. A review of female gang members in three cities found that 6.4% of the girls (largely African American) described themselves as being in all-girl gangs, 57.3% as being in mixed-gender gangs, and 36.4% as being affiliates or auxiliaries of male gangs.[77] Most girls who join gangs do so earlier than boys, and many of them simply "grow into" the gang as a natural process of neighborhood friendship patterns rather than formally "join" it; they also "age out" of gangs earlier than boys.[78] Even though many girls may just grow into a gang, their formal acceptance usually involves some sort of painful initiation rite such as being "beaten in" (fighting a number of gang members at once), getting tattoos, participating in a drive-by shooting, or having sex with multiple male gang members.[79] This latter ritual is known as "pulling a train," in which "the boy's rank in the gang determined whether he was the engine, the caboose, or somewhere in between."[80]

▲ **Photo 4.7**   Young female members of a Los Angeles girls' gang flash gang signs. Many urban youth grow up in areas in which criminal activity is routine.

Despite sensationalized media accounts of tough, angry, and violent teenage girl "gangstas" high on crack and shooting up the neighborhood, the vast majority of female gang delinquency consists of nonviolent property and status offenses. For instance, among the 345 gang-related homicides committed in Chicago over a 4-year period, only 1 was committed by a female, and only 6 of 204 gang homicide victims were female.[81] In another study of 1,072 gang-related homicides in three cities, females committed only 8 (0.7%).[82] The overall delinquency rate of gang females is lower than that of gang males but higher than nongang females and even higher than nongang males.[83]

⌧ Evaluation of Social Structural Theories

We have already noted the problems associated with the early social structural theories that have been addressed by others working in the same tradition. Shaw and McKay's ecological theory brought home to us one of the most universal demographic characteristics of crime, namely, its concentration in socially disorganized areas inhabited by economically deprived people. But causal direction has always been a problem; are neighborhoods rundown and criminogenic because people with personal characteristics conducive to both crime and poverty populate them, or do neighborhoods somehow "cause" crime independent of the characteristics of people living there? After all, when formerly blighted areas become "gentrified" and middle-class people move in, the neighborhood is no longer "criminogenic."

The difficulty inherent in using aggregate-level data to explain individual-level behavior (the ecological fallacy) has been addressed by contemporary criminologists, who have attempted to assess the independent effects of people and places simultaneously. The consensus appears to be that there are neighborhood effects, but these effects are mediated by the characteristics of neighborhood residents to a significant extent, and both individual and neighborhood effects feed back on one another, making both worse than they might otherwise be.

A related problem is that ecological theory cannot account for why the majority of people in disorganized neighborhoods do not commit crimes or why, among those who do, a very small minority commit the majority of them. We cannot answer questions such as this without examining individual differences. Defenders of the theory will reply that these are not questions the theory was designed to answer. Rather, the theory was designed to identify characteristics of *neighborhoods* that consistently evidence high crime and delinquency rates *regardless* of the characteristics of those residing there. "Kinds of people" questions are dealt with at a different level of analysis.

Likewise, the strain theories of Merton as well as Messner and Rosenfeld claim to explain particular types of crimes in terms of their prevalence in society and not why one individual becomes criminal and another does not. Because of the excessive emphasis on monetary success in the United States, anomie/strain theory should best explain rational crimes netting perpetrators' monetary gain. As Bartol and Bartol have written, the theory's strength lies in its "ability to explain why utilitarian crime rates are so high in one society (e.g., the United States) and so low in another (e.g., England)."[84] Unfortunately for this argument, ever since the mid-1980s, England has had higher reported rates of many kinds of utilitarian crimes (e.g., burglary, auto theft) than the United States.[85] It is nonutilitarian crimes such as murder, rape, and assault that are more common in the United States than in England, which supports Cohen's contention that much of American lower-class crime is nonutilitarian and malicious rather than rationally instrumental.

Agnew's general strain theory has been criticized as reductionist because of its emphasis on attempting to explain how people subjectively perceive and react to strain.[86] However, scientists and philosophers are fairly unanimous in their opinion that reductionism (attempting to *explain* something, previously only *described,* by examining the actual mechanisms underlying a phenomenon) is how the vast majority of progress in any science is made.[87] Agnew does not undermine the structural aspects of anomie/strain theory anyway but rather complements them, which is what all reductionist accounts of anything do.

The subcultural theories of Cohen as well as Cloward and Ohlin augment both ecological and anomie/strain theories by introducing the idea of subculture. Subcultures are patterned ways of life, a mini-world whose members set themselves apart and pride themselves in their distinctiveness. It is this patterned way of life that sustains delinquent values and goals once they are set in motion.

One of the major problems with these theories is that others have cast doubt as to whether there are distinct lower-class subcultures in this sense. It is difficult to imagine that lower-class subculture arose in reaction to the larger culture by deliberately taking steps to take middle-class conduct norms and turn them on their head, as Cohen's reaction formation hypothesis supposes. A number of studies have found that most lower-class youths, and even many gang members, support middle-class goals and values.[88] But supporting middle-class goals and values and actually following them are birds of a different feather. There do seem to be areas in our cities in which middle-class values are disdained, not because they are defined as middle class but rather because they demand self-control, delayed gratification, and the disciplined application of effort.[89]

Because Miller's research on focal concerns was conducted in African American neighborhoods, he has attracted charges of racial insensitivity and that he should have framed his work in terms of social class rather than race.[90] However, similar anthropological work by African American Elijah Anderson[91] supports Miller's contention regarding lower-class values in African American areas without attracting such charges. It has also been found that allegiance to focal concern values is related to self-reported delinquency in all social classes, although allegiance is more prevalent in lower-class neighborhoods.[92]

If Miller is correct about the role of fate in lower-class life, then the whole anomie/strain argument about blocked opportunities may be off base. If lower-class individuals perceive their opportunities in a fatalistic "live-for-the-moment" way, then they or the visions of reality imparted by their subculture are doing the blocking, not the "system." Opportunities are things we must seek out and grab when we find them; they are not things that randomly tap most of us on the shoulder and invite us to play. As an old saying goes, "A wise man will make more opportunities than he finds."

⬚ Policy and Prevention: Implications of Social Structural Theories

If social disorganized life in ethnically heterogeneous slum neighborhoods is the "root cause" of crime, what kinds of feasible policy strategies might you recommend to public policy makers? One of the first things you might want to suggest would be the strengthening of community life, but things get difficult when somebody says, "Fine, OK; so where do we start?" Clifford Shaw had ideas about where to start and was able to secure funding for his famous **Chicago Area Project** (CAP). Shaw believed that treating individual offenders would be less effective than treating the communities from which they came. To that end, he and his staff organized a number of programs aimed at generating or strengthening a sense of community within neighborhoods with the help and cooperation of schools, churches, recreational clubs, trade unions, and businesses. Athletic leagues, various kinds of clubs, summer camps, and many other activities were formed to busy the idle hands of the young. "Street corner" counselors were hired to offer advice to youths and to mediate with the police on their behalf when they got into trouble. Older neighborhood residents were encouraged to form democratic committees to resolve neighborhood problems.

The money and energy investing in the CAP, which lasted from 1932 to 1957, should have produced meaningful reductions in crime and delinquency. However, despite the longevity and scope of the program, its effects were never evaluated in any systematic way. Similar programs in other cities yielded results that were also disappointing.[93] Such projects had a number of positive outcomes, but their impact on crime and delinquency rates was negligible. Even positive outcomes tended to occur in communities that needed help the least.[94] Writing about the overall impact of CAP-type programs, Rosenbaum, Lurigio, and Davis concluded that there were "few positive program effects. The local programs did not affect official crime rates and in some cases were associated with adverse change in survey-based victimization rates."[95]

If anything, the neighborhoods in South Chicago with which Shaw and McKay were most concerned, despite the heroic efforts of CAP, are worse today (both in terms of physical deterioration and crime/delinquency rates) than they ever were. Although these phenomena are occurring in urban slum areas, the concepts of classical ecology theory are inadequate to account for them. The hardening of poverty among the underclass means that the most crime-ridden neighborhoods have become stable in terms of their population composition

Table 4.1	Summarizing Social Structural Theories		
Theory	**Key Concepts**	**Strengths**	**Weaknesses**
Social Disorganization	Poverty concentrates people of different cultural backgrounds and generates cultural conflict. The breakdown of informal social controls leads to social disorganization, and peer group gangs replace social institutions as socializers.	Explains high crime rates in certain areas. Accounts for intergenerational transmission of deviant values and predicts crime rates from neighborhood characteristics.	Cannot account for individuals and groups in the same neighborhood who are crime free or why a few individuals commit a highly disproportionate share of crime.
Anomie (Durkheim)	Rapid social change leads to social deregulation and the weakening of restraining social norms. This unleashes "insatiable appetites," which some seek to satisfy through criminal activity.	Emphasizes the power of norms and social solidarity to restrain crime and points to situations that weaken them.	Concentrates on whole societies and ignores differences in areas that are differentially affected by social deregulation.
Anomie/Strain (Merton)	All members of American society are socialized to want to attain monetary success, but some are denied access to legitimate means of attaining it. These people may then resort to crime to achieve what they have been taught to want.	Explains high crime rates among the disadvantaged and how cultural norms create conflict and crime. Explains various means of adapting to strain.	Does not explain why individuals similarly affected by strain do not react (adapt) similarly.
Institutional Anomie	America is literally organized for crime due to its overweening emphasis on the economy and material success. All other institutions are devalued and must accommodate themselves to the requirements of the economy.	Explains why crime rates are higher in America than in other capitalist societies. Points to decommodification as crime reduction strategy.	Concentrates on single cause of crime. Should predict high rates of property crime in America rather than violent crime, but the opposite is true.
General Strain	There are multiple sources of strain, and strain differs along numerous dimensions. Strain is the result of negative emotions that arise from negative relationships with others as well as from sociocultural forces. Individual characteristics help us to cope poorly or well with strain.	Reminds us that strain is multifaceted and that how we cope with it is more important than its existence. Adds individual characteristics to theory.	Criticized by structural theorists as reductionist because it fails to explore structural origins of strain.
Subcultural	Much delinquency is short-run hedonism rather than utilitarian. Lower-class youths cannot live up to middle-class measuring rods and thus develop status frustration. They seek status in ways peculiar to the	Extends the scope of anomie theory and integrates social disorganization theory. Focuses on processes by which lower-class youths	Explains subcultural crime and delinquency only. There is some question as to whether a distinct lower-class culture exists in the

(Continued)

Table 4.1	(Continued)		
Theory	**Key Concepts**	**Strengths**	**Weaknesses**
	subculture. Subcultural youths do not have equal illegitimate opportunities for attaining success. Those who do join criminal gangs; those who don't join retreatist and conflict gangs and engage in mindless violence and vandalism.	adapt to their disadvantages and shows that illegitimate opportunities are also denied to some. Explains the patterned way of life that sustains delinquent values and goals.	sense that it is supported by prescriptive values that require antisocial behavior.
Focal Concerns	Lower-class youths live their lives according to the focal concerns of the neighborhoods they find themselves in. These focal concerns lead to conflict with the mainstream culture because they generate antisocial behavior.	Identifies the core values of lower-class culture and how they generate and perpetuate antisocial behavior.	Explains only lower-class antisocial behavior. Ignores the structural origin of the focal concerns.

rather than transitional. According to ecological theory, this stability should have resulted in reduced crime rather than the high levels we actually see.

The ideas of strain theory had tremendous impact on public policy via President Lyndon Johnson's War on Poverty. If the cause of crime is a disjunction between cultural values emphasizing success for all and a social structure denying access to legitimate means of achieving it to some, then the cure for crime is to increase opportunities or to dampen aspirations. The latter option would be ideologically unacceptable to policy makers of either the right or the left, so we are left with the task of trying to increase opportunities.

Following in the footsteps of Clifford Shaw's CAP, Richard Cloward and Lloyd Ohlin developed a delinquency prevention project known as **Mobilization for Youth** (MFY), which concentrated on expanding legitimate opportunities for disadvantaged youths via a number of educational, training, and job placement programs. MFY programs received generous private, state, and federal funds and served as models for such federal programs as Head Start, the Job Corps, the Comprehensive Employment and Training Act (CETA), affirmative action, and many others.[96]

Undoubtedly, some unknown number of people was diverted from a life of crime by opportunities presented to them by one or more of these government programs, but unfortunately, their heyday occurred at the same time that the United States was undergoing a huge jump in crime from 1965 to 1980. This is not to say that the correlation between expanding opportunities and expanding crime rates is causative, for many other things affecting crime rates were occurring at this time, but it did provide conservatives with arguments against the use of social welfare policies to combat crime.

The policy recommendations flowing from institutional anomie theory would be those that tame the power of the market via decommodification. For instance, the decision to have children could be freed from economic considerations by granting government-guaranteed maternity leave benefits and family allowances/income supports, and higher education could be accessible to all people with talent without regard for the financial ability to pay. In other words, policies that ensure an adequate level of material well-being that is not so completely dependent on an individual's performance in the marketplace. These programs are not utopian since they have been in place for decades in other advanced capitalist societies.

Any policy recommendations derived from subcultural theories would not differ in any significant way from those derived from ecological or anomie/strain theories. Changing a subculture via policy is extremely difficult. Insofar as a subculture is a patterned way of life, we cannot attack the problem in parts and expect to change the whole. Perhaps one possible strategy would be to disperse "problem families" throughout a city rather than concentrating them in block-type projects as is typically done. But even if this was politically feasible, rather than breaking up the subculture and its values, it may result in its displaced carriers "infecting" areas previously insulated from deviant values.

Our examination of the gang problem offers obvious policy recommendations in theory, such as increasing low-skill work opportunities by preventing American companies from moving them overseas and strengthening the other social institutions for which gangs are a substitute. This brings us back to the same kinds of recommendations that IAT suggests. Gangs will always be a problem, while legitimate social institutions in our poorest areas are too weak to provide all young people with their basic needs.

SUMMARY

Social structural theories of crime emphasize the social forces influencing people to commit criminal acts. The ecological theory emphasizes "deviant places" alleged to cause delinquent and criminal behavior regardless of the personal characteristics of individuals residing there. Such areas are characterized by social disorganization, which results from diverse cultural traditions within slum areas. Social disorganization leads to the breakdown of social institutions that traditionally serve to control antisocial behavior. Areas of social disorganization are found in *zones of transition,* located nearest a city's central core. One of the most interesting early findings of this perspective is that the same slum areas continued to have the highest crime rates in a city regardless of the ethnic or racial composition of its inhabitants. More recent ecological studies have focused on the question of whether people living in these areas commit more criminal acts because they live there or whether people who tend to commit crime also tend to aggregate in such areas. Neighborhoods do have effects independent of the people who live in them, but most effects are mediated by individual differences.

Anomie/strain theories focus on the frustration generated by society's emphasis on success goals for which all should strive, coupled with its denial of access to legitimate opportunities to achieve it to some. Merton's strain theory focuses on the ways people adapt to this situation via conformity, ritualism, retreatism, rebellion, and innovation (the modes of adaptation). Although the latter four modes are "deviant," they are not all criminal. The innovator and the retreatist modes are considered the most criminal.

Institutional anomie theory more forcefully argues that the United States is literally organized for crime because the institutional balance of power strongly favors the economy. All other American institutions are subordinate to our highly competitive economy, and the competition would be meaningless if there were not both winners and losers.

General strain theory argues that there are many other sources of strain other than Merton's disjunction between goals and means. These strains result in negative emotions that adversely affect relationships with others and may lead to crime. The important thing is not strain, however, but how people cope with it. Among the many attributes Agnew lists as coping resources are temperament, intelligence, and self-esteem.

Subcultural strain theories have slightly different emphases. Albert Cohen also sees that lower-class people are frustrated by denial of opportunities, but he concentrated on the emergence of subcultures as a reaction to this frustration. Lower-class boys, knowing that they cannot live up to the middle-class measuring rod, form oppositional gangs that perpetuate an oppositional subculture. These gangs usually reject both the goals and the means of middle-class society, as gauged by the malicious and nonutilitarian nature of many of their crimes. Walter Miller augments Cohen's assertion that lower-class culture is oppositional to middle-class culture with his theory of focal concerns. Focal concerns—trouble, toughness, smartness, excitement, fate, and autonomy—are behavioral norms of lower-class culture that command strong emotional attention. Finally, Cloward and Ohlin emphasize that people have differential access to illegitimate, as well as legitimate, means to success and that sociological and psychological factors limit a person's access to both.

Youth gangs have been noted throughout recorded history. The prevalence of gangs in the United States is greater than ever before and has been attributable to the deindustrialization of America. Deindustrialization has affected minorities the most and has tended to leave a sizable number of them marginalized from mainstream society and living in disorganized neighborhoods. The gang becomes an attractive option to many of these youths because it offers them many of the things that the ineffective social institutions in those neighborhoods do not. This is true both for girls and boys.

The policy recommendations flowing from social structural theories have not fared well, although they enjoyed widespread implementation via President Johnson's War on Poverty. The famous Chicago Area Project (and others like them) and the Mobilization for Youth had little or no impact on delinquency or crime rates.

On Your Own

Log on to the web-based student study site at http://www.sagepub.com/criminologystudy for more information about the vignettes and materials presented in this chapter, suggestions for activities, study aids such as review quizzes, and research recommendations including journal article links and questions related to this chapter.

EXERCISES AND DISCUSSION QUESTIONS

1. What is your position on the "kinds of people versus kinds of places" argument in ecological theory?

2. Is the American stress on material success a good or bad one overall? Is greed "good"? Does it drive the economy? Would we be better off psychologically with less?

3. Are lower-class delinquents reacting against middle-class values, as Cohen contends, or is there a lower-class culture with its own set of values and attitudes to which delinquents are conforming, as Miller contends?

4. Agnew believes that the addition of individual characteristics such as IQ and temperament would improve strain theory. Do you or don't you agree and why?

5. Would you like to see the "decommodification" recommendations such as paid maternal leave, more vacation time, and family allowances implemented in the United States? If so, what price in the form of taxes are you prepared to pay?

6. In your opinion, why were the various programs recommended by ecological and strain theories unsuccessful?

7. Go to http://www.iuscrim.mpg.de/forsch/krim/ortmann1_e.html and read *On the Anomie Theories of Merton and Durkheim* from a German psychologist's perspective. What does he say is the major difference, and what version of the theory does he favor?

KEY WORDS

Anomie
Chicago Area Project
Collective efficacy
Consensus or functionalist perspective
Conformity
Decommodification
Ecological fallacy
Focal concerns

General strain theory
Institutional anomie theory
Institutional balance of power
Mechanical solidarity
Middle-class measuring rods
Mobilization for youth
Modes of adaptation

Opportunity structure theory
Organic solidarity
Short-run hedonism
Social ecology
Social disorganization
Social structure
Status frustration
Transition zone

REFERENCES

1. Durkheim, E. (1982). *Rules of sociological method.* New York: Free Press.
2. Durkheim (1982, p. 10).
3. Durkheim (1982, pp. 106–107).
4. Durkheim (1982, p. 101).
5. Durkheim, E. (1951). *The division of labor in society.* Glencoe, IL: Free Press. (Quote on p. 251)
6. Durkheim (1951, p. 247).
7. Durkheim (1951, p. 246).
8. Shaw, C., & McKay, H. (1972). *Juvenile delinquency and urban areas* (Rev. ed.). Chicago: University of Chicago Press.
9. Sampson, R. (2004). Neighbourhood and community: Collective efficacy and community safety. *New Economy, 1070,* 106–173. (Quote on p. 108)
10. Osgood, D., & Chamber, J. (2003, May). Community correlates of rural youth violence. *Juvenile Justice Bulletin.* (Quote on p. 1)
11. Osgood and Chamber (2003, p. 6).
12. Bursik, R. (1988). Social disorganization and theories of crime and delinquency: Problems and prospects. *Criminology, 26,* 519–552.

13. Robinson, W. S. (1950). Ecological correlations and the behavior of individuals. *American Sociological Review, 15,* 351–357.
14. Shaw and McKay (1972).
15. Vold, G., & Bernard, T. (1986). *Theoretical criminology.* New York: Oxford University Press.
16. Kornhauser, R. (1978). *Social sources of delinquency: An appraisal of analytical methods.* Chicago: University of Chicago Press. (Quote on p. 104)
17. Wikstrom, P., & Loeber, R. (2000). Do disadvantaged neighborhoods cause well-adjusted children to become adolescent delinquents? A study of male juvenile serious offending, individual risk and protective factors and neighborhood context. *Criminology, 38,* 1109–1142.
18. Stewart, E., Simons, R., & Conger, R. (2002). Assessing neighborhood and social psychological influences on childhood violence in an African-American sample. *Criminology, 40,* 801–824.
19. Baumer, E., Horney, J., Felson, R., & Lauritsen, J. (2003). Neighborhood disadvantage and the nature of violence. *Criminology, 41,* 39–71.

20. Ludwig, J., Duncan, G., & Hirschfield, P. (2001). Urban poverty and juvenile crime: Evidence from a randomized housing-mobility experiment. *Quarterly Journal of Economics, 116,* 655–680.

21. Merton, R. (1938). Social structure and anomie. *American Sociological Review, 3,* 672–682.

22. Featherstone, R., & Deflem, M. (2003). Anomie and strain: Context and consequences of Merton's two theories. *Sociological Inquiry, 73,* 471–489.

23. Messner, S., & Rosenfeld, R. (2001). *Crime and the American Dream* (3rd ed.). Belmont, CA: Wadsworth.

24. Messner and Rosenfeld (2001, p. 5, emphasis added).

25. Messner and Rosenfeld (2001, p. 9).

26. Messner and Rosenfeld (2001, p. 68).

27. Messner and Rosenfeld (2001, p. 70).

28. Messner, S., & Rosenfeld, R. (1997). Political restraint of the market and levels of criminal homicide: A cross-national application of institutional anomie theory. *Social Forces, 75,* 1393–1416. (Quote on p. 1394)

29. Messner and Rosenfeld (1997).

30. Messner and Rosenfeld (2001, p. 107).

31. Maume, M., & Lee, M. (2003). Social institutions and violence: A sub-national test of institutional anomie theory. *Criminology, 41,* 1137–1172.

32. Batton, C., & Jensen, G. (2002). Decommodification and homicide rates in the 20th-century United States. *Homicide Studies, 6,* 6–38.

33. Agnew, R. (2002). Foundation for a general strain theory of crime. In S. Cote (Ed.), *Criminological theories: Bridging the past to the future* (pp. 113–124). Thousand Oaks, CA: Sage.

34. Agnew (2002, p. 119).

35. Agnew (2002, p. 123).

36. Agnew, R. (1997). Stability and change in crime over the lifecourse: A strain theory explanation. In T. Thornberry (Ed.), *Developmental theories of crime and delinquency* (pp. 101–132). New Brunswick, NJ: Transaction.

37. Agnew (1997, p. 103).

38. Agnew (1997, p. 106).

39. Curran, D., & Renzetti, C. (2001). *Theories of crime* (2nd ed.). Boston: Allyn & Bacon.

40. Cohen, A. (1955) *Delinquent boys.* New York: Free Press.

41. Cohen (1955, p. 66).

42. Rowe, D. (1996). An adaptive strategy theory of crime and delinquency. In J. Hawkins (Ed.), *Delinquency and crime: Current theories* (pp. 268–314). Cambridge, UK: Cambridge University Press. (Quote on p. 305)

43. Katz, J. (1988). *Seductions of crime: Moral and sensual attractions in doing evil.* New York: Basic Books.

44. Sutton, W., & Linn, E. (1976). *Where the money was: Memoirs of a bank robber.* New York: Viking. (Quote on p. 120)

45. Sampson, R., & Laub, J. (2005). A general age-graded theory of crime: Lessons learned and the future of life-course criminology. In D. Farrington (Ed.), *Advances in criminological theory* (Vol. 14, pp. 165–181). Piscataway, NJ: Transaction. (Quote on p. 173)

46. Gove, W., & Wilmoth, C. (2003). The neurophysiology of motivation and habitual criminal behavior. In A. Walsh & L. Ellis (Eds.), *Biosocial criminology: Challenging environmentalism's supremacy* (pp. 227–245). Hauppauge, NY: Nova Science.

47. Cloward, R., & Ohlin, L. (1960). *Delinquency and opportunity.* New York: Free Press.

48. Cloward and Ohlin (1960, p. 96).

49. Cloward and Ohlin (1960, p. 73).

50. Miller, W. (1958). Lower-class culture as a generating milieu of gang delinquency. *Journal of Social Issues, 14,* 5–19.

51. Miller (1958, p. 14).

52. Schmalleger, F. (2004). *Criminology today.* Upper Saddle River, NJ: Prentice Hall. (Quote on p. 223)

53. Porter, M. (1995). The competitive advantage of the inner city. *Harvard Business Review, 73,* 63–64.

54. Walinsky, A. (1997). The crisis of public order. In M. Fisch (Ed.), *Criminology 97/98* (pp. 6–14). Guilford, CT: Dushkin. (Quote on p. 11)

55. Western, B. (2003). *Incarceration, employment, and public policy.* New Jersey Institute for Social Justice. Retrieved from http://www.njisj.org/reports/western_report.html

56. Hurst, C. (1995). *Social inequality: Forms, causes, and consequences.* Boston: Allyn & Bacon.

57. Thernstrom, S., & Thernstrom, A. (1997). *America in black and white: One nation indivisible.* New York: Simon & Schuster.

58. Klein, M. (1971). *Street gang and street workers.* Englewood Cliffs, NJ: Prentice Hall. (Quote on p. 111)

59. Pearson, G. (1983). *Hooligan: A history of reportable fears.* New York: Schocken. (Quote on p. 188)

60. Shelden, R., Tracy, S., & Brown, W. (2001). *Youth gangs in American society* (2nd ed.). Belmont, CA: Wadsworth.

61. Egley, A., & Major, A. (2004). *Highlights of the 2002 National Youth Gang Survey* (OJJDP Fact Sheet). Washington, DC: U.S. Department of Justice, Office of Juvenile Justice and Delinquency Prevention.

62. Moore, J., & Hagedorn, J. (2001). Female gangs: Focus on research. *OJJDP Juvenile Justice Bulletin.*

63. Wilson, J. (1987). *The truly disadvantaged.* Chicago: University of Chicago Press.

64. Egley, A. (2002). *National youth gang survey trends from 1996 to 2000* (OJJDP fact sheet). Washington,

DC: U.S. Department of Justice, Office of Juvenile Justice and Delinquency Prevention.

65. Shelden et al. (2001).

66. Spergel, I. (1995). *The youth gang problem: A community approach.* New York: Oxford University Press. (Quote on pp. 108–109)

67. Perkins, U. (1987). *Explosion of Chicago's Black street gangs: 1900 to the present.* Chicago: Third World Press.

68. Padilla, F. (1992). *The gang as an American enterprise.* New Brunswick, NJ: Rutgers University Press.

69. Bing, L. (1991). *Do or die.* New York: HarperCollins. (Quote on p. 12)

70. Hall, S. (2002). Daubing the drudges of fury: Men, violence and the piety of the hegemonic masculinity thesis. *Theoretical Criminology, 6,* 35–61.

71. Hayslett-McCall, K., & Bernard, T. (2002). Attachment, masculinity, and self-control: A theory of male crime rates. *Theoretical Criminology, 6,* 5–33.

72. Ember, M., & Ember, C. (1998, October). Facts of violence. *Anthropology Newsletter,* pp. 14–15.

73. Moore and Hagedorn (2001).

74. Moore and Hagedorn (2001).

75. Moore and Hagedorn (2001).

76. Shelden et al. (2001).

77. Miller, J. (2002). The girls in the gang: What we've learned from two decades of research. In R. Huff (Ed.), *Gangs in America* (pp. 175–197). Thousand Oaks, CA: Sage.

78. Shelden et al. (2001).

79. Shelden et al. (2001).

80. Sikes, G. (1997). *Eight ball chicks.* New York: Anchor. (Quote on p. 103)

81. Spergel (1995).

82. Shelden et al. (2001).

83. Moore and Hagedorn (2001).

84. Bartol, C., & Bartol, A. (1989). *Juvenile delinquency: A systems approach.* Englewood Cliffs, NJ: Prentice Hall. (Quote on p. 110)

85. van Kesteren, J., Mayhew, P., & Nieuwbeerta, P. (2000). Criminal victimization in seventeen industrialised countries: Key findings from the 2000 International Crime Victims Survey. The Hague, the Netherlands: Ministry of Justice.

86. Shoemaker, D. (1996). *Theories of delinquency: An examination of explanations of delinquent behavior* (3rd ed.). New York: Oxford University Press.

87. Wilson, E. O. (1998). *Consilience: The unity of knowledge.* New York: Knopf.

88. Siegel, L. (2006). *Criminology* (9th ed.). Belmont, CA: Wadsworth.

89. Anderson, E. (1999). *Code of the street: Decency, violence, and the moral life of the inner city.* New York: Norton.

90. Shoemaker, D. (1984). *Theories of delinquency: An examination of explanations of delinquent behavior.* New York: Oxford University Press.

91. Anderson (1999).

92. Cernkovich, S. (1978). Value orientations and delinquency involvement. *Criminology, 15,* 443–458.

93. Curran and Renzetti (2001).

94. Bartol and Bartol (1989).

95. Rosenbaum, D., Lurigio, A., & Davis, R. (1998). *The prevention of crime: Social and situational strategies.* Belmont, CA: West/Wadsworth. (Quote on p. 214)

96. LaFree, G., Drass, K., & O'Day, P. (1992). Race and crime in postwar America: Determinants of African-American and white rates. *Criminology, 30,* 157–185.

5

SOCIAL PROCESS THEORIES

The social structural theories discussed in the previous chapter only explain part of the possible reason that Kody Scott chose the path in life he did. Not all who experience the same conditions turn out the same way. Indeed, only one of Kody's brothers ran afoul of the law, for drug trafficking. The social process theories discussed in this chapter take us a step further in understanding Kody's choices. Two of the theories in this chapter tell us that criminal behavior is learned in association with peers and that we choose to repeat behaviors that are rewarding to us. After he shot and killed the Blood gang members in his initiation, Kody tells us that he lay in bed that night feeling guilty and ashamed of his actions and that he knew they were wrong. Nevertheless, when the time came to do the same thing again, he chose to do what his peers told him to do because he valued their praise and approval more than anything else in life. His fellow Crips also provided him with rationales and justifications for his actions that neutralized his guilt. Another theory in this chapter tells us that labels have the power to make us live up to them; we have seen how Kody proudly accepted the label of "Monster" and how he did his best to live up to it. Other theories stress the importance of attachment to the family and other social institutions, but he tells us that his "homeboys" were his only family and that his only commitment and involvement were to and with them and their activities.

On a personal level, he plainly lacked self-control; he was impulsive, hedonistic, and angry. Theorists in this chapter tell us that self-control is developed by consistent parental monitoring, supervision, and discipline, but his weary single mother lacked the time, resources, or incentive to provide Kody with proper parenting. From the youngest age, he came and went as he pleased. His autobiography makes it plain that he was something of a "feral child," big enough, mean enough, and guiltless enough to be free to satisfy any and all urges as they arose. This chapter details many of the social processes by which Kody came to be the monster he claims himself to be.

◪ The Social Process Tradition

Sometimes social structural theories are examined as if social structure exists apart from day to-day human activity and as if human perceptions are irrelevant. Social process criminologists, on the other hand, operate from a general sociological perspective known as **symbolic interactionism**. Symbolic interactionists focus on how people interpret and define their social reality and the meanings they attach to it in the process of interacting with one another via language (symbols)—hence the phrase *symbolic* interaction. Social process theorists believe that if we wish to understand social behavior, we have to understand how individuals subjectively perceive their social reality and how they interact with others to create, sustain, and change it. This perspective may be summarized in the so-called **Thomas theorem:** "If men [and women] define situations as real, they are real in their consequences."[1] For example, witches flying around on broomsticks and casting evils spells do not exist, but that objective fact was of no comfort to the thousands of women burned as witches in the past because they were defined by their cultures as real and treated accordingly.

The social processes most stressed in this chapter are the socialization and cultural conflict processes. We are all socialized, but not in the same way, and although conflict is an ever-present part of social life, its casualties are not evenly distributed across society. Social process theories seek to describe the process of criminal and delinquent socialization (how antisocial attitudes and behavior are learned) and how the process of social conflict "pressures" individuals into committing antisocial acts. Some process theories focus on the reverse process of learning prosocial attitudes and behavior in the face of temptations to do otherwise. The first theory we examine, after addressing the contribution of the early social process positivist sociologist, Gabriel Tarde, stresses the relationship between social conflict and the learning of antisocial attitudes and behavior, with special emphasis on socialization by delinquent companions.

Gabriel Tarde and the Laws of Imitation

Gabriel Tarde,[2] French sociologist and contemporary of Durkheim, was one of the few pioneers whose primary interest was criminology. Tarde believed that criminal behavior is intrinsic to society, not inherent in people, and that it is learned mainly by imitation. Tarde laid out three **laws of imitation,** the first of which states that people imitate one another in direct proportion to physical and psychological closeness of contact, as well as the frequency of such contact. In other words, we imitate those with whom we interact frequently and whom we respect, admire, and find worthy.

The second law of imitation deals with changes in social customs and fashions and posits that imitation flows downward from the "superior" to the "inferior" classes or persons most of the time. The influence of the superior over the inferior is proportional to the degree of superiority/inferiority and to the physical and psychological distance between persons and classes. Fashions include new kinds of crimes or, at least, crimes that gain a new popularity for one reason or another or new ways of committing them. As examples of crime fashions, Tarde gives the substitution of the gun for the knife and the fad for "cutting women to pieces" (a reference to Jack the Ripper).

The third law addresses the insertion of new fashions into the fabric of society. Fashions may be short-lived, but they may also become embedded over time and take on the quality of a custom. Sometimes different currents of imitation may evolve from a common fashion.

Tarde cites the Industrial Revolution as an event (fashion) that created increased acquisitiveness. By doing so, it generated industriousness and ambition, but it also generated criminal behavior as some individuals sought to acquire their increased wants by illegitimate means (a tinge of Merton's anomie/strain theory here).

Tarde attempted to reconcile positive science with moral obligation and personal responsibility. Criminal behavior may have a number of causes, but identifying them does not absolve the criminal from blame. According to Tarde, persons are responsible for their behavior as long as they are their habitual social selves, and insofar as there is a "similarity" between the self and its social surroundings. A person cannot be held fully responsible for wrongful acts if he or she, at the time of the act, was not identical with the self, as he or she habitually knows that self. Madness, epilepsy, and a sudden and profound change in the habitual way of life (e.g., immigration) are examples of occurrences that take the person "out" of his or her habitual identity and diminish the similarity between the self and its social surroundings.

Tarde has never been as popular as Durkheim among criminologists, perhaps because he actively opposed Durkheim's overdetermined sociological approach.[3] Tarde constantly reminded others that the relationship between social facts and crime is not a direct one, but rather one that is mediated by the interpretation of those facts by those whom they touch most. In recognizing that individuals do not respond mechanistically to social factors, Tarde provided "a happy marriage of psychology and sociology."[4] All social process theories represent the joining of these two disciplines to varying extents, even if they explicitly deny that this is the case.

Differential Association Theory

Differential association theory is the brainchild of America's most famous criminologist, Edwin Sutherland. Sutherland's ambition was to arrive at a theory that could explain both individual criminality and aggregate crime rates by identifying conditions that must be present for crime to occur and that are absent when crime is absent. Although he explicitly denied the role of psychology in understanding crime and delinquency, his theory is true to the Thomas theorem in that it focuses on the process of becoming delinquent via differential definitions of reality and attitude formation.

Differential association theory takes the form of nine propositions outlining the process by which individuals come to acquire attitudes favorable to criminal or delinquent behavior, as well as the specific techniques involved in it. Sutherland and his long-time collaborator, Donald Cressey,[5] list these propositions as follows:

1. Criminal behavior is learned.

2. Criminal behavior is learned in interaction with other persons in a process of communication.

3. The principal part of learning criminal behavior occurs within intimate personal groups.

4. When criminal behavior is learned, the learning includes (a) techniques of committing the crime . . . (b) the specific direction of motives, drives, rationalizations, and attitudes.

5. The specific direction of motives and drives is learned from definitions of the legal code as favorable or unfavorable.

6. A person becomes delinquent because of an excess of definitions favorable to violations of law over definitions unfavorable to violations of law.

7. Differential associations may vary in frequency, duration, priority, and intensity.

8. The process of learning criminal behavior by association with criminal and anti-criminal patterns involves all of the mechanisms that are involved in any other learning.

9. While criminal behavior is an expression of general needs and values, it is not explained by [them] since noncriminal behavior is an expression of the same needs and values.

The first three principles assert that criminal behavior is learned in the process of social interaction, particularly within intimate personal groups (note the debt to Tarde's first law of imitation here). By emphasizing learning, Sutherland was attempting to guide criminologists away from the notion that criminal behavior is the result of biological or psychological abnormalities or is invented anew by each criminal. Sutherland believed that criminality is not the

▲ **Photo 5.1** Youthful racist skinheads in London give the fascist salute. Differential association theory would argue that if the people you spent most of your time with espouse deviant values, you are likely to adopt these as well.

result of individual traits; nor, for the most part, is it learned from impersonal communication from movies or magazines and the like. The learning of criminal behavior involves the same mechanisms involved in any other learning and includes specific skills and techniques for committing crimes, as well as the motives, rationalizations, justifications, and attitudes of criminals.

The theory asserts that humans take on the hues and colors of their environments, blending in and conforming with natural ease. We view the world differently according to the attitudes, beliefs, and expectations of the groups around which our lives revolve. If you think about it, it could hardly be otherwise, particularly in our formative years.

The key proposition in the theory is number 6: "*A person becomes delinquent because of an excess of definitions favorable to violations of law over definitions unfavorable to violations of law.*"[6] Learning criminal conduct is not just a matter of "monkey see, monkey do"; it is a process of modeling the self after and becoming identified with individuals we respect and value and who happen to hold an excess of procriminal definitions over noncriminal definitions. **Definitions** refer to meanings our experiences have for us, how we see things, and our attitudes, values, and habitual ways of viewing the world.[7]

Definitions become favorable or unfavorable to law violation according to the *weight* granted the definitions by individuals, not simply their excess. Weights are assigned to our definitions in our associations with others, and these associations vary in *frequency, duration, priority, and intensity.* That being the case, the earlier we are exposed to criminal norms of conduct, the more often we are exposed to them, the longer those exposures last, and the more strongly we are attached to those who supply us with the definitions favorable to law violation, the more likely we are to commit criminal acts when opportunities to do so present themselves.

In addition to the socialization process, Sutherland's theory is also about conflict. He was well aware of the findings of the Chicago school regarding neighborhood effects but found the phrase *social disorganization* to be insulting to lower-class people and substituted **differential social organization.** He agreed with Walter Miller that lower-class neighborhoods are not disorganized or pathological but rather just "different," with integrity of their own. Whatever we call them, however, if we find ourselves in one of them, we will be surrounded by "definitions favorable to law violation" and cannot help being influenced by them, regardless of our individual characteristics. The concept of differential social organization thus allows differential association theorists to adequately account for the associations people have without reference to individual differences. Differential association theory is presented in diagrammatic form in Figure 5.1.

Ronald Akers's Social Learning Theory

Sutherland's differential association theory is a learning theory of crime, but beyond looking at frequency, priority, duration, and intensity, the theory says nothing about the mechanisms by which "definitions favorable" to crime are learned. Robert Burgess (a psychologist) and Ronald Akers (a sociologist) rectified this omission by applying the concepts of operant psychology to the vague "definitions favorable" concept in their **social learning theory.**[8] The formulation of the theory relies on psychological principles, which suggests that it could be classified as a psychological theory, but Akers[9] insists that his theory is in the same sociological tradition of symbolic interaction as differential association. Social learning theory is an example of how borrowing from one field of inquiry can enhance another.

Figure 5.1	Diagrammatic Presentation of Differential Association Theory

Differential social	→	Normative conflict leads	→	Differential association	→	Crime and
organization in		to definitions favorable		with others holding such		delinquency
lower-class areas		to law violation		definitions		

Operant psychology is a perspective on learning that asserts that behavior is governed and shaped by its consequences. An *operant* is any behavior emitted that results in some consequence that affects future behavior. Operant conditioning is thus active in that it depends on the actor's operations (behavior), is cognitive in nature, and forms an association between a person's behavior and its consequences. In other words, people receive feedback in response to their behavior from others in their environment, which they interpret in terms of positive or negative consequences. A conditioned behavior may have emerged initially by imitation, modeling, or even spontaneously, but how well that behavior is learned and whether or not it is repeated depends on how others in the immediate social environment react to it.

Behavior has two general consequences; it is reinforced or punished. Behavior that has positive consequences for the actor is said to *reinforce* that behavior, making it more likely that the behavior will be repeated in similar situations. Behavior that is punished is less likely to be repeated. **Reinforcement** is either positive or negative. The loot from a burglary and the status achieved by killing a member of a rival gang are criminal examples of *positive reinforcement*. *Negative reinforcement* occurs when some aversive condition is avoided or removed, such as the removal of a negative street reputation as a "chicken" or "punk" following some act of criminal bravado.

Punishment, which leads to the weakening or eliminating of the behavior preceding it, can also be positive or negative. *Positive punishment* is the application of some aversive stimulus, such as a prison term. *Negative punishment* is the removal of a pleasant stimulus, such as the loss of status in a street gang. The acquisition of Sutherland's "definitions favorable" to antisocial behavior (or prosocial behavior, for that matter) thus depends on each individual's history of reinforcement and punishment. The processes of reinforcement and punishment are illustrated in Figure 5.2.

Things are not really this simple; we cannot just add and subtract observable rewards and punishments and expect to understand complex human behavior. Rewards and punishments are differentially valued and thus differentially influential in shaping our behavior. They are differentially valued and influential according to the meaning they have for us and according to their source. What is reinforcing for some may be punishing for others. For teens who value the approval of their parents and teachers, an arrest and probation placement is punishment. For teens who would rather gain the approval of antisocial peers, such an outcome may be a reinforcer since it marks them officially as a "bad ass." The social context is thus an extremely important component of social learning theory. As Akers puts it, "Most of the learning relevant to deviant behavior is the result of social interactions or exchanges in which the words, responses, presence, and behavior of other persons make reinforcers available, and provide the setting for reinforcement."[10]

Figure 5.2	Illustrating Types of Reinforcement and Punishment

Reinforcement Increases Behavior	*Punishment Decreases Behavior*
Positive Reinforcement	**Positive Punishment**
(something rewarding received)	(something punishing applied)
Negative Reinforcement	**Negative Punishment**
(something punishing avoided)	(something rewarding lost)

Discrimination is another important component of social learning theory. Whereas reinforcements or punishments are stimuli that *follow* behavior, discriminative stimuli are present *before* the behavior occurs. Discriminative stimuli are clues that signal whether a particular behavior is likely to be followed by reward or punishment. In other words, discrimination involves learning to distinguish between stimuli that have been reinforced or punished in the past with similar stimuli you expect will result in the same response in the future.

We all have images in our heads about the nature of certain people and situations and about how we should respond to them. Consider what your possible responses might be if yelled at by a child, your brother, a police officer, or a hulking tattooed biker with an attitude. Your response would represent what you have learned personally or vicariously about those people or others like them. What about your response to an unlocked car with the keys in it? For the criminal mind, it is a discriminative stimulus that signals "immediate reward"; for you, it probably signals nothing other than how foolish the owner is because you have never previously been rewarded for stealing a car. Besides, your conscience wouldn't let you anyhow, and you are probably more concerned with the long-term rewards of a prosocial lifestyle than any immediate rewards from stealing the car or any of its contents.

Social Control Theories

If society is to be possible, individuals with different and often conflicting interests must enjoy peaceful and predictable coexistence. To ensure such coexistence, mechanisms have been devised to minimize nonconformity and deviance that we may collectively refer to as **social control.** Social control essentially means any action on the part of others, deliberate or not, that facilitates conformity to social rules. In many senses, both Durkheim's anomie and Shaw and McKay's structural theories were also control theories. Both pointed to situations or circumstances (anomie or social disorganization) that lessened control of individuals' behavior. Social control may be direct, formal, and coercive, as exemplified by uniformed symbols of the state. But indirect and informal social control is preferable because it produces prosocial behavior, regardless of the presence or absence of external coercion. Obeying society's rules of proper conduct because we believe that the rules are right and just, not because we fear formal sanctions, means that we have our own internalized police officer and judge in the form of something called a conscience.

Walter Reckless's Containment Theory

Walter Reckless's **containment theory** is an early control that sought answers to why some people in similar environments are immune to criminal temptations and others are not.[11,12] Reckless recognized that we all experience both outer and inner pushes and pulls

FOCUS ON . . .

Self-Esteem and Crime

The concepts of self-concept and self-esteem are not synonyms. The self-concept involves two separate motives: the motive to think well of the self (*self-esteem*) and the motive to protect the self from change (the *self-consistency* motive).[13] No one should have to face life carrying around a picture of themselves as worthless failures, but we have a built-in bias against changing our self-image, even if we do not like the image. People need a sense of order and consistency in their lives, so what they have become used to doing and thinking becomes habitual and comfortable because they surround themselves with a cognitive protective belt around their self-images.

The relationship between self-esteem and criminal behavior has been traditionally viewed from the perspective that criminals do not feel worthy, and this lack of self-esteem gets them into trouble with the law. They take drugs and alcohol in vain attempts to feel better, and they seek out all other manner of deviant ways to bolster damaged self-esteem. However, the link between self-esteem and offending is ambiguous. Robert Vermerian and his colleagues[14] point out that there are subtypes of self-esteem based on the source and that its effects on behavior depend on the type being examined. In other words, there are social situations in which you feel good about yourself and those in which you don't. In Vermerian and colleagues' study of juveniles in Belgium, self-esteem gained from academic competence was negatively related to offending (the higher the academic competence, the lower the offending), but self-esteem based on perceived peer popularity was positively related (the higher the self-esteem gained from this source, the greater the offending). David and Kistner[15] report similar findings.

There is a dark side to the conventional wisdom that high self-esteem is conducive to prosocial behavior and that low self-esteem is conducive to antisocial behavior. Highly antisocial individuals, especially psychopaths, tend to have greatly exaggerated opinions of their self-worth,[16] and many criminals have a god-like attitude that they are the center of the universe.[17] It has been frequently found that most male/male assaults and homicides arise not from low self-esteem but from trivial incidents that threaten bloated opinions of the perpetrator's self-worth.[18,19] The kind of self-esteem earned on the streets ("juice") does not tolerate being "dissed" and is therefore dangerous self-esteem.[20] We can always claim that such bloated self-esteem is really egotism, narcissism, and conceit rather than "true" self-esteem and that people with "true" self-esteem would be immune to minor assaults on their self-worth. But this is a value judgment based on middle-class opinions about how "true" self-worth "should" be earned. Any theory based on self-image, then, must be careful that it does not confuse the sources of that construct. Sociology does psychology a service by pointing to the social developmental contexts of constructs such as the self-concept.

toward delinquent and criminal behavior. Outer pushes and pulls may include poverty, delinquent peers, and so on, and inner pushes and pulls may include various strains, needs for excitement, or any other number of things. Those of us who resist antisocial temptations (at least most of the time) are "contained" by two overlapping forms of containment: outer and inner.

Outer containment is the social pressure on individuals brought to bear by the family and other important individuals and groups to abide by community rules. This pressure is exerted via the socialization process and by the threat of social disgrace if one does not live up to the standards imparted by that process. Inner containment is the most important kind of containment because it is self-containment.

Inner containment (or self-control), says Reckless, relies heavily on how persons see themselves—their **self-concept.** Reckless assumes that persons with a negative self-concept are more likely to become criminal and delinquent, and persons with a positive self-concept are insulated from the pushes and pulls drawing them to crime and delinquency. He further asserts that the self-concept is essentially formed by the age of 12. Persons with positive self-concepts have high tolerance for frustration (they cope well with strain), are goal oriented (they have realistic legitimate career aspirations), and identify with prosocial norms and values. Persons with negative self-concepts are saddled with the opposite traits and values. However, it is unclear if these traits and values precede or follow the formation of a self-concept or even whether Reckless considered them components or merely correlates of the self-concept.

Travis Hirschi's Social Bonding Theory

There are other varieties of control theory, but by far the most popular and enduring is Travis Hirschi's social control, or social bonding, theory,[21,22] a theory that places primary importance on the family. Separate surveys in the 1980s[23] and 1990s[24] showed that Hirschi's social control theory is the most popular theory among contemporary criminologists. Surveys of laypersons have also consistently shown that they emphasize family factors when asked their opinions about the causes of crime.[25,26]

Social control theory is very much in the constrained vision camp. Except for neoclassical theories, previous theories we have examined assume that crime is something that is learned by good people living in bad environments. Under this assumption, it makes sense to ask, "What causes crime?" Control theorists believe that this question is based on a faulty understanding of human nature and that the real question is not why some people behave badly but why most of us behave well most of the time. After all, children who are not properly socialized hit, kick, bite, steal, whine, scream, and otherwise behave obnoxiously whenever the mood strikes them. They have to be taught not to do these things, which, in the absence of training, "come naturally." In this tradition, it is society that is "good" and human beings, in the absence of the proper training, who are "bad." Crime is natural (note the agreement with Durkheim here), and the criminal is just the unsocialized self-centered child grown strong. Gwynn Nettler said it most colorfully: "If we grow up 'naturally,' without cultivation, like weeds, we grow up like weeds—rank."[27] Social control theory is thus about the role of social relationships that bind people to the social order and prevent antisocial behavior.

Hirschi's theory is consistent with what we know with reasonable certainty about the personal and demographic characteristics of criminals. He starts with the correlates of the "typical" criminal and finds him to be a young male who grew up in a fatherless home in an urban slum, who has a history of difficulty in school, and who is unemployed. Having defined the typical criminal, Hirschi makes a series of logical deductions, beginning with the observation that criminal activity is contrary to the wishes and expectations of others. From this, he deduces that those most likely to commit crimes are least likely to be concerned with the wishes and expectations of others. Criminal activity is also contrary to the law and involves the risk of punishment. Therefore, those who commit crimes are least likely to be concerned with the risk of punishment (because they have little to lose) and least likely to accept the moral beliefs underlying the law. Finally, criminal acts take time and are thus most likely to be engaged in by those who have the time required to commit them (the unemployed).[28]

▲ **Photo 5.2** These students purchased similar jackets to display their solidarity and bonding to the group. Social control theory would predict that despite their quirky behavior as displayed here, they would not become involved in serious criminal behavior.

The Four Social Bonds

From these observations, Hirschi makes the assumptions that the typical delinquent or criminal lacks *attachment* to prosocial others, that he lacks *commitment* to a prosocial career and *involvement* in a prosocial lifestyle, and that he does not *believe* in the validity of the mainstream moral order. Attachment, commitment, involvement, and belief are *social bonds* that exist in the lives of noncriminals, restraining them from criminal activity, and are absent or weak in the lives of criminals.

Attachment is the emotional component of conformity. It refers to the emotional bonds existing between the individual and key social institutions, such as the family and the school. Attachment to conventional others is the foundation for all other social bonds because it leads us to feel valued, respected, and admired and to value the favorable judgments of those to whom we are attached. Sociologists use the concepts of significant other and reference group to refer to the people we consider important to us and whose good opinions we value. Significant others are close family members and friends, and reference groups are groups of people who we admire and seek to emulate. These are the people to whom we look for guidance in our behavior. Much of our behavior can be seen as attempts to gain favorable judgments from our reference groups and significant others.

Parents are for many years the most important behavior-orienting significant others. Children who do not care about parental reactions are those who are most likely to behave in ways contrary to their wishes. Risking the good opinion of another is of minor concern when that good opinion is not valued. Parental opinion may not be valued if parents have not earned the love and respect of their children because of physical and/or emotional neglect and abuse, the lack of intimate communication, erratic and unfair disciplinary practices, emotional coldness, or perhaps because their appearance, demeanor, or social status is embarrassing to the child.[29] Lack of attachment to parents and lack of respect for their wishes easily spills over into a lack of attachment and respect for the broader social groupings of which the child is a part. Much of the controlling power of others outside the family lies in the threat of reporting juvenile misbehavior to parents. If the child has little fear of parental sanctions, the control exercised by others has little effect because parental control has limited effect.

Commitment is the rational component of conformity and refers to a lifestyle in which one has invested considerable time and energy in the pursuit of a lawful career. Unlike Merton's negative view of aspirations (they sometimes induce strain), Hirschi[30] contends that they tie individuals to the social order. People who have heavily invested in a lawful career have a valuable stake in conformity and are not likely to risk it by engaging in criminal activity. The cost/benefit ratio renders the cost of crime prohibitive for such a person. Poor students, truants, dropouts, and the unemployed do not have much of an investment in conventional behavior and therefore risk less in any cost/benefit comparison. Acquiring a stake in conformity requires disciplined application to tasks that children do not relish but complete to gain approval from parents. If children's efforts are not valued, they may busy themselves in tasks more congenial to their natural inclinations, which for most of them almost certainly do not include algebra or English grammar. Attachment is thus the essential foundation for commitment to a prosocial lifestyle.

Involvement is a direct consequence of commitment; it is a part of an overall conventional pattern of existence: "Many persons undoubtedly owe a life of virtue to lack of opportunity to do otherwise."[31] Involvement is a matter of time and energy constrictions placed on us by the demands of our lawful activities that reduce exposure to illegal opportunities. Conversely, noninvolvement in lawful activities increases the possibility of exposure to illegal activities: "Idle hands are the devil's workshop."[32]

Belief refers to the acceptance of the social norms regulating conduct. Individuals free of the constraints on their behavior imposed by attachment, commitment, and involvement evolve a belief system shorn of conventional morality. A belief system empty of conventional morality is concerned only with narrow self-interest. Hirschi does not view a criminal belief system as a motivator of criminal behavior as Sutherland did; criminals simply act according to their urges and then rationalize their behavior. Likewise, crime is not motivated by the absence of any of the social bonds; their absence merely represents social deficiencies that result in a reduction of the potential costs of committing it. Hirschi's social control theory is presented in diagrammatic form in Figure 5.3.

For social control theorists, then, antisocial and criminal behavior will emerge automatically if social controls are lacking; it needs no special motivating factors since human beings are assumed to be naturally self-centered. But criminal behavior is influenced by both push-and-pull factors, and we should consider both the restraining and motivating factors

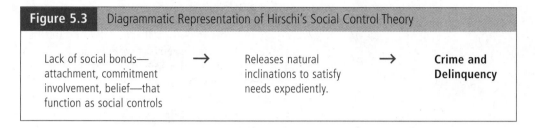

Figure 5.3   Diagrammatic Representation of Hirschi's Social Control Theory

Lack of social bonds—
attachment, commitment
involvement, belief—that
function as social controls   →   Releases natural
inclinations to satisfy
needs expediently.   →   **Crime and
Delinquency**

associated with it. One study, based on a large national sample of boys, found that social control variables "work" better to explain delinquency if low social control leads to anger and frustration (strain) and to association with delinquent peers.[33] However, weak social bonds do not *necessarily* lead to strain and/or association with delinquent peers, and just because a youth associates with delinquent peers and/or is strained does not mean that social bonds are lacking. Strain can also lead to the weakening of social bonds just as well as the other way around. The next stage in the research agenda might be to identify what is different about youths with weak social bonds who do and do not develop strain and associations with delinquent peers. The next theory we discuss goes part way to doing this.

From Social to Self-Control:
Gottfredson and Hirschi's Low Self-Control Theory

With colleague Michael Gottfredson, Hirschi has moved away from explaining crime and delinquency in terms of social control toward explaining it in terms of self-control. *Self-control* is defined as the "extent to which [different people] are vulnerable to the temptations of the moment."[34] The theory accepts the classical idea that crimes are the result of the natural human impulse to enhance pleasure and avoid pain: "Whatever the mechanisms of restraint they employ [either social or self-control], control theories assume that lack of restraints frees people to follow their human nature, to do whatever it is that brings them pleasure."[35]

Following an unrestrained path to pleasure often leads to crimes, which Gottfredson and Hirschi define as "acts of force or fraud undertaken in pursuit of self-interest."[36] Most crimes, they assert, are spontaneous acts requiring little skill and earn the criminal minimal, short-term satisfaction. People with low self-control possess the following personal traits that put them at risk for criminal offending:

◆ They are oriented to the present rather than to the future, and crime affords them immediate rather than delayed gratification.
◆ They are risk taking and physical as opposed to cautious and cognitive, and crime provides them with exciting and risky adventures.
◆ They lack patience, persistence, and diligence, and crime provides them with quick and easy ways to obtain money, sex, revenge, and so forth.
◆ They are self-centered and insensitive, so they can commit crimes without experiencing pangs of guilt for causing the suffering of others.[37]

▲ **Photo 5.3** These two lovers, Paul Bernardo and Karla Homolka, enjoyed committing rape and murder as part of their passion for one another. As individuals, each demonstrates low self-control, while together, they reinforce that it's OK to harm others, a neutralization technique often employed by groups.

The Origin of Self-Control

According to the theory, low self-control is established early in childhood, tends to persist throughout life, and is the result of incompetent parenting. It is important to realize that children do not learn low self-control; low self-control is the default outcome that occurs in the absence of adequate socialization. If children are to be taught self-control, their behavior must be strictly and consistently monitored, and parents and/or caregivers must recognize deviant behavior when it occurs and punish it. Parental concern for the well-being of their children is central to the rearing of self-controlled children. Warmth, nurturance, vigilance, and the willingness to practice "tough love" are necessary parental attributes that forge self-control in their offspring. Other family-related factors that may lead to low self-control include parental criminality (criminals are not very successful in socializing their children), family size (the larger the family, the more difficult it is to monitor behavior), single-parent family (two parents are generally better than one), and working mothers, which negatively affect the development of children's self-control if no substitute monitor is provided.[38]

Gottfredson and Hirschi argue that children acquire or fail to acquire self-control in the first decade of life, after which the attained level of control remains stable across the life course. Subsequent experiences, situations, and circumstances have little independent effect on the probability of offending because the level of self-control acquired in childhood heavily influences these experiences. Low self-control is thus considered a stable component of a criminal personality, which is why most criminals typically fail in anything that requires long-term commitment and compromise, such as school, employment, and marriage, because such commitments and compromises get in the way of immediate satisfaction of their desires.

Opportunity Gottfredson and Hirschi assert that low self-control is a necessary but not sufficient determinant of criminal offending. Once a person's level of self-control is established and remains stable across the life course, we cannot explain different levels of criminal involvement by different levels of self-control (this appears to imply that all offenders have the same low level of self-control), and then we need something else to account for different levels of offending. What accounts for different levels of offending, according to Gottfredson and Hirschi, are the different opportunities criminals encounter that are conducive to committing crimes. By virtue of differential placement in the social structure, some individuals are exposed to more criminal opportunities than others. Offending is thus the result of people with low self-control meeting a criminal opportunity. A criminal **opportunity** is a situation that presents itself to an offender by which he or she can immediately satisfy needs with minimal mental or physical effort.[39] Gottfredson and Hirschi's descriptions of what they see as typical criminal incidents suggest that most of them are environmental events (an open door, an unlocked car, a young woman walking alone down a dark alley) witnessed by someone ready to take advantage of them.

The impulsive nature of the typical crime is supported by Wolfgang, Thornberry, and Figlio's Philadelphia cohort study[40] in which they found that 83% of offenders claimed that the crimes for which they were first arrested were unplanned and "just happened." Eleven percent said they planned the crime on the day it was committed, and only 6% said they planned their crimes 1 or more days in advance. Further supporting Gottfredson and Hirschi's claim, this same study found that the impulsive tendency is remarkably stable. When asked about their *last* crime, 83% of those who had not planned their first crime also had not planned their last, while 60% of those who had planned their first crime had not planned their last. The theory is outlined diagrammatically in Figure 5.4.

Self-control theory appears to be an effort to answer additional questions suggested by social control theory by shifting the level of analysis from social to self-control. The assumption of a self-interested person anxious to experience pleasure and avoid pain is still there, but the theory tries to account for why some people pursue their self-interest in legitimate ways and others do not, with primary emphasis on socialization practices that do or do not produce children capable of reining in their natural instincts.

Labeling Theory: The Irony of Social Reaction

Do you believe that there is any truth to the old saying, "Give a dog a bad name and he'll live up to it"? There are those who do, and one school of criminological thought takes seriously the power of bad labels to stigmatize and, by doing so, evoke the very behavior the label signifies. The school is known as the *labeling* or *societal reaction* school. Other theories may recognize that the stigma of a criminal label can have unintended consequences, but only this theory grants the labeling process a central role in explaining crime and deviance. The labeling perspective is interesting and provocative because, unlike other criminological theories, it does not ask why crime rates vary or why individuals differ in their propensity to commit antisocial acts. Rather, it asks, "Why are some behaviors labeled criminal and not others?" and "Why is there variation in societal reaction to criminal and other forms of antisocial behavior?" Labeling theory thus shifts the focus (and the blame) from the actor (the criminal) to the reactor (agents of the criminal justice system).

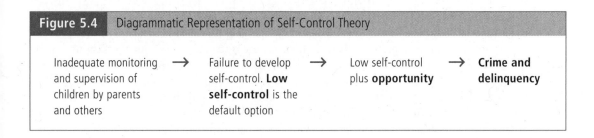

Figure 5.4   Diagrammatic Representation of Self-Control Theory

Inadequate monitoring and supervision of children by parents and others → Failure to develop self-control. **Low self-control** is the default option → Low self-control plus **opportunity** → **Crime and delinquency**

The origin of labeling theory is traditionally traced to Frank Tannenbaum's *Crime and the Community,* published in 1938.[41] In this book, Tannenbaum emphasized that a major part in the making of a criminal is the process of identifying and labeling a person as such or, in his own words, the process of "dramatizing evil."[42] Tannenbaum viewed the labeling of a delinquent or criminal as "bad" or "evil" as amounting to a self-fulfilling prophesy (a false definition of a situation or person that becomes true if the prophesy is believed and acted upon), which means that catching and punishing criminals has an effect completely opposite of that which was intended. That is, the violator's experience of being processed through the criminal justice system, rather than serving to deter future criminal behavior, may embed them further in the criminal lifestyle.

The Nature of Crime

The labeling perspective lay dormant until the 1960s, at which time the intellectual climate of questioning all mainstream assumptions was ripe for it. One of the assumptions questioned was that crime and other forms of deviance have an objective reality like "disease" or "gravity." Labeling theorists asserted that crime is defined into existence rather than discovered. For them, there is no crime independent of cultural values and norms, which are embodied in the judgments and reactions of others. To put it simply, no act is by its "nature" criminal because acts do not have natures until they are witnessed, judged good or bad, and reacted to as such by others.

Based on self-report studies of delinquency, criminologists of this period began to seriously question many of the statistics reported in the *Uniform Crime Reports (UCR).* These official statistics typically show much higher arrest rates for minorities and lower-class Whites than for middle-class Whites, but self-report data tended to show small or even no significant differences in race or class in rates of offending. Taking these self-report data at face value (and ignoring the distinction between serious crime and the minor infractions typically asked about and admitted to in self-reports), labeling theorists suggested that it is the race and class prejudice of criminal justice agents that is responsible for the arrest figures reflected in the *UCR,* not any real race or class differences in actual offending.[43]

Primary and Secondary Deviance

Edwin Lemert,[44] the most influential labeling theorist, distinguished between primary deviance and secondary deviance. **Primary deviance** is the initial nonconforming act that comes to the attention of the authorities. Lemert accepted that primary delinquent and criminal behavior could arise for a wide variety of reasons, but they were of little interest to him because they had only marginal effects on the offender's self-concept as a criminal or noncriminal, and it is the individual's self-concept that is crucial in labeling theory. In fact, primary deviance is of interest to labeling theorists only insofar as it is detected and reacted to by individuals with the power to pin a stigmatizing label on the rule breaker.

It may appear strange that labeling theorists are unconcerned about the origins of primary deviance, and you might wonder why. It all boils down to their views on crime and criminality. Since self-report studies have consistently shown that almost everyone has committed some kind of illegal act, labeling theorists reason that there are no objective causes to be concerned about. Their belief that crime is simply the successful application of a label rather than a quality of the act or of the actor leads them to conclude that primary deviance is of little concern. Being caught in an act of primary deviance is either the result of police bias or sheer bad luck; the real criminogenic experience comes *after* a person is caught and labeled. The central concern of labeling theory is thus to explain the behavioral consequences of being labeled.

Secondary deviance is deviance that results from society's reaction to offenders' primary deviance. The stigma of a criminal label may result in people becoming more criminal than they would have been had they not been caught. This may occur in two related ways. First, labeled persons may alter their self-concepts in conformity with the label ("yes, I am a criminal, and I will act more like one in future"). Second, the label may exclude them from conventional employment opportunities and lead to the loss of conventional friends. Stigmatizing and segregating offenders leads them to seek illegitimate opportunities to fulfill their financial needs and to seek other criminals to fulfill their friendship needs, which further strengthens their growing conception of themselves as "really" criminal. The criminal label becomes a self-fulfilling prophesy because it is a more powerful label than other social labels, such as father, sister, bowler, ex-soldier, and plumber, that offenders may claim. The criminal label operates as a "master status" governing most of the offender's social interactions by blinding others to his or her other statuses.[45]

The most important consideration, however, is the change of an offender's identity that supposedly results from the formal application of a deviant label. If the criminal label is successfully applied to the actor, it leads to the actor's reevaluation of his or her self-concept as a criminal, which then increases the probability of further criminal activity (secondary deviance). Labeling theorists do not assert that this process is inevitable; there are many exceptions to the "rule." Some offenders resist labeling by denying or downplaying the seriousness of their actions and may be successful at disavowing their deviance, even if formally labeled. At the opposite pole, there are others who actively seek the criminal or delinquent label as a badge of pride.[46] In addition, those who are already largely excluded from legitimate opportunities and prosocial friends, whether for psychological or social reasons, will not be affected by the labeling process in the same way that un-excluded individuals may be.

Extending Labeling Theory

In his book *Crime, Shame, and Reintegration,* John Braithwaite[47] noted that nations with low crime rates (and nations that formerly enjoyed low crime rates) are those where shaming has great social power. Shaming was defined as "all processes of expressing disapproval which have the intention or effect of invoking remorse in the person being shamed and/or condemnation by others who become aware of the shaming."[48] At first blush, this seems to be diametrically opposed to labeling theory, which recommends that we avoid shaming and condemnation at all costs lest it launch stigmatized and condemned individuals into full-blown criminal careers.

Braithwaite agrees that the kind of shaming and condemnation received by offenders in the criminal justice system, a kind he calls **disintegrative shaming,** is counterproductive because it is based on "power assertion and injury."[49] The kind of shaming he recommends, which he terms **reintegrative shaming,** is different. Reintegrative shaming is a method of condemning the offender's *acts* without condemning his or her personhood. (Alcoholics Anonymous [AA] is an example of such shaming. Alcoholics in AA must acknowledge their

| Figure 5.5 | Diagrammatic Presentation of Labeling Theory |

Primary deviance $\rightarrow$ Apprehension and $\rightarrow$ Offenders may $\rightarrow$ **Secondary**
flowing from a   labeling as   come to accept   **deviance**
variety of causes   criminal or   labels and change   delinquency and
that are of no   delinquent. Person   their self-concepts   crime consequent
concern to labeling   is stigmatized with   to fit those labels. to changed
theorists.   a "master status."   self-concept.

alcoholic status, but they do so in an atmosphere of empathy and acceptance.) According to Braithwaite, the criminal justice system cannot ignore wrongdoing, and it must rebuke wrongdoers, but condemnation must be done in the spirit of strong disappointment that such a "good person" as the offender would do such a bad thing. Having been rebuked in a "degradation ceremony," offenders, after a suitable time, should undergo another formal ceremony stressing forgiveness and their decertification as deviants.[50]

As appealing as reintegrative shaming is, it is a difficult concept to apply when, as Braithwaite himself agrees, one of the few things many people are ashamed of in the modern world is being ashamed.[51] Shame has gone the way of other "anachronisms" in modern society, such as honor, civility, and courtesy. How do we shame people who have no shame, and how do we reintegrate people who were never integrated in the first place? Shaming is most effective when we are shamed by people who matter most to us.[52] What if no one who matters to us has prosocial values and ridicules everything that middle-class society considers good and decent? Many of our worst criminals have no one at all who matters in the least to them and consider any sign of "true" remorse to be a weakness.

Sykes and Matza's Neutralization Theory

Sykes and Matza's techniques of neutralization theory[53] run counter to many of the theories we have encountered in both this and the previous chapter. They run counter to labeling theory because they show how delinquents resist being tagged with labels rather than passively accepting them. They also run counter to subcultural theories that leave us with the impression that delinquent behavior is endowed with positive value and condoned as morally right in certain areas. It is difficult to believe that people who commit bad acts do not know "deep down" that they are wrong. According to Charis Kurbin and Ronald Weitzer, "Rather than condoning crime members of these communities instead have a degree of fatalism or 'moral cynicism' about crime. Crime is viewed as inevitable in high crime neighborhoods, and is thus less vigorously condemned by residents."[54]

Sykes and Matza agree and write, "If there existed in fact a delinquent subculture such that the delinquent viewed his [or her] behavior as morally correct," he or she would show no shame when caught but would instead show "indignation or a sense of martyrdom."[55] Their **techniques of neutralization** theory suggests that although delinquents know that

▲ **Photo 5.4** In our society, the homeless are frequently stigmatized and labeled as lazy, willing to live off the handouts of others, which they use to buy alcohol or drugs, rather than get a job. The irony of this photo, taken in Boston of a homeless man sleeping near the JFK Building on a very cold morning, is that JFK fought to end poverty in America.

their behavior is wrong, they justify it as "acceptable" on a number of grounds. In other words, they neutralize (render inoperative) any sense of shame or guilt for having committed some wrongful act, which, for Sykes and Matza, meant that they are at least minimally attached to conventional norms. Sykes and Matza identify the following five techniques of neutralization:

1. *Denial of responsibility.* This technique involves shifting the blame for a deviant act away from the actor: "I know she's only 6, but every time she would come over she would sit on my knee and wiggle about. So it was she who seduced me."

2. *Denial of injury.* This technique involves the offender's claim that no "real" offense occurred because no one was harmed: "He got his car back, didn't he, and his insurance covers the damage, doesn't it?"

3. *Denial of victim.* This technique is very much like the first one but implies that the victim got what he or she deserves: "I guess I did smash her face, but I was drunk and she kept nagging; hell, she asked for it!"

4. *Condemnation of the condemners.* This technique refers to attempts by the offender to share the shame and guilt with the condemners (parents, police, probation officers) by

asserting that their behavior is just bad as his or hers is: "You drink booze, I smoke grass; what's the difference?"

5. *Appeal to higher loyalties.* This technique elevates the offender's moral integrity by claiming altruistic motives: "I took the money to help pay for my grandmother's surgery" and "I have to cover my homies' backs, don't I"?

The motive behind the employment of these techniques is assumed to be the maintenance of a noncriminal self-image on the part of individuals who have committed a criminal act and who have been asked to explain why. Such individuals "define the situation" in a way that mitigates the seriousness of their acts and simultaneously protects the image they have of themselves as noncriminals. A less benign interpretation of the use of these techniques is that rather than trying to protect their self-images, they are seeking to mitigate their punishment or, at least, to "share" it with some convenient other. Conversely, intensive interviews with hardcore criminals indicate that they strive to maintain an image consistent with inner-city street codes, not with conventional ones (i.e., "they neutralize being good rather than being bad").[56]

What comes first, attitudes or behavior? If we start engaging in behavior that we consider morally wrong but find that behavior rewarding, we tend to develop a form of psychological discomfort called **cognitive dissonance.** It is this contradiction—belief in the validity of the moral order coupled with noncompliance with it—that generates cognitive dissonance or, in this context, guilt and shame. The elimination of uncomfortable inconsistencies between attitudes and behavior (cognitive dissonance) becomes a powerful motive to change one or the other. Psychologists tell us that we tend to find it a lot easier to make our attitudes consistent with our behavior than to change the behavior to conform with our attitudes if the behavior is rewarding.[57]

Techniques of neutralization are both ways of easing uncomfortable feelings of guilt and shame after a person has committed some wrong and ways of loosening moral constraints, thus making repetition of the behavior more probable. Rather than viewing techniques of neutralization as behavioral prescriptions, Sykes and Matza view them as functioning initially to reduce guilt and shame following an antisocial act and *then* becoming an integral part of offenders' repertoires of self-justifications, which they may eventually accept as valid. Neutralization techniques might be instrumental in increasing the probability of further antisocial behavior if offenders start to believe their own excuses. If this happens, it is a short step to believing that they have been treated unfairly by the criminal justice system ("I explained to them that it wasn't my fault, but the judge sent me to jail anyway") to feelings of frustration, alienation, and loss of control over one's life, which might provide motivation to commit new crimes.[58] Sykes and Matza may have thus hit on the cognitive process by which delinquents come to possess an excess of "definitions favorable" to law violation.

✉ Evaluation of Social Process Theories

Differential association theory plainly shares the unconstrained vision in that it assumes that antisocial behavior is learned and is not something that comes naturally in the absence of prosocial training. Critics of the theory (no doubt holders of the constrained vision) stress that antisocial behavior comes naturally to the unsocialized individual: "What is there to be learned about simple lying, taking things that belong to another, fighting and sex play?" asked an early critic.[59] Individuals certainly learn to get better at doing these things because of their associations with other like-minded individuals, but do they have to be taught them? Many critics of the theory say no; what they have to be taught is how to curb them, what constitutes moral behavior, and how to consider the rights and feelings of others.

Differential association theory also has to contend with the criticism that it ignores individual differences. In fact, in the 1939 formulation of his theory, Sutherland did recognize that individual differences influence relationship patterns: "Individual differences in respect to personal characteristics or social situations cause crime only as they affect differential association or frequency and consistency of contacts with criminal patterns."[60] Sutherland was saying that individual differences sort people in different relationship patterns—as numerous studies of relationship patterns attest (reviewed in Rodkin, Farmer, Pearl, and Van Acker[61])—and thus they are important. It may be a case of birds of a feather flocking together and that their flocking merely facilitates and accentuates their activities rather than "causes" them. Perhaps recognizing this as an impediment to his goal of a purely sociological theory, Sutherland dropped this reference to individual differences from subsequent formulations.

Defenders of the theory might reply that factors other than personal preferences influence our associations with others. As children, we all associated, played, and became friendly with other children in the neighborhoods in which we found ourselves. As the social ecology folks remind us, neighborhoods matter, and choice opportunities available to us are different in different neighborhoods.

Finally, although he firmly supports Sutherland's contention that peer group associations are of prime importance in explaining juvenile delinquency, Mark Warr criticizes him for having only a singular vision of peer influence. Warr makes a distinction between two approaches to the influence of delinquent peers among group members—*private acceptance* and *compliance*.[62] Compliance refers to public conformity with group behavior ("going through the motions") without privately accepting the appropriateness of what they are doing. Private acceptance refers to both public and private acceptance of the attitudes valued and the behavior of the delinquent group. Warr's criticism is that differential association "was built squarely on the idea of private acceptance."[63] Private acceptance implies that pro-offending attitudes become an integral part of the person's psyche and lifestyle. Thus, once a delinquent career is initiated, the person will continue offending across the life span. The problem with this is that we know that the great majority of delinquents limit their offending to adolescence (are temporary compliers) and do not become adult criminals.[64]

Akers's **social learning theory** adds some meat to differential association theory by specifying how definitions favorable to law violation are learned using psychology's powerful theory of operant conditioning, although it neglects the role of individual differences in the ease or difficulty with which persons learn. Some people find general hell-raising more exciting (and thus more intrinsically reinforcing) than others. Some people are more susceptible to short-term rewards because they are especially impulsive, and some are better able to appreciate the long-term rewards of behaving well. Some are more ready to engage in aggressive behavior than others because of the nature of their temperaments and will find such behavior is reinforced in delinquent areas. As Gwynn Nettler put it, "Constitutions affect the impact of environment. What we learn and how well we learn it depends on constitution. . . . The fire that melts the butter hardens the egg."[65]

Hirschi's social control theory is not only the most popular theory among contemporary criminologists, but it has also been the most tested and among the best empirically supported.[66,67] All versions of control theory agree that the family is central to the control and developmental mechanisms that affect criminal behavior, and because of this, they have been criticized for neglecting social structure.[68] Critics feel that if the family is so important, the social, economic, and political factors that impede stable and nurturing families should be addressed.[69] However, whatever those things may be, they are not within the purview of control theorists who wish to explain the *consequences* of weak and disrupted families, not why they are disrupted. All theories of behavior neglect some things and focus on others.

One interesting study conducted by Freda Adler, based on the social control model, looked at two countries, each from Western Europe (Switzerland, Ireland) and Eastern Europe (East Germany and Bulgaria), Asia (Japan and Nepal), Latin America (Costa Rica and Peru), and the Middle East (Algeria and Saudi Arabia), with the lowest crime rate in their respective regions. These countries are an odd mixture; some are advanced democracies, some are authoritarian, some are religious and others not, and some are rural and some urban. Adler set out to determine what they had in common besides low crime rates and found that it was a strong social control system—that is, an informal *social* control system, not a formal *legal* control system. These controls included strong family ties and supports, encouragement of communal activities (especially for youths), shared religious values, and the fostering of a powerful commitment to advancing the interests of the community as opposed to fostering self-interest. Adler concluded that these societies enjoyed a condition opposite of anomie, which she called *synnomie* ("with norms").[70]

The major criticism of self-control theory arises from Gottfredson and Hirschi's claim that it is a *general* theory meant to explain *all* crime. Although many crimes are impulsive spontaneous acts, many others are not. White-collar criminals, terrorists, and even serial killers provide ample evidence that their acts follow careful planning. So many criminal acts fall outside the purview of the theory that perhaps it is fair to say that Gottfredson and Hirschi claim too much for their theory and that it should be limited to explaining run-of-the-mill street crime only.[71]

Another criticism of self-control theory is that it attributes variation in self-control solely to variation in parental behavior and ignores child effects.[72] The child development literature is unequivocal in its assertion that socialization is a two-way street in which parental behavior is shaped by the evocative behavior of the child just as much as the child's behavior is shaped by its parents.[73,74] Low self-control (impulsiveness) may be something that children bring with them to the socialization process rather than its simply being a product of the failure of that process. A number of studies have found a strong genetic component to low self-control.[75–77]

Others have criticized the theory's assertion that crime proneness can be explained by the single tendency of self-control as simplistic, and at the very least, it should be augmented with something called "negative emotionality" or irritability[78,79] (more about this trait in Chapter 7). But when all the criticisms have been chewed and digested, we can still say that Hirschi's contribution has been to connect the most fundamental institution of society—the family—to individual differences in the propensity to commit illegal acts and thus, like Tarde and Agnew, has provided a happy marriage of sociology and psychology.[80]

Labeling theory comes dangerously close to claiming that the original "causes" (primary deviance) do not matter. This upset more than a few criminologists, including those who shared labeling theory's emphasis on power/conflict, who saw this position as denying the importance of the social conditions that they felt led to crime. If the causes of primary deviance do not matter, then efforts to control crime via various structural changes would be abandoned in favor of reliance on labeling theory's "radical noninterventionism" ("Leave the kids alone; they'll grow out of it"). This advice may be prudent for teenage pot smokers or runaways but hardly wise for teenage robbers and rapists. Nevertheless, labeling theory advises that such delinquents should be "treated" rather than "punished." But since labeling theorists insist that there is nothing intrinsically bad about any action, what is the point of treatment, and what is it that is to be treated? If they only mean that there is nothing intrinsically bad about the kinds of minor behaviors they surveyed, perhaps they should limit their theory to minor misbehaviors, for which the "causes" may indeed be irrelevant.

Criminologists from the left and right have criticized labeling theory, which may not be too surprising since it sits ideologically between both camps. Curran and Renzetti point out that labeling theory is "often seen as a bridge or link from the traditional [consensus] theories to contemporary radical theories."[81] This is useful for our purposes in transitioning to the critical theories presented in the next chapter.

One of the positive elements of neutralization theory is that it eliminates much of the overdetermined image of subcultural values implied in subcultural theories. Many delinquents are no more completely committed to antisocial values than they are to prosocial values. Neutralization techniques are not viewed as "causes" of antisocial behavior; rather, they are a set of justifications that loosen moral constraints and allow offenders to drift in and out of antisocial behavior because they are able to "neutralize" these constraints.

One of the major problems with the theory is that it says nothing about the origins of the antisocial behavior the actors seek to neutralize. To be a causal theory of criminal behavior rather than an explanation of the post hoc process of rationalization, it would have to show that individuals *first* neutralize their moral beliefs and *then* engage in antisocial acts. Some studies have found that neutralization techniques were able to explain future deviance,[82] but this should not surprise anyone since persons in a position where they have to explain their offending behavior are more likely than those not in such a position to offend in the future—past is prolog regardless our explanations of it. Perhaps Robert Agnew said it best when he wrote that neutralizing techniques "may be used as both after-the-fact excuses and before-the-fact justifications."[83]

▧ Policy and Prevention: Implications of Social Process Theories

Very few policy recommendations not already implicit in ecological and strain theories can be gleaned from differential association theory or social learning theory. Whether we call it social disorganization or differential social organization, the bottom line for all subcultural theories is that lower-class neighborhoods harbor values and attitudes conducive to criminal behavior. Thus, if learning crime and delinquency within a particular culture is the problem, then changing relative aspects of that culture would appear to be the answer. However, we have already seen that attempts to do that have met with only meager success at best.

Because differential association concerns itself with the influence of role models in intimate peer groups, the provision of positive (prosocial) role models to replace negative (antisocial) ones is an obvious thought. Probation and parole authorities have long recognized the importance of keeping convicted felons away from each other, even making it a probation- or parole-revocable offense to "associate with known felons." As every probation and parole officer knows, however,

Table 5.1	Summarizing Social Process Theories		
Theory	**Key Concepts**	**Strengths**	**Weaknesses**
Differential Association	Crime is learned in association with peers holding definitions favorable to law violation. Most likely to occur in differentially organized (lower-class) neighborhoods.	Explains the onset of offending and the power of peer pressure.	Neglects possibility of like seeking like (birds of a feather). Does not make distinction between private accepters and temporary compliers.
Social Learning	Definitions favorable to law violation depend on history of reinforcement and punishment. Excess rewards for criminal behavior perpetuate it.	Adds powerful concepts of operant psychology to explain how people learn criminal behavior. Links sociology to psychology.	Neglects individual differences affecting what is reinforcing to whom and the ease or difficulty with which one learns.
Social Bonding	Bonds to social institutions prevent crime, which otherwise comes naturally. The bonds are attachment, commitment, involvement, and belief.	The most popular and empirically supported theory. Emphasizes importance of the family and provides workable policy recommendations.	Neglects structural variables contributing to family instability and to loss of occupational opportunities. Neglects differences in the ease with which attachment is achieved.
Self-Control	Low self-control explains all crime and analogous acts. Low self-control occurs in the absence of proper parenting. Exposure to criminal opportunities explains differences in criminal behavior among low self-control individuals.	Identifies a single measurable trait to be responsible for many antisocial behaviors. Accords well with the impulsive nature of most criminal behavior. Links sociology to psychology.	Claims too much for a single trait. Neglects child influences on parenting behavior and the effects of genes on low self-control.
Labeling	Crime has no independent reality. Original primary deviance is unimportant; what is important is the labeling process, which leads to secondary (continuing) deviance. Labeling people criminal leads them to organize their self-concepts around that label.	Explains consequences of labeling with a "master status." Identifies the social construction of crime and points to the power of some (the powerful) to criminalize the acts of others (the powerless).	The neglect of causes of primary deviance. Advice that criminals should be treated, not punished, contradicts the theory that says that there is nothing intrinsically bad about crime and therefore there is nothing to "treat."
Neutralization	Delinquents and criminals learn to neutralize moral constraints and thus their guilt for committing crimes. They drift in and out of crime.	Emphasizes that criminals are no more fully committed to antisocial attitudes than they are to prosocial attitudes. Shows how criminals handle feelings of guilt.	Says nothing about the origins of behavior being neutralized. More a theory of antisocial rationalization than of crime.

this is easier said than done. Programs that bring youths together for prosocial purposes, such as sports leagues and community projects, might be high on the agenda of any policy maker using differential association as a guide. But the lure of "the streets" and of the friends they have grown up with remains a powerful countervailing force retarding rehabilitation. The good news is that with maturity, most delinquents will desist as they mature, and the breakup of the friendship group by the incarceration, migration, death, or marriage of some of its members will break the grip of antisocial behavior for many of the remaining members.[84]

The policy implications derivable from social control and self-control theories have to do with the family. Given the importance of nurturance and attachment, both versions of control theory support the idea of early family intervention designed to cultivate these things. Based largely on studies suggesting positive neurological consequences of extended mother/infant contact, the Canadian government, in common with most European countries, passed legislation in 1979 guaranteeing paid maternal leave to all new mothers.[85] Also in common with most European nations, Canadian families receive family support via family allowances paid to families with children. Neither of these programs exists in the United States, which again shows that politics and ideology dictate the direction of criminal justice policy more than criminological theory.

Other attempts to increase bonding to social institutions other than the family would concentrate on increasing children's involvement in a variety of prosocial activities centered in and around the school. These would include various sporting activities, clubs such as 4H and Junior Achievement, cub and scout programs, and church-sponsored activities outside of the school. These programs provide prosocial models; teach conventional moral beliefs such as the value of work, responsibility, and working with others; and keep youths busy in meaningful and challenging ways. Social control theory might recommend more vocationally oriented classes to keep less academically inclined students bonded to school. For youths who lack interest or ability in academics, the probability of failure, shame, anger, hostility, and dropping out is built into our high schools with their college preparation orientation. Vocational classes are recommended only for the maintenance of social bonds.

Neither version of control theory would advise increased employment opportunities as a way to control crime. The assumption of control theory is that people who are attached and who possess self-control will do fine in the job market as it is, and increasing job opportunities for those lacking attachment and self-control will have minimal effect.

Because low self-control is the result of the absence of inhibiting forces typically experienced in early childhood, Gottfredson and Hirschi[86] are pessimistic about the ability of less powerful inhibiting forces (such as the threat of punishment) present in later life to deter crime. They also see little use in seeking to reduce crime by satisfying the wants and needs alleged by other theories to cause crime (reducing poverty, improving neighborhoods, etc.) because crime's appeal is its provision of immediate gains and minimal cost. In short, "society" is neither the cause nor the solution to the crime problem.

Self-control theory emphasizes opportunity as well as self-control, and thus Gottfredson and Hirschi[87] advocate some of the same policies (e.g., target hardening) advocated by rational choice and routine activities. However, the most important policy recommendation is to strengthen families and improve parenting skills, especially skills relevant to teaching self-control. It is only by working with and through families that society can do anything about crime in the long run. Gottfredson and Hirschi are forthright about the policy recommendations of their theory: "Delaying pregnancy among unmarried girls would probably do more to affect the long-term crime rates than all the criminal justice programs combined."[88]

Labeling theory had an effect on criminal justice policy far in excess of what its empirical support warrants. If it is correct that official societal reaction to primary deviance amplifies and promotes more of the same, the logical policy recommendation is that we should ignore primary deviance for the sake of alleviating secondary deviance. Labeling theory recommends that we allow offenders to protect their self-images as noncriminals by not challenging their "techniques of neutralization." Juveniles must be particularly protected from labeling. Under a policy of "radical nonintervention," sociologist Edwin Schur[89] proposed that only the most serious of crimes warrant formal intervention, that juvenile correctional facilities should be abolished, and that treatment programs should be entirely voluntary. Such recommendations fell on receptive ears in more liberal times and generated what came to be known as the "4D revolution": diversion, due process, decriminalization, and deinstitutionalization.[90]

Diversion refers to efforts to avoid stigmatizing juveniles by "diverting" them from formal probation to informal voluntary programs, as well as the extension of probation programs in the adult system to keep adult offenders away from the "hardening" effects of imprisonment. Juvenile diversion programs increased in the 1970s, but they may have actually pulled more people into the criminal justice system than may have been there without them. The net widening made possible by adding another component to the juvenile court meant that cases that formerly may have been dismissed were now brought into the system.[91]

Due process refers to the legal revolution of the 1960s that greatly extended the rights of criminal defendants. During this period, the U.S. Supreme Court extended due process rights to juveniles, who were previously denied them. Although labeling theory cannot take the credit for the due process revolution, it provided much of the theoretical justification.[92]

Decriminalization refers to efforts to restrict the reach of the criminal justice system by making legal certain behaviors that were illegal. Abortion and pornography became legal in the early 1970s, and the decriminalization of the possession of small amounts of marijuana and the extension of gambling rights became realities. However, efforts to decriminalize many other activities deemed by mainstream society to be antisocial have not been very successful.

Deinstitutionalization refers to the movement to remove prison inmates and mental patients, as far as was deemed practical, from institutions and place them in community care. This movement led to the expansion of probation services and community mental health clinics.

The only policy implication of neutralization theory is that criminal justice agents charged with managing offenders (probation/parole officers, etc.) should strongly challenge their excuse making. If offenders come to truly believe their own rationalizations, rehabilitative efforts will become more difficult. Thus, offenders must be shown that their thinking patterns have negative long-term consequences for them.

SUMMARY

Social process theories emphasize how people perceive their reality and how these perceptions structure their behavior. Differential association theory is a learning theory that emphasizes the power of peer associations and the definitions favorable to law violation found within them to be the cause of crime and delinquency. Social learning theory adds to differential association theory by stressing the mechanisms (operant psychology) by which "definitions favorable" are learned. Behavior is either reinforced (rewarded) or punished. Behavior that is rewarded tends to be repeated, and behavior that is punished tends not to be. What is reinforcing or punishing, however, depends on the person's social attachments and his or her social situation. Discriminative stimuli provide signals for the kinds of behaviors that are likely to be rewarding or punishing and are based on what we have learned about those stimuli in the past.

Although classified as social process theories, control theories are in many ways the opposite of differential association and social learning theories because they don't ask why people commit crimes but why most of us do not. Crime comes naturally to those who are not either socially or self-controlled. Reckless speaks of outer (social) and inner (self) containment and claims that our self-concepts lead us into conforming or deviant behavior. Hirschi speaks of the social bonds (attachment, commitment, involvement, and belief) that keep us on the straight and narrow. These are not causes of crime; rather, they are bonds, the absence of which allows our natural impulses to emerge. Gottfredson and Hirschi's self-control theory moves the focus from social to self-control, although our experiences within the family are still vital to learn self-control. Self-control must be paired with a criminal opportunity for crime to occur.

Labeling theory also does not ask why some people commit crimes, believing that the only thing that differentiates delinquents and criminals from the rest of us is that they have been caught and labeled. The initial nonconforming act (primary deviance) is of no consequence for the theory; the real problem is the affixing of a deviant label because it changes the labelee's self-concept, and he or she then engages in secondary deviance in conformity with the label. Sykes and Matza's neutralization theory is contrary to labeling theory because it focuses on individuals' attempts to resist being labeled a delinquent or criminal by offering justifications or excuses for their behavior.

On Your Own

Log on to the web-based student study site at http://www.sagepub.com/criminologystudy for more information about the vignettes and materials presented in this chapter, suggestions for activities, study aids such as review quizzes, and research recommendations including journal article links and questions related to this chapter.

EXERCISES AND DISCUSSION QUESTION

1. Write a two-page report indicating which theory in this chapter appeals most to you and why.

2. Compare and contrast differential association theory with control theory (any version) in terms of their respective assumptions about human nature. Which assumption makes more sense to you?

3. Is a delinquent or criminal label applied to someone, which is sufficient in most cases to change a person's self-concept, enough to lead him or her to continue offending? Why or why not?

4. Gottfredson and Hirschi claim that parents are to blame for an individual's lack of self-control. Are there some children who are simply more difficult to socialize than others? Are they, rather than the parents, at fault for their lack of self-control?

5. Why is attachment the most important of the four social bonds?

6. What, if anything, did Sutherland add to Tarde? Is differential association merely Tarde's law of imitation expanded and rebottled in America?

7. Go to http://www.ncjrs.gov/html/ojjdp/jjbul2000_8_2/contents.html and read the *Juvenile Justice Bulletin* article "Youth Gangs in Schools." What were the main criteria for recognizing the existence of gangs in schools, according to the students?

KEY WORDS

Attachment
Cognitive dissonance
Commitment
Containment theory
Definitions
Differential association
    theory
Differential social
    organization

Discrimination
Disintegrative shaming
Laws of imitation
Social learning theory
Operant psychology
Primary deviance
Punishment
Reinforcement
Reintegrative shaming

Secondary deviance
Self-concept
Social control
Symbolic interactionism
Techniques of neutralization
Thomas theorem

REFERENCES

1. Farley, J. (1990). *Sociology.* Englewood Cliffs, NJ: Prentice Hall. (Quote on p. 71)
2. Tarde, G. (1890). *La philosophie penale.* Paris: Lyon.
3. Beirne, P. (1987). Between classicism and positivism: Crime and penalty in the writings of Gabriel Tarde. *Criminology, 25,* 785–819.
4. Vine, M. (1973). Gabriel Tarde. In H. Mannheim (Ed.), *Pioneers in criminology* (pp. 292–303). Montclair, NJ: Patterson Smith. (Quote on p. 293)
5. Sutherland, E., & Cressey, D. (1974). *Criminology* (9th ed.). Philadelphia: J. B. Lippincott.
6. Sutherland and Cressey (1974, p. 75).
7. Vold, G., Bernard, T., & Snipes, J. (1998). *Theoretical criminology* (4th ed.). New York: Oxford University Press.
8. Burgess, R., & Akers, R. (1966). A differential association-reinforcement theory of criminal behavior. *Social Problems, 14,* 128–147.
9. Akers, R. (2002). A social learning theory of crime. In S. Cote (Ed.), *Criminological theories: Bridging the past to the future* (pp. 135–143). Thousand Oaks, CA: Sage.
10. Akers, R. (1994). *Criminological theories: Introduction and evaluation.* Los Angeles: Roxbury. (Quote on p. 45)
11. Reckless, W. (1961). A new theory of delinquency and crime. *Federal Probation, 25,* 42–46.
12. Reckless, W. (1967). *The crime problem.* New York: Appleton-Century-Crofts.
13. Rosenberg, M. (1979). *Conceiving the self.* New York: Basic Books.
14. Vermeiren, R., Bogaerts, J., Ruchkin, V., Deboutte, D., & Schwab-Stone, M. (2004). Subtypes of self-esteem and self-concept in adolescent violent and property offenders. *Journal of Child Psychology, 45,* 405–411.
15. David, C., & Kistner, J. (2000). Do positive self-perceptions have a 'dark side'? Examination of the link between perceptual bias and aggression. *Journal of Abnormal Child Psychology, 28,* 227–337.
16. Hare, R. (1993). *Without conscience: The disturbing world of the psychopaths among us.* New York: Pocket Books.
17. Sharp, B. (2000). *Changing criminal thinking: A treatment program.* Lanham, MD: American Correctional Association.
18. Anderson, E. (1999). *Code of the street: Decency, violence, and the moral life of the inner city.* New York: W. W. Norton.
19. Baumeister, R., Smart, L., & Boden, J. (1996). Relation of threatened egoism to violence and aggression: The dark side of self-esteem. *Psychological Review, 103,* 5–33.
20. Barash, D., & Lipton, J. (2001). Making sense of sex. In D. Barash (Ed.), *Understanding violence* (pp. 20–30). Boston: Allyn & Bacon.
21. Hirschi, T. (1969). *The causes of delinquency.* Berkeley: University of California Press.
22. Hirschi, T. (1977). Causes and prevention of juvenile delinquency. *Sociological Inquiry, 47,* 322–341.
23. Ellis, L., & Hoffman, H. (1990). Views of contemporary criminologists on causes and theories of crime. In L. Ellis & H. Hoffman (Eds.), *Crime in biological, social, and moral contexts* (pp. 50–58). New York: Praeger.
24. Walsh, A., & Ellis, L. (1999). Political ideology and American criminologists' explanations for criminal behavior. *The Criminologist, 24*(6), 1–27.
25. Johnson, J. (1997, September). Americans' views on crime and law enforcement. *National Institute of Justice Journal,* pp. 9–14.
26. Pfeffer, K., Cole, B., & Dada, K. (1996). British and Nigerian adolescents' lay theories of youth crime. *Psychology, Crime, and Law, 3,* 21–35.

27. Nettler, G. (1984). *Explaining crime* (3rd ed.). New York: McGraw-Hill. (Quote on p. 313)

28. Hirschi (1977, p. 329).

29. Hirschi (1977, p. 333).

30. Hirschi (1969, p. 162).

31. Hirschi (1969, p. 21).

32. Hirschi (1969, p. 187).

33. Agnew, R. (1993). Why do they do it? An examination of the intervening mechanisms between social-control variables and delinquency. *Journal of Research in Crime and Delinquency, 30,* 245–266.

34. Gottfredson, M., & Hirschi, T. (1990). *A general theory of crime.* Stanford, CA: Stanford University Press. (Quote on p. 87)

35. Hirschi, T., & Gottfredson, M. (2000). In defense of self-control. *Theoretical Criminology, 7,* 55–69. (Quote on p. 64)

36. Gottfredson and Hirschi (1990, p. 15).

37. Gottfredson and Hirschi (1990, pp. 89–90).

38. Gottfredson and Hirschi (1990, pp. 100–105).

39. Gottfredson and Hirschi (1990, pp. 12–13).

40. Wolfgang, M., Thornberry, T., & Figlio, R. (1987). *From boy to man, from delinquency to crime.* Chicago: University of Chicago Press.

41. Tannenbaum, F. (1938). *Crime and community.* New York: Columbia University Press.

42. Tannenbaum (1938, p. 20).

43. Paternoster, R., & Iovanni, L. (1989). The labeling perspective and delinquency: An elaboration of the theory and an assessment of the evidence. *Justice Quarterly, 6,* 359–394.

44. Lemert, E. (1974). Beyond Mead: The societal reaction to deviance. *Social Problems, 21,* 457–468.

45. Lilly, J., Cullen, F., & Ball, R. (1995). *Criminological theory: Context and consequences.* Thousand Oaks, CA: Sage.

46. Paternoster and Iovanni (1989).

47. Braithwaite, J. (1989). *Crime, shame, and reintegration.* Cambridge, UK: Cambridge University Press.

48. Braithwaite (1989, p. 9).

49. Braithwaite (1989, p. 73).

50. Braithwaite (1989, p. 55).

51. Braithwaite, J. (1993). Beyond positivism: Learning from contextual integrated strategies. *Journal of Research in Crime and Delinquency, 30,* 383–399.

52. Braithwaite (1993).

53. Sykes, G., & Matza, D. (1957). Techniques of neutralization: A theory of delinquency. *American Sociological Review, 22,* 664–670.

54. Kubrin, C., & Weitzer, R. (2003). New directions in social disorganization theory. *Journal of Research in Crime and Delinquency, 40,* 374–402. (Quote on p. 379)

55. Sykes, G., & Matza, D. (2002). Techniques of neutralization: A theory of delinquency. In S. Cote (Ed.), *Criminological theories: Bridging the past to the future* (pp. 144–150). Thousand Oaks, CA: Sage. (Quote on p. 145)

56. Topalli, V. (2005). When being good is bad: An expansion of neutralization theory. *Criminology, 43,* 797–835. (Quote on p. 798)

57. Wood, S., & Wood, E. (1996). *The world of psychology* (2nd ed.). Boston: Allyn & Bacon.

58. Vold, G., & Bernard, T. (1986). *Theoretical criminology.* New York: Oxford University Press.

59. Glueck, S. (1956). Theory and fact in criminology: A criticism of differential association theory. *British Journal of Criminology, 7,* 92–109. (Quote on p. 94)

60. Sutherland, E. (1939). *Principles of criminology.* Philadelphia: J. B. Lippincott. (Quote on p. 8)

61. Rodkin, P., Farmer, T., Pearl, R., & Van Acker, R. (2000). Heterogeneity of popular boys: Antisocial and prosocial configurations. *Developmental Psychology, 36,* 14–24.

62. Warr, M. (2000). *Companions in crime: The social aspects of criminal conduct.* New York: Cambridge University Press.

63. Warr (2000, p. 7).

64. Moffitt, T., & Walsh, A. (2003). The adolescent-limited/life-course persistent theory of antisocial behavior: What have we learned? In A. Walsh & L. Ellis (Eds.), *Biosocial criminology: Challenging environmentalism's supremacy* (pp. 123–144). Hauppauge, NY: Nova Science.

65. Nettler (1984, p. 295).

66. Curran, D., & Renzetti, C. (2001). *Theories of crime* (2nd ed.). Boston: Allyn & Bacon.

67. Lanier, M., & Henry, S. (1998). *Essential criminology.* Boulder, CO: Westview.

68. Grasmick, H., Tittle, C., Bursik, R., & Arneklev, B. (1993). Testing the core empirical implication of Gottfredson and Hirschi's general theory of crime. *Journal of Research in Crime and Delinquency, 30,* 5–29.

69. Lilly et al. (1995).

70. Adler, F., Mueller, G., & Laufer, W. (2001). *Criminology and the criminal justice system.* Boston: McGraw-Hill.

71. Curran and Renzetti (2001).

72. Shaw, D., & Bell, R. (1993). Developmental theories of parental contributions to antisocial behavior. *Journal of Abnormal Child Psychology, 21,* 493–518.

73. Harris, J. (1998). *The nurture assumption: Why children turn out the way they do.* New York: Free Press.

74. Walsh, A. (2002). *Biosocial criminology: Introduction and integration.* Cincinnati, OH: Anderson.

75. Bernhardt, P. (1997). Influences of serotonin and testosterone in aggression and dominance: Convergence with social psychology. *Current Directions in Psychological Science, 6,* 44–48.

76. Hur, Y., & Bouchard, T. (1997). The genetic correlation between impulsivity and sensation-seeking traits. *Behavior Genetics, 27,* 455–463.

77. Goldman, D., Lappalainen, J., & Ozaki, N. (1996). Direct analysis of candidate genes in impulsive behavior. In G. Bock & J. Goode (Eds.), *Genetics of criminal and antisocial behaviour* (pp. 183–195). Chichester, UK: Wiley.

78. Caspi, A., Moffitt, T., Silva, P., Stouthamer-Loeber, M., Krueger, R., & Schmutte, P. (1994). Are some people crime-prone? Replications of the personality-crime relationship across countries, genders, races, and methods. *Criminology, 32,* 163–194.

79. Agnew, R. (2005). *Why do criminals offend? A general theory of crime and delinquency.* Los Angeles: Roxbury.

80. Weibe, R. (2004). Expanding the model of human nature underlying self-control theory: Implications for the constructs of self-control and opportunity. *Australian and New Zealand Journal of Criminology, 37,* 65–84.

81. Curran and Renzetti (2001, p. 183).

82. Thurman, Q. (1984). Deviance and the neutralization of moral commitment: An empirical analysis. *Deviant Behavior, 5,* 291–304.

83. Agnew, R. (1994). The techniques of neutralization and violence. *Criminology, 32,* 555–580. (Quote on p. 572)

84. Sampson, R., & Laub, J. (1999). Crime and deviance over the lifecourse: The salience of adult social bonds. In F. Scarpitti & A. Nielsen (Eds.), *Crime and criminals: Contemporary and classical readings in criminology* (pp. 238–246). Los Angeles: Roxbury.

85. Walsh, A., & Ellis, L. (1997). The neurobiology of nurturance, evolutionary expectations, and crime control. *Politics and the Life Sciences, 16,* 42–44.

86. Gottfredson and Hirschi (1990, p. 255).

87. Gottfredson, M., & Hirschi, T. (1997). National crime control policies. In M. Fisch (Ed.), *Criminology 97/98* (pp. 27–33). Guilford, CT: Dushkin.

88. Gottfredson and Hirschi (1997, p. 33).

89. Schur, E. (1973). *Radical non-intervention: Rethinking the delinquency problem.* Englewood Cliffs, NJ: Prentice Hall.

90. Lilly et al. (1995).

91. Klein, D. (1986). Labeling theory and delinquency policy: An experimental test. *Criminal Justice and Behavior, 13,* 47–79.

92. Lilly et al. (1995).

6

CRITICAL THEORIES: MARXIST, CONFLICT, AND FEMINIST

*A*t the heart of the theories in this chapter is social stratification by class, power, and race
and how it generates conflict. They are about how those at the top of the social heap pass
laws to maintain their privileged position and how those at the bottom often violate
these laws to improve their position. These theories are thus the most "politicized" of all criminological theories. Sanyika Shakur, AKA Kody Scott, came to embrace this politicized view of society
as he grew older and was converted to Afrocentric Islam. Shakur was very much a member of the
class Karl Marx called the "lumpenproletariat," which is the very bottom of the class hierarchy.
Many critical theorists would view Shakur's criminality as justifiable rebellion against class and
racial exploitation. Shakur wanted all the material rewards of American capitalism, but he perceived that the only way he could get them was through crime. He was a thoroughgoing egoist, but
many Marxists would excuse this as a trait in him as nourished by capitalism, the "root cause" of
crime. From his earliest days, he was on the fringes of a society he plainly disdained. He frequently
referred to Whites as "Americans" to emphasize his distance from them, and he referred to Black
cops as "Negroes" to distinguish them from the "New African Man." He called himself a "student
of revolutionary science," referred to the 1992 L.A. riots as "rebellion," and advocated a separate
Black nation in America.

Even at a less politicized level, conflict concepts dominated Shakur's life as he battled the
Bloods and other Crip "sets" with interests at odds with his set. It is easy to imagine his violent
acts as the outlets of a desperate man struggling against feelings of class and race inferiority.
Perhaps he was only able to achieve a sense of power when he held the fate of another human
being in his hands. His fragile narcissism often exploded into violent fury whenever he felt himself being "dissed." How much of Shakur's behavior and the behavior of youth gangs in general is

explained by the concepts of critical theories? Is violent conflict a justifiable response to class and race inequality, or are there more productive ways to resolve such conflicts?

The Conflict Perspective of Society

Although all sociological theories of crime necessarily contain elements of underlying conflict, the theories discussed in the previous chapter are broadly characterized as consensus theories. They are consensus theories because they tend to judge alternative normative systems from the point of view of mainstream values and because any policy recommendations flowing from them do not require a major restructuring of the social system. While consensus theorists may criticize certain aspects of contemporary society, they do not attack it in its totality. A number of theories presented in this chapter do just that and tend to concentrate on power relations as explanatory variables and to exclude almost everything else. They view criminal behavior, the law, and the penalties imposed for breaking it as originating in the deep inequalities of power and resources existing in society.

Where consensus theorists see at least a fair degree of orderliness, fairness, and harmony in society and claim that society's institutions are functional despite their ills, critical theorists see society riddled with dissension, inequality, and conflict. Critical theorists argue that any apparent consensus in society is maintained by overt (the criminal justice system) and covert (ideological) coercion. They denounce the current social distribution of resources as unjust and favor a more equal distribution. Critical theorists are aware that both conflict and consensus exist in all societies and that conflict and consensus are two sides of the same coin. Which side of the coin criminologists emphasize depends more on their ideology than on compelling empirical evidence.

Critical criminology is an umbrella term we have chosen for a variety of theories united only by the assumption that conflict and power relations between various classes of people best characterize the nature of society. Adherents of these diverse theories are not of one mind; they quarrel among themselves, and they coin new names for their theories such as "conflict," "radical," "critical," "new criminology," "radical human rights criminology," "Marxist," "neo-Marxist," and "left realists." It is fair to say that there is far more agreement among them about what they are against (the status quo) than what they are for.[1] These theories differ in subtle philosophical and theoretical ways within the general framework of the conflict model of society.

A survey of criminologists' favored theories found that those favoring Marxist theories defined themselves as radicals, and all favoring conflict theory identified themselves as liberal or radical.[2] You don't have to be a radical or even a liberal to acknowledge that great inequalities exist and that the powerful and wealthy classes always have the upper hand in all things. History is replete with class struggles that even defenders of the status quo have acknowledged. Plutarch wrote of the disparity of wealth in Athens in 594 B.C. and of the dangerous conflicts it generated,[3] and U.S. President John Adams wrote that American society in the late 18th century was divided into a small group of rich men and a great mass of poor engaged in a constant class struggle.[4]

Probably the major differences within the various critical theories is the degree to which they integrate the ideas of Karl Marx or Max Weber into their thinking and whether they are reformist or revolutionary in their policy recommendations. The more radical theorists favor Marx and revolution; the more liberal theorists favor Weber and reform. For the sake of clarity, we will refer to the radical schools as "Marxist" and reserve the term *conflict theory* for the more liberal schools.

Karl Marx and Revolution

Karl Marx was born in Germany in 1818 and died in London in 1883. The core of Marxist philosophy is the concept of **class struggle.** For Marx, the history of all societies is a history of class struggles: "Freeman and slave, patrician and plebian, lord and serf, guildmaster and journeyman, in a word, oppressor and oppressed, stood in constant opposition to one another."[5] In Marx's time, the oppressors were the wealthy owners of the means of production (the **bourgeoisie**), and the oppressed were the working class (the **proletariat**). The bourgeoisie strives to keep the cost of labor at a minimum, and the proletariat strives to sell its labor at the highest possible price. These opposing goals are the major source of conflict in a capitalist society. The bourgeoisie enjoys the upper hand because capitalist societies typically have large armies of unemployed workers anxious to secure work at any price, thus driving down the cost of labor. According to Marx, these economic and social arrangements—the material conditions of people's lives—determine what they will know, believe, and value and how they will behave.

The ruling class always develops ideologies to justify and legitimize their exploitation, which the subordinate classes are led to accept as valid because the ruling class controls all institutions (the schools, churches, government, and the law) that teach and support those ideologies. Marx called the workers' acceptance of ideologies that ran counter to their interests *false consciousness.* False consciousness deflects anger away from the ruling class and thus prevents change. Marx believed that capitalist competition would drive the less able capitalists into the ranks of the proletariat, and it is they who would provide the intellectual leadership that would overthrow capitalism and help the workers to understand how they had been duped. In time, false consciousness would be replaced by *class consciousness*—that is, the recognition of a common class condition and the development of a common unity in opposition to capitalist exploitation. This would set the stage for revolution and the "dictatorship of the proletariat," marking the end of exploitation and social conflict and the beginning of universal brotherhood and sisterhood.[6]

Marx and Engels on Crime

Unlike Durkheim's view of crime as a natural part of social life, Marx and his collaborator, Friedrich Engels, saw it as a social cancer that had to be cut out. Although some modern Marxist criminologists tend to romanticize criminals as victims rather than victimizers, Marx and Engels made plain their disdain for criminals, calling them "the dangerous class, the social scum, that rotting mass thrown off by the lowest layers of the old society."[7] According to Marx and Engels, criminals came from a third class in society—the **lumpenproletariat**—who would play no decisive role in the expected revolution. It is probably for this reason that Marx and Engels only wrote about crime to illustrate the bitter fruits of capitalism and produced no coherent theory of crime. Crime was the product of unjust, alienating, and demoralizing social conditions that denied productive labor to masses of unemployed—"the struggle of the isolated individual against the prevailing conditions."[8]

Marx and Engels's statement about the origin of crime has come to be known as the **primitive rebellion hypothesis.** One of the best modern statements of this hypothesis is given by Bohm: "The class struggle and exploitation . . . produce crime, income or property inequality,

▲ **Photo 6.1** Marx and Engels did not find it surprising that the poorest of society would have to do whatever it takes to survive, including committing crimes. Here a Montreal woman quickly sifts through the trash, looking for food.

poverty, and many other problems that are characteristic of a capitalist society . . . crime in capitalist societies is often a rational response to the circumstances in which people find themselves."[9] Marx and Engels did not excuse or justify crime because criminals had suffered such social conditions; after all, criminals were victimizing the honest laboring class, or "providing demoralizing services such as prostitution and gambling."[10]

Marx and Engels stressed that the rich and powerful in every age made the rules favoring themselves and subordinating the classes below them. Capitalist societies pass laws that criminalize any action that jeopardizes private property and tend to overlook many socially injurious activities viewed as economically beneficial ("normal business practices") for the ruling class. This view was stated in the United States as early as 1822 by lawyer and legislator Edward Livingston, who wrote, "Everywhere, with few exceptions, the interest of the many has, from the earliest ages, been sacrificed to the power of the few. Everywhere penal laws have been framed to support this power."[11] It is for this reason that radical criminologists look to the analysis of lawmaking, white-collar crime, and differential criminal sanctioning to buttress arguments about the evils of capitalism and the unjustness of the criminal justice system.[12]

Willem Bonger: The First Marxist Criminologist

Willem Bonger (1876–1940) was a Dutch criminologist credited with the first work completely devoted to a Marxist analysis of crime. Originally published in 1905, his book, *Criminality and Economic Conditions,* supported the view that the roots of crime lay in the exploitive and alienating conditions of capitalism.[13] Bonger believed that some individuals are at greater risk for criminality than others because people varied in their "moral qualities . . . according to the intensity of their innate social sentiments."[14] The social sentiments that concerned him were *altruism*—an active concern for the well-being of others—and its opposite, *egoism,* a concern only for one's own selfish interests.

Whether altruism or egoism is the dominant sentiment in society depends on how it produces its material life (its mode of production). Capitalism, by its very nature, generates egoism and blunts altruism[15] because it relies on competition for wealth, profits, status, and jobs, setting person against person and group against group, leaving the losers to their miserable fates. Such a moral climate generates alienation, greed, and crime. According to Bonger, all individuals in capitalist societies are infected by egoism because they are alienated from authentic social relationships with their fellow human beings, and all are thus prone to crime—the poor out of economic necessity, the rich from pure greed.

Even among those who are relatively successful in a capitalist society, the logic of market-based economies dictates that envy, dissatisfaction, and greed be generated to keep the economy buzzing along. Note the Mertonian "American Dream" theme in Bonger's example of how capitalism creates dissatisfaction and want among the public:

> Modern industry manufactures enormous quantities of goods without the outlet for them being known. The desire to buy, then, must be excited in the public. Beautiful displays, dazzling illuminations, and many other means are used to attain the desired end. [In the modern department store] the public is drawn as a moth to a flame. The result of these tactics is that the cupidity of the crowd is highly excited.[16]

On the other hand, among "primitive" peoples, altruism was the predominant sentiment because the ideas of profit and social classes did not exist. They enjoyed a different mode of production (hunting, gathering, and rudimentary agriculture) and were too occupied with obtaining the basics of life to worry about being drawn into any competitions for goods of no practical value (needless to say, most of the things we want and compete for today did not exist in those days). Being part of relatively small bands or tribes, they also enjoyed a uniformity of existence and thus had common interests. Such an existence (Durkheim's mechanical solidarity) is conducive to a general altruistic sentiment, regardless of any innate variability in the sentiment among the population.

To be sure, the "root cause" of crime is the capitalist mode of production, but unlike many contemporary Marxist criminologists, Bonger was careful to delineate the mechanisms by which he believed capitalist-generated egoism translated into criminal behavior. He believed that poverty was the major cause of crime but traced its effects on family structure (broken homes, illegitimacy) and on parental inability to properly supervise their children. He also wrote about "the lack of civilization and education among the poorer classes."[17] Although Bonger has been criticized by other Marxists as non-Marxist[18] because of his emphasis on family structure and what he saw as the moral deficits of the poor, he firmly believed that only by transforming society from a capitalist to a socialist mode of production would it be possible to regain the altruistic sentiment and thus reduce crime.

Modern Marxist Criminology

Marxist ideas in criminology began to surface in the United States during the 1960s and 1970s. Because Marx wrote so little about crime, it is probably better to characterize modern Marxist criminologists as radicals for whom Marxism serves as a philosophical underpinning and to refer to them as *neo-Marxists* rather than Marxists. According to many of its critics, neo-Marxist criminology is little more than maudlin sentimentality for criminals. William Chambliss,[19] for instance, views some criminal behavior to be "no more than the 'rightful' behavior of persons exploited by the extant economic relationships," and Ian Taylor[20] sees the convict as "an additional victim of the routine operations of a capitalist system—a victim, that is of 'processes of reproduction' of social and racial inequality." David Greenberg has even turned Marx on his head by elevating Marx's despised lumpenproletariat to the status of revolutionary leaders: "Criminals, rather than the working class, might be the vanguard of the revolution."[21] Many neo-Marxist criminologists appear to view the class struggle as the *only* source of *all* crime and to view "real" crime as violations of human rights, such as racism, sexism, imperialism, and capitalism.[22] Others accuse mainstream criminology of focusing on "nuts, sluts, and perverts"[23] at the expense of analyzing "real crime" (war, imperialism, poverty, racism, sexism, and classism) and claim that criminological studies have been used by the state to oppress the powerless, thus putting criminologists in the position of being parties to this oppression. One Marxist criminologist, Tony Platt, went so far as to write that "it is not too far-fetched to characterize many criminologists as domestic war criminals."[24] Other neo-Marxists are faithful to Marx's view and are critical of common street crime as an activity preventing the formation of proletarian class consciousness.[25]

Left Realism—Taking Crime Seriously

The argument that the "real" crime is committed by politicians and the wealthy upper classes, while not without merit, is not an argument for taking street crime any less seriously or for romanticizing it. Lower-class crime is overwhelmingly directed at lower- and working-class victims and hardly ever touches the wealthy. It was this point more than any other that led to a new movement among radical criminologists called left realism.

Left realist criminologists believe that the path of least resistance is to work within the system. They had to acknowledge that predatory street crime is a *real* source of concern among the working class, who are the primary victims of it, and they have to translate their concern for the poor into practical, *realistic* social policies. In a statement that could have been made by any neoclassical criminologist, left realist Steven Box asserted that people *choose* to act criminally, and "their choice makes them responsible, but the conditions make the choice comprehensible."[26] Box is saying that people make choices for which they must be held accountable, but a variety of conditions make some choices more probable and understandable than others. This theoretical shift signals a move away from the former singular emphasis on the political economy to embrace the interrelatedness of the offender, the victim, the community, and the state in the causes of crime. It also signals a return to a more orthodox Marxist view of criminals as people whose activities are against the interests of the working class, as well as against the interests of the ruling class. Although unashamedly socialist in orientation, left realists have been criticized by more traditional Marxists, who see left realism's advocacy of solutions to the crime problem within the context of capitalism as a sellout.[27]

⊠ Conflict Theory: Max Weber, Power, and Conflict

Max Weber (1864–1920), a German lawyer and sociologist, shared with Marx an interest in the social changes wrought by the Industrial Revolution and in social conflict. Weber wrote even less about crime (at least about the causes of crime) than Marx did, with his contribution to criminology being his ideas on the nature and function of conflict. Although Weber agreed with Marx on some things, in many of his writings, he was in direct opposition to Marx.[28] Whereas Marx saw a culture's ideas as molded by its mode of production (its economic system), Weber saw a culture's economic system being molded by its ideas. They also differed in their ideas about class and conflict, with Marx emphasizing economic conflict between two social classes and Weber holding a pluralistic view of conflict. Also, unlike Marx, who envisioned the end of social conflict with the destruction of capitalism, Weber contended that social conflict has always existed and always will, regardless of the social, economic, or political nature of society.

Weber and Marx also differed in their view of social class. For Marx, social class was determined solely by a person's position in relationship to the means of production, either owner or worker, while for Weber, it was determined by *class* (wealth), *status* (prestige), and *power* (the ability to impose one's will regardless of opposition). Rather than emphasizing a single monumental struggle between workers and owners, conflict theorists emphasize that there are multiple sources of conflict among multiple social groups. Weber viewed the various class divisions in society as normal, inevitable, and acceptable, as do many contemporary liberal and conservative conflict theorists.[29] Individuals and groups enjoying wealth, prestige, and power have the resources necessary to impose their values and vision for society on others with fewer resources. Weber agreed with Marx that the law is a resource by which the powerful are able to impose their will on the less powerful and the powerless by criminalizing acts that are contrary to their class interests. Because of this power, wrote Weber, "criminality exists in all societies and is the result of the political struggle among different groups attempting to promote or enhance their life chances."[30]

From Individual Violators to Group Struggles

The Chicago school first developed the concept of cultural conflict as an explanation for criminal behavior in promulgating the view that crime was produced by social disorganization. As we have seen, much of this disorganization was a function of the invasion of ethnic outsiders bringing with them norms and values that conflicted with those already established in the neighborhood and with mainstream middle-class values, many of which have been codified into law. Examples include differing codes of conduct relating to such things as gambling, drug use, sexual behavior, and dealing with "matters of honor" and intrafamily conflict. The essence of the cultural conflict thesis is that in certain situations, members of ethnic groups who conform to rules of conduct that have been criminalized by the mainstream culture may be labeled criminals.

George Vold's version of conflict theory provides a transition from the Chicago school to modern conflict theory. Vold moved conflict away from an exclusive emphasis of value and normative conflicts to include *conflicts of interest.* Vold saw social life as a continual struggle to maintain or improve one's own group's interests in a constant clash of antagonistic actions—workers against management, race against race, ecologists against land developers, and the young against adult authority. The list could go on endlessly, for interest groups are continually being formed and disbanded as conflicts arise and are resolved.

The conflicts between youth gangs and adult authorities are of particular concern to criminologists. Youth gangs are in conflict with the values and interests of just about every other interest group, including those of other gangs. These gangs are examples of *minority power groups,*[31] or groups whose interests are sufficiently on the margins of mainstream society that just about all their activities are criminalized. People whose interests and values conflict with those of the gang's have the power to make criminals out of gang members in the same way that factory owners were able to criminalize union activities for many decades in the United States. In short, Vold's conflict theory concentrates entirely on the clash of individuals loyally upholding their differing group interests and has no interest in explaining crime unrelated to group conflict.[32]

Vold's thinking about conflict is in the Weberian tradition, which views conflict not only as normal but also as socially desirable. Conflict is a way of ensuring social change, a way of generating group solidarity, and, in the long run, a way of ensuring social stability. A society that stifles conflict in the name of order stagnates and has no mechanisms for change short of revolution. Since social change is inevitable, it is preferable that it occurs peacefully and incrementally (evolutionary) rather than violently and concurrently (revolutionary). Even 19th-century arch conservative British philosopher Edmund Burke saw that conflict is functional in this regard, writing that "a state without the means of some change is without means of its conservation."[33]

The Social Reality of Crime

The conflict perspective favors what we have called the moving target concept of crime—crime is not simply a function of the behavior of those who commit it but also a function of those who react to it by criminalizing it. Simply put, the *ultimate cause of crime is the law!* If no one group or confederation of groups possesses sufficient power to criminalize the activities of other groups, those activities remain legally permissible and may be engaged in without fear of interference. In common with labeling theorists, conflict theorists see that no act is intrinsically criminal. An act only becomes criminal when its performance is contrary to the interests of groups with the power to pass laws forbidding it. Thus, crime has no real objective existence that can be discovered; it is socially defined reality.[34] It is the imposition of codes of conduct imposed by what Austin Turk[35] calls the *authorities* (individuals in powerful, dominant social positions) on *subjects* (individuals in subordinate, relatively powerless social positions).

This perspective also shares with labeling theory the idea that it does not make sense to ask, "Why do criminals do it?" "Criminal" behavior, they say, is normal behavior (in the sense that it is part of the potential behavioral repertory of all humans) subject to criminalization and decriminalization, depending on the power relationship existing between those who "do it" and those who don't want them to. Conflict criminology differs from neo-Marxist criminology in that it concentrates on the *processes* of value conflict and lawmaking rather than on the social structural elements underlying them. It is also relatively silent about how the powerful got to be powerful or how authorities and subjects are formed. Also, unlike neo-Marxists, conflict theorists make no value judgments about whether crime is socially harmful, the actions of revolutionaries, or violations of human rights; they simply analyze the power relationships underlying the act of criminalization.

Although labeling theorists also use the "social construction of crime" argument, the difference between labeling and conflict theory here is that while labeling theory concerns itself with the application of deviant labels on the powerless and the consequences that follow, it does not necessarily concern itself with the process of how particular labels come to be stigmatized. There is quite a difference between tagging an *individual* with a criminal label that is already available for use and labeling a previously permissible *act* as criminal.[36] However, conflict criminology has more in common with labeling theory than with the various Marxist theories with which it is often confused. Given this confusion, a summary of the differences between them is presented in Table 6.1.

Conflict theorists tend to share neo-Marxism's fondness for research illustrating some principle of their perspective rather than for formulating hypotheses from it and putting them to the test. It is difficult to rigorously test the process of criminal, regulatory, and administrative lawmaking to find out if wealth, status, and power differentials determine the outcome. In a sense, it would be testing the obvious anyway. Justly or unjustly, the democratic political process is designed to be responsive to the groups bringing the most pressure to bear on lawmakers.

Table 6.1	Comparing Marxist and Conflict Theory on Major Concepts	
Concept	**Marxist**	**Conflict**
Origin of conflict	The powerful oppressing the powerless (e.g., the bourgeoisie oppressing the proletariat under capitalism).	It is generated by many factors regardless of the political and economic system.
Nature of conflict	It is socially bad and must and will be eliminated in a socialist system.	It is socially useful and necessary and cannot be eliminated.
Major participants in conflict	The owners of the means of production and the workers are engaged in the only conflict that matters.	Conflict takes place everywhere between all sorts of interest groups.
Social class	Only two classes defined by their relationship to the means of production, the bourgeoisie and proletariat. The aristocracy and the lumpenproletariat are parasite classes that will be eliminated.	There are a number of different classes in society defined by their relative wealth, status, and power.
Concept of the law	It is the tool of the ruling class that criminalizes the activities of the workers harmful to its interests and ignores its own socially harmful behavior.	The law favors the powerful, but not any one particular group. The greater the wealth, power, and prestige a group has, the more likely the law will favor it.
Concept of crime	Some view crime as the revolutionary actions of the downtrodden, others view it as the socially harmful acts of "class traitors," and others see it as violations of human rights.	Conflict theorists refuse to pass moral judgment because they view criminal conduct as morally neutral with no intrinsic properties that distinguish it from conforming behavior. Crime doesn't exist until a powerful interest group is able to criminalize the activities of another less powerful group.
Cause of crime	The dehumanizing conditions of capitalism. Capitalism generates egoism and alienates people from themselves and from others.	The distribution of political power that leads to some interest groups being able to criminalize the acts of other interest groups.
Cure for crime	With the overthrow of the capitalist mode of production, the natural goodness of humanity will emerge, and there will be no more criminal behavior.	As long as people have different interests and as long as some groups have more power than others, crime will exist. Since interest and power differentials are part of the human condition, crime will always be with us.

Postmodernist Theory

Postmodernist criminology is firmly in the critical/radical tradition in that it views the law as an oppressive instrument of the rich and powerful, but unlike other critical approaches, it rejects the "modernist" view of the world. The modernist view of criminology is a scientific

The Supreme Court and Class Conflict

There is perhaps no better example to illustrate the central position of conflict theory than the history of class conflict in the United States as fought in the U.S. Supreme Court. The die seems to have been set by the prophetic statement of John Jay, the first chief justice, when he announced that "the people who own the country ought to govern it."[37] The Supreme Court does not have the power of the sword or of the purse, but it wields a tremendous amount of power, which it has used most often against the least powerful members of U.S. society in the service of the most powerful.

All democratic societies engage in certain reform activities designed to temper the overwhelming power of great wealth. They have attempted to do this by allowing for trade union activity, by regulating the activities of big business, and by implementing a system of progressive taxation.[38] These reforms have been resisted everywhere they have been attempted, but nowhere in the democratic world more successfully than in the United States, thanks to the Supreme Court.

The freedom of contract clause of the Constitution and Section I of the 14th Amendment have been tools frequently used by the Court to protect the rights of property against the "covetous depredations of the lower classes."[39] The 14th Amendment was a response to the Black Codes passed by Southern states during Reconstruction and was designed to protect former slaves. Ironically, the courts used the amendment to protect business interests against the demands of workers. The courts found that they could use the amendment, the relevant part of which reads " . . . nor shall any state deprive any person of life, liberty, or property, without due process of law," to issue injunctions against striking workers. Formerly, the courts had protected business against strikers under criminal conspiracy laws but found convictions difficult to obtain. Now they could issue injunctions and imprison workers who ignore them for contempt of court, thus bypassing "messy" trials in front of juries reluctant to convict fellow workers. Using freedom of contract and the 14th Amendment, between 1889 and 1929, the U.S. Supreme Court invalidated 50 acts of Congress and more than 400 state laws that would have benefited workers.[40] These included a series of decisions in the 1930s that undermined much of President Roosevelt's efforts to help the poor during the Great Depression.

The Sherman Anti-Trust Act was yet another tool ostensibly designed to regulate business that the Court turned against the workers instead. In *United States v. E. C. Knight* (1895), the Court ruled that manufacturing was not commerce, thus denying Congress the right to regulate it. In a remarkable display of doublespeak, on the *very same day* that it decided that manufacturing was not commerce, the Court, in *Re Debs* (1895), decided that trade union activity *was* and, therefore, could be regulated. The Court upheld the conviction of union leader Eugene Debs for leading his union in the famous Pullman strike of 1894 and for ignoring the injunction, issued under the Sherman Act, against doing so. Although the Court's appetite for protecting conservative business interests against those of the working class became less ravenous after the 1930s, many subsequent cases have revealed that it is still very healthy.[41,42]

The third method used by democratic governments to attempt to thwart excessive concentrations of wealth and power is to redistribute some of the wealth via progressive taxation. In another 1895 case, the Supreme Court denied the government the right to impose an income tax. Galloway views these three 1895 cases as "tantamount to a systematic judicial assault on the methods available to the poor in their quest for greater justice."[43]

Although unions are now legal, business is regulated, and we all groan under the weight of taxation, the Court still seems to have an infernal itch to protect the wealthy whenever their interests are in conflict with the poor. In the 1970s and 1980s, the Court rendered OSHA (Occupational Safety and Health Administration) impotent to enforce rules to protect workers from harm, refused to require companies to insure pension payments for retired workers, and allowed companies to unilaterally breach collective bargaining contracts and to permanently replace striking workers.[44] A federal judge imposed a $5 million fine against the striking United Mine Workers in 1975, plus $100,000 for every day the strike lasted, yet the maximum fine for violating the Sherman Anti-Trust Act was a mere $50,000 until 2004 (it is now $100 million).[45] If there is any "ruling class," broadly construed, in the United States, it may be the legal rule of this priestly class sitting on the U.S. Supreme Court.

view aimed at understanding, explaining, predicting, and controlling crime. Postmodernists reject the notion that the scientific view is any better than any other view, and they disparage the claim that any method of understanding can be objective. All knowledge, they assert, is socially constructed and has no independent reality apart from the minds of those who create it: "Post-modernism questions whether we can ever 'know' something objectively; so called neutral science is considered a sham and criminology's search for causes is bankrupt because even the question is framed by androcentric [male centered], sexist, classist, and racist definitions of crime, criminality, and cause."[46] Not all postmodernists reject the scientific view, but they all appeal for a diversity of views in which none are disparaged and all are legitimized.

The main point of postmodernism is that all worldviews are mediated by language. By this, they do not mean the common mode of expression used by people in a particular society (i.e., English, French, etc.) but rather a particular specialized vocabulary that mediates our perceptions of the world. The language of the modernist worldview is science, and rather than liberating people, the forces it produced, such as industrialism and modern weaponry, have oppressed people because they have "extended and amplified the scope of violence in the world."[47]

Postmodernism has substituted "ownership of the means of communication" for Marx's "ownership of the means of production." Postmodernists claim that the dominant language (sometimes referred to as a *discourse*) of society is the language of the rich and powerful, and by virtue of "owning" the dominant language, their point of view is privileged. For example, the views of reality shared by criminals and the mentally challenged are rejected and replaced by the views of the criminal justice and medical systems because the latter have the power to enforce their view of reality, and "this replacement of languages eclipses reality as lived and spoken by others."[48] High on the postmodernist agenda is the exposure of the dominant language system as a source of oppression and then to "deconstruct" and supplant it with "replacement discourses." These replacement discourses are supposed to authenticate all of society's pluralistic viewpoints and to privilege none.

Peacemaking Criminology

Peacemaking criminology is another recent addition to the growing number of theories in our discipline. It is situated squarely in the postmodernist tradition and has drawn a number of disillusioned former Marxists into its fold. It relies heavily on "appreciative relativism" (i.e., all points of view, including criminals', are relative, and all should be appreciated) in its peacemaking endeavors. It is a compassionate and spiritual criminology that has much of its philosophical roots in humanistic religion.

Peacemaking criminology's basic philosophy is similar to the 1960s Hippie adage, "Make love, not war," without the sexual overtones. It shudders at the current "war on crime" metaphor and wants to substitute "peace on crime." The idea of making peace on crime is perhaps best captured by Kay Harris in writing that we "need to reject the idea that those who cause injury or harm to others should suffer severance of the common bonds of respect and concern that binds members of a community. We should relinquish the notion that it is acceptable to try to 'get rid of' another person whether through execution, banishment, or caging away people about whom we do not care."[49] While recognizing that many criminals should be incarcerated, peacemaking criminologists aver that an overemphasis on punishing criminals escalates violence. Marxist-cum-peacemaker Richard Quinney has called the American criminal justice system the moral equivalent of war and notes that war naturally invites resistance by those it is waged against. He further adds that when society resists criminal victimization, it "must be in compassion and love, not in terms of the violence that is being resisted."[50]

In place of imprisoning offenders, peacemaking criminologists advocate **restorative justice,** which is basically a system of mediation and conflict resolution. Restorative justice is "every

▲ **Photo 6.2** Peacemaking criminology focuses on the sources of strife, both personal and political, in the world today with an emphasis on eliminating its root causes. Here a banner has been put up announcing a mass rally in Trafalgar Square, London, to protest the visit of U.S. President George Bush shortly after the start of the Iraq War in 2003. Protestors hoped that peace rather than war would prevail.

action that is primarily oriented toward justice by repairing the harm that has been caused by the crime" and "usually means a face-to-face confrontation between victim and perpetrator, where a mutually agreeable restorative solution is proposed and agreed upon."[51] Restorative justice has been applauded because it humanizes justice by bringing victim and offender together to negotiate a mutually satisfying way to correct the wrong done. Although developed for juveniles and primarily confined to them, restorative justice has also been applied to nonviolent adult offenders in a number of countries as well as the United States.[52] The belief behind restorative justice is that, to the extent that both victim and victimizer come to see that justice is attained when a violation of one person by another is made right by the violator, the violator will have taken a step to reformation and the community will be a safer place in which to live.

◪ Feminist Criminology

Broadly defined, feminism is a set of theories and strategies for social change that takes gender as their central focus in attempting to understand social institutions, processes, and relationships. Like Marxism, feminism is both a social movement and a worldview of which criminology is but a small part. Mainstream feminism holds that women suffer oppression and discrimination in a society run for men by men who have passed laws and created customs to perpetuate their privileged position.[53] Feminist criminologists take these core elements and apply them to criminology.

There are as many varieties of feminist criminology as there are of "male" critical criminology, and they are just as hard to capture with a single stroke of the pen. These varieties—liberal, radical, socialist, and Marxist—have at least one thing in common with each other and with "male" neo-Marxist criminology: They are largely opposed to mainstream ("male-stream?") culture. The extent of the opposition varies according to the faction. Feminist criminology is therefore conflict oriented, but it shifts emphasis to issues of gender and power rather than class and power, although feminists, especially Marxists, make use of the class concept. Marxism's class-based conflict in the context of the capitalist mode of production gives way to gender-based conflict within the context of a patriarchal (male-dominated) society as the major orienting concept. The "bourgeoisie" and "powerful interest groups" of neo-Marxist and conflict theories become gendered and defined as "rich white *men*."[54] Feminists see women as being doubly oppressed by gender inequality (their social position in a sexist culture) and by class inequality (their economic position in a capitalist society). For many feminists, the only answer to their oppression is the overthrow of the two-headed monster—capitalism and patriarchy.

But what does all this have to do with crime? Since crime is overwhelmingly a male activity, why should criminologists bother with examining any effects that capitalism and patriarchy may have on female-specific crime? For those females who do become criminals, why should their paths differ from those taken by male criminals? Are females' social experiences and ways of thinking so different that we need "special" theories of crime causation for them? These are questions often asked by feminist criminologists, and their answers are complex.

One of the reasons we need a feminist criminology is that female crime has been virtually ignored by mainstream criminology, which tends to assume that what is good for the rooster is also good for the hen. Feminists want to put women on the criminological agenda, and they especially want to be able to interpret female crime from a feminist perspective. In postmodernist terms, feminists would like an appreciative relativism for their approach to criminology.

Feminist criminology has two major concerns: Do traditional male-centered theories of crime apply to women and, if not, why not? This is known as the **generalizability problem.** The second concern is the following: What explains the universal fact that women are far less likely than men to involve themselves in criminal activity? This is known as the **gender ratio problem.**[55]

The Generalizability Problem

The theories we have discussed thus far have been formulated on the basis of information about mostly male offenders. Although this is reasonable given that the crime problem is essentially a male problem, these theories may not "translate" to female offenders. Eileen Leonard[56] has examined many of the sociological theories of crime causation to see if they can be applied to female criminality, starting with anomie theory.

Anomie Anomie theory views crime and delinquency in terms of innovative adaptations to strain generated by cultural pressures to achieve financial success. Leonard says that this theory cannot be applied to women because women are socialized to be successful in relationships, to get married, and to raise families, not for financial success. There is no one cultural success goal for all to strive for; there are two cultural success goals, one for men and one for women. The failure to succeed in either goal is productive of strain, but even if male crimes are innovative means of attaining their *success* goals, it is illogical to view female crimes as innovative means to their *relationship* goals. Anomie is thus very much a male-centered theory since it only addresses the difficulties faced by males in attaining their goals. It may only be workable for women if their goals shift more toward male goals.

Subcultural Theories Subcultural theories of Cohen, Cloward and Ohlin, and Miller are also inadequate explanations of female crime. Unlike Merton, Cohen recognized that males and females have different goals (financial success versus relationship success). Female goals are supposedly easier to achieve, and thus the problems leading to the establishment of delinquent subcultures are fundamentally male problems. Boys seek vindication of their male status in delinquent gangs, but according to Cohen, not only is delinquent gang activity irrelevant to vindication of a girl's female status, but participation also threatens it.

Miller's focal concern talks about lower-class culture in general but is exclusively a male-centered theory of criminality. His focal concerns are male concerns and have little salience for females and are thus not amenable to considerations of gender.

Because Cloward and Ohlin's theory considered the availability of both legitimate and illegitimate opportunities, Leonard sees more hope for it. Cloward and Ohlin stated that women are frequently excluded from delinquent and criminal activities, even within subcultures that support it for males. However, Cloward and Ohlin still emphasized common (not gender-related) cultural goals, and their theory cannot explain why women who have achieved their relationship goals commit crimes. Some theorists assert that female crime rises as their participation in the workforce increases, but according to the differential opportunity perspective, the provision of legitimate opportunities is supposed to prevent crime. In short, Leonard finds that subcultural theories are of little use in explaining female crime.

Differential Association Differential association theory asserts that crime and delinquency results from an excess of definitions favorable to law violation over definitions unfavorable to law violation learned in intimate personal groups. Males are more likely than females to attach themselves to groups holding antisocial definitions, and females are more likely to attach themselves to the family, where they will learn fewer definitions favorable to law violation. Leonard is more positive toward differential association theory than toward the other theories because it "reminds us that women are not permitted the same associations as men" and are taught different things.[57] She sees the theory as better for explaining why females commit less crime than men but not as one that explains female crime on its own terms.

Labeling One of labeling theory's propositions is that social control agents with the power to apply stigmatizing labels do not associate certain groups with crime. Women (because the traditional stereotype sees them as dependent, passive, nurturing, and so forth) are among those less likely to be labeled. Labeling theorists might posit that women may have crime rates more closely matching those of males, but because they are not officially labeled, they *appear* to be far less criminal. Leonard dismisses this as thoroughly rejected by research. She also rejects the entire labeling perspective as lacking an explanation of why people engage in deviance in the first place and because it lacks an analysis of the structures of power and oppression impinging on women.

Marxism Although sympathetic to the Marxist perspective, Leonard also criticizes it for its neglect of gender issues. Marxism's emphasis on power relations and on the exploitation and oppression of one group by another fits in well with the feminist agenda, but its strict reliance on a class analysis does not allow it to account for female crime. Working-class women experience the same capitalist exploitation as men, but they still commit far less crime.

The Gender Ratio Problem

Along with many other feminist criminologists, Leonard concludes that male-centered theories have limited applicability to females. Nevertheless, there is little argument that most female offenders are found in the same places as their male counterparts (i.e., among single-parent families located in poor, socially disorganized neighborhoods). Male and female crime rates march in lockstep across different nations and across communities in the same nation (as male rates increase, so do female rates, and vice versa), indicating that females are broadly responsive to the same environmental conditions as males.[58] Given this evidence, Daly and Chesney-Lind ask, "Why do similar processes produce a distinctive, gender-based [male] structure to crime and delinquency?"[59]

Most feminist criminologists have attempted to answer this question using only traditional sociological concepts that view gender differences as mostly products of differential socialization. Men are socialized to be assertive, ambitious, career oriented, and dominant, and women are socialized to be nurturing, passive, and home and family oriented. This viewpoint suggests that if females were socialized in the same way as males and had similar roles and experiences, their rates of criminal offending would be roughly the same.

The Masculinization and Emancipation Hypotheses: Adler and Simon

The first serious attempt at a feminist criminology adopted this assumption. In her book *Sisters in Crime*, Freda Adler[60] attributed the rise in female crime rates in the 1960s and 1970s

▲ **Photo 6.3** While females are no longer excluded from certain workplaces and careers, their numbers in certain professions remain disproportionate. Note that the depicted roll call of NYPD beat cops has only one female officer.

to an increasing number of females adopting "male" roles and, by doing so, increasingly masculinizing their attitudes and behavior (the **masculinization hypothesis**). Adler argued that "determined women are forcing their way into the world of crime," adding that "increasing numbers are women are using guns, knives, and wits to establish themselves as full human beings, as capable of violent aggression as any man."[61]

Adler's thesis was not well received by many feminists who did not share her opinion of how women might establish their humanity, perceiving it as providing ammunition for those who oppose women's liberation (more women in the workforce equals more crime). Nor has the thesis been supported by research. Female crime in the United States has increased over the past 30 years, but as a proportion of total arrests, the female arrest rate has not varied by more than 5 percentage points, and the male/female gap—which is the real issue—has remained essentially unchanged.[62]

Rita Simon offered a different view in her book *Women and Crime.*[63] Simon claimed that increased participation in the workforce affords women greater opportunities to commit job-related crime (the **emancipation hypothesis**). Women could thus commit crime without first undergoing Adler's masculinization of attitudes. This hypothesis has intuitive appeal (apart from the obvious fact that one must be employed to commit job-related crime). International data have shown that women are from 5 to 50 times less likely to be arrested than males, depending on the country.[64] In general, the arrest ratio is lower in countries that afford females greater levels of equality with men. However, when comparisons are made within or across countries with similar levels of development, the majority of studies actually support the *opposite* of the emancipation hypothesis—that is, as the trend toward gender equality has increased, females have tended to commit fewer rather than more crimes relative to males.[65]

More recently, it has been proposed that the gender ratio exists because the genders differ in exposure to delinquent peers, males are more influenced by delinquent peers than females, and there is greater inhibitory morality in females.[66] This has been called nothing more than claiming that "boys will be boys" and "girls will be girls" because it begs the questions of why males are more "exposed" and more "influenced" than females and why females have a stronger sense of morality.[67] The standard answers to these questions are in the form sex role socialization: Females are socialized more strongly to conformity. While these factors certainly affect the behavior of both genders, controlling for supervision level results in the same large gender gap in offending.[68] Furthermore, a meta-analysis of 172 studies found a slight tendency for girls to be *less* strictly supervised than boys.[69] Many others studies have shown that large sex differences in antisocial behavior exist regardless of the level of supervision and whether or not the family is patriarchal (implying strict control of females) or egalitarian (implying more equal treatment of boys and girls).[70] As Dianna Fishbein has summed up the gender ratio issue, "Cross cultural studies do not support the prominent role of structural and cultural influences of gender-specific crime rates as the type and extent of male versus female crime remains consistent across cultures."[71]

Female-Centered Theory: Criminalizing Girls' Survival and Victim-Precipitated Homicide

Because of the difficulty in accounting for the generalizability and gender ratio problems, feminist scholars have tended to focus more on men's victimization of women and to concentrate on case histories.[72] Rather than developing general theories of female crime, feminist theorists have developed a series of models cataloging the responses of girls and women to situations more or less specific to their gender that result in them committing *specific* criminal acts. For instance, a typical female role is that of shopping, and females are usually arrested for shoplifting (a criminal extension of a traditional female role) more often than males.[73] Because women are said to exchange sex for financial security in marriage, some feminists also view prostitution as an illegitimate extension of a legitimate role.[74]

Meda Chesney-Lind combines this "role extension" idea with structural patriarchy to develop a model she calls *criminalizing girls' survival.* She describes a sequence of events related to efforts of parents and social control agents to closely supervise the lives of girls. She notes that girls are more likely than boys to be reported to the authorities for status offenses (offenses that would not be crimes if committed by adults) and takes this as evidence that girls are given less leeway than boys.

Chesney-Lind also notes that girls are more likely to be sexually victimized than boys, their assailants are more likely to be family members, and a likely response is to run away from home. The first runaway offense will probably result in the girl being returned to the very conditions she sought to escape. This both reinforces her feelings of "nobody cares" and strengthens her resolve not to get caught again. When a girl is on the streets, she has to do something to survive: steal money, food, or clothing; use and sell drugs; and possibly engage in prostitution. These behaviors learned on the streets may then become lifetime patterns of behavior. Chesney-Lind's point is that girls' victimization and their response to it are shaped by their status in a patriarchal society in which males dominate the family and define their daughters and stepdaughters as sexual property. When girls run away from such homes, they are returned by paternalistic juvenile authorities who feel it is their duty to "protect" them. Thus, patriarchy (as expressed in family dynamics) combines with paternalism (as expressed in official reactions to female runaways) to force girls to live "lives of escaped convicts."[75]

Along the same lines as Chesney-Lind's analysis is the concern for explaining female homicide. Homicide is a crime that is mostly *intra*sexual for men but *inter*sexual for women, which suggests that the causes of homicidal behavior might be quite different for men and women. It has been pointed out that African American women are second only to African American men in the frequency of arrest for homicide.[76,77] Feminist criminologists have explained this using the concept of *victim-precipitated homicide*, which is a homicide in which the murder victim initiates the sequence of events that leads to his or her death. Most instances of Black female homicide (for White female homicide also) involve women killing their husbands or boyfriends in self-defense situations.[78] Black females may be more reluctant to report battering than White females due to an alleged greater acceptance of violence in the Black subculture, and they may be less willing or less able to make use

▲ **Photo 6.4** Did serial killer nurse Kristen Gilbert poison her patients as acts of mercy killing or from other motivations? What might the radical feminist perspective have to say on this?

of agencies dealing with spousal abuse.[79] The greater victimization of Black women relative to women of other races, as well as barriers preventing their escape from the situation, may lead them to resort to violent solutions to protect themselves more often than other women, who presumably have more non-violent options available to them.

Radical Feminist Explanations

Radical feminists take a "radically" different approach from mainstream feminists. They agree with Gwynn Nettler, who notes that "environments—good or bad, and whichever facet of them is considered—affect males, the less viable of the sexes, more strongly than they do females."[80] It takes more to push females over the line from conforming to nonconforming behavior, a fact that has led some theorists to look for crime-resistant characteristics that are gender related (not gender specific) to explain the gender ratio problem. Radical feminists argue that because the magnitude of the gender gap varies across time and space and yet still remains constantly wide at all times and in all places, biological factors *must* play a large part. For radical feminists, the root of the gender ratio lies in fundamental differences between the genders, not in socialization practices. If social factors alone accounted for gender differences, there should be a set of cultural conditions under which crime rates would be equal for both sexes or even under which female rates would be higher, but no such conditions have ever been discovered anywhere. Robust sex differences in dominance and aggression are noted in all human cultures from the earliest days of life. These differences are underscored during the teen years and are observed in all primate and most mammalian species, for which no one would evoke socialization as an explanation.[81,82]

Neuroscientists have long known that gender-typical behavior (and sex-typical behavior in all mammals) requires that hormones organize the brain in male or female directions during sensitive prenatal periods.[83] Biosocial criminologists claim that this process organizes male brains in such a way that males become more vulnerable to the various traits associated with antisocial behavior via the regulation of brain chemistry.[84,85] According to neuropsychologist Doreen Kimura, males and females come into this world with "differently wired brains," and these brain differences "make it almost impossible to evaluate the effects of experience [the socialization process] independent of physiological predisposition."[86] The major biological factor said to underlie gender differences in dominance, aggression, violence, and general antisocial behavior is testosterone.[87,88] Note that biosocial theorists are *not* saying that testosterone is a major or even minor cause of crime and general mayhem, only that it is the major factor that underlies gender *differences* in crime and general mayhem.

Brain and hormonal differences provide a proximate-level explanation of the genders' "differently wired brains," but why do these differences exist in the first place? Feminist psychologist Anne Campbell[89] has attempted to account for them at the ultimate level using the logic of evolutionary theory in her **staying alive hypothesis.** Evolutionary logic is all about passing on genes that prove useful in the struggle for survival and reproductive success to future generations over the eons of time in which our most human characteristics were being formed. We still carry those characteristics around with us regardless of whether they are still useful to us and regardless of our awareness of them.

Biologists note that sex differences in aggression and dominance seeking are related to parental investment, not biological sex per se. It is parental investment that provokes evolutionary pressures for the selection of the mechanisms that underlie these behaviors. In some bird and fish species, males contribute greater parental investment (e.g., incubating the eggs and feeding the young) than females, and females take more risks, are more promiscuous and aggressive in courtship, and engage in violent competition for mates.[90,91] In these species, sex-related characteristics are the opposite of those found in species in which females assume all or most of the burden of parenting (the vast majority of species).

Campbell argues that because the *obligatory* parental investment of females is greater than that of males, and because of the infant's greater dependence on the mother, a mother's presence is more critical to offspring survival than is a father's. Offspring survival is more critical to a female's reproductive success than it is to a male's because of the limits placed on female reproduction by long periods of gestation and lactation (male reproductive success is only limited by his access to willing females). Campbell argues that because offspring survival is so enormously important to their reproductive success, females evolved a propensity to avoid engaging in behaviors that pose survival risks. The practice of keeping nursing children in close proximity in ancestral environments posed an elevated risk of injuring the child as well as herself if the mother placed herself in risky situations. Thus, Campbell says, it became adaptive for females to experience many different situations as fearful. Campbell shows that there are no sex differences in fearfulness *unless* a situation contains a significant risk of physical injury, and it is this fear that accounts for the greater tendency of females to avoid or remove themselves from potentially violent situations and to employ low-risk strategies in competition and dispute resolution relative to males.

Striving for status and dominance was a risky business in evolutionary environments, and it still is in some environments today. Nature exerted less evolutionary pressure on females for the selection of mechanisms useful for status/dominance seeking than for males because dominance and status are less reproductively consequential for females.[92] Females do engage in competition with one another for resources and mates, but it is rarely violent competition in any primate species. Most of it is decidedly low key, low risk, and chronic as opposed to high key, high risk, and acute male competition. Evolutionary theorists assert that the female assets most pertinent to reproductive success are youth and beauty, which one either has or does not. Male assets are the resources that females desire for their reproductive success and, unlike youth and beauty, can be achieved in competition with other males. Males are willing to incur high risks to achieve the status and dominance that bring them resources and thus access to more females.

Campbell shows that when females engage in crime, they almost always do so for instrumental reasons, and their crimes rarely involve risk of physical injury. There is no evidence, for instance, that female robbers crave the additional payoffs of dominance that male robbers do or seek reputations as "hard-asses." Any woman with a reputation as a "hard-ass" would not be very desirable as a mate. Thus, Campbell notes that while women do aggress and do steal, "they rarely do both at the same time because the equation of resources and status reflects a particularly masculine logic."[93]

⊠ Evaluation of Critical Theories

It is often said that Marxist theory has very little that is unique to add to criminology theory: "When Marxist theorists offer explanations of crime that go beyond simply attributing the causes of all crime to capitalism, they rely on concepts taken from the same 'traditional' criminological theories of which they have been so critical."[94]

Marxist theories also tend to be philosophically hostile to empiricism, the method usually applied to theory testing.[95] Citing Marx's famous lines—"Philosophers have only interpreted the world . . . the point is to change it"—Marxist criminologists tend to be action oriented rather than science oriented. Marxist research is historical, descriptive, and illustrative. The tendency to romanticize criminals as revolutionaries has long been a major criticism, although Marxist criminologists are less likely to do this today.

Since Marxism's causal variable is a society's mode of production, a simple empirical test of its thesis would be to compare crime rates in capitalist and socialist societies. Socialist countries do tend to have less crime than capitalist countries, and crime rates in former socialist countries soared with the breakdown of the socialist system and the implementation of capitalist economic principles.[96] Can Marxists claim empirical support for their contention that capitalism causes crime and socialism "cures" it on this evidence? That capitalism is *associated* with higher crime rates than socialism is uncontested, but the question we have to ask is whether the Marxist *interpretation* of this fact is correct. It is probably true that capitalism promotes egoism to a greater extent than does socialism. However, analyses of previously secret crime figures from the former Soviet Union reveal that crime rates there fluctuated over the years almost as much as they did in capitalist societies, and crime started to increase significantly there even before the implementation of the liberalization policies of the late 1980s.[97] The lower crime rates in socialist societies probably have more to do with repressive law enforcement practices than with any altruistic qualities intrinsic to socialism.[98]

Much of Marxist criminology also appears to be in a time warp in that it assumes that the conditions prevailing in Marx's time still exist in the same form today in advanced capitalist societies. People from all over the noncapitalist world have risked life and limb to get into capitalist countries because it is in those countries where human rights are most respected and human needs and wants most readily satisfied. Even before the collapse of the Soviet system, left realists realized that utopia would be a long time coming and that it would be more realistic to work within the system to achieve reforms. Left realism is thus more the reform-minded "practical" wing of Marxism than a theory of crime that has anything special to offer criminology.

Conflict theory brought a breath of fresh air to criminology in the 1960s. Simply being opposed to the consensus theory of society made it both challenging and refreshing, and its efforts to identify power relationships in society have applications that go beyond criminology. However, there are several problems with it that make it less than an adequate theory of criminal behavior. It has even been said that "conflict theory does not attempt to explain crime; it simply identifies social conflict as a basic fact of life and a source of discriminatory treatment."[99]

Conflict theory's assumption that crime is just a "social construct" without any intrinsic properties minimizes the suffering of those who have been assaulted, raped, robbed, molested, and otherwise victimized. These acts *are* intrinsically bad (mala in se) and are not arbitrarily criminalized because they threaten the privileged world of the powerful few. As we saw in Chapter 1, there is wide agreement among people of various classes in the United States about what crimes are—laws exist to protect everyone, not just "the elite."

This highlights another problem with conflict criminology, that of using mala prohibita crimes to make a point about all crimes—a classic "bait-and-switch" tactic. For instance, William Chambliss studied how the vagrancy laws in 12th-century England were implemented by the elite for the elite and concluded, "What is true of the vagrancy laws is also true of the criminal law in general."[100] Thus, in common with Marxist theorists, many conflict theorists prefer case studies to the empirical methods of mainstream criminologists. Such case studies can be very useful as long as the conclusions drawn from them are not stretched to the breaking point.

Although postmodernism has been useful in challenging traditional criminological theories to rethink some of their assumptions, it offers no viable alternative except to advance the notion that "crime can be abated by changing the way that people think and talk about it."[101] Postmodernist criminology has thus tended toward an "appreciative relativism" and "communal celebration . . . to the extent that it 'appreciates' or 'celebrates' the actions of criminals when they victimize other people."[102] Postmodernists counsel that we "appreciate" the excuses (techniques of neutralization) criminals may offer for their actions as having as much validity as the views held by their victims and by the criminal justice system.

Partly because of this, and partly because of the incomprehensibility of much of its prose, many criminologists have dismissed postmodernist criminology as "a pretentious intellectual fad."[103] Lanier and Henry point out that "postmodernism has been sharply criticized by mainstream criminologists and even critical criminologists . . . as (1) difficult to understand, not the least because of its language; (2) nihilistic and relativistic, having no standards to judge anything as good or bad; and (3) impractical and even dangerous to disempowered groups."[104]

Many of the criticisms aimed at postmodernism apply to peacemaking criminology since the latter springs from the former. It urges us to make peace on crime, but what does such advice actually mean? As a number of commentators have pointed out, "being nice" is not enough to stop others from hurting us.[105] It is undoubtedly true (almost by definition) that the reduction of human suffering and achieving a truly just world will reduce crime, as peacemaking advocates contend, but they never offer us any notion of how this can be achieved beyond counseling that we should appreciate criminals' points of view and not be so punitive. It will only be when the public and the criminal justice system give up the violence of punishment that we can expect criminals to also give up violence.[106] If this were true, we would see countries with the harshest punishments suffering the most crime and those with the most lenient punishments reaping the harvest of low crime rates. In general, we see the opposite of this. For instance, justice is swift and severe (use of the death penalty, whippings, and limb amputations) in Islamic countries, where crime is low, and even among democracies, crime appears to creep upwards when penalties become more lenient.[107]

The separate strands of feminist theory have reminded us all that women and girls commit crimes and delinquent acts too. Bringing females into the criminological agenda has done the discipline a huge favor. However, despite the best efforts of many, there is still no gender-specific theory of crime. Feminist scholars have even pointed out that no such theory is possible.[108]

In common with other critical theorists, feminist theorists have been content to focus on descriptive studies or on crime-specific "mini-theories" such as criminalizing girls' survival.

When all is said and done, maleness is without doubt the best single predictor of criminal behavior. This leaves feminist theorists without much left to explain in *specific* female terms about female offending. Nevertheless, females constitute at least one half of the world's population, and they are confronted by a different social reality than males. Thus, an explication of female-specific criminality would be most useful in its own right, and as a bonus, it may help us to better understand the more serious problem of male crime.

Campbell's staying alive/high-fear hypothesis is an example, since it is the female equivalent of the low-fear/high-sensation seeking theories (to be discussed later) based on mostly male samples.[109] Indicative of a growing disciplinary integration in criminology, only 4 of the 27 invited commentators on Campbell's target article argued that strictly social theories better accounted for gender differences in crime. It nevertheless remains true that we can never fully understand any social phenomenon such as crime outside its cultural context. Any assumed evolved behavioral disposition is exquisitely sensitive to environmental context. We have noted that African American females tend to have higher homicide rates than White males because of cultural context. However, this does not negate the basic gender ratio argument because *within* the African American community, the gender ratio is generally higher than it is in the White community (e.g., there is a bigger gap between the homicide rates of Black males and females than there is between the homicide rates of White males and females).[110]

◪ Policy and Prevention: Implications of Critical Theories

The policy implications of Marxist theory are straightforward: overthrow the capitalist system and crime will be reduced. Marxist criminologists realize today that the abolition of capitalism is not supported by the masses, a fact underlined for them by the collapse of Marxist economies across Eastern Europe. They also realized that their emphasis on a single cause of crime (the class struggle) and the romanticizing of criminals by the so-called "left idealists" was naive and unrealistic.[111]

Rather than throw out their entire ideological agenda, left realists decided to temper their views so as to deny conservative criminology a monopoly on the crime problem, while at the same maintaining their critical stance toward the "system." Policy recommendations made by left realists have many things in common with those made by ecology, anomie, and routine activities theorists. Community activities, neighborhood watches, community policing, dispute resolution centers, and target hardening are among the policies suggested.

Because crime is viewed as the result of conflict between interest groups with power and wealth differences, and since many conflict theorists view conflict and the existence of social classes as normal, it is difficult to recommend policies *specifically* derived from conflict theory. We might logically conclude from this view of class and conflict that if these things are normal and perhaps beneficial, then so is crime in some sense.

If we do want to reduce crime, equalizing the distribution of power, wealth, and status will reduce the ability of any one group to dictate what is criminalized, and thus there will be less crime. The widening gap between rich and poor in the United States must be countered by passing legislation mandating a livable minimum wage, job creation, and workplace democracy, which is not utopian "because many other nations have done it."[112] Conflict theory would predict, however, that the income gap would not be closed until powerful interest groups arise from the unprivileged classes to force the issue. Only labor unions have been able to organize previously unorganized aggregates of powerless individuals into a force to be reckoned with, but the power of unions is rapidly declining in the United States. Generally speaking, conflict theorists favor programs such as minimum wage laws, sharply progressive taxation, a government-controlled comprehensive health care system, maternal leave, and a national policy of family support as a way of reducing crime.[113]

The policy recommendations of feminist theory range from the liberal's affirmative action programs to the Marxist's revolutionary overthrow of capitalism. The former has been relatively successful in moving women into what had formerly been "male" occupations, and the latter is hardly likely to occur. There are all sorts of other recommendations in between, the major one being the reform of our patriarchal society. Other recommendations include the more equal (less paternalistic) treatment of girls and boys by juvenile authorities, increased educational and occupational choices for women so that those in abusive relationships can leave them, more day care centers, and so forth. Feminist theory suggests that gender sensitivity education in the schools and workplaces may lead men to abandon many of their embedded sexist ideas pertaining to the relationship between the sexes.

Feminists insist that the elimination of patriarchy would benefit both men and women in a number of ways, thus leading to a reduction in crime. The implication that women are owned by men, which is embedded in our cultural values, as we have seen, often leads to male abuse of females (criminal acts), which sometimes leads to violent retaliation (criminal acts) by females. Greater financial equality between males and females should, according to some feminist theorists, also lead to a reduction in females' crimes committed out of financial necessity, destructiveness, egoism, and competitiveness.[114]

The major impact of feminism on criminal justice policy to date has been to push the plight of victims into the light of day. Rape law reforms, the involvement of victims in various stages of criminal processing (especially at sentencing and parole hearings), victim counseling, and a variety of other victim-benefiting services have been a major legacy of feminist interest in criminal justice.

SUMMARY

Critical criminology is a generic term encompassing many different theoretical positions united by the common view that society is best characterized by conflict and power relations rather than by value consensus. Neo-Marxist criminologists follow the theoretical trail of Karl Marx, who posited the existence of two conflicting classes in society: the bourgeoisie and the proletariat. While some modern Marxists have a tendency to romanticize criminals as heroic revolutionaries, Marx considered them "social scum" who preyed upon the working class. Nevertheless, he saw their activities as stemming from class oppression and alienated social relations.

Willem Bonger is credited with being the first Marxist criminologist. He was concerned with two opposite "social sentiments": altruism and egoism. The sentiment of altruism is killed in a capitalist social system because it generates competition for wealth, status, and jobs. Thus, capitalism produces egoism, which leads to criminal behavior on the part of both the poor and the rich. Bonger advocated the abolition of capitalism as the answer to the crime problem.

Neo-Marxists tend to view capitalism as the only cause of crime, and they insist that class and class values are generated by the material conditions of social life, not the other way around. Thus, they discount subcultural explanations of crime as being generated by values because the material origins of those values are ignored in subcultural explanations. Because only the material conditions of life really matter, the only way to make any serious impact on crime is to eliminate the capitalist mode of production and institute a Marxist social order. Left realists realize that such a radical transformation is highly unlikely in modern times, and although they maintain a critical stance toward the system, they work within it in an effort to influence social policy and to deny conservative criminologists a monopoly in the discipline.

Conflict theorists share some sentiments with neo-Marxists but view conflict in pluralistic terms and as intrinsic to society, not something that can be eliminated. They also view social classes as not necessarily bad, although the causes of crime are linked to class and conflict. Crime is the result of the ability of powerful interest groups to criminalize the behavior of other, less powerful interest groups when that behavior is contrary to their interests. Conflict criminological research tends to focus on the differential treatment by the criminal justice system of individuals who are members of less powerful groups such as minorities, women, and working-class Whites. It is difficult to make policy recommendations from conflict theory except to call for the reduction of power differentials in society.

Feminist criminology focuses on trying to understand female offending from the feminist perspective, which contends that women are faced with special disabilities living in an oppressive sexist society. They contend that mainstream criminological theories have ignored the special situations faced by women, and some believe that these theories are not able to explain female offending. They also fail to provide adequate explanations for the universal fact that women commit far less crime, especially violent crime, than men.

Early attempts to explain female crime from the feminist tradition emphasized the "masculinization" of attitudes as females increasingly adopted "male" roles, or simply that as women move into the workforce in greater numbers, they found greater opportunities to commit job-related crimes. Many feminists rejected both positions, pointing out that such theorizing provided ammunition for those who opposed the women's movement and that, regardless of any increase in female offending, the male/female gap remains as wide as ever.

The size and universality of the gender gap suggests to some that the most logical explanation for it must lie in some fundamental differences between the sexes rather than socialization. It has been repeatedly found that the female threshold for crossing the line from conforming to criminal behavior is set much higher than it is for males.

Female-specific crime theories tend to be models of specific crimes rather than theories per se (e.g., criminalizing girls' survival and victim-precipitated homicide). The infancy of feminist criminology means that there is as yet no real body of empirical literature assessing its usefulness. However, the feminist concern is not so much with generating a body of empirical evidence as it is in awakening mainstream criminology to the fact that women exist and should be included. Feminists have also been concerned with issues of fighting sexism, patriarchy, and paternalism in society and in the criminal justice system, and they have done much to advance the cause of victims' rights. Feminist criminologists insist that greater gender equality will reduce crime and delinquency for both men and women.

On Your Own

Log on to the web-based student study site at http://www.sagepub.com/criminologystudy for more information about the vignettes and materials presented in this chapter, suggestions for activities, study aids such as review quizzes, and research recommendations including journal article links and questions related to this chapter.

EXERCISES AND DISCUSSION QUESTIONS

1. Do you think that the "material conditions of life" largely determine what we will know, believe, and value and how we will behave?

2. Can social classes ever be eliminated? Should they be? What purposes do they serve?

3. Do you believe that social conflict is inevitable? In what ways is conflict a good thing?

4. If capitalism encourages egoism and blunts altruism, what can we do to change this?

5. Do we really need a feminist criminology, or do the traditional theories suffice to explain both male and female criminality?

6. What are the main contributions of feminist criminology?

7. Go to the Web site of the Critical Criminology Division of the American Society of Criminology at http://www.critcrim.org. Click on the paper by Gregg Barak on race, gender, and class. What does he conclude about the treatment of minorities, women, and lower socioeconomic status members? How would you argue with him?

KEY WORDS

Bourgeoisie
Class struggle
Critical criminology
Emancipation hypothesis
Generalizability problem
Gender ratio problem

Left realist criminology
Lumpenproletariat
Masculinization
 hypothesis
Peacemaking criminology
Postmodernist criminology

Primitive rebellion
 hypothesis
Proletariat
Restorative justice
Staying alive hypothesis

REFERENCES

1. Hill, R., & Robertson, R. (2003). What sort of future for critical criminology? *Crime, Law, & Social Change, 39,* 91–115.

2. Walsh, A., & Ellis, L. (2004). Ideology: Criminology's Achilles' heel? *Quarterly Journal of Ideology, 27,* 1–25.

3. Durant, W., & Durant, A. (1968). *The lessons of history.* New York: Simon & Schuster.

4. Adams, J. (1971). *In defense of the Constitution of the United States* (Vol. 1). New York: De Capo. (Original work published 1778)

5. Marx, K., & Engels, F. (1948). *The Communist Manifesto.* New York: International. (Quote on p. 9)

6. Ritzer, G. (1992). *Sociological theory* (3rd ed.). New York: McGraw-Hill.

7. Marx and Engels (1948, p. 22).

8. Marx, K., & Engels, F. (1965). *The German ideology.* London: Lawrence and Wishart. (Quote on p. 367)

9. Bohm, R. (2001). *A primer on crime and delinquency* (2nd ed.). Belmont, CA: Wadsworth. (Quote on p. 115)

10. Bernard, T. (1981). The distinction between conflict and radical criminology. *Journal of Criminal Law and Criminology, 72,* 362–379. (Quote on p. 365)

11. Livingston, E. (1968). *The complete works of Edward Livingston on criminal jurisprudence.* Montclair, NJ: Patterson Smith. (Original work published 1822; quote on p. 45)

12. Curran, D., & Renzetti, C. (2001). *Theories of crime* (2nd ed.). Boston: Allyn & Bacon.

13. Bonger, W. (1969). *Criminality and economic conditions.* Bloomington: Indiana University Press. (Original work published 1905)

14. Bonger (1905/1969, p. 88).

15. Bonger (1905/1969).

16. Bonger (1905/1969, p. 108).

17. Bonger (1905/1969, p. 195).

18. Taylor, I., Walton, P., & Young, J. (1973). *The new criminology.* New York: Harper & Row.

19. Chambliss, W. (1976). *Criminal law in action.* Santa Barbara, CA: Hamilton. (Quote on p. 6)

20. Taylor, I. (1999). Crime and social criticism. *Social Justice, 26,* 150–168. (Quote on p. 151)

21. Greenberg, D. (1981). *Crime and capitalism: Readings in Marxist criminology.* Palo Alto, CA: Mayfield. (Quote on p. 28)

22. Platt, T. (1975). Prospects for a radical criminology in the USA. In I. Taylor, P. Walton, & J. Young (Eds.), *Critical criminology* (pp. 95–112). Boston: Routledge & Kegan Paul.

23. Liazos, A. (1972). The poverty of the sociology of deviance: Nuts, sluts and perverts. *Social Problems, 20,* 103–120.

24. Siegel, L. (1986). *Criminology.* Belmont, CA: Wadsworth. (Quote on p. 276)

25. DeKeseredy, W., & Schwartz, M. (1991). British and U.S. left realism: A critical comparison. *International Journal of Offender Therapy and Comparative Criminology, 35,* 248–262.

26. Box, S. (1987). *Recession, crime and punishment.* Totowa, NJ: Barnes & Noble. (Quote on p. 29)

27. Bohm (2001).

28. Ritzer (1992).

29. Curran and Renzetti (2001).

30. Bartollas, C. (2005). *Juvenile delinquency* (7th ed.). Boston: Allyn & Bacon. (Quote on p. 179)

31. Vold, G., & Bernard, T. (1986). *Theoretical criminology.* New York: Oxford University Press.

32. Vold and Bernard (1986).

33. Walsh, A., & Hemmens, C. (2000). *From law to order: The theory and practice of law and justice.* Lanham, MD: American Correctional Association. (Quote on p. 214)

34. Quinney, R. (1975). Crime control in capitalist society: A critical philosophy of legal order. In I. Taylor, P. Walton, & J. Young (Eds.), *Critical criminology* (pp. 181–202). Boston: Routledge & Kegan Paul.

35. Turk, A. (1969). *Criminality and the legal order.* Chicago: Rand McNally.

36. Triplett, R. (1993). The conflict perspective, symbolic interactionism, and the status characteristics hypothesis. *Justice Quarterly, 10,* 541–556.

37. Walsh, A. (1988). 'The people who own the country ought to govern it': The Supreme Court, hegemony, and its consequences. *Law and Inequality, 5,* 431–451. (Quote on p. 431)

38. Galloway, R. (1982). *The rich and the poor in Supreme Court history.* Greenbrae, CA: Paradigm.

39. Pfeffer, L. (1965). *This honorable court.* Boston: Beacon. (Quote on p. 41)

40. Abadinsky, H. (1991). *Law and justice.* Chicago: Nelson-Hall.

41. Galloway (1982).

42. Walsh (1988).

43. Galloway (1982, p. 95).

44. Walsh (1988).

45. Wikipedia. (2005). *Sherman Anti-Trust Act.* Retrieved from http://www.answers.com/topic/

46. Pollock, J. (1999). *Criminal women.* Cincinnati, OH: Anderson. (Quote on p. 146)

47. Schwartz, M., & Friedrichs, D. (1994). Postmodern thought and criminological discontent. *Criminology, 32,* 221–246. (Quote on p. 224)

48. Arrigo, B., & Bernard, T. (2002). Postmodern criminology in relation to radical and conflict criminology. In S. Cote (Ed.), *Criminological theories: Bridging the past to the future* (pp. 250–257). Thousand Oaks, CA: Sage. (Quote on p. 251)

49. Harris, K. (1991). Moving into the new millennium: Toward a feminist view of justice. In H. Pepinsky & R. Quinney (Eds.), *Criminology as peacemaking* (pp. 83–97). Bloomington: Indiana University Press. (Quote on p. 93)

50. Vold, G., Bernard, T., & Snipes, J. (1998). *Theoretical criminology.* New York: Oxford University Press. (Quote on p. 274)

51. Champion, D. (2005). *Probation, parole, and community corrections* (5th ed.). Upper Saddle River, NJ: Prentice Hall. (Quote on p. 154)

52. Crowe, A. (1998). Restorative justice and offender rehabilitation: A meeting of the minds. *Perspectives, 22,* 28–40.

53. Yoder, J., & Khan, A. (1992). Toward a feminist understanding of women and power. *Psychology of Women Quarterly, 16,* 381–388.

54. Sokoloff, N., & Price, B. (1995). The criminal law and women. In B. Price & N. Sokoloff (Eds.), *The criminal justice system and women: Offenders, victims, and workers* (pp. 11–29). New York: McGraw-Hill. (Quote on p. 14)

55. Daly, K., & Chesney-Lind, M. (2002). Feminism and criminology. In S. Cote (Ed.), *Criminological theories: Bridging the past to the future* (pp. 267–284). Thousand Oaks, CA: Sage.

56. Leonard, E. (1995). Theoretical criminology and gender. In B. Price & N. Sokoloff (Eds.), *The criminal justice system and women: Offenders, victims, and workers* (pp. 54–70). New York: McGraw-Hill.

57. Leonard (1995, p. 61).

58. Campbell, A. (1999). Staying alive: Evolution, culture, and women's intrasexual aggression. *Behavioral and Brain Sciences, 22,* 203–214.

59. Daly, K., & Chesney-Lind, M. (1996). Feminism and criminology. In P. Cordella & L. Siegel (Eds.), *Readings in contemporary criminological theory* (pp. 340–364). Boston: Northeastern University Press. (Quote on p. 349)

60. Adler, F. (1975). *Sisters in crime: The rise of the new female criminal.* New York: McGraw-Hill.

61. Adler (1975, p. 15).

62. Campbell (1999).

63. Simon, R. (1975). *Women and crime.* Lexington, MA: Lexington Books.

64. Wilson, J., & Herrnstein, R. (1985). *Crime and human nature.* New York: Simon & Schuster.

65. Ellis, L., & Walsh, A. (2000). *Criminology: A global perspective.* Boston: Allyn & Bacon.

66. Mears, D., Ploeger, M., & Warr, M. (1998). Explaining the gender gap in delinquency: Peer influence and moral evaluations of behavior. *Journal of Research in Crime and Delinquency, 35,* 251–266.

67. Walsh, A. (2002). *Biosocial criminology: Introduction and integration.* Cincinnati, OH: Anderson.

68. Gottfredson, M., & Hirschi, T. (1990). *A general theory of crime.* Stanford, CA: Stanford University Press.

69. Lytton, H., & Romney, D. (1991). Parents' differential socialization of boys and girls: A meta-analysis. *Psychological Bulletin, 109,* 267–296.

70. Chesney-Lind, M., & Shelden, R. (1992). *Girls' delinquency and juvenile justice.* Pacific Grove, CA: Brooks/Cole.

71. Fishbein, D. (1992). The psychobiology of female aggression. *Criminal Justice and Behavior, 19,* 99–126. (Quote on p. 100)

72. Vold et al. (1998).

73. Smart, C. (1976). *Women, crime and criminology: A feminist critique.* London: Routledge & Kegan Paul.

74. Morris, A. (1987). *Women and criminal justice.* Oxford, UK: Basil Blackwell.

75. Chesney-Lind, M. (1995). Girls, delinquency and juvenile justice: Toward a feminist theory of young women's crime. In B. Price & N. Sokoloff (Eds.), *The criminal justice system and women: Offenders, victims, and workers* (pp. 71–88). New York: McGraw-Hill.

76. Barak, G. (1998). *Integrating criminologies.* Boston: Allyn & Bacon.

77. Mann, C. (1995). Women of color and the criminal justice system. In B. Price & N. Sokoloff (Eds.), *The criminal justice system and women: Offenders, victims, and workers* (pp. 118–119). New York: McGraw-Hill.

78. Mann, C. (1988). Getting even? Women who kill in domestic encounters. *Justice Quarterly, 5,* 33–51.

79. Rasche, C. (1995). Minority women and domestic violence: The unique dilemmas of battered women of color. In B. Price & N. Sokoloff (Eds.), *The criminal justice system and women: Offenders, victims, and workers* (pp. 246–261). New York: McGraw-Hill.

80. Nettler, G. (1982). *Explaining criminals.* Cincinnati, OH: Anderson. (Quote on p. 138)

81. Archer, J. (1996). Sex differences in social behavior: Are the social role and evolutionary explanations compatible? *American Psychologist, 51,* 909–917.

82. Geary, D. (1998). Functional organization of the human mind: Implications for behavioral genetic research. *Human Biology, 70,* 185–198.

83. Amateau, S., & McCarthy, M. (2004). Induction of PGE2 by estradiol mediates developmental masculinization of sex behavior. *Nature Neuroscience, 7,* 643–650.

84. Ellis, L. (2003). Genes, criminality, and the evolutionary neuroandrogenic theory. In A. Walsh & L. Ellis (Eds.), *Biosocial criminology: Challenging environmentalism's supremacy* (pp. 12–34). Hauppauge, NY: Nova Science.

85. Lopreato, J., & Crippen, T. (1999). *Crisis in sociology: The need for Darwin.* New Brunswick, NJ: Transaction.

86. Kimura, D. (1992). Sex differences in the brain. *Scientific American, 267,* 119–125. (Quote on p. 119)

87. Archer (1996).

88. Kanazawa, S. (2003). A general evolutionary psychological theory of criminality and related male-typical behavior. In A. Walsh & L. Ellis (Eds.), *Biosocial criminology: Challenging environmentalism's supremacy* (pp. 37–60). Hauppauge, NY: Nova Science.

89. Campbell (1999).

90. Barash, D., & Lipton, J. (2001). Making sense of sex. In D. Barash (Ed.), *Understanding violence* (pp. 20–30). Boston: Allyn & Bacon.

91. Betzig, L. (1999). When women win. *Behavioral and Brain Sciences, 22,* 217.

92. Barash and Lipton (2001).

93. Campbell (1999, p. 210).

94. Akers, R. (1994). *Criminological theories: Introduction and evaluation.* Los Angeles: Roxbury. (Quote on p. 167)

95. Lynch, M. (1987). Quantitative analysis and Marxist criminology: Some old answers to a dilemma in Marxist criminology. *Crime and Social Justice, 29,* 110–127.

96. Butler, W. (1992). Crime in the Soviet Union: Early glimpses of the true story. *British Journal of Criminology, 32,* 144–159.

97. Butler (1992).

98. Klockars, C. (1980). The contemporary crises of Marxist criminology. In J. Inciardi, *Radical criminology: The coming crisis* (pp. 92–123). Beverly Hills, CA: Sage.

99. Adler, F., Mueller, G., & Laufer, W. (2001). *Criminology and the criminal justice system.* Boston: McGraw-Hill.

100. Nettler, G. (1984). *Explaining crime* (3rd ed.). New York: McGraw-Hill. (Quote on p. 197)

101. Cote, S. (2002). Critical perspectives in crime and criminology. In S. Cote (Ed.), *Criminological theories: Bridging the past to the*

future (pp. 227–234). Thousand Oaks, CA: Sage. (Quote on p. 229)

102. Vold et al. (1998, p. 274).
103. Vold et al. (1998, p. 270).
104. Lanier, M., & Henry, S. (1998). *Essential criminology.* Boulder, CO: Westview. (Quote on p. 285)
105. Lanier and Henry (1998).
106. Vold et al. (1998, p. 274).
107. Becker, G. (1997). The economics of crime. In M. Fisch (Ed.), *Criminology 97/98* (pp. 15–20). Guilford, CT: Dushkin. (Quote on p. 223)
108. Daly and Chesney-Lind (2002).
109. Kanazawa (2003).
110. Laub, J., & McDermott, M. (1985). An analysis of serious crime by young Black women. *Criminology, 23,* 89–98.
111. DeKeseredy and Schwartz (1991, p. 248).
112. Currie, E. (1989). Confronting crime: Looking toward the twenty-first century. *Justice Quarterly, 6,* 5–25. (Quote on p. 16)
113. Currie (1989).
114. Williams, F., & McShane, M. (1994). *Criminological theory.* Englewood Cliffs, NJ: Prentice Hall.

PSYCHOSOCIAL THEORIES: INDIVIDUAL TRAITS AND CRIMINAL BEHAVIOR

L ittle Jimmy Caine, a pug-nosed third-generation Irish American, is an emotionless, guiltless, walking id, all 5' 5" and 130 pounds of him. By the time he was 26, Jimmy had accumulated one of the worst criminal records the police in Toledo, Ohio, had ever seen: burglary, aggravated assault, robbery, rape—name it, Jimmy had probably done it. This little tear-away had been arrested for the brutal rape of a 45-year-old barmaid. Jimmy entered an unlocked bar after closing time to find the lone barmaid attending to some cleaning chores. Putting a knife to the terrified woman's throat, he forced her to strip and proceeded to rape her. Because she was not sexually responsive, Jimmy became angry and placed her head over the kitchen sink and tried to decapitate her. His knife was a dull as his conscience, which only increased his anger, so he picked up a bottle of liquor and smashed it over her head. While the woman lay moaning at his feet, he poured more liquor over her, screaming, "I'm going to burn you up, bitch!" The noisy approach of the bar's owner sent Jimmy scurrying away. He was arrested 45 minutes later while casually eating a hamburger at a fast-food restaurant.

Jimmy didn't fit the demographic profile of individuals who engage in this type of crime. Although he had a slightly below-average IQ, he came from a fairly normal, intact middle-class home. However, Jimmy had been in trouble since his earliest days and had been examined by a variety of psychiatrists and psychologists. Psychiatrists diagnosed him with something called *conduct disorder as an 8-year-old and as having antisocial personality disorder at 18. Jimmy's case reminds us that we have to go beyond factors such as age, race, gender, and socioeconomic status to explain why individuals commit criminal acts. In this chapter, we look at many of the traits that psychologists and psychiatrists have examined to explain individual criminality. These explanations do not compete with sociological explanation; rather, they strengthen and complete them.*

Psychological theories of criminal behavior were in vogue before sociology got into the picture and were more interested in individual differences in the propensity to commit crimes than in environmental conditions assumed to facilitate it. These theories looked at how certain personality traits were conducive to criminal behavior, with emphasis placed strongly on intelligence and temperament. The assumption was that low intelligence hampers the ability to properly calculate the pleasures and pains involved in undertaking criminal activity and that certain types of temperament tend to make the person impulsive and difficult to socialize. As with all other individual characteristics, low IQ should be considered a single risk factor among many others and as neither a necessary or sufficient cause of criminal behavior.

One of the earliest works emphasizing low intelligence was Richard Dugdale's "*The Jukes*": *A Study of Crime, Pauperism, Disease, and Heredity*.[1] Dugdale studied the lineage of a rural upstate New York family known for its criminal activity, to which he gave the fictitious name of "Jukes." He traced the family lineage to a colonial-era character named "Max." Generations of Max's descendents remained in relative isolation and largely propagated themselves through intermarriage. Dugdale eventually traced 1,200 of Max's descendents, among whom he found numerous cases of crime, pauperism, illegitimacy, feeblemindedness, disease, sexual promiscuity, and prostitution. Dugdale's work was widely interpreted as further evidence of the hereditary nature of criminal behavior, although Dugdale himself was a firm believer that moral education could override biological propensities.

Another early study was conducted by Henry Goddard and published in a book titled *The Kallikak Family: A Study in the Heredity of Feeble-mindedness*.[2] This study traced two family lineages of a Revolutionary War soldier named "Martin Kallikak Sr," who dallied with a feebleminded tavern girl with whom he fathered an illegitimate, feebleminded son. From this lineage there issued a variety of individuals of unsavory character. Martin produced another line of descendants with a woman from a good Quaker family, from whose lineage there emerged a number of prominent people and very few of unsavory character. From these two families with a common male ancestor and two female ancestors, one "defective" and the other "respectable," Goddard concluded that "degeneracy" was the result of "bad blood."[3]

⬚ Modern Psychology and Intelligence

The root word of *intelligence* is *intelligo*, which means "to select among." Thus, intelligence is the ability to select from among a variety of elements and analyze, synthesize, and arrange them in ways that provide satisfactory and sometimes novel solutions to problems the elements pose. David Wechsler (who devised many of the IQ tests in use today) defined intelligence as "the aggregate or global capacity of the individual to act purposefully, to think rationally, and to deal effectively with his [or her] environment."[4] Intelligence is arguably the trait that most sharply separates humans from the rest of the animal kingdom and, as such, has to be of tremendous importance in all manner of human affairs.

While not seriously questioning the existence of individual differences in intelligence, some social scientists question our ability to measure it accurately and claim that tests designed to do so are biased in favor of the White middle class. However, no studies designed to detect bias in IQ tests have found evidence of bias against any racial/ethnic group or lower socioeconomic (SES) individuals.[5] This impressive record led the National Academy of Sciences,[6] the overwhelming majority of 1,020 Ph.D.-level experts surveyed by Snyderman and Rothman,[7] and the American Psychological Association's (APA) Task Force on Intelligence[8] to conclude that IQ tests are not biased against any group.

Intelligence, Genes, and the Environment

While scientists who study intelligence agree that IQ levels are substantially influenced by genes,[9,10] the environment also greatly influences it, as the so-called **Flynn effect**[11] has demonstrated. This effect refers to an upward creep in average IQ scores that has been taking place across the last four generations in all countries examined (the largest IQ gains are concentrated at the lowest IQ levels). These IQ gains must be attributed to environmental factors because the gene pool cannot possibly have changed appreciably over the time period involved. The environmental effects are the result of the increase in the complexity of the modern world and of better nutrition and pre- and postnatal care.[12]

Any genetic advantage may not be overly large, but individuals born with a genetic advantage are likely to enjoy an environmental advantage as well (bright children tend to have bright parents). This double advantage sets a child on a trajectory in which there is constant interplay between his or her innate ability and an environment conducive to its development. Dickens and Flynn[13] call this a *multiplier effect*. Children who show an interest in learning will please their intellectually prone parents, who will encourage and reward such behavior. In the school environment, teachers will also note and encourage the child's intellectual gifts. It is this constant interplay of innate ability and an encouraging environment that magnifies small genetic advantages into large advantages over time. Genes and environments are matched in the opposite direction also. Individuals lacking the initial genetic push toward scholarly endeavors will find themselves in environments indifferent (or even hostile) to intellectual pursuits and on a downward spiral with respect to the development of their intellectual abilities. Thus, a small initial genetic disadvantage may be amplified into a large disadvantage over time.

The IQ-Crime Connection

A number of studies find an IQ gap between offenders and nonoffenders of between 9 and 14 points, and reviews of the IQ-crime relationship find it to be robust.[14,15] There are methodological problems that tend to give the impression that IQ is less strongly related to crime and delinquency than it actually is. Simple comparisons of average IQ levels of offenders and the average IQ of the general population may underestimate the effects of IQ because the population average includes offenders as well as nonoffenders and individuals with such low IQs that they are largely incapable of committing crimes. Thus, the difference in average IQ between offenders and intellectually normally functioning nonoffenders must be greater than the 8 to 10 points usually reported.[16]

Another problem is that boys who limit their offending to their teenage years and commit only minor delinquent acts are lumped together with boys who will continue to seriously and frequently offend into adulthood. Simple arithmetic tells us that pooling these two groups hides the magnitude of IQ differences between nonoffenders and serious offenders if the latter have lower IQs than the former. Casual and less serious offenders differ from nonoffenders by about 1 point, while serious persistent offenders differ from nonoffenders by about 17 points.[17]

Intellectual Imbalance

Intellectual imbalance refers to a significant difference between verbal and performance IQ scores. IQ scores are typically given in terms of a *full-scale* score, obtained by averaging the scores on *verbal* (VIQ) and *performance* (PIQ) IQ subscales. Most people have VIQ and PIQ scores that closely match, with a population average of 100 on each subscale. People who have either VIQ or PIQ subscale scores 12 or more points greater than the other (VIQ > PIQ or PIQ > VIQ) are considered intellectually imbalanced. Offender populations are almost always found to have significantly lower VIQ scores, but not lower PIQ scores, than nonoffenders. As Miller remarks, "This PIQ>VIQ relationship was found across studies, despite variations in age, sex, race, setting, and form of the Wechsler [IQ] scale administered, as well as in differences in criteria for delinquency."[18]

Averaged across a number of studies, VIQ > PIQ boys are underrepresented in delinquent populations by a factor of about 2.6, and PIQ > VIQ boys are overrepresented by a factor of about 2.2.[19] A VIQ > PIQ profile appears to be a major predictor of prosocial behavior, especially among adults, given the finding that only 0.9% of 1,792 prison inmates had a VIQ > PIQ profile compared to 18% of the general male population, a ratio of 20:1.[20] The research on intellectual imbalance provides another example of how the role of IQ in understanding criminal behavior may be underestimated if we rely solely on full-scale IQ.

Explaining the IQ-Offending Relationship

There are a number of different routes by which IQ may be related to offending. Perhaps high-IQ people are just as likely to break the law as low-IQ people, but only the less intelligent get caught. If this is the case, low IQ is related to criminal offending only insofar as it leads to a greater probability of detection. This argument is known as the **differential detection hypothesis.** A test of this hypothesis, based on a large birth cohort, found no support for it.[21] Subjects were asked to self-report delinquent activity, which was compared with official police records. This provided three distinct groups: (1) self-reported delinquents with a police record, (2) self-reported delinquents with no police record, and (3) nondelinquents, as assessed both by self-reports and police records. Comparing IQ scores among the groups, it was found that the full-scale, verbal, and performance IQ means of Groups 1 and 2 did not significantly differ from one another, meaning that undetected delinquents were no brighter than their less fortunate detected peers. Both groups had significantly lower full-scale and VIQ means, but not lower PIQ means, than nondelinquents.

Another argument is that crime rates fluctuate greatly while IQ averages do not. If crime rises irrespective of IQ changes, something other than IQ must be responsible for the rise. This is true; low IQ is simply a risk factor differentially expressed under different social conditions. A generation or two ago, when most families were intact, when there was a higher level of moral conformity, and when entry into the workforce demanded less academic preparation, people with relatively low IQs were more insulated from crime by social control mechanisms. Social conditions are different today, and low-IQ individuals are less insulated from crime. This is an example of individuals with different risk factors crossing the crime threshold boundary according to shifting social conditions (see Figure 1.3).

Others argue that the link between IQ and criminality simply reflects the links between SES, IQ, and criminality—that is, low SES causes low IQ *and* crime, and thus the IQ-criminality relationship is simply a consequence of the SES-criminality relationship. SES does affect the relative contributions of genes and environments, but when SES is completely controlled by examining the relationship between IQ and crime *within* families, we find that criminal siblings average 10 IQ points lower than their noncriminal full siblings.[22]

IQ and School Performance

The most usual explanation is that low IQ leads to antisocial behavior via poor school performance.[23] That is, low IQ sets individuals on a trajectory, beginning with poor school performance, which results in a number of negative interactions with other people in the school environment, leading them to drop out of school and associate with delinquent peers. The notion that IQ influences offending via its influences on school performance has much to commend it. Ellis and Walsh's review[24] of 158 studies linking IQ to criminal and delinquent behavior found that 89% based on official statistics and 77.7% based on self-reports found a significant link. On the other hand, all 46 studies exploring the link between grade point average (GPA) and antisocial behavior did so. Actual performance measures of academic achievement such as GPA are thus probably better predictors of antisocial behavior than IQ. Academic achievement is a measure of intelligence plus many other personal and situational characteristics, such as conscientious study habits and supportive parents.

Finally, it would be a mistake to regard IQ as an indicator of social worth rather than as representing a limited set of cognitive traits. High-IQ miscreants can do much more damage than their low-IQ counterparts due to the greater deviousness made possible by high IQ. The IQs of Nazi war criminals remind us not to confuse IQ with worth. Herman Goring, Franz von Papen, and Albert Speer had IQ scores of 138, 134, and 128, respectively.[25] We have no record of Hitler's IQ, but he has been repeatedly described as an evil genius.[26] Many serial killers such as Ted Bundy (124) and Edward Kemper (136) score high on IQ as well.[27]

FOCUS ON . . .

The Impact of High and Low IQ on Life Outcomes

IQ is related to a wide range of life outcomes that are themselves related to criminal and antisocial behavior such as poverty, lack of education, and unemployment. The data presented below come from 12,686 White males and females in the National Longitudinal Study of Youth (NLSY). This study began in 1979, when subjects were 14 to 17 years old; the data were collected in 1989, when the subjects were 24 to 27 years old. The bottom 20% on IQ had scores of 87 and below; the top 20% had scores 113 and above. Note the large ratios between the two groups on all outcomes. For instance, 31 low-IQ subjects were ever interviewed in jail or prison for every 1 high-IQ subject ever interviewed in jail or prison. Low IQ thus affects many areas of life that increase the probability of offending.

(Continued)

(Continued)

IQ Level

Social Behavior	Bottom 20% (%)	Top 20% (%)	Ratio
Dropped out of high school	66	2	33.0:1
Living below poverty level	48	5	9.6:1
Unemployed entire previous year[a]	64	4	16.0:1
Ever interviewed in jail or prison	62	2	31.0:1
Chronic welfare recipient	57	2	28.5:1
Had child out of wedlock[b]	52	3	17.3:1

SOURCE: NLSY data taken from various chapters in Herrnstein, R., & Murray, C. (1994). *The bell curve: Intelligence and class structure in American life*. New York: Free Press.

a. Males only.
b. Females only.

⊠ The Role of Temperament

It is obvious that low intelligence alone cannot explain criminal behavior. Most individuals with a below-average IQ do not commit crimes, and many people with an above-average IQ do. Environmental factors presumably outside the individual's control are extremely important, of course, but we are not concerned with such factors in this chapter. Rather, we want to look at what other personal factors are considered important for understanding criminal behavior by psychologically inclined criminologists.

According to many of the early psychological positivists, criminal behavior is the result of the interaction of low intelligence and a particular kind of temperament: A "feebleminded" person with weak impulses and a quiet temperament may never stoop to crime unless duped by others or forced by necessity to do so, but an excitable and impulsive person of low intelligence "is almost sure to turn in the direction of criminality."[28] As we have seen, IQ and temperament are given prominent roles as factors influencing how a person copes with strain, and thus how insulated he or she is from criminal behavior, in Robert Agnew's general strain theory.[29,30] Temperament and IQ are thus spilling over from psychological theories into theories considered primarily sociological.

Temperament is an individual characteristic identifiable as early as infancy that constitutes a habitual mode of emotionally responding to stimuli. Temperamental components include *mood* (happy/sad), *sociability* (introverted/extraverted), *activity level* (high/low), *reactivity* (calm/excitable), and *affect* (warm/cold), among others. These various components make it easy or difficult for others to like us and to get along with us. Temperamental differences are largely a function of different genetic predispositions in nervous system functioning governing physiological arousal patterns.[31] The genetic underpinning of temperament ensures that it will be reasonably stable across the life course, although environmental input can strengthen or weaken innate propensities. Different temperamental components emerge at different junctures as arousal systems are fine-tuned by experience.[32]

Temperamental differences in children make them variably responsive to socialization. Some children are easy to socialize; others are difficult. A child's unresponsiveness to socialization is made worse by the fact that the temperaments of parents and children are usually similar; that is, warm, happy, and easygoing children tend to have warm, happy, and easygoing parents, and cold, melancholic, and difficult children tend to have parents who share those same traits. Children with difficult temperaments tend to have parents who are poor disciplinarians, irritable, impatient, and unstable, just the opposite of what is required to adequately socialize difficult children. Temperamentally difficult children are thus typically (but not always) saddled with both a genetic and an environmental liability.[33,34]

Children who throw temper tantrums, react negatively to new situations and people, and who reject warm overtures from others may adversely affect the quality of parent-infant interactions regardless of their parents' temperaments, thus leading to poor parent-child attachment and all the negative consequences that result. Numerous studies have shown that parents, teachers, and peers respond to children with disinhibited and irritable temperaments negatively, and such children find acceptance only in association with others with similar dispositions.[35]

Personality: In the Beginning Was Freud

Personality is the relatively enduring, distinctive, integrated, and functional set of psychological characteristics that result from people's temperaments interacting with their cultural and developmental experiences. There are many different components of personality that psychologists call *traits,* some of which are associated with the probability of committing antisocial acts.

No discussion of personality can proceed without acknowledging the role of the father of psychoanalysis and the grandfather of positivist psychology, Austrian physician Sigmund Freud. Freud offered a broad, sweeping theory of personality, and although he wrote little about crime, his ideas stimulated many criminologists.

Early psychological theories never labored over what mental processes might intervene between the assumed cause and criminal behavior. Just *how does* "feeblemindedness," "atavism," or any other assumed cause influence persons to commit criminal acts? If all people are hedonistic, why do only some commit crimes? If criminals are feebleminded, why don't all low-IQ people commit crimes? The psychological answer to such questions is that individuals possess different personalities, and these different personalities lead them to respond differently to identical situations.

According to Freud, the basic human personality is a composite of three interacting components, each having separate purposes: the *id, ego,* and *superego.* The *id* is the biological raw material of our temperament and personality; it represents our drives and instincts for acquiring life-sustaining necessities and life's pleasures. Like a spoiled child, the id demands instant gratification of its desires and cares not whether the means used to satisfy them are appropriate or injurious to self or to others. The id obeys the *pleasure principle,* but since it lacks the ability to engage in the hedonistic calculus, it is often dangerous to itself. The selfish, immoral, uncaring, antisocial id is the only aspect of the personality we are born with, so in a Freudian sense, we might say that we are all Lombroso's "born criminals."

The *ego* and the *superego* are formed from the raw material of the id in the process of socialization. With the correct moral training, energy from the id is appropriated to form the ego, or the aspect of the personality we think of as "me" or "I." The ego obeys the *reality principle;* it realizes that the desires and demands of the id, although necessary, must be satisfied in socially appropriate ways if one is to avoid negative consequences. It is the ego that performs the hedonistic calculus; it does not deny the pleasure principle but simply adjusts it to the demands of reality. Freud analogized the interaction of the ego and the id in terms of a rider and a horse. The horse (the id) supplies the raw locomotive power, while the rider (the ego) supplies the goals and the direction.[36]

The superego strives for the ideal and is thus just as irrational as the id. It represents all the moral and social prescriptions and proscriptions (the "dos and don'ts") internalized by the person during the process of socialization and may be summed up as the human conscience. The superego tries to suppress all the normal urges arising from the id by generating guilt because many urges have been defined as wrong or sinful. It is the ego's function to sort out the conflict between the antisocial demands of the id and the overly conformist demands of the censorious superego.

The normal personality is one in which the ego is successful in working out compromises between its irrational partners. An abnormal personality results when either the id or the superego overwhelms the ego, resulting in psychic energy being drained from the weaker components to strengthen the stronger component. If the id is "in command" of the personality, the result is a conscienceless and impulsive individual who seeks to satisfy personal needs regardless of the expense to others.

Personality Traits Associated With Criminal Behavior

We will now briefly examine personality traits that have consistently been associated with criminal behavior. Keep in mind that all of these traits are the result of different kinds of temperaments meeting different kinds of developmental experiences and that they are continuous, not dichotomous. That is, people differ only on the strength of these traits; they are not characteristics that some people possess and others do not.

Impulsiveness refers to people's varying tendencies to act on matters without giving much thought to the consequences (not looking before you leap). Impulsiveness varies from person to person according to the circumstances involved, and one can be impulsive without ever crossing the noncrime/crime threshold. Nevertheless, impulsive individuals are found more often among criminal populations than among the population at large. Not surprisingly, impulsive people also have elevated probabilities of being diagnosed with psychopathy.[37] A review of 80 studies examining the relationship between impulsivity and criminal behavior found that 78 of them (97.5%) were positive, and the remaining 2 were nonsignificant.[38] Although impulsiveness is a potent risk factor for criminality in its own right, it becomes more potent if negative emotionality is added to the mix.[39]

Negative emotionality (or *negative affect*) is a personality trait that refers to the tendency to experience many situations as aversive and to react to them with irritation and anger more readily than with positive affective states.[40] Caspi and his colleagues[41] contend that criminality is defined (at a minimum) by both low self-control (which they call *low constraint*) and negative emotionality. Constraint is inversely related to negative emotionality; that is, people who are low on constraint tend to be high on negative emotionality. Individuals high on negative emotionality but also high on self-control are able to hold their anger and irritability in check.

▲ **Photo 7.1**   Depicted is the couch used by a large number of Freud's patients in Vienna. Freud theorized that early childhood events and traumas in particular caused his patients to exhibit emotional and personality problems as adults. By putting them through the process of psychoanalysis and recovering these early childhood memories, Freud hoped to restore his patients.

In the absence of strong social controls, people high on negative affect and low on self-control usually cannot.

Negative emotionality is strongly related to self-reported and officially recorded criminality "across countries, genders, races, and methods."[42] Caspi and his colleagues state that low levels of a brain chemical called serotonin (more about this chemical in the next chapter) underlie both high levels of negative emotionality and low levels of constraint (high impulsivity). They also claim that low serotonin may represent a constitutional predisposition for a personality characterized by high levels of negative affect and low levels of constraint, and this generates vulnerability to criminal behavior. Although some individuals may be at genetic risk for high negative emotionality and low self-control, both traits are influenced by environmental factors, particularly by family dynamics that include emotional and physical abuse and neglect.[43]

Sensation seeking refers to the active desire for novel, varied, and extreme sensations and experiences, often to the point of taking physical and social risks to obtain them.[44] Sensation seekers skydive, bungee jump, race cars, and go on adventure safaris if they are well off; if they are not, their kicks might just be criminal in nature. Sensation seekers with normal to above-normal IQs and who are properly socialized will probably want to work as firefighters, police officers, or any other job that provides physical activity, variety, and excitement. Low-IQ and unsocialized individuals do not have those legitimate options available to them. Ellis and Walsh's review[45] found that 58 of 59 (98.4%) studies reported a statistically significant relationship between sensation seeking and various kinds of antisocial behavior.

The more impulsive a person is, the more sensation seeking he or she tends to be. A Canadian study found that measures of impulsivity and sensation seeking in male preschoolers are the best available predictors of delinquency at age 13.[46] A longitudinal study using both physiological and psychological measures of sensation seeking that looked at high and low sensation seekers who were and were not seriously involved in delinquency found some interesting results.[47] High sensation-seeking delinquents were significantly more impulsive, had significantly lower IQs, and were lower in socioeconomic status than high sensation-seeking control subjects. Among the low sensation seekers, only low IQ differentiated delinquents (average IQ = 85.5) from nondelinquents (average IQ = 102.8). However, 33% of the serious delinquents were low sensation seekers—low sensation seekers can be seriously involved in delinquency, too. The fact that 54% of the nondelinquents were high sensation seekers shows that high sensation seeking requires the addition of other factors (high impulsivity, low IQ, and low SES in this study) to result in serious delinquent behavior. Criminal behavior is almost always the result of a constellation of risk factors rather than of any one single factor.

Conscientiousness is a primary trait composed of several secondary traits such as well organized, disciplined, scrupulous, responsible, and reliable at one pole and disorganized, careless, unreliable, irresponsible, and unscrupulous at the other. It is easy to see from this list how conscientiousness could be directly related to crime, but it might be a more useful discussion to tie it to Merton's anomie theory. Recall that Merton tells us that all Americans are exhorted to strive for the American Dream, but some of us are denied access to attaining it legitimately. Isn't it just as possible that those who do not pursue the dream legitimately cannot do so because they lack the requisite qualities for occupational success? Vold, Bernard, and Snipes thought so when they wrote, "It is not merely a matter of talented individuals confronted with inferior schools and discriminatory hiring practices. Rather, a good deal of research indicates that many delinquents and criminals are untalented individuals who cannot compete effectively in complex industrial societies."[48]

Conscientiousness is highly associated with upward social mobility, and employers obviously favor high levels of conscientiousness in their employees.[49] In a study that followed subjects from early childhood to retirement, Judge and his colleagues[50] found that conscientiousness predicted occupational success better than any other factor they examined. In other words, it may be that persons with certain kinds of temperament do not develop the personal qualities needed to apply themselves to the long and arduous task of achieving financial success legitimately and, as a consequence, may attempt to obtain it illegitimately through crime. A review of the genetic literature indicated that genes account for an average of about 66% of the difference in conscientiousness among individuals.[51]

Empathy is the emotional and cognitive ability to understand the feelings and distress of others as if they were your own—to be able to "walk in another's shoes." The emotional component of empathy allows you to "feel" the other person's pain, and the cognitive component allows you to understand that person's pain and why he or she is feeling it. Individuals differ in their ability to empathize, with some people shouldering the pains of the world at one end of the continuum and others caring less about even their closest relatives at the other. Most criminals will fall closer to the latter than to the former for obvious reasons—you are less likely to victimize someone if you have a tendency to feel and understand what the consequences may be for them. A number of studies show that offenders are significantly less empathetic than nonoffenders.[52] Baron and Byrne[53] cite evidence that genetic factors account for about one third of the difference among people in empathy.

Altruism can be thought of as the action component of empathy; if you feel empathy for someone, you will probably feel motivated to take some sort of action to alleviate that person's distress if you are able. Altruism may thus be defined as an *active* concern for the well-being of others, and in many ways, it is a synonym for prosocial behavior. Thus we have another continuum, with extremely altruistic individuals at one end and extremely selfish people at the other. There are no prizes for guessing on which side of the line most criminals will fall. In fact, the lack of empathy and altruism is considered one of the most salient characteristics of psychopaths, the worst of the worst among criminals.[54] A review of 24 studies of those traits found that 23 of them were statistically significant in the predicted direction; that is, the lower the level of empathy/altruism, the more antisocial the behavior.[55]

Moral reasoning is another personal characteristic that psychologists find to be linked to antisocial behavior. Studies have repeatedly shown that a strong relationship exists between moral reasoning and the ability and/or inclination to empathize with and come to the aid of others.[56] Not all immoral behavior is criminal, of course, but they do have certain things in common. Both forms of behavior violate social expectations and ignore the obligations we all have toward one another.

To measure moral reasoning, subjects are read a series of scenarios containing moral dilemmas to which they are asked to verbally respond. Most of these dilemmas involve the ability to put oneself in another's shoes (empathy) and to devise a course of action to help that person (altruism). Ten studies assessing the link between moral reasoning and empathy and altruism revealed that the higher the empathy and altruism, the greater the moral reasoning.[57] The same reviewers also found that 16 of 17 studies found IQ to be positively related to moral reasoning level.[58] Moral reasoning is thus a function of empathy and altruism, as well as knowledge and understanding of, and agreement with, culturally defined standards of right and proper behavior. Consciousness of one's own moral standards and conduct, as well as the feeling of obligation to live up to those standards, is the stuff of conscience.

Classical Conditioning and Conscience

Ever since human groups first established rules, people have been tempted to violate them. Many of us have been prevented from doing so by fear of punishment and by the bite of our consciences. **Conscience** is a complex mix of emotional and cognitive mechanisms that we acquire by internalizing the moral rules of our social group in the ongoing socialization process. Those of us with strong consciences will feel guilt, shame, stress, and anxiety when we violate, or even contemplate violating, these rules. In other words, we have emotional reactions that vary from person to person based on innate physiological arousal patterns and how they have been molded by experience.

Differences in the emotional component of conscience are observed as early as 18 months, long before children are able to cognitively reflect on their behavior as morally right or wrong. These differences reflect variation in **autonomic nervous system** arousal patterns.[59] The autonomic nervous system (ANS) is part of the body's *peripheral nervous system* (as opposed to the central nervous system [CNS], which consists of the brain and spinal column). The ANS carries out the basic housekeeping functions of the body by funneling messages from the environment to the various internal organs so that they may keep the organism in a state of biological balance. Most of these messages elicit only reflexive responses (adjusting pupil size, signaling digestive enzymes, shivering or sweating in response to temperature, etc.) and never reach our conscious awareness. Messages that influence ANS functioning and that do reach our awareness are important for the acquisition of conscience.

To understand why, we have to briefly describe what psychologists call **classical conditioning.** Classical conditioning is a form of learning that is more visceral (felt in the internal organs) than cognitive. If you have taken Psych 101, you will have read about Russian psychologist Ivan Pavlov's experiment in which he conditioned dogs to salivate at the sound of a bell. Salivation is a natural ANS response to the expectation of food; food is an unconditioned stimulus to an unconditioned (innate, hardwired) salivation response. A bell has no intrinsic properties that would make dogs salivate at its sound, and thus the bell is a neutral stimulus with respect to salivation. Because Pavlov consistently paired the sound of the bell with food, the dogs learned (were conditioned) to associate the sound of the bell with food, and the sound itself became enough to make them salivate even when not paired with food. Figure 7.1 illustrates this process.

It is necessary to briefly differentiate classical from operant conditioning. Operant conditioning is active (it depends on the actor's behavior), is cognitive in nature, and forms an association between a person's behavior and its consequences. Classical conditioning is mostly passive (it depends more on the level of ANS arousal than on anything the actor does) and is visceral in nature; it simply forms an association between two paired stimuli.

We have all been conditioned in various ways to respond viscerally to neutral stimuli via their association with unconditional stimuli. As children, how did you feel when the school bell rang for recess or when the bells announced the arrival of the ice cream truck? In both cases, we expect that you responded with some pleasure, not because you love the sound of bells, but because they signaled something that you did love.

It is by way of these kinds of associations that we develop the "gut-level" emotions of shame, guilt, and embarrassment that make up the emotional ("feeling") superstructure of our consciences. These emotions are the *social* or *secondary* emotions that are retrofitted to the same neurophysiological machinery that drives the hardwired *primary* emotions of fear, anger, sadness, and joy that are common to all animals. After the primary emotions are elaborated and refined by cognition during socialization, we fear the pain of punishment and the shame of rejection when we transgress and welcome the joy of acceptance and affection when we behave well.

Children must learn which behaviors are acceptable and which are not (the knowledge part of our conscience). If John is spanked and sent to his room for sticking pins in the cat, he will experience a variety of unpleasant physiological events. The degree to which these emotions affect John will depend on the severity of the reprimand interacting with the responsiveness of his ANS.[60] Assuming John's ANS is adequately responsive to discipline, he will eventually name similar behaviors that generate the same ANS responses as bad or wrong, and he will feel guilt if he even contemplates doing them. If John refrains from such behavior in the future, it is not because he has rationally calculated the cost/benefit ratio involved but

Figure 7.1	Illustrating Classical Conditioning

BEFORE CONDITIONING	BEFORE CONDITIONING
Unconditioned → Unconditioned Stimulus Response (food) (salivation)	Neutral → No Response Stimulus (bell)
Unconditioned stimulus produces an unconditioned response.	Neutral stimulus produces no response.
CONDITIONING PROCESS	AFTER CONDITIONING
Unconditioned → Unconditioned Stimulus (food) Response + Neutral (salivation) Stimulus (bell)	Conditioned → Conditioned Stimulus Response (bell) (salivation)
Unconditioned stimulus paired with neutral stimulus produces an unconditioned response.	Neutral stimulus becomes a conditioned stimulus that now produces a conditioned response.

rather because his internal response system (the emotional component of his conscience) strongly discourages it by generating unpleasant feelings.

People differ greatly in the responsiveness of their ANSs. Individuals with a readily aroused ANS are easily socialized—they learn their moral lessons well. They do so because ANS arousal ("butterflies in the stomach") is subjectively experienced as fear and anxiety. We soon learn that when we behave ourselves, we do not incur the wrath of our socializers, and fear and anxiety do not appear. A hyperresponsive ANS (one that is easily aroused and generates high levels of fear and anxiety) is a protective factor against antisocial behavior. Studies have shown that males with *hyper*arousable ANSs living in environments that put them at high risk for antisocial behavior were less involved with antisocial behavior than males living in low-risk communities with *hypo*arousable (slow to arouse) ANSs.[61] This constitutes yet another example of how personal characteristics interact with environments to mold behavior.

Individuals with relatively unresponsive ANSs are difficult to condition (to socialize) and are relatively fearless. These individuals experience little fear, shame, guilt, or embarrassment when they transgress, even when discovered and punished, and thus have no built-in visceral restraints against further transgressions. Various measures of ANS underarousal (electroencephalographic activity, resting heart rate, and skin conductance) in childhood enable researchers to correctly classify about three quarters of their subjects as "criminals" or "noncriminals" in adulthood.[62] In other words, across a wide variety of subjects and settings, it is consistently found that antisocial individuals evidence relatively unresponsive ANSs, and the reason for this is that hypoarousable ANSs do not allow for adequate conditioning of the social emotions. Having knowledge of what is right or wrong without that knowledge being paired with emotional arousal is rather like knowing the words to a song but not the music.

☒ Modern Psychosocial Theories

Arousal Theory

Arousal theory (sometimes called *suboptimal arousal theory*) focuses on central nervous system (brain) arousal rather than peripheral system (ANS) arousal. The theory is rooted in the commonsense observation that people vary greatly in their sensitivities and preferences for environmental stimulation and on established psychological findings that different levels of physiological arousal correlate with different personality and behavioral patterns. In identical environmental situations, some people are underaroused and other people are overaroused, and both levels are psychologically uncomfortable. Arousal levels are normally (bell curve shaped) distributed with very few people being extremely under- or overaroused, with most people being optimally aroused under the normal range of environmental conditions (neither too constant nor too varied). What is an optimal level of environmental stimulation for most of us will be stressful for some and boring for others. If you've ever taken your grandpa to a punk rock concert or he has taken you to a chamber music recital, you'll know what we mean.

The regulator of neurological arousal (sleep, wakefulness, attention) is the *reticular activating system* (RAS). The RAS is a little finger-size bundle of brain cells situated at the top of the spinal cord and can be thought of as the brain's filter system determining what incoming stimuli the higher brain centers will pay attention to. Some individuals possess an RAS that is highly sensitive to incoming stimuli (more information is taken in and processed), and others possess an RAS that is unusually insensitive. We call the former *augmenters* and the latter *reducers*. There is no conscious attempt to augment or reduce incoming stimuli; as is the reactivity of the ANS, augmentation or reduction is solely a function of differential physiology. RAS augmenters tend to be the people with hyperactive ANSs, and reducers tend to be people with hypoactive ANSs. Underarousal of the ANS is associated with fearlessness, and underarousal of the RAS is associated with sensation seeking. We can readily appreciate that sensation seeking and fearlessness are correlated since sensation seeking is aided by fearlessness.[63]

Augmenters prefer more constancy than variety in their world and seek to tone down environmental stimuli that most people find to be "just right." Such people quickly learn to avoid engaging in behavior that raises the intensity of stimuli to levels they find unpleasant and are rarely found in criminal populations. Reducers are easily bored with "just right" levels of stimulation and continually seek to boost stimuli to what are for them more comfortable levels. They also require a high level of punishing stimuli before learning to avoid the behavior that provokes it. According to arousal theory, the latter are the individuals who are unusually prone to criminal behavior. A number of studies have shown that relative to the general population, criminals, especially those with the most serious records, are chronically underaroused, as determined by electroencephalography (EEG) brainwave patterns, resting heart rate, and skin conductance.[64]

EEG brainwaves reflect the electrical "chatter" of billions of our brain cells. Clinicians recognize four bands to classify EEG brainwaves: *alpha, beta, theta,* and *delta*. Beta waves followed by alpha waves are the most rapid, and they signal when a person is alert and focused. Theta waves are emitted when the person is in a drowsy mental state, and delta waves are the slowest of them all and signal deep sleep. Most studies (about 75%) show that EEG readouts of criminals reveal that their brains are less often in the alert and focused range than are the brains of people in general.[65]

Resting heart rate and skin conductivity are more measures of ANS than RAS arousal. Resting heart rates measured during childhood has emerged as a very good predictor of delinquent and criminal behavior later in life.[66] A review of 23 studies found that slow resting heart rate is significantly related to delinquent/criminal behavior in all studies.[67]

Skin conductivity is measured by a meter attached to various parts of the body that records electrical responses to sweat. Sweat contains high levels of salt, and salt water is an excellent electrical conductor. In temperature-controlled environments, increased sweating (even though the sweating may not be enough for the person to notice that he or she is sweating) occurs in response emotions. This is the basis of polygraph testing. The polygrapher asks suspects questions that evoke emotions such as guilt, shame, or embarrassment that are detected (or rather skin conductivity is detected) by the monitor. Chronic criminals tend to have lower levels of these emotions as well as lower levels of ANS arousal, so they are least likely to show sweat responses to threatening questions. Thus, low skin conductivity and criminal behavior are expected to be related. Seventeen of 19 studies (89.5%) did find this relationship, with the remaining 2 (both for childhood conduct disorder) not significant.[68]

▲ **Photo 7.2**   Arousal theory states that human beings have varying internal "thermostats," which explains why people differ on the levels of arousal or stimulation they need to feel comfortable. Those already set on "high" may attempt to avoid noise, activity, or crowds. On the other hand, those who crave stimulation might climb mountains, go to loud parties, or watch slasher movies.

◀ **Photo 7.3**   The so-called lie detector (or polygraph) is composed of several physiological measures of emotional stress. Here a subject is demonstrating one of the most common stress indicators used in polygraphs—known as the Galvanic skin response (GSR). The GSR monitors sweating of the palms and fingertips, as shown in this photograph. Several studies have shown that offenders exhibit less sweating when under stress than do nonoffenders. This is considered evidence in favor of the theory that criminals tend to be suboptimally aroused.

Wilson and Herrnstein's Net Advantage Theory

James Q. Wilson and Richard Herrnstein's **net advantage theory**[69] is based on reinforcement and conditioning principles and adds rational choice and individual differences into the theoretical mix. *Net advantage* refers to the fact that any choice we make rests on the cognitive and emotional calculations we make before deciding on a course of action relating to the possible positive and negative consequences that may result from choices such as what to do when we see unlocked cars with keys in the ignition. If our calculations of the costs and benefits of a given behavior point to a net advantage for us, we will make the choice in favor of engaging in that behavior; if our calculations point to a negative outcome, we will not.

Unlike differential association and social learning theories, this theory goes a step beyond to identify individual differences in the likelihood of understanding and appreciating the long-term consequences of a chosen course of behavior. According to Wilson and Herrnstein, there is little difference among people in their ability to appreciate the immediate short-term positive or negative consequences of their behavior, but there is a difference in the ability to appreciate long-term consequences because people differ in the tendency to discount the negative consequences of their behavior to themselves and to others. People who discount negative consequences have a greater probability of antisocial behavior being experienced as reinforcing.

Net advantage theory is anchored in the constrained vision camp in its assumption that crime is inherently rewarding to human beings (because it usually means getting something for little or no cost) and that most of us would commit crime if we were not externally and internally restrained from doing so. External restraints consist of the kinds of social controls present because of the social bonds we enjoy with others, as well as the more formal controls represented by law enforcement. Individuals with a tendency to discount the negative consequences of their behavior do so because their inhibitions are weak, and their inhibitions are weak because they are impulsive, have learning difficulties, are present rather than future oriented, and lack the bite of conscience. Such people are reinforced by the immediate rewards of criminal activity rather than the more distant rewards of a noncriminal lifestyle. They also fail to take into account the punitive consequences of their behavior, and/or they do not fear those consequences.

Net advantage theory adds valuable insights into Akers's theory because it takes into account how the learning process (what is reinforcing and what is not and what serves as discriminative stimuli) is influenced by individual traits and characteristics. Another interesting fact about this theory is that it takes into consideration both classical and operant conditioning, as well as almost every personality trait and characteristic that psychologists have identified as risk factors for criminal behavior. The theory is illustrated diagrammatically in Figure 7.2.

Glen Walters's Lifestyle Theory

Lifestyle theory was formulated by Glen Walters,[70] a senior psychologist at the U.S. Penitentiary at Leavenworth, Kansas, a position that has provided him with a great deal of insight into the criminal mind. The term *lifestyle* implies that Walters believes that criminal behavior is a general criminal pattern of life. Lifestyle criminals are characterized by

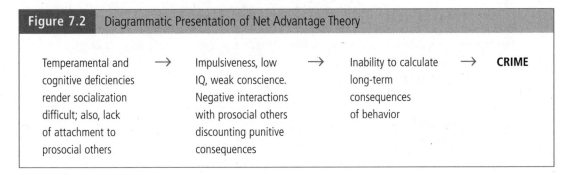

Figure 7.2 Diagrammatic Presentation of Net Advantage Theory

Temperamental and cognitive deficiencies render socialization difficult; also, lack of attachment to prosocial others $\rightarrow$ Impulsiveness, low IQ, weak conscience. Negative interactions with prosocial others discounting punitive consequences $\rightarrow$ Inability to calculate long-term consequences of behavior $\rightarrow$ **CRIME**

irresponsibility, impulsiveness, self-indulgence, negative interpersonal relationships, and the chronic willingness to violate society's rules. Walters views criminal behavior as a choice conditioned by the interaction of individual traits and environmental circumstances. The main distinguishing features of Walters's theory are (1) it is a theory that concentrates on criminal thinking patterns rather than on how those patterns developed, and (2) it was designed more to guide counselors in their efforts to change criminal thinking rather than to add to the body of criminological knowledge.

Lifestyle theory contains three key concepts: *conditions, choice,* and *cognition.* A criminal lifestyle is the result of *choices* criminals make, although Walters acknowledges that these choices are made "within the limits established by our early and current biologic/environmental *conditions.*"[71] Thus, various biological and environmental conditions lay the foundation of future choices. In common with the long psychological tradition, Walters stresses impulsiveness and low IQ as the most important choice biasing conditions at the individual level and attachment to significant others as the most important environmental condition.

The third concept, *cognition,* refers to cognitive styles that people develop as a consequence of their biological/environmental conditions and the pattern of the choices they have made in response to them. According to this theory, lifestyle criminals display eight major cognitive features or **thinking errors** that make them what they are.[72,73] Examples of criminal thinking errors are *cutoff* (the ability to discount the suffering of their victims), *entitlement* (the world owes them a living), *power orientation* (viewing the world in terms of weakness and strength), *cognitive indolence* (orientation to the present; concrete in thinking), and *discontinuity* (the inability to integrate thinking patterns). According to Walters, little can be done to change criminal behavior until criminals change their pattern of thinking.

These thinking errors lead to four interrelated behavioral patterns or styles that almost guarantee criminality: *rule breaking, interpersonal intrusiveness* (intruding into the lives of others when not wanted), *self-indulgence,* and *irresponsibility.* Criminality is thus the result of irrational behavior patterns (all of which are antisocial but not necessarily criminal). These behavioral patterns are the result of faulty thinking patterns, which arise from the consequences (reward and punishment) of choices in early life, which are themselves influenced by biological and early environmental conditions.

Note the similarity with Sutherland's differential association theory: *Cognition* (how we think) *causes conduct.* The major difference between the two theories is that lifestyle theory stresses that cognitions are caused by individual choices, which are in turn caused by early biological and environmental conditions that are assumed to be detrimental to the individual's moral development. Differential association theory explicitly denies biological variables and considers environmental (cultural) conditions to be simply different rather than deviant. Likewise, Sutherland does not invest his "definitions favorable" with any evaluative or moral connotations, whereas Walters does, calling them "thinking errors." Figure 7.3 illustrates lifestyle theory.

Figure 7.3	Diagrammatic Presentation of Criminal Lifestyle Theory		
Conditions	**Choices**	**Cognition**	**Behavior**
Early biological and environmental experiences and personal traits. $\rightarrow$	Choices resulting from conditions. $\rightarrow$	Cognitive style formed by choices; "thinking errors." $\rightarrow$	Pattern of behavior: $\rightarrow$ **CRIME** rule breaking, impulsiveness, egocentrism, etc.

✉ The Antisocial Personalities

Depending on whom you ask, *antisocial personality disorder, psychopathy,* and *sociopathy* are terms describing the same constellation of traits or separate concepts with fuzzy boundaries. Psychopathic behavior was once referred to as *manie sans delire* (insanity without delirium), meaning that while psychopaths are "insane," they could function normally, if not morally, in society. Some researchers in this area believe that there is a subset of psychopaths (so-called primary psychopaths) whose behavior is biological in origin, as well as a more numerous group (secondary psychopaths) whose behavior is the result of genetics and adverse environments.[74] Primary psychopaths constitute a small group of individuals whose numbers remain fairly stable across cultures and time periods and may come from any social class, family type, or racial or ethnic group. The number of secondary psychopaths, on the other hand, fluctuates with environmental conditions; they come primarily from the lower social classes, from dysfunctional families, and from disadvantaged groups.[75]

Other researchers view **psychopathy** as a continuous construct rather than as a dichotomy. In other words, psychopathy is not something one is or isn't; rather, it is a name that we have applied to the most serious and chronic criminal offenders. Researchers do have cutoff points on scales measuring psychopathy (discussed below) that put someone in the "primary" psychopath category and others in a "borderline" or "secondary" category, but these cutoff points are rather arbitrary. Other researchers devise all sorts of names for subtypes of psychopaths based on small differences among them, but we will continue to view psychopathy as a continuous variable here.

Antisocial Personality Disorder (APD)

Antisocial personality disorder (APD) is described in the fourth edition of the *Diagnostic and Statistical Manual of Mental Disorders* (*DSM-IV*) by the American Psychiatric Association (APA) as "a pervasive pattern of disregard for, and violation of, the rights of others that begins in childhood or early adolescence and continues into adulthood."[76] APD is an umbrella term applied to the various antisocial types mentioned above. It is a clinical/legal label that psychiatrists apply to someone if he or she consistently shows three or more of the following behavioral patterns since reaching the age of 15:

1. failure to conform to social norms with respect to lawful behaviors indicated by repeatedly performing acts that are grounds for arrest;

2. deceitfulness, as indicated by repeated lying, use of aliases, or conning others for personal profit or pleasure;

3. impulsivity or failing to plan ahead;

4. irritability and aggressiveness, as indicated by repeated physical fights or assaults;

5. reckless disregard for safety of self or others;

6. consistent irresponsibility, as indicated by repeated failure to sustain consistent work behavior or honor financial obligations;

7. lack of remorse, as indicated by being indifferent to or rationalizing having hurt, mistreated, or stolen from another.

The individual must also be at least 18 years old, must have been diagnosed with conduct disorder prior to age 15, and his or her antisocial behavior must not occur exclusively during a schizophrenic or manic episode.

Astute readers may have noted that you would have to search a long time to find any criminal that *didn't* consistently evidence three or more of these criteria, although the requirement that the person must have been diagnosed with conduct disorder as a child prevents APD from being synonymous with criminal behavior. Having to be at least 18 years old is also problematic because it leaves out thousands of teenage murderers, rapists, and robbers (the age criterion is more for legal than clinical reasons). Finally, the diagnosis is made purely on the basis of behavior. Criminologists generally want to define individuals according to criteria that are independent of their behavior and then determine in what ways those so defined differ from individuals not so defined.

The most widely used measure of psychopathy is the Psychopathy Checklist—Revised (PCL-R), which was devised by Robert Hare, the leading expert in psychopathy in the world today.[77] With this checklist, clinicians rate patients as either having or not having each of 20 behavior/personality traits such as those listed earlier. The ratings for each trait are made on a 3-point scale, with 0 meaning subjects lack the particular trait, 1 meaning that they have it to some degree, and 2 meaning that they have it to an extreme degree. Persons who receive a total score of 30 or higher are given a diagnosis of psychopathy, and people scoring in the 20s receive a diagnosis of "borderline psychopathy."[78] It is thus convenient to refer to the former as primary psychopaths and the latter as secondary psychopaths while at the same time remembering that we are actually referring to a continuum ranging from 0 to 40.

What Causes Psychopathy?

Recall that primary psychopaths are said constitute a relatively stable portion of any population and can be from any social/environmental background. They can be successful entrepreneurs, CEOs, lawyers, cult leaders, or politicians who, while they may exploit and manipulate others, may never commit any violation of the penal code. The stability of the prevalence of psychopathy over time, as well as its existence across class lines, has led to the virtual dismissal of social or developmental causal explanations of primary psychopathy by psychopathy researchers.[79–81] As Robert Hare remarks, "I can find no convincing evidence that psychopathy is the direct result of early social or environmental factors."[82]

Cesare Lombroso probably had psychopaths in mind with his "morally insane" born criminals (i.e., those "who appear normal in physique and intelligence but cannot distinguish good from evil").[83] Researchers who believed that primary psychopaths are "born that way" have come full circle to evolutionary explanations, but with the advantage of more than a century's worth of research behind us, our understanding of evolutionary mechanisms is much more sophisticated than Lombroso's. We no longer talk of criminals as evolutionary throwbacks whose behavior is "unnatural." Rather, many scientists view psychopaths as behaving exactly as they were designed by natural selection to behave.[84,85] This does not mean that their behavior is acceptable or that we cannot consider it *morally* pathological and punish it accordingly; the naturalistic fallacy warns us that the fact that something is natural (i.e., designed by nature) does not make it acceptable or morally right.

Psychopathy and the Social Emotions

If psychopathy is a strategy forged by natural selection, there must be a number of identifiable markers that distinguish psychopaths from the rest of us. One of the most consistent physiological findings about psychopaths is their inability to "tie" the brain's cognitive and emotional networks together, which translates into the inability (or, at least, the greatly reduced ability) to experience the social emotions of shame, embarrassment, guilt, empathy, and love.[86,87] The social emotions are distinguished from the *primary* emotions such as anger, joy, and happiness, all of which psychopaths experience as strongly as other people. The social emotions have evolved as integral parts of our social lives that serve to provide clues about the kinds of relationships (cooperative vs. uncooperative) that we are likely to have with others.[88] Social emotions focus and modify brain activity in ways that lead us to choose certain responses over others. Feelings of guilt, shame, embarrassment, and empathy prevent us from doing things that might be to our immediate advantage (steal, lie, cheat) but would cost us in reputation and future positive relationships if discovered. Thus, the positive and negative feelings we experience when we survey the possible consequences of our actions keep most of us on the straight and narrow most of the time. The weaker we feel them, the more likely we are to exploit others; the stronger we feel them, the less likely we are to exploit others. This is the emotional component of our consciences coming into play.

Emotional responses are typically studied using EEG data reflecting the brain's arousal levels in response to the person's thoughts and emotions. The example presented in Figure 7.4

Figure 7.4	Comparison of Electroencephalographs of Psychopaths and Nonpsychopaths on Emotionally Neutral and Emotionally Laden Words

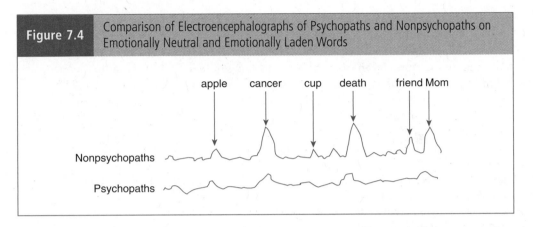

is adapted from an experiment conducted by Robert Hare and shown in an educational video titled *The Psychopath*. Hare presented psychopaths and nonpsychopaths with a list of emotionally neutral and emotionally laden words while they were hooked up to an EEG. When nonpsychopaths see an emotionally neutral word (e.g., *apple, cup*) we see that their waves show a small spike indicating that they have recognized the word and visualized an apple or cup. When presented with emotionally laden words (*cancer, death, Mom*), there is a much higher spike indicating that they have recognized the word and made associations pairing the cognition with emotions (the reason for the higher spike). When psychopaths are presented with those same emotional words, they tend to process them in ways similar to processing *apple* or *cup*. That is, they chew over the word, recognize it, and pass on to the next word without involving the emotions. This and hundreds of other studies using many different methods have revealed over and over that the defining characteristic of psychopaths is their inability to "tie" the brain's cognitive and emotional networks together.[89]

Psychopaths can thus pursue cold-blooded selfish interests without being distracted by the emotional signals of conscience. Let us not forget that defining traits of chronic offenders evolved not for the purposes of carjacking, stock market fraud, arson, or any other act we call criminal but for successful mating effort: Cads and crooks are woven from the same evolutionary cloth.

Environmental Considerations

We have to go beyond individual characteristics, however, to understand the full range of the psychopathy spectrum. Lykken colorfully describes secondary psychopaths (what he calls sociopaths) as "feral creatures, undomesticated predators, stowaways on our communal voyage who have never signed the Social Contract."[90] According to Mealey, these folks are individuals who employ a "cheating strategy not as clearly tied to genotype (as is that of the primary psychopath)."[91] Lykken holds a similar view, stating that their behavior is "traceable to deviant learning histories interacting, perhaps, with deviant genetic predilections."[92]

A number of researchers claim that one of the biggest factors contributing to psychopathy is poor parenting, and they see increasing levels of poor parenting as a function of the increase in the number of children being born out of wedlock.[93,94] However, the relationship between unwed motherhood and criminal behavior cannot be simply traced to family structure (single parent versus intact home). According to a study of 1,524 sibling pairs from different family structures taken from the National Longitudinal Survey of Youth, Cleveland and his colleagues[95] found that genetic traits associated with antisocial behavior select individuals into different family structures, and these traits are then passed on to offspring. It was found that, on average, unmarried mothers have a tendency to follow an impulsive and risky lifestyle and to have a number of antisocial personality traits, be more promiscuous, and have a below-average IQ. Families headed by single mothers with children fathered by different men were found to be the family type that put offspring most at risk for antisocial behavior. A two-parent family with full siblings placed offspring at lowest risk. It was also found that genetic differences accounted for 94% of the difference on an antisocial subscale between the most at-risk group (single parent, half siblings) and the least at-risk group (two parents, full siblings). Similar findings and conclusions from a large-scale British behavior genetic study have been reported.[95a]

According to David Rowe, the important factor in understanding the relationship between out-of-wedlock birth and criminal behavior is the genetically transmitted traits of fathers. He emphasizes the traits of the "feckless boyfriends" who abandon their pregnant girl-friends rather than the traits of mothers. The traits of these males include "strong hypermasculinity, early sexuality, absence of pair bonding capacity, and . . . other hallmarks of 'psychopaths'—are all passed on genetically to offspring."[96] Studies of fathers of illegitimate children have found that they are more than twice as likely to be involved in delinquent and criminal behavior as nonfathers in the same neighborhoods.

Given the many and severe deficits faced by many children born out of wedlock, it is no surprise that Gottfredson and Hirschi concluded that "delaying pregnancy among unmarried girls would probably do more to affect the long-term crime rates than all the criminal justice programs combined."[97] This view is shared by the Office of Juvenile Justice and Delinquency Prevention (OJJDP), which claims that delaying pregnancy until 20 to 21 years of age would lead to a 30% to 40% reduction in child abuse and neglect and could potentially save $4 billion in law enforcement and corrections costs because offspring of teenage mothers are 2.7 times more likely than offspring of adult mothers to be incarcerated.

✄ Evaluation of the Psychosocial Perspective

Psychologists are always happy to point out that whatever social conditions may contribute to criminal behavior, they must influence individuals before they affect crime. Social factors matter and may well "prepare the scene" for crimes, but real flesh-and-blood people commit them. The psychosocial perspective points out that individuals are differentially vulnerable to the criminogenic forces existing in the environment because they differ on the personality traits. We have already quoted Gwynn Nettler's descriptive phrase "The heat that melts the butter hardens the egg"; what psychologists do is largely take the heat (the environment) for granted and look for how the butter and eggs of our differing constitutions relate to the heat. In other words, psychologists focus on the horizontal line of Figure 1.3, whereas sociologists focus on the vertical line.

By titling this chapter *psychosocial* approaches rather than *psychological,* we reveal our bias against strictly separating social and psychological perspectives. To the extent that a theory specifically addresses both social conditions conducive to crimes and psychological preparedness on the part of individuals to commit them, we can only call the theory sociological or psychological artificially by noting where the primary emphasis is placed. Social process theories such as self-control theory and social learning theory are only labeled sociological because the theories' originators are sociologists. Sociologist Gregg Barak even insists that all social process theories are psychological theories "because of the way in which human nature interacts with desire, translated as appetites, and aversions, motives and emotions."[98]

One of the most pervasive criticisms of psychological theories is that they focus on "defective" or "abnormal" personalities.[99] This may have been true of older psychoanalytic perspectives, but psychologists maintain that our personalities consist of normal variation in traits we all possess and that they are the products of the interaction of our temperaments and our developmental experiences. If, by "abnormal," critics mean *statistical* abnormality (below or above the average on a variety of traits), however, then by definition, all theories of criminality focus on abnormality.

Psychosocial theories do have their problems and limitations, of course, such as paying insufficient attention to the social context of offending. Just as some people are at risk for offending in almost any environment, some environments are such that almost everyone is at risk for offending. In addition, very few psychologists specialize in criminology, so fewer studies are available to enable us to assess the validity of their theories.

As noted already, the relationship between IQ and criminal behavior has always been contentious among sociologically trained criminologists. Adler, Mueller, and Laufer[100] voice the familiar criticism that IQ tests are culturally biased despite the findings of the National Academy of Sciences and the APA's Task Force on Intelligence cited earlier. They also cite the "debate" over whether genetics or the environment "determines" intelligence. This implies that an either/or answer is possible, but since scientists involved in the study of intelligence are unanimous that all traits (human or otherwise) are *necessarily* the result of both genes and environment, it is a monumental nondebate.[101] The multiplier effect outlined by Dickens and Flynn earlier says much about the importance of the environment to intelligence levels.

- ◆ Net advantage theory is essentially an extremely broadened version of social learning and rational choice theories. The very broadness of the theory makes it difficult to test and, therefore, to evaluate. Nevertheless, it has all the strengths and weaknesses of both social learning and rational choice theories.
- ◆ Lifestyle theory is more thoroughly psychological than the other theories outlined in this chapter because it focuses squarely on how criminals think, with only passing reference to why they do so. This constitutes a weakness in terms of criminological theorizing, but the theory's strength lies in its policy implications for treating offenders.

The section on antisocial personalities is about *types* of offenders rather than theories of crime. Both syndromes have been extensively studied, and there appears to be an emerging consensus about the causes of these syndromes, especially of psychopathy. These syndromes clearly exist, and the only weakness we have to contend with at the present time is

Table 7.1	Summarizing Psychosocial Theories		
Theory	**Key Concepts**	**Strengths**	**Weaknesses**
Arousal	Because of differing ANS and RAS physiology, people differ in arousal levels they consider optimal. Underarousal under normal conditions poses an elevated risk of criminal behavior because it signals fearlessness, boredom, and poor prospects for socialization.	Allows researchers to use "harder" assessment tools such as EEGs to measure traits. Ties behavior to physiology. Explains why individuals in "good" environments commit crimes and why individuals in "bad" ones do not.	May be too individualistic for some criminologists. Puts all the "blame" on the individual's physiology. Ignores environmental effects.
Net advantage	Crime is inherently rewarding. People make rational choices to commit crimes, but there are individual differences in the ability to calculate the long-term consequences of their behavior because of temperamental and cognitive deficiencies.	Combines many sociological, psychological, and biological concepts into a coherent theory and adds rational choice.	May be too complex because it integrates too many concepts. Focus on internal constraints against crime ignores social inducements and constraints.
Lifestyle	Crime is a patterned way of life (a lifestyle) rather than simply a behavior. Crime is caused by errors in thinking, which results from choices previously made, which are the results of early negative biological and environmental conditions.	Primarily a theory useful for correctional counselors dealing with their clients. Shows how criminals think and how these errors in thinking lead them into criminal behavior.	Concentrates only on thinking errors. Does talk about why they exist but pays scant attention to these reasons.
Antisocial personality	There are a small, stable group of individuals who may be biologically obligated to behave antisocially (psychopaths) and a larger group who behave similarly but whose numbers grow or subside with changing environmental conditions.	Concentrates on the scariest and most persistent criminals in our midst. Uses theories from evolutionary biology and "hard" brain imaging and physiological measures to identify psychopaths.	There is often a confusion of terms, and arguments about the nature of psychopathy abound. Offers no policy recommendations.

technological rather than theoretical—that is, how can we better measure these syndromes? The physiological and neurological measures we have now do differentiate between psychopaths and nonpsychopaths, but the antisocial personality needs a more precise method of diagnosis because the dangers of false-positive definitions (defining someone as a psychopath who is not) and false-negative definitions (defining someone as nonpsychopathic who is) are obvious.

⊠ Policy and Prevention: Implications of Psychosocial Theories

The best anticrime policies are doubtless environmental since they are aimed at reducing the prevalence of crime in the population. But because such policies have had little, no, or even adverse effects on the crime problem in the past,[102] perhaps it is wise at present to focus our efforts on those who are already committing crimes rather than on conditions external to them. A variety of such programs aimed at rehabilitating offenders operate under the assumption that they are rational beings who are, however, plagued by ignorance of the long-term negative consequences of their offending behavior.[103]

How well do rehabilitative programs work? There is wide disagreement on this issue and even about what the criteria are for success. Reviews of studies with strict criteria for determining success find recidivism rates lowered by between 8% and 10%.[104] A major review of a large number of studies found lowered recidivism rates in the 10% to 20% range.[105] A nationwide evaluation of state and local corrections programs identified what is known about successful and unsuccessful programs. Effective programs use multiple treatment components; are structured and focus on developing social, academic, and employment skills; use directive cognitive-behavioral counseling methods; and provide substantial and meaningful contact between treatment personnel and offenders.[106]

Glen Walters's theory deals with what correctional psychologists call "stinkin' thinkin'"; these psychologists see their task as guiding offenders to realize how destructive that thinking has been in their lives. The counselor sees offenders' problems as resulting from illogical and negative thinking about experiences that they reiterate in self-defeating monologs. Empathizing with the offenders' definition of reality (or granting it "appreciative relevance" in postmodernist terms) serves to reinforce faulty thinking and is counterproductive. The counselor's task is to strip away self-damaging ideas (such as techniques of neutralization) and beliefs by attacking them directly and challenging offenders to reinterpret their experiences in a growth-enhancing fashion. The cognitive-behavioral counselor operates from the assumption that no matter how well offenders come to understand the remote origins of their behavior, if they are unable to make the vital link between those origins and current behavioral problems, it is of no avail.

Psychopaths are poor candidates for treatment. Robert Hare states that because they are largely incapable of the empathy, warmth, and sincerity needed to develop an effective treatment relationship, treatment often makes them worse because they learn how to better push other people's buttons.[107] Old age seems to be the only "cure" for the behaviors associated with this syndrome.

SUMMARY

Psychological criminology focuses largely on intelligence and temperament as the most important correlates of criminal behavior. Low intelligence, as measured by IQ tests, is thought to be linked to crime because people with low IQ are said to lack the ability to correctly calculate the costs and benefits of committing crimes, and temperament is linked to crime largely in terms of impulsiveness. Intelligence is the product of both genes and environment. Genes appear to be more important in explaining IQ differences among people in high-SES environments, and environmental factors appear to be more important in low-SES environments.

The role of IQ in understanding criminal behavior has been underestimated for at least three reasons. (1) The average population IQ includes offenders and individuals with such low IQs that they are largely incapable of committing crimes, and thus the difference between offenders and nonoffenders on IQ is most likely greater than usually reported. (2) Serious and persistent offenders are lumped together with minor and temporary offenders, and although minor and temporary offenders do not significantly differ from nonoffenders on IQ, there is a large gap between serious and persistent offenders and nonoffenders. (3) Comparisons are almost always made of full-scale IQ averages rather than of the separate VIQ and PIQ subscales. Criminals do not typically differ from noncriminals on PIQ, but they do on VIQ.

Various explanations of why IQ is related to criminal behavior were discussed. Although the differential detection hypothesis has intuitive appeal, studies indicated that detected and undetected delinquents do not differ significantly on IQ. We dismissed the criticism of the role of IQ based on fluctuating crime rates (crime rates change rapidly, but IQs do not) as a theoretical misinterpretation of how individual factors interact with environmental conditions by raising or lowering individual thresholds for crossing the criminal behavior threshold. The criticism that the IQ-crime relationship simply reflects the SES-crime relationship was countered by providing evidence that criminal siblings within the same families (thus completely controlling for SES effects) average about 10 IQ points lower than noncriminal siblings. We concluded that IQ is probably related to crime and delinquency through its effect on poor school performance.

Temperament constitutes a person's habitual way of emotionally responding to stimuli. The kind of temperament we inherit makes us variably responsive to socialization, although patient and caring parents can modify a difficult temperament. Our personalities are formed from the joint raw material of temperament and developmental processes. A number of personality traits are associated with the probability of engaging in antisocial behavior, particularly being high on impulsiveness, negative emotionality, and sensation seeking, as well as being low on conscientiousness, empathy, altruism, and moral reasoning.

Classical conditioning via the autonomic nervous system is the emotional component of conscience and precedes the cognitive component. Behavior can be thought of as the outcome of both classical and operant conditioning, although people will differ greatly in their behavior depending on their innate temperaments, their developmental and other environmental experiences, and their personality traits that emerge from these processes.

Net advantage theory is based on conditioning principles and adds individual differences to account for the outcome of conditioning. People are differentially responsive to rewards and punishment, and they differ in what they find to be rewarding or punishing. People who are impulsive, have learning difficulties, and have not developed an adequate conscience focus on immediate rewards from crime without concern for the hurt they cause others while discounting punishment for themselves.

Lifestyle theory views criminal behavior as a lifestyle rather than just another form of behavior. The lifestyle begins with biological and environmental conditions that lead criminals to make certain choices, which in turn lead to criminal cognitions. The theory focuses on these cognitions, or "thinking errors." Thinking errors lead criminals into behavioral patterns that virtually guarantee criminality. The theory was devised primarily to assist correctional counselors to change criminal thinking patterns.

Psychopaths and sociopaths are at the extreme end of the antisocial personality continuum and appear to constitute a stable proportion of any population. Most researchers regard the psychopathy syndrome as biological in origin, whereas sociopaths are formed both by genetics and the environment, with the environment playing the larger role. Many hundreds of studies have shown that psychopaths have limited ability to tie the rational and emotional components of thinking together.

Some researchers assert that the primary cause of psychopathy is inept parenting by single-parent mothers. This puts children at a greatly increased risk for growing up in poor neighborhoods and for abuse and neglect. Other theorists point to the fact that children born to such mothers also receive genes advantageous to antisocial behavior from both parents in addition to an environment conducive to its expression.

On Your Own

Log on to the web-based student study site at http://www.sagepub.com/criminologystudy for more information about the vignettes and materials presented in this chapter, suggestions for activities, study aids such as review quizzes, and research recommendations including journal article links and questions related to this chapter.

EXERCISES AND DISCUSSION QUESTIONS

1. Write a two-page paper applying Dickens and Flynn's multiplier effect to basketball prowess. How did this exercise help you to more fully understand the principle of the gene/environment correlation as it is applied to intellectual prowess?

2. Discuss how the reverse of the multiplier effect may affect children born and raised in poor, disorganized neighborhoods.

3. Since psychologists have long identified different temperaments as something that makes it easy or difficult to socialize children, why do you think Gottfredson and Hirschi ignored it in their self-control theory?

4. Honestly rate yourself from 1 to 10 on the traits positively associated with antisocial behavior (impulsiveness, negative emotionality, and sensation seeking) and then on the traits negatively related with antisocial behavior (conscientiousness, empathy, and altruism). Subtract the latter from the former. If the difference is a positive number greater than 10 or a negative number less than–10, does this little exercise correspond to your actual behavior?

5. Look up *cognitive behavioral therapy* in a book or on the Internet and report how a therapist using this method would approach offenders using Walters's "stinkin' thinkin'."

6. What is the primary difference between psychopaths and sociopaths according to modern researchers?

7. Explain how low arousal of the autonomic nervous system and the reticular activating system plays a role in psychopathy.

8. Go to http://www.crimelibrary.com/criminal mind/psychology/robert_hare/ index.html, where you will find an excellent profile of Dr. Robert Hare, the world's foremost expert on psychopaths. What does he say about the possibility of change in psychopaths?

KEY WORDS

Altruism
Antisocial personality
    disorder
Arousal theory
Autonomic nervous system
Classical conditioning
Conscience
Conscientiousness

Differential detection
    hypothesis
Empathy
Flynn effect
Impulsiveness
Intellectual imbalance
Lifestyle theory
Negative emotionality

Net advantage theory
Personality
Psychopathy
Sensation seeking
Temperament
Thinking errors

REFERENCES

1. Dugdale, R. (1895). *"The Jukes": A study in crime, pauperism, disease, and heredity.* New York: Putnam. (Original work published 1877)

2. Goddard, H. (1931). *The Kallikak family: A study in the heredity of feeble-mindedness.* New York: Macmillan. (Original work published 1912)

3. Goddard (1912/1931).

4. Matarazzo, J. (1976). *Weschler's measurement and appraisal of adult intelligence.* Baltimore: Williams & Wilkins. (Quote on p. 79)

5. Gordon, R. (1997). Everyday life as an intelligence test: Effects of intelligence and intelligence context. *Intelligence, 24,* 203–320.

6. Seligman, D. (1992). *A question of intelligence: The IQ debate in America.* New York: Birch Lane.

7. Snyderman, M., & Rothman, S. (1988). *The IQ controversy, the media and public policy.* New Brunswick, NJ: Transaction.

8. Neisser, U., Boodoo, G., Bouchard, T., Boykin, A., Brody, N., Ceci, S., Halpern, D., Loehlin, J., Perloff, R., Sternberg, R., & Urbina, S. (1995). *Intelligence: Knowns and unknowns: Report of a task force established by the board of scientific affairs of the American Psychological Association.* Washington, DC: American Psychological Association.

9. Grigorenko, E. (2000). Heritability and intelligence. In R. Sternberg (Ed.), *Handbook of intelligence* (pp. 53–91). Cambridge, UK: Cambridge University Press.

10. Neisser et al. (1995).

11. Flynn, J. (1987). Massive gains in 14 nations: What IQ tests really measure. *Psychological Bulletin, 101,* 171–191.

12. Dickens, W., & Flynn, J. (2001). Heritability estimates versus large environmental effects: The IQ paradox resolved. *Psychological Review, 108,* 346–349.

13. Dickens and Flynn (2001).

14. Lynam, D., Moffitt, T., & Stouthamer-Loeber, M. (1993). Explaining the relation between IQ and

delinquency: Class, race, test motivation, school failure, or self control? *Journal of Abnormal Psychology, 102,* 187–196.

15. Ellis, L., & Walsh, A. (2003). Crime, delinquency and intelligence: A review of the worldwide literature. In H. Nyborg (Ed.), *The scientific study of general intelligence: A tribute to Arthur Jensen* (pp. 343–365). Amsterdam: Pergamon.

16. Herrnstein, R. (1989). *Biology and crime* (National Institute of Justice Crime File, NCJ 97216). Washington, DC: U.S. Department of Justice.

17. Moffitt, T. (1993). Adolescent-limited and life-course-persistent antisocial behavior: A developmental taxonomy. *Psychological Review, 100,* 674–701.

18. Miller, L. (1987). Neuropsychology of the aggressive psychopath: An integrative review. *Aggressive Behavior, 13,* 119–140. (Quote on p. 120)

19. Walsh, A. (2003). Intelligence and antisocial behavior. In A. Walsh & L. Ellis (Eds.), *Biosocial criminology: Challenging environmentalism's supremacy* (pp. 105–124). Hauppauge, NY: Nova Science.

20. Barnett, R., Zimmer, L., & McCormack, J. (1989). P>V sign and personality profiles. *Journal of Correctional and Social Psychiatry, 35,* 18–20.

21. Moffitt, T., & Silva, P. (1988). IQ and delinquency: A test of the differential detection hypothesis. *Journal of Abnormal Psychology, 97,* 330–333.

22. Jensen, A. (1998). *The g factor: The science of mental ability.* Westport, CT: Praeger.

23. Ward, D., & Tittle, C. (1994). IQ and delinquency: A test of two competing explanations. *Journal of Quantitative Criminology, 10,* 189–212.

24. Ellis, L., & Walsh, A. (2000). *Criminology: A global perspective.* Boston: Allyn & Bacon.

25. Seligman (1992).

26. Blain, M. (1988). Fighting words: What can we learn from Hitler's hyperbole? *Symbolic Interactionism, 11,* 257–276.

27. Sears, D. (1991). *To kill again: The motivation and development of serial murder.* Wilmington, DE: Scholarly Resources.

28. Goddard, H. (1979). Feeble-mindedness. In J. Jacoby (Ed.), *Classics of criminology* (pp. 96–102). Oak Park, IL: Moore Publishing. (Original work published 1914; quote on p. 101)

29. Agnew, R. (1992). Foundations for a general strain theory of crime and delinquency. *Criminology, 30,* 47–87.

30. Agnew, R. (1997). Stability and change in crime over the lifecourse: A strain theory explanation. In T. Thornberry (Ed.), *Developmental theories of crime and delinquency* (pp. 101–132). New Brunswick, NJ: Transaction.

31. Rothbart, M., & Ahadi, S. (1994). Temperament and the development of personality. *Journal of Abnormal Psychology, 101,* 55–66.

32. Rothbart, M., Ahadi, A., & Evans, D. (2000). Temperament and personality: Origins and outcomes. *Journal of Personality and Social Psychology, 78,* 122–135.

33. Lykken, D. (1995). *The antisocial personalities.* Hillsdale, NJ: Lawrence Erlbaum.

34. Moffitt, T. (1996). The neuropsychology of conduct disorder. In P. Cordella & L. Siegel (Eds.), *Readings in contemporary criminological theory* (pp. 85–106). Boston: Northeastern University Press.

35. Caspi, A. (2000). The child is the father of the man: Personality continuities from childhood to adulthood. *Journal of Personality and Social Psychology, 78,* 158–172.

36. Freud, S. (1976). The ego and the id. In J. Strachey (Ed. & Trans.), *The complete psychological works of Sigmund Freud* (V01.19, pp. 5–30). New York: Norton. (Original work published 1923)

37. Sher, K., & Trull, T. (1994). Personality and disinhibitory psychopathology: Alcoholism and antisocial personality disorder. *Journal of Abnormal Psychology, 103,* 92–102.

38. Ellis and Walsh (2000).

39. Agnew, R. (2005). *Why do criminals offend? A general theory of crime and delinquency.* Los Angeles: Roxbury.

40. McGue, M., Bacon, S., & Lykken, D. (1993). Personality stability and change in early adulthood: A behavioral genetic analysis. *Developmental Psychology, 29,* 96–109.

41. Caspi, A., Moffitt, T., Silva, P., Stouthamer-Loeber, M., Krueger, R., & Schmutte, P. (1994). Are some people crime-prone? Replications of the personality-crime relationship across countries, genders, races, and methods. *Criminology, 32,* 163–194.

42. Caspi et al. (1994).

43. Caspi et al. (1994).

44. Zuckerman, M. (1990). The psychophysiology of sensation-seeking. *Journal of Personality, 58,* 314–345.

45. Ellis and Walsh (2000).

46. Tremblay, R., R. Pihl, Viaro, F., & Dobkin, P. (1994). Predicting early onset of male antisocial behavior from preschool behavior. *Archives of General Psychiatry, 51,* 732–739.

47. Gatzke-Kopp, L., Raine, A., Loeber, R., Stouthamer-Loeber, M., & Steinhauer, S. (2002). Serious delinquent behavior, sensation seeking, and electrodermal arousal. *Journal of Abnormal Child Psychology, 30,* 477–486.

48. Vold, G., Bernard, T., & Snipes, J. (1998). *Theoretical criminology* (4th ed.). New York: Oxford University Press. (Quote on p. 177)

49. Kyl-Heku, L., & Buss, D. (1996). Tactics as units of analysis in personality psychology: An illustration using tactics of hierarchy negotiation. *Personality and Individual Differences, 21,* 497–517.

50. Judge, T., Higgins, C., Thoresen, C., & Barrick, M. (1999). The big five personality traits, general mental ability, and career success across the lifespan. *Personnel Psychology, 52,* 621–652.

51. Lynn, R. (1996). *Dysgenics: Genetic deterioration in modern populations.* Westport, CT: Greenwood.

52. Covell, C., & Scalora, M. (2002). Empathetic deficits in sexual offenders: An integration of affective, social, and cognitive constructs. *Aggression and Violent Behavior, 37,* 251–270.

53. Baron, R., & Byrne, D. (2000). *Social psychology* (9th ed.). Boston: Allyn & Bacon.

54. Fishbein, D. (2001). *Biobehavioral perspectives in criminology.* Belmont, CA: Wadsworth.

55. Ellis and Walsh (2000).

56. Campbell, R., & Christopher, J. (1996). Moral development theory: A critique of its Kantian presuppositions. *Developmental Review, 16,* 1–47.

57. Ellis and Walsh (2000).

58. Ellis and Walsh (2000).

59. Kochanska, M. (1991). Socialization and temperament in the development of guilt and conscience. *Child Development, 62,* 1379–1392.

60. Pinel, J. (2000). *Biopsychology* (4th ed.). Boston: Allyn & Bacon.

61. Brennan, P., Raine, A., Schulsinger, F., Kirkegaard-Sorenen, L., Knop, J., Hutchings, B., Rosenberg, R., & Mednick, S. (1997). Psychophysiological protective factors for male subjects at high risk for criminal behavior. *American Journal of Psychiatry, 154,* 853–855.

62. Raine, A. (1997). Antisocial behavior and psychophysiology: A biosocial perspective and a prefrontal dysfunction hypothesis. In D. Stoff, J. Breiling, & J. Maser (Eds.), *Handbook of antisocial behavior* (pp. 289–304). New York: John Wiley.

63. Raine (1997).

64. Ellis, L. (2003). Genes, criminality, and the evolutionary neuroandrogenic theory. In A. Walsh & L. Ellis (Eds.), *Biosocial criminology: Challenging environmentalism's supremacy* (pp. 12–34). Hauppauge, NY: Nova Science.

65. Ellis and Walsh (2000).

66. Raine (1997).

67. Ellis and Walsh (2000).

68. Ellis and Walsh (2000).

69. Wilson, J. Q., & Herrnstein, R. (1985). *Crime and human nature.* New York: Simon & Schuster.

70. Walters, G. (1990). *The criminal lifestyle.* Newbury Park, CA: Sage.

71. Walters, G., & White, T. (1989, April). The thinking criminal: A cognitive model of lifestyle criminality. *Criminal Justice Research Bulletin.* (Quote on p. 3)

72. Walters (1990).

73. Walters and White (1989).

74. Mealey, L. (1995). The sociobiology of sociopathy: An integrated evolutionary model. *Behavioral and Brain Sciences, 18,* 523–559.

75. Lykken (1995).

76. American Psychiatric Association (APA). (1994). *Diagnostic and statistical manual of mental disorders* (4th ed.). Washington, DC: Author. (Quote on p. 645)

77. Bartol, C. (2002). *Criminal behavior: A psychosocial approach* (6th ed.). Upper Saddle River, NJ: Prentice Hall.

78. Harris, G., Rice, M., & Quinsey, V. (1994). Psychopathy as a taxon: Evidence that psychopaths are a discrete class. *Journal of Consulting and Clinical Psychology, 62,* 387–397.

79. Kinner, S. (2003). Psychopathy as an adaptation: Implications for society and social policy. In R. Bloom & N. Dass (Eds.), *Evolutionary psychology and violence* (pp. 57–81). Westport, CT: Praeger.

80. Pitchford, I. (2001). The origins of violence: Is psychopathy and adaptation? *Human Nature Review, 1,* 28–38.

81. Mealey (1995).

82. Hare, R. (1993). *Without conscience: The disturbing world of the psychopaths among us.* New York: Pocket Books.

83. Gibson, M. (2002). *Born to crime: Cesare Lombroso and the origins of biological criminology.* Westport, CT: Praeger. (Quote on p. 25)

84. Harris, G., Skilling, T., & Rice, M. (2001). The construct of psychopathy. In M. Tonry (Ed.), *Crime and justice: A review of research* (pp. 197–264). Chicago: University of Chicago Press.

85. Quinsey, V. (2002). Evolutionary theory and criminal behavior. *Legal and Criminological Psychology, 7,* 1–14.

86. Scarpa, A., & Raine, A. (2003). The psychophysiology of antisocial behavior: Interactions with environmental experiences. In A. Walsh & L. Ellis (Eds.), *Biosocial criminology: Challenging environmentalism's supremacy* (pp. 209–226). Hauppauge, NY: Nova Science.

87. Weibe, R. (2004). Psychopathy and sexual coercion: A Darwinian analysis. *Counseling and Clinical Psychology Journal, 1,* 23–41.

88. Mealey (1995).

89. Scarpa and Raine (2003).

90. Lykken (1995, p. 22).

91. Mealey (1995, p. 539).

92. Lykken (1995, p. 23).

93. Lykken (1995).

94. Rowe, D. (2002). *Biology and crime.* Los Angeles: Roxbury.

95. Cleveland, H., Wiebe, R., van den Oord, E., & Rowe, D. (2000). Behavior problems among children from different family structures: The influence of genetic self-selection. *Child Development, 71,* 733–751.

95a. Moffitt, T., & The E-Risk Study Team (2002). Teenage mothers in contemporary Britain. *Journal of Child Psychology and Psychiatry, 43,* 1–16.

96. Rowe, D. (1997). Are parents to blame? A look at *The antisocial personalities. Psychological Inquiry, 8,* 251–260. (Quote on p. 257)

97. Gottfredson, M., & Hirschi, T. (1997). National crime control policies. In M. Fisch (Ed.), *Criminology 97/98* (pp. 27–33). Guilford, CT: Dushkin. (Quote on p. 33)

98. Barak, G. (1998). *Integrating criminologies.* Boston: Allyn & Bacon. (Quote on p. 128)

99. Akers, R. (1994). *Criminological theories: Introduction and evaluation.* Los Angeles: Roxbury.

100. Adler, F., Mueller, G., & Laufer, W. (2001). *Criminology and the criminal justice system.* Boston: McGraw-Hill.

101. Carey, G. (2003). *Human genetics for the social scientists.* Thousand Oaks, CA: Sage.

102. Rosenbaum, D., Lurigio, A., & Davis, R. (1998). *The prevention of crime: Social and situational strategies.* Belmont, CA: West/Wadsworth.

103. Walsh, A. (2006). *Correctional assessment, casework, and counseling* (4th ed.). Lanham, MD: American Correctional Association.

104. Andrews, D., & Bonta, J. (1998). *The psychology of criminal conduct.* Cincinnati, OH: Anderson.

105. Cullen, F., & Gendreau, P. (2000). Assessing correctional rehabilitation: Policy, practice, and prospects. In *Criminal justice 2000.* Washington, DC: National Institute of Justice.

106. Sherman, L., Gottfredson, D., McKenzie, D., Eck, J., Reuter, P., & Bushway, S. (1997). *Preventing crime: What works, what doesn't, what's promising.* Washington, DC: U.S. Department of Justice.

107. Hare (1993).

CHAPTER 8

BIOSOCIAL APPROACHES

*I*n February 1991, Stephen Mobley walked into a Domino's Pizza store in Georgia to rob it. *After getting the money, Mobley forced store manager John Collins onto his knees and shot him execution style. After committing several other robberies and bragging to friends about Collins's murder, he was apprehended by Atlanta police, charged with aggravated murder, and sentenced to death. In the automatic appeal to the Georgia Supreme Court to get his sentence commuted to life in prison, his primary defense boiled down to claiming that his "genes made me do it." In support of this defense, Mobley's lawyers pointed to a Dutch study of an extended family in which for generations, many of the men had histories of unprovoked violence. The researchers took DNA samples from 24 male members of the family and found that those with violent records had a marker for a mutant or variation of a gene for the manufacture of monoamine oxydase, an enzyme that regulates a lot of different brain chemicals. Mobley's lawyers found a similar pattern of violent behavior and criminal convictions among his male relatives across the generations and requested the court for funds to conduct genetic tests on Mobley to see if he had the same genetic variant.*

The court wisely denied the defense motion. Even if it were found that Mobley had the same genetic variant, it would not show that he lacked the substantial capacity to appreciate the wrongfulness of his acts or to conform to the requirements of the law. Mobley's lawyers were hoping to mitigate his sentence by appealing to a sort of genetic determinism that simply does not exist. As we shall see in this chapter, genes don't "make" us do anything; they simply bias us in one direction rather than another and do differently in different environments. Except in cases of extreme mental disease or defect, we are always legally and morally responsible for our behavior. Cases such as Mobley's underline the urgent need for criminologists to understand the role of genes in human behavior as that role is understood by geneticists.

Because humans have brains, genes, hormones, and an evolutionary history, biosocial criminologists believe that disciplines that study these things provide us with rich new insights into the familiar and exciting ways of discovering things previously overlooked.[1] Biosocial scientists are aware that we cannot explain behavior genetically, evolutionarily, neurologically, or hormonally without understanding the complementary influence of the environment and dismiss naive nature *versus* nurture arguments in favor of nature *via* nurture. *Any* trait, characteristic, or behavior of *any* living thing is *always* the result of biological factors interacting with environmental factors.[2] In many ways, the early positivists were biosocial in approach because they explicitly envisioned biological and environmental interaction. Their ideas and methods were primitive by today's standards, but then, so were the ideas and methods of most sciences in the 19th century. Evolutionary ideas about the behavior of all animals (especially the human animal) were poorly understood; genes were unheard of, and the brain was still a mysterious locked black box.

⊠ Behavior Genetics

Behavior genetics is a branch of genetics that studies the relative contributions of heredity and environment to behavioral and personality characteristics. Human behavioral and personality characteristics are observable and measurable components of a person's **phenotype,** which is the detectable expression of a person's **genotype** interacting with his or her environment. Genes and environments work in tandem to develop any phenotypic trait—height, weight, IQ, impulsiveness, blood sugar levels, blood pressure, and so on—the sum of which constitutes the person.

What Are Genes?

Genes are strands of DNA that code proteins. Although some of the proteins genes produce, such as neurotransmitters and hormones, have a lot to do with how we behave or feel, they do not *cause* us to behave or feel; they simply *facilitate* our behavior and our feelings. Genes produce tendencies or dispositions to respond to the environments in one way rather than in another; they do not code for responses in any deterministic fashion. That is to say, there are no blueprints by which genes construct certain kinds of brains, which in turn produce certain kinds of behavior. There are no genes "for" criminal behavior, but there are genes that lead to particular traits such as low empathy, low IQ, aggression, and impulsiveness that increase the probability of criminal behavior when combined with the right environments.

How Do Behavior Geneticists Do Research on Criminal Behavior?

Behavior geneticists conduct research much like any other behavioral scientist. The big difference is that if they are to discover genetic effects, they must sample pairs of individuals with a known degree of genetic relatedness such as identical (monozygotic—MZ) twin pairs and same-sex fraternal (dizygotic—DZ) twin pairs. In other words, rather than sampling single isolated individuals, they must sample *pairs* of individuals such as twins, adoptee/biological sibling pairs, child/parent pairs, and so forth. Having done this, they can then calculate the central concept of behavior genetics—heritability.

We have previously talked about such and such a percentage of the difference in traits associated with criminal behavior being attributable to genes; calculating heritability coefficients is how geneticists are able to make such statements. **Heritability** (symbolized as h^2) refers to a number ranging between 0 and 1 indicating the extent to which variance in a trait in a *population,* not in an individual, is due to genetic factors. Since any differences (variance) among individuals can only come from two sources—genes or environment—heritability is also a measure of environmental effects ($1—h^2$ = environmental effects). All cognitive, behavioral, and personality traits are heritable to some degree.[3]

Heritability estimates the proportion of variance in a trait attributable to *actualized* genetic potential (what we actually observe in the phenotype); whatever the unactualized potential may be, it cannot be inferred from h^2.[4] It does not set limits on creating new environments that may influence the trait in ways that differ from those of the environment on which it was calculated. Think of identical seeds from prize-winning roses planted (a) in an English garden and (b) in the Nevada desert, and then think about where the full potential of the seeds will be observed. Middle-class environments are like the English garden, and poor environments are like the Nevada desert— environments matter!

Even if $h^2 = 1.0$ for a trait, it does *not* mean that the environment doesn't matter; genes cannot be expressed at all without an environment. High heritability tells us that the *present environment at the present time* accounts for very little variance in the trait; it does not tell what other environments *may* affect variance in the trait. Without both genes and environment, there is no you to think and behave, just as without both hydrogen and oxygen there is no water, and without both height and width, there is no area.

The Twin Method

▲ **Photo 8.1** Former major league baseball player Jose Canseco is sworn in at a U.S. House of Representatives baseball steroids hearing. Canseco presents a fascinating case for biosocial theories. Jose had a fraternal twin brother, Ozzie, who also chose a career in baseball. However, in comparison with Jose's 462 home runs and over 1,400 RBI, Ozzie had only a "cup of coffee" in the major leagues. He came to bat only 65 times over 3 seasons and never hit a home run. Had he been an identical rather than a fraternal twin, might Ozzie have performed more like his brother? After finishing his baseball career, Jose wrote a book (Juiced) in which he admitted using steroids for most of his playing career and claimed that 85% of other player in his era did likewise. Because of his steroid use, many baseball experts predict Jose will never be elected to the baseball Hall of Fame, though his career numbers exceed those of many current hall of fame players.

Behavior geneticists calculate the heritability of human traits by comparing correlations for a trait between MZ and DZ twin pairs. They can do this because MZ twins are genetically identical and because DZ twins, on average, share half of their genes. If genes are an important source of variation in a trait, then it is logical that individuals who are more genetically similar should be more alike on that trait than individuals who are less genetically similar.

As well as sorting out genetic from environmental effects on a trait, behavior genetic studies enable us to examine the effects of environments that people share and those they do not. Just as shared genes make those who share them more alike and nonshared genes make them different, shared environments make people similar, and nonshared environments make them different. Shared environment refers to the environment experienced by children reared in the same family, such as sharing parental socioeconomic status (SES), religion, values, attitudes, family size, and neighborhood. Nonshared environments can also be experienced in the family and be indicated by such variables as gender, birth order, illness, and parental treatment. Nonshared variables outside the family include having different peer groups and teachers; experiencing a different historical period; and any other idiosyncratic experiences.

Some environmental features may be difficult to describe as either shared or nonshared. All children in the family may share the same objective street address, but under the same roof, there are many subjective rooms. Parenting style may not be the same for all siblings, but rather more a function of parents responding to the behavioral style of each child, and thus a nonshared rather than shared feature. Thus, just as there is environmental mediation of genetic effects, there is genetic mediation (e.g., child's temperament mediating parenting style) of environmental effects.

The Adoption Method

The adoption method allows us to hold genes constant to investigate the effect of environments, as well as to hold environments constant to observe the effect of genes. Trait similarities between genetically unrelated children reared together must be entirely a function of their common environment, and any similarities between genetically related children reared in different homes must be a function of their shared genes. This method also allows us to compare trait similarities between adopted children and both their biological and adoptive parents. Adopted children more closely resemble their biological parents than their adopted parents on all measures of personality and cognitive functioning.[5]

Gene-Environment Interaction and Correlation

Gene-environment (G-E) interaction and G-E correlation describe people's active transactions with their environment and are important concepts for us to understand. The concept of the **gene-environment interaction** involves the notion that people are differentially sensitive to identical environmental influences and will thus respond in different ways to them. For instance, a relatively fearless and impulsive child is more likely to seize opportunities to engage in antisocial behavior than is a fearful and constrained child. **Gene-environment correlation** simply means that genotypes and the environments they find themselves in are related.[6] In effect, this means that genetic factors influence complex psychosocial traits by influencing the range of individuals' experiences. The concept thus enables us to conceptualize the indirect way (there is no direct way) that genes help to determine what aspects of the environment will and will not be important to us. There are three types of G-E correlation: passive, reactive, and active.

Passive G/E correlation refers to the association between genotypes and their environments in children's earliest years. The association exists because biological parents provide children with genes for certain traits and an environment favorable for their expression. Children born to intellectually gifted parents, for instance, are likely to receive genes for above-average intelligence and an environment in which intellectual behavior is modeled and reinforced, thus setting them on a trajectory independent (passively) of their actions.

Reactive G-E correlation refers to the way parents, siblings, teachers, peers, and others react to the individual on the basis of his or her evocative behavior. The treatment of children by others is as much a function of children's evocative behavior as it is of the interaction style of those who respond to them. Children bring traits with them to situations that increase or decrease the probability of evoking certain kinds of responses from others. A pleasant and well-mannered child will evoke different reactions than will a bad-tempered and ill-mannered child. Socialization is not something adults do to children; it is a reciprocal process that adults and children do together. Some children may be so resistant to socialization that parents may resort to coercive parenting or simply give up, either of which is likely to worsen any antisocial tendencies they may have and drive them to seek environments where their behavior is accepted. Reactive G-E correlation thus serves to magnify phenotypic differences by funneling individuals into like-minded peer groups ("birds of a feather flock together").

Active G-E correlation refers to the active seeking of environments compatible with our genetic dispositions. Active G-E correlation becomes more pertinent as we mature and acquire the ability to take greater control of our lives because, within the range of possibilities available in our cultures, our genes help to determine what features of the environment will and will not be attractive to us. The power of active G-E correlation is apparent in studies showing that the intelligence, personalities, and attitudes of MZ twins tested as adults are virtually unaffected by whether they were reared together or apart. In fact, MZ twins reared apart construct their environments in ways far more similarly than DZ twins reared together.[7]

The concept of G-E correlation is liberating because it tells us that our minds and personalities are not simply products of external forces and that our choices are not just passive responses to social forces and situations. We are active "niche-picking" agents who create our own environments just as they help to create us. Genes imply human self-determination because, after all, our genes are *our* genes. As Colin Badcock put it, "Genes don't deny human freedom; they positively guarantee it."[8]

Behavior Genetics and Criminal Behavior

Studies using genetically sensitive methods almost invariably show some genetic influence on antisocial behavior. A review of 72 such studies conducted up to 1997 found that 67 (93%) were supportive of the genetic hypothesis, 3 were inconclusive, and 2 ran counter.[11] Nevertheless, there are no behavior genetic theories of criminal behavior per se. What behavior genetics does for us is to make more sense of traditional criminological theories by pointing out the genetic underpinnings of some of their favored causal variables and providing us with fresh ways to understand and interpret their findings. The MAO/abuse-neglect and crime study in the next "Focus On . . . " (page 204) helps us to understand, for instance, why the majority of abused and neglected children do not become violent offenders. We also saw in Chapter 7 that two large behavior genetic studies conducted in the United States[12] and the United Kingdom[13] showed that genetic factors play a large part in sorting individuals into different family structures (broken vs. intact homes), a variable often linked to antisocial behavior. In addition, a variety of traits and characteristics that feature prominently in many criminological theories such as altruism, aggression, empathy, self-control, impulsiveness, and

Gene-Environment Interaction: MAO, Abuse/Neglect, and Crime

An excellent example of G-E interaction is the interaction of monoamine oxidase (MAO) and abuse/neglect as joint biosocial risk factors for criminal behavior. MAO is a type of enzyme, and enzymes are chemical substances that bring about or accelerate chemical reactions such as breaking down food to provide us with energy. MAO acts in the brain to maintain the balance of several different neurotransmitters by breaking them down and recycling the excess. It plays an important role in neurotransmission by clearing the synaptic gap from much of the chemical debris that might otherwise interfere with subsequent transmissions.

Animal and human studies have consistently linked low levels of MAO to violence and aggression.[9] A particularly instructive study of a male birth cohort followed from birth to age 26 looked at the joint effects of MAO and maltreatment (G-E interaction) on future antisocial behavior.[10] Low MAO was not able to predict antisocial behavior by itself, but powerful findings emerged when maltreatment was taken into consideration. Among those maltreated as children and who had low MAO, 85% had antisocial histories and showed antisocial personality traits in adulthood. These subjects were 9.8 times more likely to have been arrested for a violent crime than other subjects in the study. Almost all maltreated children who had high levels of MAO, however, showed no antisocial behavior. The combination of maltreatment and MAO predicted the following four antisocial outcomes:

1. Psychiatric diagnoses of adolescent conduct disorder (persistent fighting, bullying, lying, stealing, cruelty to people or animals, and vandalism)

2. Official court records of conviction for violent offenses (assault, robbery, rape, domestic violence, homicide)

3. Aggressive personality traits (willingness to harm others for own advantage, interest in and enjoyment of violent material)

4. Symptoms of adult antisocial personality disorder (a long-term history of repeated law violations, deceitfulness, conning, impulsivity, physical aggression, and irresponsibility with respect to jobs, spouse, or children, along with a lack of remorse)

This study shows how genes can moderate children's sensitivity to abusive environments and underscores the importance of taking both biological and environmental variables and their interaction into account if we are to really understand human behavior. It also helps to explain why not all victims of maltreatment grow up to victimize others. Note that neither maltreatment nor low MAO alone was sufficient to produce antisocial outcomes and that the risk of antisocial behavior posed by low MAO was only manifested in conjunction with childhood maltreatment.

negative emotionality, as well as the neurohormonal substances that underlie them, such as serotonin and testosterone, are heritable with coefficients of 0.50 or higher.[14]

Adoption studies can help us to determine if children at genetic risk for antisocial behavior pattern experience more environmental risks for it than children not at genetic risk.

O'Connor and his colleagues[15] classified a number of adopted children as either being or not being at genetic risk for antisocial behavior on the basis of their biological mothers' self-reported antisocial behavior. It was found that children at genetic risk consistently received more negative parenting from their adoptive parents than did children not at genetic risk. This is an example of reactive G-E correlation, in which the poor behavior of the children evoked negative reactions from their adopted parents, which may in turn further magnify their children's antisocial proclivities.

Another study compared the antisocial history of adopted children, who were separated at birth from biological mothers with verified antisocial histories, to that of other adoptees with biological mothers with no antisocial history.[16] It was found that adverse adoptive home environments such as divorce, parental substance abuse, and neglect/abuse led to significant increases in antisocial behavior for adoptees at genetic risk but not for adoptees without genetic risk. This study provides an example of G-E interaction in that both genes and environments operating in tandem (interacting) were required to produce antisocial behavior, while neither was powerful enough to produce the effect by itself. In other words, genetically at-risk children reared in positive family environments did not display antisocial behavior, and children not at genetic risk did not become antisocial in adverse family environments. Only children with both a genetic risk *and* an adverse environment displayed antisocial behavior.

Another study showing how behavior genetics can strengthen criminological theories is Wright and Beaver's test[17] of Gottfredson and Hirschi's assumption[18] that parents are primarily responsible for their children's self-control or lack thereof. Using a sample of 310 twin pairs and 1,000 other children, they found that when genes were not taken into account, parental socialization techniques had a modest relationship with children's level of self-control, but when genetically informed methods were used, parental effects disappeared. In other words, not using genetically informed methods leads researchers to misidentify important causal influences. Self-control is strongly related to a brain chemical called serotonin, levels of which are heritable in the .55 to .66 range.[19] Wright and Beaver conclude that "for self-control to be a valid theory of crime it must incorporate a more sophisticated understanding of the origins of self-control."[20]

The Modest Heritability of Criminality

Unlike the relatively strong genetic influences discovered for most human traits, genetic influences on antisocial behavior are rather weak, especially during the teenage years, when influences to be discussed in the next chapter are operating. A study of 3,226 twin pairs found that genes accounted for only 7% of the variance in antisocial behavior among juvenile offenders, with 62% accounted for by the nonshared environment and 31% by the shared environment.[21] This same study found that genes accounted for 43% of the variance in adult offenders, with 52% accounted for by the nonshared environment and only 5% by the shared environment. A meta-analysis of 51 studies found an average heritability of 0.40 for combined adolescent and adult antisocial behavior.[22]

The majority of delinquents probably have little if any genetic vulnerability to criminal behavior, while a small minority may have considerable vulnerability. Pooling these two groups has the effect of elevating estimates of the overall influence of genes while minimizing it for those most seriously involved. For instance, Mednick, Gabrielli, and Hutchings's study[23] found a weak overall pattern of genetic effects for delinquency among a large number of young males. However, the 37 males (1.0% of the cohort) who had biological fathers with three or more criminal convictions accounted for fully 30% of all convictions in it. This suggests that genetic influences on juvenile antisocial behavior beneath some unknown threshold may be weak to nonexistent, while above that threshold, they may be very strong. Genetic effects on antisocial behavior appear most likely to be found among chronic offenders who begin offending prior to puberty and who continue to do so across the life course.[24]

⊠ Evolutionary Psychology

Evolutionary psychology is a way of thinking about human behavior using an evolutionary theoretical framework. The evolutionary perspective seeks to explain human behavior with reference to human evolutionary history but emphasizes that evolved behavior is always expressed according to current environmental circumstances. Criminologists operating within the evolutionary framework explore how certain behaviors that society now calls criminal may have been adaptive in ancestral environments.

Evolutionary psychology complements behavior genetics because it informs us how the genes of interest came to be present in our species in the first place. The primary difference between the two disciplines is that while behavior genetics looks for what makes people different, evolutionary psychology focuses on what makes us all the same. Another basic difference is that evolutionary psychology looks at ultimate-level "why" questions (what evolutionary problem did this behavioral mechanism evolve to solve?), and behavioral geneticists look at proximate-level "how" questions (to what extent is this behavioral mechanism influenced by genes in this population at this time?).

Evolution by Natural Selection

Evolution may be very simply defined as changes in a population's gene pool over time in response to environmental conditions. Evolution by natural selection is the only scientifically viable explanation for the origin of *basic* behavioral design we have available to us. Evolutionary psychologists do not dismiss the fine nuances in behavior that are generated by culture; they simply ask us to remember that "psychology underlies culture and society, and biological evolution underlies psychology."[25]

The basic point of Charles Darwin, the father of evolutionary theory, was that populations of animals grow until they strain the ability of the environment to support them all. This results in a struggle for existence in which the "fittest" survive. Darwin noted that individuals within populations exhibit a considerable degree of *variation* in their traits and characteristics, some of which gave their possessors an edge in their ability to avoid predators, parasites, and other environmental risks, as well as to secure needed resources. Whatever the edge happened to be, those possessing it would be more likely than those not possessing it to survive and reproduce, thus passing the genes underlying it to future generations. When this occurs, the trait variant has been *selected* from among other variants for preservation because it best "fits" its possessors into the environmental conditions existing *at the time*. Darwin called this process of selecting the "fittest" **natural selection** because it is nature (the environment) that "selects" the favorable variants and preserves them in later generations.

Natural selection is evolution's mover and shaker because it continuously adjusts populations to their environments; we call these adjustments **adaptations.** Adaptations may be anatomical, physiological, or behavioral. Adaptive traits are not selected *in order* to fit their possessors into their environments; there is no "purpose" to evolution for nature cannot anticipate future needs. Environmental conditions set evolution on a particular "trial-and-error" course, but if environments change drastically, some adaptations may become maladaptive.

Darwin had no idea what the source of that variation was or how it was passed on. Today, we know that trait variation is caused by the reshuffling of genes when the sex cells divide (meiosis) and by advantageous mutations. Biologists now view evolution as changes in the genetic composition of a population across the generations, and they use the term *fittest* to mean the most prolific reproducers. The most reproductively successful organisms leave behind the largest number of offspring and hence the greatest number of genes. In evolutionary terms, survival means nothing if survivors do not pass on the traits that helped them to survive. The genes underlying traits that contributed to reproductive success will therefore be found more frequently in subsequent generations.

Thinking Evolutionarily: Direct Versus Indirect Motivation and the Naturalistic Fallacy

Evolutionary logic, while scientifically impeccable, sometimes leads to confusion. Two points of confusion we want to guard against are the confusion of direct versus indirect motivation and the confusion of natural with good. Evolutionary logic does not dictate that evolved adaptive behaviors are *directly* and consciously motivated by concerns of reproductive success. Adaptations move us to seek the immediate means of achieving specific goals, not ultimate evolutionary ends.[26] No behavior is derived from conscious motives to increase fitness. Who thinks about pushing their genes into the future while enjoying sex, even if attempting to start a family? Who worries about their genetic representation in future generations when nurturing and loving their children? Parents love their children because they just do. Ultimately, they love their children because ancestral parents who loved theirs saw more of them grow to reproductive age and pass on the genes underlying love and nurturance. The mechanisms conducive to love and nurturing are adaptations because they went a long way to solving the problem of offspring survival.[27]

When we use the term *natural,* we often use it to mean *good* or *desirable* ("She has a *natural* beauty"). When thinking in evolutionary terms, we should not confuse *natural* with *good,* for what is natural is not always good (think disease and death). To use these terms synonymously is to commit what philosophers of science call the **naturalistic fallacy,** the fallacy of confusing *is* with *ought*. Nature simply *is;* what *ought* to be is a moral judgment. Scientists must always maintain the distinction between establishing facts and morally evaluating them.

The Evolution of Criminal Behavior: Crime Is Normal

Evolutionary psychologists agree with most criminologists that although it is morally regrettable, crime is normal behavior for which we all have the potential.[28] Evolutionary logic tells us that if criminal behavior is normal, it must have conferred some evolutionary advantage on our distant ancestors. Because criminal behavior is mostly maladaptive today (it can land you in prison for a long time, which is not very conducive to reproductive success), it does not mean that mechanisms that underlie it are not evolved adaptations. Modern environments are so radically different from the hunter-gatherer environments in which we evolved that many traits selected for their adaptive value at the time may not be adaptive today. It is important to realize that it is the *traits* underlying criminal behavior, not the specific acts, that are the alleged adaptations; genes do not code themselves for burglarizing a house or stealing a car.

Criminal behavior is a way to acquire valued resources by exploiting and deceiving others. Evolutionary psychologists refer to such behavior (whether it is defined as criminal or not) as *cheating* and think of individual traits associated with it such as impulsiveness, aggression, and low empathy, in terms of normal distributions dispersed around adaptive species averages. Whether exploitation occurs depends on environmental triggers interacting with individual differences and with environmental constraints.

Although we all have the potential to exploit and deceive others, we are a highly social and cooperative species with minds forged by evolution to form cooperative relationships built on trust.[29] Cooperation is typically contingent on the reciprocal cooperation of others and is thus a tit-for-tat strategy favored by natural selection because of the benefits it confers. We cooperate with our fellows because we feel good when we do and because it identifies us as reliable and trustworthy, which confers valued social status on us.

Cooperation Creates Niches for Cheats

Because cooperation occurs among groups of other cooperators, it creates niches for noncooperators to exploit.[30] **Cheats** are individuals in a population of cooperators who gain resources from others by signaling their cooperation but then failing to follow through. In the absence of internal (guilt, shame) or external (punishment, ostracism) deterrents, it is in an individual's interests to obtain resources from others under the assumption of reciprocity and then to default. Such "social parasitism" has been observed among numerous animal species,[31] which implies that it has had positive fitness consequences. In the human species, criminal behavior may be viewed as an extreme form of defaulting on the rules of cooperation or reciprocity. But cheating comes at a cost, so before deciding to do so, the individual must weigh the costs and benefits of cooperating versus defaulting. This concept is illustrated in the *prisoner's dilemma* game.[32]

Suppose two criminal accomplices—Bill and Frank—are being held in jail as suspects of a crime. The evidence against them is weak, so the prosecutor offers each a deal: If one testifies against the other, he will go free and his accomplice will get 10 years. If both agree to testify, both will receive a reduced sentence of 5 years. If neither testifies, both will be convicted of a minor crime and receive 1 year in prison. The dilemma is that they cannot communicate with one another, and doubts about the trustworthiness of the other and the temptation to default creep in. Bill's best strategy is to testify regardless of what Frank does because it will either get him released if Frank does not testify or 5 years if Frank does. Both outcomes are far better than the 10 years he will receive if he does not default but Frank does not. The same holds true for Frank. Each man following his own best interests testifies against the other and receives 5 years. The paradox is that although the *payoff for cheating is high when the other actor does not cheat, if both cheat, they are both worse off than if they cooperate*. By not cooperating with the other, each man behaved entirely rationally under the circumstances—that is, there is a positive fit between the end they both desired (minimizing their punishment) and the means used to achieve it (defaulting).

But if cheating is so rational, how did cooperation come to be predominant in social species? The answer is that cheating is only rational in circumstances of limited interaction and communication. Frank and Bill might never see each other again and thus may not fear any repercussions arising from their cheating. Had Bill and Frank belonged to an organized gang, been good friends, or were related in some way, it is unlikely that they would have defaulted, and each would have benefited from not doing so. Frequent interaction and communication breeds trust and bonding, and cheating becomes a less rational strategy because cooperators remember and retaliate against those who have cheated them. Cheating ruins reputations, invites retaliation, and results in punishment.

Cheats can only prosper in a population of pure cooperators who continue to extend benefits to those who have cheated them (evolutionists call them *suckers*). Cheats would soon drive a population of suckers to extinction, leaving only cheats to interact with cheats. A population of cheats could not exist for long any more than a population of suckers could, and selection for cooperation would occur rapidly.[33] Evolutionary processes ensure that pure suckers or pure cheats are not likely to exist in large numbers in any social species.

The vast majority of social animals, including human beings, are conditional cooperators (evolutionists call them *grudgers*). Grudgers can be suckered because they believe in mutual trust and cooperation and expect the same from others, but if victimized, they retaliate by not cooperating with their victimizer in the future and perhaps repaying the cheat in kind. Cheaters interact with grudgers in a *repeated* game of prisoner's dilemma, in which players adjust their strategies according to their experience with other players.[34] Under these circumstances, cooperation is the rational strategy because each player reaps in the future what he or she has sown in the past.

If this is so, why do we continue to see cheating behavior despite threats of exposure and retaliation? Exposure and retaliation are threats only if cheats are constrained to operate within the same environment in which their reputations are known. Cheats can move from location to location, meeting and cheating a series of grudgers who are unaware of their reputation. This is the pattern of many career criminals who move from place to place, job to job, and relationship to relationship, leaving a trail of misery behind them before their reputation catches up. This is why cheats are more likely to prosper in large cities in modern societies than in small traditional communities, where the threat of exposure and retaliation is great.[35]

The Evolution of Criminal Traits

There are a number of evolutionary theories of crime, all of which focus on sexuality as the prime mover of human behavior. This is not surprising because from a biological point of view, the evolutionary imperative of all living things is reproductive success. Members of any animal species can follow two strategies to maximize reproductive success: *parenting effort* and *mating effort*.[36] **Parenting effort** is that proportion of the total reproductive effort invested in rearing offspring, and **mating effort** is that proportion allotted to acquiring sexual partners. Reproductive strategies vary tremendously across species, with some species laying thousands of eggs every month and engaging in no parenting, while others may only produce a single offspring every 2 to 4 years and engage in extensive parenting. Because humans are born more dependent than any other animal, parenting effort is particularly important to our species. The most useful traits underlying parenting effort are altruism, empathy, nurturance, and intelligence.[37]

Humans invest more in parenting effort than any other species, but there is considerable variation within the species. Gender constitutes the largest division due to different levels of obligatory parental investment between the genders. As we saw in Chapter 6, female parental investment necessarily requires an enormous expenditure of time and energy, but the only *obligatory* investment of males is the time and energy spent copulating. Reproductive success for males increases in proportion to the number of females to whom they have sexual access, and thus males have an evolved propensity to seek multiple partners. Mating effort emphasizes quantity over quality (maximizing the number of offspring rather than nurturing a few), although maximizing offspring numbers is obviously not a conscious motive of any male seeking sex. The proximate motivation is sexual pleasure, with more offspring being a natural consequence (in precontraceptive days) when the strategy proved successful.

Ancestral females could not increase their reproductive success by mating with multiple partners given the low likelihood of males to invest in females with a reputation for promiscuity. A female could increase her success by mating with multiple partners in some circumstances, not by increasing the number of offspring but rather by obtaining resources from each partner, thus increasing the probability that offspring she already has will survive to reproductive age.[38] Thus, reproductive success among our ancestral females rested primarily on their ability to secure mates to assist them in raising offspring in exchange for exclusive sexual access, and thus human females evolved a much more discriminating attitude about sexual behavior.[39,40]

According to evolutionary biologists, the inherent conflict between the reckless and indiscriminate male mating strategy and the careful and discriminating female mating strategy drove the evolution of traits such as aggressiveness and low levels of empathy and constraint, which have helped males to overcome both male competitors and female reticence. The important point to remember is that *although these traits were designed by natural selection to facilitate mating effort, they are also useful in gaining nonsexual resources via illegitimate means.* In other words, the neurohormonal processes underlying these traits were selected to foster reproductive success, not criminality, but once the mechanisms are in place, they can serve purposes other than those for which they were designed.[41,42]

The reverse is also true—traits that facilitate parenting effort are conducive to other forms of prosocial activity: "Crime can be identified with the behaviors that tend to promote mating effort and noncrime with those that tend to promote parenting effort."[43] Because female reproductive success hinges more on parenting effort than mating effort, females have evolved higher levels of the traits that facilitate it (e.g., empathy and altruism) and lower levels of traits unfavorable to it (e.g., aggressiveness, sensation seeking) than males. Of course, both males and females engage in both mating and parenting strategies, and most of both genders follow a mixed mating strategy. It is only claimed that mating behavior is more typical of males and parenting effort is more typical of females.

Empirical research strongly supports the notion that an excessive concentration on mating effort is linked to criminal behavior. A review of 51 studies examining the relationship between number of sex partners and criminal behavior found 50 of them to be positive. In addition, age of onset of sexual behavior is also negatively related to criminal behavior (the earlier the age of onset, the greater the criminal activity) in all 51 studies.[44] A cohort study of more than 1,100 British twin pairs found that the most antisocial 10% of males in the cohort fathered 27% of the children,[45] and anthropologists tell us that there are striking differences in behavior between members of cultures that emphasize either parenting or mating strategies. Cultures emphasizing mating effort the world over exhibit behaviors (low-level parental care, hypermasculinity, transient bonding) considered antisocial in Western societies.[46,47]

⊠ The Neurohormonal Sciences

Whether the source of our behavior comes from within us or from our environment, it is necessarily funneled through transmitted nerve impulses in the brain, the most wonderful and complicated structure in the universe. Although the brain is only about 2% of body mass, it consumes 20% of the body's energy as it perceives, evaluates, and responds to its environment.[48] This 3-pound marvel of evolutionary design is the CEO of all that we think, feel, and do, which makes it advisable for us to know some basic neuroscience.

Some Basic Concepts and Terminology

The most primitive part of the brain has been referred to as the *reptilian system* to emphasize its ancient evolutionary origins.[49] The reptilian system consists of the spinal cord, brainstem, and the reticular activating system, among other things. Wrapped around the reptilian system like a protective claw is the *limbic system*, which evolved in conjunction with the evolutionary switch from a reptilian to a mammalian lifestyle. The mammalian lifestyle includes the addition of nursing and parental care, vocal communication, and play to the reptilian system, which is only concerned with the most primitive of biological tasks.[50] The limbic system is especially concerned with emotion, and as we saw in Chapter 7, the emotions perform many functions vital to social and cultural evolution.

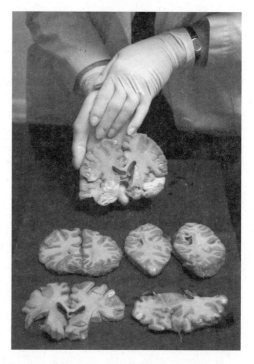

▲ **Photo 8.2** Harkening back to the 19th century, when postmortem examinations of the brains of criminals were a frequent phenomenon, the brain of serial killer John Wayne Gacy was dissected after his execution. The attempt to locate an organic explanation of his monstrous behavior was unsuccessful.

Surrounding the limbic system and forming the bulk of the human brain is the *neomammalian system* (the cerebrum), the most recent evolutionary addition. The cerebrum is divided into two hemispheres, each with its own specialized functions: The right hemisphere is for perception and the expression of emotion, and the left hemisphere is for language and analytical thinking. The outer layer of the cerebrum is the cerebral cortex; it is the "thinking" brain that organizes and analyzes information from other brain areas and structures and relays it back to them for appropriate response.

The **prefrontal cortex** (PFC) occupies approximately one third of the cerebrum and has extensive connections with other cortical regions, as well as with deeper structures in the limbic system. Because of its many connections with other brain structures, it is generally considered to play the major integrative and supervisory roles in the brain and is especially vital for mediating emotions.[51] Major parts of the brain of interest to criminologists and discussed in this chapter (reticular activating system, limbic system, and the prefrontal cortex) are presented in Figure 8.1.

Figure 8.1	Major Parts of the Brain of Concern to Criminologists

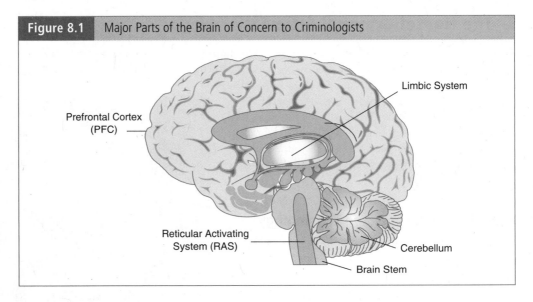

Illustration by Peter A. Collins

Connecting all these brain structures are hundreds of billions of nerve cells called **neurons.** All our thoughts, feelings, emotions, and behavior are the results of communication networks of neurons, each of which consists of the cell body (soma), an axon, and a number of dendrites. The soma carries out the metabolic functions of the neuron, the axons are transmitters that send signals to other neurons, and dendrites are receivers that pick up messages from neighboring neurons. Each of our 100 billion or so communicating neurons makes thousands of connections with other neurons, making the potential combination of connections in the human brain "hyper-astronomical."[52] Most lower-level brain structures such as the brainstem come with their connections fairly complete at birth ("hardwired"), but development of the higher brain areas depends a lot on environmental "software" downloaded after birth.

Sending and receiving messages is accomplished in microscopic fluid-filled gaps between axons and dendrites called **synapses.** Information from our sense organs is carried via the afferent nerves for processing in the brain cells. The brain cells pass the information along the axon electrically until it reaches the *synaptic knob* at the end of a dendrite, at which time it is translated into chemistry as tiny vesicles burst open and spill out one or more of a variety of chemicals called **neurotransmitters.** These neurotransmitters cross the synaptic gap to make contact with postsynaptic receptor sites, where the message is translated back into an electrical one for further transportation or inhibition. When they have passed on their messages, excess amounts of neurotransmitter are pumped back up into the presynaptic knob or degraded by enzymes. Figure 8.2 illustrates the process of neurotransmission from presynaptic neuron to postsynaptic neuron.

Scientists have identified some 400 different neurotransmitters, all of which are genetically activated according to the kind of environmental stimuli the person is experiencing. The most important of these neurotransmitters for criminologists to understand are dopamine, serotonin, and norepinephrine (or noradrenaline) because they regulate our reward and arousal systems, our impulsiveness/constraint, and our fear responses.[53]

Figure 8.2	The Process of Synaptic Transmission. Sketch of two neurons at the top with an enlargement at the bottom showing the release of an unspecified transmitter into the synaptic cleft.

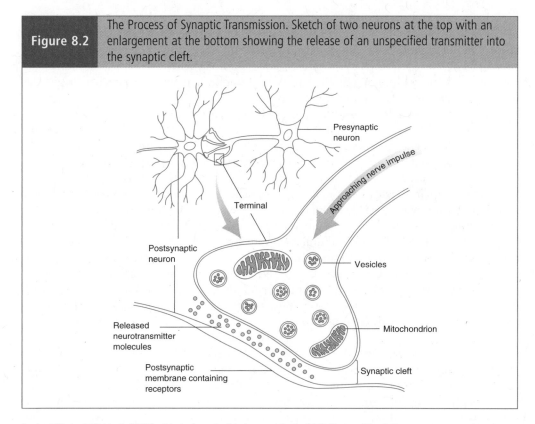

SOURCE: Ellis, L., & Walsh, A. (2000). *Criminology: A global perspective* (p. 288). Boston: Allyn & Bacon.

Softwiring the Brain

Neuroscientists argue about how much brain development depends on processes intrinsic to the brain (the genes) relative to processes extrinsic to it (environmental), but not in naive nature *or* nurture terms. About 50% to 60% of our genes are involved in brain development specifying its architecture, building its cells, and synthesizing the brain chemicals.[54] Genes carry an immense amount of information but are few in number (25,000 to 30,000) relative to the billions of neurons and the trillions of connections they may make with one another. If only genes specified neuronal connections, we would be hardwired drones responding stereotypically to stimuli and incapable of adapting to novel situations. Human environments are too varied and too complex for hardwired brains. Debates in neuroscience are thus not about "*whether* the environment thoroughly influences brain development, but *how* it does."[55] The message neuroscience is shunting along our synapses is that *we and the experiences we encounter largely determine the patterns of our neuronal connections and thus our ability to successfully navigate our lives.*

Neuroscientists identify two brain developmental processes that *physically* capture environmental events in a person's lifetime just as genes captured environmental events in the genome during the life span of the species: **experience-expected** and **experience-dependent brain development.**[56] Both processes use environmental input to facilitate synaptic production.

Experience-expected mechanisms are hardwired and reflect the evolutionary history of the species, and experience-dependent mechanisms reflect each person's unique developmental history. To put it another way, every person inherits the same brain structures and functions because he or she is produced by a common pool of human genetic material, but individuals will vary in brain functioning as their genes interact with their environments to put the finishing touches on their neurological development.[57]

Experience-expected processes have evolved as preparedness to integrate environmental information that is vital to normal development. Natural selection has recognized that certain processes such as sight, speech, depth perception, affectionate bonds, mobility, and sexual maturation are vital, and it has provided for mechanisms (adaptations) designed to take advantage of experiences occurring naturally within the normal range of human environments. The brain structures controlling these processes are hardwired so that we will respond consistently and stereotypically to environmental stimuli that trigger the proper development of them.[58]

Much of the variability in the brain-wiring patterns of different individuals depends on the kinds of physical, social, and cultural environments they will encounter. This experience-dependent process enables us to understand personality as a dynamic construct forged as genes and environmental experiences collaborate across the life span. Experience-dependent development reflects what neuroscientists call brain *plasticity,* which is another way of saying that the brain is molded, changed, and calibrated by what it experiences. Brain plasticity is greatest in infancy and early childhood, but a certain degree is maintained as long as the brain is active. Every time we learn something, we shape and reshape the brain in ways that could never have been preprogrammed.

The process of wiring the brain is known as **synaptogenesis.** The newborn's cerebral cortex contains neurons with underdeveloped dendrites, but during the first few months, dendrites proliferate and axons begin the process of *myelination. Myelin* is a fatty substance that coats the axons and makes for speedier transmission of electrical impulses. The process of myelination and dendrite and axon growth proceeds at an explosive rate during infancy and toddlerhood; the number and density of synaptic connections are higher at 8 months of age than they ever will be again.[59] The primitive regions are the first to be myelinated since they are the most vital regions in terms of sheer survival, and some "higher" brain areas (especially the PFC) are not fully myelinated until adulthood.[60]

Although the brain creates and eliminates synapses throughout life, creation exceeds elimination in the first 2 or 3 years, when about half the synaptic connections are eliminated. Production and elimination are roughly balanced thereafter until adolescence, after which elimination again exceeds production.[61] The process of selection and elimination has been termed **neural Darwinism** by Gerald Edleman,[62] who posits a selection process among competing synapses. In order for synaptic selection to take place, there must be an excess of synapses available, just as an excess of genetic variation is required for natural selection. Neuron populations thus evolve by selective retention and elimination in the person's lifetime much as species evolve in evolutionary time.

Retention of synapse networks is a use-dependent process governed by the strength and frequency of experience and is biased in favor of the neuron populations that are most stimulated during early development.[63] Experiences with strong emotional content are accompanied by especially strong nerve impulses. If these impulses are both strong and frequent, the neurons involved become more sensitive and responsive to similar stimuli in the future and become primed to fire at lower stimulus thresholds in the future.

Bonding, Attachment, and the Brain

The importance of social science concepts such as attachment and bonding receives strong support from the neurosciences. Humans have powerful neurological and hormonal structures that demand the formation of affectionate bonds, and there are many negative consequences associated with the failure to form them. But why are such bonds important, and what are the consequences relevant to criminal behavior of not forming them? A number of theorists trace the human need for strong bonding to two conflicting evolutionary trajectories: selection for intelligence and selection for upright walking. Greater intelligence means a bigger brain and bigger skull to carry it around; cranial capacity almost tripled from our earliest hominid ancestors to modern *Homo sapiens*.[64] Bigger skulls were being selected for at the same time that the female pelvis was being shaped to satisfy upright posture and bipedalism (which has the effect of narrowing the birth canal) more than for increased fetal brain size.[65] The increased skull size of babies, coupled with the narrowing pelvises of their mothers, placed a huge reproductive burden on human females, which resulted in many maternal deaths.[66]

The mechanism that partially solved the conflict was for infants to be born at earlier and earlier stages of development as cerebral mass increased. Human infants experience 25% brain growth inside the womb (*uterogestation*) and 75% growth outside the womb (*exterogestation*), which is a much greater percentage than for any other animal and thus ensures a greater role for the environment in its development than is true for any other animal. A species giving birth to highly dependent young must evolve mechanisms designed to ensure that they are nurtured for as long as is necessary; we call these mechanisms love and nurturing. Children who fail to receive love and nurturing often fall prey to developmental problems that may lead to criminal behavior.

Abuse, Neglect, and the Developing Brain

Neuronal pathways forged from negative early experiences among nonhuman primates have been identified for decades.[67] It is known that chronic stress can produce neuron death via the frequent production of stress hormones[68] and that children with chronic high levels of these hormones experience cognitive, motor, and social development delays.[69] The lack of nurturing and attachment during early development may result in a brain that will adversely affect the child's ability to interact with his or her world adaptively because, as Perry and Pollard point out, "Experience in adults *alters* the *organized* brain, but in infants and children it *organizes* the *developing* brain."[70] Brains organized by stressful and traumatic events tend to relay events along the same neural pathways laid out by those early events because pathways laid down early in life are more resistant to pruning than pathways laid down later in life. A brain organized by negative events is ripe for antisocial behavior.

The Evolutionary Neuroandrogenic Theory

A recently developed biosocial theory of criminal behavior that incorporates numerous interrelated variables is the evolutionary neuroandrogenic (ENA) theory.[71] ENA theory asserts that evolutionary, neurological, and hormonal factors, like social environment factors, are all involved in crime causation.

The theory has two fundamental assumptions. The first is that males have been naturally selected for engaging in resource procurement and status striving, especially after the onset of puberty. To explain why males do so, the theory asserts that over countless generations, females who have chosen mates based on a male's ability to obtain resources will have left more offspring in subsequent generations than females who use other criteria for selecting mates.

The mechanism that inclines males to be more competitive and prone toward status striving is addressed in the second assumption. The second assumption asserts that fetal exposure of male brains to hormones known as *androgens,* the most important of which is testosterone (see Chapter 9), makes them more prone to competitive status striving than females. While the theory assumes that status striving is largely unlearned, the techniques for doing so must be learned. Consequently, the initial expressions of status striving are often crude, and many of the crudest expressions come in the form of antisocial behavior. More sophisticated expressions of status-striving tendencies that are culturally acceptable (noncriminal) are learned by most people as they mature biologically and socially.

ENA theory thus asserts that criminality is part of a continuum of activities involving status striving in which males are the main offenders. Males who transition most slowly from the crude to the sophisticated end of this continuum are those who have the greatest difficulty learning. Slow-transitioning males often struggle with societal rules and institutions well into adulthood, are prone to fall afoul of the law, and will fare poorly in the economy as well.

ENA theory explains sex and age variations in criminality and can account for why persistent criminality is concentrated in the lower socioeconomic strata. In terms of biological factors, the theory is supported by several studies linking persistent criminality with high levels of testosterone, especially for violent offenses.[72] The theory is also consistent with evidence that success in business is positively correlated with testosterone levels.[73]

Reward Dominance Theory and Criminal Behavior

Reward dominance theory is a neurological theory based on the proposition that behavior is regulated by two opposing mechanisms, the **behavioral activating system** (BAS) and the **behavioral inhibition system** (BIS). The BAS is associated chemically with the neurotransmitter dopamine and anatomically with pleasure areas in the limbic system.[74] The BIS is associated with serotonin and with limbic system structures such as the hippocampus (the seat of memory) that feed into the prefrontal cortex.[75] Dopamine facilitates goal-directed behavior, and serotonin generally modulates behavior.[76]

The BAS is sensitive to reward signals and can be likened to an accelerator motivating a person to seek rewarding stimuli. The BIS is sensitive to threats of punishment and can be likened to a brake that stops a person from going too far too fast. The BAS motivates us to seek all kinds of pleasure, and the BIS tells us when we have had enough for our own good. A normal BAS combined with a faulty BIS, or vice versa, may lead to a very impulsive person with a "craving brain" that can lead him or her into all sorts of physical, social, moral, and legal difficulties, such as obesity, gambling, sex addiction, and alcohol and drug addiction.[77]

Most people are more or less equally sensitive to both reward and punishment because we are in a state of dopamine/serotonin equilibrium most of the time, but for some people, one system might dominate the other most or all of the time.[78] BIS/BAS theory asserts that criminals, especially chronic criminals, have a dominant BAS, which tends to make them overly sensitive to reward cues and relatively insensitive to punishment cues.[79] Reward dominance theory provides us with hard *physical* evidence relating to the concepts of sensation seeking, impulsiveness, and low self-control that we have previously discussed since each of these traits is underlain by either a sticky accelerator (high dopamine) or faulty brakes (low serotonin).

Although the "set points" of BIS/BAS functioning are genetically influenced, human brain plasticity leads many neuroscientists to think that early experience may be important for altering those set points during critical developmental periods.[80] It has also been shown that poor parenting is associated with low serotonin levels in children, although the causal direction is unclear—that is, did poor parenting lead to low serotonin, or did children's impulsive behavior driven by low serotonin lead to poor parenting?[81]

A third system of behavior control is the **flight/fight system** (FFS). The FFS refers to ANS mechanisms that mobilize the body for vigorous action in response to threats by pumping out epinephrine (adrenaline). Fear and anxiety at the chemical level is epinephrine shouting its warning: "Attention, danger ahead; take action to avoid!" Having a weak FFS (low epinephrine) that whispers rather than shouts combined with a BAS (high dopamine) that keeps shouting "Go get it," along with a BIS (low serotonin) too feeble to object, is obviously very useful when pursuing all kinds of criminal and antisocial activities.[82]

Prefrontal Dysfunction (PFD) Theory and Criminal Behavior

As previously noted, the PFC is responsible for a number of uniquely human attributes such as making moral judgments, planning for the future, analyzing, synthesizing, and modulating emotions. The PFC provides us with knowledge about how other people see and think about us, thus moving us to adjust our behavior to consider their needs and concerns as well as their expectations of us. All these PFC functions are collectively referred to as *executive functions*. These functions are clearly involved in prosocial behavior, and if they are compromised in some way via damage to the PFC, they can result in antisocial behavior. PFC damage does not have to be anatomically discernible to negatively affect its behavior modification functions; it can be at the cellular level and result from such things as maternal substance abuse during pregnancy.[83]

Positron emission tomography (PET) and functional magnetic resonance imaging (fMRI) studies find links between PFC activity and impulsive criminal behavior. A PET study comparing impulsive murderers with murderers whose crimes were planned found that the former showed significantly lower prefrontal and higher limbic system activity (indicative of emotional arousal) than the latter and control subjects.[84] Nonimpulsive murderers had PFC functioning similar to the control subjects. Tying reward dominance and PFC dysfunctions together, a large-scale study of incarcerated and nonincarcerated California youths found that seriously delinquent offenders have slower resting heart rates and performed poorly relative to nondelinquents on various cognitive functions mediated by the PFC.[85] Finally, a review of 17 neuroimaging studies showed conclusively that impulsive violent behaviors are associated with PFC deficits.[86] The authors interpreted the findings in the context problems with the PFC's regulation of negative emotionality.

◩ Evaluation of the Biosocial Perspective

Biosocial theories have been tarred with labels such as *racist, sexist,* and *classicist* in the past because they were interpreted as theories implying a Lombrosian biological inferiority of criminals. These kinds of attacks have become rarer as social scientists have become more sophisticated in their thinking about the interaction of biological and environmental factors in producing behavior.[87] There are still people who fear that "biological" theories can be used for eugenic or racist ends, but as Bryan Vila remarks, "Findings can be used for racist or

Table 8.1	Summarizing Biosocial Perspectives and Theories		
Theory	**Key Concepts**	**Strengths**	**Weaknesses**
Behavior genetics perspective	Genes affect behavior in interaction with environmental influences. Heritability estimates the relative contribution of genetic and environmental factor traits affecting criminality. All individual traits are at least modestly influenced by genes.	Looks at both the genetic and environmental risk factors for criminal behavior Understanding genetic contributions also identifies the complementary contributions of environmental factors.	Requires twin samples of twins and/or adoptees, which are difficult to come by. While general environmental factors are identified, behavior genetics does not specify what they are.
Evolutionary psychology perspective	Human behavior is rooted in evolutionary history. Natural selection has favored victimizing tendencies in humans, especially males. These tendencies arose to facilitate mating effort but are useful in pursuing criminal behavior as well. Criminals emphasize mating effort over parenting effort more than males in general.	Ties criminology to evolutionary biology. Mating effort helps to explain why males are more criminal than females and why criminals tend to be more sexually promiscuous than persons in general. Emphasizes that crime is biologically "normal" (although regrettable) rather than pathological.	Gives some the impression that because crime is considered "normal," it is justified or excused. Makes assumptions about human nature that may or may not be true. While recognizing that culture is important, it tends to ignore it.
Neuroscience perspective	Whatever their origin, all stimuli are channeled through the brain before given expression in behavior. The development of the brain is strongly influenced by early environmental experiences, especially those involving nurturance and attachment.	Shows how environmental experiences are physically "captured" by the brain. Emphasizes the importance of nurturing for optimal development of the brain. Uses sophisticated technology and provides "harder" evidence.	High cost of neuroimaging studies is a drawback. Very small samples of known criminals are often used, thus limiting generalizations. Linking specific brain areas to specific behaviors is problematic.
Evolutionary neuroandrenic theory	Androgens alter the brains of males to make them more prone toward status striving, especially following puberty. Crime is a crude expression of status striving.	Integrates evolutionary and neuroscience concepts. Explains why sex, age, and social status are related to violent and property crimes, as most studies have shown.	Does not explain most forms of victimless crimes. Does not pay sufficient attention to specific environmental factors.
Reward dominance theory	Behavioral activating system (BAS) and behavioral inhibiting system (BIS) are dopamine and serotonin driven, respectively. Among criminals, the BAS tends to be dominant over the BIS. This BIS/BAS imbalance can lead to addiction to many things, including crime.	Explains why low serotonin is related to offending (low serotonin = low self-control). Explains why criminality is persistent in some offenders because they develop a taste for the "thrill of it all."	The neurological underpinnings of the BAS and BIS have been difficult to precisely identify. Studies difficult and expensive to conduct.
Prefrontal dysfunction theory	Frontal lobes control long-term planning and temper emotions and their expressions. Criminals have frontal lobes that fail to function as they do in most people, especially in terms of inhibiting actions that harm others.	Explains why moral reasoning is inversely related to involvement in persistent criminality. Explains why criminality has been linked to frontal lobe damage and to abnormal brainwaves.	Dysfunction of the prefrontal lobes remains difficult to precisely measure, even with fMRI scans. Same sampling difficulties noted for the neurosciences in general.

eugenic ends only if we allow perpetuation of the ignorance that underlies these arguments."[88] Bigots and hate-mongers will climb aboard any vehicle that gives their prejudices a free ride, and they have done so for centuries before genes were ever heard of.

The strength of biosocial approaches lies in their ability to incorporate biological factors into their theories and to physically measure many of them via various chemical, electrophysiological, and neuroimaging methods. These strengths, however, become weaknesses in terms of generalizing from samples to populations. Many biosocial studies of criminality consist of small samples and may often consist of incarcerated subjects. Neuroimaging studies are extremely expensive to conduct, and many of them may only consist of 20 identified criminals matched with a control group of similar size. Furthermore, if we want genetic information, we cannot simply go to the nearest high school and survey a few hundred students. Behavior genetic studies require comparing samples consisting of pairs of MZ and DZ twins and/or adopted twins, and these are extremely difficult to find. There are some wonderfully informative studies coming from around the world, however, from scientists lucky enough to have access to large twin and adoption databases. The best strategy for biosocial theory advancement appears to be for criminologists to attach themselves to large longitudinal multidisciplinary studies such as the study from which the MAO/abuse data were gathered.

Given these problems, the greatest contribution of biosocial theories at this point in time is to complement and strengthen existing sociological theories and to serve as a reality check for them. These theories must acknowledge the following proposition: "Genes and environments both contribute to individual differences in human behavior is as close to a universal statement as one can get in the behavioral sciences."[89] We will continue to misinterpret many of our findings if we do not simultaneously take into account the social, psychological, and biological forces impinging on the quicksilver of human behavior.

⬙ Policy and Prevention: Implications of Biosocial Theories

The policy issues suggested by the biosocial perspective are midway between the macro-level sociological suggestions aimed at whole societies or communities and the micro-level suggestions of psychological theories aimed at already convicted criminals. Mindful of the great importance of nurturing for the human species, many biosocial criminologists have advocated a wide array of "nurturant" strategies such as pre- and postnatal care for all women, monitoring infants and young children through the early developmental years, paid maternal leave, nutritional programs, and a whole host of other interventions.[90–92] Whether such programs are feasible in the political climate in the United States at present is another matter.

The above interventions are attempts at prevention rather than "cures" for those already afflicted. Biosocial criminologists are typically in the forefront in advocating treatment over punishment, and toward this end, they have favored indeterminate sentences over fixed sentences.[93] Pharmacological treatments in conjunction with psychosocial treatments have proven time and time again to be superior to psychosocial treatment alone for syndromes (alcoholism, drug addiction, etc.) associated with criminal behavior.[94] Of course, there are always dangers of seeking simple medical solutions to complex social problems such as crime. Requiring sex offenders to take anti-androgen treatment to reduce the sex drive raises both medical and legal/ethical issues regardless of how effective the treatment is. Prescribing selective serotonin reuptake inhibitors such as Prozac and Zoloft should help curb the low self-control and irritability of offenders characterized by those traits, but there is always the temptation to treat everyone the same regardless of their serotonin levels.

Some behavioral scientists tend to feel that identifying biological risk factors will lead to cessation of efforts to reduce crime through environmental improvement because such factors are wrongly thought to be intractable. But biosocial studies provide information about *both* environmental and biological risk factors and, as such, are "more likely to refine social policies by better specification of environmental factors than to divert funds from environmental crime prevention strategies."[95] In other words, they will enable us to better pinpoint environmental factors that may or may not prove fruitful in our crime prevention efforts.

A final policy suggestion comes from data showing that a great deal of delinquent and criminal behavior is intrinsically rewarding via the "high" it produces. Providing challenging and risky legal alternatives to the excitement of antisocial behavior may be part of a useful preventative package. According to Wood, Gove, and Cochran, "The key to preventing some crime may depend on finding alternative activities that both produce a neurophysiological 'high' and which are symbolically meaningful to the persons performing the crimes."[96]

SUMMARY

Behavior geneticists study the genetic underpinning of traits and characteristics in populations by calculating heritability coefficients. There are no genes "for" any kind of complex human behavior; genes simply make proteins that interact with other proteins and the environment in complicated ways. Genes do not cause behavior, they simply bias trait values in one direction or another and are activated by environmental information, including information that originates in our own thoughts and feelings. This view is respectful of human dignity because it implies self-determinism: our genes are *our genes;* they manufacture the proteins that facilitate the traits that modulate our personal responses to the variety of situations we encounter or fashion for ourselves.

Behavior geneticists also examine shared and nonshared environmental effects. Shared environments make people who share them more alike, and nonshared environments make them different. Gene-environment interaction tells us that the impact that the environmental situation (i.e., living in a crime-ridden neighborhood) has on us depends on who we are, and gene-environment correlation tells us that who we are is a product of our unique genotype and the environments we find ourselves in.

Genes have practically no influence on juvenile delinquency, probably because of the high base rate of delinquency. There are genetic effects for chronic and serious delinquents, but these few individuals tend to get "lost" in studies that combine them with those who limit their offending to adolescence. Adult criminality is much more influenced by genes. One of the reasons that we find only modest genetic effects in criminality when the traits that underlie it are strongly influenced by genes is that parents have control over their children's behavior but little or none over the underlying traits.

Evolutionary psychology focuses on why we have the traits we do and is more interested in their universality than in their variability. Crime is viewed as a normal but regrettable response to environmental conditions. By this it is meant that many human adaptations forged by natural selection in response to survival and reproductive pressures are easily co-opted to serve morally wrong purposes.

In common with all sexually producing species, humans are preeminently concerned with our own survival and reproductive success. The traits designed to assist males in their mating efforts include many that can also assist them to secure other resources illegitimately; traits designed to assist females in their parenting efforts are conducive to prosocial behavior. Mating versus parenting effort is not an either/or thing. Males and females engage in both at various times in their lives; it is just that mating effort is more typical of males, and parenting effort is more typical of females.

Socially cooperating species create niches that cheats can exploit to their advantage by signaling cooperation but then defaulting. As illustrated in the prisoner's dilemma, cheating is a rational strategy in the short term but invites retaliation in the long term. This is why chronic criminals rarely have successful relationships with others and why they typically die broke.

Neuroscience tells us that genes have surrendered control of human behavior to the brain. Following genetic wiring to jump-start the process, the brain literally wires itself in response to environmental input. Neurons can make trillions of connections with one another, with each connection reflecting our experiences (experience-dependent brain development). But this does not mean that the human mind is a blank slate at birth; there must be hardwired programs guiding our responses to the environment that are too important to be left to the vagaries of learning (experience-expected brain development).

The selection process involving neuronal pathways (neural Darwinism) is an electrochemical process that depends on the frequency and intensity of early experiences. Adverse experiences can literally physically organize the brain so that we experience the world negatively, which is why nurturing, love, and attachment are so important to the healthy development of humans.

This proposition was examined within BIS/BAS and prefrontal dysfunction theories of criminal behavior. Most people have BIS and BAS systems (underlain by serotonin and dopamine neurotransmitter, respectively), but criminals tend to have either an overactive BAS or an underactive BIS, and thus their behavior is dominated by reward cues is relatively unaffected by punishment cues. Early experiences may possibly influence the BIS/BAS balance. Likewise, early experiences may adversely affect prefrontal lobe functioning by influencing neuron pathways.

ENA theory integrates a number of evolutionary, neuroscience, and social concepts and asserts that androgens alter the male brain and incline males toward status striving. As anomie theory also maintains, crime is a crude expression of status striving.

On Your Own

Log on to the web-based student study site at http://www.sagepub.com/criminologystudy for more information about the vignettes and materials presented in this chapter, suggestions for activities, study aids such as review quizzes, and research recommendations including journal article links and questions related to this chapter.

EXERCISES AND DISCUSSION QUESTIONS

1. If it could be shown with high scientific confidence that some young children inherit a genetic variant that puts them at 85% risk for developing antisocial proclivities, what do you think should be done? Should their parents be warned to be especially vigilant

and to seek early treatment for their children, or would such a warning tend to stigmatize children? What are the costs and benefits of each option?

2. Recalling what has been said about "genetic determinism," should persons at presumed high genetic risk for criminal behavior receive more lenient treatment if they commit crimes?

3. If some people are constitutionally more prone to criminal behavior, how would you explain much higher crime rates in large urban areas versus rural areas? Are city folks more constitutionally prone than urban folks, or is something else operating—gene-environment interaction, for example?

4. We know that males, especially young males, are more likely to perpetrate and be victimized by violent crimes. Provide a plausible evolutionary explanation for this other than Campbell's staying alive hypothesis discussed in Chapter 6.

5. Search the Internet or library for one of the theories presented in this chapter and write a two-page paper adding to the information given in this chapter.

6. Discuss how reward dominance theory might add strength and coherence to low self-control theory discussed in Chapter 5.

7. The best Internet source of research and information about biosocial criminology is *Crime Times*. Go to this source at http://crimetimes.org and click on any of the topics discussed in this chapter that may interest you. These are only short abstracts, so click on five or six and report your general impressions.

KEY WORDS

Adaptations
Behavioral activating system
Behavioral inhibition system
Behavior genetics
Cheats
Evolutionary psychology
Experience-dependent brain development
Experience-expected brain development

Flight/fight system
Gene-environment interaction
Gene-environment correlation
Genes
Genotype
Heritability
Mating effort
Natural selection

Naturalistic fallacy
Neural Darwinism
Neurons
Neurotransmitters
Parenting effort
Phenotype
Prefrontal cortex
Reward dominance theory
Synapse
Synaptogenesis

REFERENCES

1. Freese, J., Li, J., & Wade, L. (2003). The potential relevance of biology to social inquiry. *Annual Review of Sociology, 29*, 233–256.

2. Cartwright, J. (2000). *Evolution and human behavior.* Cambridge: MIT Press.

3. Carey, G. (2003). *Human genetics for the social sciences.* Thousand Oaks, CA: Sage.

4. Bronfenbrenner, U., & Ceci, S. (1994). Heredity, environment, and the question "how": A first approximation. In R. Plomin & G. McClearn (Eds.), *Nature, nurture, and psychology* (pp. 313–324). Washington, DC: American Psychological Association.

5. Carey (2003).

6. Plomin, R. (1995). Genetics and children's experiences in the family. *Journal of Child Psychology and Psychiatry, 36,* 33–68.

7. Rowe, D. (2002). *Biology and crime.* Los Angeles: Roxbury.

8. Badcock, C. (2000). *Evolutionary psychology: A critical introduction.* Cambridge, UK: Polity. (Quote on p. 71)

9. Ellis, L. (1991). Monoamine oxydase and criminality: Identifying an apparent biological marker for antisocial behavior. *Journal of Research in Crime and Delinquency, 28,* 227–251.

10. Caspi, A., McClay, J., Moffitt, T., Mill, J., Martin, J., Craig, I., Taylor, A., & Poulton, R. (2002). Evidence that the cycle of violence in maltreated children depends on genotype. *Science, 297,* 851–854.

11. Ellis, L., & Walsh, A. (2000). *Criminology: A global perspective.* Boston: Allyn & Bacon.

12. Cleveland, H., Wiebe, R., van den Oord, E., & Rowe, D. (2000). Behavior problems among children from different family structures: The influence of genetic self-selection. *Child Development, 71,* 733–751.

13. Moffitt, T., & the E-Risk Study Team. (2002). Teen-aged mothers in contemporary Britain. *Journal of Child Psychology and Psychiatry, 43,* 1–16.

14. Walsh, A. (2002). *Biosocial criminology: Introduction and integration.* Cincinnati, OH: Anderson.

15. O'Connor, T., Deater-Deckard, K., Fulker, D., Rutter, M., & Plomin, R. (1998). Genotype-environment correlations in late childhood and early adolescence: Antisocial behavioral problems and coercive parenting. *Developmental Psychology, 34,* 970–981.

16. Cadoret, R., Yates, W., Troughton, E., Woodworth, G., & Stewart, M. (1995). Genetic-environmental interaction in the genesis of aggressivity and conduct disorders. *Archives of General Psychiatry, 52,* 916–924.

17. Wright, J., & Beaver, K. (2005). Do parents matter in creating self-control in their children? A genetically informed test of Gottfredson and Hirschi's theory of low self-control. *Criminology, 43,* 1169–1202.

18. Gottfredson, M., & Hirschi, T. (1990). *A general theory of crime.* Stanford, CA: Stanford University Press.

19. Hur, Y., & Bouchard, T. (1997). The genetic correlation between impulsivity and sensation-seeking traits. *Behavior Genetics, 27,* 455–463.

20. Wright and Beaver (2005, p. 1190).

21. Lyons, M., True, W., Eusen, S., Goldberg, J., Meyer, J., Faraone, S., Eaves, L., & Tsuang, M. (1995). Differential heritability of adult and juvenile antisocial traits. *Archives of General Psychiatry, 53,* 906–915.

22. Rhee, S., & Waldman, I. (2002). Genetic and environmental influences on antisocial behavior: A meta-analysis of twin and adoption studies. *Psychological Bulletin, 128*(3), 490–529.

23. Mednick, S., Gabrielli, W., & Hutchings, B. (1984). Genetic influences in criminal convictions: Evidence from an adoption cohort. *Science, 224,* 891–894.

24. Moffitt, T., & Walsh, A. (2003). The adolescence-limited/Life-course persistent theory and antisocial behavior: What have we learned? In A. Walsh & L. Ellis (Eds.), *Biosocial criminology: Challenging environmentalism's supremacy* (pp. 125–144). Hauppauge, NY: Nova Science.

25. Barkow, J. (1989). *Darwin, sex and status: Biological approaches to mind and culture.* Toronto: University of Toronto Press. (Quote on p. 635)

26. Symons, D. (1992). The use and misuse of Darwinism in the study of human behavior. In J. Barkow, L. Cosmides, & J. Tooby (Eds.), *The adapted mind: Evolutionary psychology and the generation of culture* (pp. 137–159). New York: Oxford University Press.

27. Fisher, H. (1998). Lust, attraction, and attachment in mammalian reproduction. *Human Nature, 9,* 23–52.

28. Kanazawa, S. (2003). A general evolutionary psychological theory of criminality and related male-typical behavior. In A. Walsh & L. Ellis (Eds.), *Biosocial criminology: Challenging environmentalism's supremacy* (pp. 37–60). Hauppauge, NY: Nova Science.

29. Allman, W. (1994). *The stone age present.* New York: Simon & Schuster.

30. Tibbetts, S. (2003). Selfishness, social control, and emotions: An integrated perspective on criminality. In A. Walsh & L. Ellis (Eds.), *Biosocial criminology: Challenging environmentalism's supremacy* (pp. 83–101). Hauppauge, NY: Nova Science.

31. Alcock, J. (1998). *Animal behavior: An evolutionary approach* (6th ed.). Sunderland, MA: Sinauer Associates.

32. Axelrod, R. (1984). *The evolution of cooperation.* New York: Basic Books.

33. Machalek, R. (1996). The evolution of social exploitation. *Advances in Human Ecology, 5,* 1–32.

34. Raine, A. (1993). *The psychopathology of crime: Criminal behavior as a clinical disorder.* San Diego: Academic Press.

35. Ellis, L., & Walsh, A. (1997). Gene-based evolutionary theories in criminology. *Criminology, 35,* 229–276.

36. Rowe, D. (1996). An adaptive strategy theory of crime and delinquency. In J. Hawkins (Ed.), *Delinquency and crime: Current theories* (pp. 268–314). Cambridge, UK: Cambridge University Press.

37. MacDonald, K. (1992). Warmth as a developmental construct: An evolutionary analysis. *Child Development, 63,* 753–773.

38. Hrdy, S. (1999). *Mother Nature: A history of mothers, infants, and natural selection.* New York: Pantheon.

39. Fisher (1998).

40. Geary, D. (2000). Evolution and proximate expression of human paternal investment. *Psychological Bulletin, 126,* 55–77.

41. Walsh, A. (2006) Evolutionary psychology and criminal behavior. In J. Barkow (Ed.), *Missing the revolution: Darwinism for social scientists* (pp. 225–268). Oxford, UK: Oxford University Press.

42. Quinsey, V. (2002). Evolutionary theory and criminal behavior. *Legal and Criminological Psychology, 7,* 1–14.

43. Rowe (1996, p. 270).

44. Ellis and Walsh (2000).

45. Jaffee, S., Moffitt, T., Caspi, A., & Taylor, A. (2003). Life with (or without) father: The benefits of living with two biological parents depend on the father's antisocial behavior. *Child Development, 74,* 109–126.

46. Harpending, H., & Draper, P. (1988). Antisocial behavior and the other side of cultural evolution. In T. Moffitt & S. Mednick (Eds.), *Biological contributions to crime causation* (pp. 293–307). Dordrecht, The Netherlands: Martinus Nyhoff.

47. Ember, M., & Ember, C. (1998, October). Facts of violence. *Anthropology Newsletter,* pp. 14–15.

48. Shore, R. (1997). *Rethinking the brain: New insights into early development.* New York: Families and Work Institute.

49. MacLean, P. (1990). T*he triune brain in evolution: Role in paleocerebral functions.* New York: Plenum.

50. Buck, R. (1999). The biological affects: A typology. *Psychological Review, 106,* 301–336.

51. Sowell, E., Thompson, P., Holmes, C., Jernigan, T., & Toga, A. (1999). In vivo evidence for post-adolescent brain maturation in frontal and striatal regions. *Nature Neuroscience, 2,* 859–861.

52. Edelman, G. (1992). *Bright air, brilliant fire.* New York: Basic Books.

53. Munafo, M., Clark, T., Moore, L., Payne, E., Walton, R., & Flint, J. (2003). Genetic polymorphisms and personality in healthy adults: A systematic review and meta-analysis. *Molecular Psychiatry, 8,* 471–484.

54. Pinel, J. (2000). *Biopsychology* (4th ed.). Boston: Allyn & Bacon.

55. Quartz, S., & Sejnowski, T. (1997). The neural basis of cognitive development: A constructivist manifesto. *Behavioral and Brain Sciences, 20,* 537–596. (Quote on p. 579)

56. Black, J., & Greenough, W. (1997). How to build a brain: Multiple memory systems have evolved and only some of them are constructivist. *Behavioral and Brain Sciences, 20,* 558–559.

57. Depue, R., & Collins, P. (1999). Neurobiology of the structure of personality: Dopamine, facilitation of incentive motivation, and extraversion. *Behavioral and Brain Sciences, 22,* 491–569.

58. Black and Greenough (1997).

59. Rakic, P. (1996). Development of the cerebral cortex in human and non-human primates. In M. Lewis (Ed.), *Child and adolescent psychiatry: A comprehensive textbook* (pp. 9–30). New York: Williams & Wilkins.

60. Sowell et al. (1999).

61. Sowell et al. (1999).

62. Edelman (1992).

63. Levine, D. (1993). Survival of the synapses. *The Sciences, 33,* 46–52.

64. Bromage, T. (1987). The biological and chronological maturation of early hominids. *Journal of Human Evolution, 16,* 257–272.

65. Buck (1999).

66. Bromage (1987).

67. Glaser, D. (2000). Child abuse and neglect and the brain: A review. *Journal of Child Psychology and Psychiatry, 41,* 97–116.

68. Teicher, M., Ito, Y., Glod, C., Schiffer, F., & Gelbard, H. (1997). Early abuse, limbic system dysfunction, and borderline personality disorder. In J. Osofsky (Ed.), *Children in a violent society* (pp. 177–207). New York: Guilford.

69. Gunnar, M. (1996). *Quality of care and the buffering of stress physiology: Its potential in protecting the developing human brain.* Minneapolis: University of Minnesota Institute of Child Development.

70. Perry, B., & Pollard, R. (1998). Homeostasis, stress, trauma, and adaptation: A neurodevelopmental view of childhood trauma. *Child and Adolescent Psychiatric Clinics of America, 7,* 33–51. (Quote on p. 36, emphasis added)

71. Ellis, L. (2006). Sex, status, and criminality: A theoretical nexus. *Social Biology, 53,* 144–160.

72. Ellis, L. (2005). A theory explaining biological correlates of criminality. *European Journal of Criminology, 2,* 287–315.

73. White, R., Thornhill, S., & Hampson, E. (In press). Entrepreneurs and evolutionary biology: The relationship between testosterone and new venture creation. *Organizational Behavior and Human Decision Processes.*

74. Gove, W., & Wilmoth, C. (2003). The neurophysiology of motivation and habitual criminal behavior. In A. Walsh & L. Ellis (Eds.), *Biosocial criminology: Challenging environmentalism's supremacy* (pp. 227–245). Hauppauge, NY: Nova Science.

75. Pinel (2000).

76. Depue and Collins (1999).

77. Ruden, R. (1997). *The craving brain: The biobalance approach to controlling addictions.* New York: HarperCollins.

78. Ruden (1997).

79. Lykken, D. (1995). *The antisocial personalities.* Hillsdale, NJ: Lawrence Erlbaum.

80. Depue and Collins (1999).

81. Pine, D., Coplan, J., Wasserman, G., Miller, L., Fried, J., Davies, M., et al. (1997). Neuroendocrine response to fenfluramine challenge to boys: Associations with aggressive behavior and adverse rearing. *Archives of General Psychiatry, 54,* 839–846.

82. Gray, J. (1994). Three fundamental emotional systems. In P. Ekman & R. Davidson (Eds.), *The nature of emotion: Fundamental questions* (pp. 243–247). New York: Oxford University Press.

83. Pihl, R., & Bruce, K. (1995). Cognitive impairment in children of alcoholics. *Alcohol, Health and Research World, 19,* 142–147.

84. Raine, A., Meloy, J., Bihrle, S., Stoddard, J., LaCasse, L., & Buchsbaum, M. (1998). Reduced prefrontal and increased subcortical brain functioning assessed using positron emission tomography in predatory and affective murderers. *Behavioral Sciences and the Law, 16,* 319–332.

85. Cauffman, E., Steinberg, L., & Piquero, A. (2005). Psychological, neuropsychological and physiological correlates of serious antisocial behavior in adolescence: The role of self-control. *Criminology, 43,* 133–175.

86. Bufkin, J., & Luttrell, V. (2005). Neuroimaging studies of aggressive and violent behavior. *Trauma, Violence, and Abuse, 6,* 176–191.

87. Robinson, M. B. (2005). *Why crime? An integrated systems theory of antisocial behavior.* Upper Saddle River, NJ: Prentice Hall.

88. Vila, B. (1994). A general paradigm for understanding criminal behavior: Extending evolutionary ecological theory. *Criminology, 32,* 311–358. (Quote on p. 329)

89. Carey (2003, p. 295).

90. Jeffrey, C. R. (1993). Obstacles to the development of research in crime and delinquency. *Journal of Research in Crime and Delinquency, 30,* 491–497.

91. Vila, B. (1997). Human nature and crime control: Improving the feasibility of nurturant strategies. *Politics and the Life Sciences, 16,* 3–21.

92. Walsh, A., & Ellis, L. (1997). The neurobiology of nurturance, evolutionary expectations, and crime control. *Politics and the Life Sciences, 16,* 42–44.

93. Lanier, M., & Henry, S. (1998). *Essential criminology.* Boulder, CO: Westview.

94. Walsh (2002).

95. Morley, K., & Hall, W. (2003, October). Is there a genetic susceptibility to engage in criminal acts? *Trends and Issues in Crime and Criminal Justice,* pp. 1–10. (Quote on p. 5)

96. Wood, P., Gove, W., & Cochran, J. (1994). Motivations for violent crime among incarcerated adults: A consideration of reinforcement processes. *Journal of the Oklahoma Criminal Justice Consortium, 1,* 63–80. (Quote on pp. 75–76)

DEVELOPMENTAL THEORIES: FROM DELINQUENCY TO CRIME TO DESISTANCE

*K*athleen Holmes was a sweet child born to an "all-American" family in Boise, Idaho. Her parents sent her to a Catholic girls' school, where she did well in her studies. All seemed to be going well for Kathy until she was 16 years old, when she agreed to go to a local Air Force base with two older friends from the neighborhood to meet one of the girl's boyfriends. The boyfriend brought along two of his friends, and the six of them partied with alcohol, drugs, and sex. It was Kathy's first time experiencing any of these things, and she discovered that she liked them all. Thus began a 9-year spiral into alcohol, drugs, and sex addiction, along with all the crimes associated with these conditions, such as drug trafficking, robbery, and prostitution.

When she was 25 years old, she was involved in a serious automobile accident in which she broke her pelvis, both legs, and an arm and suffered a concussion. She was charged with drunken driving and possession of methamphetamine for sale. Kathy spent 10 months recuperating from her injuries, during which she was drug, alcohol, and sex free. Because of her medical condition, she was placed on probation. Her parole officer (PO) was a real "knuckle-dragger," who, while brooking no nonsense, became something of a father figure to her. While she was recuperating, she was often taken care of by a male nurse she described as "nerdy but nice." Her parents, who had been estranged from her for some time, became reacquainted with her, and her PO and nurse taught her to trust men again. She also occupied her time taking online college courses on drug *addiction and counseling. She eventually married her "nerdy nurse" with her parents' blessing, and one of the honored guests was the "knuckle-dragger."*

Kathy's story illustrates some core ideas in this chapter. No matter how low a person sinks into antisocial behavior, he or she is not destined to continue the downward spiral. Certain so-called turning points in life can have a dramatic impact on a person's life. The auto accident and meeting the tough PO and the tender nurse would certainly qualify as significant turning points, as most certainly would marriage and the decision to continue her education. Before she became involved with "the wrong crowd," she had accumulated what is called "social capital" in the form of a good relationship with her family and a good academic preparation. Although she spent most of her social capital, there was sufficient left to get her back on the right track.

In previous chapters, we have examined a variety of theories attempting to explain criminal behavior that have implicitly assumed that their favored causes are applicable across the life span and tend to neglect "the continuity from childhood to adulthood in offending and antisocial behavior and the importance of biological and psychological factors."[1] Another problem is that they imply that criminal behavior is self-perpetuating and continuous once initiated and say little about the process of desisting from it. In contrast to these somewhat static views, developmental theories are dynamic in that they emphasize that individuals develop along different pathways, and as they develop, factors that were previously meaningful to them (say, acceptance by antisocial peers) no longer are, and factors that previously meant little to them (say, marriage and a career) suddenly become meaningful. These theories are concerned with the onset of offending, its acceleration and deceleration, and finally desisting from offending. Because these theories are developmental, they tend to be more integrative than other theories; that is, they look at social, psychological, and biological factors simultaneously. We begin by looking at the early stages of offending.

⚒ Juvenile Delinquency

Delinquency is a legal term that distinguishes between youthful (juvenile) offenders and adult offenders that has its origins in the concept of culpability. Culpability describes the degree to which persons are responsible for their criminal actions. The minimum legally defined age of criminal responsibility is defined in common law as 7 and is the age of responsibility in most states, but it ranges from 6 in North Carolina to 10 in Arkansas, Colorado, Kansas, Pennsylvania, and Wisconsin.[2]

Except in rare instances in which a juvenile commits murder and is waived (transferred) to adult court, juvenile offenders are not referred to as criminals. Acts that are forbidden by law are called delinquent acts when committed by juveniles. The term *delinquent* comes from a Latin term meaning to "leave undone" (as in, "You are delinquent in your car payment"), with the connotation being that juveniles have *not done* something that they were supposed to (behave lawfully) rather than *done* something they were not supposed to. This subtle difference reflects the rehabilitative rather than punitive thrust of the juvenile justice system.

Juveniles have a special status in society. They are expected not to do a number of things adults have a right to do such as smoke, drink, leave home, and stay out late, and they are expected to do things that adults may ignore, such as attend school, obey curfews, and obey their parents. If juveniles violate any of these, they can be charged with a *status offense*—an act of commission or omission applicable only to juveniles. Status offenses are the most frequently dealt with offenses in the juvenile system.[3] The special status of juveniles in the justice system rests on the concept of *parens patriae* ("father of his country"), under which the state may take over the supervision of a delinquent child from his or her parents "in the best interests of the child." The juvenile courts do not have trials—they have "hearings," and the child does not plead guilty or not guilty but rather "admits" or "denies" the charge. Except in rare instances when a juvenile is transferred to adult court, he or she is never found "guilty," but rather the court makes "a finding of fact" indicating that he or she is or is not delinquent. Children found delinquent are never "sentenced"; rather, the courts "dispose" of the matter and seek rehabilitative rather than punitive remedies.[4]

The Extent of Delinquency

As is the case with many other things, the public image of juvenile offenders is fueled by sensationalized media accounts of atypical cases.[5] It is true, however, that juveniles do commit a disproportionate percentage of the *Uniform Crime Reports* (*UCR*) Part I index crimes. Krisberg[6] indicates that we have actually witnessed a steady decline in juvenile offending since 1994 and that youths younger than 18 account for "only" 13% of arrests for violent crime. However, youths younger than 18 comprise only about 6% of the American population,[7] and thus they are overrepresented among those arrested for violence. In 2003, youths younger than 18 accounted for 15.5% of Part I index violent crimes and 28.9% of Part I index property crimes and thus account for about 2.5 times their "fair share" of violent crimes and about 4.5 times their "fair share" of property crimes.[8]

Juvenile misbehavior occurs everywhere and at all times. William Shakespeare wrote in *The Winter's Tale*, "I would there be no age between ten and three-and-twenty, or that youth would sleep out the rest; for there is nothing in the between but getting wenches with child, wronging the ancientry, stealing, fighting" (Act III, Scene III). Figure 9.1 presents four graphs showing arrest rates by age in various countries during various time periods. Although the height of the peaks in graphs (the height indicates the prevalence—the proportion of the population—committing crimes; the higher the peak, the greater the prevalence) will change across time periods and across cultures, the same pattern (i.e., a sharp rise beginning around puberty and rising steadily until the mid-teens and then falling off) is always present.

Why we consistently see this pattern of behavior suddenly appear at puberty and then slowly burn itself out after reaching its peak between 16 and 18 has long been a mystery to criminologists. Some theories attempt to explain the rise in antisocial behavior by pointing to the increase in peer involvement in adolescence and the decline in antisocial behavior thereafter by the decreasing influence of peers and the increasing influence of girlfriends, wives, children, and employers.[9] However, this describes situations that co-occur with the probable beginning and the end of delinquent behavior. It does no explain *why* the period between these events is so filled with it or *why* associations with peers so often lead to negative behavior. As Shavit and Rattner point out, the age peak in delinquency remains "unexplained by any known set of sociological variables."[10] Gottfredson and Hirschi[11] share this opinion and appear to be saying that because the age effect is constant across time and place, criminologists should accept it as a fact and go on from there. After all, *age* in this context is not a personal characteristic but rather an index of a certain developmental stage (puberty) we all go through. But just because we all go through it does not mean that age effects can be ignored. There must be something special requiring its own explanations going on during this period of life that dramatically, albeit temporarily, increases the probability of antisocial behavior.

| Figure 9.1 | Illustrating the Age Curve in Different Countries at Different Times |

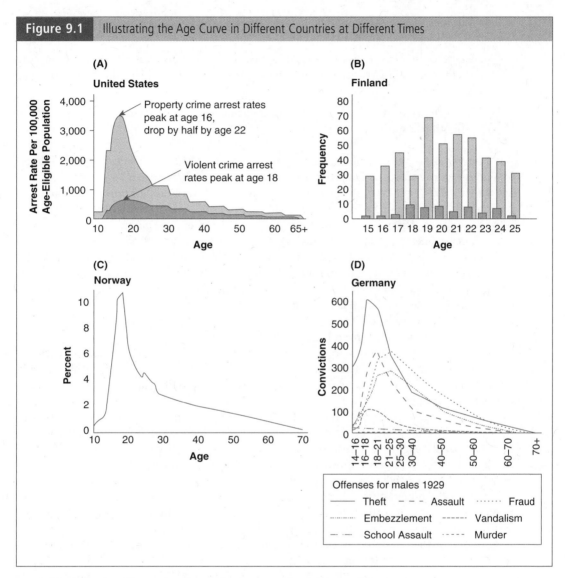

Source: Ellis, L., & Walsh, A. (2000). *Criminology: A global perspective* (p. 109). Boston: Allyn & Bacon.

Puberty, Adolescence, and Change

Aaron White[12] provides us with four key messages from the 2003 conference of the New York Academy of Sciences, which focused on adolescent brain development:

1. Much of the behavior characterizing adolescence is rooted in biology intermingling with environmental influences to cause teens to conflict with their parents, take more risks, and experience wide swings in emotion.

2. The lack of synchrony between a physically mature body and a still maturing nervous system may explain these behaviors.

3. Adolescents' sensitivities to rewards appear to be different than in adults, prompting them to seek higher levels of novelty and stimulation to achieve the same feeling of pleasure.

4. With the right dose of guidance and understanding, adolescence can be a relatively smooth transition.

Puberty is a developmental stage that marks the onset of the transition from childhood to adulthood, preparing us for procreation. The onset of puberty occurs around 11 years of age for girls and 12 for boys, although there is considerable variation for both onset and completion. When undergoing these changes, many happy and loveable children suddenly morph into malcontents acting like they should be in Pampers rather than pants.

Whereas puberty is a defined biological *event* (or series of events), adolescence is a *process* that begins at puberty and ends with adulthood. The term *adulthood* is both vague and variable because it is a socially defined status. The legally defined adult age of 18 rarely matches socially defined adulthood today. Socially defined adulthood typically means taking on socially responsible roles such as acquiring a steady job and starting one's own family, roles that mark one as an independent member of society. Adolescence is thus a period of limbo in which individuals no longer need parental care but are not yet ready to take on the roles and responsibilities of adulthood. For all its alleged "storm and stress," adolescence is a perfectly normal and very necessary period in the human life span.[13] There is much to learn about being an adult, and adolescence is a time to experiment with a variety of social skills before having to put them into practice in earnest.

To encourage all this experimentation, natural selection has provided adolescents with the necessary tools, the first of which is the 10- to 20-fold increase in testosterone that accompanies puberty.[14] Figure 9.2 illustrates the ebb and flow of testosterone across the life span for males and females. Testosterone organizes the male brain during the second trimester of pregnancy so that it will respond in male-typical ways when the brain is activated in that direction by the pubertal surge.[15] Note from Figure 9.2 that after sex-related brain organization takes place, there is little difference in levels of male and female testosterone until puberty, at which time males have approximately 10 times the female levels. Testosterone is most responsible for the development of male characteristics, including behavioral characteristics such as aggression and dominance seeking.[16]

Adolescents are also experiencing changes in the ratios of excitatory and inhibitory neurotransmitters. Dopamine (the "go get it" transmitter we met in Chapter 8) and another excitatory transmitter, called glutamate, peak during adolescence, while the inhibitory transmitters gamma-aminobutyric acid and serotonin are reduced.[17–19] Given that adolescents have been provided with all the biological tools needed to increase novelty seeking, sensation seeking, status seeking, risk taking, and competitiveness, we can conclude that the behaviors manifested in adolescence (or rather the mechanisms underlying them) are adaptations forged by natural selection.[20,21] Evolutionary biologists stress that natural selection favors the most adventurous and dominant males because such characteristics typically result in more mating opportunities and thus greater reproductive success. As among all primate species, mid-adolescence and early adulthood is a period of intense competition among males for

| Figure 9.2 | Testosterone Levels of Human Males and Females Across the Lifespan |

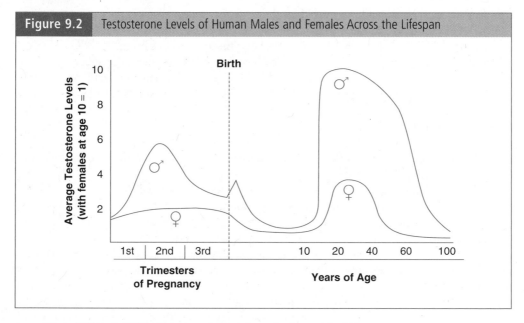

SOURCE: Ellis, L., & Walsh, A. (2000). Criminology: *A global perspective.* Boston: Allyn & Bacon.

dominance and status aimed ultimately at securing more mating opportunities than the next male.[22] As Martin Daly puts it, "There are many reasons to think that we've been designed [by natural selection] to be maximally competitive and conflictual in young adulthood."[23]

In addition, the adolescent brain is also going through an intense period of physical restructuring. The pubertal hormonal surges prompt the increase of gene expression in the brain; the expressed genes then play their parts in slowly refining the neural circuitry to its adult form.[24] Magnetic resonance imaging (MRI) studies reveal that the prefrontal cortex undergoes a wave of synaptic overproduction just prior to puberty, which is followed by a period of pruning during adolescence and early adulthood.[25,26] Recall that the prefrontal cortex (PFC) serves functions such as modulating emotions from the limbic system and making reasoned judgments and plans. Because the selective retention and elimination of synapses depend on input from the environment, adolescence is a critical stage of development in which to provide opportunities for youths to test themselves with prosocial activities that are as exciting and challenging for them as raising hell.[27]

The adolescent PFC is also less completely myelinated (myelin is the fatty substance that coats and insulates axons) than the adult PFC,[28] and a less myelinated brain results in a larger "time lapse" between the onset of an emotional event in the limbic system and a person's rational judgment of it. In other words, there are *physical* reasons for the greater ratio of emotional to rational responses evidenced by many teens. The physical immaturity of the adolescent brain, combined with a "supercharged" physiology, facilitates the tendency to assign faulty attributions to situations and the intentions of others. In other words, a brain on "go slow" superimposed on a physiology on "fast forward" explains why many teenagers find it difficult to accurately gauge the meanings and intentions of others and to experience more stimuli as aversive during adolescence than they did as children and will do so when they are adults.[29] As neurologist Richard Restak so well puts it, "The immaturity of the adolescent's behavior is perfectly mirrored by the immaturity of the adolescent's brain."[30]

Several studies show generally that the earlier the onset of puberty, the greater the level of problem behavior for both girls and boys.[31,32] Juveniles who enter puberty significantly earlier than their peers must confront their "raging hormones" with a brain that is no more mature than those of their peers. In one study, testosterone level predicted future problem behavior, but only for boys who entered puberty early.[33] Felson and Haynie[34] found that boys who experience early onset of puberty were more likely to commit a number of delinquent and other antisocial acts than other boys, but they were also more autonomous, were better psychologically adjusted, and had more friends.

What about when adolescence is over and adulthood is attained? We talk about "aging out" of crime, but this is just as empty as saying adolescence "ages in" crime without knowing what the mechanisms are. Around about the age of 20, the exicatory transmitters start to decrease and the inhibitory transmitters start to increase.[35] With a more bio-balanced brain on board, more adult-like personality traits emerge. McCrae and his colleagues[36] report findings from five different countries showing age-related decreases in personality traits positively related to antisocial behavior and increases in personality traits positively related to prosocial behavior. The fine-tuning of neurological and endocrine (hormonal) systems occurs across the life span and thankfully results in personality traits in adulthood conducive to prosocial behavior for the great majority of individuals. These changes lay the foundations for the acquisition of responsible social roles that help us stay on the straight and narrow.

Patterns of Serious Delinquency

The developmental model devised by Terrence Thornberry, David Huizinga, and Rolf Loeber[37] focuses on the escalation of the seriousness of delinquent acts being committed as boys age, not on why they commit such acts. The model is based on three longitudinal studies that include more than 4,000 subjects followed since 1987. What has emerged from these three studies is an image of three developmental pathways of offending, as noted in Figure 9.3.

The *authority conflict* pathway starts before age 12 with simple stubborn behavior, followed by defiance and authority avoidance. Some boys in this pathway move into the second stage (*defiance/disobedience*) and a few more into the *authority avoidance* stage. At this point, some boys progress to one of the other two pathways, but many will go no further. The *covert* pathway starts after puberty and involves minor offenses in Stage 1 that become progressively more serious for a few boys who enter Stage 3 on this pathway. The *overt* pathway progresses from minor aggressive acts in Stage 1 to very serious violent acts in Stage 3. The more seriously involved delinquents in the overt and covert pathways may switch back and forth between violent and property crimes. The overall take-home lesson of this model is that as boys get older, their crimes become more serious, but happily there are far fewer of them.

Risk and Protective Factors for Serious Delinquency

There are individuals who go beyond the normal adolescent hell-raising to commit serious crimes. An examination of the risk and protective factors presented in Table 9.1 for violent offending, gleaned from hundreds of studies by the Office of the Surgeon General of

What Role Do Genes Play in Delinquency?

Genes obviously play a huge role in turning on and controlling the processes of puberty, but what role do they play beyond that? A large number of studies have found large heritability coefficients (ranging from .58 to .82 for the various traits associated with delinquent and criminal behavior such as fearlessness, aggressiveness, sensation seeking, empathy, and impulsiveness) (reviewed in Moffitt & Walsh[38]). These high estimates contrast with the low heritability estimate of .40 for adolescent and adult antisocial behavior from a meta-analysis of 51 studies.[39] We may ask why the heritability for delinquent and criminal behavior is so small compared with the traits that are its constituent parts. One reason is that the constituent parts are *traits,* whereas criminality is *behavior* expressing those traits.[40] Parents have a greater deal of control over their offspring's behavior but little or none beyond the genes they bequeathed them over their personality traits; behavior is more subject to environmental influences than are personality traits.

Lykken[41] asks us to imagine two hypothetical populations, one in which all parents are equally incompetent and negligent in their parental duties and the other in which all parents are equally diligent and skilled. If the only environmental factor that mattered was parenting quality (which of course it isn't, but Lykken is trying to make a point), then the only factor that could account for differences in antisocial behavior within each population would be genes (because in each case, the environments are constants), and the heritability coefficient would be 1.0. Although genes would account for 100% of the variance in both environments, there would be much more antisocial behavior in the first one because incompetent and negligent parents have created a situation in which only the most fearful, nonaggressive, and conscientious children would refrain from antisocial behavior. In the second environment, only the most fearless, aggressive, and impulsive children would become antisocial. In the real world, there is a wide variation in the quality of parenting and thus wide variation in the control parents have over their children's behavior. This is why the heritability of all forms of antisocial behavior is less than the basic psychological traits that are its constituent parts. Parenting matters, and that is what the last of the four key messages from the 2003 conference of the New York Academy of Sciences ("With the right dose of guidance and understanding, adolescence can be a relatively smooth transition") conveys.[42]

the United States (OSGUS), help us to understand why.[43] A **risk factor** is something in individuals' personal characteristics or their environment that increases the probability of violent offending. These factors are dynamic rather than static, meaning that their predictive value changes according to what stage of a person's development they occur in, the presence of other risk and protective factors, and the immediate social circumstances. For instance, low socioeconomic status (SES) is a family risk factor, but a person with a high IQ who enjoys a warm relationship with both parents is protected from the risks low SES poses. Similarly, low SES exposes a child to medical problems such as low birth weight and birth complications due to poor maternal health, maternal smoking, drinking, drug taking, and so on. These problems can lead to low IQ, which leads to poor school performance, which can lead to offending.

| Figure 9.3 | Three Pathways to Boys' Disruptive Behavior and Delinquency |

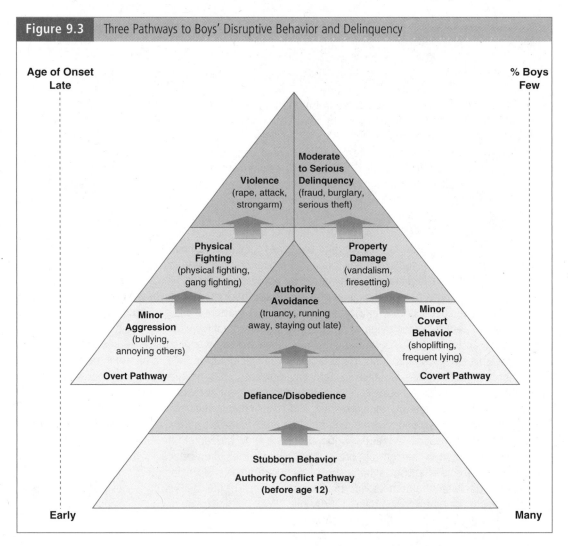

Source: Thornberry, T., Huizinga, D., & Loeber, R. (2004). The causes and correlates studies: Findings and policy implication. *Juvenile Justice, 9*, 3–19.

It is typical for risk (and protective) factors to cluster together because the tendency is for miseries to multiply and advantages to aggregate. A broken home (single-parent family), for instance, is a risk factor that can lead to low SES and the financial necessity to reside in a neighborhood with many other similarly situated families, and thus children are exposed to social disorganization and antisocial peers. Risk factors also vary greatly in intensity. Some children are more impulsive than others, some are more severely abused, and some neighborhoods are more disorganized than others. The OSGUS report[44] indicates that a 10-year-old child with six or more risk factors is approximately 10 times more likely than a 10-year-old child with only one risk factor to be violent by the age of 18.

We have already examined many of these risk factors (low IQ, poverty, social disorganization, parental supervision or abuse, etc.) and will not do so again here. We can also ignore those risk factors labeled "general offenses" and "problem (antisocial) behavior" since these are precisely the things we want to explain. Other risk factors (aggression, substance abuse) will be examined in subsequent chapters. We will only examine those individual level factors here that have their onset early in life and become more salient in adolescence.

Table 9.1	Delinquency Risk Factors by Domain		
Domain	**Early Onset (Ages 6–11)**	**Late Onset (Ages 12–14)**	**Protective Factors**

Individual	Being male
	ADHD/impulsivity
	Medical, physical problems
	Aggression
	Low IQ
	General offenses
	Problem (antisocial behavior)
	Substance abuse
	Exposure to TV violence
	Antisocial attitudes, beliefs
	Dishonesty[a]
		Restlessness
		Difficulty concentrating[a]
		General offenses
		Risk taking
		Aggression[a]
		Being male
		Physical violence
		Antisocial attitudes, beliefs
		Crimes against persons
		Low IQ
		Substance abuse
			Intolerant attitude toward
			  deviance
			High IQ
			Being female
			Positive social orientation
			Perceived sanction for
			  transgressions

Family	Low socioeconomic status
	Antisocial parents
	Poor parent-child relationship
	Harsh, lax, or inconsistent
	  parenting
	Broken home
	Separation from parents
	Abusive parents
	Neglect
		Poor parent-child
		  relationship
		Low socioeconomic status
		Harsh, lax, or inconsistent
		  parenting
		Poor monitoring, supervision
		Antisocial parents
		Broken home
		Abusive parents
		Family conflict [a]
			Warm, supportive relationship
			  with parents and other
			  adults
			Parent's positive evaluation of
			  child's peers
			Parental monitoring

School	Poor attitude, performance	Poor attitude, performance Academic failure	Commitment to school Recognition for involvement in conventional activities
Peer group	Weak social ties Antisocial peers	Weak social ties Antisocial, delinquent peers Gang membership	Friends who engage in conventional behavior

Community		Neighborhood crime, drugs
		Neighborhood
		  disorganization
			Stable, organized
			  neighborhood

Source: Adapted from the Office of the Surgeon General. (2001). *Youth violence: A report of the Surgeon General*. Washington, DC: U.S. Department of Health and Human Services.

a. Males only.

ADHD and CD

Among the individual-level risk factors listed in Table 9.1 are attention deficit with hyperactivity disorder (ADHD)/impulsivity, restlessness, difficulty concentrating, and aggression. These and other such risk factors can be fruitfully explored by looking at the childhood syndromes of ADHD and conduct disorder (CD). These separate but often linked syndromes are neuropsychological and temperamental deficits that can lead to a lifetime of antisocial behavior.

Attention deficit with hyperactivity disorder is a chronic neurological condition that is behaviorally manifested as constant restlessness, impulsiveness, difficulty with peers, disruptive behavior, short attention span, academic underachievement, risk-taking behavior, and extreme boredom. As with any other syndrome, the symptoms vary widely in their severity and frequency of occurrence. Most healthy children will manifest some of these symptoms at one time or another, but they cluster together to form a syndrome in ADHD children (8 out of 14 symptoms are required for diagnosis) and are chronic and more severe than simple high spirits.[45] Numerous brain-imaging studies have found many differences (albeit small ones) in brain anatomy and physiology between ADHD and non-ADHD children.[46,47]

ADHD affects somewhere between 2% and 9% of the childhood population and is four or five times more prevalent in males than in females.[48] Although the precise cause of ADHD is not known, it is known that genes play a large role.[49] Heritability values in the .75 to .95 range are consistently found regardless of whether ADHD is considered to be a categorical (something a person has or does not have) or continuous (a matter of degree) trait.[50] Environmental factors that play a role in the etiology of ADHD are fetal exposure to drugs, alcohol, and tobacco; perinatal complications; and head trauma.[51] Subsequent environmental factors such as family, school, and peer variables appear not to have any causal impact on it, although they can exacerbate its symptoms.[52] ADHD symptoms generally decline in their severity with age, although about 90% of ADHD sufferers continue to display some impairment into adulthood.[53]

Some, but not all, children diagnosed with ADHD show electroencephalogram (EEG) patterns of underarousal (slow brainwaves) similar to adult psychopaths.[54] Such a brainwave pattern is experienced subjectively as boredom, which motivates the person to seek or create environments containing more excitement. ADHD behavior can be normalized temporarily by administering methylphenidate (Ritalin), a mild stimulant drug. Stimulant drugs have the effect of *increasing* activity for non-ADHD individuals but have a calming or normalizing effect on suboptimally aroused individuals by raising the activity of the brain's sensory mechanisms to normal levels. This relieves feelings of boredom because the brain is now able to be more attentive to features of the environment that it could not previously capture. When on medication, children with ADHD are less disruptive, become less obnoxious to peers, and can focus more on schoolwork.

Given the range of symptoms associated with ADHD, it is not surprising that it is consistently found to be related to a wide variety of antisocial behaviors. A review of 100 studies found that 99 of them reported a positive relationship between ADHD and various antisocial behaviors.[55]

ADHD delinquents are more likely than non-ADHD delinquents to persist in their offending as adults, but this probability rises dramatically for ADHD children also diagnosed with **conduct disorder** (CD). CD is defined as "the persistent display of serious antisocial actions that are extreme given the child's developmental level and have a significant impact on the rights of others."[56] ADHD and CD are found to co-occur in 30% to 50% of cases (reviewed in Lynam[57]). Conduct disorder has an onset at around 5 years of age. It remains at a steady rate for girls (about 0.8% of all girls) and rises to about 2.8% at age 15, but it rises steadily in boys from about 2.1% age 5 to about 5.5% at age 15.[58] Conduct disorder also appears to be a neurological disorder with substantial genetic effects.[59]

Terrie Moffitt[60] has proposed that verbal deficits are what place children at risk for CD. Moffitt indicates that neurological evidence suggests that the left frontal lobes contain the mechanisms by which children process their parents' instructions ("No!" "That's naughty"). These instructions then become the child's internalized verbally based basis of self-control. Children with deficits in frontal lobe mechanisms do not profit from verbal instructions and tend to develop a present-oriented and impulsive cognitive style. Lacking normal levels of abstract reasoning, such children may have to learn lessons through the more painful process of trial and error and may thus experience more frequent punishments for their lack of compliance with instructions. Moffitt also hypothesizes that the PIQ > VIQ intellectual imbalance profile discussed in Chapter 7 may be an index of this deficiency given that items on the performance scale require mostly manual responses and make little use of language skills.

Many of the cognitive and temperamental symptoms of children with CD and ADHD are similar. Children with CD, but not children with ADHD, tend to score below average in intelligence and are highly overrepresented in impoverished family environments.[61] As mentioned, the co-occurrence of ADHD and CD represents the greatest risk for serious delinquency and adult criminality. Markus Krueisi and his colleagues[62] propose that ADHD is a product of a deficient behavioral inhibition system (BIS), and CD is a product of an oversensitive behavioral activating system (BAS) (see Chapter 8). If this is the case, then those afflicted with both ADHD and CD suffer a double disability because not only does their oversensitive BAS incline them to seek high levels of stimulation, but their faulty BIS also leaves them with little sense of when to put a stop to their search. The co-occurrence of ADHD and CD puts a heavy burden on parents and may lead them to adopt coercive rearing practices that further enhance the risk of offending. Academic failure will also increase frustration, as will the peer rejection that is a feature of ADHD.

ADHD does not represent a hopeless pathology that leads its victims down the road to inevitable criminality, particularly when CD is not present. Perhaps it should not even be called a disorder but rather a natural variant of human diversity. While acknowledging that ADHD is problematic in modern society, that it has real neurological foundations, and that parents are probably right in the current social context to choose to medicate their children with ADHD, Jaak Panksepp[63] asserts that ADHD-like behaviors are observed in the young of all social species, and it is called "rough-and-tumble" play. ADHD-like behaviors may have even been adaptive in our evolutionary history when restless boldness and curiosity meant exploring beyond known boundaries.[64] If the "true" rate of ADHD is as high as reported, then genes underlying it have survived natural selection, which means that they must have conferred some benefits in evolutionary environments even if they do not in evolutionarily novel classroom environments. Many individuals with ADHD have above-average IQs and are creative, so perhaps the symptoms of ADHD are only problematic in the modern context in which children are expected to sit still for long periods trying to learn subjects that they find boring.

⊠ Major Developmental Theories

Having highlighted the major biological developmental changes from childhood through early adulthood and having identified the various risk factors for offending, we can now explore developmental theories. As noted at the beginning of this chapter, developmental theories are dynamic theories concerned with the frequency, duration, and seriousness of offending behavior from onset to desistance. Some theories assume that a **latent trait**—a "master trait" such as low self-control—influences behavioral choices across time and situations, while others do not. All theories maintain that although a criminal career may be initiated at any time, it is almost always begun in childhood, with only about 4% being initiated in adulthood.[65] The duration of a criminal career may be limited to one offense or can (rarely) last well into old age, and the frequency and seriousness of offending can vary widely. All of these factors (onset, frequency, duration, seriousness, and desistance) depend on a variety of interacting individual and situational factors that vary across the life course. Developmental theories therefore require longitudinal studies in which the same cohort of people is continually interviewed and assessed over long periods of time. We begin with Agnew's general theory.

Robert Agnew's General or "Super Traits" Theory

Robert Agnew has narrowed down his search for traits conducive to criminal behavior in his new general theory of crime. Recall from Chapter 4 that in his general strain theory, Agnew began by adding a number of individual traits to Merton's anomie/strain theory. In **Agnew's super traits theory** (our name for it to distinguish it from Gottfredson and Hirschi's general theory), Agnew identifies five so-called *life domains* that contain possible crime-generating factors: *personality, family, school, peers,* and *work*. It is a developmental theory because these domains interact and feed back on one another across the life span. Agnew suggests that personality traits set individuals on a particular developmental trajectory that influence how other people in the family, school, peer group, and work domains react to them. In other words, personality variables "condition" the effect of social variables on crime.

Noting that personality traits cluster together, Agnew identifies the latent traits of *low self-control* and *irritability* as "super traits" that encompass many of the traits we discussed in Chapter 7 such as sensation seeking, impulsivity, poor problem-solving skills, inattentiveness, and low empathy. People saddled with low self-control and irritable temperaments are likely to evoke negative responses from family members, school teachers, peers, and workmates that feed back and exacerbate those tendencies (reactive gene-environment correlation).

We have already discussed low self-control and impulsiveness/low constraint at length in earlier chapters. From Agnew's description of irritability, it appears to be what we identified as negative emotionality in Chapter 7. Agnew states that "biological factors [autonomic nervous system and brain chemistry] have a direct effect on irritability/low self-control and an indirect effect on the other life domains through irritability/low self-control,"[66] although he favors parental treatment as the primary reason children are irritable and lack self-control.

Agnew claims that his theory can explain gender, racial, and age effects in criminality and can also account for the differences between individuals who limit their offending to the adolescent years and those who offend across the life course. In terms of gender differences, Agnew says that males are more likely to inherit irritability/low self-control than females, perhaps because in evolutionary terms, these traits have aided male reproductive success by enhancing male aggressiveness and competitiveness.[67] In terms of race differences, Agnew argues that Blacks are more likely to be poor and to receive discriminatory treatment. This and other factors may significantly increase irritability, and perceptions of poor job prospects may also lead to the adoption of an impulsive "live-for-the-day" lifestyle among some African Americans.

Agnew notes that neuroscience claims that the immaturity of adolescent behavior is closely tied to the immaturity of the adolescent brain, with adolescents tending to become more irritable because their brains are undergoing a period of intense "remodeling." At the same time their brains are changing, adolescents are experiencing massive hormonal surges that tend to facilitate aggression and competitiveness. Thus, says Agnew, the neurological and endocrine changes during adolescence *temporarily* increase irritability/low self-control among adolescents who limit their offending to that period, while for those who continue to offend, irritability/low self-control is a *stable* characteristic.

Robert Agnew is one of the world's most prominent criminologists, and as such, it is gratifying to see how he has neatly integrated concepts and research from behavior genetics, evolutionary psychology, and the neurosciences into his theory, as well as showing how the various components (domains) influence each other developmentally across the life span. Figure 9.4 summarizes Agnew's theory.

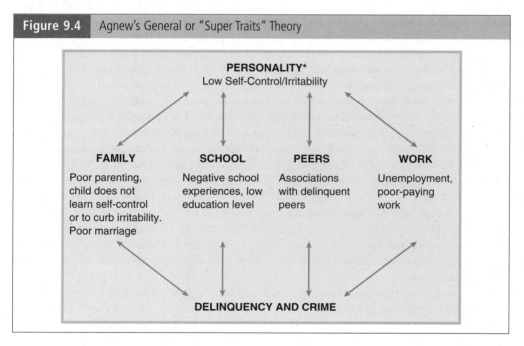

Figure 9.4   Agnew's General or "Super Traits" Theory

*These five domains interact and feed back on one another.

Sampson and Laub's Age-Graded Developmental Theory

Sampson and Laub's age-graded developmental theory[68,69] (they prefer to call it a life course theory rather than a developmental theory) is based on data collected in the 1930s through the 1960s by Sheldon and Eleanor Glueck.[70] The Gluecks sampled 500 delinquents from two correctional schools in Massachusetts and a control group of 500 boys who grew up in the same economically deprived areas as the delinquents. Few boys escaped any sort of antisocial behavior, but the delinquents were found to have lower IQs and to be more impulsive, extroverted, hostile, and destructive than the boys from the control group. The Gluecks were concerned with the power of social bonds as constraining factors rather than with individual differences, however, and found that among both groups, those more strongly bonded to jobs and spouses were significantly less likely to be arrested between the ages of 17 and 32. Seventy-four percent of the delinquents with low job stability were arrested versus 32% with high job stability; the corresponding percentages for the control group were 36% and 9%. Similarly, 76% of the delinquents with weak spousal bonding were arrested versus 34% with high spousal bonding; the corresponding percentages for the control group were 39% and 12%. Although individual personality factors clearly differentiated *between* the two groups, strong social bonds clearly differentiated individuals *within* each group.

Sampson and Laub added to the Gluecks' data by locating a small number of the original delinquent group and conducting further interviews with them up to age 70. Age-graded theory is essentially a social control theory extended into adulthood to include adult bonds. While the bonds to parents and school are very important during childhood and to peers during adolescence, they become less important in adulthood when new situations offer opportunities to form new social bonds that constrain offending behavior.

As with all control theories with their classical assumptions about human nature, the task of age-graded theory is not to explain why people commit crimes but why people do not. The theory does not assume any latent trait and posits that factors such as low IQ, difficult temperament, SES, and broken home have only indirect affects on offending via their influence on the ease or difficulty with which bonding and socialization take place. Thus the theory places emphasis on the process of desisting rather than on risk factors for offending.

People who bond well with conventional others build social capital. **Social capital** refers to a store of positive relationships in social networks built on norms of reciprocity and trust developed over time upon which the individual can draw for support. People who have opened their social capital "accounts" early in life (bonding to parents and school), even though they may spend it freely as adolescents, build quite a nest egg by the time they reach adulthood. They can then gather more interest in the form of a successful career and marriage (bonding to a career and a family of one's own). This accumulation of social capital provides people with a powerful stake in conformity, which they are not likely to risk by engaging in criminal activity.

All is not lost for people who enter adulthood with little social capital, however. Life is a series of transitions (or life events) that may change a person's life trajectory in prosocial directions. Sampson and Laub call such events **turning points** and consider this concept the most important contribution of their theory.[71] Important turning points include getting married, finding a decent job, moving to a new neighborhood, or entering military service. Of course, turning points are processes rather than events and, rather than promoting change, may accentuate antisocial tendencies. According to Gottfredson and Hirschi, the problem is that "the offender tends to convert these institutions [marriage, jobs] into sources of satisfaction consistent with his previous criminal behavior."[72] In other words, they expand their antisocial repertoire into domestic abuse and workplace crime. Nevertheless, Laub and Sampson[73] have shown that obtaining a good job and a good marriage (emphasis on quality) does reduce offending among previously high-rate offenders.

Although a person may be disadvantaged by the past (miseries multiply just as advantages accumulate), he or she does not have to be a prisoner to the past. Age-graded theory strongly emphasizes human agency—"the purposeful execution of choice and individual will"[74]—and some people freely chose a life of crime because they find it seductive and rewarding despite

▲ **Photo 9.1**   From this series of family images taken over time, can you discern the behavioral and life course paths of the individuals depicted? One became a teen delinquent but then went on to be law-abiding adult and, ultimately, a minister. One dropped out of a teen job to move away to marry a federal inmate, who had sold a number of types of drugs. Another started a career in sales but became involved in possible "Ponzi" schemes. One became a criminologist.

Figure 9.5	Sampson and Laub's Age-Graded Developmental Theory

Childhood	Adolescence	Early Adulthood	Late Adulthood
Low SES, low IQ, difficult temperament, family disruption →	Poor bonds to parents and school →	Serious → delinquency	Poor marriage, → poor job	Continued → Gradual offending desisting from offending

		Social Capital		Turning Points
Lower level of → risk factors	Good bonds to → parents and school.	Minor → Delinquency	Good marriage, → good job	Desist from offending

NOTE: Top trajectory = high-risk delinquents; bottom trajectory = low-risk delinquents.

having full knowledge of the negative consequences. Nevertheless, all members of the Gluecks' original delinquent sample that Sampson and Laub were able to locate ($N = 52$) had desisted from offending by age 70, regardless of whether they were defined as high risk or low risk as children and regardless of the level of social capital they had managed to accumulate. Figure 9.5 presents the theory in schematic form representing the life course trajectories of high- and low-risk delinquents.

David Farrington's Integrated Cognitive Antisocial Potential (ICAP) Theory

Farrington's integrated cognitive antisocial potential (ICAP) theory is based on a longitudinal cohort study of 411 boys born in deprived areas (thus putting all boys at environmental risk) of London in 1953. The key concepts in the theory are *antisocial potential* (AP), which is a person's risk or propensity to engage in crime, and *cognition,* which is the "thinking or decision-making process that turns potential into actual behavior."[75] AP (a latent trait) is ordered on a continuum (as in Figure 1.3), with relatively few people with very high levels, but levels vary over time and across life events and peak in adolescence.

Farrington distinguishes between *long-term* AP and *short-term* AP. Individuals with long-term AP tend to come from poor families; be poorly socialized, low on anxiety, impulsive, and sensation-seeking; have low IQs; and fail in school.[76] Short-term AP individuals suffer few or any of these deficits but may temporarily increase their AP in response to certain situations or inducements. Farrington indicates that we all have "desires for material goods, status among intimates, excitement, and sexual satisfaction," and people choose illegitimate ways of satisfying them when they lack legitimate means of doing so or when bored, frustrated, or drunk.[77]

The teenage years are particularly potent years for temporarily increasing AP because not only are they years in which the desires Farrington identifies are particularly strong, but they are also the years in which many teenagers lack prosocial means of satisfying them. As we have seen, they are also the years in which teens lack full integration of the cognitive means that enable persons to make wise choices.

Short-term AP can turn into long-term AP over time as a consequence of offending. This can happen if individuals find offending to be reinforcing either in material terms or in psychological terms by gaining status and approval from peers. Such outcomes lead to changes in cognition such that AP is more likely to turn into actual criminal behavior in the future. Offending can also lead to criminal labeling and incarceration, which limits future opportunities to meet one's needs legitimately. Thus offending can be self-perpetuating and cognition changing, as labeling theorists aver. Thus, long-term AP can develop even in the absence of most or all of the risk factors said to predict chronic offending across the life course.

ICAP theory is also interested in the process of desisting from offending. Desistance occurs for both social and individual reasons and occurs at different rates (fairly abruptly or gradually) according to a person's level of AP. As people age, they tend to become less impulsive and less easily frustrated. They also experience turning points such as marriage, steady employment, and moving to new areas, thus shifting their patterns of interaction from peers to girlfriends, wives, and children. These events (1) decrease offending opportunities by shifting routine activities such as drinking with male peers, (2) increase informal controls in terms of having family and work responsibilities, and (3) change cognition in the form of reduced subjective rewards of offending because the costs of doing so are now much higher than before (the risk of losing their hard-earned stake in conformity) as potential peer approval becomes the potential disapproval of wives.[78]

One advantage that sets Farrington's work above others in this chapter is that it is the only one that is multigenerational: It studied the parents of the boys (Generation 1) born in 1953 (Generation 2) and the offspring of these boys (Generation 3). The basic finding across the generations is that having antisocial parents more than doubles the risk that their offspring will also be antisocial.[79] This is particularly likely when children are the offspring of antisocial fathers *and* antisocial mothers, and given the concept of assortative mating (like seeking like), this is highly likely. A variety of studies show strong correlations between number of convictions and antisocial personality traits between husbands and wives.[80] Assortative mating is active gene-environment correlation in the parental generation and passive gene-environment correlation in the offspring generation because children receive genes linked to antisocial traits from both parents and an environment conducive to their development. In such cases, nature and nurture "become a tightly tied bundle."[81]

Terrie Moffitt's Dual-Pathway Developmental Theory

Moffitt's dual-pathway developmental theory is based on findings from an ongoing longitudinal study of a New Zealand birth cohort (in its 30th year as of 2005). It has become perhaps the most empirically supported theory in the literature, and Charles Tittle has called it "the most innovative approach to age-crime relationships and life-course patterns."[82] One of the advantages it has over other developmental theories is that the data available to Moffitt and her colleagues come from collaborative efforts by scientists in medicine and the various biological subdisciplines such as genetics, neuroscience, and endocrinology, as well as psychologists and other social scientists. These rich data have enabled the study team to test biosocial hypotheses such as the MAO/maltreatment hypothesis discussed in Chapter 8.

It has long been known that the vast majority of youth who offend during adolescence desist and that a small number of them continue to offend in adulthood. Moffitt calls the former adolescents limited offenders and the latter life course persistent offenders. This is simply a convenient typology, and it is not meant to imply that all offenders fit nicely into one category or the other. The term *life course persistent* is also a convenient and descriptive term and is not meant to imply that these offenders commit crimes across the entire life course—we rarely see 60-year-old muggers.

Life course persistent offenders (LCPs) are individuals who begin offending prior to puberty and continue well into adulthood. LCP offenders are saddled with high rates of Farrington's AP because of neuropsychological and temperamental deficits that are manifested in low IQ, hyperactivity, inattentiveness, negative emotionality, slow heart rate, and low impulse control. These problems arise from a combination of genetic and environmental effects on central nervous system development. Environmental risk factors include being the offspring of a single teenage mother, low SES, abuse/neglect, and inconsistent discipline.[83] These related individual and environmental impairments initiate a cumulative process of negative person-environment interactions that result in a life course trajectory propelling individuals toward ever hardening antisocial attitudes and behaviors.

Moffitt describes the antisocial trajectory of LCP offenders as one of "biting and hitting at age 4, shoplifting and truancy at age 10, selling drugs and stealing cars at age 16, robbery and rape at age 22, fraud and child abuse at age 30; the underlying disposition remains the same, but its expression changes form as new social opportunities arise at different points of development."[84] This age-consistent behavior is matched by cross-situational behavioral consistency. LCP offenders "lie at home, steal from shops, cheat at school, fight in bars, and embezzle at work."[85] Given this antisocial consistency across time and place, opportunities for change and for legitimate success become increasingly unlikely for these individuals.

Although LCP offenders constituted only 7% of the cohort, they were responsible for more than 50% of all delinquent and criminal acts committed by it.[86,87] Note the consistency of these figures with other cohort data indicating that serious and frequent offending is concentrated among a very small percentage of offenders, the majority of whom began offending prior to puberty. These repeat, persistent, chronic offenders are often referred as career criminals.[88] Moreover, whereas adolescent-limited offenders tend to commit relatively minor offenses such as petty theft, LCP offenders tend to be convicted of more serious crimes, such as assault, robbery, and rape.[89]

Adolescent limited (AL) offenders have a different developmental history that places them on a prosocial trajectory that is temporarily derailed at adolescence (short-term AP). They are not burdened with the neuropsychological problems that weigh heavily on LCP offenders, and they are adequately socialized in childhood by competent parents. AL offenders are "normal" youths adapting to the transitional events surrounding adolescence and whose offending is a social phenomenon played out in peer groups and does not reflect any stable personal deficiencies.[90] At least 90% of offenders are AL.

According to Moffitt, many more teens than in the past are being diverted from their prosocial life trajectories because better health and nutrition have lowered the average age of puberty, while the average time needed to prepare for participation in the economy has increased. These changes have resulted in about a 5- to 10-year **maturity gap** between puberty and entry into the job market. Thus, "adolescent-limited offending is a product of an interaction between age and historical period."[91] Filled with youthful energy, strength, and confidence, as well as a strong desire to shed the restrictions of childhood, AL offenders are attracted to the excitement of antisocial peer groups typically led by experienced LCP delinquents. Once initiated into the group, juveniles learn the attitudes and techniques of offending through mimicking others and gain reinforcement in the form of much desired group approval and acceptance for doing so, as social learning theorists argue.

Moffitt maintains that adolescent antisocial behavior is adaptive because it offers opportunities to gain valuable resources they could not otherwise obtain. Teenagers, still dependent on their parents for so many things, turn their envious eyes on LCP offenders who already have many of the things that signal independence and mature status, such as cars, nice clothes, and access to sex partners. It is no accident that disruptive and belligerent antisocial youths in school become "central members of prominent classroom cliques."[92] In the eyes of their admirers, the behavior of LCP offenders brings them positive results, and many see no reason why similar behavior cannot bring them the same results. LCP and AL youths reinforce one another; LCP youths are rewarded with the admiration of their AL peers, and AL youths receive reinforcement by being accepted by LCP youths.

Figure 9.6 compares the life course trajectories for LCP and AL offenders. Note the role of association with delinquent peers in the two trajectories. In the case of LCP offenders, *stable* antisocial characteristics precede association with delinquent peers. This exemplifies the active gene-environment (G-E) correlation that like seeks like. For AL offenders, association with delinquent peers precedes the development of *temporary* antisocial characteristics. This suggests that association with delinquent peers may be necessary to initiate delinquency for AL offenders and that there is little or no genetic influence on AL delinquency. Teens have a limited ability to choose their environments, so even those at low risk for delinquency may succumb to it under the influence of their more daring peers, whom they temporarily admire and seek to emulate at a time in life when peer influence is tremendously important.

Desisting

As AL offenders mature, they begin to realize that an adult criminal record will severely limit their future options. They also begin to realize that they are freer now to structure their environments consistent with their innate preferences. For some AL offenders, desistance from antisocial behavior is abrupt; for others, it is a slower process. Much depends on a combination of how well they were integrated into the antisocial peer group, what prosocial opportunities become available to them, and personal characteristics. AL offenders have accumulated a store of positive attachments (they elicit positive responses from prosocial others) and academic skills (they stayed in school and did reasonably well) before they started offending and even while they were offending. These attachments and skills can be called upon to provide them with prosocial opportunities such as a good marriage and a good job.

| Figure 9.6 | Moffitt's Dual-Developmental Pathways |

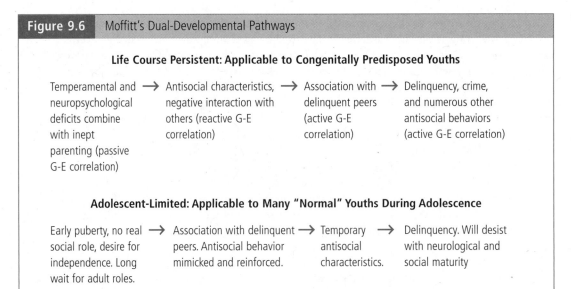

Life Course Persistent: Applicable to Congenitally Predisposed Youths

Temperamental and → Antisocial characteristics, → Association with → Delinquency, crime, neuropsychological negative interaction with delinquent peers and numerous other deficits combine others (reactive G-E (active G-E antisocial behaviors with inept correlation) correlation) (active G-E correlation) parenting (passive G-E correlation)

Adolescent-Limited: Applicable to Many "Normal" Youths During Adolescence

Early puberty, no real → Association with delinquent → Temporary → Delinquency. Will desist social role, desire for peers. Antisocial behavior antisocial with neurological and independence. Long mimicked and reinforced. characteristics. social maturity wait for adult roles.

In Moffitt's words, AL offenders desist from offending because they are "psychologically healthy," and "Healthy youths respond adaptively to changing contingencies."[93]

Sampson and Laub also showed that obtaining a stable job and a spouse are important protective factors for preventing continuing criminal behavior but do not differentiate between LCP and AL offenders (indeed, they deny the existence of such a typology). They do say that social capital is the result of prior social investment, but only AL offenders seem to accumulate such capital. Because LCP offenders burn their prosocial bridges early in life, Sampson and Laub may be referring only to AL offenders (or Farrington's short-term AP offenders) who become involved in adult offending for social reasons only. Only 15% of the boys in the New Zealand cohort with early onset of offending had escaped all adjustment problems by the age of 26,[94] although future studies of the cohort will doubtless find accelerated desistance as it ages. Given the many differences between late- and early-onset boys discovered in numerous longitudinal studies, it is difficult to disagree with C. Ray Jeffery's statement that the early-onset persistent offender is "biologically different from the adolescent offender who stops at age 18–21."[95]

What About Adolescents Who Abstain From Delinquency Altogether?

Moffitt's cohort contained only a small group of males who avoided virtually any antisocial behavior during adolescence. Those who did not engage in such behavior were extremely self-controlled, fearful, interpersonally timid, socially inept, and mostly virginal at age 18. Subsequent studies at age 26 confirmed that abstainers had not become late-onset offenders. They were mostly settled into marriage, were delaying having children, and were likely to be college educated and to hold high-status jobs.[96] Such inhibited and introverted personality characteristics are consistent with studies of autonomic nervous system (ANS) arousal and criminality. As we saw in Chapter 7, individuals with a hyperarousable ANS are easily conditioned, and those with a hypoarousable ANS are conditioned with difficulty. Given the personality profiles of abstainers, it is probable that they are individuals located at the hypertail of the ANS arousal distribution and thus have excessive guilt feelings and excessive fear of the negative consequences of nonconformity.[97]

✖ Evaluation of Developmental Theories

Textbook authors have different opinions about which theories are developmental and which are not, but in our discussion, we focus only on the leading theories that address changes in the propensity to commit crimes across the life span. Developmental theories offer many advantages over theories previously discussed because of their dynamic nature. It is not only consideration of the differential impact of risk factors at

▲ **Photo 9.2** Life course theories attempt to uncover points of desistance, critical events that may change a person's life path from deviant behavior back to law-abiding status. Getting married is considered one of those events. Once one is married, free time to hang out with one's friends tends to disappear.

different junctures across the life span that distinguishes developmental theories; it is also their focus on the process of desisting from crime. Both these contributions are extremely important.

Robert Agnew's "super traits" theory marks an advance on his earlier general strain theory because it parsimoniously (a fancy scientific term describing the frugal use of concepts to succinctly explain a phenomenon) ties together life domains and how they are affected by and affect traits that individuals bring with them to those domains. It is also a major improvement on Gottfredson and Hirschi's self-control theory because it adds the important dimension of negative emotionality (irritability) and links these traits to family, school, peer, and work domains. Agnew is a major figure in criminology, and this new theory seems to have few flaws, although such flaws may emerge as it undergoes testing.

With the exception of Agnew's theory, all developmental theories discussed in this chapter are based on longitudinal cohort data so that theorists can examine the links between risk factors and crime among the same individuals at every developmental stage of their lives. The "youngest" of these cohorts is Moffitt's, but this cohort has the benefit of the participation of scientists from many different disciplines. Such data are hard to come by, however, and some theorists argue that cross-sectional studies (research that studies a sample at a single moment in time) are adequate and that longitudinal studies are an expensive and unnecessary luxury. Individuals making such claims are those who identify a latent trait (e.g., self-control) that is considered stable throughout life. Thus, cross-sectional studies capture characteristics of individuals at any one time, making multiyear studies redundant. Such a position ignores the interaction of this supposed stable latent trait with vastly different life experiences.

Whatever other advantages longitudinal studies may offer, their main advantage is that they allow us to actually identify causes rather than mere correlates because temporal order (which factor came first) can be established among the correlates, something that cross-sectional studies cannot do. For example, if we followed a birth cohort for 40 years theoretically guided by Agnew's super traits theory, we could measure the relationship between serotonin levels (recall that low serotonin underlies both low self-control and negative emotionality) and patterns of offending at different developmental stages. We could then observe how these behavior patterns affected relationships in the family, school, peers, and work. We could ask questions such as the following:

- Did subjects initially determined to be low on self-control and high on irritability become more so because of the magnifying effect brought about by the reactions of others to subjects' traits?
- Are there important transitional events in people's lives that have the effect of increasing/decreasing criminal behavior regardless of their traits?
- Is the marriage effect a matter of self-selection into a stable marriage based on individual traits rather than the effects of social bonding?
- Which environmental factors are strongest in strengthening or weakening low self-control and irritability?

Questions such as these can only be answered with longitudinal data.

In short, if there is a "gold standard" for criminological theory, developmental theories would have to be it because (1) they generally integrate and consider sociological, psychological, and biological factors as a coherent whole; (2) they follow the same individuals over long periods of time, a strategy that allows for cause/effect analysis; (3) they do not rely on "convenience samples" from high schools and colleges; and (4) they can identify characteristics that lead to onset, persistence, and desistance from crime in the same individuals. One useful addition to all developmental theories considering continuity/desistance of antisocial behavior and the age-crime curve in general is the integration of the neurochemical data because these phenomena "may have a strong basis in normal neurochemistry."[98]

⊠ Policy and Prevention: Implications of Developmental Theories

Policies designed to prevent and reduce crime derived from developmental studies do not differ from other theories but rather encompass them all and suggest a broad array of strategies. Because of the emphasis on latent traits that set individuals on a particular life trajectory, developmental theories support the same kind of family-based nurturant strategies supported

Table 9.2	Summarizing Key Points, Strengths, and Differences of Developmental Theories		
Theory	**Key Points**	**Key Strengths**	**Key Differences**
Agnew's general or super traits theory	Low self-control and irritability set people on a trajectory leading to negative interactions with others in the family, school, peers, work, and in marriage. These different domains interact and feed back on one another.	Parsimoniously integrates concepts from psychology, sociology, and biology and shows how each affects and is affected by all others. Theory states that low self-control and irritability are temporarily increased during adolescence.	Does not address the process of desisting from offending. Does not explicitly address different trajectories as in Moffitt and, to a lesser extent, in Farrington and Sampson and Laub.
Sampson and Laub's age-graded theory	Power of informal social controls across the life course. Assumes classical notions of why people commit crimes, and therefore there is no need to dwell too much on risk factors. Turning points in life and human agency are important. These turning points are made easier if one has accumulated significant social capital.	Emphasis on the power of life events to turn trajectories around and to facilitate desistance. Also emphasis on human agency is refreshing. All offenders will eventually desist regardless of risk factors or lack of social capital.	Unlike other theories, there is little emphasis on risk factors setting people on a particular trajectory other than bonding strength. Emphasis on inhibiting (bonding, social capital) rather than facilitating factors.
Farrington's ICAP theory	People have varying levels of antisocial propensity (AP) due to a variety of environmental and biological factors. Few people have long-term AP, but these people tend to offend across the life course. Short-term AP tends to occur in adolescence and can change to long-term AP under some circumstances.	Shows how people think (cognition) translates AP into actual offending behavior. As with Moffitt's AL offenders, AP is said to increase temporarily during adolescence, but it can lead to long-term AP if someone is caught and labeled a criminal because such a label limits future opportunities.	Not so much emphasis on desisting as age-graded theory, but more so than Agnew and Moffitt. Less emphasis than Agnew and Moffitt on latent traits, but more than Sampson and Laub. Unlike Moffitt, AP is considered a continuum rather than a distinct two-type typology.
Moffitt's dual-pathway theory	There are two main pathways to offending—LCP and AL. LCP offenders have neurological and temperamental difficulties that are exacerbated by inept parenting. LCP offenders offend across time and situations, begin prior to puberty, and continue well into adulthood. AL offenders are "normal" individuals temporarily derailed during adolescence.	Identifies two distinct pathways to offending rather than assuming all people are similarly affected by similar factors. Shows how the social bonds so important to age-graded theory are formed or not formed according to the characteristics of individuals.	Emphasizes a larger number of individual differences that affect offending behavior than all other theories. Also attempts to explain prevalence of offending with reference to the modern maturity gap. Differences between the two trajectory groups more defined than they are in other theories.

by biosocial and social and self-control theories. Regardless of any traits children may bring with them to the socialization process, however, these traits can be muted by patient and loving parenting, and as such, many developmental theories suggest family interventions as early as possible to help nurture bonds between children and their parents.

The Nurse-Family Partnership program has attempted to do this. The program began in 1978 with a sample of 400 at-risk women and girls and their infants. All mothers were unmarried, most were living in poverty, and 48% were younger than age 15. The women were randomly assigned to four different groups, with one group (the experimental group) receiving extensive care from nurses in the form of multiple prenatal and postnatal home visitations in which the nurses gave help and advice on a variety of child care matters. The other groups received less comprehensive care for shorter periods. A 15-year follow-up study by Olds and his colleagues[99] found that the program had many beneficial outcomes for the experimental group children and their mothers relative to the subjects in the other groups. For the mothers, there was less substance abuse, fewer subsequent illegitimate births, fewer legal difficulties, and 79% fewer verified instances of child abuse/neglect relative to the control groups. For the children, there was less substance abuse, fewer arrests, better school performance, and better all-around social adjustment.

A very interesting school-based program that has been implemented in several countries and explicitly based on the assumptions of developmental theories is the Fast Track Project.[100] Through multistage screening of more than 10,000 kindergarten children in 1991–1993, 891 were identified as being at risk for antisocial behavior. These children were impulsive, had difficult temperaments, and came from unstable families living in low-income, high-crime neighborhoods. The children were divided into experimental ($n = 445$) and control ($n = 446$) groups. The experimental group was given a curriculum designed to lead to development of social understanding and emotional communication skills and improvement in self-control and problem-solving skills. They were also placed in so-called *friendship groups* and *peer pairing* designed to increase social skills and enhance friendships. Their parents received parenting effectiveness training and home visits to foster their problem-solving skills and general life management.

The program is evaluated periodically and has been found to have modest but positive outcomes. By the end of the third grade, 37% of the experimental group was judged to be free of conduct problems as opposed to 27% of the control group. By eighth grade, 38% of the experimental group had been arrested as opposed to 42% of the control group. Although these differences are modest at best, they still reflect a good number of people saved from criminal victimization if the improvements hold in the future. If programs such as the Fast Track Project could be combined with programs like the Nurse-Family Partnership, we should see improved results since even kindergarten intervention may be too late in some cases. Yet developmental theories tell us that human life is characterized by dynamism, and people can change at any time. This is a note of optimism for crime control/prevention strategies.

SUMMARY

Developmental theories are dynamic and integrative and examine offending across the life course. Juvenile offending has been noted across time and cultures. A sharp rise in offending following puberty and a steady decline thereafter have been noted always and everywhere. Brain and hormonal scientists explain the age effect with respect to the brain and hormonal processes occurring during adolescence. At puberty, a huge surge in testosterone levels is experienced, the brain is undergoing a process of intensive pruning, myelination of the higher brain centers is yet to be completed, and the balance of excitatory to inhibitory neurotransmitters is tipped in favor of the excitatory transmitters. Evolutionary theorists maintain that all these changes are evolved adaptations that prepare adolescents for adulthood, and with all negative outcomes notwithstanding, teens are behaving exactly as they were designed to act.

A wide variety of factors put some teens more at risk for delinquent behavior than others. The factors we focused on in this chapter were ADHD and CD, which are highly heritable. The co-occurrence of ADHD and CD is a particularly strong risk factor, and children so afflicted show many resemblances to psychopaths. Nevertheless, ADHD by itself may have been adaptive in evolutionary environments, and perhaps we need to find prosocial outlets for the excessive activity requirement of children with ADHD.

Developmental theories follow individuals across the life course to determine the differential effect of risk factors for offending at different junctures. Robert Agnew stresses the constant interaction of low self-control/irritability with other life domains across the life course. Sampson and Laub's age-graded theory is less concerned with individual traits and more concerned with the power of informal social control (bonds) to prevent offending. Farrington's ICAP theory stresses antisocial potential and cognition and how these things are shaped in prosocial and antisocial directions at different times and in different situations. Moffitt's theory is probably the best known and best researched of these theories. Moffitt posits a dual-pathway model consisting of adolescent limited (AL) offenders, who limit their offending to the adolescent years, and life course persistent (LCP) offenders, who offend across the life course. LCP offenders have neurological and temperamental difficulties that set them on a developmental trajectory that leads to antisocial behavior at all ages and social situations. AL offenders do not suffer these disabilities and have accumulated sufficient social capital so that they can resettle into a prosocial lifestyle once neurological and social maturity has been reached.

Overall, we are very positive about developmental theories because of their dynamic (as opposed to static) and integrative (the inclusion of biological, psychological, and sociological concepts) as opposed to single-discipline explanations, and they are longitudinal as opposed to cross-sectional "snapshots."

On Your Own

Log on to the web-based student study site at http://www.sagepub.com/criminologystudy for more information about the vignettes and materials presented in this chapter, suggestions for activities, study aids such as review quizzes, and research recommendations including journal article links and questions related to this chapter.

EXERCISES AND DISCUSSION QUESTIONS

1. Why is it imperative that we understand what is going on biologically during adolescence?

2. A large number of risk factors are listed under the family domain in Table 9.1; if the family is that important, think back to the policy recommendations derivable from

control theories in Chapter 5 and argue which of those policies would best help to prevent delinquency.

3. If people age out of crime as well as into it, would it be a good idea to ignore all but the most serious of juvenile crimes so that we don't risk having children gain a "criminal" reputation?

4. If only a very small number of individuals are life course persistent offenders, shouldn't we concentrate our crime control efforts on them? If you agree with this, how do we identify them? Isn't there a danger of false-positive identification (identifying a person as someone who will continue to offend well into adulthood when in fact he or she wouldn't have)?

5. What is social capital, and how much of it do you believe that you have accumulated?

6. Go to http://www.fasttrackproject.org/fasttrackoverview.htm and read more about the Fast Track Program. Identify some of the specifics of the program and report to the class.

KEY WORDS

Agnew's super traits theory

Attention deficit with hyperactivity disorder (ADHD)

Conduct disorder

Delinquency

Farrington's integrated cognitive antisocial potential (ICAP) theory

Latent trait

Maturity gap

Moffitt's dual-pathway developmental theory

Puberty

Risk factor

Sampson and Laub's age-graded developmental theory

Social capital

Turning points

REFERENCES

1. Farrington, D. (2003). Developmental and life-course criminology: Key theoretical and empirical issues—The 2002 Sutherland Award address. *Criminology, 41,* 221–255. (Quote on p. 228)

2. Snyder, H., Espiritu, R., Huizinga, D., Loeber, R., & Petechuck, D. (2003). *Prevalence and development of child delinquency* (Child Delinquency Bulletin Series). Washington, DC: U.S. Department of Justice, Office of Juvenile Justice and Delinquency Prevention.

3. Heck, G. (2000). Civil law and juvenile justice. In A. Walsh & C. Hemmens (Eds.), *From law to order: The theory and practice of law and justice* (pp. 153–176). Lanham, MD: American Correctional Association.

4. Heck (2000).

5. Lawrence, R., & Mueller, D. (2004). School shooting and the man-bites-dog criterion of newsworthiness. *Youth Violence and Juvenile Justice,* 1:330–345.

6. Krisberg, B. (2005). *Juvenile justice: Redeeming our children.* Thousand Oaks, CA: Sage.

7. U.S. Bureau of the Census (2004). *Statistical abstracts of the United States.* Retrieved from http://www.census.gov/prod/2004pubs/03statab/vitstat.pdf

8. Federal Bureau of Investigation (FBI). (2004). *Crime in the United States, 2003: Uniform Crime Reports.* Washington, DC: Government Printing Office.

9. Warr, M. (2002). *Companions in crime: The social aspects of criminal conduct.* New York: Cambridge University Press.

10. Shavit, Y., & Rattner, A. (1988). Age, crime, and the early lifecourse. *American Journal of Sociology, 93,* 1457–1470. (Quote on p. 1547)

11. Gottfredson, M., & Hirschi, T. (1990). *A general theory of crime.* Stanford, CA: Stanford University Press.

12. White, A. (2004). *Substance use and the adolescent brain: An overview with the focus on alcohol.* Durham, NC: Duke University Medical Center.

13. Bogin, B. (1993). Why must I be a teenager at all? *New Scientist, 137,* 34–38.

14. Felson, R., & Haynie, D. (2002). Pubertal development, social factors, and delinquency among adolescent boys. *Criminology, 40,* 967–988.

15. Ellis, L. (2003). Genes, criminality, and the evolutionary neuroandrogenic theory. In A. Walsh & L. Ellis (Eds.), *Biosocial criminology: Challenging environmentalism's supremacy* (pp. 13–34). Hauppauge, NY: Nova Science.

16. Quadango, D. (2003). Genes, brains, hormones, and violence: Interactions with complex environments. In A. Walsh & L. Ellis (Eds.), *Biosocial criminology: Challenging environmentalism's supremacy* (pp. 167–184). Hauppauge, NY: Nova Science.

17. Spear, L. (2000). Neurobehavioral changes in adolescence. *Current Directions in Psychological Science, 9,* 111–114.

18. Collins, R. (2004). Onset and desistance in criminal careers: Neurobiology and the age-crime relationship. *Journal of Offender Rehabilitation, 39,* 1–19.

19. Walker, E. (2002). Adolescent neurodevelopment and psychopathology. *Current Directions in Psychological Science, 11,* 24–28.

20. Spear (2000).

21. White (2004).

22. White (2004).

23. Daly, M. (1996). Evolutionary adaptationism: Another biological approach to criminal and antisocial behavior. In G. Bock & J. Goode (Eds.), *Genetics of criminal and antisocial behaviour* (pp. 183–195). Chichester, England: Wiley. (Quote on p. 193)

24. Walker (2002).

25. Giedd, J., Blumenthal, J., Jeffries, N., Castellanos, F., Liu, H., Zijenbos, A., et al. (1999). Brain development during childhood and adolescence: A longitudinal MRI study. *Nature Neuroscience, 2,* 861–863.

26. Sowell, E., Thompson, P., Holmes, C., Jernigan, T., & Toga, A. (1999). In vivo evidence for postadolescent brain maturation in frontal and striatal regions. *Nature Neuroscience, 2,* 859–861.

27. Giedd et al. (1999).

28. Sowell et al. (1999).

29. Walsh, A. (2002). *Biosocial criminology: Introduction and integration.* Cincinnati, OH: Anderson.

30. Restak, R. (2001). *The secret life of the brain.* New York: Dana Press/Joseph Henry Press. (Quote on p. 76)

31. Caspi, A., Henry, B., McGee, R., Moffitt, T., & Silva, P. (1995). Temperamental origins of child and adolescent behavior problems: From age three to age fifteen. *Child Development, 66,* 55–68.

32. Felson and Haynie (2002).

33. Drigotas, S., & Udry, J. (1993). Biosocial models of adolescent problem behavior: Extensions to panel design. *Social Biology, 40,* 1–7.

34. Felson and Haynie (2002).

35. Collins (2004).

36. McCrae, R., Costa, P., Ostendorf, F., Angleitner, A., Hrebickova, M., Avia, M., et al. (2000). Nature over nurture: Temperament, personality, and life span development. *Journal of Personality and Social Psychology, 78,* 173–186.

37. Thornberry, T., Huizinga, D., & Loeber, R. (2004). The causes and correlates studies: Findings and policy implication. *Juvenile Justice, 9,* 3–19.

38. Moffitt, T., & Walsh, A. (2003) The adolescence-limited/life-course persistent theory of antisocial behavior: What have we learned? In A. Walsh & L. Ellis (Eds.), *Biosocial criminology: Challenging environmentalism's supremacy* (pp. 125–144). Hauppauge, NY: Nova Science.

39. Rhee, S., & Waldman, I. (2002). Genetic and environmental influences on antisocial behavior: A meta-analysis of twin and adoption studies. *Psychological Bulletin, 28,* 490–529.

40. Lykken, D. (1995). *The antisocial personalities.* Hillsdale, NJ: Lawrence Erlbaum.

41. Lykken (1995).

42. White (2004, p. 4).

43. Office of the Surgeon General. (2001). *Youth violence: A report of the Surgeon General.* Washington, DC: U.S. Department of Health and Human Services. Retrieved from www.surgeongeneral.gov/library/youthviolence

44. Office of the Surgeon General (2001).

45. Durston, S. (2003). A review of the biological bases of ADHD: What have we learned from imaging studies? *Mental Retardation and Developmental Disabilities, 9,* 184–195.

46. Raz, A. (2004, August). Brain imaging data of ADHD. *Neuropsychiatry,* pp. 46–50.

47. Sanjiv, K., & Thaden, E. (2004, January). Examining brain connectivity in ADHD. *Psychiatric Times,* pp. 40–41.

48. Levy, F., Hay, D., McStephen, M., Wood, C., & Waldman, I. (1997). Attention-deficit hyperactivity disorder: A category or a continuum? Genetic analysis of a large- scale twin study. *Journal of the American Academy of Child and Adolescent Psychiatry, 36,* 737–744.

49. Coolidge, F., Thede, L., & Young, S. (2000). Heritability and the comorbidity of attention deficit hyperactivity disorder with behavioral disorders and executive function deficits: A preliminary investigation. *Developmental Neuropsychology, 17,* 273–287.

50. Levy et al. (1997).

51. Durston (2003).

52. Coolidge et al. (2000).

53. Willoughby, M. (2003). Developmental course of ADHD symptomatology during the transition from childhood to adolescence: A review with recommendations. *Journal of Child Psychology and Psychiatry, 43,* 609–621.

54. Lynam, D. (1996). Early identification of chronic offenders: Who is the fledgling psychopath? *Psychological Bulletin, 120,* 209–234.

55. Ellis, L., & Walsh, A. (2000). *Criminology: A global perspective.* Boston: Allyn & Bacon.

56. Lynam (1996, p. 211).

57. Lynam (1996).

58. Maughan, B., Rowe, R., Messer, J., Goodman, R., & Meltzer, H. (2004). Conduct disorder and oppositional defiant disorder in a national sample: Developmental epidemiology. *Journal of Child Psychology and Psychiatry, 43,* 609–621.

59. Coolidge et al. (2000).

60. Moffitt, T. (1996). The neuropsychology of conduct disorder. In P. Cordella & L. Siegel (Eds.), *Readings in contemporary criminology* (pp. 85–106). Boston: Northeastern University Press.

61. Lewis, D. (1991). Conduct disorder. In M. Lewis (Ed.), *Child and adolescent psychiatry: A comprehensive textbook* (pp. 561–583). Baltimore: Williams & Wilkins.

62. Krueisi, M., Leonard, H., Swedo, S., Nadi, S., Hamburger, S., Lui, J., et al. (1994). Endogenous opioids, childhood psychopathology, and Quay's interpretation of Jeffrey Gray. In D. Routh (Ed.), *Disruptive behavior disorders in childhood* (pp. 207–219). New York: Plenum.

63. Panksepp, J. (1998). Attention deficit hyperactivity disorders, psychostimulants, and intolerance of childhood playfulness: A tragedy in the making. *Current Directions in Psychological Science, 7,* 91–98.

64. Crawford, C. (1998). The theory of evolution in the study of human behavior: An introduction and overview. In C. Crawford & D. Krebs (Eds.), *Handbook of evolutionary psychology: Ideas, issues, and applications* (pp. 3–42). Mahwah, NJ: Lawrence Erlbaum.

65. Elliot, D., Huizinga, D., & Menard, S. (1989). *Multiple problem youth: Delinquency, Substance abuse, and mental health problems.* New York: Springer-Verlag.

66. Agnew, R. (2005). *Why do criminals offend? A general theory of crime and delinquency.* Los Angeles: Roxbury. (Quote on p. 213)

67. Agnew (2005).

68. Sampson, R., & Laub, J. (1999). Crime and deviance over the lifecourse: The salience of adult social bonds. In F. Scarpitti & A. Nielsen (Eds.), *Crime and criminals: Contemporary and classical readings in criminology* (pp. 238–246). Los Angeles: Roxbury.

69. Sampson, R., & Laub, J. (2005). A life-course view of the development of crime. *Annals of the American Academy of Political and Social Sciences, 602,* 12–45.

70. Glueck, S., & Glueck, E. (1950). *Unraveling juvenile delinquency.* New York: Commonwealth Fund.

71. Sampson and Laub (2005).

72. Gottfredson and Hirschi (1990, p. 141).

73. Laub, J., & Sampson, R. (2003). *Shared beginnings, divergent lives: Delinquent boys to age 70.* Cambridge, MA: Harvard University Press.

74. Sampson and Laub (2005, p. 37).

75. Farrington (2003, p. 231).

76. Farrington (2003).

77. Farrington (2003, p. 231).

78. Farrington (2003).

79. Smith, C., & Farrington, D. (2004). Continuities in antisocial behavior and parenting across three generations. *Journal of Child Psychology and Psychiatry, 45,* 230–247.

80. Walsh (2002).

81. Krueger, R., Moffitt, T., Caspi, A., Bleske, A., & Silva, P. (1998). Assortative mating for antisocial behavior: Developmental and methodological implications. *Behavior Genetics, 28,* 173–185. (Quote on p. 183)

82. Tittle, C. (2000). Theoretical developments in criminology. In *National Institute of Justice 2000: Vol. 1. The nature of crime: Continuity and change* (pp. 51–101). Washington, DC: National Institute of Justice. (Quote on p. 68)

83. Moffitt and Walsh (2003).

84. Moffitt, T. (1993). Adolescent-limited and life-course-persistent antisocial behavior: A developmental taxonomy. *Psychological Review, 100,* 674–701. (Quote on p. 679)

85. Moffitt (1993, p. 679).

86. Jeglum-Bartusch, D., Lynam, D., Moffitt, T., & Silva, P. (1997). Is age important? Testing general versus developmental theories of antisocial behavior. *Criminology, 35,* 13–48.

87. Henry, B., Caspi, A., Moffitt, T., & Silva, P. (1996). Temperament and familial predictors of violent and non-violent criminal convictions: From age 3 to age 18. *Developmental Psychology, 32,* 614–623.

88. DeLisi, M. (2005). *Career criminals and society.* Thousand Oaks, CA: Sage.

89. Moffitt and Walsh (2003).

90. Moffitt (1993).

91. Moffitt (1993, p. 692).

92. Rodkin, P., Farmer, T., Pearl, R., & Van Acker, R. (2000). Heterogeneity of popular boys: Antisocial and prosocial configurations. *Developmental Psychology, 36,* 14–24. (Quote on p. 21)

93. Moffitt (1993, p. 690).

94. Moffitt and Walsh (2003).

95. Jeffrey, C. (1993). Obstacles to the development of research in crime and delinquency. *Journal of Research in Crime and Delinquency, 30,* 491–497. (Quote on p. 494)

96. Moffitt, T. E., Caspi, A., Harrington, H., & Milne, B. (2002). Males on the life-course persistent and adolescence-limited antisocial pathways: Follow-up at age 26. *Development & Psychopathology, 14,* 179–206.

97. Moffitt and Walsh (2003).

98. Collins (2004, p. 12).

99. Olds, D., Hill, P., Mihalic, S., & O'Brien, R. (1998). *Blueprints for violence prevention, book seven: Prenatal and infancy home visitation by nurses.* Boulder, CO: Center for the Study and Prevention of Violence.

100. Fast Track Project (2005). *Fast track project overview.* Retrieved from http://www.fasttrack project.org/fasttrackoverview.htm

ALTERED MINDS AND CRIME: ALCOHOL, DRUGS, AND MENTAL ILLNESS

B oth Joe Alladyce and Jared Livingston were literally born drunk. Their mothers were heavy drinkers who continued to drink during their pregnancies, and if mothers drink, so do their fetuses. During the third trimester of pregnancy, the fetal brain starts to wire itself, and because alcohol (and other noxious substances) interferes with this process, many things go awry. If the fetus survives this assault, it is highly likely to be born with a severe problem condition called fetal alcohol syndrome (FAS). Symptoms of FAS, which range from moderate to severe, include neurological abnormalities, intellectual impairment, behavioral problems, and various bodily and facial imperfections that set its victims visually apart.

Joe and Jared were made wards of the court and sent to a special institution where teachers, physicians, and social workers did their best to educate and care for them. The boys formed a close bond with each other and soothed each other's increasing feelings of anger and depression. When they were both 17, they walked away from the home and made their way to the nearest town, where they robbed a convenience store and went on a drinking binge. Walking down the street in a semi-stupor, they came across Mr. and Mrs. Wheelan and little 7-year-old Angela walking toward them. Angela made a remark about their behavior and appearance and started to giggle. Enraged, Jared smashed Angela over the head with the beer bottle he was carrying, and Joe did the same thing to her father when he tackled Jared. Both boys mercilessly beat and kicked all three family members to death. The boys were picked up by the police about an hour later and charged with the murders.

This tragic story illustrates the insidious nature of alcohol abuse. Joe and Jared didn't ask to be born with incurable disabilities and, according to many FAS experts, could no more be held responsible for their actions than a blind person is for not recognizing faces. They have brains incapable of appreciating right from wrong and of linking cause and effect. Their mothers not only ruined their own lives but also the lives of their sons and the lives of the surviving members of the Wheelan family. In this chapter, you will learn of the huge cost to society caused by what has been aptly named "the beast in the bottle" and by other substances and circumstances that tear the rationality from our brains and replace it with all manner of monsters.

⊠ The Scope of the Alcohol/Crime Problem

We humans have an infernal love of ingesting substances that alter our moods from states we consider undesirable to states we consider desirable. We swallow, sniff, inhale, and inject with relish, suggesting that sobriety is a difficult state for us to tolerate. Unfortunately, "desirable" moods attained this way don't last long, and the excessive ingestion of the substances used to bring them about has consequences that in the long run are anything but desirable. Alcohol has always been humankind's favorite way of temporarily escaping reality. We drink this powerful drug to loosen our tongues, to be sociable, to liven up our parties, to feel good, to sedate ourselves, and to anesthetize the anxieties and pains of life. Many centuries before the birth of Christ, the ancient Sumerians and Egyptians were singing the praises of beer, wine, and the various spirits but also warning about the consequences of excessive use.[1]

Of all the substances used to alter mood and consciousness, alcohol is the one most directly linked to crime, especially violent crime.[2] The notion that drinking leads to violence is ancient folk wisdom that is as old as alcohol itself.[3] It has been estimated that at least 70% of American prison inmates[4] and 60% of British inmates[5] are alcohol and/or drug addicted. Alcohol is linked to about 110,000 deaths a year versus the "mere" 19,000 fatalities attributable to other drugs,[6] although this should be interpreted in light of the fact that many more people drink alcohol than take illicit drugs.

Police officers spend more than half of their time on alcohol-related offenses, and it is estimated that one third of all arrests (excluding drunk driving) in the United States are for alcohol-related offenses.[7] About 75% of robberies and 80% of homicides involve a drunken offender and/or victim, and about 40% of other violent offenders in the United States had been drinking at the time of the offense.[8] A study of the link between alcohol consumption and homicide/attempted homicide in Russia found that more than 66% of the offenders and about 40% of the victims were intoxicated at the time of the offense.[9] The U.S. Department of Health and Human Services[10] estimates the cost of alcohol abuse to society in terms of crime, health, sickness, property damage, and family and occupational disruption to be a staggering $185 billion. Of the total costs to society of both drug and alcohol abuse, the National Institute on Alcohol Abuse and Addiction[11] estimates that alcohol abuse accounts for 60% and drug abuse the remaining 40%.

The following are the major conclusions regarding alcohol consumption in the United States from the 2001 National Household Survey on Drug Abuse (NHSDA). The NHSDA interviewed approximately 70,000 people age 12 years or older, in every state, over a 12-month period.[12]

◆ The rate of alcohol use and the number of drinkers increased between 2000 and 2001. Almost half of all Americans age 12 or older, 48.3% or 109 million persons, were current drinkers in the 2001 survey. This estimate was roughly 5.0 million higher than 2000, when 46.6% of those 12 years or older reported current alcohol use. Comparing 2000 and 2001, no significant changes were found in heavy or binge drinking.

◆ About 10.1 million persons ages 12 to 20 years reported current use of alcohol in 2001. This number represents 28.5% of this age group, for whom alcohol is an illicit substance. Of this number, nearly 6.8 million or 19.0% were binge drinkers, and 2.1 million or 6.0% were heavy drinkers.

◆ In 2001, more than 1 in 10 Americans or 25.1 million persons reported driving under the influence of alcohol at least once in the 12 months prior to the interview. The rate of driving under the influence of alcohol increased from 10.0% to 11.1% between 2000 and 2001. Among young adults ages 18 to 25 years, 22.8% drove under the influence of alcohol.

The Direct Effects of Alcohol on Behavior

The effects of alcohol (or any other drug) on behavior are a function of the interactions of the pharmacological properties of the substance, the individual's physiology and personality, and the social and cultural context in which the substance is ingested. In terms of its pharmacological properties, alcohol is a depressant drug that inhibits the functioning of the higher brain centers. As more and more alcohol is drunk, behavior becomes less and less inhibited as the rational cortex surrenders its control of the drinker's demeanor to the more primitive limbic system, the seat of emotion. When this occurs, we often see the expression of raw emotions unmodified by the guiding hand of the prefrontal cortex. In Freudian terms, this means a weakening of superego functioning and the release of the dreaded id.

What's going on in the drinker's brain to cause this? Although alcohol is a brain-numbing depressant, at low dosages, it is actually a stimulant because it raises dopamine levels.[13] At the same time that it raises dopamine, it decreases serotonin, which we know by now reduces impulse control and increases the likelihood of aggression.[14] Alcohol also reduces inhibition by affecting the neurotransmitter gamma-aminobutyric acid (GABA), which is a major inhibitor of internal stimuli such as fear, anxiety, and stress.[15] Increasing GABA production results in "reduced anxiety about the consequences of aggressive behavior [or any other behavior not normally evoked when sober]."[16] Alcohol's direct effects on the brain can thus help us to reinvent ourselves as "superior" beings: the fearful to become more courageous, the self-effacing to become more confident, and the timid to become more assertive.

Contextual Factors

As powerful a behavioral disinhibitor as alcohol is, it is not sufficient by itself to change anyone's behavior, especially in the direction of serious law violations. Most people don't become violent or commit any kind of criminal offense when drinking or even when they are "over the limit." Alcohol is a releaser of behaviors that we normally want to keep under control but that we may be prone to exhibit when control is weakened. Hence, we may become silly, amorous, melancholic, maudlin, and even aggressive and violent when our underlying propensity to be these things is facilitated by alcohol and the social context in which it is drunk. In some social contexts, drinking may lead to violence but not in others. A major nationwide British study

◀ **Photo 10.1**
Many alcohol researchers compare societies in which drinking alcohol is considered normal behavior from an early age with American society, in which youth alcohol drinking is illegal. In the United States, many teens drink anyway, and binge drinking rather than moderate use is a potential problem.

found that one third of violent incidents between strangers took place in or around drinking establishments in which both victims and perpetrators had been drinking.[17] Other contextual factors for eliciting violence are skid row bars, bars frequented by groups of males rather than by single males or couples, bars with an "anything-goes" atmosphere (unrestricted swearing, sexual activity, drug use, prostitution, etc.), and bars with a low staff to customer ratio.[18]

Placing separate groups of young males into the kinds of bars described above is a recipe for trouble. Experimental research has shown that drinking increases males' fantasies of power and domination and that men who are the heaviest drinkers were the most likely to have such fantasies.[19] With loosened inhibitions, such fantasies might lead to males flirting with the girl-friends of males from another group and then not backing off when challenged or interpreting some comment or gesture as threatening. Lower levels of physical coordination will result in more people bumping into one another and spilling drinks, which may lead to aggressive responses. If a person values a reputation as a macho tough guy, then aggressive responses are more likely when his friends are present and the responder is looking to validate his reputation. There's an old saying among heavy drinkers: "It's not how many beers you drink, it's who you drink them with." Anyone who has ever frequented rowdy bars can doubtless think of many other barroom situations that can lead to trouble.

There are also cultural factors to be considered when evaluating the alcohol-crime relationship. Two major cultural factors influence the relationship between alcohol consumption and criminal behavior. One defines "a drinking occasion as a 'time-out' period in which controls are loosened from usual behavior."[20] and the other is "a willingness to hold a person less responsible for their actions when drinking than when sober by attributing the blame to alcohol."[21] If one's culture defines alcohol as a good-time elixir—the unfortunate (but often subjectively experienced as enjoyable) by-product of which is a loss of control over behavioral inhibitions—then one is granted cultural "permission" to do just that. In addition, if culture tells me that I'm less responsible for my behavior when "under the influence," this too may grant me permission to do something I might not otherwise do, intoxicated or sober. There is some weak evidence that an intoxication excuse may mitigate the severity of a sentence a convicted person may receive.[22] Perhaps judges and probation officers may reason that he or she would not have committed the crime if sober, and thus a probation sentence coupled with a treatment order would be in order.[23]

Binge drinkers frequently consume anywhere between 5 and 10 drinks in a few hours' time and are particularly likely to define drinking as a time-out period. Binge drinkers are typically college-age single young adults who drink solely to get drunk. An American study found that 40% of college students reported at least one episode of binge drinking in the previous 2 weeks,[24] and a Russian nationwide study found that almost one third of the men admitted binge drinking at least once a month.[25] The cultures of both American college students and Russians in general have a high level of tolerance for engaging in heavy drinking. Robinson and Berridge's nationwide British study[26] found that 39% of binge drinkers admitted a criminal offense in the previous 12 months, whereas 14% of other regular drinkers and 8% of occasional or nondrinkers did. The corresponding percentages for a violent crime were 17%, 4%, and 2%. The 2003 Arrestee Drug Abuse Monitoring (ADAM) program's survey of 180,455 male and 3,664 female arrestees in major U.S. cities found that 47.9% of the males and 34.9% of the females reported that that they had engaged in binge drinking on at least one occasion in the 30 days preceding their arrest.[27]

The unanswered question in many studies of this kind is whether heavy drinking plus social context per se causes an increased probability of engaging in antisocial behavior. It could well be that certain kinds of people are more prone to drink heavily, to be attracted to social contexts in which violence is most likely to occur, and to commit antisocial acts. In this view, antisocial propensities are simply exacerbated under the influence of alcohol and social setting.[28] Heavy alcohol intake certainly has a greater disinhibiting effect on behavior than heavy tea intake, so alcohol-induced disinhibition may be considered a cause of antisocial acts. Likewise, violence and other antisocial behaviors are assuredly more likely to occur in a biker bar than in a tearoom, and thus social context may be considered a cause as well. But a stricter standard of causation may want to consider that perhaps the substance and the setting are secondary in causal importance to the traits of individuals drinking the beverage of their choice in the settings of their choice. To explore this line of thinking, we will examine the disease of alcoholism, a disease strongly related to criminal behavior.

Alcoholism: Type I and Type II

Alcoholism is a chronic disease condition marked by progressive incapacity to control alcohol consumption despite psychological, spiritual, social, or physiological disruptions. Alcoholics are physically dependent on alcohol, meaning that their bodies have developed a metabolic demand for alcohol and rebel violently when they are denied it. Alcoholism is a state of altered cellular physiology caused by the repetitive consumption of alcohol that manifests itself in physical disturbances (withdrawal symptoms) when alcohol use is suspended (alcohol withdrawal can be more life threatening than withdrawal from narcotics). Heavy drinkers who are not alcoholics are able to stop self-destructive drinking patterns in the face of compelling life circumstances such as marital problems, poor job performance, or various alcohol-related health problems, but the alcoholic will be unable to sustain control over time unless treated.[29]

We don't want to give you the impression that alcoholism and criminality are synonymous; many, perhaps most, alcoholics do not get into serious trouble with the law. However, numerous theorists have hypothesized that the two phenomena are linked because they share a common cause.[30–32] One link is the reward dominance concept in criminology and the "craving brain" concept in alcoholism theory. Recall from Chapter 8 that the behavioral activating system (BAS) is primarily dopamine driven, that the behavioral inhibiting system (BIS) is primarily serotonin driven, and that the two systems are "biobalanced" in most people most of the time. Alcoholics have an old saying that one drink is too many and a hundred drinks are not enough. This seemingly contradictory statement informs us that a single drink activates the pleasure centers in the nucleus accumbens by activating dopamine, but one drink leads to such a craving for more that even a hundred drinks will not satiate. The saying is a metaphor for what is called the *craving brain*.[33] It appears that both alcoholics and serious criminals are "reward dominant" in terms of their neurophysiology. Figure 10.1 shows the major brain areas affected by alcohol. The reward system includes the ventral tegmental area and nucleus accumbens, which use dopamine, and includes the other structures shown, all of which use GABA as a neurotransmitter.

Just as Terrie Moffitt[34] has shown us that there are at least two different types of offenders (adolescent limited and life course persistent), alcoholism researchers have shown that there are two different types of alcoholics. These types have been termed *Type I* and *Type II* alcoholics. Crabbe describes the two types in this way: "**Type I alcoholism** is characterized by mild abuse, minimal criminality, and passive-dependent personality variables, whereas **Type II alcoholism** is characterized by early onset, violence, and criminality, and is largely limited to males."[35] Type II alcoholics are similar to Moffitt's life course persistent offenders because they start drinking (and using other drugs) at a very early age, rapidly become addicted, and have many character disorders and behavioral problems that *precede* their alcoholism. Type I alcoholics are similar to Moffitt's adolescent limited offenders in that they start drinking later

| Figure 10.1 | The Alcohol Reward System and Other Areas Affected by Alcohol |

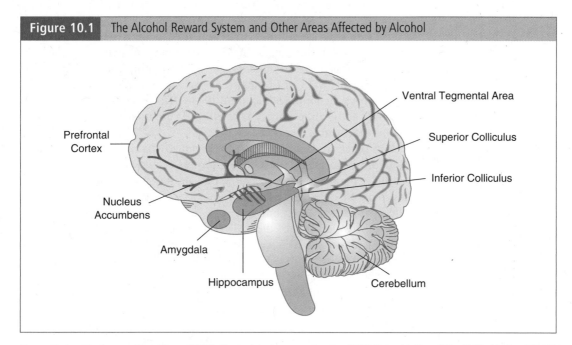

Source: National Institute on Drug Abuse. (1996). *The brain's drug reward system* (NIDA Notes 11: Tearoff Sheet). Washington, DC: U.S. Department of Health and Human Services.

in life than Type II alcoholics and progress to alcoholism slowly. Type I alcoholics typically have families and careers, and if they have character defects, these are typically induced by alcohol and are not permanent.[36]

Heritability estimates are about 0.90 for Type II alcoholism and about 0.40 for Type I alcoholism,[37] indicating that environmental factors are much more important to understanding Type I alcoholism than Type II alcoholism.[38] The genetic influence on alcoholism reflects genetic regulation of neurotransmitters such as GABA, dopamine, and serotonin[39] and/or their enzyme regulation.[40] Fishbein[41] proposes that Type II alcoholics have inherited abnormalities of the serotonin and dopamine systems that may be driving both their drinking and their antisocial behavior.

✉ Illegal Drugs and Crime

The Extent of the Illicit Drug Problem

The use of illegal drugs to alter consciousness is probably as old as the use of alcohol to accomplish the same thing. Alcohol use is a legal and socially acceptable way of drugging oneself, but substances discussed in this section are not. But this was not always the case, for many of these drugs have been legitimately used in religious rituals, for medical treatment, and for recreational use around the world and across the ages. There is a reference to the opium poppy as "the plant of joy" in Mesopotamia from around 3000 B.C.; the early Egyptians used opium in their religious ceremonies, and an early Spanish missionary in Peru estimated that in 1571, the Peruvian coca (the plant from which cocaine is made) traffic was worth the equivalent of half a million dollars.[42]

Up until 1914, drugs now considered illicit were legally and widely used in the United States for medicinal purposes. Sigmund Freud was an avid proponent of the "miraculous" medicinal properties of cocaine for a period of time and used it himself for depression. Because society was not fully aware of the dangers of addiction, many substances were openly advertised and sold as cures for all sorts of ailments and for refreshing "pick-me-ups." The most famous of these refreshments was Coca-Cola, which was made with the coca leaf (used to process cocaine) and kola nuts (hence the name) until 1903. Many patented medicines such as Cocaine Toothache Drops and Mother Barley's Quieting Syrup, used to "soothe" infants and young children, contained cocaine, morphine, or heroin.

Attitudes toward drug usage in America gradually began to change as physicians and lawmakers began to more fully understand the addictive powers of many of these substances. Although there were earlier federal and state acts aimed at specific practices and substances (such as opium smoking in opium dens), the Harrison Narcotic Act of 1914 was the benchmark act for changing America's concept of drugs and their use. According to Richard Davenport-Hines, "By the early 1920s, the conception of the addict changed from that of a middle-class victim accidentally addicted through medicinal use, to that of a criminal deviant using narcotics (or stimulants) for pleasure."[43] The Harrison Act did reduce the number of addicts (estimated at around 200,000 in the early 1900s), but it also spawned criminal black market operations (as did the Volstead Act prohibiting the production and sale of alcohol in 1919) and ultimately many more addicts. Just 3 years after the passing of the Harrison Act, a congressional report found that "the 'dope peddlers' appeared to have established a national organization, smuggling the drugs in through seaports or across the Canadian or Mexican borders. . . . The wrongful use of narcotic drugs has increased since the passage of the Harrison Act."[44]

   Figure 10.2 shows percentages of individuals participating in the 2004 NHSDA who admitted the use of any illicit drug during the month prior to being interviewed. Note the similarity of the graph to the graphs in Chapter 9, which show the relationship between age and crime. As with delinquency and crime, drug use rises to a peak in the age 18 to 20 category and then drops precipitously. The use of illicit drugs by most adolescents probably reflects experimentation (adolescent limited use), while their continued use in adulthood (life course persistent use) reflects a far more serious antisocial situation. Some highlights from the NHSDA data on illegal drug use are presented as follows.

◆   22.5 million Americans aged 12 or older in 2004 were classified with past year substance dependence or abuse (9.4 percent of the population), about the same number as in 2002 and 2003. Of these, 3.4 million were classified with dependence on or abuse of both alcohol and illicit drugs, 3.9 million were dependent on or abused illicit drugs but not alcohol, and 15.2 million were dependent on or abused alcohol but not illicit drugs.

◆   In 2004, 19.9 percent of unemployed adults aged 18 or older were classified with dependence or abuse, while 10.5 percent of full-time employed adults and 11.9 percent of part-time employed adults were classified as such. However, most adults with substance dependence or abuse were employed either full or part time. Of the 20.3 million adults classified with dependence or abuse, 15.7 million (77.6 percent) were employed.

◆   In 2004, 3.8 million people aged 12 or older (1.6 percent of the population) received treatment in the past 12 months for a drug or alcohol use problem. Of these, 2.3 million received treatment at a specialty facility for substance use treatment, including 1.7 million at a rehabilitation facility as an outpatient, 947,000 at a rehabilitation facility as an inpatient, 775,000 at a hospital as an impatient, and 982,000 at a mental health center as an outpatient. Nonspecialty treatment locations were self-help groups (2.1 million persons), private doctor's offices (490,000 persons), emergency rooms (453,000 persons), and prisons or jails (310,000 persons). (Note that the estimates of treatment by location include persons reporting more than one location.)

◆   Persons dependent on or abusing a substance in the past 12 months, or who received specialty treatment for a substance use problem within the past 12 months, are classified as needing treatment. In 2004, the number of persons aged 12 or older needing treatment for an alcohol or illicit drug use problem was 23.48 million (9.8 percent). Of these, 2.33 million received treatment at a specialty facility in the past year. Thus, 21.15 million people needed but did not receive treatment at a specialty facility in 2004. The number needing but not receiving treatment did not change significantly from 2002 to 2004.

◆   Of the 21.1 million people who needed but did not receive treatment in 2004, an estimated 1.2 million (5.8 percent) reported that they felt they needed treatment for their alcohol or drug use problem. Of the 1.2 million persons who felt they needed treatment, 441,000 (35.8 percent) reported that they made an effort but were unable to get treatment, and 792,000 (64.2 percent) reported making no effort to get treatment.

◆   Among people who needed but did not receive treatment and felt they needed treatment for a substance use problem, the most often reported reasons for not receiving treatment were not ready to stop using (40.0 percent) and cost or insurance barriers (34.5 percent). However, among the people who made an effort but were unable to get treatment, 42.5 percent reported cost or insurance barriers, and only 25.3 percent reported that they were not ready to stop using. These results are based on 2003 and 2004 combined data.

Sources: U.S. Department of Health and Human Services. (2000). *Results from the 2001 National Household Survey on Drug Abuse: Vol. I. Summary of National Findings.* Washington, DC: Government Printing Office. National Institute on Alcohol Abuse and Alcoholism. (1998). *Economic costs of alcohol and drug abuse estimated at $246 billion in the United States.* Retrieved from http://www.niaaa.nih.gov/press/1998/economics.htm

Table 10.1 presents data from the same survey indicating the percentage of individuals who admitted using a variety of illegal substance over different periods of time. Note that although almost half of the nationwide sample admitted usage during their lifetime, very few had taken any substance over the previous year and even fewer over the past month. We have to remember, however, that such surveys are not likely to have sampled individuals seriously involved in drugs.

Drug Addiction

All addictive drugs mimic the actions of normal brain chemistry by inhibiting or slowing down the release of neurotransmitters, stimulating or speeding up their release, preventing their reuptake after they have stimulated neighboring neurons, or breaking transmitters down more quickly. Virtually all illegal drugs "have common effects on a single pathway deep within the brain, the mesolimbic reward system."[45] Drugs hijack the brain and produce more powerful, rapid, and predictable effects on our pleasure centers than are naturally obtained by the action of neurotransmitters in response to non-drug-induced pleasant experiences.

People turn to illegal drugs for many of the same reasons that people turn to alcohol—to be "with it," to be sociable, to conform, to induce pleasure, to escape stress, or to escape

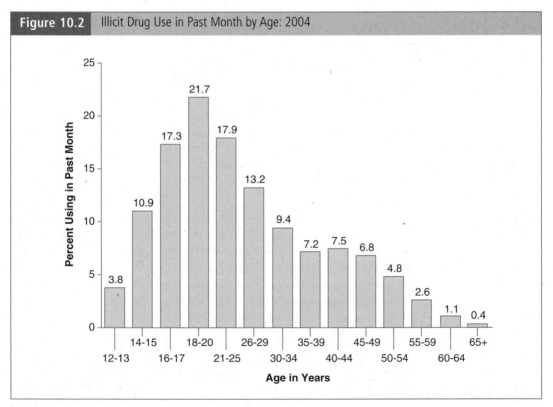

Figure 10.2 | Illicit Drug Use in Past Month by Age: 2004

SOURCE: U.S. Department of Health and Human Services. *National survey on drug use and health,* (2005). Washington, DC: Author.

chronic boredom. Among those who experiment with drugs, there are some who are genetically predisposed to develop addiction to their substance(s) of choice just as others are "sitting ducks" for alcoholism.[46] The Drug Enforcement Administration (DEA) defines **drug addiction** as "compulsive drug-seeking behavior where acquiring and using a drug becomes the most important activity in the user's life" and estimates that 5 million Americans suffer from drug addiction as they define it.[47] **Physical dependence** on a drug refers to changes to the body that have occurred after repeated use of it and necessitate its continued administration to avoid withdrawal symptoms. Physical dependence is not synonymous with addiction, as commonly thought, but **psychological dependence** (the deep craving for the drug and the feeling that one cannot function without it) is synonymous with addiction. Detoxified addicts have drug-free bodies and have ceased to experience withdrawal symptoms, but they frequently return to drugs because of psychological, not physical, compulsion.[48]

Regardless of the type of drug, addiction is not an invariable outcome of drug usage any more than alcoholism is an invariable outcome of drinking. The DEA[49] estimates that about 55% of today's youths have used some form of illegal substance, but few descend into the hell of addiction.[50] Genetic differences are undoubtedly related to a person's chances of becoming addicted given identical levels of usage and an identical period of time using. People differ in the degree of pleasure obtained by a drug, the rate of tolerance, and the type of effect produced.[51] For instance, individuals with attention deficit with hyperactivity disorder (ADHD) are at double the risk for serious substance abuse than non-ADHD individuals, particularly abuse of stimulant drugs such as cocaine and the amphetamines, because these drugs reduce the chronic level of underarousal that is characteristic of individuals with ADHD.[52]

Drug Classification

Several drug classification schemes are determined by the purpose for which the classification is being made. We will discuss the most popularly abused illegal drugs according to their pharmacological effects and their DEA schedule classification. This classification scheme divides chemical substances into five categories, or schedules. Schedule I substances are those that have high abuse liability and no medical use in the United States, such as heroin, peyote, and LSD. Schedule II substances have equally high (or higher) abuse liability but have some approved medical usage, such as opium or cocaine. Schedule III and IV substances have moderate to moderately high abuse liability and are legally available with prescription, and Schedule V substances can be purchased without prescription.

The Narcotics

Narcotic drugs are those that reduce the sense of pain, tension, and anxiety and produce a drowsy sense of euphoria. All drugs in this category have the potential for physical and psychological dependence, and all produce **tolerance** (the tendency to require larger and larger doses to produce the same effects after the body adjusts to lower dosages) and induce **withdrawal** symptoms (adverse physical reactions that occur when the body is deprived of the drug). The most insidious of the narcotics is heroin, the drug that leads to full-blown addiction in about 23% of those who try it.[53]

Heroin is a Schedule I substance and is a derivative of morphine that wafts the individual into a euphoric state of sweet indifference, a state that heroin users describe as "the floats." Intravenous injection of heroin ("mainlining") used to be the most popular method of

| Table 10.1 | Illicit Drug Use in Lifetime, Past Year, and Past Month Among Persons Age 12 or Older: Percentages, 2003 and 2004 |

	TIME PERIOD					
	Lifetime		Past Year		Past Month	
Drug	2003	2004	2003	2004	2003	2004
ILLICIT DRUG[1]	46.4	45.8	14.7	14.5	8.2	7.9
Marijuana and Hashish	40.6	40.2	10.6	10.6	6.2	6.1
Cocaine	14.7	14.2	2.5	2.4	1.0	0.8
Crack	3.3	3.3	0.6	0.5	0.3	0.2
Heroin	1.6[a]	1.3	0.1	0.2	0.1	0.1
Hallucinogens	14.5	14.3	1.7	1.6	0.4	0.4
LSD	10.3	9.7	0.2	0.2	0.1	0.1
PCP	3.0	2.8	0.1	0.1	0.0	0.0
Ecstasy	4.6	4.6	0.9	0.8	0.2	0.2
Inhalants	9.7	9.5	0.9	0.9	0.2	0.3
Nonmedical Use of Psychotherapeutics[2]	20.1	20.0	6.3	6.1	2.7	2.5
Pain Relievers	13.1	13.2	4.9	4.7	2.0	1.8
OxyContin®	1.2	1.3	—	0.5	—	0.1
Tranquilizers	8.5	8.3	2.1	2.1	0.8	0.7
Stimulants	8.8	8.3	1.2	1.2	0.5	0.5
Methamphetamine	5.2	4.9	0.6	0.6	0.3	0.2
Sedatives	4.0	4.1	0.3	0.3	0.1	0.1
ILLICIT DRUG OTHER THAN MARIJUANA[1]	29.9	29.4	8.5	8.2	3.7	3.4

SOURCE: SAMHSA, Office of Applied Studies, National Survey on Drug Use and Health, 2003 and 2004.

*Low precision; no estimate reported.

—Not available.

a. Difference between estimate and 2004 estimate is statistically significant at the 0.05 level.
b. Difference between estimate and 2004 estimate is statistically significant at the 0.01 level.

1. Illicit Drugs include marijuana/hashish, cocaine (including crack), heroin, hallucinogens, inhalants, or prescription-type psychotherapeutics used nonmedically. Illicit Drugs Other Than Marijuana include cocaine (including crack), heroin, hallucinogens, inhalants, or prescription-type psychotherapeutics used nonmedically.
2. Nonmedical use of prescription-type pain relievers, tranquilizers, stimulants, or sedative; does not include over-the-counter drugs.

administering the drug among hard-core addicts. This produces the famous *rush*, a warm skin flush and orgasmic feeling, after which the user drifts off into a carefree world for anywhere up to 12 hours. Because of the increasing awareness of the dangers (AIDS, hepatitis, etc.) of sharing contaminated "works," many heroin addicts now snort or smoke heroin. It is possible to achieve about the same effect as mainlining using these methods because of the increased potency of the heroin available today.[54]

The brain produces its own painkilling substances called endorphins (for "endogenous morphine-like substances") that do for us naturally, if far less effectively, what heroin does artificially. The presence of these naturally occurring analgesics provides clues to the addictive process. Frequent use of heroin negatively affects the body's natural capacity to produce and release endorphins in response to the pains and stresses of life. If the brain has opiates running around from the outside, it is fooled into stopping the production of its own natural endorphins, and the addict may then be totally reliant on heroin to dull the pains of life.[55]

The Stimulants

The stimulants have effects opposite to those of the narcotics. *Cocaine* is a Schedule II substance because it has legitimate medical uses as a local anesthetic. Cocaine works by blocking the reuptake of excitatory neurotransmitters at the synaptic terminals, thus keeping the body in an extended state of arousal. Cocaine is taken up by the brain quickly, producing the familiar euphoric rush, and when it is taken intravenously, the "rush" or "flash" takes only about 15 seconds.

Smokeable cocaine (*crack*) produces intense craving and may be the most addictive substance known. Crack is manufactured by combining cocaine, baking soda, and water; heating the mixture, which is then allowed to cool; and breaking it into tiny pieces or "rocks." Crack produces the same high as powdered cocaine. It only lasts 5 to 10 minutes, but its relatively low price makes it attractive to those who formerly resisted the more expensive powder. Crack prices range from $5 to $25 for a rock compared with about $200 for a gram (about the amount of artificial sweetener contained in the typical Equal packet) of powdered cocaine.

Crack is a real shortcut to the nucleus accumbens, arriving there within seconds of being inhaled. Cocaine works by blocking the reuptake of dopamine into the sending synaptic knob, thus keeping the "joy juice" active for longer periods of time. Neurotransmitters not pumped back into the sending knob eventually are broken apart and cleared away by enzymes that balance their production and use. Because cocaine blocks all reuptake, enzymes eventually, with chronic use, destroy so much dopamine trapped between synapses that the brain's supply is depleted and the addict is unable to experience any kind of pleasure without cocaine.[56]

A comparison of persons arrested testing positive for cocaine (mostly crack) has dropped dramatically since 1990.[57] This decrease may be due to a number of factors, such as severe penalties for the sale and possession of crack and the danger from others trafficking in the market. It may also be that many individuals have decided not to try crack in the first place after seeing its consequences. Many inner-city youths have apparently determined that crack is not "cool" anymore, and this emerging norm has been attributed to the *younger brother syndrome*. This syndrome essentially means that these youths have seen relatives and friends serving long prison sentences, killed or permanently disabled in drug deals gone wrong, and others sick and dying because of their addiction.[58]

Methamphetamine is the strongest form of a class of stimulants called *amphetamines*, all of which accentuate and accelerate the visual, tactile, auditory, and olfactory impulses. The amphetamines are chemically similar to epinephrine (adrenaline), the hormone that provides the body with its "fight-or-flight" energy.[59] They all act on the brain by stimulating the release of norepinephrine and dopamine and preventing their reuptake. While the stimulant effects of methamphetamine are slower in coming than are cocaine's, they last longer. Methamphetamine is the poor man's cocaine, enabling users to go on a "run" of several days at a cost of only a few hundred dollars compared with a few thousand for a cocaine run of similar duration. Chronic abuse of methamphetamine may produce schizophrenic-like effects (paranoia, auditory and visual hallucinations, picking at one's skin, and a preoccupation with one's inner thoughts) that can last for months or years after withdrawal from the drug.[60]

Hallucinogens

Hallucinogenic drugs are mind-altering drugs such as lysergic acid diethylamide (LSD) and peyote, and they are classified by the DEA as Schedule I. *LSD* is a clear, odorless, and tasteless liquid that is sold soaked in sugar cubes or on saturated blotting paper (microdots). LSD is produced from acid found in a fungus called ergot, which grows on grains such as rye. It is a drug primarily favored by inward lookers who seek to increase awareness rather than to escape it. It causes hyperawareness and greatly enhances appreciation of stimuli in the user's perceptual field, disabling the brain's filtering system by inhibiting serotonin production, thus releasing the user's perceptual brakes.[61] This flood of stimuli sometimes induces psychotic-like behavior. LSD does not cause physical dependence, but psychological dependence may occur, and the drug rapidly produces tolerance.

Some classification systems include *marijuana* (Spanish for Mary Jane) among the hallucinogens, while others classify it separately under *cannabis,* which also includes hashish. As noted in Table 10.1, marijuana is by far the most widely used illicit drug in the United States. Despite its classification as a Schedule I substance, it is only mildly hallucinogenic, moderately addictive, and available in some states for the treatment of glaucoma and for the effects of chemotherapy. Today's marijuana is much stronger than that available in the days of the hippie pot smoker. Unlike alcohol, which is water soluble and quickly metabolized and excreted from the body, tetrahydrocannabinol, or THC (the active chemical in marijuana), is fat soluble, which means that it penetrates the fatty areas of the body and may remain there for months or even years. There are many THC receptors in areas of the brain that influence not only pleasure but also concentration, memory, and coordination.[62] Marijuana users might want to consider the facts that there are 421 different chemicals in cannabis and that there is about four times the carcinogenic tar in marijuana smoke as in tobacco smoke.[63]

Synthetic look-alike or designer drugs fall into the general family of psychoactive substances. Designer drugs are synthesized by underground chemists from nonprescription substances. A well-known drug that fits this category is *ecstasy,* one of the street names for 3, 4 methylenedioxymethylamphetamine (MDMA). MDMA is a popular drug among the young attending dance parties ("raves") because its effects are similar to those produced by both psychedelic drugs such as LSD (mild hallucinations) and stimulants such as methamphetamine (increased sensual arousal). Experiments with nonhuman primates have shown that exposure to MDMA for only 4 days causes damage to the serotonin system that has been found to last up to 7 years.[64]

The Drugs/Violence Link

Scholars researching the link between illegal drugs and crime tend to rely heavily on Paul Goldstein's tripartite framework.[65] According to this framework, illegal drugs are associated with violence in three ways: (1) *pharmacological,* (2) *economic-compulsive,* and (3) *systemic.* Although Goldstein's framework focuses on violent crime, it can include other forms of crime also. The systemic link is by far the strongest, and thus we will begin with it.

Goldstein[66] defines **systemic violence** as violence associated with "traditionally aggressive patterns of interaction within the system of drug distribution and use." In other words, it is violence committed as part of "doing business" (the growing, processing, transporting, and selling of drugs) in the criminal drug culture. There is so much systemic violence because the drug business is tremendously lucrative for those involved in it, and there is much competition for a slice of that business. Davenport-Hines quotes a United Nations estimate of the annual worth of the international illicit drug trade at $400 billion—about the same worth as the oil industry.[67]

As with the oil industry, the illicit drug industry consists of several levels of business between extracting the product from the ground and selling it to the eventual consumer. Cocaine and heroin both begin as natural products grown in fields, cocaine as the coca leaf and heroin as the poppy flower. According to the U.S. Department of State,[68] the number of acres used for coca cultivation in 2004 in South America was 60,787, down from 552,763 in 2001. This huge reduction was accomplished mainly by the aerial spraying of the coca crop with herbicides. On the down side, it was also reported that Afghanistan had 510,756 acres (798 square miles) devoted to cultivating poppies, up from a mere 4,164 acres under cultivation during the last full year (2001) of the Taliban regime.

After the crop has been picked, the raw material must be processed, packaged, and smuggled via various "pipelines" into the countries in which the customers for the product reside. Figure 10.3 show the trafficking routes for cocaine and heroin from points of origin to eventual destination. Once it is at its destination, it is "cut" (mixed with various other substances) to increase its volume and then distributed to street-level outlets for sale to drug users. Profit is made along each step of the way. In 2000, for instance, a kilogram (about 2.2 pounds) of heroin cost an average of $2,720 in Pakistan but sold for an average of $129,380 on the streets in the United states, and a kilogram of coca base cost an average of $950 in Colombia in 1997 and sold for $25,000 in the United States.[69] Figure 10.4 shows the five-stage flow of the illegal drug trade from grower to market.

Systemic violence and other criminal activity begin with the bribery and corruption of law enforcement officials and political figures, or their intimidation and assassination, in the countries where raw materials are grown and through which the processed product is transported. On the streets of the United States, systemic violence is most closely linked with gang battles over control of territory (control of drug markets). Goldstein and his colleagues found that just over half of a sample of 414 murders committed in New York in 1988 was drug related, with 90% of them involving cocaine. The National Institute of Justice[70] estimated that about 80% of the homicides in the District of Columbia in 1988 were drug related, a huge increase from the 1985 estimate of 21%. In fact, the dramatic increase in criminal homicides beginning in the mid-1980s (see Chapter 11) has been attributed to the emergence of crack cocaine in the inner city and the subsequent recruitment of young males to sell it.[71]

In addition to homicides directly related to the drug trade, the emergence of the crack trade led to an increase in criminal homicides that were not directly related to the drug trade. Street-level crack dealers found it necessary to arm themselves for protection against

Figure 10.3 Global Cocaine and Heroin Trafficking Routes: Countries of Origin and Major Countries of Destination.

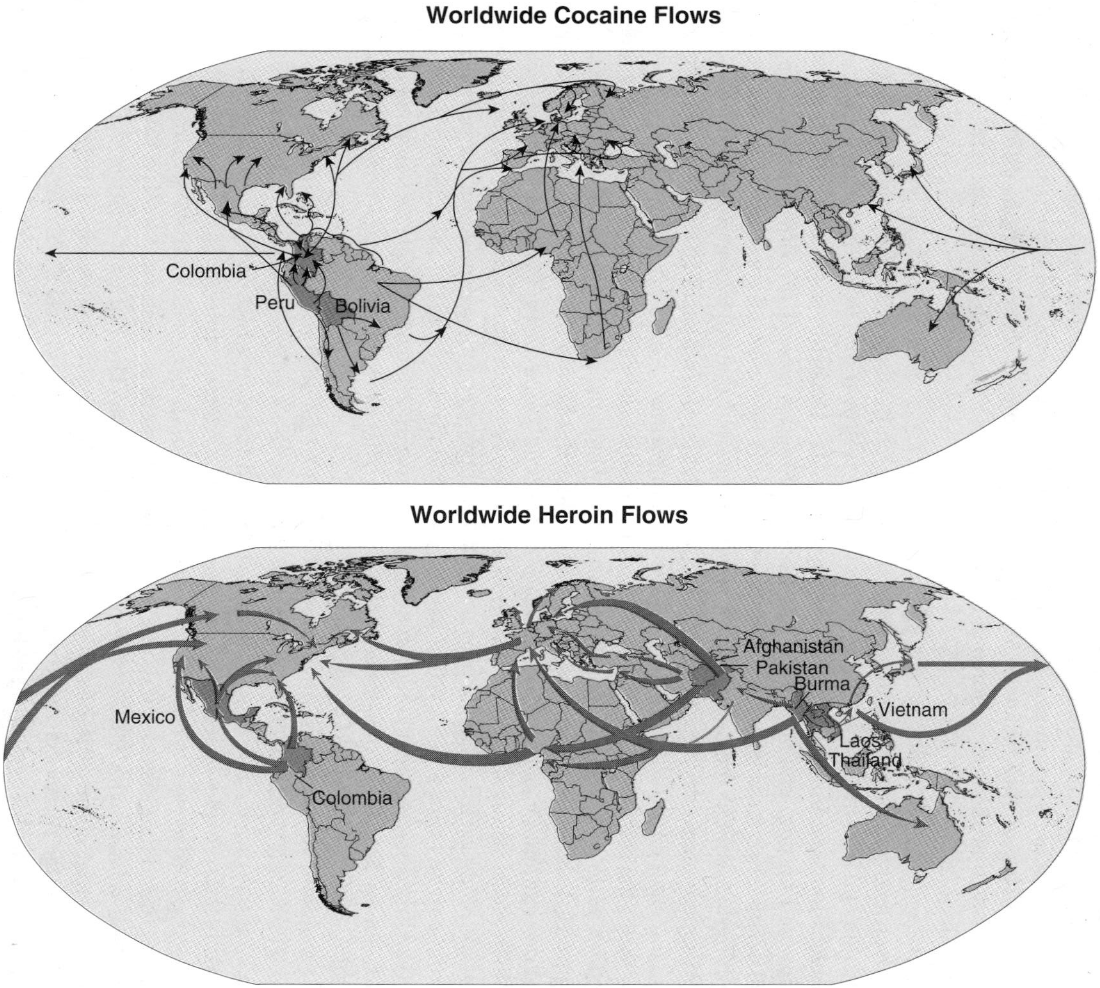

Worldwide Cocaine Flows

Worldwide Heroin Flows

Source: *The National Drug Control Strategy: 2000 Annual Report.* Washington, DC: U.S. Government Printing Office.

rival gang members competing for the same business and from individuals who might rob them for their money and their product. According to Blumstein,[72] the habit of carrying guns "diffused" to other youths inhabiting the same neighborhoods as perceptions regarding the necessity of arming oneself for protection grew. The carrying of a "piece" soon became a highly rated status symbol in those communities, further increasing the incentive to acquire one. The dramatic decline in homicides in the United States beginning in the early 1990s may have a lot to do with the consolidation of drug gangs (particularly those in the lucrative crack market) and the subsequent end to the territorial wars.[73]

Economic-compulsive violence is violence associated with efforts to obtain money to finance the high cost of illicit drugs. Addicts are not typically wage earners, and even if they were, few occupations pay enough to cover the cost of illicit drugs, which can be anything up to $400 a day for some drugs. The drugs most associated with this type of criminal activity are heroin and cocaine because they are the drugs most likely to lead to addiction among their users and the most expensive.[74] Crimes committed to obtain drug money run the gamut from shoplifting, robbery, and prostitution to trafficking in the very substance the addict craves. A study of newly incarcerated drug users found that 72% claimed that they committed their latest crime to obtain drug money.[75]

Pharmacological violence is violence induced by the pharmacological properties of the drug itself. Violence induced by illicit drug uses is rare compared with violence induced by alcohol, the legal drug. One criminal victimization survey found that less than 5% of victims of violent crimes perceived their assailants to be under the influence of illicit drugs versus 20% who perceived them to be under the influence of alcohol.[76] Pharmacologically induced violence is most likely to occur *after* the effects of the drugs have worn off, leaving the users stressed, irritable, and paranoid.[77]

Offenders dependent on methamphetamine are especially dangerous after the run is over. They find themselves in deep posthigh depressions, their nerves are badly frayed, and they are in desperate need of sleep. They become very argumentative and are susceptible to explosive violence. Any confrontation worsens the depression and leads them on a desperate search for more speed to alleviate the feeling. They will do almost anything to get the next fix and start the vicious cycle spinning again.

Figure 10.4	Illegal Drug Marketing from Grower to Market			
Grower →	**Processor** →	**Transporter** →	**Wholesaler** →	**Retailer**
Farmers plant and harvest poppy, coca, and marijuana crops	Use of chemicals such as motor oil, sulfuric acid, kerosene, and insecticides to refine product	Smugglers use planes, boats, trucks, and many other methods to get product to wholesaler	Organized criminal groups cut product and distribute it to dealers	Deals directly with consumer in crack houses or on street

▲ **Photo 10.2**   A teenager drinks alcohol from a bottle. Alcohol and/or other substance abuse is often associated with other forms of juvenile delinquency and involvement in status offenses.

What Causes Drug Abuse?

Sociological explanations of drug abuse mirror almost exactly their explanations for crime. This is best illustrated in Gottfredson and Hirschi's bold statement that "crime and drug usage are the same thing—that is, manifestations of low self-control."[78] Erich Goode also illustrates the almost indistinguishable explanations offered for the causes of crime and drug abuse in his book *Drugs in American Society*.[79] In terms of anomie theory, drug abuse is a retreatist adaptation of those who have failed in both the legitimate and illegitimate opportunity structures, and drug dealing is an innovative adaptation. In social control theory, drug abusers lack attachment to prosocial others and lack a stake in conformity, and in self-control theory, drug abuse is the hedonistic search for immediate pleasures. Likewise, social learning and subcultural theories stress that drug abuse reflects differential exposure to individuals and groups in which it is modeled and reinforced.

Goode favors conflict theory most as an explanation. As the rich get richer, the poor get poorer, and economic opportunities shrink for the uneducated and the unskilled, drug dealers have taken firm root among the increasingly demoralized, disorganized, and politically powerless "underclass." He notes that most members of this class do not succumb to addiction, but enough do "to make the lives of the majority unpredictable, insecure, and dangerous."[80] Goode maintains that conflict theory applies "more or less exclusively to heavy chronic, compulsive use of heroin or crack."[81] Of course, neither conflict theory nor any other theory can account for the middle- and upper-class user or even the occasional recreational user of any class. Such people simply chose to take drugs for the pleasures they afford them and ignore the long-term consequences.

Does Drug Abuse Cause Crime?

The National Institute of Justice attempts to monitor the extent to which drug use and crime are associated through its ADAM program, which currently operates in large urban jails in 25 states.[82] ADAM collects urine samples from arrestees and tests it for the presence of drugs. Table 10.2 shows the percentage of male and female adult arrestees in some of our largest cities who tested positive for illicit drugs. These jail data, averaged over all cities, mirror the finding that 67% of state and 56% of federal prison inmates indicated regular drug use prior to imprisonment.[83] Note that the majority of both male and female arrestees tested positive for at least one drug, and the majority of males tested positive for multiple drugs. Clearly, these data show that illicit drug abuse is strongly *associated* with criminal behavior, but is the association a *causal* one? From our discussion of the identical nature of the explanations for crime and drug abuse discussed above, neither causes the other, and both are caused by factors they share. In terms of developmental theories, we have already seen that drug usage follows the same age-graded pattern that offending does and that both are largely adolescent limited. But what comes first, drugs or crime?

A large body of research indicates that drug abuse does not appear to *initiate* a criminal career, although it does increase the extent and seriousness of one.[84,85] Drug abusers are not "innocents" driven into a criminal career by drugs, although this might occasionally be true. Rather, chronic drug abuse and criminality are part of a broader propensity of some individuals to engage in a variety of deviant and antisocial behaviors. A large number of studies have shown that traits characterizing antisocial individuals, such as ADHD with conduct disorder, impulsiveness, and high scores on the Hare Psychopathy Checklist, also characterize drug addicts.[86,87] The reciprocal (feedback) nature of the drugs/crime connection is explained by Menard, Mihalic, and Huizinga as follows: "Initiation of substance abuse is preceded by initiation of crime for most individuals (and therefore cannot be a cause of crime). At a later stage of involvement, however, serious illicit drug use appears to contribute to continuity in serious crime, and serious crime contributes to continuity in serious illicit drug use."[88]

▧ Mental Disorders and Crime

Alcoholics and drug addicts ingest substances that alter the functioning of their brains in ways that interfere with their ability to cope with everyday life, although their brains may be quite normal when not befuddled by these substances. Mentally disordered (or mentally ill) persons also have brains that limit their capacity to cope, but that limitation is intrinsic to their brains and not attributable to the ingestion of intoxicating substances. The World Health Organization defines **mental disorders** as "clinically significant conditions characterized by alterations in thinking, mood (emotions), or behaviour associated with personal distress and/or impaired functioning" and adds that they "are not variations within the range of 'normal,' but are clearly abnormal or pathological phenomena."[97] A 1999 Bureau of Justice study found that 16% of prison and jail inmates suffer some sort of mental disorder as defined above and that 547,000 mentally ill offenders were on probation or parole.[98]

| Table 10.2 | Male and Female Adult Arrestees Testing Positive for Various Drugs (in Percentages) |

MALES

City	Any of Five Drugs[a]	Multiple Drugs	Cocaine	Heroin	Metham-phetamine	Marijuana
Atlanta	72.4	73.5	49.8	3.0	2.0	41.8
Chicago	86.0	86.0	50.6	24.9	1.4	53.2
Dallas	62.3	63.8	32.5	6.9	5.8	39.1
Houston	61.7	61.9	22.6	5.7	2.1	47.5
Los Angeles	68.6	68.9	23.5	2.0	28.7	47.5
New York	67.7	72.7	35.7	15.0	0.0	43.1
Philadelphia	67.0	68.8	30.3	11.5	0.6	45.8
Phoenix	74.1	76.8	23.4	4.4	38.3	45.8
San Diego	66.8	71.2	10.3	5.1	36.2	41.6
Washington	65.6	65.8	26.5	9.8	0.7	37.4

FEMALES[b]

City	Any of Five Drugs[a]	Multiple Drugs	Cocaine	Heroin	Metham-phetamine	Marijuana
Albany, NY	60.9	65.2	34.8	4.3	0.0	34.8
Chicago	61.1	66.7	33.3	22.2	0.0	38.9
Denver	69.1	24.9	52.5	6.1	5.0	34.3
Honolulu	74.5	27.7	8.5	6.4	57.4	29.8
Los Angeles	59.3	63.0	25.9	2.1	18.5	36.7
New York	67.7	72.7	35.7	15.0	0.0	43.1
New Orleans	58.8	17.8	37.3	13.3	0.8	30.3
Phoenix	74.6	78.5	16.8	6.1	41.6	31.6
San Diego	69.1	72.6	15.2	8.7	47.1	29.1
Washington	61.1	66.7	30.9	10.3	0.0	29.1

SOURCE: Adapted from the Arrestee Drug Abuse Monitoring Program.

a. The five drugs are cocaine, marijuana, methamphetamine, opiates, and phencyclidine (PCP).

b. Atlanta, Dallas, Houston, and Philadelphia did not sample female arrestees; Albany, Denver, Honolulu, and New Orleans were substituted.

c. Multiple drugs are any of nine drugs that include the basic five plus barbiturates, methadone, benzodiazepines, and propoxyphene.

We cannot conduct a comprehensive overview of mental illness here, so we concentrate on the disorders most associated with criminal offending (psychopathy is not considered an illness since psychopaths are able to function well, if not morally, in society). These two psychiatric conditions are schizophrenia and bipolar disorder, with special attention being given to schizophrenia. Together, these conditions account for more criminal offenses than all other mental patients combined[99] and are the two conditions "most strongly due to genetic inheritance."[100]

Treatment for Substance Abuse in the Criminal Justice System

Given the strong links between alcohol and drug abuse and crime, it is not surprising that the criminal justice system makes a significant effort to treat the problem. Treatment for the alcoholic includes both medical treatment and psychosocial counseling, with the goal being *recovery*, as defined by abstinence, sobriety, and normal social functioning. The major tool available to community corrections for the treatment of alcoholism is Alcoholics Anonymous (AA), which has been called by the World Health Organization as "one of the great success stories of our century."[89] AA is a mutual self-help support group composed of alcoholics who recognize that sobriety is a one-day-at-a-time process rather than a treatment per se. Rational Recovery (RR) and Secular Sobriety (SS) are alternative support groups for those who object to the quasi-spiritual nature of AA.

Sometimes, medication is needed to supplement a person's efforts to maintain sobriety. One of the oldest medical treatments is the use of disulfiram (Antabuse). Antabuse treatment is a form of aversion therapy that "punishes" the drinker by strongly accentuating "hangover" symptoms. Another form of medical treatment is naltrexone (ReVia), which has great promise for offenders in their struggle against relapse. It has been claimed that this drug reduces relapse episodes by up to 50% by reducing craving in abstinent persons and blocking the reinforcing effects of alcohol among those who are drinking, thus lessening the probability of them returning to heavy drinking.[90]

Drug abuse and addiction is also a huge problem the correctional system tries to address. There are also self-help support groups for drug abusers modeled after AA, such as Narcotics Anonymous (NA) and Cocaine Anonymous (CA). As a former director of the National Institute on Drug Abuse said about drug addiction, it is "a psychobiological illness," and treatment "must include biological, behavioral, and social context components."[91] Nalrexone has been used to treat a variety of types of substance abuse. A study of more than 1,600 cocaine addicts in 11 U.S. cities found that 77% were cocaine free a year after treatment.[92] A study of federal probationers found that one third who received nalrexone plus counseling relapsed compared with two thirds who received counseling only.[93] Two reviews of the U.S.[94] and U.K.[95] literature on drug treatment for offenders surprisingly concluded that there were greater reductions in abuse among offenders ordered into programs than among voluntary participants.

Therapeutic communities (TCs) are very useful self-help treatment modalities. They are programs that rely on learning processes fostered by positive peer pressure in a highly structured residential environment. In these TC settings, residents rely on one another to stay on the straight and narrow, resocialize themselves, build self-images that do not include drugs, and learn to become more responsible as they gradually return to the larger community. A successful drug-free reentry into society depends quite a bit on the length of stay in the TC, which in turn depends quite a bit on the kind of person the TC resident is. In one evaluation of a prison-based TC, only 45.5% relapsed by 6 months after completion compared with 65.5% in a work release comparison group. On a more positive note, only 9.9% who completed the TC program *and* were part of a postrelease outreach program relapsed.[96] Beating the hell of alcoholism or drug addiction is possible.

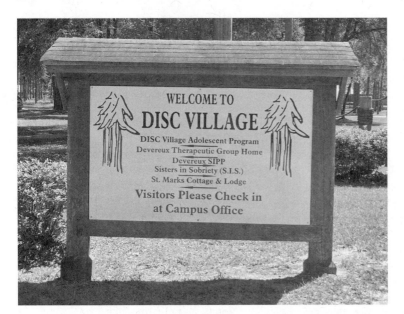

◄ **Photo 10.3** The depicted treatment facility runs five different programs. Some are residential and others day treatment programs. A number of clients sent to programs such as these come from court-ordered diversion or other judicial intervention.

▲ **Photo 10.4** Because the teens in this drug treatment facility are still of school age, the facility must offer a full educational curriculum. The small class sizes and individualized attention do assist these teens, who are often alienated from school, to return to their own high schools upon release.

Schizophrenia is the most widespread of the psychotic disorders (disorders in which the person loses contact with reality), affecting about 1% of the world's population.[101] Following concerns about psychiatric patients' rights and the accompanying movement to deinstitutionalize them, many schizophrenics who would previously have been hospitalized are now living on the streets. In the United States in 1955, for instance, there were 339 per 100,000 individuals in state mental hospitals, but in 2001, there were only 20 per 100,000.[102] This approximately 1,600% decrease in hospitalized patients leaves only jails and prisons as surrogate mental hospitals to absorb much of the mentally ill population. Robinson[103] reports that there are now about three-and-one-half times more mentally ill people in American prisons and jails as there are in psychiatric hospitals. Only the most severely mentally impaired patients are hospitalized today, with most others being able to function minimally in the community.[104]

Schizophrenia comes in a variety of subtypes that are categorized according to the symptoms that patients manifest. Some schizophrenics are rigid and unresponsive (catatonic), some are frenetic and wild (hebephrenic), some are hostile and distrusting (paranoid), and some are placed under various other subcategories. The disease has most recently come to the attention of the American public through the movie and book (*A Beautiful Mind*) about the life of John Nash, a brilliant mathematician, and Andrea Yates, the mother who drowned her five children in a bathtub to "save them from the devil."[105] Both Nash and Yates were schizophrenics, yet both had radically different life outcomes.

Most schizophrenic disorders develop insidiously over a long period of time and are characterized by an early inability to function normally, to make friends, to handle schoolwork, and to behave acceptably, but it is not typically diagnosed until the teen years. There is also a second type, called *reactive schizophrenia,* which develops in individuals without a history of psychological and social dysfunction. Their descent into schizophrenia is usually marked by the onset of an acutely stressful experience, such as being incarcerated for the first time.[106]

Schizophrenia, as well as psychosis in general, is so far removed from the everyday experience of most of us that we have to resort to talking about dreams and what the brain is doing when we dream to give you some sort of insight into the schizophrenic experience. Think of the scariest and most vivid dreams you have ever had, and then think about how you would feel if you experienced them when you knew that you were awake. When we are dreaming, our neurons are making random connections unrelated to any external stimuli.[107] During sleep, there are no external stimuli, so the brain does the best it can to generate order from the random chaos by drawing on past experiences stored in its memory banks, but because the brain impulses are haphazard, randomly darting from one memory to another, the images generated are less than coherent.

Think of the schizophrenic state as evoked from a very private reality, an often scary and quite incoherent reality. When we awake, we are aware that we were dreaming and begin to respond normally to stimuli outside of our private worlds, but schizophrenics must remain in their private worlds with their brain trying to make sense of a neurochemical cascade that has little or no connection with external reality. With this neural activity going on, schizophrenics experience delusions and hallucinations and, as a consequence, have difficulties filtering information and focusing their attention on "real" environmental stimuli.[108] Delusions are strongly held beliefs with no basis in reality, such as the belief that aliens are trying to control the person via radio waves or that he or she is Napoleon or Cleopatra. Hallucinations are severe auditory and visual perceptual distortions, such as actually hearing those alien voices or actually seeing the aliens.

Bipolar disorder (which used to be known as manic depression) is a disorder in which individuals alternate between the poles of extreme elation or euphoria (mania) and deep depression. These symptoms are experienced with varying degrees of severity, with periods of relative normality in between. The most severe form of this disorder is known as *bipolar disorder I;* the less severe form, in which individuals have a less severe form of mania called hypomania, is known as *bipolar disorder II.* Hypomania does not include schizophrenic-like delusions or hallucinations, but full-blown mania does. The prevalence of bipolar disorder in the general population is about 1.6% and is slightly higher in females than in males.[109]

Causality: The Diathesis/Stress Model

Before psychiatry became more sophisticated, it was fashionable to blame mental disorders on negative relationships within the family or even to dismiss the whole concept of mental illness as a myth, or simply a labeling process by which the powerful controlled the "eccentric" behavior of the powerless (e.g., Szasz[110]). It evidently did not occur to researchers that many of the negative parental events observed among families of the mentally ill were more likely to be effects of mental illness, not its cause. Even the most loving of parents may become frustrated and eventually turn away when their mentally ill children continually rebuff their best efforts to nurture them.

Today we know that schizophrenia and bipolar disorder are real identifiable entities that we can "see" with the use of positron emission tomography (PET) and functional magnetic resonance imaging (fMRI) scans. PET and fMRI scans provide information about brain functioning and produce distinct neurological maps of normal, schizophrenic, and bipolar individuals.[111] The genetic basis of schizophrenia and bipolar disorder is well established, although how strong the genetic effect is relative to nongenetic effects remains an open question. Behavior genetic studies of schizophrenia show a concordance rate of about 50% for monozygotic twins and about 12% for dizygotic twins.[112,113] Thus, if one of a pair of identical twins has schizophrenia, the co-twin will also have it about half of the time, but if one of a pair of fraternal twins has it, the co-twin has only about a 12% risk. Both percentages are considerably greater than the 1% risk rate of schizophrenia in the general population. The concordance rate for bipolar disorder is even greater—80% for monozygotic twins and 16% for dizygotic twins.[114]

Both schizophrenia and bipolar disorder are primarily disorders of brain chemistry; schizophrenia is typically seen as a problem involving an excess of dopamine,[115] and bipolar disorder is seen as a cyclical pattern of too much (the manic phase) or too little (the depressive phase) norepinephrine.[116] Clues to the neurchemical basis for these disorders came with the advent of the antipsychotic drugs such as haloperidol and clozapine, which work by blocking the neurotransmitter dopamine at the synapse. Antipsychotic drugs work more effectively for symptoms such as hallucinations, delusions, and incoherence, which represent *increased* neural activity, than for symptoms such as *decreased* neural activity, such as withdrawal, lack of warmth, and blunted emotions.[117]

The **diathesis/stress model** is a biosocial model that now dominates schizophrenia and bipolar research. This biosocial model maintains that although mental illnesses reflect an underlying genetic vulnerability (diathesis), they are often the products of multiple other factors interacting with this vulnerability. If only half of a genetically identical twin pair typically falls afoul of schizophrenia, then there must have been something in the environment of the afflicted twin that was not in the environment of the other that precipitated the onset of schizophrenia: "Genetic factors determine predispositions to schizophrenia, but environmental factors are required for expression of the illness."[118] The list of potential environmental stressors is seemingly endless: genetic mutation occurring during embryonic development, rubella, maternal influenza, birth complications such as oxygen deprivation, abuse and neglect, and traumatic environmental events.[119,120]

It has long been known that people with mental disorders are disproportionately from the lower socioeconomic (SES) classes of society and from urban as opposed to rural areas. This can be interpreted in at least two ways. First, those with a predisposition are exposed to many more stresses than they can handle living in urban areas, especially if they have access to limited financial resources. It is also possible that such persons are more likely than higher SES persons to have been exposed prenatally to noxious substances that can negatively affect the developing brain such as drugs, tobacco, and alcohol.[121] In addition, people in urban areas are exposed to more infectious diseases, pollutants, toxins, and crime than are people living in rural areas. On the other hand, there is ample research support that shows that lower SES is a consequence, not a cause, of mental illness; that is, becoming mentally ill precipitates a downward spiral in the SES of the sufferer relative to the SES of his or her parents.[122] Both explanations of the SES/mental illness relationship may be valid depending on the individual cases being examined.

FOCUS ON . . .

Portrait of a Schizophrenic

Greg was a frail, good-looking man of twenty-four when I first met him. He had two prior convictions for misdemeanor vandalism and was in my office now convicted of felony vandalism. Greg had this nasty habit of throwing chunks of rock through plate glass windows.

He was extremely difficult to interview for he manifested all the classic symptoms of the schizophrenic. He sat staring at me with flat affect, his hygiene was poor, and he did not particularly care what I had to say to him. I was able to find out that his life revolved around the TV set, in front of which he spent practically every waking hour. He wasn't fussy about which programs he watched, but he was concerned that whatever channel it happened to be, it must not be changed. Each of his vandalism charges stemmed from arguments with his mother or some other family member over changing channels. The upshot of those arguments was that his mother would throw him out of the house. When that occurred, Greg would proceed to the closest business establishment with a big glass window, put a brick through it, and sit down among the debris to await the arrival of the police. This tactic yielded him a place to sleep and another TV at which he could stare.

(Continued)

(Continued)

I took Greg back home after the presentence investigation interview since he had just been released from the county jail and was penniless. I also wanted to get a feel for his environment. Upon meeting his mother, I soon formed an opinion of her as a dominating, egocentric, and manipulative shrew. She flatly informed me that the only reason that her son was welcome in her house was his $200 monthly disability check. His four brothers were likewise unfriendly and cruel. Since Greg was much smaller than his brothers, and a "wacko" to boot, he was a convenient target for their verbal and physical aggression. It seemed to me that rather than involving himself with those who rejected him and offered him no love, Greg had withdrawn into a semicatatonic world of dials and plastic people. The characters on the screen could not rebuff him as real people could. I came to view his reactions to channel switching as an attempt to protect somehow the existence of those benign characters on the screen.

I learned that Greg was seeing a psychiatrist at a local center who was prescribing Thorazine for him. Unfortunately, family members never made it much of their business to make sure that Greg took his medication as directed. I was able to persuade his mother to request that his psychiatrist place him on Prolixin if medically advisable, arguing that for a small investment of her time (driving Greg to the center for his injection twice a month) she could enjoy a semblance of peace in the house. And, more important for her, she could be assured of the uninterrupted flow of his disability checks. I also suggested that to avoid future problems she might consider buying Greg his own TV set.

Greg's mother did both of these things, and peace reigned for about nine months. Greg reported at my office on time twice a month and was fairly agreeable. Visits to his home revealed that things were still the same in terms of the family's treatment of Greg. He still was picked on and rejected, even beaten, by other family members, even though his own behavior had improved rather remarkably.

Then, I received a call from the mental health center informing me that Greg had missed his last two appointments with them. He was also a week late reporting to me. I decided to go to his home to find out what was happening. I was informed that two weeks prior to my visit Greg had gotten into a fight with his older brother and had stabbed him. Although the wound was superficial and the police had not been called, Greg panicked and fled from the house. I never heard from Greg again. Had he remained in my city, he surely would have been arrested again and I would have seen him. As far as I know, Greg is still out there somewhere among the hordes of loveless and rejected individuals who aimlessly wander the streets of our big cities. Greg's case is an example of how one's best efforts can sometimes come to less than an ideal ending. We have to accept failures as well as successes and learn from them both.

SOURCE: Walsh, A. (2006). *Correctional assessment, casework, and counseling* (4th ed.). Lanham, MD: American Correctional Association. Reprinted with permission from the American Correctional Association.

The Link Between Mental Illness and Crime

After several decades of denying the link between mental illness and crime, the psychiatric community has reversed its stance. Older studies that concluded that there was no link between crime and mental illness were conducted during the period when individuals with serious mental illnesses were routinely institutionalized, sometimes even for life. The deinstitutionalization movement in the 1960s shifted many such persons into the community, which resulted in greater visibility and higher arrest rates for the mentally ill.[123,124] Even now there is some reluctance to affirm the link between crime and mental illness out of fear of further stigmatizing an already highly stigmatized group, although the link cannot be ignored.[125]

A review of 86 studies examining the mental illness and criminal/antisocial behavior relationship found that 79 (92%) of them found it to be positive, 6 studies were nonsignificant, and only 1 study was negative; that is, mental illness was associated with lower levels of criminal and antisocial behavior in this study.[126] After controlling for many demographic factors, 2 studies found that the incidence of violence was up to 5 times greater among people with serious mental problems (mostly people with schizophrenia and bipolar disorder) than among people with no mental illness.[127,128] Researchers in Denmark, looking at more than 300,000 individuals followed to age 43, found that persons with histories of psychiatric hospitalization were 3 to 11 times more likely to have criminal convictions than people with no psychiatric history.[129] A Swedish study reported that people with psychosis are about 4 times more likely to have a criminal record than members of the general population,[130] and an American study[131] found that those with schizophrenia were far more likely to be imprisoned for assaultive crimes than for any other type of crime. Similarly, a British study found that male schizophrenics had 3 times as many convictions for violent crimes as nonpsychotic criminals in a control group,[132] and an Israeli study found that people with schizophrenia and bipolar disorder were about 3 times more likely than members of the general population to report engaging in fighting over a 5-year period.[133]

However, the majority of the mentally ill are nonviolent, and because of their vulnerability, they are more likely to be victims of violence than perpetrators. One study found that they were more likely to harm themselves than others and are up to six times more likely to be victims of a crime than people in the general population.[134] The mentally ill most at risk for committing violent acts are the homeless, those who use alcohol and other drugs, and those who do not take their antipsychotic medication.[135] Unfortunately, more than half of mentally ill persons also have histories of serious substance abuse.[136] As with sex offenders, juvenile delinquents, or any other disvalued groups, mentally ill persons are usually defined by the worst among them. Mentally ill persons who remain connected to other human beings, who do not abuse alcohol or drugs, and who faithfully take their medication may be less dangerous than the average person.[137]

Although the mentally disordered are at greater risk for committing crimes, especially violent crimes, than the average person, they are few in number, and thus their crimes constitute only a very small proportion of all crimes committed. After reviewing evidence pertaining to the link between mental illness and violence, Marzuk summed up the issue as follows:

We must recognize that the link is a real one and that it persists even after controlling for demographic . . . variables. The link appears strongest for the severe mental illnesses, particularly those involving psychosis, and, as for those persons without diagnosed mental illness, it is increased by the use of alcohol and other psychoactive substances. It is likely that active symptoms, particularly distorted perceptions, faulty reasoning, and distorted modulation of affect are more important than the label of a specific diagnosis.[138]

SUMMARY

Alcohol has always been humankind's favorite way of drugging itself and has always been associated with criminal and antisocial behavior. It reduces the inhibiting neurotransmitters and thus reduces impulse control. These chemical responses are not the only things we have to consider; contextual factors also play their part in producing the kinds of obnoxious behavior associated with drinking too much alcohol. So-called binge drinking is a major contextual problem.

Alcoholism is a problem associated with an overactive BAS in which frequent drinking leads to a "craving brain." There are two types of alcoholism: Type I and Type II. Type I is associated with mild abuse, minimal violence, moderate heritability, and character disorders that result from the alcoholism, whereas Type II is characterized by early onset, violence, criminality, high heritability, and character disorders that precede the alcoholism. Type II alcoholics may have inherited disorders of the serotonin/dopamine systems that drive both their alcoholism and their criminality.

Illicit drug use is also a major problem, although it has become much worse since drug usage became criminalized in 1914. Like delinquency, drug usage increases at puberty and drops off in early adulthood to almost zero by the age of 65. Drug addiction is fairly similar to alcoholism in terms of brain mechanisms. Drugs hijack the nucleus accumbens and make addicts crave drugs to gain any sort of pleasures at all. The various types of drugs—narcotics, stimulants and hallucinogenics—were discussed. Most people who try drugs do not become addicted.

Drugs are associated with violence in the following ways: pharmacological, economic-compulsive, and systemic, with the latter having the strongest association. It does so because violence is part of "doing business" in the lucrative illicit drug business. The economic-compulsive link with violence is the result of addicts' efforts to gain money to purchase drugs, and the rarest link, pharmacological, is violence induced by ingested drugs. Most people arrested for a crime test positive for drugs, but this does not mean that drugs cause crime. Drug abuse is part of a broader propensity of some individuals to engage in all kinds of antisocial behavior, and such behavior is usually initiated before drug abuse behavior. Drug abuse does exacerbate criminal behavior, however.

A mental disorder is an impairment of the ability to function adaptively in society. The two disorders most associated with criminal behavior are schizophrenia and bipolar disorder. Following the movement to deinstitutionalize mentally ill patients, it has fallen largely on the criminal justice system to deal with them. The most popular model for explaining these disorders is the diathesis/stress model, meaning that an inherited propensity is exacerbated by stressful environmental experiences to produce them.

The link between schizophrenia and bipolar disorder and criminal behavior is a fairly strong one found by studies in many countries. It is particularly strong if the disorders are combined with substance abuse. However, the majority of the mentally ill are nonviolent, and because of their vulnerability, they are more likely to be victims of violence than perpetrators. Mentally ill persons who remain connected to other human beings, who do not abuse alcohol or drugs, and who faithfully take their medication may be less dangerous than the average person.

On Your Own

Log on to the web-based student study site at http://www.sagepub.com/criminologystudy for more information about the vignettes and materials presented in this chapter, suggestions for activities, study aids such as review quizzes, and research recommendations including journal article links and questions related to this chapter.

EXERCISES AND DISCUSSION QUESTIONS

1. Discuss with classmates how each of you act—silly, aggressive, lusty, maudlin, and so on—when you have "gone over the limit" drinking alcohol. Why do you think that the same substance "makes" different people react differently?

2. Why do some people binge drink when they know that it is dangerous and can lead them into a lot of trouble?

3. Discuss the issue of whether alcoholism is a disease or a character defect.

4. Examine Figure 10.2 and Figure 9.1 and comment on the similarities. What's going on?

5. Given what you know about the history of drug laws in the United States and the link between drug abuse and violence (and crime in general), would legalizing drugs be the lesser of two evils? Give reasons why or why not.

6. Did the deinstitutionalization of mentally ill patients do more harm than good? Is there a more humane way of treating them than locking them up? What is it?

7. Go to the Web site of the National Institute on Drug Abuse at http://www.clubdrugs.org/ and report on the dangers of using the popular party drug, ecstasy.

KEY WORDS

Alcoholism
Bipolar disorder
Binge drinkers
Diathesis/stress model
Drug addiction

Economic-compulsive violence
Mental disorder
Pharmacological violence
Physical dependence
Psychological dependence

Schizophrenia
Systemic violence
Tolerance
Type I alcoholism
Type II alcoholism
Withdrawal

REFERENCES

1. Burns, E. (2004). *The spirits of America: A social history of alcohol.* Philadelphia: Temple University Press.

2. Martin, S. (2001). The Links between alcohol, crime and the criminal justice system: Explanations, evidence and interventions. *American Journal on Addictions, 10,* 136–158.

3. Volavka, J. (2002). *Neurobiology of violence* (2nd ed.). Washington, DC: American Psychiatric Publishing.

4. Wanberg, K., & Milkman, H. (1998). *Criminal conduct and substance abuse treatment: Strategies for self-improvement.* Thousand Oaks, CA: Sage.

5. McMurren, M. (2003). Alcohol and crime. *Criminal Behaviour and Mental Health, 13,* 1–4.

6. Robinson, M. (2005). *Justice blind: Ideals and realities of American criminal justice.* Upper Saddle River, NJ: Prentice Hall.

7. Mustaine, E., & Tewksbury, R. (2004). Alcohol and violence. In S. Holmes & R. Holmes (Eds.), *Violence: A contemporary reader* (pp. 9–25). Upper Saddle River, NJ: Prentice Hall.

8. Martin (2001).

9. Pridemore, W. (2004). Weekend effects on binge drinking and homicide: The social connection between alcohol and violence in Russia. *Addiction, 99,* 1034–1041.

10. U.S. Department of Health and Human Services. (2000). *Results from the 2001 National Household Survey on Drug Abuse: Vol. I. Summary of National Findings.* Washington, DC: Government Printing Office.

11. National Institute on Alcohol Abuse and Alcoholism. (1998). *Economic costs of alcohol and drug abuse estimated at $246 billion in the United States.* Retrieved from http://www.niaaa.nih.gov/press/1998/economics.htm

12. U.S. Department of Health and Human Services. (2002). *National household survey on drug abuse.* Washington, DC: Author.

13. Ruden, R. (1997). *The craving brain: The biobalance approach to controlling addictions.* New York: HarperCollins.

14. Martin (2001).

15. Buck, K., & Finn, D. (2000). Genetic factors in addiction: QTL mapping and candidate gene studies implicate GABAergic genes in alcohol and barbiturate withdrawal in mice. *Addiction, 96,* 139–149.

16. Martin (2001, p. 141).

17. Richardson, A., & Budd, T. (2003). Young adults, crime and disorder. *Criminal Behaviour and Mental Health, 13,* 5–17.

18. Martin (2001).

19. Martin (2001).

20. Martin (2001).

21. Martin (2001, p. 146).

22. Martin (2001).

23. Walsh, A. (2006). *Correctional assessment, casework and counseling* (4th ed.). Lanham, MD: American Correctional Association.

24. Johnson, L., O'Malley, P., & Bachman, J. (2000). *Monitoring the future National Survey Results on drug use, 1975–1999.* Bethesda, MD: National Institute of Drug Abuse.

25. Pridemore (2004).

26. Robinson, T., & Berridge, K. (2003). Addiction. *Annual Review of Psychology, 54,* 25–53.

27. Zang, Z. (2004). *Drug and alcohol use and related matters among arrestees, 2003.* Washington, DC: National Institute of Justice.

28. Bartol, C. (2002). *Criminal behavior: A psychosocial approach.* Englewood Cliffs, NJ: Prentice Hall.

29. Walsh (2006).

30. Fishbein, D. (1998). Differential susceptibility to comorbid drug abuse and violence. *Journal of Drug Issues, 28,* 859–891.

31. Gove, W., & Wilmoth, C. (2003). The neurophysiology of motivation and habitual criminal behavior. In A. Walsh & L. Ellis (Eds.), *Biosocial criminology: Challenging environmentalism's supremacy* (pp. 227–245). Hauppauge, NY: Nova Science.

32. Martin (2001).

33. Ruden (1997).

34. Moffitt, T. E. (1993). Life-course-persistent and adolescence-limited antisocial behavior: A developmental taxonomy. *Psychological Review, 100,* 674–701.

35. Crabbe, J. (2002). Genetic contributions to addiction. *Annual Review of Psychology, 53,* 435–462. (Quote on p. 449)

36. DuPont, R. (1997). *The selfish brain: Learning from addiction.* Washington, DC: American Psychiatric Press.

37. McGue, M. (1999). The behavioral genetics of alcoholism. *Current Directions in Psychological Science, 8,* 109–115.

38. Crabbe (2002).

39. Buck and Finn (2000).

40. Demir, B., Ucar, G., Ulug, B., Ulosoy, S., Sevinc, I., & Batur, S. (2002). Platelet monoamine oxidase activity in alcoholism subtypes: Relationship to personality traits and executive functions. *Alcohol and Alcoholism, 37,* 597–602.

41. Fishbein (1998).

42. Davenport-Hines, R. (2002). *The pursuit of oblivion: A global history of narcotics.* New York: W. W. Norton.

43. Davenport-Hines (2002, p. 14).

44. Casey, E. (1978). *History of drug use and drug users in the United States.* Schaffer Library of Drug Policy. Retrieved from http://www.druglibrary.org/schaffer/History/CASEY1.htm (Quote on p. 11)

45. Leshner, A. (1998). Addiction is a brain disease—and it matters. *National Institute of Justice Journal, 237,* 2–6. (Quote on p. 4)

46. Robinson and Berridge (2003).

47. Drug Enforcement Administration. (2003). *Drugs of abuse.* Arlington, VA: U.S. Department of Justice. (Quote on p. 13)

48. Pinel, J. (2000). *Biopsychology* (4th ed.). Boston: Allyn & Bacon.

49. Drug Enforcement Administration (2003).

50. Kleber, H. (2003). Pharmacological treatments for heroin and cocaine dependence. *American Journal on Addictions, 12,* S5–S18.

51. Pinel (2000).

52. Restak, R. (2001). *The secret life of the brain.* New York: Dana Press/Joseph Henry Press.

53. Kleber (2003).

54. Drug Enforcement Administration (2003).

55. Alexander, R., & Pratsinak, G. (2002). *Arresting addictions: Drug education and relapse.* Lanham, MD: American Correctional Association.

56. Alexander and Pratsinak (2002).

57. Walsh (2006).

58. Witkin, G. (1998, May 25). The crime bust. *U.S. News and World Report.*

59. Alexander and Pratsinak (2002).

60. Drug Enforcement Administration (2003).

61. Alexander and Pratsinak (2002).

62. National Institute on Drug Abuse. (2004). *Marijuana.* Washington, DC: U.S. Department of Health and Human Services.

63. Alexander and Pratsinak (2002).

64. National Institute on Drug Abuse. (2005). *LSD* (NIDA Notes). Washington, DC: U.S. Department of Health and Human Services.

65. Goldstein, P. (1985). The drugs/violence nexus: A tripartite conceptual framework. *Journal of Drug Issues, 15,* 493–506.

66. Goldstein (1985, p. 497).

67. Davenport-Hines (2002).

68. U.S. Department of State (2005). *International narcotics control strategy report.* Washington, DC: Author.

69. Davenport-Hines (2002).

70. National Institute of Justice. (1991). *Annual report on adult arrestees: Drugs and crime in America's cities.* Washington, DC: U.S. Department of Justice.

71. Blumstein, A. (1995). Youth violence, guns, and the illicit-drug industry. *Journal of Criminal Law and Criminology, 86,* 10–36.

72. Blumstein (1995).

73. Witkin (1998).

74. Parker, N., & Auerhahn, K. (1998). Alcohol, drugs, and violence. *Annual Review of Sociology, 24,* 291–311.

75. Lo, C., & Stephens, R. (2002). The role of drugs in crime: Insights from a group of incoming prisoners. *Substance Use and Misuse, 37,* 121–131.

76. Parker and Auerhahn (1998).

77. Walsh (2006).

78. Gottfredson, M., & Hirschi, T. (1990). *A general theory of crime.* Stanford, CA: Stanford University Press. (Quote on p. 239)

79. Goode, E. (2005). *Drugs in American society* (6th ed). Boston: McGraw-Hill.

80. Goode (2005, p. 77).

81. Goode (2005, p. 74).

82. Zang (2004).

83. Seiter, R. (2005). *Corrections: An introduction.* Upper Saddle River, NJ: Prentice Hall.

84. McBride, D., & McCoy, C. (1993). The drugs-crime relationship: An analytical framework. *The Prison Journal, 73,* 257–278.

85. Menard, S., Mihalic, S., & Huizinga, D. (2001). Drugs and crime revisited. *Justice Quarterly, 18,* 269–299.

86. Fishbein, D. (2003). Neuropsychological and emotional regulatory processes in antisocial behavior. In A. Walsh & L. Ellis (Eds.), *Biosocial criminology: Challenging environmentalism's supremacy* (pp. 185–208). Hauppauge, NY: Nova Science.

87. McDermott, P. A., Alterman, A. I., Cacciola, J. S., Rutherford, M. J., Newman, J. P., & Mulholland, E. M. (2000). Generality of Psychopathy Checklist—Revised factors over prisoners and substance-dependent patients. *Journal of Consulting and Clinical Psychology, 68*(1), 181–186.

88. Menard et al. (2001, p. 295).

89. Walsh (2006, p. 313).

90. Walsh (2006).

91. Leshner (1998).

92. Simpson, D., Joe, G., Fletcher, B., Hubbard, R., & Anglin, D. (1999). A national evaluation of treatment outcomes for cocaine dependence. *Archives of General Psychiatry, 56,* 505–514.

93. Kleber (2003).

94. Farabee, D., Pendergast, M., and Anglin, M. (1998). The effectiveness of coerced treatment for drug-abusing offenders. *Federal Probation, 109,* 3–10.

95. Barton, A. (1999). Breaking the crime/drugs cycle: The birth of a new approach? *The Howard Journal, 38,* 144–157.

96. Hooper, R., Lockwood, D., & Inciardi, J. (1993). Treatment techniques in corrections-based therapeutic communities. *The Prison Journal, 73,* 290–306.

97. Brookman, F. (2005). *Understanding homicide.* Thousand Oaks, CA: Sage. (Quote on p. 87)

98. Ditton, P. (1999). *Mental health and treatment of inmates and probationers.* Washington, DC: Bureau of Justice Statistics.

99. Palermo, G., Gumz, E., & Liska, F. (1992). Mental illness and criminal behavior revisited. *International Journal of Offender Therapy and Comparative Criminology, 36,* 53–61.

100. Escamilla, M., & Walss-Bass, C. (2004). Genetic mapping studies of schizophrenia and bipolar disorder. *Salud Mental, 27,* 1–7. (Quote on p. 2)

101. Mueser, S., & McGurk, S. (2004). Schizophrenia. *The Lancet, 363,* 2063–2073.

102. Lamb, H., Weinberger, L., & Gross, B. (2004). Mentally ill persons in the criminal justice system. *Psychiatric Quarterly, 75,* 107–126.

103. Robinson (2005).

104. Lurigio, A. (2001). Effective services for parolees with mental illness. *Crime and Delinquency, 47,* 446–461.

105. Javitt, D., & Coyle, J. (2004). Decoding schizophrenia. *Scientific American, 290,* 48–56.

106. Walker, E., Kestler, L., Bollini, A., & Hochman, K. (2004). Schizophrenia: Etiology and course. *Annual Review of Psychology, 55,* 401–430.

107. Peterson, C. (1997). *Psychology: A biopsychosocial approach.* New York: Longman.

108. Pinel (2000).

109. Kessler, R., McGonagle, K., Zhao, S., Nelson, C., Hughes, M., Eshleman, S., et al. (1994). Lifetime and 12-month prevalence of DSM-III-R psychiatric disorders in the United States: Results from the national comorbidity survey. *American Journal of Psychiatry, 51,* 8–19.

110. Szasz, T. (1961). *The myth of mental illness.* New York: Harper & Row.

111. Walker et al. (2004).

112. Mueser and McGurk (2004).

113. Walker et al. (2004).

114. Durand, V., & Barlow, D. (2000). *Abnormal psychology: An introduction.* Scarborough, Ontario: Wadsworth.

115. Pinel (2000).

116. Wood, S., & Wood, E. (1996). *The world of psychology.* Boston: Allyn & Bacon.

117. Buckley, P. (2004, October). Pharmacological options for treating schizophrenia with violent behavior. *Psychiatric Times,* Supplement, 1–8.

118. Buckley, P., Buchanan, R., Schulz, S., & Tamminga, C. (1996). Catching up on schizophrenia: The Fifth International Congress on Schizophrenia Research, Warm Springs, Virginia, April 8-12, 1995. *Archives of General Psychiatry, 53,* 456–462. (Quote on p. 458)

119. Buckley (2004).

120. Mueser and McGurk (2004).

121. Wood and Wood (1996).

122. Thaker, G., Adami, H., & Gold, J. (2001). Functional deterioration in individuals with schizophrenia spectrum personality symptoms. *Journal of Personality Disorders, 15,* 229–234.

123. Bartol (2002).

124. Marzuk, P. (1996). Violence, crime, and mental illness: How strong a link? *Archives of General Psychiatry, 53,* 481–486.

125. Feldman, T. (2001). Bipolar disorder and violence. *Psychiatric Quarterly, 72,* 119–129.

126. Ellis, L., & Walsh, A. (2000). *Criminology: A global perspective.* Boston: Allyn & Bacon.

127. Link, B., Andrews, H., & Cullen, F. (1992). The violent and illegal behavior of mental patients reconsidered. *American Sociological Review, 57,* 275–292.

128. Swanson, J. (1994). Mental disorder, substance abuse, and community violence. In J. Monahan & H. Steadman (Eds.), *Violence and mental disorders: Developments in risk assessment* (pp. 101–136). Chicago: University of Chicago Press.

129. Hodkins, S., Mednick, S., Brennan, P., Schulsinger, F., & Engberg, M. (1996). Mental disorder and crime: Evidence from a Danish birth cohort. *Archives of General Psychiatry, 53,* 489–496.

130. Tuninger, E., Levander, S., Bernce, R., & Johansson, G. (2001). Criminality and aggression among psychotic in-patients: Frequency and clinical correlates. *Acta Psychiatrica Scandinavica, 103,* 294–300.

131. Buckley (2004).

132. Beck, J., & Wencel, H. (1998). Violent crime and axis I pathology. *Annual Review of Psychiatry, 17,* 1–27.

133. Stueve, A., & Link, B. (1997). Violence and psychiatric disorders: Results from an epidemiological study of young adults in Israel. *Psychiatric Quarterly, 68,* 327–342.

134. Hioeh, U., Appleby, L., Mortensen, P., & Dunn, G. (2001). Death by homicide, suicide, and other unnatural causes in people with mental illness: A population-based study. *The Lancet, 358,* 2110–2112.

135. Buckley (2004).

136. Hartwell, S. (2004). Triple stigma: Persons with mental illness and substance abuse problems in the criminal justice system. *Criminal Justice Policy Review, 15,* 84–99.

137. Bartol (2002).

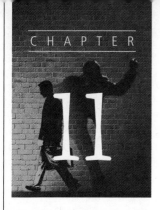

CRIMES OF VIOLENCE

O
n April 20, 1999, the 110th anniversary of Adolf Hitler's birthday, Columbine High School, located in the small White middle-class town of Littleton, Colorado, became the site of one of the worst cases of teen terrorism in U.S. history. Eric Harris, 18, and Dylan Klebold, 17, entered the school at 11:35 that morning and began their murderous rampage through the halls and corridors that lasted for 55 minutes. During this period, they shot 13 people dead and seriously wounded 25 others. Harris and Klebold hated the world, but they singled out athletes and people they knew to be religious as special targets. After running out of targets, they either both committed suicide or Harris killed Klebold and then himself as the police closed in.

Both boys came from intact middle-class homes, so what made them worshipers of Hitler, guns, and violence? Some accounts of their lives paint them as nerds picked on by jocks, others that they were bullies themselves with a history of threatening violence and of trouble with the police. It is plain that their parents exercised very little control over them. Diaries and computer Web sites revealed that they had planned the attack to celebrate Hitler's birthday a full year before it occurred. In the meantime, they amassed an arsenal of weapons, including handguns, shotguns, a 9-mm carbine, and a number of homemade bombs that they had learned to make on the Internet. They were clearly deeply disturbed young men with a dark fascination with violence.

We will learn in this chapter that the potential for violence is in us all, waiting to be ignited by environmental sparks. The vast majority of us will never come into close contact with such sparks, even though they are all around us. We have to ask ourselves what kind of a society we are that glorifies violence in its entertainment, that allows young boys to gain access to deadly weapons and to instructions on how to build bombs, and that does not provide its young with meaningful moral lessons and activities to fill their time. These are among the environmental sparks that should be kept well clear of combustible material like Harris and Klebold.

Just as every generation in its youth seems to think it discovered sex, every generation in its maturity seems to feel that it is in the midst of an unprecedented wave of violent crime. If we had lived in 16th-century Rome, we really would have had something to complain about, as this short description will attest: "Crimes of violence were innumerable. Assassins could be bought almost as cheaply as indulgences. The palaces of Roman nobles swarmed with thugs ready to kill at a nod. Everyone had a dagger, and brewers of poison found many customers; at last the people of Rome could hardly believe in the natural death of any man of prominence or wealth."[1] London in the 14th century had a murder rate of 44 per 100,000,[2] which is larger than any American city's rate in 2004, with the exception of New Orleans. In the city of Nuremberg, Germany, the homicide rate fluctuated between 20 and 65 per 100,000 from 1292 to 1392, which compares very poorly with the rate of 4.7 for the same city in 1984.[3] The homicide rate in medieval Europe doubtless had a lot to do with the combination of the habit of bearing arms, alcohol-induced quarrels, the absence of effective medical treatment for wounds that would be considered minor today, the absence of effective police power, and the absence of a trusted system of neutral justice.

Researchers in different disciplines ask different questions about violence. Sociologists might ask what it is about the social structure of a society or the norms of a subculture within it that leads to high rates of violence. Psychologists might ask what personality features, situations, or developmental experiences increase the risk of violence. Behavioral geneticists inquire about the mix of genetic and environmental factors associated with violence in a particular population at a particular time. Neuroscientists will focus questions about the brain structures and neurotransmitters associated with violence. And finally, evolutionary psychologists will want to know why humans have a propensity for violence in the first place and what adaptive purposes did/does it serve. Table 11.1 presents 2004 violent crime rates for all 50 states, with total violent crimes ranked from highest to lowest (District of Columbia not included in ranking); where does your state rank?

⊠ Murder

The Federal Bureau of Investigation (FBI) defines **murder** as "the willful (non-negligent) killing of one human being by another."[4] There were 16,137 murders in the United States in 2004, a rate of 5.5 per 100,000, which is a decrease of 3.3% over the 2003 figure[5] and almost half of the all-time high rate of 10.2 in 1980. Louisiana had the highest rate of any state (12.7), and three states—Maine, New Hampshire, and North Dakota—shared the honor of having the lowest homicide rate (1.4). For cities with populations greater than 100,000, New Orleans (56) had the highest rate, followed by Detroit (42.1) and Washington, D.C. (35.8). Gary, Indiana, which had the highest rate (67) in 2003, did not report 2004 statistics. A number of cities with populations over 100,000 had zero murders in 2004; the biggest city with a population over 100,000 and zero murders was Boise, Idaho. For an international comparison in 2004, try Medellin, Colombia, with a homicide rate of around 71 per 100,000.[6]

For known offenders, 90.1% were males, 50% were Black, 47.6% were White, and 2.4% were of other races (*Hispanic* is not a race; about 93% of Hispanics are classified as White, and thus the *White* category includes both Anglos and Hispanics). For single-victim/single-offender incidents, 92.2% of Black victims were slain by Black offenders, and White offenders killed 84.8% of White victims. Male victims were killed by other males 89.8% of the time, and

Table 11.1   Violent Crime Rates and State Rank in 2004

State	Rank	Total Violent Crime	Murder	Rape	Robbery	Aggravated Assault
Alabama	(22)	426.6	5.6	38.5	133.4	249.1
Alaska	(7)	634.5	5.6	85.1	68.2	475.6
Arizona	(13)	504.1	7.2	33.0	134.4	329.4
Arkansas	(15)	499.1	6.4	42.4	86.2	364.1
California	(9)	551.8	6.7	26.8	172.1	346.3
Colorado	(25)	373.5	4.4	42.5	81.5	245.1
Connecticut	(34)	286.3	2.6	20.7	120.5	142.6
Delaware	(12)	568.4	2.0	41.5	146.7	378.1
District of Columbia		1,371.2	35.8	40.1	578.5	716.9
Florida	(2)	711.3	5.4	38.0	172.4	495.5
Georgia	(19)	455.5	6.9	27.0	154.7	266.8
Hawaii	(39)	254.4	2.6	26.4	74.8	150.7
Idaho	(42)	244.9	2.2	40.9	17.2	184.6
Illinois	(10)	542.9	6.1	33.2	177.2	326.4
Indiana	(29)	325.4	5.1	28.9	102.2	189.2
Iowa	(37)	270.9	1.6	26.7	38.0	204.5
Kansas	(24)	374.5	4.5	40.4	66.3	263.4
Kentucky	(41)	244.9	5.7	29.9	78.8	130.5
Louisiana	(6)	638.7	12.7	35.8	145.4	444.9
Maine	(49)	103.5	1.4	23.9	21.9	56.3
Maryland	(3)	700.5	9.4	23.7	229.6	437.8
Massachusetts	(18)	458.8	2.6	28.0	116.4	311.7
Michigan	(17)	490.2	6.4	54.2	111.9	317.7
Minnesota	(38)	269.6	2.2	41.6	79.8	146.0
Mississippi	(32)	295.1	7.8	40.0	86.2	161.1
Missouri	(16)	490.5	6.2	25.7	115.2	343.4
Montana	(33)	293.8	3.2	29.5	25.1	236.0
Nebraska	(30)	308.7	2.3	35.5	65.1	205.8
Nevada	(8)	615.9	7.4	40.9	210.1	357.6
New Hampshire	(47)	167.0	1.4	35.3	38.5	91.8
New Jersey	(26)	355.7	4.5	15.3	150.3	185.6
New Mexico	(5)	687.3	8.9	54.6	108.3	515.5
New York	(21)	441.6	4.6	18.8	174.3	244.0
North Carolina	(20)	447.8	6.2	27.4	137.9	276.2
North Dakota	(50)	79.4	1.4	25.1	6.1	46.8

(Continued)

Table 11.1	(Continued)					
State	Rank	Total Violent Crime	Murder	Rape	Robbery	Aggravated Assault
Ohio	(28)	341.8	4.5	40.5	153.1	143.6
Oklahoma	(14)	500.5	5.3	44.2	87.7	363.3
Oregon	(31)	298.3	2.5	35.7	76.5	183.6
Pennsylvania	(23)	411.1	5.2	28.5	148.9	288.4
Rhode Island	(40)	247.4	2.4	29.6	67.6	147.7
South Carolina	(1)	784.2	6.9	40.9	129.7	606.7
South Dakota	(46)	171.5	2.3	43.8	14.8	110.5
Tennessee	(4)	695.2	5.9	37.6	149.8	501.8
Texas	(11)	540.5	6.1	37.3	159.3	339.9
Utah	(43)	236.0	1.9	39.1	51.7	143.3
Vermont	(48)	112.0	2.6	24.4	12.2	72.7
Virginia	(35)	275.6	5.2	23.7	92.6	154.1
Washington	(27)	343.8	3.1	46.1	94.6	200.2
West Virginia	(36)	271.2	3.7	17.6	42.3	207.6
Wisconsin	(45)	209.6	2.8	20.6	73.8	112.4
Wyoming	(44)	229.6	2.2	22.1	13.2	192.1

SOURCE: Federal Bureau of Investigation (2005). *Crime in the United States, 2004: Uniform Crime Reports.* Washington, DC: Government Printing Office.

NOTE: We did not include District of Columbia for ranking purposes.

female victims were killed by males 90.4% of the time. Firearms (mostly handguns) were used in 70.3% of homicides and cutting instruments in 13.4%, with the remainder being divided among blunt objects, personal weapons (hands or feet), poison, arson, and narcotics. These figures were based on the Supplementary Homicide Reports data containing 14,121 cases rather than the total 16,137 murders.

Of the total number of murders in 2004, 62.6% were cleared. Despite increases in law enforcement's use of high-powered technology, the clearance rate seemingly decreases yearly. In 1968, for instance, long before computerized databases, DNA testing, and all the other marvels of modern forensic science, the murder clearance rate in the United States was 86%.[7]

Homicide Trends in the United States in the 20th Century

Figure 11.1 shows a graph of homicide rates in the United States in the 20th century. The graph looks like a rugged mountain range with steep peaks and valleys that represent wide fluctuations in sociocultural factors that move the homicide rate up or down. The 1900 rate of 1.0 per 100,000 is highly suspect given the descriptions of life in such cities as New York and Boston at the turn of the century, as well as the still semi-civilized condition of much of the

---

Figure 11.1 | Homicide Rates in the United States in the 20th Century

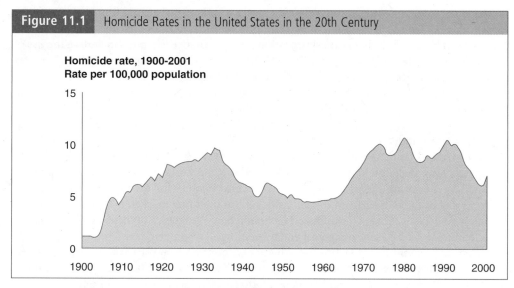

Homicide rate, 1900-2001
Rate per 100,000 population

SOURCE: National Center for Health Statistics. (2002). *Vital statistics.* Washington, DC: U.S. Department of Health and Human Services.

NOTE: The 2001 rate includes deaths attributed to the 9/11 terrorism attacks.

western United States. We should never take national statistics at face value unless we are very sure of their quality, and national reporting of crime statistics was in an abysmal state in the early part of the 20th century.

The homicide statistics of individual cities are more reliable. The boisterous western mining towns in the middle of the 19th century had huge homicide rates. Nevada County, California, had a rate of 83 per 100,000 from 1851 to 1856; Aurora, Nevada, had a rate of 64 from 1861 to 1865; and Bodie, California, had one of 116 from 1878 to 1882.[8] We can attribute these huge rates to the same sort of social conditions we attributed the huge European rates of earlier centuries—that is, the lack of effective law enforcement, drunken quarrels, and the absence of effective medical treatment. To this, we can add a new and more powerful weapon—the gun—to the equation, as well as the virtual absence of the civilizing influence of women in these mining towns; about 95% of the populations of these mining towns were men, and mostly young men at that.[9]

With the advent of the *Uniform Crime Reports* (*UCR*) in 1930, national data became somewhat more reliable. The homicide rate started a steep climb after the Volstead Act, prohibiting the production and sale of alcohol, was passed in 1920 as gangs fought over the lucrative illegal alcohol market. The rate started to fall with the repeal of the Volstead Act in 1933 and during the Great Depression. It dropped even further during World War II, when most young men were in uniform and overseas; showed a sharp rise when they returned; and then settled into a relatively peaceful period during the 1950s to early 1960s.

How do you think Emile Durkheim would explain the steep rise in the rate beginning in the late 1960s? Perhaps he would point out that the late 1960s to early 1970s was a period of tumultuous changes in American society. Opposition to the Vietnam War, combined with the civil rights and feminist movements, led to the widespread questioning of many of the fundamental values of American society. When values and norms are questioned, they become weaker in their ability to regulate behavior, and we have Durkheim's anomie. Behavioral deregulation led to all kinds of experimentation with alternative lifestyles, including the use of drugs. The emergence of crack cocaine in the early 1980s led to a period of gang wars over territory, just like the gang wars over alcohol did in the 1920s. Crack cocaine is easier to make, conceal, and sell than barrels of beer or bottles of whiskey, so crack dealing is more of an "equal-opportunity" enterprise than supplying illegal alcohol was. Numerous young "gang-bangers" took advantage of the opportunity for easy money, sparking a decade-long street war with other like-minded individuals.

This decrease in the homicide rate in the early 1990s can be attributed to several factors, including a large decrease in the crack market and in gang warfare as territories became consolidated by the strong pushing out the weak. Severe penalties for the sale and possession of crack, as well as the danger from others trafficking in the same market, may have also driven out many dealers. According to Anthony Harris and his colleagues,[10] perhaps the biggest factor in the homicide drop has been medical and technological improvements. They claim that U.S. homicide rates would be up to five times higher without those improvements, which means that we may have experienced 80,685 murders in 2004 rather than the 16,135 that we did if medicine and technology were at the same level that they were in 1960. Cell phones for reporting incidents are everywhere, and emergency medical technicians are alerted and dispatched swiftly. Once hospitalized, victims have the benefit of all that medicine learned from treating violent traumas since the Vietnam War. Many other factors known and unknown have contributed to the fluctuations in the homicide rate that we have observed over the course of the 20th century.

International Comparisons

We often hear statements to the effect that the United States is a terribly violent place or even *the* most violent place in the world, but how true is this? Any sort of criminal violence is unacceptable, but relative to most other countries in the world, the United States is a fairly safe place to live. Table 11.2 presents World Health Organization (WHO) homicide data among "youths" 10 to 29 years of age in the 10 most violent countries and the 10 safest countries in the world, with the United States added for comparison purposes. There are a number of other countries both above and below the United States in terms of their "youth" homicide rates; we simply chose to present the 10 highest and 10 lowest.

Of special interest is that, except for the United States, all countries (including those not shown in Table 11.2) with homicide rates above 10 per 100,000 were either Third World or developing counties or countries experiencing rapid social and economic changes (e.g., Russia). All low-homicide countries are high income and politically stable, and except for Japan, which stands out as the safest country in the world, they are Western European countries.

It is also interesting that the male/female ratio is highest in countries with high overall homicide rates (e.g., Colombia's ratio of 13.1:1) and lowest in countries with low overall homicide rates (e.g., Spain's ratio of 1.6:1). The Hungarian ratio of 0.9:1 is totally anomalous (higher rate for females than for males, but the WHO provides no explanation for it). It is also noteworthy that the variation in the female homicide rate across all countries is considerably less than it is among males, and females in high-rate murder cultures have higher homicide rates than males in low-rate homicide cultures.

| Table 11.2 | Homicide Rates Among Youths Ages 10 to 29 in the 10 Most Violent and 10 Safest Countries With the United States Added for Comparison | | | |

| Country | Total | Homicide Rate Per 100,000 Population | | |
		Male	Female	Male/Female Ratio
Colombia	84.4	156.3	11.9	13.1
South Africa	51.0	—	—	—
El Salvador	50.2	94.8	6.5	14.6
Brazil	32.5	59.6	5.2	11.5
Jamaica	32.0	—	—	—
Albania	28.2	53.5	5.5	9.8
Venezuela	25.0	46.4	2.8	16.5
Russia	18.0	27.5	8.0	3.4
Ecuador	15.9	29.2	2.3	12.4
Mexico	15.3	27.8	2.8	9.8
United States	**11.0**	**17.9**	**3.7**	**4.8**
Netherlands	1.5	1.8	1.2	1.6
Hungary	1.4	1.4	1.5	0.9
Belgium	1.4	1.8	—	—
Portugal	1.3	1.3	—	—
Czech Republic	1.2	1.2	1.4	—
United Kingdom	0.9	1.4	0.4	3.9
Germany	0.8	1.0	0.6	1.6
Spain	0.8	1.2	0.4	2.9
France	0.6	0.7	0.4	1.9
Japan	0.4	0.5	0.3	1.7

SOURCE: Krug, E., Dahlberg, L., Mercy, J., Zwi, A., & Lozano, R. (2002). *World report on violence and health.* Geneva, Switzerland: World Health Organization.

Categories of Murder

Not all murders are considered equally serious, although the victims are equally dead. In traditional common law, murder in the first degree, or *aggravated murder,* required that the act be committed with malice and aforethought, deliberation, and premeditation. *Malice* is essentially synonymous with *mens rea* or "evil mind," and *aforethought* is synonymous with planning, as in deliberation and premeditation. This being the case, we hear first-degree murder being defined today as the intentional unlawful killing of one human being by another with "premeditation and deliberation." In other words, the killer had a purposeful and evil intention (malice) to kill the victim and had thought about and planned it (premeditation) with full awareness of the consequences (deliberation).

First-degree murder is the only kind of murder for which a convicted murderer can be executed in states that have the death penalty, although a special type of murder, called felony murder, may also carry that penalty, especially when an agent of the criminal justice system is the victim. *Felony murder* does not require the intention to kill but rather the intention to commit some other felony, such as robbery, rape, burglary, or arson, during the commission of which a victim was killed. If, for instance, a burglar rapes a women, kills her, and then sets fire to her home to cover up the crime, he could be charged with two counts of aggravated murder (murder in the commission of a rape and murder in the commission of arson), even though there is only one victim and even though he entered the victim's home only with the intention of burglarizing it. Of the murders committed in 2004 for which a motive is known, 14.8% were felony murders.[11]

Voluntary manslaughter (called second-degree murder in some states) is the intentional killing of another human being without premeditation and deliberation. It is murder committed in response to the mistaken belief that self-defense required the use of deadly force or in response to adequate provocation while in the heat of passion. The term *passion* can mean fear, anger, or outrage and can result from such provocations as being threatened in a bar or catching your spouse in bed with someone else. In other words, voluntary manslaughter is usually charged when the suspect had temporarily been in such a high state of emotional arousal that his or her rational faculties were impeded.

Involuntary manslaughter is a criminal homicide where an unintentional killing results from a reckless act. In such cases, the defendant is charged with consciously disregarding a substantial risk that he or she should know puts others in danger of losing their lives. The most obvious example of this is driving under the influence of alcohol or some other drug. **Negligent manslaughter** is an unintentional homicide that is charged when a death or deaths arise from some negligent act that carries a substantial risk of death to others. Note that involuntary manslaughter is charged when defendants do something they should not have (drive drunk), and negligent homicide is charged when they neglect to do something they should have. Doing something they should not have can range widely from driving an unsafe vehicle that should have been fixed to failing to comply with safety regulations in a work setting.

Stranger, Acquaintance, Family Member: Who Kills Whom?

Just as we are not all equally likely to murder, we are not equally likely to be murdered. Looking at Figure 11.2, which gives homicide victimization rates from 1976 to 2002, we see that young people ages 18 through 24, male or female, Black or White, are the most likely to be killed. By race, we see that young Black males are about nine times more likely to be murdered than young White males and that young Black females are about six times more likely to be murdered than young White females. The same pattern is also observed for perpetrators; that is, the "typical" homicide victim and perpetrator is a young (18 to 24 years old) Black male living in a large urban center.

We previously noted that females killed males and other females in only about 10% of the cases in the United States in 2004. When females kill males, it is typically a spouse, ex-spouse, or boyfriend in a self-defense situation.[12] The low rate of female/female murder is found around the world, although the American rate of female/female homicide is high compared with that found in other countries. Daly and Wilson[13] examined data on same-sex nonrelative murders from 3 U.S. cities, 4 countries, and 13 ethnic cultures in various nations around the world and found that females killing females constituted only 2.5% of the total number of murders for which the sex of both the victim and the perpetrator was known. Even going back to England in the 13th century, Given[14] found that female/female murder accounted for only 4.9% of the total murders.

In 2004, 42.9% of homicide perpetrators knew their victims, 12.9% were committed by strangers, and in the remaining 44.1%, the relationship between victim and offender was

| Figure 11.2 | Homicide Victimization for Years 1976-2002 by Age, Gender, and Race |

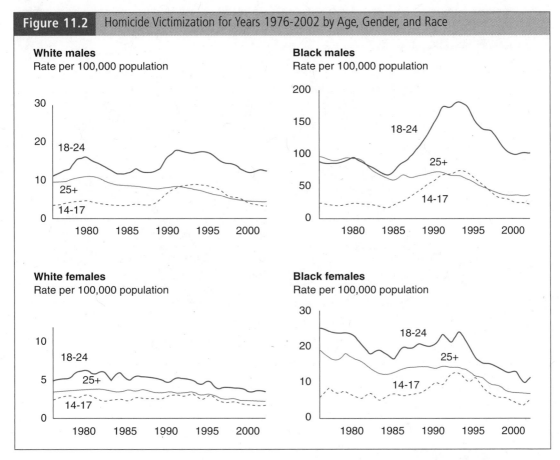

Source: Homicide trends in the U.S. Bureau of Justice Statistics. (2004). *Homicide trends in the U.S.* Retrieved from http://www.ojp.gov/bjs/homicide/tables/varstab.htm

unknown. In the known category, 12.5% of the homicides were within the family. These intrafamily homicides have provided some interesting data for evolutionary theorists because who kills whom within the family conforms to evolutionary logic. The typical explanation for intrafamily homicide is that family members are in danger of being assaulted by other family members simply because they are frequently in "striking distance" of one another. However, if homicide probability simply followed the striking distance rule, genetically and nongenetically related family members would be equally at risk, but they are not. Nongenetically related family members such as spouses, stepchildren, and stepparents are at hugely elevated risk for victimization relative to genetically related family members.[15] The 2004 *UCR* data show that wives were the most likely to be killed (32%) in the family, with husbands constituting only 8.2% of victims. One large-scale study found that a child living with a nonbiological male caregiver (typically a stepfather or live-in boyfriend) is approximately 65 times more likely to be fatally abused than is a child living with both biological parents.[16] Although stepparenting elevates the risk of fatal abuse, the vast majority of stepparents do not kill or abuse their stepchildren.

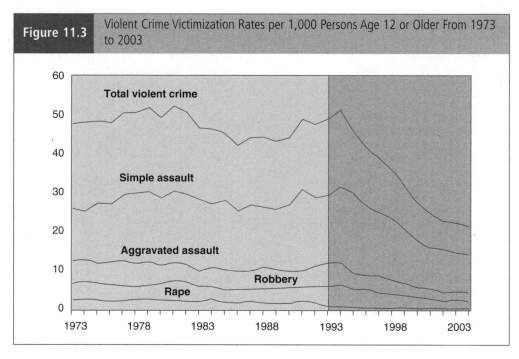

Figure 11.3 | Violent Crime Victimization Rates per 1,000 Persons Age 12 or Older From 1973 to 2003

NOTE: Data collected before the National Crime Victimization Surveys (NCVS) redesign was implemented during 1992 (the lightly shaded area) have been made comparable to the postdesign NCVS. Data were reestimated to account for the effects of the redesign. Rape does not include sexual assault for this trend analysis.

Other Violent Crimes

Although murder is the most serious of the violent crimes, it is the rarest. Figure 11.3 presents victimization trends for all violent crimes except murder from 1973 to 2003 from the National Crime Victimization Surveys (NCVS).[17] Note that all violent crimes have decreased substantially.

☒ Rape and Rapists

Forcible rape is "the carnal knowledge of a female forcibly and against her will."[18] This definition includes attempts to commit rape but excludes statutory rape (consensual sex with an underage female) and the rape of males. Rapes of males are classified as either assaults or other sex offenses, depending on the circumstances of the crime and the extent of physical injury. The National Incident-Based Reporting System (NIBRS) and NCVS definitions of rape include male victims. A sexual assault may also be defined as rape in some jurisdictions if nonvaginal (oral or anal) penetration was accomplished or if vaginal penetration was made with an inanimate object. According to the 2005 *UCR*, there were 94,635 reported rapes in 2004, which is a rate of 63.5 per 100,000 females. The clearance rate for forcible rape in 2004 was 41.8. By race, 65.3% of those arrested for rape were White, 32.2% were Black, and the remaining 2.5% were other races.

The 2004 NCVS survey[19] reported 209,880 cases of rape, 6,200 (2.95%) of which were against males. The survey reports that just over two rapes were committed for every one reported to the police that year. However, see the discussion in Chapter 2 regarding problems with comparing the *UCR* and NCVS data on rape.

By race, it was found that people reporting two or more races had the highest rate (2.4 per 1000), follows by Blacks (1.7), Whites (0.8), and finally Hispanics (0.6). Most rapes are *intra*racial, but a study of rape based on victimization surveys in 26 U.S. cities found that African Americans chose White victims 41.3% of the time[20] and that the number of White offender/Black victim rapes was too small (approximately 1%) to be included in the analysis, which is typically the case in other studies of interracial rape.[21,22]

The 16 to 19 and 20 to 24 age groups were most likely to be victimized (a rate of 2.5) and the 65 and older age group the least (0.1). Women with household incomes less than $7,500 per year were most likely to be victimized (2.4) and women in the highest income categories the least likely (a rate of 0.6). Women who were divorced or separated were most likely to be victimized (2.0) and married women least (0.2).

Some Facts About Rape

Some major findings from 20 years of NCVS surveys on rape include the following:

- About half of all rapes are committed by someone known to the victim.
- The offender was armed in about 20% of the cases. Stranger rapists were more likely to be armed (29%) than were rapists known to the victim.
- Among the victims who fought their attackers or yelled and screamed, more reported that it helped the situation rather than made it worse.
- Slightly more than half of the victims report the assault to the police. Victims are more likely to report the incident if the perpetrator was armed or if they sustained physical injuries (in Ellis and Walsh[23]).

Rape Internationally

Rape rates vary considerably from country to country; the *reported* rape rate in the United States is typically 4 times higher than that of Germany, 13 times higher than Britain's, and 20 times higher than Japan's.[24] We emphasize *reported* because determining "true" rape rates is extremely difficult, and comparing international rape rates is more difficult yet. Some countries include statutory rape in their rape reports (which would inflate the number of rapes in those countries relative to those in the United States), others do not, and some do not differentiate between rape and other sexual offenses (which would also inflate their rates). We also have to be sensitive to the degree of stigma attached to rape victims in different cultures. For instance, Egypt, a nation of about 54 million people, reported just three rapes to Interpol in 1991, while France, with approximately the same population, reported 4,582.[25] Accusing someone of rape in some Islamic countries is not taken lightly. Proof requires the sworn eye-witness testimony of two males of good Muslim character (or four Muslim women). As if the stigma of being raped that attaches to women in Islamic countries is not reason enough to forgo reporting the crime, if eyewitness testimony is not forthcoming, the accuser may herself be punished with 100 lashes for making a "false accusation."[26]

FOCUS ON . . .

Characteristics of Rapists

A rapist may be any man, but studies have found that about 75% of convicted rapists are younger than age 30, about 80% are either unemployed or blue-collar workers, and only about 20% have a high school education or better. About 80% of males convicted of rape have previous convictions, a small number have prior rape convictions, and about one third have prior convictions for other violent crimes. Compared with other men, rapists are more likely to be hostile toward women, to hold traditional sex role attitudes, to be easily sexually aroused, to be more irresponsible, to lack social conscience and interpersonal social skills, and to have a history of substance abuse.[27–30]

Compared to date rapists, stranger rapists have significantly more serious criminal histories, are significantly younger and lower class, and are more likely to use a weapon, to be drug and/or alcohol addicted, and to cause physical harm to their victims.[31] In most instances of date rape, force is used only after a variety of nonviolent tactics (getting the victim drunk, verbal pressures, false pledges of love, threatening to terminate the relationship, and so on) have been tried.[32,33] One of the strangest yet consistently found findings related to date rape is that "a significant percentage [of rape victims] continue to date a date rapist after the rape" and that "a larger percentage of women continue to date the perpetrator of a *completed* rape than of an *attempted but uncompleted* rape."[34]

Several typologies of rapists have been developed, with Nicholas Groth's being the best known.[35] Groth views rape as an aggressive act symptomatic of psychological dysfunction, labeling his three categories of rape as *anger, power,* and *sadistic,* depending on what he views the rapist's primary motivation to be. This typology was formulated and the motivations inferred by noting the characteristics of the assault rather than the *known* motives of the assailant.

The *anger rapist* is thought to be mad at the world in general and at women in particular. He uses a great deal more force than is necessary to make his victim comply and then forces her into a variety of acts designed as much to degrade and humiliate his victim as to satisfy himself. Groth estimates that 40% of the rapists treated by his agency—the Connecticut Sex Offender Program (CSOP)—are anger rapists.

Power rapists are interested more in establishing complete dominance and control over their victims rather than humiliating and degrading them, although they will use considerable force if their victims fail to comply with their demands. Power rapists may kidnap and hold their victims captive so as to further assert their authority, mastery, and dominance. The power rapist is satisfied to the degree to which he can establish the complete submission of his victim. He is seen as having a poor self-image and as feeling a need to prove his masculinity. Groth indicates that the power rapist is the most common type (55%) treated at CSOP.

The *sadistic rapist* achieves sexual arousal by torturing and otherwise mistreating his victims. He is a combination of the anger and power rapist, except that his goal is to physically hurt and injure his victim rather than just humiliating her. Many sadistic rapists choose women who symbolize something they consider to be "bad," such as prostitutes, and use rape to punish them. The sadistic rapist is about one step away from becoming a serial killer and is the most dangerous of the three types of rapists. Groth estimates that only about 5% of convicted rapists are of this type.

◀ **Photo 11.1** Some males excuse their inappropriate behavior with women by adopting rape myths. For example, girls who dress provocatively or consume significant amounts of alcohol are sometimes considered to be "asking" to be victimized. Even the police and courts appear to be less sympathetic toward sex crime victims who do not take "all precautions" to avoid situations in which males might assume a female is not truly saying "No!"

Theories of Rape

The three main theories of rape are the *feminist, social learning,* and *evolutionary.* Each theory provides some of the puzzle of rape, and none should be uncritically embraced or summarily dismissed. As always, you should realize that there is no single feminist, social learning, or evolutionary theory and that our presentation represents what we believe to be the most accepted versions of these theories.

Feminist Theory of Rape

The fundamental assumption of the **feminist theory of rape** is that rape is motivated by power, not sexual desire. It is viewed as a crime of violence and degradation designed to intimidate and keep women "in their place."[36] According to most versions of feminist theory, to understand rape, we have to understand three things about gender relations:

1. There are large social, legal, and economic power differentials between the genders.
2. These power differentials affect all social interactions between men and women, as well as the actions of individual men and women.
3. Males enjoy the advantages of these power differentials and use any and all means to control women. Men use a variety of control tactics without necessarily being consciously aware of the "true" intent of these tactics.

Feminist theories maintain that males are indirectly socialized to rape via gender role messages asserting male authority and dominance over women. Rape is the major weapon males have used to establish and maintain both the general social patriarchy and the dominance of individual men over individual women. Feminists maintain that rape and the threat of rape forces a woman to seek male protection from the predations of other men, thus forcing her into permanent subjugation. As Susan Brownmiller puts it, rape "is nothing more or less than a conscious process of intimidation by which *all* men keep *all* women in a state of fear."[37] It is for this reason that many feminists view rape as a violent *political* act, not a sexual act.

Given this view of rape, many feminist theorists are of the opinion that rape is not an act committed by a few psychologically unhealthy men. Rather, as the master symbol of women's oppression, it is an act that practically all men may commit and is indicative of a general hatred of women that characterizes the behavior of "normal" adult men.

Social Learning Theory of Rape

The **social learning theory of rape** is similar to the feminist theory. According to both theories, rape is caused by differences in the way women and men are sexually socialized, which implies that if women were socialized like men, they would be equally likely to use sexually coercive tactics, and if men were socialized like women, they would be equally unlikely. The major difference between the two theories is that social learning theory places less emphasis on sexual politics and is generally agnostic about what the "ultimate" purpose of rape is (e.g., to "keep women in their place"). Social learning theorists are also unlikely to view rapists as "normal" men, as Groth's social learning typology discussed earlier indicates.

Social learning theorists agree with feminists that the negative images of women as the sexual playthings of men, promulgated in advertising and pornography, play a critical role in rape causation. Studies have shown that sex offenders are about three times more likely to own pornography than "normal" male controls.[38] The cumulative effect of pairing women with eroticized violence and impersonal sex is that people become immune to the suffering inherent in the content of these images. Men come to "objectify" women and to view them as "things" useful only insofar as they can be used to satisfy sexual needs. A major difference between the feminist and social learning theories is that feminist theory is a social structural theory that emphasizes structural factors that put *all* men at risk for committing rape, while social learning theory attempts to explain rape at the individual level by asking "what are the characteristics of *specific individuals* who have actually committed rape?"

Evolutionary Theory of Rape

Some **evolutionary theories of rape** hold the view that coercive sexuality is a "normal" male strategy designed by natural selection. Because of the negative moral implications of this position (if rape is normal, aren't we justifying it or excusing it?), we remind you again of the naturalistic fallacy of confusing *is* with *ought*. Many leading evolutionary theorists are feminists who condemn rape just as strongly as any social learning or feminist theorist and are among the first to denounce rape as a crime in need of severe punishment precisely *because* they view it as a potential behavior of all men requiring strong environmental deterrents.[39]

Evolutionary theorists point out that forced copulation is observed in many animal species and that the key to understanding rape is the wide disparity in parental investment between the sexes. Having no *necessary* parental investment other than insemination, males have evolved a propensity to seek copulations with multiple partners, while the enormous parental investment of females has resulted in their being more inclined to resist casual copulations than men. Thus, two conflicting reproductive strategies arise from different levels of parental investment for males and females: the careful and discriminating female strategy and the reckless and indiscriminate male strategy. Rape is sometimes the result of this discrepancy, that is, a maladaptive consequence of the general mating strategy of men.[40]

Evolutionists agree with feminists on at least two points: (1) All men are *potential* rapists, and (2) men who employ coercive tactics do so because of environmental factors. The factors stressed by evolutionary theorists are differences in male status and ability to obtain resources. Because older males monopolize females by virtue of their control over resources valued by females, forced copulation throughout much of the animal kingdom is a strategy employed primarily by young, resource-poor males.[41] Human females have been found cross-culturally to prefer to mate with males of high status or who at least have the potential of achieving high status.[42] Many young low-status males may be denied the opportunity to mate legitimately with the most attractive females, and thus evolutionary theory predicts that most rapists will be young males of low socioeconomic status, a prediction that is confirmed with data from around the world.[43]

Evaluation of the Theories

The main contribution of feminist theory is political and legal in that it has made us more aware of the horrible nature of rape, and it has challenged stereotypes associated with rape

▲ **Photo 11.2**   A male elephant seal attacks and sexually assaults a female as she attempts to flee to open ocean after a long stay on shore without eating. Such assaults are fairly common among young males who do not yet control harems (as many fully adult males do). Photograph provided by Sara Mesnick.

and rape victims. The major problematic area in both the feminist and social learning theories is the insistence that rape is a pseudo-sexual act (although Susan Brownmiller's seminal work[44] on the feminist theory said that rape *was* a sexual act in several places). Critics argue that while it is obvious that rape is a violent act, it is also obvious that it is a sexual act. Most clinicians engaged in the treatment of rapists insist that rape is primarily sexually motivated,[45] and very few laypersons (about 9% of males and 18% of females) believe that power and anger are the primary motives for rape.[46] Some feminist writers recognize the sexual, as well as the violent, nature of rape but insist that the "not-sex" argument was necessary initially to emphasize that women received no sexual pleasure from being raped.[47] Other theorists even consider the "not-sex" belief to be dangerous because it prevents us from learning more about the causes of rape at the expense of an increased number of victims.[48]

Because few social scientists are familiar with it and because of the human tendency to subscribe to the naturalistic fallacy, evolutionary theory draws the most severe criticism. Its emphasis on reproductive success has led to the criticism that it cannot explain instances of rape in which there is no possibility of reproduction, such as rapes involving males, children, and postmenopausal women, as well as rapes that do not include vaginal intercourse.[49] In response, evolutionists might reply that nonreproductive sex can be likened to the diffusion of human nurturance to animals, which has no fitness-promoting advantage at all for the nurturer. Both nonreproductive sex and animal nurturance provide us with pleasurable effects that are wholly irrelevant to the effects responsible for their evolutionary selection.[50]

Biosocial Theory of Rape

The **biosocial theory of rape** incorporates the most empirically supportable claims of feminist, social learning, and evolutionary theories and adds neurohormonal variables to the mix.[51] The theory contains four propositions:

1. *The sex drive and the drive to possess and control motivates rape.* All sexually producing organisms possess an unlearned sex drive, although the manner in which it is expressed is open to learning. The contention that rape is sexually motivated rests on many kinds of evidence. Perhaps the most compelling is that nonstranger rapists are likely to use force only when other tactics such as the use of alcohol, pleading, false claims of love, and so on have failed. The rapist's preliminary use of nonforceful tactics to gain sexual access makes it difficult to claim that rape is "nonsexual." In addition, the existence of forced copulation in other animal species makes it difficult to claim that similar behavior among humans is motivated by hatred of females, that rape occurs because males and females are differentially socialized, or that rapists are subconsciously protecting the privileged political and economic positions of males.

   Animals also possess a strong drive to possess and control, as evidenced by the catching, hoarding, burying, and protection of resources needed to survive and attract mates. The drive to possess and control is especially strong where sex partners are concerned. Among humans, there is plentiful evidence that men and women are extremely possessive of one another. We can be sure that ancient humans who were inclined to be nonchalant about who had access to their resources and mates are not among our ancestors. Jealousy and male sexual proprietariness are responsible for a huge percentage of domestic violence and spousal and lover homicides around the world.[52,53]

2. *The average sex drive of men is stronger than the average sex drive of women.* Among the many facts called upon to support this proposition are that males commit the vast majority of sexual crimes, consume the vast majority of pornography, constitute practically all the customers of both male and female prostitutes, masturbate more frequently, and have a much greater interest in casual sex with multiple partners.[54,55] Not only are these and many other indices of gender differences in strength of sex drive found across cultures but also among other species. Opposing the male tendency to readily learn forceful tactics to obtain sex is the evolved female tendency to resist them.

3. *Although the motivation for rape is unlearned, the specific behavior surrounding it is learned.* Rape is learned via operant conditioning, and individuals with the strongest sex drives will learn rape behavior more readily. Men who have successfully used "pushy" (but not necessarily forceful) tactics to gain sexual favors in the past have learned that those tactics may pay off. A male's initial payoff may be little more than a necking or petting session, but if he finds that each time he escalates his pushiness he succeeds in gaining greater sexual access, his behavior will be gradually shaped by reinforcement in ways that could lead to rape.

4. *Because of neurohormonal factors, people differ in the strength of their sex drives and in their sensitivity to threats of punishment.* The sex drive is primarily a function of testosterone, a hormone that is at least 10 times more prevalent in adult males than in adult females. Testosterone and other androgen hormones masculinize the male brain while in the womb, and different levels of these hormones lead to varying intensities of the sexual drive. Exposure to fetal androgens also results in lessened male sensitivity to environmental stimuli. Males in many species are less sensitive on average to noxious stimuli than females, leading them to be more likely to discount the consequences of antisocial behavior for themselves and for their victims. Unfortunately, individuals with the strongest sex drives are usually the same individuals who are the most insensitive to environmental stimuli because the same neurohormonal factors are responsible for both. These are the individuals who are most likely to rape and to be engaged in criminal activity in general.

▧ Robbery and Robbers

The *UCR* defines **robbery** as "the taking or attempted taking of anything of value from the care, custody, or control of a person or persons by force or threat of force or violence and/or putting the victim in fear."[56] The primary motive of robbers is to take property that does not belong to them, so why isn't robbery defined as a property crime rather than as a violent crime? The reason is that robbers confront their victims and take their property from their "care, custody, or control" by violent or threatened violent means. Robbery carries a more serious penalty than grand theft or burglary in every state in the union because the act of taking property from someone who has it in his or her custody entails a greater risk of violence. Note that a pickpocket takes personal assets from a person's care, custody, or control, but there is no force or threat of force because the person is not usually aware of the theft until later. The offense of pocket picking is classified as a larceny/theft.

In 2004, there were 401,326 reported robberies in the United States, a rate of 136.7 robberies per 100,000 inhabitants. This rate is down 4.1% from the 2003 rate and down almost

50% from the peak rate of 272.7 in 1991. Most robberies (52%) occurred on the street/highway, followed by commercial houses (taverns, hotels, motels, restaurants, etc.) (12.4%), private residences (12.57%), convenience stores (6.2%), gas or service stations (1.7%), and banks (1.5%). The remaining 17% occurred at miscellaneous locations. Firearms were used in 40.6% of all reported robberies, followed by strong-arm (hands, fists, feet) tactics (41.4%), knives and other cutting instruments (8.9%), and "other weapon" (9.4%). Victims were murdered in 988 of the robberies in 2004, which, excluding crimes specifically motivated by the desire to harm the victim, makes robbery by far the crime most likely to lead to murder.[57]

The FBI[58] estimates that $525 million was taken in robbery incidents in 2004, for an average of $1,308 per robbery. Bank robberies averaged $4,221 per robbery, commercial houses $1,529 per robbery, and residential homes $1,488. Street and highway robberies averaged $923 per robbery. The surprisingly high figure for street/highway is doubtless the result of some highly atypical "professional" robberies. Many street robberies ("muggings") are not reported to the police, especially if no injury and minimal loss is incurred, and most offenders who specialize in robbery tend to prey on other criminals, especially drug dealers, who, for obvious reasons, do not report their victimization to the police.[59]

The Robbers

Law enforcement cleared 26.2% of the reported robberies committed in 2004. Of those arrested, 60.1% were younger than 25 years of age, and 89.0% were male. By race, 53.6% of robbery arrestees were Black, 43.9% were White, and the remaining 1.5% were of other races.

Robbery is a high-risk crime because of the danger posed by resisting victims and in terms of the severe penalties attached to committing it, suggesting that criminals who commit it may be among the most daring and dangerous of all criminals. Interviews of active street robbers[60,61] show them to be the least educated, least conscientious, most fearless, most impulsive, and most hedonistic of criminals. Obtaining legitimate work is simply not an option that street robbers see as viable; they live for the moment, and the work and the discipline that it entails would put a severe crimp in their "every night is Saturday night" lifestyles.

These studies find that the robbers themselves view robbery as the quickest and safest way to gain quick cash. Burglary takes time and requires the burglar to find buyers for stolen property, and burglars never know who or what they might run into inside a house. Drug selling means dealing with a lot of people, the risk of being robbed oneself, and, most important, coping with the temptation of being one's own best customer. Robbery, on the other hand, allows the robber to pick the time, place, and victim at leisure and then complete the job in a matter of minutes and seconds. It is the perfect crime for those with a pressing and constant need for fast cash to feed a hedonistic lifestyle and who enjoy the rush that the crime affords them. Robbery, along with flaunting the material trappings signaling its successful pursuit, is seen ultimately as a campaign for respect and status in the street culture in which most robbery specialists participate.[62] As James Messerschmidt has put it, "The robbery setting provides the ideal opportunity to construct an 'essential' toughness and 'maleness'; it provides a means with which to construct that certain type of masculinity—hardman. Within the social context that ghetto and barrio males find themselves, then, robbery is a rational practice for 'doing gender' and for getting money."[63]

With the exception of rape, robbery is the most "male" of all crimes, but women constituted 11% of the robbery arrestees in 2004. Most female robbers share the same street culture with their male counterparts. A favorite ploy for female robbers is to appear sexually available (prostitution or otherwise) to a male victim and then, either alone or with the help of an accomplice, rob him. Female robbers will seldom rob males without an accomplice but will practice their "art" mostly on other females. Much like their male counterparts, female robbers are totally educationally or motivationally unprepared for legitimate work and prefer their hedonistic "money for nothing" lifestyles.[64]

Why are so few women involved in robbery compared with their involvement in other crimes of resource acquisition? The female percentage of arrests for larceny/theft in 2004, for instance, was 38.3%, or almost four times their proportion in arrests for robbery.[65] From an evolutionary perspective, Anne Campbell supports Messerschmidt's analysis explaining that while women need resources as much as men, the difference is that men seek status and dominance and the reputation as a "hardman," as well as the resources expropriated from their victims, and this "reflects a particularly masculine logic."[66]

▶ **Photo 11.3** Gang members brandish a handgun. Unlike back in the days of *Westside Story,* when gangs fought with knives and pipes, from the mid-1980s, urban youth gangs started to carry both handguns and automatic weapons. Partly, this was to protect the drug distribution networks these gangs became part of at that time.

◪ Aggravated Assault

The FBI defines **aggravated assault** as "an unlawful attack by one person upon another for the purpose of inflicting severe or aggravated bodily injury."[67] As opposed to simple assault, aggravated assault is an assault in which a weapon such as a knife or gun is used, although the use of personal weapons such as hands and feet can result in a charge of aggravated assault if they cause great bodily harm. Aggravated assault is the most common felony violent crime, accounting for 62.5% of all Part I violent crimes in 2004. Each incident of aggravated assault carries the potential threat of becoming a murder; thus, everything we have said about murder victims and offenders applies equally to aggravated assault. Indeed, without the speedy access to modern medicine we enjoy today, many aggravated assaults would have turned into murders.[68]

The FBI indicates that 854,911 aggravated assaults were reported to the police in the United States in 2004. This translates into a rate of 291.1 per 100,000, which is a 34% drop from the all-time high of 441.8 reported in 1992. This number grossly underestimates the actual number of aggravated assaults since many people decline to report them, particularly if the assault took place in a family context. The NCVS reported 1,030,080 aggravated assaults in 2004.[69] Personal weapons were used in 26.6% of the *UCR* cases, firearms in 19.3%, and knives or other cutting instruments in 18.6%, with the remaining 35.6% being other miscellaneous weapons such as clubs, tire irons, and so forth. Law enforcement cleared 55.6% of reported aggravated assaults in 2004. About 40% of those arrested for aggravated assault were younger than age 25, 79.3% were male, 64.5% were White, 33.1% were Black, and 2.3% were other races/ethnicities. We now explore possible reasons for why violent behavior is disproportionately found in certain areas.

Explaining Violence Sociologically: The Subculture of Violence Thesis

According to Cao, Adams, and Jensen, the subculture of violence thesis, formulated by criminologists Wolfgang and Feracutti in 1967, "remains *the* definitive argument for society's role in creating violent criminal behavior."[70] A **subculture of violence** is a subculture in which the norms, values, and attitudes of its members legitimize the use of violence to resolve conflicts. The thesis reminds us that violence is not evenly distributed among all groups and in all locations in society, and it is necessary to find out why it is more prevalent in some areas and among some groups than in others. Wolfgang and Feracutti reasoned that "by identifying the groups with the highest rates of homicide, we should find in the most intense degree a subculture of violence."[71] They found such a culture in Philadelphia's Black community in the mid-1950s, where the homicide rate for young males was 27 times higher than for young White males, and the female rate was 23 times greater than for White females.[72]

Figure 11.4 presents violent crime data for Asians, Whites, and Blacks. The Asian rate is set at 1.0, with the Black and White rates rendered as multiples of the Asian rate. In 2001, the Asian, White, and Black murder rates were 1.7, 2.83, and 18.18 per 100,000, respectively, rendering the White/non-Black Hispanic rate 1.66 times greater than the Asian rate and the Black rate 10.7 times greater than the Asian rate. The subculture of violence thesis attempts to explain these wide racial disparities.

Violent subcultures are supported by a set of conduct norms that favor the use of violence to settle differences over other methods: "In the most impoverished pockets of the inner city, interpersonal relations are now governed by informal rules that emphasize the threat and use of violence rather than civility."[73] Violence is especially likely to be used in situations that threaten a male's status or reputation on the street. Violent subcultures are not limited to the United States or to African Americans within it. As the data on homicide around the world clearly show, they exist in many countries where the people living in them do not trust the legal system to protect them.

Subcultural practices cannot be properly examined or understood without reference to the structural factors present in the larger society that led to their formation. Wolfgang and Ferracutti believed that such subcultures could have begun as a "negative reaction [to a mainstream culture] that turned into regularized, institutionalized patterns of prescription."[74] Our explanation is consistent with this and with Richard Wright's argument made long ago: "The Negro's conduct, his personality, his culture, his entire life flow naturally and inevitably out of the conditions imposed upon him by white America."[75]

A number of African American scholars have traced the subculture of violence to the odious institution of slavery.[76–79] Slavery can be likened to what has been called a *total institution*[80] to describe prisons. A total institution is one in which a large group of people live together under

Figure 11.4	2001 *UCR* Violent Crime Rates by Race

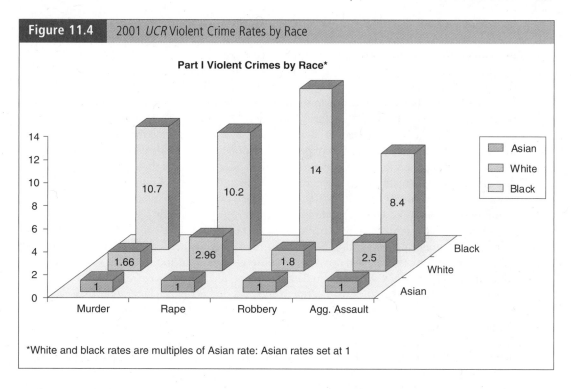

Part I Violent Crimes by Race*

*White and black rates are multiples of Asian rate: Asian rates set at 1

the restricted and coercive control of others and in which controllers and controlled are physically and psychologically isolated from one another by mutual distrust and hostility. To adjust to life in prison, inmates develop an *inmate code* that is contrary to the code of the prison staff to guide their behavior toward each other and toward their controllers. The inmate code includes prohibitions against cooperating with guards beyond the level necessary to avoid trouble, against showing subservience and friendliness toward staff unless you can use them for your own ends, and against ratting on other inmates (be a man and settle your own beefs). Compliance with the code is necessary to become a good convict and to be accepted by other inmates.[81]

Likewise, African Americans developed their subculture in response to slavery without much reference to what Whites (their "jailers") considered acceptable. Although slavery has long gone, the subculture born of it remains just as the inmate code remains a part of the psychology of the long-term convict long after release. Clarke[82] points out that slaves did everything in their power to deceive their masters, even considering it their "duty" to do so. Cultural norms developed among slaves that lauded thievery and deception and warned about treacherous Whites.

These lawless ways were reinforced by White indifference to Black-on-Black crime. Blacks who committed crimes against other Blacks were granted leniency and protection from prosecution, particularly if powerful Whites employed the perpetrators.[83] Valuable and submissive Blacks secured immunity from punishments for a variety of serious offenses, which led to many Blacks having "extraordinary liberty to do violent things to other Negroes."[84] This situation generated a tradition of settling differences without involving the authorities. A 1930s commentator wrote that because Blacks had no faith in the police to protect them, they resorted to "the ready use of firearms in trivial matters. . . . Negroes are often allowed without interference from the police, to commit crimes on one another, which, when committed against white people, result in severe [punishments]. Many Southern leaders, white and Negro feel strongly that the inadequate police protection provided within Negro communities virtually breeds crime."[85]

Being left to their own devices and building on a tradition of rule challenging, Blacks did not look to White standards to determine their worth. Like convicts, African Americans were expected by their cultural code to settle matters "like a man" and to take care of their own beefs (don't involve the power structure). "Taking care of business" often involves violence in a subculture where it is not viewed as illicit. It is part of the street code that "emerges where the influence of the police ends and where personal responsibility for one's safety is felt to begin."[86] The successful application of aggression—as a manifestation of subcultural values *and* as a disavowal of mainstream cultural values—is a source of pride.[87] Kenneth Stampp's classical work on slavery similarly concluded that in the Black community, "success, respectability, and morality were measured by *other* standards, and prestige was won in *other* ways."[88]

Other social scientists may attribute the extraordinary level of violence in the inner cities to a culture of poverty rather than a culture of violence per se. They may point out that while White poverty is dispersed across many different neighborhoods, Black poverty is highly concentrated in racially segregated single neighborhoods. This concentration has been called hyper-ghettoization.[89] In other words, the problem is one of social class rather than race.

However, the class/poverty argument implies that violent subcultures only exist among the poor and that the subculture of violence thesis is about race. It is categorically not about race per se; Wolfgang and Ferracutti[90] used Black neighborhoods in Philadelphia to illustrate their theory because that is where they found the best contemporary example of their thesis. Subcultures of violence have always existed and have also been referred to as honor subcultures. **Honor subcultures** are defined as "communities in which young men are hypersensitive to insult, rushing to defend their reputation in dominance contests."[91] Cultural norms that allowed duels over trivial matters of "honor" were common among the most polished and cultivated "gentlemen" of Europe and the American South until fairly recently in history. Such duels over "matters of honor" enhanced the duelists' reputations and provided them with public validation of their self-worth.[92] Only with the establishment of modern law was dueling as a way to settle disputes brought into disrepute. Far from acting in pathological ways, males in our modern honor subcultures are acting in historically and evolutionarily normative ways. This does not make such behavior morally acceptable, but it makes it understandable.

Hormones, Brains, and Violence

Testosterone Young males are swimming in testosterone, a substance consistently linked with aggressive behavior.[93] Testosterone energizes male competition for status in all animals and for the mating opportunities that accompany its attainment. No one claims that testosterone *causes* criminal or status-striving behaviors, only that it facilitates them. Testosterone is like fuel in your gas tank—it does not cause you to go to the big city on Saturday night, but it helps to make the trip possible once you have decided that is what you want to do.

Testosterone levels have an average heritability coefficient of 0.60,[94] which means that at least 40% of the variation is accounted for by environmental factors. African Americans may have higher average levels of testosterone than other races,[95] but it is unclear whether these differences reflect true base-level differences or feedback environmental effects. Testosterone levels fluctuate up and down in response to environmental circumstances. Sports participants experience a rise in testosterone if they win and a decrease if they lose, and even spectators experience these fluctuations according to their teams' fortunes.[96] This means that variation in testosterone levels is often the *consequence* of successful or failed aggression and not necessarily its cause.

If testosterone is responsive to sporting competition and even to vicarious competition, it must be more so in response to real-life competitive challenges such as challenges to a person's status in honor subcultures.[97] Allan Mazur's study[98] of 4,462 army veterans found significant racial differences in testosterone levels overall, but no differences were found among older males, college graduates, and males raised outside violent subcultures. Younger Black males with little education who had participated in violent subcultures in civilian life largely accounted for the significantly higher testosterone levels in Blacks relative to Whites. Similarly, a laboratory study found that administering insults generated testosterone surges among men raised in honor cultures but not among men not raised in one.[99] This shows how important it is for males living in an honor subculture to respond to challenges and how the body is calibrated to produce the chemical means to do so.

Serotonin The relationships between low levels of serotonin and aggression and impulsivity have been called "perhaps the most reliable findings in the history of psychiatry."[100] Although serotonin levels are highly heritable, most of the one third to one half of the variation attributable to environmental effects may reflect our social position in local status hierarchies. Researchers have experimentally shown that serotonin underlies primate status hierarchies.[101] The highest ranking males have the highest levels of serotonin, and the lowest ranking have the lowest. Low-ranking males in established hierarchies defer with little fuss to the demands of higher ranking males, suggesting that lowering serotonin levels for those at the bottom of the social heap may be nature's way of preventing them from challenging those at the top when a successful challenge is unlikely. When the hierarchy is disrupted, however, it is the impulsive low-serotonin males who become the most aggressive in the competition for available resources. Living on the ground floor of the status hierarchy is not at all pleasant, and natural selection has built in us a penchant for revolting when possibilities exist to reverse our fortunes. Males who succeed in rising up to a new status hierarchy find that their serotonin rises to levels commensurate with their new position.[102]

Experiments with rhesus monkeys have shown that peer-raised monkeys have lower concentrations of serotonin than parentally raised monkeys.[103,104] In the case of humans, read this as "fatherless, gang-raised children." Such children are especially prone to be abused and neglected and to be raised in poverty-stricken honor subcultures. We have also seen that low self-control and negative emotionality are affected by child abuse and neglect and that serotonin levels underlie both those traits.[105] Abused and neglected children raised in honor subcultures are thus likely to experience both elevated levels of testosterone *and* lowered levels of serotonin, a combination especially likely to result in violence.[106] High-testosterone/low-serotonin males in violent subcultures who "try their luck" in elevating their status do so against others with similar chemical profiles and status aspirations, which means that the potential for violent confrontation is always present.[107]

The Brain As we saw in Chapter 8, the brain *physically* captures our experiences by molding and shaping neuronal circuitry in ways that make our behavior adaptive in the environments in which we find ourselves. The neurological literature is consistent with the serotonin literature in suggesting that impulsiveness is the proximate behavioral expression of a brain wired by consistent exposure to violence.[108,109] If our brains develop in violent environments, we expect hostility from others and behave accordingly. By doing so, we invite the very hostility we are on guard for, thus confirming our belief that the world is a dangerous and hostile place and setting in motion a vicious circle of negative expectations and confirmations.

How much violence do children in our inner cities witness? In one study in Chicago, 33% of schoolchildren had witnessed a homicide, and 66% had witnessed a serious assault.[110] Another study found that 32% of children from Washington, D.C., and 51% of children from New Orleans had been victims of violence, and 72% of children from Washington, D.C., and 91% percent of children from New Orleans had witnessed violence.[111] Witnessing and experiencing so much violence cannot help but put a stamp on the neural circuitry of these children that the world is a dangerous place in which one must be prepared to protect one's interests by violent means, if necessary. It is in this sense that violence begets violence.

⬚ Evolutionary Considerations: What Is Violence For?

When evolutionary biologists explore the behavioral repertoire of any species, their first question is, "What is the adaptive significance of this particular behavior?" With regard to violence, they want to know how violence was adaptive in evolutionary environments, what its function is, and what environmental circumstances are likely to evoke it. Evolutionary biologists assume that violence evolved to solve some set of adaptive problems; if it didn't solve some such problems, it wouldn't be part of our behavioral repertoire. The bloody history of humanity attests to how easily we are moved to create situations that lead to violence with alarming frequency.

Violence (at least credible threats of violence) is intimately related to reproductive success in almost all animal species through its role in attaining status and dominance, and thus access to more resources and to more females. Reacting violently when some brute tries to steal your bananas or your wife could be very useful in evolutionary environments when you just couldn't call 911 to have someone else settle your problem. Having a reputation for violence would be even better because others would be aware of it and avoid your bananas and your wife in the first place. In other words, in environments in which one is expected to take care of one's own beefs, violence or the threat of violence works to let any potential challenger know that it would be in his best interests to avoid you and your resources and look elsewhere. All this is why a "bad ass" reputation is so valued in honor subcultures, why those with such a reputation are always looking for opportunities to validate it, and why it is craved to such an extent that "many inner city young men . . . will risk their lives to attain it."[112]

Violence also imposes a cost on those who use it. They could be killed or severely injured in a violent conflict, so perhaps some alternative strategy would be better, such as sharing your bananas and your wife with any who may covet them. Sharing your bananas is OK, but you can be sure that any male who shared his wife so nonchalantly is not among our ancestors. Anyway, what would happen to you if the other guy wants it all and resorts to violence to assert his claim in a subculture in which calling 911 is not an option? If you are unprepared to match violence with violence, you may lose your life as well as your resources. Natural selection has provided us with the ability to switch to a violence mode quickly when we have reason to believe that things we value may be taken from us.[113] This propensity is most useful today in disorganized neighborhoods in which a tradition of settling one's own quarrels without involving the authorities is entrenched—that is, in neighborhoods in which social institutions that control, shape, and sublimate violent tendencies are absent or enfeebled.

Individuals living in "respectable" areas who have faith in the fairness of the criminal justice system rarely have to resort to violence to gain what they want or to protect what they have. Violence is maladaptive for them—violence may be *in* the nature of human males, but it is not *the* nature of human males. Natural selection has favored flexibility over fixity of human behavior, which is why behaving violently is very much contingent on environmental instigation. The evolutionary point of view shares the neuroscience point of view that the major long-term factor in violence instigation is how much violence a person has been exposed to in the past. As Caulin and Burney explain, when many acts of violence are observed, "there is a feedback effect; each violent act observed makes observers feel more at risk and therefore more likely to resort to preemptive violence themselves."[114]

FOCUS ON . . .

Evolutionary Considerations of Inequality and Violence

Natural selection has not strongly favored violent competition over access to resources in long-lived species such as ours because males in long-lived species have plenty of time to move up status hierarchies and acquire them in more peaceful ways.[115] High-risk battles over access to food, territory, and females take place mostly in polygynous and short-lived species. But what if everything we see and have experienced tells us that we don't have "plenty of time" and that we cannot advance in life through peaceful means? We have frequently noted that impulsivity and discounting the future are maladaptive, but psychologists Margo Wilson and Martin Daly suggest that discounting the future "may be a 'rational' response to information that indicates an uncertain or low probability of surviving to reap delayed benefits, for example, and 'reckless' risk taking can be optimal when the expected profits from safer courses of action are negligible."[116] In other words, when the young perceive little opportunity for legitimate success and when many people they know die at an early age, then living for the present and engaging in risky violence to obtain resources makes excellent evolutionary sense. Males compete for status by whatever means are available to them in the cultural environments in which they live.

Wilson and Daly tested their assumption with homicide, income inequality, and life expectancy data from the 77 neighborhoods in Chicago for the years 1988 through 1995. They hypothesized that neighborhoods with the lowest income levels and the shortest life expectancies (excluding homicides) would have the highest homicide rates. Life expectancy (effects of homicide mortality removed) ranged from 54.3 years in the poorest neighborhood to 77.4 years in the wealthiest, and the attending homicide rates ranged from 1.3 to 156 per 100,000, a huge 120-fold difference. Wilson and Daly appeal to evolutionary logic to interpret these data, viewing them as reflecting escalations of risky competitive tactics that make sense from an evolutionary point of view, given the conditions in which people in disadvantaged and disorganized neighborhoods live. As Bob Dylan sang, "When you ain't got nothin,' you got nothin' to lose."

We remind you again not to confuse an *explanation* of the facts with a *moral evaluation* of them. Wilson and Daly are saying that natural selection has equipped us to respond to high levels of inequality and expectations of a short life by creating risky, high-stakes male-male competitions that all too frequently result in homicide. From a moral point of view, this is obviously something to be condemned, but to the extent that such contingent responses are the products of natural selection, they are not pathological from the point of view of evolutionary biology. A policy suggestion from this perspective is to provide inner-city males with more legitimate routes to status and resources, which is a standard liberal crime control prescription. As Robert Wright has remarked, it is surprising "how far to the left one can be dragged by a modern Darwinian view of the human mind."[117]

SUMMARY

Murder rates have been significantly higher in the past than they are today, primarily because of the lack of effective law enforcement and adequate medical attention. Homicide trends in the United States have fluctuated wildly over the years, with modern-day rates being relatively small compared with the past. In international comparisons, the United States homicide rate is situated somewhere in the middle. In terms of who kills whom in the United States, both the typical perpetrator and the typical victim of homicide are young Black males living in an urban center. It was also noted that female/female homicide is very rare worldwide.

Feminist and evolutionary theories maintain that all men have a propensity to rape, but the typical convicted rapist is a young, uneducated, and poor male with a record of other types of crimes. There are a variety of types of rapists, with anger rapists being the most prevalent. Social learning and feminist theories maintain that rape is the result of male socialization, while evolutionary theory maintains that it is a maladaptive consequence of generally adaptive male reproductive strategy. The biosocial theory integrates the most empirically supported features of each theory.

Robbery is a violent crime in which perpetrators seek to gain something from their victims by force or threat of force. Robbers tend to be the most impulsive, hedonistic, daring, and dangerous of all criminals, as well as the least educated and least conscientious. Robbery is considered by those who practice it to be the quickest and easiest way to obtain money. It is also considered an excellent way to prove a certain kind of "manliness" in some areas. Some women also specialize in robbery, mostly working with male accomplices, but may also work alone robbing other women.

Aggravated assault is the most frequently committed of the violent Part I crimes. Each such incident carries the threat of ending up as a criminal homicide, and but for speedy access to medical treatment, many of them would have done so.

The subculture of violence thesis attempts to explain why violent crime rates are so high in African American neighborhoods. It was argued that this subculture is a legacy of slavery and its aftermath and the ways in which ex-slaves adapted to White attitudes and behavior toward them. As long as Blacks committed crimes against other Blacks, Whites cared little. African Americans were afforded little or no protection against predators from law enforcement and developed a system of "taking care of business" themselves and not involving "the man." These attitudes coalesced into what is known as honor subcultures in which young males are hypersensitive to status and to their reputations to the point that they will risk their lives to protect them.

Testosterone and serotonin are often tagged as facilitators (not causes) of violent behavior. Both chemicals are responsive to environmental input. Testosterone levels rise to meet environmental challenges and energize the body. Serotonin appears to be responsive to social hierarchies, and low levels are associated with impulsively violent behavior. The combination of high testosterone and low serotonin is one particularly vulnerable to violence. We also saw that neurological studies substantiate the role of low serotonin in explaining violence, as well as the role of the prefrontal cortex.

Any behavior that is frequently found across species and across cultures must have been useful in evolutionary environments. Violence was useful in certain circumstances when one had to protect resources from others intent on depriving one of them. Of course, we have developed social institutions to prevent such things occurring today, but in relatively lawless areas, such as honor subcultures, having a reputation for being willing to use violence if need be can be very useful. We saw that engaging in risky competitive tactics can be adaptive in circumstances in which people have little or nothing to lose.

On Your Own

Log on to the web-based student study site at http://www.sagepub.com/criminologystudy for more information about the vignettes and materials presented in this chapter, suggestions for activities, study aids such as review quizzes, and research recommendations including journal article links and questions related to this chapter.

EXERCISES AND DISCUSSION QUESTIONS

1. Locate the violent crime rate in your state from Table 11.1. What do you think accounts for the different rates between your state, the most violent state, and the least violent state?

2. Look at Table 11.2; what could possibly explain (1) the difference in homicides rates between Colombia and the United States and (2) the difference in homicide rates between Japan and the United States?

3. Why is female/female homicide so rare, and why is this the case around the world?

4. Which theory of rape makes the most and least sense to you? Give your reasons.

5. What do you think of the idea that rape is not about sex but rather about something else?

6. Does the subculture of violence thesis for explaining the high rates of violent crime in certain African American communities make sense to you? If not, what else might explain them?

7. We have seen theorists of many persuasions talking about the role of impulsiveness, low constraint, or low self-control throughout this book. Here it pops up again in yet another context. Do you think that the relationship has been established in so many different ways that we can talk about it as "settled science"?

8. Explain in your own words the idea that risky, competitive, and violent behavior can be rational (adaptive) in communities such as honor subcultures.

9. Go to http://human-nature.com volume 3, 2005 and find the article by Todd Shackelford ("An Evolutionary Psychological Perspective on Cultures of Honor"). In what ways is this explanation similar and different from the subculture of violence explanation?

KEY WORDS

Aggravated assault
Biosocial theory of rape
Evolutionary theory of rape
Feminist theory of rape
Forcible rape

Honor subcultures
Involuntary manslaughter
Negligent manslaughter
Murder
Robbery

Social learning theory
 of rape
Subculture of violence
Voluntary manslaughter

REFERENCES

1. Durant, W. (1953). *Caesar and Christ.* New York: Simon & Schuster. (Quote on p. 590)
2. Hanawalt, B. (1979). *Crime and conflict in English communities, 1300–1348.* Cambridge, MA: Harvard University Press.
3. Schussler, M. (1992). German crime in the later Middle Ages: A statistical analysis of the Nuremberg outlawry books, 1285–1400. In L. Knafla (Ed.), *Criminal justice history: An international annual* (Vol. 13). Westport, CT: Greenwood.
4. Federal Bureau of Investigation (FBI). (2005). *Crime in the United States, 2004: Uniform Crime Reports.* Washington, DC: Government Printing Office. (Quote on p. 15)
5. FBI (2005).
6. Griswold, E. (2005). Medellin's mean streets. *National Geographic, 207,* 72–91.
7. Federal Bureau of Investigation (FBI). (1968). *Crime in the United States, 1967: Uniform Crime Reports.* Washington, DC: Government Printing Office.
8. Cartwright, D. (1996). Violence in America. *American Heritage, 47,* 36–47.
9. Cartwright (1996).
10. Harris, A., Thomas, S., Fisher, G., & Hirsch, D. (2002). Murder and medicine: The lethality of criminal assault 1960–1999. *Homicide Studies, 6,* 128–166.
11. FBI (2005).
12. Mann, C. (1990). Black female homicides in the United States. *Journal of Interpersonal Violence, 5,* 176–201.
13. Daly, M., & Wilson, M. (2000). Risk-taking, intersexual competition, and homicide. *Nebraska Symposium on Motivation, 47,* 1–36.
14. Given, J. (1977). *Society and homicide in thirteenth-century England.* Stanford, CA: Stanford University Press.
15. Ketelar, T., & Ellis, B. (2000). Are evolutionary explanations unfalsifiable? Evolutionary psychology and the Lakatosian philosophy of science. *Psychological Inquiry, 11,* 1–21.
16. Daly, M., & Wilson, M. (1996). Violence against stepchildren. *Current Directions in Psychological Science, 5,* 77–81.
17. Catalano, S. (2005). *Criminal victimization, 2003.* Washington, DC: Bureau of Justice Statistics.
18. FBI (2005, p. 27).
19. Catalano (2005).
20. South, S., & Felson, R. (1990). The racial patterning of rape. *Social Forces, 69,* 71–93.
21. LaFree, G. (1982). Male power and female victimization: Toward a theory of interracial rape. *American Sociological Review, 45,* 842–854.
22. Walsh, A. (1987). The sexual stratification hypothesis and sexual assault in light of the changing conceptions of race. *Criminology, 25,* 153–173.
23. Ellis, L., & Walsh, A. (2000). *Criminology: A global perspective.* Boston: Allyn & Bacon.
24. Schwartz, B. (1995). Characteristics and typologies of sex offenders. In B. Schwartz & H. Cellini (Eds.), *The sex offender: Corrections, treatment, and legal practice.* Kingston, NJ: Civic Research Institute.
25. Interpol. (1992). *International crime statistics.* Lyons, France: Author.
26. Walsh, A., & Hemmens, C. (2000). *From law to order: The theory and practice of law and justice.* Lanham, MD: American Correctional Association.
27. Bartol, C. (2002). *Criminal behavior: A psychosocial approach.* Englewood Cliffs, NJ: Prentice Hall.
28. Emmers-Sommer, T., Allen, M., Bourhis, J., Sahlstein, E., Laskowski, K., Falato, W., et al. (2004). A meta-analysis of the relationship between social skills and sexual offenders. *Communication Reports, 17.*
29. Hanson, R. (2002). Recidivism and age: Follow-up data from 4,673 sexual offenders. *Journal of Interpersonal Violence, 17,* 1046–1062.
30. Testa, M., & Dermen, K. (1999). The differential correlates of sexual coercion and rape. *Journal of Interpersonal Violence, 14,* 548–561.
31. Figueuredo, A., Sales, B., Russel, K., Becker, J., & Kaplan, M. (2002). A Brunswickian evolutionary-developmental theory of adolescent sex offending. *Behavioral Sciences & the Law, 18,* 309–329.
32. Ellis, L. (1991). A synthesized (biosocial) theory of rape. Journal of Consulting and Clinical Psychology, 59, 631–642.
33. Mealey, L. (2003). Combating rape: Views of an evolutionary psychologist. In R. Bloom & N. Dess (Eds.), *Evolutionary psychology and violence* (pp. 83–113). Westport, CT: Praeger.
34. Mealey (2003, p. 91).
35. Groth, A. (1979). *Men who rape.* New York: Plenum.
36. Gilmartin, P. (1994). *Rape, incest, and child sexual abuse: Consequences and recovery.* New York: Garland.
37. Brownmiller, S. (1975). *Against our will: Men, women, and rape.* New York: Simon & Schuster. (Quote on p. 5)
38. Walsh, A., & Walsh, G. (1993). *Viva la difference: A celebration of the sexes.* Buffalo, NY: Prometheus.
39. Mealey (2003).
40. Mealey (2003).
41. Smuts, B. (1992). Male aggression against women: An evolutionary perspective. *Human Nature, 3,* 1–44.
42. Buss, D. (1995). *Evolutionary psychology: The science of the mind.* Boston: Allyn & Bacon.

43. Ellis, L., & Walsh, A. (1997). Gene-based evolutionary theories in criminology. Criminology, 35, 229–276.

44. Brownmiller (1975, p. 5).

45. Barbaree, H., & Marshall, W. (1991). The role of male sexual arousal in rape: Six models. *Journal of Consulting and Clinical Psychology, 59,* 621–630.

46. Hall, E. (1987). Adolescents' perceptions of sexual assault. *Journal of Sex Education and Therapy, 13,* 37–42.

47. Gilmartin (1994).

48. Palmer, C. (1988). Twelve reasons why rape is not sexually motivated: A skeptical examination. *Journal of Sex Research, 25*(4), 512–530.

49. Lloyd, E. (2001). Science gone astray: Evolution and rape. *Michigan Law Review, 99,* 1536–1559.

50. Lykken, D. (1995). *The antisocial personalities.* Hillsdale, NJ: Lawrence Erlbaum.

51. Ellis, L. (1991). A synthesized (biosocial) theory of rape. *Journal of Consulting and Clinical Psychology, 59,* 631–642.

52. Daly, M., & Wilson, M. (1988). Homicide. New York: Aldine de Gruyter.

53. Lepowsky, M. (1994). Women, men, and aggression in egalitarian societies. *Sex Roles, 30,* 199–211.

54. Geary, D. (2000). Evolution and proximate expression of human paternal investment. *Psychological Bulletin, 126,* 55–77.

55. Oliver, M., & Hyde, J. (1993). Gender differences in sexuality: A meta-analysis. *Psychological Bulletin, 14,* 29–51.

56. FBI (2005, p. 31).

57. FBI (2005).

58. FBI (2005).

59. Wright, R., & Decker, S. (1997). *Armed robbers in action.* Boston: Northeastern University Press.

60. Jacobs, B., & Wright, R. (1999). Stick-up, street culture, and offender motivation. *Criminology, 37,* 149–173.

61. Wright and Decker (1997).

62. Jacobs and Wright (1999).

63. Messerschmidt, J. (1993). *Masculinities and crime.* Lanham, MD: Rowman & Littlefield. (Quote on p. 107)

64. Miller, J. (1998). Up it up: Gender and the accomplishment of street robbery. *Criminology, 36,* 37–65.

65. FBI (2005).

66. Campbell, A. (1999). Staying alive: Evolution, culture, and women's intrasexual aggression. *Behavioral and Brain Sciences, 22,* 203–214. (Quote on p. 210)

67. FBI (2005, p. 37).

68. Harris et al. (2002).

69. Catalano (2005).

70. Cao, L., Adams, A., & Jensen, V. (1997). A test of the Black subculture of violence thesis: A research note. *Criminology, 35,* 367–369. (Quote on p. 367)

71. Wolfgang, M., & Ferracutti, F. (1967). *The subculture of violence: Towards an integrated theory in criminology.* London: Tavistock. (Quote on p. 153).

72. Wolfgang and Ferracutti (1967).

73. Ismaili, K. (2001). Codes of the streets: Decency, violence, and the moral life of the inner city. *Justice Quarterly, 18,* 233–238. (Quote on p. 233)

74. Wolfgang and Ferracutti (1967, p. 162).

75. Thernstrom, S., & Thernstrom, A. (1997). *America in Black and White: One nation indivisible.* New York: Simon & Schuster. (Quote on p. 51)

76. Frazier, E. (1939). *The Negro family in the United States.* Chicago: University of Chicago Press.

77. Ogbu, J. (1991). Low performance as an adaptation: The case of Blacks in Stockton, California. In M. Gibson & J. Ogbu (Eds.), *Minority status and schooling* (pp. 249–285). New York: Grand Publishing.

78. Petterson, O. (1998). *Rituals of blood: Consequences of slavery in two American centuries.* Washington, DC: Civitas/Counterpoint.

79. Wilson, W. (1987). *The truly disadvantaged: The inner city, the underclass, and public policy.* Chicago: University of Chicago Press.

80. Goffman, E. (1961). *Asylums.* Garden City, NY: Anchor.

81. Walsh, A. (2006). *Correctional assessment, casework and Counseling* (4th ed.). Lanham, MD: American Correctional Association.

82. Clarke, J. (1998). *The lineaments of wrath: Race, violent crime, and American culture.* New Brunswick, NJ: Transaction Publishers.

83. Dollard, J. (1988). *Caste and class in a southern town.* Madison: University of Wisconsin Press. (Original work published 1937)

84. Dollard (1937/1988, p. 201).

85. Clarke (1998, p. 212).

86. Anderson, E. (1999). *Codes of the streets: Decency, violence, and the moral life of the inner city.* New York: W. W. Norton. (Quote on p. 33)

87. Anderson (1999).

88. Stampp, K. (1956). *The peculiar institution: Slavery in the antebellum South.* New York: Vintage. (Quote on p. 334, emphasis added)

89. Sampson, R., & Wilson, W. J. (2000). Toward a theory of race, crime, and urban inequality. In S. Cooper (Ed.), *Criminology* (pp. 149–160). Madison, WI: Coursewise.

90. Wolfgang and Ferracutti (1967).

91. Mazur, A., & Booth, A. (1998). Testosterone and dominance in men. *Behavioral and Brain Sciences, 21,* 353–397. (Quote on p. 362)

92. Baumeister, R., Smart, L., & Boden, J. (1996). Relation of threatened egoism to violence and aggression: The dark side of self-esteem. *Psychological Review, 103,* 5–33.

93. Mazur and Booth (1998).

94. Harris, J., Vernon, P., & Boomsma, D. (1998). The heritability of testosterone: A study of Dutch adolescent twins and their parents. *Behavior Genetics, 28,* 165–171.

95. Ellis, L., & Nyborg, H. (1992). Racial/ethnic variations in male testosterone levels: A probable contributor to group differences in health. *Steroids, 57,* 72–75.

96. Kemper, T. (1990). *Social structure and testosterone: Explorations of the socio-biosocial chain.* New Brunswick, NJ: Rutgers University Press.

97. Mazur and Booth (1998).

98. Mazur, A. (1995). Biosocial models of deviant behavior among army veterans. *Biological Psychology, 41,* 271–293.

99. Nisbet, R., & Cohen, D. (1996). *Culture of honor: The psychology of violence in the South.* Boulder, CO: Westview.

100. Fishbein, D. (2001). *Biobehavioral perspectives in criminology.* Belmont, CA: Wadsworth. (Quote on p. 15)

101. Wrangham, R., & Peterson, D. (1996). *Demonic males: Apes and the origins of human violence.* Boston: Houghton Mifflin.

102. Brammer, G., Raleigh, M., & McGuire, M. (1994). Neurotransmitters and social status. In L. Ellis (Ed.), *Social stratification and socioeconomic inequality: Vol. 2. Reproductive and interpersonal aspects of dominance and status* (pp. 75–91). Westport, CT: Praeger.

103. Bennett, A., Lesch, K., Heills, A., Long, J., Lorenz, J., Shoaf, S., et al. (2002). Early experience and serotonin transporter gene variation interact to influence primate CNS functioning. *Molecular Psychiatry, 7,* 118–122.

104. Kreamer, G., Ebert, M., Schmidt, D., & McKinney, W. (1998). A longitudinal study of the effect of different social rearing conditions on cerebrospinal fluid norepinephrine and biogenic amine metabolites in rhesus monkeys. *Neuopsychopharmacology, 2,* 175–189.

105. Caspi, A., Moffitt, T., Silva, P., Stouthamer-Loeber, M., Krueger, R., & Schmutte, P. (1994). Are some people crime-prone? Replications of the personality-crime relationship across countries, genders, races, and methods. *Criminology, 32,* 163–194.

106. Fox, R. (1998). Testosterone is not alone: Internal secretions and external behavior. *Behavioral and Brain Sciences, 21,* 375–376.

107. Bernhardt, P. (1997). Influences of serotonin and testosterone in aggression and dominance: Convergence with social psychology. *Current Directions in Psychological Science, 6,* 44–48.

108. Niehoff, D. (2003). A vicious circle: The neurobiological foundations of violent behavior. *Modern Psychoanalysis, 28,* 235–245.

109. Volavka, J. (2002). *Neurobiology of violence* (2nd ed.). Washington, DC: American Psychiatric Publishing.

110. Osofsky, J. (1995). The effects of exposure to violence on young children. *American Psychologist, 50,* 782–788.

111. Osofsky (1995).

112. Anderson, E. (1994). The code of the streets. *The Atlantic Monthly, 5,* 81–94. (Quote on p. 89)

113. Caulin, S., & McBurney, D. (2001). *Psychology: An evolutionary approach.* Upper Saddle River, NJ: Prentice Hall.

114. Caulin and McBurney (2001, p. 83).

115. Alcock, J. (1998). *Animal behavior: An evolutionary approach* (6th ed.). Sunderland, MA: Sinauer Associates.

116. Wilson, M., & Daly, M. (1997). Life expectancy, economic inequality, homicide and reproductive timing in Chicago neighborhoods. *British Medical Journal, 314,* 1271–1274. (Quote on p. 1271)

117. Wright, R. (1995). The biology of violence. *The New Yorker, 71,* 68–78. (Quote on p. 69)

SERIAL, MASS, AND SPREE MURDER

I *n April 1973, Edmund Kemper, a 6'9", 300-pound, 25-year-old hate machine, crept into his*
mother's bedroom and bludgeoned her to death, decapitated her, had sex with her headless
body, and played darts with the head. He then invited his mother's best friend over for a
"surprise" dinner to honor his mother. When she arrived, Kemper bludgeoned and decapitated her
also. This hulk of a man had already killed his grandparents when only a boy of 15, telling the
police matter-of-factly, "I just wondered what it would be like to shoot grandma." After his release
to his mother's care from a psychiatric hospital, he began trolling the highways for victims. He
killed at least six young women, and he also decapitated and sexually assaulted their headless
corpses. On at least two occasions, he preserved their heads so that he could use them later for
perverse sexual activity. He even ate the flesh of some of his victims, cooking it into a macaroni
casserole. Kemper's biggest thrill, however, was not sex, murder, or cannibalism; it was the act of
decapitation. In Kemper's own words, "You hear that little pop and pull their heads off and hold
their heads up by the hair. Whipping their heads off, their body sitting there. That'd get me off."[1]
Kemper is just one of the many people we will meet in this chapter to receive pleasure from the act
of killing.

⬚ What Is Multiple Murder?

This chapter deals with the most bizarre and horrific of all criminal activities, the slaughter of
the innocent by the seemingly insane. Because most such crimes are considered to lack rational motivation,[2] we exclude from consideration multiple murders committed for political or
financial reasons. The kinds of mass murderers we focus on are individuals for whom the act
of murder is its own reward and from which other gains are neither desired nor expected.
Thus, we exclude people such as professional "hit men" and crimes committed for ostensibly
political reasons, such as the biggest mass murder in American history of Americans by an

American—the bombing of the Murrah Federal Building in Oklahoma City by Timothy McVeigh in April 1995, which took the lives of 169 people and injured more than 500 others.

When we exclude murders committed for some instrumental purpose, we are left with murders seemingly committed for their own sake—that is, committed because the offender enjoys it and seeks no other reward from it beyond the psychological satisfaction it affords him. Although murder is usually considered the most serious crime a person can commit, murder for revenge or for personal gain is understandable because such motives have rational if not moral elements. While we still condemn such murders, we can all think of circumstances under which we might commit them. The gruesome bloodlust of killers such as Edmund Kemper, however, baffle and terrify us because they lack any objectively rational motivation with which the rest of us can identify.

Despite our revulsion, these killers also hold a dark fascination for us, as the number of books and movies devoted to them attest. In 1988, the media marked the centennial of the Jack the Ripper case with a slew of heavily watched movies and television docudramas. The legend that grew around the Ripper case probably had a lot to do with its "novelty" (Jack is often falsely considered to be the first serial killer). Or it may have had a lot to do with the fact that Jack's six or so murders constituted a little over 3% of England's murders in 1888.[3] Many serial killers both before and after Jack have far surpassed him in the number of their victims and the sadistic brutality of their actions, thus making the study of the phenomenon an important item on the criminological agenda.

Mass and Spree Murder

The primary characteristic differentiating mass, spree, and serial murder is the time frame in which the murders take place. **Mass murder** is the killing of several people at one location. Such incidents typically begin and end within a few minutes or hours. **Spree murder** is the killing of several people at different locations over a period of several days. Research suggests that the time frame involved is the only factor that differentiates mass and spree killers and that both mass and spree killers are different from the serial killer.

There are relatively few generalities we can make about mass and spree killers. Most research on these individuals is necessarily retrospective (interviews with families and friends and sometimes notes left by the offender) because they typically commit suicide or are killed by police at or near the scene of their crime. The exceptions to this rule are felony-related and gang-related mass murder. However, reviews of the literature on mass murder from the 1960s to the late 1990s[4–6] note several commonalities shared by mass and spree murderers:

+ They are "typically" White males with an age range broader than that of serial killers.
+ African Americans are overrepresented in terms of their proportion in the population.
+ They have previously displayed impulsive, violent, frustrated, depressed, alienated, and anti-authoritarian behavior, probably arising from a deep sense of having been wronged.
+ They tend to have a morbid fascination with guns and to own many of them.
+ Their behavior at the time of the crime, as well as the fact that it is typically committed in public places, makes it obvious that they are unconcerned about their own death, leading some researchers to view this type of murder as an elaborate suicide attempt. This is not true of felony- and gang-related mass murderers.

- They seem to contemplate committing murder and prepare for the act, although the time and place where it takes place is not generally preestablished.
- Spree and mass murders increased considerably in the United States during the 1960s through the 1990s.
- Young, non-White males predominate in felony-related (58.3%) and gang-related (100%) mass murder incidents.
- The average age of all mass murderers over the past 40 years is 29.

Mass murderers can be roughly divided into two types: (1) those who chose specific targets whom the killers believe to have caused them stress (e.g., disgruntled workers attacking supervisors and other company representatives) and (2) those who attack targets having no connection with the killer but who belong to groups the killer dislikes. For instance, James Huberty disliked Hispanics and children and selected them as his targets in a McDonald's restaurant in San Ysidro, California, killing 21 mostly Hispanic children and wounding 19 before being gunned down by police. In a similar scenario, woman-hater George Hennard drove his pickup truck through a cafeteria window in Killeen, Texas, in 1991 and killed 22 people, 14 of whom were women, before committing suicide. Another woman-hater, Canadian Marc Lepine, entered a classroom in the engineering building at the University of Montreal in 1989, ordered all the men out, and began shooting women, killing 14 and wounding 13 others.[7]

The stereotype of the mass murderer as someone who suddenly "snaps" into a psychotic rage and starts shooting at anyone at random is far from accurate. Most mass murderers are motivated by a hatred that simmers until some specific incident provides the flame that brings it to a boil. Lepine, for instance, had been denied admission into the engineering school and sought revenge on the women who had taken his place in a "man's profession."[8] Likewise, Colin Ferguson, who killed 6 people and wounded 19 others on a Long Island commuter train in 1993, hated Whites. He claimed that "Black rage" at what he saw as society's mistreatment of Blacks led him to his rampage.[9] Both men thus methodically and selectively chose their victims on the basis of some alleged wrong done to them by a group that their targeted victims represented.

Spree murder involves the killing of a number of victims at different locations over a period of several days or even weeks. Spree killers move from victim to victim in fairly rapid succession and, like mass murderers, make little effort to hide their activities or avoid detection, moving from victim to victim as if driven by some frenzied compulsion. Two particularly notorious spree murder cases that illustrate a common pattern are the cases of Mark Essex and Christopher Wilder. Mark Essex was a frustrated African American who hated Whites, especially White cops. Essex was raised in a hardworking two-parent family in Emporia, Kansas, and apparently enjoyed a normal childhood. Racial insults suffered in the navy led Essex to join a Black Muslim militant group, where he received urban guerrilla warfare training. His spree began on New Year's Eve of 1974, when he ambushed and shot two police officers right outside the New Orleans Police Department building, after which he ambushed and killed another officer responding to a burglary alarm. The next day, he killed a grocery store manager and three other people in a hotel. Essex held responding officers at bay for most of the night before he was finally gunned down. When it was all over, Essex had killed 9 people and seriously wounded 10 others.[10]

Australian-born Christopher Wilder, owner of a prosperous construction company and race car driver, was a spree killer who showed that a person does not have to be a failure in life to engage in spree killing. On a wild cross-country ride from California to the East Coast, Wilder killed at least eight women before being gunned down near the Canadian border by a state trooper in 1984. Wilder was also suspected in a number of states and in Australia of the murders of several women prior to his final cross-country spree.[11]

Spree killing is rare, but spree-killing teams are even rarer and are typically composed of a dominant leader and a submissive lover. The most recent spree killer team is the sniper team of John Muhammad and Lee Malvo. Muhammad and Malvo were accused of killing 13 random individuals and wounding 6 others in the Washington, D.C., area and are suspected of killings and other crimes in Alabama, Georgia, and Louisiana. Although the team killed both Whites and Blacks, men and women, Muhammad belonged to the Black separatist group, the Nation of Islam, which may have provided ideological impetus to his vicious spree.[12] Muhammad was sentenced to death, and Malvo was given a life sentence.

Perhaps the youngest spree killer team in American history is that of 19-year-old Charles Starkweather and 14-year-old Caril Fugate. Starkweather, a high school dropout with a minor speech impediment and bowed legs, was raised in impoverished conditions and was an angry and alienated young man. The Starkweather/Fugate spree began with the murder of Caril's mother, stepfather, and young half-sister on January 21, 1958 (Starkweather had committed his first murder in a robbery early in December of the previous year). Before they were captured just 8 days later, Starkweather and Fugate had killed 11 people.[13] Starkweather, whose exploits gave birth to a number of movies and books, was executed in 1959; Fugate was sentenced to life in prison and was paroled in 1976.

Alton Coleman and Debra Brown are African American counterparts of Starkweather and Fugate. Like Starkweather, Coleman was raised in poverty and was often the butt of cruel jokes (he was nicknamed "pissy" because he often wet his pants). Coleman began his criminal career very early in life, running with street gangs and committing a variety of crimes. After a series of arrests for mostly sex crimes (he was a "polymorphous pervert," being sexually attracted to men, women, and children), Coleman began his spree of rapes, kidnappings, and murders. In the company of his female accomplice, Debra Brown, he began the spree with the rape and murder of a 9-year-old girl late in May 1984. The Coleman/Brown crime spree in the Midwest ended with their capture on July 20, 1984. During their 7-week spree, the couple killed at least seven people and committed a number of other crimes, including kidnapping, attempted murder, and rape.[14] Coleman was executed in Ohio in 2002; Brown is serving life in prison.

Spree and mass murders have increased steadily in the United States since the middle of the 20th century. In the 1950s, there were just four cases of spree or mass murder, and in the 1960s, there were only seven. During the period from 1977 to 1991, such incidents increased 10-fold. The Justice Department lists 157 incidents of mass murder, in which 964 people were killed, and 112 incidents of spree murder, in which 483 people were killed during that period.[15] This amounts to about one incident of spree or mass murder every 20 days in the United States over the 15-year period compared to one every 912 days in the 1950s. More recent data for the first 3 years of the 21st century reveal even bigger increases, with 84 incidents in 2000, an astounding 368 in 2001, and 115 in 2002.[16]

Serial Murder

The FBI's *Crime Classification Manual*[17] lists three criteria for defining a killer as a serial killer. He or she must (1) kill in three or more separate events, (2) kill at three or more separate locations, (3) and engage in an emotional "cooling-off" period between murders.

▶ **Photo 12.1** Random massacres, such as Charles Whitman's shooting spree from the University of Texas tower, attract the greatest media attention yet are the rarest forms of mass murder. In comparison, some examples of genocide have gone on for significant periods of time without major attention being paid.

▶ **Photo 12.2** Not unlike disgruntled employees who return to the workplace to take out their wrath, students Dylan Klebold and Eric Harris were captured on closed-circuit video as they sought victims, from among those they felt had snubbed them, in the school cafeteria at Columbine High School.

The first criterion separates serial from mass killings, such as Richard Speck's killing of eight student nurses in Chicago in one horrific event in 1966. The second criterion is problematic because it would eliminate killers such as John Wayne Gacy and Travis Maury, who killed only in their own homes. The third criterion is highly subjective because we do not know how long the cooling-off period must be before a spree killer becomes a serial killer or whether a serial killer can become a spree killer and then revert to serial killing again. Richard Speck, for instance, killed four females in separate incidents before his massacre of eight in a single

◀ **Photo 12.3**   Spree killer or serial killer? Lee Malvo leaves court after being convicted of sniper killings in and around the Washington, D.C., region. Ten people were killed and three others critically injured by Malvo and his associate over a several-week period.

incident, and as already noted, Christopher Wilder was suspected of serial killing a number of women prior to embarking on his spree. Thus, there are those who feel that the addition of the spree killing definition "needlessly complicates multiple homicide classification."[18] Although we have differentiated between serial and spree killers, this complication should be kept in mind.

The general consensus among criminologists is that **serial murder** is the killing of three or more victims over an extended period of time.[19] We usually hear about spree or mass murders after they are over and the perpetrator is dead or in police custody, but a serial killer can haunt a community for months or years. In addition to this time frame distinction, several generalities differentiate the serial killer from spree and mass killers, as well as from the "typical" (nonmultiple) murderer:

- ◆ Whereas spree and mass killers almost invariably use firearms and kill their victims quickly, serial killers generally prefer to stalk and often torture their victims.
- ◆ The "typical" serial killer is a White male who is older than the "typical" homicide perpetrator.
- ◆ African Americans are overrepresented among known serial killers, and Asian Americans and women of all races are greatly underrepresented.
- ◆ Researchers have identified four general types of serial killers: visionary, mission oriented, hedonistic, and power/control.
- ◆ Since 1977, the prevalence of serial murderers has been more than twice that of spree or mass murderers and has accounted for more than twice the number of victims.[20–23]

The Extent of the Problem

The true extent of the serial killer problem is difficult to gauge. One ambitious effort estimated the number of serial killers operating in the United States from 1860 to 1995 to be 3,000.[24] The sensational nature of the serial killing phenomenon has led to many exaggerated claims, however. A figure often quoted is that about 20% of the murders in the United States each year (about 3,000–4,000) are committed by serial killers.[25] Holmes and DeBurger's justification for this figure has been the steady rise in uncleared murder cases since the 1960s, noted in Chapter 10.

Murder is considered the most easily solved of all crimes because it is usually committed by someone with a transparent motive and who is known to the victim, but a randomly chosen murder victim with no previous connection to the killer often leaves the police literally "clueless." With the continual drop in clearance rates noted in successive *Uniform Crime Reports* (*UCR*) since 1968, it became common to equate "motiveless" and "uncleared" murder with "serial murder." However, many victims of uncleared murders are sexually unmolested adult males (not the typical targets of serial killers), and the "gangbanging" and territorial wars among drug dealers in the 1980s and 1990s may have more to do with the increase in uncleared murders than serial killers. From a variety of data sources, it was estimated that serial killers account for no more than 300 to 400 murders each year (about 2% of all murders), which, while a horrible toll on innocent human lives, falls far short of sensationalized claims. Some unknown percentage of uncleared homicides must doubtless be attributable to serial killers, however.

Figure 12.1 presents the number and rates of serial killers in the United States between 1795 and 2004. These figures are gross estimates, and the true number of serial killers operating in any time period can probably never be known. The increase in the rate of killers from 1925–1944 to 1980–2004 is probably only partly a real increase in the number of serial killers. An unknown portion of the increase may be attributed to improved law enforcement methods (discussed later) initiated during the latter period. The increase in other forms of homicide, including spree and mass murder during the same period, however, leads us to conclude that part of the reported increase in serial killers represents a real increase.

A Typology of Serial Killers

Although all serial killers have the same killing goal, they have different psychological motives. Among a number of typologies of serial killers, that of Holmes and DeBurger[26] has perhaps gained the widest acceptance. Their typology divides serial killers into four broad types: *visionary, mission oriented, hedonistic, and power/control.* These are ideal types, not definitive categories; many serial killers may evidence aspects of all types at various times, and there is considerable overlap of categories from killer to killer.

The **visionary serial killer** feels impelled to commit murder by visions or "voices in my head." These visions or voices may be thought of as coming from God, from demons, from a dead parent, or even from a howling dog, as initially claimed by David Berkowitz (the "Son of Sam"), but all command the person to kill. Visionary killers are typically out of touch with reality and may be diagnosed as psychotic or schizophrenic. The sexual assault of victims is not usually a component of the visionary killer's pattern. Berkowitz, for instance, shot most of his victims (young women and their male companions parked in "lover's lanes" in New York) and then fled the scene.

Mission-oriented serial killers feel it to be their mission in life to kill certain kinds of people. Unlike visionary killers, they do not have visions or hear voices: They define their own

| **Figure 12.1** | Estimated Number and Rate per 10 Million of Serial Killers Operating in the United States from 1795 to Mid-2004 |

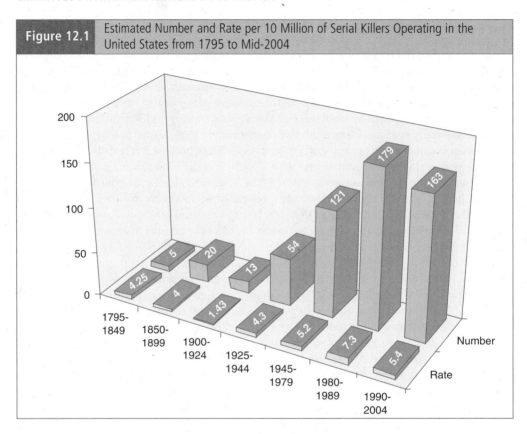

SOURCES: U.S. Justice Department figures as reported by Jenkins, P. (1994). *Using murder: The social construction of serial homicide.* New York: Aldine de Gruyter. Updated figures are from Hickey, E. (2006). *Serial murderers and their victims* (4th ed.). Belmont, CA: Wadsworth; Walsh, A. (2005). African Americans and serial killing in the media: The myth and the reality. *Homicide Studies, 9,* 271–291. Rates per 10 million population computed by authors.

"undesirables" and set out to eliminate as many as they can. Prostitutes and homosexuals are frequent targets of mission-oriented serial killers, but targets may also be people of particular races, religions, or ethnic groups. Although most serial killers operate alone, groups of individuals sometimes act together. An example of a mission-oriented serial killing group is a Black Muslim group, operating in Southern California during the early 1970s, called the Angels of Death (the "Zebra killers"). Each member, the most notable of whom included Larry Green and Jesse Cooks, was to kill at least four "evil blue-eyed devils" (Whites). Although convictions were obtained for only 23 of the murders, Angels of Death may have killed more people in the early to mid-1970s than all the other serial killers operating during that period combined.[27] Clark Howard[28] identifies 270 victims, although a different source[29] indicates that the police believed them to have killed about 80. Angels of Death killings often involved long torture sessions. Sexual assault is typically not involved in mission-oriented killings.

Hedonistic serial killers kill for the pure thrill and joy of it. The hedonistic killer is such a self-centered psychopath that he considers someone's life less important than the achievement of his orgasm. Most serial killers are hedonistic killers.[30] Killing, along with the cruel and perverted sexual activity that is part of it, becomes the greatest of pleasures for these people. Torture, cannibalism, necrophilia, and other bizarre activities are central to the hedonistic killer's pattern of sexuality. Edmund Kemper is an example of this kind of killer (although Kemper had been institutionalized and found to be psychotic after killing his grandparents, he never claimed that "voices" made him do what he did). Many hedonistic killers are sexually dysfunctional and only achieve satisfactory orgasm while "penetrating" their victims with a knife (picquerism). Killing becomes an addiction among hedonistic killers, and it becomes amalgamated into their lifestyles in much the same way that obtaining and using drugs dominate the lifestyles of drug addicts.[31]

The **power/control serial killer** gains more satisfaction from exercising complete power over his victims than from "bloodlust," although sexual activity is almost always involved. Like the hedonist killer, the power/control killer frequently suffers from some form of sexual inadequacy. Ted Bundy was of this type. Bundy would keep the bodies of some of his victims for several days before disposing of them, during which time he would frequently wash and groom them like dolls. The prime example of this type is Jeffrey Dahmer, who tried to create sex slaves of some of his victims (all males) by performing "lobotomies" on them by drilling holes in their heads and pouring acid into them. Dahmer's goal was to exert complete control over mindless human beings; even his acts of cannibalism may be viewed as attempts to fully possess at least parts of his victims.

▲ **Photo 12.4** Most serial killers don't look like monsters, though their behavior often is monstrous. John Wayne Gacy was a respected member of his community and was employed as a clown at children's birthday parties.

Race and Multiple Murder

While the typical serial killer is a White male, it is little known that African Americans are over-represented among serial killers relative to their proportion of the American population. A study of 337 serial killers operating since 1825 found that 22% were African American,[32] and a study that included mass and spree murderers with serial killers put the figure at 38.2%.[33] A sample of 413 serial killers operating from 1945 to mid-2004 in the United States found that African Americans constituted 22% of the total,[34] and Hickey[35] claims that about 44% of the serial killers operating between 1995 and 2004 have been Black.

Pre–World War II Black serial killers, such as Jarvis Catoe, Jake Bird, and Clarence Hill, were among those claiming the largest number of victims.[36] Bird was particularly prolific with 44, a number just 4 victims short of Gary Ridgway's 48 victims, which is the record number of *verified* victims in the annals of American serial killing. Coral Watts and Milton Johnson are two of the most notorious examples of African American serial killers of the early post–World War II years. Watts, known as the "Sunday Morning Slasher," confessed to 13 murders and was linked to at least 8 others between 1978 and 1983, and Milton Johnson was responsible for at least 17 murders in the 1980s.

More contemporary African American serial killers include Henry Louis Wallace, who raped and strangled at least 9 women from 1993 until his capture in 1996. All of Wallace's victims were acquaintances, which, according to FBI experts, makes him unique among serial killers, who almost always seek strangers.[37] Another recent example is Kendall Francois, who was indicted in 1999 for the murders of 16 women, all but 1 of whom were White.[38] The sibling serial killer team of Anthony and Nathaniel Cook, who also only targeted Whites, is another recent example. Both men pled guilty in 2000 in Lucas County, Ohio, of eight murders and were suspected of committing others outside Lucas County's jurisdiction.[39]

The most chilling of recent African American serial killers was Maury Travis. Travis had a secret torture chamber in his basement, where police found bondage equipment and videotapes of his rape and torture sessions when they arrested him in 2002. Travis hanged himself in jail after confessing to killing 17 women.[40] Among the most recent African American serial killers are Derrick Todd Lee, Lorenzo Gilyard, and Daniel Jones. Lee was arrested in Atlanta in 2003 for the murder of 5 women in Louisiana and is a suspect in many other murders, rapes, and assaults going back to 1992.[41] Gilyard and Jones were both arrested in Kansas City, Missouri, in 2004 for the murders of 12 and 4 women, respectively.[42]

Although the number of victims claimed by these African American killers fall short of those attributed to White killers such as Ted Bundy or John Wayne Gacy, they exceed the figures attributed to more publicized killers such as David Berkowitz and Jeffrey Dahmer.[43] The extensive media coverage of the Bundy, Gacy, and Berkowitz cases has made these killers almost household names, but African Americans such as Watts, Johnson, and Travis are practically unknown.

Philip Jenkins[44] suggests that Black serial killers do not attain the notoriety of their White counterparts because the media tend to ignore them. For instance, two very similar cases occurred in Philadelphia in the mid-1980s, one involving a White killer and the other a Black killer. Both men kidnapped and imprisoned women and shackled them in their basements, where they tortured and killed them. Gary Heidrick, the White killer, received widespread national attention and became the subject of books and television shows, while African American Harrison Graham received virtually no media attention, despite having been convicted of seven murders, four more than Heidrick.[45]

Jenkins also claims that until relatively recently, law enforcement agencies have been less likely to take Black crimes seriously unless the victims were White. Given this relative lack of interest, Jenkins is of the opinion that Black serial killers may be more "hidden" and thus more prevalent than the record indicates, especially during earlier periods of the century, when the police paid little attention to Black-on-Black crime.[46] The notorious White serial killer Albert Fish preyed exclusively on Black children during the early part of the 20th century and was not caught until he crossed the race line and killed a White child. Black serial killers operating exclusively in the Black community may have likewise escaped notice by the police and thus are not known to us today.[47]

Curiously, the only *known* Asian American serial killer operating in the United States during the 20th century is Charles Ng. Ng and his White partner, Leonard Lake, tortured and killed at least 19 people in the early 1980s. Lake was arrested in 1984, but Ng fled to Canada, where he was arrested for shoplifting in 1985. Legal maneuvers delayed Ng's extradition to the United States until 1991, and further maneuvers led to the longest and most expensive criminal trial in California's history. Ng was sentenced to death in 1999.[48] If there have been other

Asian American serial killers and if, like African Americans, they confined their crimes to their own communities, they also may have been shielded from exposure by lower levels of public and police concern for non-White victims characteristic of earlier times.

There have, of course, been Asians who have committed serial killing in their own countries; Hickey[49] lists 82 operating in Japan since 1880. One of the most brutal Asian killers was Li Wenxian, China's Jack the Ripper. As with the legendary Jack, Wenxian preyed on prostitutes, sexually assaulting, killing, and mutilating them. Unlike Jack, Wenxian left one of his victims alive, and she was able to identify him. He was charged and found guilty of 13 murders and was executed in 1996.[50] Yoshio Kodaira (11 female victims) and Raman Raghave (41 male, female, and child victims) are examples from Japan and India, respectively.[51] There are almost certainly many others that have not come to the attention of the Western press.

Female Serial Killers

In 1991, Aileen Wuornos was arrested and charged with the shooting deaths of seven males whom had she had picked up while working as a prostitute. She became an instant hero in some radical feminist and lesbian circles, where she is viewed as a sacrificial lamb, condemned to die by a patriarchal society for defending herself against brutal male johns.[52] The FBI and the media dubbed Wuornos "America's first woman serial killer" because she fit the definition of a "true" serial killer as a person who kills for no rational motive.[53]

However, Wuornos was by no means the first female serial killer. Indeed, nursing home proprietor Amy Archer-Gilligan may have murdered up to 100 patients in her charge (including 5 whom she married) between 1907 and 1914 and may be among the most prolific serial killers in American history.[54] Archer-Gilligan killed for strictly instrumental reasons. She induced her clients to pay her $1,000 up front to provide them with lifetime care and then made sure that her obligation was quickly met by cutting short their lives. The key distinction between male and female serial killers may thus be that "there are no female counterparts to a Bundy or a Gacy, to whom sex or sexual violence is a part of the murder pattern."[55] For example, an in-depth study of 14 female serial killers[56] revealed that none of the 62 victims of these women had been tortured, sexually assaulted, or mutilated, and none had been victims of stalking. Poisoning accounted for most (57%) of the killings, followed by smothering (29%), firearms (11%; all by Wuornos), and "other" (3%). About half of the women had instrumental and the other half affective (emotional) goals such as "mercy" killings.

Hungarian princess Erzsebet Bathory, who lived between 1560 and 1614, is a notable exception to this generality. The bisexual Erzsebet's imagination for torture and killing rivaled any man's. She enjoyed biting chunks of flesh from her victims' faces and searing their vaginas with hot irons. Her servants kept her supplied with victims from among the peasantry for years, but her undoing was when she shifted from them to the daughters of the minor aristocracy. News of her behavior eventually reached the king, and she was arrested in 1610. She was charged with 80 counts of murder, but historical counts place the number of her victims anywhere from 300 to 650.[57] Two of her servant accomplices were executed, and Erzsebet was placed in solitary confinement for the remainder of her life.

Women serial killers such as Erzsebet are exceptions to the "rule" that females kill for instrumental reasons or from twisted notions of mercy. Thus, they do not fit the definition of predatory killers who seek out strangers and kill for the sake of killing.[58] This is what made the

Wuornos case so interesting: She did seek strangers (or, at least, she allowed herself to be sought), and she killed them without apparent motive. Sex was certainly not her motive; she was a lesbian who hated men.[59] Wournos also reversed the male killer/prostitute victim relationship, and her victims were straight males as opposed to the more vulnerable female, child, or gay victims of male serial killers.

A more contemporary example of a female killer who apparently killed for its own sake is that of ex-wrestler Juana Barraza. Dubbed the "old lady killer," Barraza was arrested in January 2006 while running away from the murder of an 82-year-old woman in Mexico City. A number of elderly women had been found strangled to death in Mexico City since the early 1990s by a person who witnesses described as a "mannish woman." Fingerprint evidence has linked Barraza to 10 killings and one attempt, although she may be responsible for up to 30 similar cases. Like many male serial killers, Barraza took "trophies" from her victims, although there is no hint of sexual activity involved.[60]

In other cases, females have killed random strangers without any apparent motive but at the instigation of male companions. Female "disciples" of Charles Manson such as Susan Atkins and Patricia Krenwinkle boasted to authorities about their part in the Tate (five victims) and LaBianca (two victims) murders in 1969. Another example is Carol Bundy, who helped her lover, Douglas Clark, decapitate and sexually assault at least six females and one male in the early 1980s.

Multiple Murder Overseas

Excluding acts of terrorism, mass or spree murder is relatively rare in developed countries outside the United States. Other countries have their "crazies" and their disgruntled, but strict gun control laws often deny them the tools that are practically essential to the commission of such acts. But mass and spree murder does occur overseas. Michael Ryan killed 14 people and wounded 16 before committing suicide in Hungerford, England, in 1987, and 16 were gunned down by Eric Borel in Toulon, France, in 1995. In March 1996, Thomas Hamilton gunned down 16 elementary schoolchildren and their teacher in Scotland before killing himself, and in May of the same year, Martin Bryant killed 35 and wounded 15 in Tasmania, Australia, before being captured by police.[61]

Strict gun controls may help to prevent some would-be mass or spree killers overseas, but they do not prevent serial killers, who prefer to use more "hands-on" weapons. The United States has more than its fair share of serial killers: Norris[62] claims that the United States has produced 75% of the world's known serial killers, and Michael Newton[63] indicates that the United States has accounted for 74% of the world's known serial killers in the 20th century. Note that we say *known* serial killers. Since the writers making this claim are Americans, it is reasonable to assume that they are in a better position to document American serial killers than foreign serial killers. It has been noted that foreign writers document larger numbers of serial killers in their own countries than do American writers.[64]

Some of these foreign killers are profiled in Table 12.1. The first two columns of the table list the killer's name, number of victims, and the apparent motive. The next column briefly describes the killer and his case. Note that the killers come from all walks of life and vary greatly in status. They include a marshal of France, a physician, an engineer, an ex-police officer, a law student, several "ordinary" workingmen, and a number of drifters. The next column indicates the country and time period in which the cases occurred, which dispels the notion that serial killing is largely a modern American phenomenon.

Table 12.1	Some Notorious Serial Killers in History		
Killer and Number of Victims	**Apparent Motive**	**Brief Description**	**Country and Period**
Gilles de Rais, 140–300	Hedonistic bloodlust; practice of black magic	Gilles de Rais was marshal of France and hero of the 100-year war with England. Mostly enjoyed killing young boys in his castle, where he would sodomize them before and after death. He was hanged and burned in 1440.[65]	France, 15th century
"Jack the Ripper," 5–6	Hedonistic bloodlust, probable cannibalism, self-aggrandizement	Preyed only on prostitutes. He enjoyed dismembering his victims and neatly laying the parts around the corpses. Made no attempts to hide his victims and enjoyed taunting the police. "Jack" may have felt himself to be on a mission to rid society of prostitutes. He was never found or identified.[66]	England, late 19th century
H. H. Holmes, 200+	Hedonism and sadism. Also killed for profit	A physician who made a fortune in the drugstore business. He owned a "torture castle" in which he rented rooms to unwary visitors. He often skinned his victims and experimented with their bodies. Killed many men, women, and children in various insurance scams. Police found the remains of more than 200 people in the burned ruins of Holmes's castle. He was hanged in 1896.[67]	United States, late 19th century
Pedro Alonzo Lopez, 300+	Hedonistic bloodlust	The "monster of the Andes" killed many young girls in Colombia, Ecuador, and Peru. Kicked out of his home at age 8 and repeatedly sodomized on the streets and in prison, Pedro took his hatred out on girls he considered "gentle, trusting, and innocent." Pedro, who was executed in 1983, was probably the deadliest serial killer in history.[68]	Ecuador, Peru, and Colombia, late 20th century
Henry Lee Lucas and Ottis Toole, 200+ (many doubt this claim)	Hedonistic bloodlust, sadism	A serial-killing tag team. Lucas killed his prostitute mother and raped her corpse. After release from prison in 1976, he teamed up with Toole (a transvestite who was psychotic and retarded) to begin a spree of killing across the country. Lucas was a sadist and necrophiliac, while Toole was more interested in cannibalism. Toole died in prison of cirrhosis of the liver in 1996; Lucas died of natural causes in prison. Both men were unemployed drifters.[69]	United States, late 20th century
Bruno Ludke, 85	Hedonistic bloodlust	Ludke, a laundry delivery man, began killing in 1927 at the age of 18. Arrested in 1936 for rape and castrated, he continued his deadly business until rearrested in 1944. He was used as a guinea pig in Nazi experiments before execution in the same year.[70]	Germany, early 20th century

(Continued)

Table 12.1	(Continued)		
Andrei Chikatilo, 50+	Hedonistic bloodlust, cannibalism	Chikatilo, a part-time school teacher and engineer, murdered women, boys, and girls between 1978 and 1990. A cannibal and sexual sadist, he found most of his victims in train and bus stations. He was executed in 1994.[71]	Russia, late 20th century
Anatoly Onoprienko, 50+	Visionary killer, also bloodlust and profit	Onoprienko, a forestry student and drifter, enjoyed wiping out entire families living in isolated areas during his murderous sprees, which lasted from 1989 to 1996. He claimed that "voices" made him kill, but he also often looted homes after killing the occupants. He was arrested in 1996.	Ukraine, late 20th century
John Wayne Gacy, 30+	Power control, sadism	Gacy was a building contractor, convicted child molester, and prominent member of Chicago's "do-gooder" crowd. When not volunteering to entertain kids in hospital with his clown act, Gacy was searching for young males to rape, beat, and torture to death. When police finally searched his home, they found 30 bodies decomposing in his crawlspace. Gacy was executed in 1994.[72]	United States, late 20th century
Dean Corll, 27	Hedonistic bloodlust	Corll, a.k.a. "The Candyman," would invite young males into his home to take drugs and have sex. Boys who became incapacitated found themselves chained to the wall, where they remained until death. Corll would abuse them for days and would end it all by biting off the boys' penises. Corll was shot dead by Elmer Henly, a teenager who worked to procure new victims for him.[73]	United States, late 20th century
Jeffrey Dahmer, 17	Power control, cannibalism	Dahmer searched gay bars for his victims. He would lure them to his apartment, where he would often drug and kill them. He enjoyed having sex with their corpses (using condoms) more than with their live bodies. He would keep bodies for days before cutting them up, preserving some of the parts for food.[74]	United States, late 20th century
Albert Fish, 15+	Sadomasochism, cannibalism	Fish, a house painter, enjoyed torturing children of both sexes and hearing them scream. He would sometimes make and eat a stew of their remains and at least once sent the recipe to a victim's parents. He also enjoyed pain himself; driving needles into his scrotum and stuffing alcohol-soaked cotton balls up his rectum and lighting them. He supposedly looked forward to his execution in 1936 with great excitement.[75]	United States, early 20th century

Ted Bundy, 22+	Power control	Bundy was a handsome, intelligent, and charming ex-law student and hotline counselor who liked to abduct and kill pretty young college girls. Bundy liked to have sex with their corpses because he could exert complete control over them. He was executed in 1989.[76]	United States, late 20th century
Alexander Specsivtsev, 26	Hedonistic cannibalism	When police raided Specsivtsev's apartment in 1997 in response to a neighbor's complaints of odors, they found an inventory of cooked and uncooked human body parts. His 57-year-old mother lived in the same apartment and helped him to dress and cook the parts. He was arrested, but his fate was unknown at the time of writing.[77]	Russia, late 20th century
Dennis Nilsen, 15 bodies found in his flat. May have been others.	Power control	Britain's Jeffrey Dahmer. Nilsen, an ex-London police officer, murdered homosexuals and drifters after having sex with them. Like Dahmer, Nilsen enjoyed having sex with their corpses and washing and grooming them. He disposed of his victims by cutting them up and shoving them into the plumbing system, which was his undoing. He received 25 years to life on six counts of murder.[78]	England, late 20th century.
Fritz Haarmann, 27+	Hedonistic/ power control	A lover and killer of young boys who stalked railway stations for victims. After he had killed and sodomized his victims, he would sell their clothes and their flesh (suitably disguised as beef) for profit. He was caught when the police traced a coat belonging to a missing boy to him. Haarmann boasted of killing 40 young men. He was beheaded in 1925.[79]	Germany, early 20th century
Yang Zhiya, 65+	Hedonistic/ bloodlust	China's most prolific killer, he was arrested and charged with the murder of 65 people and the rape of 23 others in 2003 on a 3-year rampage. He came from the poorest of parents in a poor village in rural China, ran away from home at age 17, and served time in prison for a variety of offenses. He claimed that his motive for killing was that he "desperately wanted to retaliate against society." Society "retaliated" against him in December 2003 by executing him.[80]	China, early 21st century
Ahnad Suradi, 40+	Visionary	Self-styled sorcerer who claimed that his father appeared to him in a dream commanding him to kill 70 women in magic rituals to increase his occult power. His initial victims were women who came to him to purchase love charms and other potions, but he later turned to prostitutes. Police unearthed 40 corpses on his property (80 local families had reported young women missing during the time Suradi was on his rampage). He was convicted and sentenced to death in 1998.	Indonesia, late 20th century

FOCUS ON . . .

Recent Long-Term Serial Killers:
The Green River and BTK Killers

One of the secrets of serial killers who remain at large for long periods of time (two or more decades) is the extraordinary ordinariness of their appearance and the behavior they present to almost everyone except their victims. Gary Ridgway (the Green River Killer) in the Seattle, Washington, area and Dennis Rader (the **B**ind, **T**orture, **K**ill killer) in the Wichita, Kansas, area are the two most recent examples. Unlike the typical violent street criminal, both were married with children, held respectable jobs, and were reliable employees, and both were even fervent church members.

Ridgway first spilled blood when he stabbed and severely wounded a 6-year-old boy in 1965 when he was only 16 because "I always wanted to know what it was like to kill somebody." Although he was identified as the attacker, he was never prosecuted. His first known killing occurred in 1982, when the body of a 16-year-old girl was found in a field, and his last known killing in 1998. Ridgway had been a suspect in the so-called Green River murders almost from the start, but inconclusive physical evidence and the fact that he passed a polygraph test prevented his prosecution. Detectives secured a saliva sample from Ridgway in 1987, but DNA identification testing was underdeveloped at that time and nothing came of it, and the investigatory task force slowly disbanded.

After the lead detective on the Green River Task Force, Dave Reichart, was elected sheriff of King County in 1997, he jump-started the case again. In 2001, DNA evidence secured in 1987 positively linked Ridgway to a number of the murders, and he was arrested. He subsequently pled guilty in 2003 to 48 murders (almost all prostitutes) for which he received 48 life sentences. This is the largest count of verified murders of any known American serial killer, and detectives suspect that he may have been responsible for more.

Dennis Rader's first known killings (a man, woman, and two of their children) occurred in 1974 when he was 29 years old; his last known killing was in 1991, although he may be responsible for others. Unlike Ridgway's focus on prostitutes, Rader went trolling for any potential female victim, describing them as his "projects." Like Ridgway, his favorite method of killing was strangulation. He would strangle his victims into unconsciousness, revive them, and repeat the experience until they died. Where Ridgway avoided any kind of police or media attention, Rader craved it, often leaving notes and contacting the media to taunt the police (it was even he who suggested he be called the BTK killer). This craving for publicity was his undoing. When a book about the BTK killer was to be released in 2004, Rader wanted the opportunity to tell his story his way. He sent a floppy disk to a TV station in Wichita, which was turned over to the police, who soon determined that the disk had been used by the Christ Lutheran Church by "Dennis." Rader was arrested and in 2005 pled guilty to 10 counts of murder for which he received 10 life sentences.

We have noted that both killers were churchgoers. Rader was president of the Congregational Council of his church and a former Cub Scout leader. Ridgway was a religious fanatic who constantly tried to convert others and was often seen crying after sermons or a Bible reading. Both were also fascinated by police work; Rader had a degree in criminal justice, and Ridgway unsuccessfully attempted to join the police.

The biggest difference between them appears to have been their sexual appetites. Ridgway's three wives and several girlfriends report that he was sexually insatiable, and all his victims had been raped. Rader, on the other hand, never raped his victims; his greatest pleasure apparently was watching them suffer, although he would masturbate on their bodies after death. Perhaps the greatest pleasure for this publicity-hungry killer was to learn that his exploits, featured in the TV movie *The Hunt for the BTK Killer*, aired in October 2005, had 9 million viewers.

SOURCES: Multiple Internet, newspaper, and magazine sources.

✎ Theories About the Causes of Serial Killing

Serial killing is not the result of any single "cause" but of several risk factors interacting in various ways, and becoming a serial killer is a long drawn-out process, not a discrete event. Any one factor or combination of factors can facilitate or expedite the onset of killing for some killers but may have little or no effect on others. You should keep in mind that when theorists attempt to explain something as bizarre as serial killing, they are offering very broad and speculative generalities and should be read with a healthy dose of skepticism.

Elliot Leyton[81] attempted to apply anomie theory to explain serial killing across the centuries. He proposed that different social classes dominate the ranks of serial killers in different historical periods because the classes are differentially exposed to high aspirations and to barriers in different historical periods. According to Leyton, in the earliest periods, only the aristocracy could aspire to greater status, and thus only they would be susceptible to the pains of anomie. In later periods, the middle classes had realistic opportunities to advance their social position and came to feel the bite of foiled aspirations.

However, the earliest documented serial killers, such as Gilles de Rais and Erzsebet Bathory, were members of the high aristocracy who did not have the possibility of advancing without royal blood, and many known serial killers in the 19th century, such as H. H. Holmes (a physician), were solid members of the bourgeoisie. Twentieth-century serial killers were drawn overwhelmingly from the ranks of ordinary men (and a few women), but then, the vast majority of participants in almost any enterprise are ordinary men and women. Leyton is certainly correct about the 20th century, but most of the few known serial killers from the 19th century were decidedly "proletarian," and we have too little information prior to that time to make any statement about the social class from which most serial killers came.

Other authors invoke certain aspects of family and developmental theories to explain the phenomenon. Because of the relative rarity of serial murder, it is especially important to differentiate between efforts to explain the prevalence (the increase or decrease in the proportion of the population engaging in the behavior) of serial murder and efforts to explain why those who commit it do so. This section examines some social, psychological, and biological explanations that have been offered by various theorists.

Social Change and Serial Killers

Significant changes in the prevalence of any behavior always require that explanations be couched in terms of sociocultural factors. The dramatic increase in the number of serial killers in the last half of the 20th century points to some very important social changes. The change in the age distribution during the period (a greater percentage of young people) cannot account for the increase in the rate of serial killing for two important reasons. First, conventional homicides during the period only doubled, but serial killing rose about five times faster.[82] Second, while the age of those arrested for conventional murder peaks in the early 20s, most serial killers begin killing in their mid to late 20s.[83]

It has been suggested that the disinhibited counterculture that arose during the 1960s and 1970s had something to do with the increased prevalence.[84] These decades were tumultuous years in which many traditional values were questioned and rejected. The countercultural ethos, despite its rhetoric of flower power and peace, was essentially an ethos of personal satisfaction ("Do your own thing") and not feeling bad about it ("Don't get hung up on guilt"). Following that period, many more people crossed the line to engage in a variety of aberrant behaviors because of what has been called society's "War against Guilt."[85] The ethos of personal satisfaction can be liberating, but taken to extremes, it can produce the worst kind of monsters. The late 1960s also saw an explosion of pornography, some of which depicted scenes of bondage, torture, and violent rape, which may have fed and shaped the sexual fantasies of some people, a proportion of whom subsequently acted them out in the name of personal satisfaction.[86]

The 1960s also marked the beginning of the decarceration movement in the mental health system. If psychiatric hospitals had housed the same proportion of the population in 1997 that they did in 1955, they would have had more than 900,000 patients rather than the 70,000 that they actually had.[87] A number of men who became "celebrated" serial killers incarcerated under the old sexual psychopath laws were released from custody, some despite the warnings of the killers themselves that they would kill if released. For example, Henry Lee Lucas, after serving 9 years for killing his mother, warned prison officials that if they let him out, he would leave them "a present on the doorstep." He did just that, leaving a young female victim dead within walking distance of the prison gates on the day of his release.[88] Many other individuals arrested early in their criminal careers, who would have been firmly locked away on compulsory commitment orders prior to the 1960s, were released to prey on the public.

Family and Developmental Factors

Whatever the social factors accounting for the increased prevalence of serial killing may be, only an infinitesimally small number of people experiencing them ever kill once, let alone become serial killers, indicating that the developmental histories of those who do should be explored. Researchers appear to be unanimous about one factor: An extreme level of maternal deprivation almost uniformly characterized the childhood experiences of serial killers. Most serial killers are children born illegitimately and/or adopted, institutionalized, or reared by mothers married three or more times[89] and may experience these things "as the ultimate form of rejection."[90] Others contend that the great majority of serial killers experienced early separation from their mothers or were "otherwise deprived of the mother's direct emotional involvement"[91] and that "the serial killer's childhood is marked by a lack of nurturing and love."[92] A Russian psychiatrist pointed out that the breakdown of the family also provides would-be serial killers with large numbers of rootless potential victims.[93] The neglect, abuse, and social isolation experienced by many serial killers in their early years leave them angry and unable to relate to others in conventional ways. After reviewing the case histories of a number of such killers, one researcher concluded, "And so insecure social bonds prevent a capacity for love and affection from being channeled into stable relationships, and the resentment lies dormant, like a volcano, waiting to be detonated into violence."[94]

Cognitive Factors

Demographic profiles, while useful, are certainly not the whole story. About one fourth of American children were born out of wedlock in 1990,[95] and while many of them may suffer greater deprivation than children born in wedlock, only a tiny handful of this multitude become serial killers. Likewise, many abused and deprived children grow up relatively healthy, which means we must explore the peculiar psychology of serial killers. Two cognitive factors commonly imputed to serial killers, especially hedonistic killers, are strong feelings of sexual inadequacy and a rich fantasy life.

Edmund Kemper's necrophilia was supposedly tied to his concerns about his small penis.[96] Henry Lucas stated that he had to kill to gain sexual release because he was impotent with a live person,[97] and Andrei Chikatilo (see Table 12.1) suffered from extreme premature ejaculation, frequently ejaculating without even attaining an erection when sexually excited.[98] With sexuality being such a central part of human life, extreme sexual dysfunction may result in deeply embedded feelings of worthlessness and powerlessness, the seeds of which may have already been implanted by childhood abuse and neglect. Serial killers may be trying to counteract these feelings by controlling, manipulating, punishing, and destroying vulnerable members of the sex (i.e., women) whom they may see as the cause of their feelings.

A study of 36 serial murderers revealed a pattern of longstanding preoccupation with fantasies devoted to sexualized violence.[99] It is often noted that children reared in abusive homes retreat into a private fantasy world where they can escape their fears and exert control, thus gaining in their minds that which is unavailable in reality.[100] Fantasies often reflect the violence children experience in their lives and, if combined with the compulsive masturbatory behavior also characteristic of serial killers, may become firmly ingrained in the killers' minds, thus fusing sexual pleasure and violence. It has been reported that some serial killers enter a semi-hypnotic state while fantasizing, which eventually leads to a "divided self," with one part being relatively normal and the other totally preoccupied with acting out the fantasy.[101] As Fox and Levin put it, "Serial killers have incredibly rich, vivid, detailed, elaborate fantasies. Through murder and mayhem, they literally chase their dreams."[102] Partly because of their isolated fantasy lives, serial killers rarely develop caring relationships with others, making it easier to view their victims simply as "things" to be used for self-gratification.

Biological Factors

Millions of men feel sexually inadequate, and millions more enjoy rich fantasy lives (including fantasies of violent sexuality) without becoming serial killers. Perhaps the sexually inadequate fantasizers who become serial killers differ in some biological ways from those who do not. Because it is not standard procedure to do biological assessments of serial killers, we know relatively little about them in this area. Among those who have received neurological assessment via magnetic resonance imaging (MRI) or positron emission tomography (PET) scan tests, a large percentage have been found to have significant damage to the frontal lobes of the brain.[103] Damage to this part of the brain can seriously undermine the person's ability to control primitive violent impulses, as well as disrupt appropriate emotional responses to all sorts of environmental stimuli.[104]

Some studies reviewed by Norris[105] led him to hypothesize that the biological component may be explained by a combination of genetic factors and abnormal fetal development of the brain and autonomic nervous system (ANS). This could be caused by maternal alcohol and/or drug abuse, along with the secretion of stress hormones resulting from protracted abuse and neglect. The abnormal development of the brain and ANS may result in individuals who require higher levels of stimulation for sexual satisfaction. A subset of these individuals may be so suboptimally aroused that only the dangers and sexual depravity of sadistic serial murder provide sufficient stimulation to "turn them on."[106] Much more study is needed

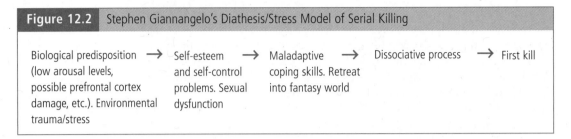

Figure 12.2   Stephen Giannangelo's Diathesis/Stress Model of Serial Killing

Biological predisposition → Self-esteem → Maladaptive → Dissociative process → First kill
(low arousal levels, and self-control coping skills. Retreat
possible prefrontal cortex problems. Sexual into fantasy world
damage, etc.). Environmental dysfunction
trauma/stress

before we can make more definitive statements about the biological profiles of serial killers, however.

An Integrated Theory

One theory that has attempted to integrate all levels of analysis to explain serial murder is the *diathesis/stress* model of Stephen Giannangelo,[107] who formulated it from in-depth case studies of serial killers on whom we have the most information (see Figure 12.2). Giannangelo believes that all serial killers have a congenital susceptibility to behave and think in ways that lead to serial killing, if combined with environmental stressors and traumas in terms of gene-environment correlation and gene-environment interaction. This combination may lead to the development of self-esteem and self-control problems and sexual dysfunction, all of which feed back upon one another. These problems lead to the development of maladaptive social skills, which may move the person to retreat into his private pornographic fantasy world. As he dwells longer and longer in this world, he enters a dissociative process (the "divided self") in which he takes his fantasies to their moral limits. At this point, the killer seeks out victims to act out his fantasies, but the actual kill never lives up to his expectations or to the thrill of the hunt, so the whole process is repeated and becomes obsessive-compulsive and ritualistic.

✑ Law Enforcement's Response to Serial Killing

Offender Profiling

Law enforcement agencies have responded to the challenge presented by serial killers in a variety of ways. The most publicized response (particularly by the movie *Silence of the Lambs*) was the establishment of the FBI's Behavioral Science Unit (BSU) in the early 1970s at Quantico, Virginia. The BSU, now called the Investigative Support Unit (ISU), is part of the National Center for the Analysis of Violent Crime (NCAVC). The ISU has developed methods of **profiling** serial killers and other violent offenders through extensive interviewing and formal psychological testing of incarcerated killers to develop a typology (the classification of offenders into different types) based on personality and other offender characteristics. Profiles are meant to narrow the range of suspects rather than to pinpoint a particular suspect.

Crime Scene Analysis

Offender profiling is augmented by crime scene analysis, which often tells experienced investigators a lot about the perpetrator's personality. Crime scene analysis involves reconstructing the sequence of events preceding, during, and after the murder. Reconstructing the events preceding the murder based on the evidence available helps investigators answer many questions, including the following:

- Was the victim carefully targeted (a specific type of victim taken in a specific manner)?
- What was the element of risk involved for the offender in selecting this victim (was she or he abducted from a public place or some more secluded place; did she or he struggle)?
- Was the crime planned (as evidenced by the presence of ropes, tape, etc., or was it apparently the result of an unexpected opportunity)?
- Does the state of the corpse (tortured, mutilated) indicate that the offender is playing out violent sexual fantasies? Is the body crudely sexually displayed for "shock" effect?
- Has the crime scene been staged to confuse the police, or is the offender an "amateur"?
- If it is reliably established that the crime was committed by a serial killer, are there indications that he is escalating (shorter time between crimes, more mutilation of the body, crime better planned), or is he getting sloppier as he seeks more frequent victims for his escalating need for gratification?

Many other clues taken from a crime scene, when combined with ISU profiles, can provide investigators with a fairly accurate picture of the kind of person they are looking for. However, profiles can be so far off the mark sometimes that they hinder rather than help. Starting with the reasonable assumption that they are looking for a White male—the "typical" serial killer—police tend to overlook females and non-White males.

The Linkage Blindness Problem

Consisting of more than 20,000 different federal, state, county, and municipal agencies, American policing is extremely decentralized and fragmented.[108] This level of decentralization often causes problems in the investigation of crimes committed in several different jurisdictions, which is sometimes the case with serial killers. Many serial murders may occur in diverse police jurisdictions, without law enforcement being able to note the connections between them. While most serial killers operate very close to home, approximately 33% are "travelers" operating in multiple jurisdictions.[109] The problem of making connections between murders committed in various jurisdictions has been termed **linkage blindness**. In response to this problem, in 1985, the FBI created the Violent Criminal Apprehension Program (VICAP), which was a national clearinghouse that collated information on unsolved violent crimes from different jurisdictions. VICAP, which is now defunct, was a computerized system that analyzes modus operandi (MOs), physical evidence, victim characteristics, crime scene analyses, suspect descriptions, and so on from crime reports submitted by police agencies from all over the United States to see if similarities exist.

The NCAVC and ISU continue to aid local investigators, but the biggest problem these programs face is similar to that faced by the National Incident-Based Reporting System (NIBRS) program—that is, the reluctance of cash-strapped police departments to provide the resources

The First Serial Killer Profile: Jack the Ripper

The following profile is claimed to be the first systematic and "scientific" profile of a serial killer. It was done in 1888 by a London physician named Thomas Bond in response to a police request to profile the person who was to become known as Jack the Ripper. Jack was never caught, and thus the accuracy of this profile cannot be assessed.

The murderer must have been a man of physical strength and great coolness and daring. There is no evidence that he had an accomplice. He must in my opinion be a man subject to periodic attacks of homicidal and erotic mania. The character of the mutilations indicated that the man may be in a condition sexually, that may be called Satyriasis [excessive sexual craving]. It is of course possible that the Homicidal impulse may have developed from a revengeful or brooding condition of mind, or that religious mania may have been the original disease, although I do not think either hypothesis is likely. The murderer in external appearance is quite likely to be a quite inoffensive looking man, probably middle-aged and neatly and respectably dressed. I think he might be in the habit a cloak or overcoat or he could have hardly escaped notice in the streets if the blood on his hands or clothes were visible.

Assuming the murderer be such a person as I have described, he would be solitary and eccentric in his habits, also he is likely to be a man without regular occupation, but with some small income or pension. He is possibly living among respectable persons who have some knowledge of his character and habits and who may have grounds for suspicion that he is not quite right in his mind at times. Such persons would probably be unwilling to communicate suspicions to the police for fear of trouble or notoriety, whereas if there were prospect of reward it might overcome their scruples.

SOURCE: Canter, D. (2004). Offender profiling and investigative psychology. *Journal of Investigative Psychology and Offender Profiling, 1,* 1–15. (Quote on p. 2)

required for collecting and reporting the extensive and complicated information on homicides requested by these programs.[110] Nevertheless, the implementation of VICAP and its successors probably accounts for a fair portion of the large increase in known serial killers noted from 1975 on compared to previous periods. Law enforcement authorities now have the ability to link a number of homicides committed in different jurisdictions to a single individual or individuals. Before computerized systems, these homicides may have been considered separate homicides committed by several different killers because of the linkage blindness problem.

SUMMARY

Spree, mass, and serial murders are irrational murders. All types have increased dramatically since the 1960s, especially serial murders, but not so dramatically as popular accounts sometimes claim. Serial murder is the murder of four or more victims over an extended period of time. A popular typology of serial killers contains visionary, mission-oriented, hedonistic, and power/control types. Visionary killers are usually psychotic, and mission-oriented killers feel that it is their duty to rid the world of people they consider undesirable. Hedonistic killers (the most common) kill for the pure joy of it, while power/control killers get more satisfaction from exerting complete control over their victims.

African Americans are slightly overrepresented in the ranks of serial killers relative to their numbers in the population. It is thought that Black serial killers are not subjected to the same scrutiny as their White counterparts because stories featuring Black characters are not likely to have wide media appeal, because the language often used to describe serial killers would be considered racist if applied to Blacks, and because there has been traditionally less police concern for Black victims.

Females are even more underrepresented among serial killers than they are among other kinds of criminals. There have been a number of women who have killed multiple times, but they have not been considered serial killers because at the core of the definition of *serial killer* is the idea of the motiveless bloodlust killing of strangers. Female killers usually have instrumental reasons for killing and usually kill someone known to them. If we define serial killing as motiveless (noninstrumental), then only Aileen Wournos fits the definition in modern times.

In trying to explain the phenomenon of serial killing, we have to explain both why the rate has increased and why those who commit it do so. Numerous social changes since the 1960s, such as the rejection of traditional morality, the mass marketing of pornography, and the decarceration movement, have been used to explain the increased prevalence of serial killing. In terms of explaining why individuals become serial killers, the one area of agreement among researchers is that such people have suffered a high degree of emotional deprivation and abuse.

Two factors commonly imputed to serial killers are strong feelings of sexual inadequacy and a rich fantasy life. These people project the blame for their sexual inadequacies onto women and fantasize about "getting even." Their fantasies are often combined with compulsive masturbation, a combination that may lead to the cognitive fusion of sex and violence, the epitome of which is the sadistic bloodlust of the serial killer.

Among the posited biological causes of such behavior is damage to certain areas of the brain, which results in difficulties controlling impulses. Some studies have shown that serial killers have hyporeactive ANSs, suggesting that only the most depraved and sadistic acts provide sufficient emotional stimulation to turn them on.

An integrated theory of serial killing (the diathesis/stress model) posits that serial killers have a biological disposition to kill, which is exacerbated by severe environmental stress during childhood. These people develop self-esteem and self-control problems as well as sexual dysfunctions, which result in maladaptive coping skills and a retreat into a fantasy world that feeds their desire to kill.

Offender profiling, crime scene analysis, and the computerized data programs have provided law enforcement with powerful tools in combating serial murder. The ability to address the linkage blindness problem probably accounts for a good part of the increase in known serial killers after such programs were implemented.

On Your Own

Log on to the web-based student study site at http://www.sagepub.com/criminologystudy for more information about the vignettes and materials presented in this chapter, suggestions for activities, study aids such as review quizzes, and research recommendations including journal article links and questions related to this chapter.

EXERCISES AND DISCUSSION QUESTIONS

1. Examine the traits and characteristics associated with psychopathy found in Chapter 10 and write a paragraph or two indicating how these same factors might be useful to serial killers.

2. Look up a story on the Internet or a newsmagazine such as *Time* or *Newsweek* on any school shooting incident committed by schoolchildren. Can you find any commonalities among all the cases in terms of the kind of kids that commit these crimes?

3. What is your explanation for why females are not represented among serial killers who kill for the joy of killing and who enjoy sexual bloodlust.

4. Which theory of criminal behavior presented in this book do you think best explains the serial killer phenomenon?

5. Mass and spree murderers almost by necessity need guns to carry out their activities. Would a ban on private ownership of weapons be an acceptable price to pay to save the lives of victims of these acts (as well as other victims of guns)?

6. Go to http://www.crimelibrary.com and click on serial killers. Write a two-page paper on any foreign serial killer not listed in this chapter. Include his number of kills and length of time operating before his capture.

KEY WORDS

Hedonistic serial killer
Linkage blindness
Mass murder

Mission-oriented serial killer
Power/control serial killer
Profiling

Serial murder
Spree murder
Visionary serial killer

REFERENCES

1. Leyton, E. (1986). *Hunting humans: Inside the minds of mass murderers.* New York: Pocket Books. (Quote on p. 42)

2. Keeney, B., & Heide, K. (1995). Serial murder: A more accurate and inclusive definition. *International Journal of Offender Therapy and Comparative Criminology, 39,* 299–306.

3. Jenkins, P. (1988). Serial murder in England 1940–1985. *Journal of Criminal Justice, 16,* 1–15.

4. Palermo, G. (1997). The berserk syndrome: A review of mass murder. *Aggression and Violent Behavior, 2,* 1–8.

5. Petee, T., Padgett, K., & York, T. (1997). Debunking the stereotypes: An examination of mass murder in public places. *Homicide Studies, 1,* 317–337.

6. Fox, J., & Levin, J. (2001). *The will to kill: Making sense of senseless murder.* Boston: Allyn & Bacon.

7. Lester, D. (1995). *Serial killers: The insatiable passion.* Philadelphia: The Charles Press.

8. Fox and Levin (2000).

9. Schmalleger, F. (2004). *Criminal justice: A brief introduction.* Upper Saddle River, NJ: Prentice Hall.

10. Leyton (1986).

11. Egger, S. (1998). *The killers among us: An examination of serial murder and its investigation.* Upper Saddle River, NJ: Prentice Hall.

12. Hurd, M. (2003). *The psychology of junior sniper Lee Malvo.* Retrieved from http://www.capmag.com

13. Leyton (1986).

14. Heise, J. (1990). We've captured the most dangerous serial killers! In A. Crockett (Ed.), *Serial murderers* (pp. 34–39). New York: Pinnacle.

15. Holmes, R., & Holmes, S. (1992). Understanding mass murder: A starting point. *Federal Probation, 56,* 53–61.

16. Federal Bureau of Investigation (FBI). (2004). *Crime in the United States: Supplemental Homicide Reports 2003*. Washington, DC: Government Printing Office, 1999.

17. Douglas, J., Burgess, A., Burgess, A., & Ressler, R. (1992). *Crime classification manual*. San Francisco: Jossey-Bass.

18. Newton, M. (2000). *The encyclopedia of serial killers*. New York: Checkmark. (Quote on p. 210)

19. Keeney and Heide (1995).

20. Fox and Levin (2000).

21. Egger (1998).

22. Jenkins, P. (1994). *Using murder: The social construction of serial homicide*. New York: Aldine De Gruyter.

23. Hickey, E. (2006). *Serial murderers and their victims* (4th ed.). Belmont, CA: Wadsworth.

24. Canter, D., Coffey, T., Huntley, M., & Missen, C. (2000). Predicting serial killers' home base using a decision support system. *Journal of Quantitative Criminology, 16*, 457–478.

25. Holmes, R., & DeBurger, J. (1998). Profiles in terror: The serial murderer. In R. Holmes & A. Holmes (Eds.), *Contemporary perspectives on serial murder* (pp. 1–16). Thousand Oaks, CA: Sage.

26. Holmes and DeBurger (1998).

27. Lubinskas, J. (2001). Remembering the zebra killings. *Frontpage Magazine*. Retrieved from www.frontpagemag.com/guestcolunists/lubinskas

28. Howard, C. (1979). *Zebra: The true account of the 179 days of terror in San Francisco*. New York: Richard Marek.

29. Newton, M., & Newton, J. (1991). *Racial and religious violence in America: A chronology*. New York: Garland.

30. Ressler, R., Burgess, A., & Douglas, J. (1988). *Sexual homicide: Patterns and motives*. New York: Lexington.

31. Norris, J. (1988). *Serial killers*. New York: Doubleday.

32. Hickey, E. (1997). *Serial murderers and their victims* (2nd ed.). Belmont, CA: Wadsworth.

33. Fox and Levin (2000).

34. Walsh, A. (2005). African Americans and serial killing in the media: The myth and the reality. *Homicide Studies, 9*, 271–291.

35. Hickey (2006).

36. Jenkins, P. (1998). African Americans and serial homicide. In R. Holmes & S. Holmes (Eds.), *Contemporary perspectives on serial murder* (pp. 17–32). Thousand Oaks, CA: Sage.

37. Powell, P. (1996, December 18). Man who admits killing 9 women baffles experts. *Idaho Statesman*, p. 15a.

38. Gado, M. (2001). *The disappeared*. Online crime library. Retrieved from http://crimelibrary.com/serial/francoise/2.httm

39. Emch, D. (2000, April 7). Black brothers admit to murdering eight Whites. *Toledo Blade*.

40. Shinkle, P. (2002, June 17). Serial killer caught by his own Internet footprint. *St. Louis Post-Dispatch*.

41. Billiot, T., & Sills, M. (2003). Serial killer Derrick Todd Lee caught in Atlanta. *The Lafayette Daily Advertiser, 28*, 1.

42. Lambe, J. (2004, May 22). Gilyard connection to suspect possible. *Kansas City Star*, p. A1.

43. Jenkins (1994).

44. Jenkins (1994).

45. Jenkins (1994).

46. Clarke, J. (1998). *The lineaments of wrath: Race, violent crime, and American culture*. New Brunswick, NJ: Transaction Publishers.

47. Warf, B., & Waddell, C. (2002). Heinous spaces, perfidious places: The sinister landscapes of serial killers. *Social and Cultural Geography, 3*, 323–345.

48. Newton (2000).

49. Hickey (2006).

50. Newton (2000).

51. Newton (2000).

52. Jenkins (1994).

53. Keeney and Heide (1995).

54. Newton (2000).

55. Segrave, K. (1992). *Women serial and mass murderers: A worldwide reference, 1580 through 1990*. Jefferson, NC: McFarland. (Quote on p. 5)

56. Keeney, B., & Heide, K. (1994). Gender differences in serial murderers: A preliminary analysis. *Journal of Interpersonal Violence, 9*, 383–398.

57. Newton (2000).

58. Keeney and Heide (1994).

59. Jenkins (1994).

60. Grillo, I. (2006). *Mexico City police detain murder suspect*. Retrieved from http://www.boston.com/news/world/latinamerica/articles/2006/01/25/mexico_city_police

61. Rufford, N. (1996, May 5). The misfit behind the massacre. *The Sunday Times*, p. 3C.

62. Norris (1988).

63. Newton, M. (1992). *Serial slaughter*. Port Washington, WA: Loompanics.

64. Lester (1995).

65. Wolf, L. (1980). *The life and crimes of Gilles de Rais*. New York: Potter.

66. Wilson, C. (1984). *A criminal history of mankind*. London: Panther.

67. Hickey (1997).

68. Hickey (1997).

69. Lester (1995).

70. Wilson (1984).

71. Hickey (1997).

72. Lester (1995).

73. Hickey (1997).

74. Lester (1995).

75. Wilson (1984).

76. Hickey (1997).

77. Saffron, I. (1997, February 2). Chance leads to capture in serial killer-cannibal case. *The Idaho Statesman*, p. 19a.

78. Egger (1998).

79. Wilson (1984).

80. People's Daily Online. (2004). Retrieved from http://English.peoplesdaily.com

81. Leyton (1986).

82. Jenkins, P. (1992). A murder 'wave'? Trends in American serial homicide 1940–1990. *Criminal Justice Review, 17,* 1–19.

83. Egger, S. (2004). Serial killers and their victims. In S. Holmes & R. Holmes (Eds.), *Violence: A contemporary reader* (pp. 159–181). Upper Saddle River, NJ: Prentice Hall.

84. Fox, J., & Leven, J. (2005). *Extreme killing: Understanding serial and mass murder.* Thousand Oaks, CA: Sage.

85. Fox and Levin (2005).

86. Sears, D. (1991). *To kill again: The motivation and development of serial murder.* Wilmington, DE: Scholarly Resources.

87. Torrey, E. (1997). The release of the mentally ill from institutions: A well-intentioned disaster. *Chronicle of Higher Education, 153,* B4–B5.

88. Norris (1988).

89. Leyton (1986).

90. Levin, J., & Fox, J. (1985). *Mass murder: America's growing menace.* New York: Plenum.

91. Norris (1988, p. 187).

92. Sears (1991, p. 79).

93. Saffron (1997).

94. Wilson (1984, p. 623).

95. Popenoe, D. (1993). American family decline, 1960–1990: A review and appraisal. *Journal of Marriage and the Family, 55,* 527–542.

96. Levin and Fox (1985).

97. Norris (1988).

98. Cullen, R. (1993). *The killer department.* New York: Pantheon.

99. Burgess, A., Hartman, C., Ressler, R., Douglas, J., & McCormack, A. (1986). Sexual homicide: A motivational model. *Journal of Interpersonal Violence, 1,* 251–272.

100. Carlisle, A. L. (1993). The divided self: Toward an understanding of the dark side of the serial killer. *American Journal of Criminal Justice, 17,* 23–26.

101. Carlisle (1993).

102. Fox and Levin (2005, p. 93).

103. Egger (1998).

104. Raine, A. (1997). Antisocial behavior and psychophysiology: A biosocial perspective and a prefrontal dysfunction hypothesis. In D. Stoff, J. Breiling, & J. Maser (Eds.), *Handbook of antisocial behavior* (pp. 289–304). New York: John Wiley.

105. Norris (1988).

106. Fishbein, D. (2003). Neuropsychological and emotional regulatory processes in antisocial behavior. In A. Walsh & L. Ellis (Eds.), *Biosocial criminology: Challenging environmentalism's supremacy* (pp. 185–208). Hauppauge, NY: Nova Science.

107. Giannangelo, S. (1996). *The psychopathology of serial murder: A theory of violence.* Westport, CT: Praeger.

108. LaGrange, R. (1993). *Policing American society.* Chicago: Nelson-Hall.

109. Hickey (2006).

110. Hickey (2006).

CHAPTER 13

TERRORISM AND TERRORISTS

O n the morning of September 11, 2001, Americans woke to horrifying images that are seared into their memories forever. Nineteen Islamic terrorists, led by Mohamed Atta, a shy 33-year-old son of a wealthy Egyptian lawyer, had hijacked four airliners and used them in coordinated attacks against the quintessential symbols of America's financial and military might. At 8:45 a.m., American Airlines Flight 11 with 92 people on board crashed into the north tower of the World Trade Center. Eighteen minutes later, as rescue workers dashed to the scene of the first impact, United Flight 175 with 64 people aboard smashed into the south tower. At 9:40, American Airlines Flight 77 carrying 64 people crashed into the Pentagon. Then at 10 a.m., United Flight 93 Carrying 45 people crashed into a Pennsylvania field, having been prevented from accomplishing its mission (apparently to destroy the Capitol building or the White House) by the courageous actions of its passengers. These actions cost the lives of close to 3,000 people from 78 different countries, making it the deadliest terrorist attack in history anywhere.[1] What were these people trying to accomplish by such a wanton act, and what drove them to sacrifice their own lives in the process? We hope to answer these questions in this chapter.

Although much less costly in lives and property damage, the killing of 340 and the wounding of at least another 700 by Islamic terrorists in Beslan, Russia, was perhaps more evil than the 9/11 attacks because the terrorists purposely targeted children. On September 3, 2004, about 30 terrorists took more than 1,000 adults and children hostage and held them tightly huddled together in a gymnasium for at least 2 days in sweltering heat, telling them that they (the terrorists) had come to die in the name of Allah and were going to take the hostages with them. They did not feed the children or allow them to use the bathrooms, and they shot and killed many of them trying to make their escapes. Some children died from dehydration or from unattended wounds, while others survived by drinking their own urine and eating flowers they had brought to school for their teachers.[2]

What kind of hatred, hostility, fanaticism, or cause could motivate individuals to board a plane or enter a school and look into the faces of innocent men, women, and children, knowing that they were to be the instruments of their deaths? And, in the case of the Beslan incident, mock and torture frightened little children? We may ask with talk show host David Letterman, speaking to a shocked nation after 9/11, "If you live to be a thousand years old . . . will that [the 9/11 attacks] make any goddamn sense?"[3]

Actions such as the mass destruction that took place on New York on September 11, 2001, and in Russia in 2004 lead us to suppose that terrorists are subhuman creatures and that terrorism is something peculiar to the modern age. Although your average terrorist will never win any humanitarian awards, and terrorism is far more prevalent and deadly today than ever before, those suppositions are incorrect.

Terrorism has a long history; it is "as old as the human discovery that people can be influenced by intimidation."[4] The term *terrorism* itself is believed to have originated with the French Revolutionary Jacobins, who instituted France's domestic Reign of Terror, killing more than 400,000 people in the process.[5] The earliest known terrorist group was a Jewish nationalist/religious group called the Sicarii. It operated against occupying Roman forces around 70 A.D., using deadly savage methods against Romans and Jews alike.[6] Another early group, the Ismailis or Assassins, responding to what they considered religious oppression, carried out a reign of intimidation throughout the Islamic world from about the 11th to the mid-13th centuries.[7] Many other terrorist groups have existed prior to modern times and have had rational motives rooted in history and politics that we must try to understand.

※ Terrorism Defined

Terrorism is like spree, mass, and serial murder rolled into one. Although revenge and hatred are usually integral to terrorist activity, the difference between it and other forms of multiple murder is that terrorism is highly organized and conducted primarily for political or religious reasons. It is estimated that up until 1995, antistate or nonstate terrorists cost the lives of 500,000 people in the 20th century,[8] with another 1,269 killed in the last 5 years of the century.[9] If we define terrorism as the murder of innocent civilians by organized killers for political or social purposes, antistate and nonstate terrorism pales in comparison with state terrorism. The former Soviet Union (62 million victims), the People's Republic of China (35 million), and Nazi Germany (21 million) stand as the bloodiest terrorist organizations in human history.[10] State-sanctioned terrorism, insidious as it may be, is not considered here. Terrorism, as we discuss it here, is the *criminal* (unsanctioned by the state) murder of innocent victims for political, religious, or social purposes. The definition of **terrorism** adopted by the FBI stresses its unlawfulness and antistate nature: "the unlawful use of force or violence against persons or property to intimidate or coerce a government, the civilian population, or any segment thereof, in furtherance of political or social goals."[11]

※ Why Terrorism?

Terrorism is a tactic used to influence the behavior of others through intimidation. The bombing of abortion clinics and the murder of those who work there, for example, are attempts by radical fringes of the pro-life movement to intimidate people who seek abortions or people who perform them. You may be horrified that some people feel it necessary to use bombs and bullets to change the minds and/or behavior of others who believe differently, but often those who resort to such tactics sincerely believe that they have no other choice and that their behavior is morally justifiable. They typically appeal to a higher moral "good," such as ethnic autonomy or some religious or political dogma to justify the killing of innocents. Some terrorist groups (e.g., the Irish Republican Army [IRA] and the Basque group ETA) embrace an ideological mixture of nationalism and Marxism, while others may invoke religious (almost exclusively Islamic) fundamentalism (e.g., the multinational al-Qaeda, Egypt's al Jihadi, or Lebanon's Hizballah). A set of moral and ideological justifications is provided to the individual terrorist by the terrorist group, which, because of its isolation from mainstream society, often becomes the sole source of comradeship, self-identity, and social support, as well as the sole definer of reality for its members.[12]

All terrorist groups see themselves and the people for whom they claim they are fighting as oppressed victims, which may have at least some truth to it, or as warriors of God seeking to free the world of the influence of religious and secular "infidels." But why strike at innocents, some of whom may be fellow "victims"? *They strike at innocents because the very essence of terrorism is public intimidation,* and the randomness of terrorist action accomplishes this better than targeting specific individuals would. Victims are incidental to the aims of terrorists; they are simply instruments in the objectives of (1) publicizing the terrorists' cause, (2) instilling in the general public a sense of personal vulnerability, and (3) provoking a government into unleashing repressive social control measures that may cost it public support.[13]

Osama bin Laden, the leader of al-Qaeda, made it clear that the latter is one of the goals of his organization. He told a reporter that in response to terrorist attacks, the U.S. government will have to restrict many of the civil liberties its citizens enjoy: "Freedom and human rights in America are doomed," he said, adding that the United States will lead people of the Western world "into an unbearable hell and a choking life."[14] President Vladimir Putin's decision to hand over sweeping new powers to the Kremlin in the wake of the Beslan attack is evidence that bin Laden may be right, for the decision has been criticized by former Russian president Boris Yeltsin as "the strangling of freedoms, the rollback of democratic rights—this can only mean that the terrorists have won."[15]

Thus, while terrorist violence may be evil and cruel, it is not "senseless" violence because it has an ultimate purpose. There is a logic to terrorism, by which evil means are justified by the ends terrorists seek. The terrorist attacks on trains in Madrid, Spain, on March 11, 2004 (exactly 911 days after 9/11 attacks in America), which took the lives of at least 200 people, led to the fall of a conservative government that supported the U.S. action in Iraq and the election of a socialist government 3 days later. The new government immediately announced that all Spanish troops would be pulled out of Iraq, which was evidently the purpose of the bombings. Every time terrorists gain an objective they have sought, the rationality of terrorism is demonstrated along with its immorality.

▧ Is There a Difference Between Terrorists and Freedom Fighters?

Do you accept the cliché that one person's terrorist is another's freedom fighter? Although many people do, this attitude has been called "sophomoric moral relativism."[16] Of course, not everyone agrees that we can draw a sharp line between terrorists and freedom fighters, and the label one chooses to affix to a group has as much to do with one's politics as anything else. After all, Drummond[17] points out that four individuals once defined as terrorists have actually been awarded Nobel Peace prizes (Sean McBride, Menachem Begin, Yasir Arafat, and Nelson Mandela), although Arafat, arguably the father of modern terrorism, continued to support terrorism until the day he died. All terrorists probably claim to be freedom fighters, but two important distinctions between terrorists and freedom fighters (or guerrillas) go beyond semantics, implying their moral equivalence. First, freedom fighters are fighters in wars of national liberation against foreign occupiers or against oppressive domestic regimes they seek to overthrow. Terrorists are typically fighting to gain some sort of ethnic autonomy, right some perceived inequity, or rid the world of some perceived evil, and they rarely have illusions of overthrowing the government they are fighting against. While guerrillas may occasionally use terrorist tactics against noncombatants, widespread use of such tactics will deprive them of the popular support they need, and thus they tend to confine their activities to fighting enemy combatants.[18]

The second important distinction is that guerrilla activity is typically confined to Third World dictatorships or one-party states, while terrorists operate mostly against liberal Western democracies. However, there are a number of Islamic terror groups operating against Islamic dictatorships such as Saudi Arabia. Because of the political contexts in which they operate, guerrillas may literally have no choice other than armed insurgence to accomplish change because they are outside the system that oppresses them. Terrorists, on the other hand, often have access to the system but spurn the ballot box in favor of the bomb. Of course, not all claims of injustice can be righted at the polling stations, and thus the distinctions we have made here may be overdrawn to some extent. They are real enough, however, to conclude that the moral conflation of *terrorist* and *freedom fighter* is probably not warranted.[19]

◀ **Photo 13.1** Is there a difference between terrorists and freedom fighters? The photo depicts a pro-Palestinian, anti-Israeli banner hung in Trafalgar Square, London. While most Westerners might consider Hamas and other Palestinian groups as terrorists, for many in the Middle Eastern world, their actions are seen as heroic.

⊠ The Extent of Terrorism

Although terrorism has ancient roots, it became far more prevalent, deadly, and destructive from the late 1960s onward. The instability experienced by many countries following World War II provided fertile soil for conflict, much like the instability and ethnic desires for autonomy that followed the breakup of the Soviet Union and Yugoslavia in the late 1980s to early 1990s. There was also a general air of discontent, protest, and alienation surrounding the 1960s as people demonstrated against the Vietnam War and for civil rights for African Americans, women, and gays. Although these protests originated in the United States, they soon spilled over into other democratic countries. The resurgence of the IRA, for instance, occurred after Catholic civil rights marchers were attacked by Protestant loyalists in 1969.

The 1960s was also the high point of conflict between the superpowers, with each having their zones of influence and with each supporting armed opposition within the other's zone. Terrorism is also much easier to accomplish than ever before. The Internet, e-mail, and cell phones give terrorists ready access to information and to each other, and economic globalization has led to open borders across which terrorists can easily flow. Modern transportation systems allow terrorists to slip in and out of areas of operation with speed and efficiency, and the same systems provide terrorists with lots of victims because they bring large numbers of people together in places such as airports and railroad stations. Modern technology also makes the terrorist's life less complicated in that it provides easily concealed and relatively cheap weapons and explosives of great destructive power. The downing of Pan American Flight 103 over Lockerbie, Scotland, in 1988 that killed 281 people was accomplished with a small amount of Semtex hidden in a cassette player. Even the enemy's technology can be turned against them. Before the advent of airplanes and the fuel to fly them, it would have taken a well-equipped army to topple structures such as the World Trade Center; certainly, 19 terrorists armed only with box cutters could not have accomplished it.

There is no better measure of the impact of modernity on the proliferation of terrorism than to note that of the 74 terrorist groups listed by the U.S. Department of State,[20] only 3 of the groups still active originated before 1960 (IRA, ETA, and the Muslim Brotherhood, an Egyptian group that has spawned other, more radical groups such as Gama' a al-Islamiya and Islamic Jihad). Terrorist incidents also rose dramatically after 1968—the year often credited with marking the advent of modern terrorism[21]—and have ebbed and flowed since then. U.S. State Department statistics, presented in Figure 13.1, show that the number of international terrorist incidents fluctuates from year to year and peaked at a high of 665 in 1987 and then dropped to a new low of 190 incidents in 2003.

Unfortunately, the Bush administration decided to eliminate the 19-year-old international terrorism report after the 2004 edition, raising disturbing charges that this was done because the 2004 statistics raised concerns about the Bush administration's frequent claims of success in the war on terrorism.[22] A separate source of information about terrorist activity—the National Counterterrorism Center (NCC)—reports a startling rise to 651 terrorist attacks in 2004 that claimed 1,907 victims.[23]

The number of incidents per se does not give an accurate picture of the damage wrought by terrorism. We are seeing fewer incidents as counterterrorism becomes more sophisticated, but those incidents that do occur today claim more victims than almost all previous terrorist attacks. In addition to the 9/11 attack, the Beslan school attack, and the Madrid train attacks already mentioned, the bomb attack in Bali, Indonesia, claimed more than 200 lives, and the

| Figure 13.1 | International Terrorist Attacks, 1982–2003 |

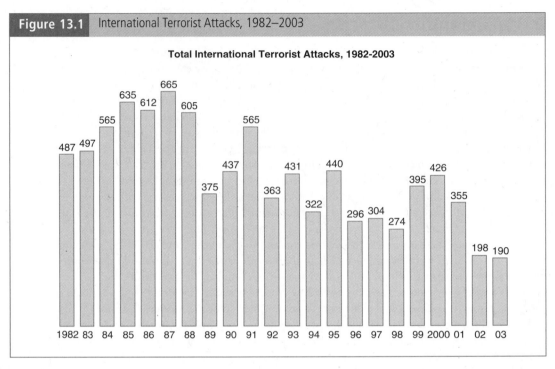

Total International Terrorist Attacks, 1982-2003

SOURCE: U.S. Department of State. (2004). *Patterns of global terrorism: 2003.* Washington, DC: Government Printing Office.

Moscow theater hostage situation, in which more than 100 people lost their lives, are 21st-century examples of mass casualties caused by determined terrorists. It is plain that just as counterterrorism is becoming more sophisticated, so is terrorism. The level of patience and planning that went into the 9/11 attacks, as well as the willingness of individual terrorists to sacrifice their own lives on a mission, does not bode well for preventing future mass killings. Counterterror operatives may thwart any number of planned attacks, but terrorists only have to outthink them once (or get lucky) and more innocent lives will be lost.

Although deaths and injuries caused by terrorists are matters of grave concern, the damage to society as a whole is more psychological than physical. The death, damage, and economic losses attributable to international terrorism are minuscule when compared to that attributable to traditional crime. To put the problem in perspective, compare the deaths *worldwide* attributable to international terrorism for the first 4 years of the 21st century to the number of homicides committed in the United States alone for those years.

⧉ Terrorism and Common Crime

Like any organization, terrorist organizations must be financed. Some funding for terrorist groups comes from governments sympathetic to their cause or hostile to the governments against which the terrorists operate. The U.S. government has designated Cuba, Iran, Iraq,

Table 13.1	International Terrorist Attacks, 1982–2003	
Year	**International Terrorism Deaths**	**Homicides in the United States**
2000	409	15,586
2001	3,547	16,037
2002	725	16,204
2003	307	16,503
2004	1,907	16,137

SOURCE: Terrorism figures for 2000–2003 from the U.S. Department of State. (2004). *Patterns of global terrorism: 2003.* Washington, DC: Government Printing Office. The 2004 figure is from the National Counterterrorism Center. Homicide figures are from the 2001 through 2005 *Uniform Crime Reports.*

Libya, Sudan, Syria, and North Korea as terrorist-sponsoring nations, with Iran the most active of them.[24] Libya renounced terrorism in 2004, and it remains to be seen what we can say of Iraq once the U.S. occupation is over. Some terrorist funding comes from private sympathizers, but most of it comes from common criminal activities such as drug trafficking, extortion, and bank robbery. As William Reid sees it, terrorists cloak "themselves in a 'crusade' that is more accurately viewed as criminal behavior. Even groups that preach against capitalism spend much of their energy raising money and using money from capitalist endeavors."[25] The IRA has raised vast sums of money by extorting "protection" money from the very people for whom they claim to be fighting. They have made so much money from this and other criminal activities that they have had to branch out into legitimate businesses and have launched money-laundering schemes.[26] Although political ideology remains an important binding link in the IRA, evidence suggests that many IRA groups now exist with the primary purpose of developing wealth for their members. Dishman calls the IRA "a prime example of a *mutated* terrorist group who invested significant energies into committing profit-driven criminal acts."[27]

Likewise, many Islamic groups obtain funding from nongovernmental organizations such as charity groups, from legitimate cover businesses, and from many kinds of criminal activities, particularly drug trafficking. Terrorist groups in South America, such as the Marxist/Maoist Shining Path of Peru, make enormous profits from drug trafficking, and European groups such as Germany's Red Army Faction and Italy's Red Brigades (both Marxist oriented and now supposedly defunct) financed their activities through bank robberies and kidnapping. The widespread involvement of terrorist groups in such pecuniary practices casts serious doubt on the ideological idealism they claim motivates their activities. The large amounts of money involved can corrupt the most dedicated ideologue in time, especially if fellow terrorists are lining their pockets. As Albanese and Pursley put it, "Gradually, the [criminal] activities become ends in themselves and terrorist groups begin to resemble ordinary criminal organizations hidden behind a thin political veneer."[28] This characterization is not true of groups motivated by Islamic fundamentalism because many members of these groups often give up more than they gain in material terms.

✄ Some Important Terrorist Groups

al-Qaeda

Very few Americans knew anything about **al-Qaeda** or its leader, Osama bin Laden, prior to the 9/11 attacks orchestrated by that group; now they are household names on par with Nazis and Adolph Hitler in a previous generation. al-Qaeda is not a single terrorist group but rather the base (*al-Qaeda* means "the base") organization for a number of Sunni Muslim terrorist groups. These groups include Jamaat Islamiyya and Islamic Jihad (Egypt), Lashkar-e-Taiba and Jaish-e-Muhammed (Kashmir), and various other groups from Uzbekistan, Algeria, Yemen, Malaysia, Philippines, and Libya. It also has cells operating in 100 countries in the world, including the United States.[29]

al-Qaeda got its start under Osama bin Laden in the late 1980s and expanded dramatically in the 1990s. Osama bin Laden, who had fought the Russians during their invasion of Afghanistan throughout the 1980s, objected to the stationing of non-Muslim troops in Saudi Arabia, the country containing the two most holy sites in Islam—Mecca and Medina—after the first Gulf War in 1991. Because of his objections, bin Laden was exiled from Saudi Arabia and went to live in Sudan, an Islamic dictatorship. It was in Sudan that bin Laden first built his worldwide terrorist network, financing much of it through his vast personal fortune, as well as through the drug trade and criminal activities in a variety of countries.[30]

After being ousted from Sudan, Osama and his henchmen moved to Afghanistan, where they found refuge and protection with the Taliban (a fanatical Islamic fundamentalist group) regime in power there. al-Qaeda set up terrorist training camps in Afghanistan from which terrorists were dispatched to wreak havoc around the world. Following the 9/11 attacks, President Bush demanded that the Taliban turn over bin Laden to U.S. authorities for trial. When the Taliban refused the demands, American and British forces, aided by Afghani groups (mostly Shiite Muslims), drove the Taliban from power and scattered al-Qaeda.

bin Laden and his organization are virulently anti-West in general and anti-American in particular. In 1998, bin Laden issued a *fatwa* (an Islamic decree or command) and called for a jihad (holy war) in which he called on Muslims everywhere to kill Americans wherever they are found, whether military or civilian, man, woman, or child, and those who support Americans. In addition to the 9/11 attacks, al-Qaeda was responsible for the 1998 bomb attacks on U.S. embassies in Nairobi, Kenya, and Dar es Salaam, Tanzania, killing or wounding more than 600 people, many of them Muslims.[31]

The malice and hatred directed against non-Muslims (and moderate Muslims), as well as the violent ideology of al-Qaeda, is made clear in a training manual seized by Manchester (England) police on a raid of an al-Qaeda member's home. Posted on the Internet by the U.S. Department of Justice (http://www.usdoj.gov/ag/trainingmanual.htm), this manual begins as follows:

In the name of Allah, the merciful and compassionate PRESENTATION

To those champions who avowed the truth day and night. . . .

And wrote with their blood and sufferings these phrases . . .

-*-The confrontation that we are calling for with the apostate regimes does not know Socratic debates, Platonic ideals, nor Aristotelian diplomacy. But it knows the dialog of bullets, the ideals of assassination, bombing and destruction, and the diplomacy of the cannon and machine gun.

> ***
>
> Islamic governments have never and will never be established through peaceful solutions and cooperative councils. They are established as they always have been
>
> > by pen and gun
> >
> > > by word and bullet
> > >
> > > > by tongue and teeth

Palestine Liberation Organization (PLO)

The **Palestine Liberation Organization** (PLO) is not a terrorist organization per se. Like al-Qaeda, it serves as an umbrella organization for several such groups serving a variety of ideologies and agendas united by Palestinian nationalism. Groups under the PLO umbrella, such as the Arab Liberation Front, al Fatah, Hamas, and the Al Aqsa Martyr's Brigade, engage in numerous terrorist acts against noncombatants, even noncombatants from neutral nations, and in guerilla warfare against the Israeli military.

The PLO was created at the first Arab Summit meeting in Egypt in 1964 with the aim of liberating Palestine from the Israelis. The irony of this aim is that Palestine did not exist until the end of World War I. Up until then, the area now called Palestine or Israel was part of the Turkish (Ottoman) Empire, organized into Jewish, Christian, and Muslim religious communities without any kind of national identity.[32] During World War I, the British promised to support Arab nationalism in the area in exchange for Arab support against the Ottoman Empire, which was allied with Germany and Austria/Hungary, but they also supported a national homeland for the Jews in the same area. After World War II, the United Nations voted to partition the area into Arab and Jewish areas under British supervision. The Arabs did not accept this, and the day after the British (who were harassed during their mandate by Israeli terror-

▲ **Photo 13.2**   Osama bin Laden, founder of the al-Qaeda terrorist movement. A Muslim fundamentalist, bin Laden's demands that must be met if he is to end his *jihad* (holy war) against the United States include the removal of all U.S. military presence from the Middle East and Saudi Arabia in particular, the return of all of Palestine to the Palestinians, and conversion of "infidels" to Islam. As his demands cannot possibly be complied with, his war on the West is likely to continue.

ist organizations such as the Irgun and the Stern Gang) left the newly proclaimed state of Israel, a number of Arab armies invaded the new country and were soundly defeated. Israel's victory and expansion of its territory became the impetus for the formation of the various Palestinian liberation groups. The latest round of terrorist activity in Israel was sparked by the ill-considered September 2000 visit (backed by military force) of Prime Minister Ehud Barak to the Muslim holy place, Haram al Sharif, designed to assert his rights to do so. Barak's visit sparked a new Palestinian *intifada* (uprising), an uprising that saw a vast increase in suicide bombers.[33] Israel's understandable military responses to these bombings perpetuate a continuous cycle of tit-for-tat violence. With the victory of the main terrorist Palestinian group Hamas ("zeal") in the January 2006 Palestinian election, with its charter claiming that Israel must be wiped off the map, the prospects for peace in the area in the short term have disappeared.

Hizballah

Hizballah ("Party of God") is the best contemporary example of a state-sponsored terrorist organization. Hizballah (sometimes spelled *Hezbollah*) ultimately owes its existence to the religious split between Sunni Muslims, who believe in the legitimacy of the secular state, and Shi'ite Muslims, who do not. It was organized by the Shi'ite religious leader Ayatollah Khomeini to fight the secular rule of the Shah of Iran. It emerged on the international stage after the Israeli invasion of Lebanon in 1982, which drove the PLO out of that country. Ironically, the PLO had been the chief opponent of the Lebanese Shi'ites prior to the invasion. Hizballah fighters were sent to Lebanon by Khomeini, ostensibly to aid in the fight against Israel, but with the long-range goal of establishing an Iranian-style Islamic regime in Lebanon. Hizballah has claimed responsibility for a number of spectacular terrorist operations that helped hasten the withdrawal of American and Israeli forces from Lebanon (something no Arab army has ever accomplished). Among these actions where the bombing of the U.S. marine barracks in 1983, killing 251 American and 56 French soldiers, and the kidnapping and/or murder of several American and European citizens.

Hizballah has a sense of engaging in a sacred mission that transcends the confines of Lebanon. Much as Christian crusaders several centuries before them saw the Muslim presence in the Holy Land as an affront to Christianity, the more radical among modern Shi'ites view the existence of a Jewish state in an area they also consider holy to be an affront to Islam.[34] They are fiercely anti-Israeli and anti-American, viewing the United States as the decadent, drug-infested, crime-ridden, sex-perverted "Great Satan" of the world. Directed and financed by Iran, Hizballah is headquartered in Lebanon and has established cells in Europe, North and South America, and Africa.[35]

After Israel withdrew from southern Lebanon in 2000, Hizballah lost its "claim to fame" that it was "standing up to Israel" and became one of Lebanon's many political parties. Hizballah's crisis came early in 2006, when other Lebanese political parties began pressuring it, as the country's last "militia" organization, to disarm. To avert having to do this, Hizballah terrorists crossed the Israeli border and killed three soldiers and kidnapped two others, knowing that Israel would retaliate and thus preserve Hizballah's "value" to Lebanon. Israel did retaliate with awesome power, doing everything in its power to destroy Hizballah's fighters, weaponry, and infrastructure. Unfortunately, these things were intentionally located among the civilian population, and the inevitable casualties ensued. Because Hizballah was fighting the Israeli invasion, it has again made itself popular among many segments of the Lebanese population (although other segments are blaming it rather than Israel for the destruction), which was evidently its intention. At the time of this writing, the war raged on as a further reminder that terrorists will do anything to achieve their objectives.

The Irish Republican Army (IRA): A Decommissioned Group?

The IRA was probably the terrorist organization best known to Americans prior to 9/11. The IRA traces its origin to the ill-fated Easter Rebellion against British rule in 1916. It began as an organization devoted to reuniting the predominantly Catholic Republic of Ireland with the predominantly Protestant Northern Ireland, which is now a part of the United Kingdom. The IRA was decimated by Irish government forces during the Irish civil war in the 1930s but reemerged in the late 1960s. The IRA has carried out terrorist activities in the Republic of Ireland, Northern Ireland, the British mainland, and against British military bases in Germany. After some bloody internal struggles in the early 1960s, some IRA members, disenchanted with the Official IRA's (OIRA) Marxist orientation and willingness to seek peace with the British, broke off to form the Provisional IRA (PIRA). The PIRA has been responsible for many hundreds of murders since the late 1960s and has done everything that it could to sabotage Anglo-Irish agreement.[36] In 1994, the PIRA agreed to join the OIRA in a cease-fire, although some PIRA units have carried out conventional robberies.

The 1994 cease-fire was shattered by two IRA bombings in London in early 1996, but peace prospects improved with the victory of the more conciliatory Labour Party in Britain in the 1997 election. When the PIRA began making tentative moves toward a peace accord, a breakaway group, calling itself the Continuity IRA (CIRA), decided to continue (hence the term *continuity*) terrorist activity. Another such breakaway group, the Real IRA (RIRA), has also continued sporadic terrorist attacks in Northern Ireland and the British mainland.[37] The 9/11 attacks in the United States and the arrest of three RIRA members who were teaching bombing techniques to narcotic terrorists in Colombia seem to have dampened support for IRA terrorism, marginalized its hard-liners, and provided impetus for the IRA to give up its weapons. In 2005, Sinn Fein (the "political" wing of the IRA) leader Gerry Adams appealed to the IRA to abandon its terrorist tactics and rely on the political process to advance their cause.[38] In July 2005, the IRA released a statement that it was ending its armed campaign, and in September 2005, international weapons inspectors supervised the disarmament of the IRA.[39]

In the IRA's decommissioning, we perhaps see some hope that terrorism is not an intractable problem that can only be solved by giving in to terrorism. It tells us that terrorism can be defeated when terrorist groups lose the moral backing of their former supporters, as well as when its less radical members are granted access to the political process, as in Sinn Fein.

Table 13.2 provides brief descriptions of some terrorist organizations not discussed in the text identified by the U.S. Department of State (USDS).[40] Of the 74 organizations listed by the USDS, 39 (52.7%) were Islamic and 18 (24.3%) were Marxist/Maoist. The remaining 17 groups were hybrids of Marxist/Islamic groups or nationalist groups.

| Table 13.2 | Some Major Terrorist Groups | | | |

Group	Description & Activities	Ideology	Strength	Funding
Abu Sayyaf	Philippine radical Islamic group motivated to gain an independent Islamic state in southern Philippines. Engages in kidnapping, bombing, and other criminal activities. Has strong links with al-Qaeda.	Nationalist/ Islamic	200 to 500	Self-financed via criminal activity + other Islamic groups.
Asbat al-Ansar	Lebanon-based Sunni Islamic group that has assassinated Lebanese Shi'ite religious leaders and bombed symbols of Western "decadence" such as nightclubs and U.S. franchise restaurants.	Islamic	About 300	International Sunni networks and al-Qaeda
Basque Fatherland and Liberty (ETA)	Founded in 1959 with the aim of creating an independent Basque homeland in northwest Spain and southwest France. Its activities have been aimed primarily at Spanish government officials and security forces, but French interests have also been attacked.	Nationalist and weakly Marxist	Unknown, but has many supporters in Basque regions	Primarily via criminal activity; has received training in Libya and Lebanon
Communist Party of Philippines/New People's Army	Military wing of the Philippine Communist Party. Carries out assassinations and kidnappings of political figures and U.S. military personnel stationed in the Philippines.	Maoist	1,000+	Criminal activity, contributions, and "revolutionary taxes" extorted from businesses
Harakat ul-Mujahidin (HUM)	Pakistani group operating primarily against Indian troops and civilians in Kashmir, territory claimed by both India and Pakistan. Has carried out airline hijackings and kidnapping of Westerners. HUM is aligned with al-Qaeda and signed bin Laden's 1998 fatwa calling for war on the United States.	Islamic	Several thousand	Donations from Saudi Arabia and other Islamic states; also donations from individuals
Islamic Movement of Uzbekistan	Coalition of a number of central Asian groups opposed to secular rule in Uzbekistan. Responsible for numerous bombing incidents and kidnapping of Westerners. Fought with the Taliban against U.S.-led invasion of Afghanistan.	Islamic	About 1,000	Support from other Islamic groups and patrons in the Middle East
Jemaah Islamiya (JI)	A Southeast Asian network with links to al-Qaeda that has the goal of creating a huge Islamic state composed of Indonesia, Singapore, the southern Philippines, and southern Thailand. JI was responsible for the Bali bombing in 2002 that killed 200 and wounded 300 others.	Islamic	About 5,000	Middle Eastern and Asian supporters and al-Qaeda

Group	Description & Activities	Ideology	Strength	Funding
Kurdistan Workers Party	Composed of Turkish Kurds seeking an independent Kurdish state in Turkey. Has attacked Turkish diplomats in many countries and attempted to disrupt tourism in Turkey by bombing hotels and historical sites and kidnapping tourists.	Marxist	4,000 to 5,000	Syria, Iraq, Iran
Liberation Tigers of Tamil Eelam (LTTE)	Composed of ethnic Tamils seeking an independent Tamil state in Sri Lanka, primarily through the use of bombings and assassinations. The LTTE has refrained from targeting Western tourists for fear of drying up funds from overseas Tamils.	Nationalism	10,000	Funds from Tamil communities overseas and some drug smuggling
Mujahedin-e Khalq	Formed in the 1960s to counter the Westernization of Iran under the Shah. It supported the overthrow of the Shah but is presently fighting against Iran's Islamic fundamentalist regime. Carries out attacks on Iranian diplomats and Iranian property.	A mixture of Marxism and Islam	Several thousand	Contributions from Iranian expatriates
National Liberation Army	Colombian Marxist group formed by urban intellectuals inspired by Fidel Castro and legendary terrorist Che Guevara. Engages in kidnapping, bombing, and extortion. Attacks foreigners and Colombian infrastructure.	Marxist	3,000 to 5,000	Criminal activity (drug trafficking and extortion) and some aid from Cuba
Sendero Luminoso (Shining Path)	Formed in late 1960s to destroy existing Peruvian institutions and replace them with a peasant revolutionary regime. Almost all Peruvian institutions have been brutally targeted in Peru and abroad.	Marxist/ Maoist	2,000+	Mostly drug trafficking and other forms of crime
Turkish Hizballah	Kurdish Sunni Islamic group that arose in opposition to the Marxist Kurdish Workers Party's (KWP's) actions against Muslims. Fights against KWP and Turkish armed forces. Bombs any establishment considered anti-Islamic. Kidnapped, tortured, and murdered at least 70 businessmen and journalists in the 1990s.	Islamic	A few hundred + several thousand supporters	Unknown

SOURCE: U.S. Department of State. (2004). *Patterns of global terrorism: 2003*. Washington, DC: Government Printing Office.

▧ Terrorism in the United States

Americans have been targeted by terrorists while overseas, but foreign terrorists found it difficult to do so within the borders of the United States, thanks largely to the great distances between

▲ **Photo 13.3** The September 11, 2001 attack on New York's Twin Towers and the Pentagon, carried out by al-Qaeda operatives, stunned the world. Ultimately, it resulted in passage of a comprehensive Patriot Act, the creation of the Department of Homeland Security, and a war with Iraq.

this country and the countries in which the terrorist groups are based. But as the bombings of the World Trade Center in 1993 and of the Oklahoma City Federal Building in 1995, as well as the horrific events of 9/11, attest, the United States is not immune to such attacks. Although the World Trade Center attacks in 1993 and 2001 were the work of foreign Islamic fundamentalists, the United States has its share of homegrown terrorists. Domestic terrorist groups are decidedly amateur compared with their foreign counterparts, but the bombing in Oklahoma City demonstrates that even the acts of amateurs can have devastating results.

Ideological: Left Wing

Left-wing terrorism in the United States became active during the turmoil of the 1960s. The most prominent group was the Weather Underground (WU). Solidly middle class, mostly White, and fiercely Marxist, the WU focused its attacks on symbols of "capitalist oppression" such as banks, corporate head-quarters, and military facilities. It was thought to be defunct after the arrest of many of its leaders in the 1970s, but it renewed its robbery and bombing campaign in the 1980s.[41] An even more radical group, The May 19 Communist Organization (M19CO), carried out bombing operations of U.S. military facilities and developed ties with foreign terrorist groups.

Another left-wing group was the Revolutionary Armed Task Force (RATF), forged from the alliance of the M19CO and the Black Liberation Army. Although this group earned its terrorist credentials by bombing a number of capitalist symbols, including the FBI's headquarters in New York, much of its activity seems to be concentrated on conventional crimes such as robbery and drug trafficking. The RATF recruits from minority prisoners and parolees, especially those who see themselves as victims of a capitalist and racist America.[42] The activities of these left-wing groups began to wane in the 1980s, and according to most experts, their organizations are now defunct.[43]

Ideological: Right Wing

Most right-wing American groups characterized as terrorist are *extremist* rather than terrorist groups in that they hold views that are to the extreme right of mainstream, but they do not necessarily translate their views into terrorist action. However, if the Oklahoma City bombing was more than the independent actions of Timothy McVeigh and Terry Nichols, both of whom espoused extreme right-wing rhetoric and had ties to various militia groups, this assessment will have to be changed. An example of such a group is the Aryan Nations, founded in the mid-1970s and headquartered in Idaho until 2001. The group espouses White supremacy, anti-Semitism, tax resistance, and radical libertarianism. The group suffered a serious blow in 2000, when it lost a $6.3 million lawsuit, which cost the group the real estate it owned in Idaho as well as automobiles and other property owned by the group.[44]

The KKK is one of the oldest terrorist groups in the world, although today it is a generic name for a number of autonomous groups ranging from those that never go beyond rhetoric and cross burning to those that actively practice terrorism.[45] At its peak, the KKK boasted a membership of 4 million, and many members engaged in murders, bombings, beatings, and cross burnings to intimidate Blacks and White civil rights workers. The KKK shares with most other American right-wing extremist/terrorist organizations an extreme Christian fundamentalism, the advocacy of paramilitary survivalist training, and a conspiratorial view of politics. They refer to the U.S. government as ZOG (Zionist Occupational Government), which they say is run by Jews, liberals, and African Americans.[46]

Special-Issue Domestic Terrorism

A number of groups in the United States employ terrorist tactics that have no grand sociopolitical agenda but rather seek to resolve special issues. These groups include environmentalists seeking to protect the environment, animal rights groups seeking to protect animals, and anti-abortion groups seeking to protect the rights of the unborn. The overwhelming majority of people who align themselves with such causes are, of course, nonviolent and seek their aims through political means. However, as with any group affiliated with almost any cause, there are extremists on the fringes who turn to illegal methods to get their point across.

The Animal Liberation Front (ALF) and the Earth Liberation Front (ELF) have emerged in the past several years as major domestic terror threats, with the ELF being declared by the FBI as America's number one domestic terrorist group.[47] This group has engaged in numerous acts of tree spiking, arson, sabotage of construction equipment, and other forms of vandalism that the Law Enforcement Agency Resource Network[48] reports have caused more than $100,000 in damage. According to the ELF Web site,[49] it sees itself as "working to speed up the collapse of industry, to scare the rich, and to undermine the foundations of the state."

The ALF has close ties with ELF because of the closeness of their respective agendas. Like ELF, ALF subscribes to the principle of "leaderless resistance," organizing itself into small autonomous cells with no centralized chain of command. This minimizes the possibility of infiltration by law enforcement.[50] According to James Jarboe,[51] the FBI estimated that ALF/ELF had committed more than 600 criminal acts between 1996 and 2001. Despite the attention given to these two groups by the FBI, there have mercifully been no deaths attributed to the activities of ALF/ELF, although Leader and Probst[52] see the groups as ready to turn to more violent tactics in the future.

▨ Theories About the Causes of Terrorism

You may have guessed from our brief discussion of domestic and foreign terrorists that from a political and historical point of view, there are as many causes of terrorism as there are terrorist groups. As our brief histories of al-Qaeda, IRA, PLO, and Hizballah make clear, terrorism cannot be understood without understanding the *specific* historical, social, political, and economic conditions behind the emergence of each terrorist group. Although certain kinds of people may be drawn to terrorism, to view terrorists as a bunch of "sicko-weirdos" wreaking havoc around the world like so many mission-oriented serial killers is to ignore the diversity of histories, purposes, causes, and people associated with terrorism. After all, if terrorism were a form of mental illness, we would have defeated it long ago. Terrorist groups take pains not to recruit anyone showing signs of mental instability because such people are not considered trustworthy and would arouse the suspicion of their intended targets.[53] The one generality we can make is that all groups originated in response to some perceived injustice.

Beyond the sociopolitical conditions and the perceived injustices, we need to seek more specific causes located within individuals and groups because the vast majority of people exposed to the same situations do not resort to terrorism. For instance, the typical Palestinian martyr bomber is a young, poor, uneducated male. Such a person is ideal material for recruitment; his lack of education makes him susceptible to brainwashing, his poverty makes the award of several thousand dollars to his family attractive, and his age and sex makes the adulation of his people most welcome.[54] But the icing on the cake is the promise of immediate ascension into heaven, where he will find "rivers of milk and wine . . . lakes of honey, and the services of 72 virgins."[55] If one truly believes such promises, then a martyr's existence in the afterlife seems a most attractive alternative to a meager existence among the living and his choice a rational one.

Roughly 20% to 25% of Palestinians are Christians who endure the same conditions said to motivate young Muslim Palestinians to blow themselves up in terrorist attacks, but we never hear of Christian Palestinians doing so. The difference must lie in ideological differences between Christianity and radical interpretations of Islam rather than in personal characteristics or objective material differences between Christian and Muslim Palestinians, all of whom are indoctrinated in schools (and most in the home as well) with anti-Israeli and anti-American propaganda from the earliest days of their lives.

Many Islamic terrorists are recruited from religious schools known as **madrasas.** Although a few of these schools teach secular subjects, they mostly focus on religious texts and stress the immorality and materialism of Western life and the need to convert all infidels to Islam.[56] The madrasas are appealing to poor Muslim families because they offer free room and board, as well as free education. Many members of the Afghani Taliban regime (*Talib* means *student* in Arabic) studied and trained in Pakistani madrasas stressing a strict form of Islam. Because many of these schools foster strong anti-Western, anti-Semitic, and anti-Christian sentiments, they have become a focus for concern for the American government. The attractiveness of these schools to poor Muslims who lack alternatives is matched with the almost complete control of what their students are exposed to, so there is little wonder that young Muslims emerge from them utterly convinced of the evilness of the non-Muslim world and the righteousness of the call to jihad against it.

Is There a Terrorist Personality?

Despite self-selection for membership in terrorist groups, no study of terrorist psychology has ever produced a psychological profile, leading most terrorist experts to suspect whether there is any such thing as a "terrorist personality."[57] On the other hand, the absence of a uniform terrorist personality does not mean that certain traits are not disproportionately present among those who join terrorist groups. For the most part, terrorist groups live on the fringes of the host society and espouse a violently radical vision of reality—factors that make it unlikely that terrorist groups attract members from across the spectrum of personality types.

Some theorists are of the opinion that we should look at what terrorist groups have to offer if we want to understand why individuals join them: "Terrorism can provide a route for advancement, an opportunity for glamour and excitement, a chance of world renown, a way of demonstrating one's courage, and even a way of accumulating wealth."[58] In other words, terrorism is much like organized crime in that it provides illegitimate ways to get what most of us would like to have—fame and fortune. Terrorists also have a bonus in that they, as well as their comrades and supporters, see themselves as romanticized warriors fighting for a just and noble cause and, in the case of religious terrorists, the favor of their God and the promise of a rewarding afterlife.

There have been efforts to psychologically pigeonhole terrorists, especially terrorist leaders. For instance, a psychoanalyst characterized Osama bin Laden as a psychotic who "wishes to be destroyed so that he can meet Allah. His fantasy of merger with his father—displaced onto the image of a divine benefactor—requires him to be punished and killed because he has such trenchant feelings of badness and self-loathing; only by being punished can he be forgiven and loved by his father."[59] A clinical psychologist sees him as a charismatic psychopath so much absorbed in his cause that he is in a permanent semi-hypnotic trance.[60] bin Laden may be all of these things or none of these things, but we can hardly get an accurate picture without his presence and cooperation.

In a study of 250 incarcerated West German terrorists, it was found that they had traits very much like those found among common criminals. Many of them had suffered the early loss of one or both parents, they were involved in frequent conflicts with authorities prior to joining their groups, and they had frequently failed in school and work endeavors. Psychologically, they were found to be stimulus seekers; to be hostile, suspicious, aggressive, defensive, and extremely dependent on the terrorist group; and to have a preference for a parasitic lifestyle and a predilection for risk taking.[61]

Some scholars view terrorists as people with marginal personalities drawn to terrorist groups because their deficiencies are both accepted and welcomed by the group.[62] These scholars also see the terrorist group as being made up of three types of individuals: (1) the *charismatic leader,* (2) the *antisocial personality,* and (3) the *follower.* The charismatic leader is socially alienated, narcissistic, arrogant, and intelligent, with a deeply idealistic sense of right and wrong. The terrorist group provides a forum for his narcissistic rage and intellectual ramblings, and the subservience of group members feeds his egoism. Antisocial (or psychopathic) individuals have opportunities in terrorist groups to use force and violence to further their own personal goals, as well as the goals of the group. For the psychopath, the group functions like an organized crime family, providing greater opportunity, action, and prestige than could be found outside the group.[63] Most terrorists, however, are simple followers who see the world purely in black ("them") and white ("us") and have deep needs for acceptance, which makes them susceptible to all sorts of religious, ideological, and political propaganda.[64]

Members of some terrorist groups defy description because, for all intents and purposes, they give up more than they gain to join them, and the groups that they join have no defensible religious or nationalistic complaints to air. Such a group is Japan's Aum Shinrikyo, the

▲ **Photo 13.4**   While international terrorism is the country's main concern, homegrown terrorism, such as the bombing of the Alfred P. Murrah Federal Building in Oklahoma City in 1995, remains a priority. The main bomber, Timothy McVeigh, stated that his actions were a response to prior government actions, such as burning down the Koresh compound in Waco, Texas, and the FBI shootings at Ruby Ridge.

group that released sarin nerve gas in the Tokyo subway system in 1995, killing 12 and injuring up to 6,000. The group began as a Buddhist sect spreading a message of peace, but ended as something completely different when its leader, Shoko Asahara, started preaching about the end of the world. Caracci points out that many of the group's members were physicists, chemists, biologists, and other scientists "who had given up promising academic careers to devote themselves to the development of mass destruction commissioned by the leader."[65] The high status of these people living in a wealthy, free, and democratic society makes it difficult to believe that we can ever arrive at a "one-size-fits-all" terrorist personality profile.

⬚ Becoming a Terrorist

Some terrorism theorists, while agreeing that terrorist groups may attract a disproportionate number of antisocial types, believe that the bulk of terrorists are probably better characterized as crusaders convinced of the moral rightness of their cause.[66] If these theorists are right, we have to explain how "normal" people are persuaded to commit brutal acts against innocent people. When moral people are required to commit immoral acts, there must be some sort of personal transformation that makes it possible. In other words, the willingness to perform terrorist acts may reflect a *process* of moral disengagement more than a manifestation of pathological and/or criminal traits the individual brings to the terrorist group.[67] If the essence of terrorism is "the complete transformation of sane human beings into brutal and indiscriminate killers,"[68] terrorist acts doubtless generate significant levels of guilt and doubt in the new recruit that must be resolved. Inconsistencies between attitudes and behavior (the stuff of cognitive dissonance) are usually resolved by changing attitudes rather than behaviors. For terrorists, this typically means deepening their belief that their cause is just, further dehumanizing their targets ("infidels," "capitalist pigs," and so on), viewing the slaughter of innocents as "collateral damage," and any of a number of other ways that humans have for exorcizing behavior-inhibiting guilt and doubt.

The gruesome barbarity behind the Beslan school incident and the beheading deaths of Daniel Pearl in Pakistan in 2002, Nicholas Berg in Iraq in 2004, and Paul Johnson in Saudi Arabia in 2004 (as well as other decapitation incidents before and after these), all videotaped and boastfully distributed, underlines the psychopathic nature of much terrorist activity. There is certainly no glory in decapitating helpless individuals or terrorizing little children, and the individuals who actually ordered and carried out the acts were likely on the psychopathic fringes of the group. Musab al-Zarqawi, the leader of al-Qaeda in Iraq who was killed by an American air strike in June 2006, almost certainly fell into that category. On September 20, 2004, al-Zarqawi's terrorist group released a grisly video in which al-Zarqawi is shown drawing a knife from his belt and cutting off the head of American hostage Eugene Armstrong. Such horrendous acts are designed to unnerve the enemy by essentially saying, "We are merciless and will stop at nothing." There is a degree of rationality underlying such evil if it accomplishes something terrorists want.

▧ Law Enforcement Response and Government Policy

There is any number of ways a democracy can respond to terrorism, ranging from making concessions to military intervention. Concessions are likely only when there is moral substance to the terrorist cause and when such concessions are reasonable. For instance, Spain has granted considerable autonomy to its Basque region in response to Basque terrorism, but Israel can hardly make concessions to Islamic terrorists whose "only" demand is the complete destruction of the state of Israel. Similarly, the West cannot make any concessions to al-Qaeda and other such groups because they are not demanding any. What these groups said they want over and over is nothing less than the Islamification of the world, starting with the purification of existing Islamic regimes (as was done in Afghanistan by the Taliban) that do not match the terrorists' ideas of what an Islamic state should be.

Military intervention may be used when the terrorist threat is too big for civilian authorities to handle. But besides being distasteful to the democratic spirit, military intervention, even though successful in the short term, may be detrimental in the long term, as Israel discovered after it invaded Lebanon in 1982. On the other hand, the use of certain military units, such as Germany's Grenzschutzgruppe 9 (GSG9) and Britain's almost legendary SAS (Special Air Service), have proved spectacularly successful.[69]

However, these units were operating against ethnically homogeneous groups with definite policies and goals; the modern Islamic terrorist threat is an altogether different proposition. The Islamic terrorist threat emanates from many nations and is fed by a constant stream of religious hatred poisoning the minds of young Muslim men. It is estimated that more than 50,000 terrorists trained in Afghanistan are now scattered around the globe and quietly have been integrated into local communities, awaiting their orders to strike.[70] U.S. Defense Secretary Donald Rumsfeld has himself expressed doubt that the West can win the broader global fight against Islamic terrorism and wonders if the various groups "are turning out newly trained terrorists faster than the United States can capture or kill them."[71] Clearly, we cannot defeat the threat by military force alone, but nobody knows of any alternative save capitulation.

International law has been applied against terrorists, sometimes successfully, but often not. The principle of international law known as *aut dedire aut punire* (Latin for *either extradite or punish*) obligates countries to either extradite terrorists to the country where their crimes were committed or to punish them themselves. Some countries neither extradite nor punish for one reason or another (they may support the terrorist's cause, or they may fear reprisals). Some countries have difficulties with the terrorist/freedom fighter distinction, and even closely allied countries (e.g., Canada, Great Britain) refuse to extradite anyone to the United States if that person faces the possibility of receiving the death penalty.[72]

The United States has a clear-cut policy to combat terrorism. According to the U.S. State Department, the government's counterterrorist policy follows three general rules:

1. Do not make deals with terrorists or submit to blackmail. We have found over the years that this policy works.

2. Treat terrorists as criminals and apply the rule of law.

3. Bring maximum pressure on states that sponsor and support terrorists by imposing economic, diplomatic, and political sanctions and urging other states to do likewise.[73]

Following the September 11 attacks, President George W. Bush issued an executive order establishing the **Department of Homeland Security** under the directorship of Governor Tom Ridge (now under the leadership of Michael Chertoff). The mission of the department is to detect, prevent, prepare for, and recover from terrorist attacks within the United States. *Detection* involves coordinated efforts on the part of federal, state, and local agencies to collect information in an attempt to identify terrorist activities within the United States. *Prevention* relates to the investigation of identified threats, the denial of entry of suspected terrorists and terrorist materials and supplies into the United States, and the arrest, detention, and deportation of individuals suspected of membership in foreign terrorist groups. *Preparedness* refers to nationwide efforts to prepare for and lessen the impact of any terrorist attack. *Recovery* refers to efforts to quickly restore critical infrastructure facilities (distribution systems, telecommunications, utilities), provide adequate medical facilities, and remove hazardous materials in the event of a successful terrorist attack.[74]

Homeland security efforts were given "legal teeth" by the passage of the congressional **USA Patriot Act** on October 11, 2001. The Patriot Act is either loved as a powerful tool that will avert terrorist plots and put terrorists in jail or feared as the beginning of the end of American civil liberties. The act grants federal agencies greater authority to track and intercept private communications, gives greater powers to the Treasury Department to combat corruption and prevent money laundering, and creates new crimes, penalties, and procedures for use against domestic and foreign terrorists.[75]

Many people feel that if the establishment of the Office of Homeland Security and the passage of the Patriot Act prevent another 9/11, it is all right with them. After all, if you are not engaged in any of the above activities, what have you to fear? While no one suggests that law enforcement is interested in intercepting e-mail exchanges of cheesecake recipes or listening to your call home asking for money, the American Civil Liberties Union (ACLU) fears that the inclusion of domestic terrorism in the Patriot Act's definition of terrorism has great potential for abuse. The ACLU claims that the definition is broad enough to encompass the activities of several legitimate activist groups such as Greenpeace, Operation Rescue, and Environmental Liberation, putting participants in some protest activities at risk for the same enhanced criminal penalties and asset forfeitures applied to genuine terrorists.[76]

The mechanisms set up by the Office of Homeland Security can only work if the men and women in the front lines of security are constantly vigilant. Security was so tight in the first months after 9/11 that this period was probably the safest period to fly in the history of aviation. But the human tendency is to grow complacent after long periods in which nothing happens, and this is terrorism's great weapon. For instance, a U.S. federal government document published in 1999 predicted that al-Qaeda would retaliate "in a spectacular way" for the cruise missile attacks against their training facilities in 1998, ordered by President Clinton in retaliation for the 1998 attacks on U.S. embassies in 1998. This document stated that "suicide bomber(s) belonging to al-Qaeda's Martyrdom Battalion could crash an aircraft packed with high explosives (C-4 and semtex) into the Pentagon, the headquarters of the Central Intelligence Agency (CIA) or the White House."[77] al-Qaeda waited patiently for 3 years before doing almost exactly as predicted, and it did it with relative ease. Thus, all the intelligence in the world is of little use unless those in the day-to-day security trenches take it as seriously every day as they did immediately after September 11, 2001.

▲ **Photo 13.5**   In the wake of 9/11, preparation drills for potential future terrorist attacks became more common. One of the targets frequently mentioned was large sports stadiums filled to capacity on game day. The depicted drill was carried out at FSU's football stadium. The simulated attack featured potential snipers, bombers, and the release of anthrax. More than 20 police, fire, emergency, and medical responders participated.

▲ **Photo 13.6** Another major terrorism concern after 9/11 is the nation's ports. Fears that a weapon of mass destruction might be brought into the country in a cargo container, or port oil facilities targeted for bombing, led to prep drills such as this one. Dive teams practice collecting evidence after a simulated disaster event, while a robot craft patrols the harbor.

▲ **Photo 13.7** The security of the extensive coastline of the United States is the mission of the U.S. Coast Guard. Prior to 9/11, the Coast Guard was heavily involved in drug interdiction efforts. After 9/11, their mission included the fight against terrorism.

SUMMARY

Terrorism is an ancient method of intimidating the public by the indiscriminate use of violence for social or political reasons. Terrorists are different from freedom fighters or guerrillas in that terrorists usually operate against democracies and freedom fighters against foreign colonialists or oppressive domestic regimes. Terrorism increased rather dramatically from the 1960s to the mid-1980s and has steadily dropped off since then. Many terrorist groups tend to evolve into organized crime groups hidden behind an ideological veneer.

al-Qaeda is a "base" organization for a number of Islamic terrorist groups and is the group of most concern to Americans. The IRA and the PLO were probably the best-known terrorist groups prior to the emergence of al-Qaeda, but the IRA has supposedly decommissioned. Hizballah, a radical pro-Iranian Islamic fundamentalist group, appears to be the most active and most deadly terrorist group presently operating not associated with al-Qaeda.

Although American terrorists are decidedly amateur in comparison with their foreign counterparts, there are a fair number of terrorist groups operating in this country. These groups may be divided into ideological (left and right wing), nationalist, and special-issue groups.

From a historical and political point of view, there are as many causes of terrorism as there are terrorist groups. Each group has its origins in some perceived social, economic, or political injustice, but only a minuscule number of people react to such conditions by joining terrorist organizations. This observation leads many researchers to look for a "terrorist personality." There is no uniform terrorist personality, although certain traits are found more frequently among terrorists than among the general population. The most common traits found are low self-esteem and a predilection for risk taking. Since most terrorists are not mentally ill, a process of moral disengagement is posited to explain their transition from sane human beings to killers.

Democracies have considerable difficulty responding to the terrorist threat because of legal restraints. The international community has evolved certain processes for dealing with terrorists, such as the passage of laws that obligate a country to either extradite terrorists in their custody to the country where the terrorism took place or punish the offenders themselves. As for the United States, it has a clear-cut policy of treating terrorists like common criminals, not making deals with them, and imposing sanctions against nations that sponsor terrorism. The threat to democracies from terrorism is great, and the United States responded after 9/11 with the establishment of the Department of Homeland Security and the USA Patriot Act.

On Your Own

Log on to the web-based student study site at http://www.sagepub.com/criminologystudy for more information about the vignettes and materials presented in this chapter, suggestions for activities, study aids such as review quizzes, and research recommendations including journal article links and questions related to this chapter.

EXERCISES AND DISCUSSION QUESTIONS

1. Do you agree or disagree that there is a moral difference between terrorists and guerillas?

2. In what respects is terrorism rational behavior?

3. Do you think that extremist Muslims hate the United States because it has troops on soil they consider holy (Saudi Arabia)? If so, why don't we take them out of there? Or does fear of losing Saudi oil keep them there?

4. Can you conceive of any circumstances under which you would commit the kinds of terrorist acts committed on 9/11 or the Beslan school, sacrificing your own life in the bargain?

5. Discuss why the Patriot Act does or does not make us safer from terrorist attacks. Are we giving up certain civil liberties for a measure of security?

6. Should the United States and other Western democracies "fight fire with fire" and pursue whatever means necessary to defeat terrorism?

7. Go to http://www.cfrterrorism.org and click on "groups." You will find a number of terrorist groups listed there with a variety of motives. Choose an Islamic group and a Marxist group and write a short paper comparing and contrasting them on their motives and methods.

KEY WORDS

al-Qaeda
Department of Homeland Security
Hizballah

Madrasas
Palestine Liberation Organization

Terrorism
USA Patriot Act

REFERENCES

1. U.S. Department of State. (2004). *Patterns of global terrorism: 2003.* Washington, DC: Government Printing Office.
2. What really happened at Beslan? (2004). Retrieved from http//us.rediff.com/cms/print.jsp?docpath=/news/2004/sep/09raman.htm
3. Feeney, D. (2002). Enhancement in Islamic fundamentalism. In C. Stout (Ed.), *The psychology of terrorism* (Vol. III, pp. 192–209). Westport, CT: Praeger. (Quote on p. 191)
4. Hacker, F. (1977). *Crusaders, criminals, crazies: Terror and terrorism in our time.* New York: Norton. (Quote on p. ix)
5. Simonsen, C., & Spindlove, J. (2004). *Terrorism today: The past, the players, the future.* Upper Saddle River, NJ: Prentice Hall.
6. Vetter, H., & Perlstein, G. (1991). *Perspectives on terrorism.* Pacific Grove, CA: Brooks/Cole.
7. Wheeler, E. (1991). Terrorism and military theory: An historical perspective. In C. McCauley (Ed.), *Terrorism research and public policy* (pp. 6–33). London: Frank Cass.

8. Rummel, R. (1992). Megamurderers. *Society, 29,* 47–52.
9. U.S. Department of State (2004).
10. Rummel (1992).
11. Smith, B. (1994). *Terrorism in America: Pipe bombs and pipe dreams.* Albany: State University of New York Press. (Quote on p. 8)
12. McCauley, C. (2002). Psychological issues in understanding terrorism and the response to terrorism. In C. Stout (Ed.), *The psychology of terrorism* (Vol. III, pp. 3–29). Westport, CT: Praeger.
13. Simonsen and Spindlove (2004).
14. Kurtz, H. (2002, February 2–3). America is "doomed" bin Laden says on tape. *International Herald Tribune,* p. 5.
15. Yeltsin warns Russia rolling back democracy in wake of Beslan crisis. (2004). Retrieved from http://www.channelnewsasia.com/stories/afp_world/view/107040/1/
16. Sederberg, P. (1989). *Terrorist myths: Illusions, rhetoric, and reality.* Englewood Cliffs, NJ: Prentice Hall.

17. Drummond, J. (2002). From the northwest imperative to global jihad: Social psychological aspects of the construction of the enemy, political violence, and terror. In E. Stout (Ed.), *The psychology of terrorism* (Vol. 1, pp. 49–95). Wesport, CT: Praeger.

18. Garrison, A. (2004). Defining terrorism: Philosophy of the bomb, propaganda by deed and change through fear and violence. *Criminal Justice Studies, 17,* 259–279.

19. Garrison (2004).

20. U.S. Department of State (2004).

21. Hoffman, C. (2002). Rethinking terrorism and counterterrorism since 9/11. *Studies in Conflict & Terrorism, 25,* 303–316.

22. Landay, J. (2005). *Bush administration eliminating 19-year-old international terrorism report.* Washington Bureau and Wire Service Sources. Retrieved from http://www.realities.com

23. National Counterterrorism Center. (2005). *A chronology of significant international terrorism for 2004.* Washington, DC: Author.

24. U.S. Department of State (2004).

25. Reid, W. (2002). Controlling political terrorism: Practicality, not psychology. In C. Stout (Ed.), *The psychology of terrorism: Public understanding* (pp. 1–8). Westport, CT: Praeger. (Quote on p. 4)

26. Dishman, C. (2001). Terrorism, crime, and transformation. *Studies in Conflict & Terrorism, 24,* 43–58.

27. Dishman (2001, p. 49).

28. Albanese, J., & Pursley, R. (1993). *Crime in America: Some existing and emerging issues.* Englewood Cliffs, NJ: Regents/Prentice Hall. (Quote on p. 100)

29. Council on Foreign Relations. (2004). Al-Qaeda. Retrieved from http://cfrterrorism.org/groups/alqaeda

30. Simonsen and Spindlove (2004).

31. Primakov, E. (2004). *A world challenged: Fighting terrorism in the twenty-first century.* Washington, DC: The Nixon Center and Brookings Institute Press.

32. Long, D. (1990). *The anatomy of terrorism.* New York: Free Press.

33. Simonsen and Spindlove (2004).

34. Kramer, M. (1990). The moral logic of Hizballah. In W. Reich (Ed.), *Origins of terrorism: Psychologies, ideologies, theologies, states of mind* (pp. 131–157). New York: Cambridge University Press.

35. U.S. Department of State. (1995). *Patterns of global terrorism: 1994.* Washington, DC: Government Printing Office.

36. Drake, C. (1991). Provisional IRA: A case study. *Terrorism and Political Violence, 3,* 43–60.

37. Simonsen and Spindlove (2004).

38. Sinn Fein leader asks IRA to give up fighting. (2005, April 7). *Idaho Statesman,* p. 2.

39. Provisional Irish Republican Army. (2005). Retrieved from http://en.wilipedia.org/wili

40. U.S. Department of State (2004).

41. Drake (1991).

42. Albanese and Pursley (1993).

43. Council on Foreign Relations. (2004). *American militant extremists.* Retrieved from http://cfrterrorism.org/groups/American_print.html

44. Law Enforcement Agency Resource Network. (2004). *Aryan Nations/Church of Jesus Christ Christian.* Retrieved from http://www.adl.org/learn/ext_us/Aryan_Nations.asp?xpicked=3&

45. White, J. (1998). *Terrorism: An introduction* (2nd ed). Belmont, CA: West/Wadsworth.

46. Vetter and Perlstein (1991).

47. Consumer Freedom. (2006). *America's number one terrorists.* Retrieved from http://consumerfreedom.com

48. Law Enforcement Agency Resource Network. (2006). Retrieved from http://www.adl.org/adl_in_action/gfiirc.pdf

49. Earth First. (2006). *Communique from the Earth Liberation Front.* Retrieved from http://www.iiipublishing.com/elf.htm

50. Leader, S., & Probst, P. (2006). *The Earth Liberation Front and environmental terrorism.* Retrieved from http://www1.umn.edu/des/earthliberationfront3pub.htm

51. Jarboe, J. (2002). *The threat of domestic terrorism.* Testimony, Congressional Committee on Forests and Forest Health. Retrieved from http://www.fbi.gov/congress/congress02/jarboe021202.htm

52. Leader and Probst (2006).

53. Hudson, R. (1999). *The sociology and psychology of terrorism: Who becomes a terrorist and why?* Washington, DC: The Library of Congress, Federal Research Division.

54. Lelyveld, J. (2001, October 28). All suicide bombers are not alike. *New York Times Magazine,* pp. 48–53, 78–79.

55. Hoffman (2002, p. 305).

56. Armanios, F. (2003). *Islamic religious schools, madrasas: Background* (Congressional Research Service, Report RS21654). Washington, DC: Library of Congress.

57. Hudson (1999).

58. Reich, W. (1990). Understanding terrorist behavior: The limits and opportunities of psychological inquiry. In W. Reich (Ed.), *Origins of terrorism: Psychologies, ideologies, theologies, states of mind* (pp. 261–279). New York: Cambridge University Press. (Quote on p. 271)

59. Piven, J. (2002). On the psychosis (religion) of terrorism. In C. Stout (Ed.), *The psychology of terrorism* (Vol. III, pp. 120–148). Westport, CT: Praeger. (Quote on p. 134)

60. Feeney (2002).

61. Reich (1990).

62. Johnson, P., & Feldman, T. (1992). Personality types and terrorism: Self-psychology perspectives. *Forensic Reports, 5,* 293–303.

63. Perlman, D. (2002). Intersubjective dimensions of terrorism and its transcendence. In C. Stout (Ed.), *The psychology of terrorism* (Vol. III, pp. 57–81). Westport, CT: Praeger.

64. Ardila, R. (2002). The psychology of the terrorist: Behavioral perspectives. In C. Stout (Ed.), *The psychology of terrorism* (Vol. I, pp. 9–15). Westport, CT: Praeger.

65. Caracci, G. (2002). Cultural and contextual aspects of terrorism. In C. Stout, (Ed.), *The psychology of terrorism* (Vol. III, pp. 57–81). Westport, CT: Praeger. (Quote on p. 68)

66. White (1998).

67. Bandura, A. (1990). Mechanisms of moral disengagement. In W. Reich (Ed.), *Origins of terrorism: Psychologies, ideologies, theologies, states of mind* (pp. 161–191). New York: Cambridge University Press.

68. Sprinzak, E. (1991). The process of delegitimization: Towards a linkage theory of political terrorism. In C. McCauley (Ed.), *Terrorism research and public policy* (pp. 50–68). London: Frank Cass. (Quote on p. 58)

69. Simonsen and Spindlove (2004).

70. Simonsen and Spindlove (2004).

71. Burns, R. (2004, June 6). Rumsfeld fearful of losing broader battle against extremists. *Idaho Statesman,* p. 5a.

72. Vetter and Perlstein (1991).

73. U.S. Department of State (1995, p. iv).

74. White House. (2001). *The Office of Homeland Security.* Retrieved from http://www.whitehouse .gov/news/release/2001/10/print

75. Doyle, C. (2002). *The USA Patriot Act: A sketch.* Washington, DC: Congressional Research Service, Library of Congress.

76. American Civil Liberties Union. (2002). *How the USA Patriot Act redefines "domestic terrorism."* Retrieved from http://www.aclu.org/National Security.cfm?ID=11437&c=111

77. Hudson (1999, pp. 7–8).

PROPERTY AND PUBLIC ORDER CRIME

J ay Scott Ballinger was a property offender on a dark mission. He admitted in court to setting fire to between 30 and 50 churches in 11 states between 1994 and 1999. A volunteer firefighter was killed in one of the blazes, which makes him a murderer too. Ballinger did not set these fires for profit or because he got some weird sexual kick from watching them burn; he did so on an anti-Christian mission. Ballinger, his girlfriend Angela Wood, and accomplice David Puckett traveled around the country seeking converts to Satanism, and churches were the sanctuaries of the enemy. The trio would burglarize and shoplift, and Woods would work as a stripper to finance their travels around the Midwest and South. It all came to an end when Ballinger was arrested after paramedics, who treated him for severe burns, wondered why he waited 2 days to seek treatment (he had burns to 40% of his body and had to receive four skin grafts). A police officer who remembered Ballinger's name from a previous investigation questioned him and then summoned ATF (Alcohol, Tobacco, and Firearms) agents, who found firesetting paraphernalia and satanic literature at Ballinger's home. Among the writings agents found were 50 "contracts" signed by teenagers in their own blood pledging their souls to the devil and to do "all types of evil" for which they would be rewarded with wealth, power, and sex, the perennial male motivators. Ballinger, aged 36 at the time of his arrest, was described as a misfit loner and high school dropout who was more comfortable with teens than people his own age. He was sentenced to 42 years in prison for his multistate arson spree.[1] As the Ballinger case shows, property crimes can sometimes morph into something as deadly as violent crimes.

Although crimes of violence against the person get the lion's share of media attention and student interest, of the 11,695,264 offenses reported to the police in 2004, only 11.7% were violent. The remaining 88.3% were property crimes. A significant number of other offenses not included in the above figure because they are based on arrests rather than reports are public-order offenses. Property crime involves the illegal acquisition of money and goods or the destruction of property for financial gain or other malicious purposes. Public-order crimes are crimes against prevailing social morality or that contribute to the breakdown of the public order. Few of us will be victimized by murder, rape, robbery, or an assault serious enough to constitute an aggravated assault during our lives, but hardly any of us will escape being victimized by a property offense or from witnessing a public-order offense. Likewise, the vast majority of us will never commit a violent crime, but few among us have never committed or will never commit a property offense of some kind such as cheating on our income tax, pilfering items from work, shoplifting, or failing to turn in money or other valuables we have found.

As is the case with violent crime, property crime has been dropping dramatically over the past two decades. Figure 14.1 shows property crime trends in the United States over the history of the National Crime Victimization Surveys (NCVS).[2] Recall from Chapter 2 that the NCVS only includes offenses against individuals and households; it does not include the huge number of offenses committed against commercial establishments (stores, garages, warehouses, factories, and so forth), thus leaving out a very large number of property offenses.

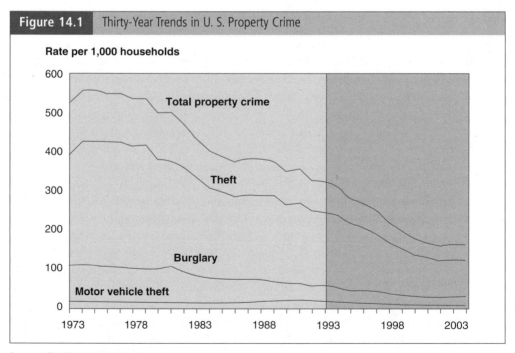

| **Figure 14.1** | Thirty-Year Trends in U. S. Property Crime |

SOURCE: NCVS 2004 Victimization Survey.

NOTE: Data collected before the NCVS redesign was implemented during 1992 (the lightly shaded area) have been made comparable to the postdesign NCVS. Data were reestimated to account for the effects of the redesign. Arson not included.

⊠ Larceny-Theft

Larceny-theft is the most common property crime committed in the United States and is defined as "the unlawful taking, leading, or riding away from the possession or constructive possession of another."[3] *Constructive possession* refers to circumstances in which a person does not have actual possession but has the power to control an asset. Examples include someone gaining access to your credit card number or car keys. He or she has constructive possession even though you still have actual possession of the card and your car is still sitting in your garage. In both cases, the person may use what rightfully belongs to you without your consent. In early English common law, larceny only applied to persons who achieved possession of goods belonging to others by stealth or force and did not cover persons who abused the trust of their victims to steal from them. For instance, if a person gave another person some money to hold in trust and that other person used it for his or her own purposes, there was no larceny because there was no wrongful taking since the first person voluntarily handed over the money. You can easily see the problems this would cause in our modern, complex society, where we voluntarily hand over our money to bank tellers and our broken vehicles and appliances to repair shops! Lawmakers responded to this by enlarging the definition of larceny to include taking by fraud and false pretenses as well as by stealth and force. Taking by stealth has evolved into other crimes such as burglary or embezzlement, and taking by force has evolved into the crime of robbery.[4]

Today, larceny-theft covers most types of theft that do not include the use of threats, violence, or force. Not included in this category is theft of a motor vehicle, forgery, passing bad checks, or embezzlement. Larceny-theft includes grand theft (a felony) and petty theft (a misdemeanor), with the distinction depending on the value of the asset stolen. The cutoff value varies from state to state, but presently it is under $1,000 in every state. It should be noted that whether a person is charged with grand or petty theft depends on the value of the item at the time it was stolen, not its replacement value. A stolen television set bought for $700 but now worth only $100 is a petty theft, but a stolen guitar bought for $100 in 1955 that has become a classic worth $10,000 today constitutes a grand theft. Because the grand theft/petty theft distinction varies across states, the *Uniform Crime Reports* (*UCR*) includes both grand theft and petty theft in its yearly larceny-theft tally.

The number of larceny-thefts reported in the United States in 2004 was 6,947,685, for a rate of 2,365.9 per 100,000 U.S. residents, down 2.2% from 2003. This crime constituted 67.3% of the nation's property crimes in 2004. The average loss due to larceny-theft was $727, for a total national loss of approximately $5.1 billion. Only 18.3% of reported larceny-thefts were cleared.

Of the 1,191,945 people arrested for larceny-theft in 2004, 61.7% were males and 38.3% were females. Whites (which we remind you again in this chapter includes non-Black Hispanics) accounted for 69.2% of larceny-theft arrests, Blacks for 27.4%, and other races the remainder. Persons younger than age 18 accounted for 27.3% of arrests for larceny-theft.

Types of Larceny-Theft

Larceny-thefts are subclassified by the FBI into shoplifting, pocket picking, purse snatching, thefts from motor vehicles (except for parts and accessories), theft of motor parts and accessories, theft of bicycles, and theft from buildings. Perhaps surprisingly, theft from motor vehicles (excluding parts and accessories) is the most common type of larceny-theft. These thefts include thefts from just about any type of motorized vehicle, such as automobiles, trucks, buses, and motor homes. The definition includes thefts from any area of the vehicle such as the trunk, glove compartment, seat, or any other enclosure whether locked or unlocked. Some state statutes may define some of these thefts as burglaries, but they must be reported to the FBI as larceny-thefts.

Shoplifting Shoplifting, which is theft by a person other than an employee of goods exposed for sale in a store, is the most studied of the subcategories of larceny-theft. Perhaps this is so because it has sometimes been defined as a psychiatric problem (kleptomania) and because we periodically hear about the rich and famous boosting items from stores that they could afford to buy lock, stock, and barrel. For instance, actress Winona Ryder was arrested in 2001 for shoplifting about $5,000 worth of goods from a Saks Fifth Avenue store in Beverly Hills. Although she consistently denied her guilt, she was found guilty and sentenced to 3 years' probation and 480 hours of community service.[5] Ryder's "five-finger discount" is one of hundreds of thousands occurring each year that cost the retail industry approximately $31 billion in 2004 (this amount included employee theft as well).[6] This loss is passed on to law-abiding customers in the form of increased prices.

People shoplift for a variety of reasons, with about 8% engaging in it as a primary source of income. These individuals have been called *boosters*[7] or *semiprofessional shoplifters*.[8] These are the individuals with the greatest level of expertise who know how to minimize the risk of being caught, target the most expensive items, and steal almost exclusively for resale. Most shoplifters, however, are amateurs classified as *snitches*[9] or *impulsive*.[10] These are individuals who shoplift relatively inexpensive items on the spur of the moment and for their own gratification, and they often tend to be poor and unemployed.[11] One self-report study is consistent with rational choice theory in that shoplifters said that they engaged in shoplifting simply because it is an easy, low-risk crime for which there are abundant opportunities.[12]

There may be a small percentage of shoplifters afflicted with **kleptomania** (Greek for "stealing madness"), which is repetitive impulsive stealing for the thrill of stealing and getting away with it. This psychiatric label may be more of an upscale "technique of neutralization" applied to affluent offenders to excuse their behavior and/or mitigate their punishment.[13] However, there is a self-help organization similar to Alcoholics Anonymous (AA) called *Cleptomaniacs And Shoplifters Anonymous* (CASA), designed to treat what CASA prefers to call addictive-compulsive shoplifting.[14] A common theme for people who engage in "nonsensical shoplifting" is that they are often depressed and have other compulsive addictions.[15]

✉ Burglary

The FBI defines **burglary** as "the unlawful entry of a structure to commit a felony or theft."[16] This simple definition belies the hodgepodge of state laws that define burglary in a variety of ways. Burglary has always been considered a very serious offense under common law dating back many centuries because of the importance attached to the sanctity of the home, as indicated by the ancient saying, "An Englishman's home is his castle." Residential burglary is one of the most traumatic crimes victims can experience, generating feelings of anger, fear, and a profound sense of invasion of privacy and vulnerability in addition to financial loss. The original common-law definition involved breaking and entering at nighttime with the intention of

▲ **Photo 14.1** Major cities and tourist areas often have problems with pickpocketing and other minor thefts. Travelers are warned constantly about not putting purses on the backs of chairs in restaurants or carrying cameras without fanny backs or other secure bags. This public service campaign in Prague, Czech Republic, warns citizens not to carry their wallets in their back pockets.

committing a felony, whether or not a felony was committed. Burglary almost always involves theft, but burglary may be charged if no theft actually took place. The definition has evolved to include any unlawful entry (entry without right or permission), and thus a forceful entry ("breaking and entering") is no longer a necessary element of burglary, although a forceful entry is obviously one method of unlawful entry. Entering through an unlocked door or open window still constitutes a burglary if the person has no legal right to be present in the structure.

Nor is nighttime entry any longer a necessary element. Nighttime entry was considered most seriously in early common law because it was assumed that home owners would most likely be at home during the night and thus at risk of violent confrontation with any intruders. This has also been recognized in modern statutes where nighttime burglaries (first-degree burglaries or aggravated burglaries) are punished more severely than daytime burglaries. Unlawful entries into motels, hotels, or vacation residences are considered residential burglaries committed against those who have temporarily rented or leased rooms in such places.

The number of burglaries reported to the police in 2004 was 2,143,456, for a rate of 7,299.5 per 100,000, a decrease of 1.5% from 2003. Of these burglaries, 65.7% were residential, and most occurred between the hours of 6:00 a.m. and 6:00 p.m. The average loss in a residential burglary was $1,607; for nonresidential burglary, it was $1,708. Of the 294,591 people arrested for burglary in 2004, 85.7% were male, 70.9% White, 27.2% Black, and the remainder other races. Persons younger than 18 accounted for 28.6% of burglary arrests.

As noted previously, burglary statutes are a hodgepodge of laws covering a variety of conduct. The unlawful entry element enables some states to define shoplifting as burglary if it can be shown that a suspect entered a store with the intention of stealing, thereby making the entry unlawful. Samaha[17] lists a variety of offending scenarios for which offenders have been charged *and* convicted of burglary. These include shoplifting, pumping gas and leaving without paying, stealing a case of cigarettes from an open trunk, stealing popcorn from a sidewalk stand, and stealing a few coins from a pay telephone. None of these offenses included "breaking," and only the shoplifter "entered" a "structure" (unless a telephone booth is so defined). Regardless of state statutes, however, all these offenses must be reported to the FBI as a larceny-theft and not burglary. The absurdity of such broad definitions of burglary is that a 15-year-old girl who shoplifts a $1.50 lipstick and a 30-year-old man who enters an occupied residence at night and steals property worth thousands of dollars could both be charged with the same crime in some states, although they obviously would not receive the same penalty.

Burglars and Their Motives

The "typical" burglar is a young male firmly embedded in the street culture to the same degree as the robbers we met in the previous chapter. They are perhaps a little less daring since there is less chance of victim contact, injury, and identification for burglary than for robbery, and the penalties and probability of arrest are much lower (recall from Chapter 2 that the clearance rate for burglary is only 12.9 versus 26.2 for robbery). Burglars are the most likely of all criminals to be reconvicted (76%) within 2 years of being released from prison, with sex offenders being the least likely (19%).[18] This is not to imply that burglars are necessary "specialists" because almost all of the 105 active burglars in St. Louis, Missouri, interviewed in depth by Wright and Decker[19] admitted to a smorgasbord of offenses they had committed in the previous 6 months. Most of Wright and Decker's "burglars" preferred to call themselves "hustlers" to reflect their proud ability to exploit the range of criminal opportunities that come their way, but most of them considered burglary their preferred crime because it offers the greatest chance of success and reward with the least amount of risk.

The basic motive for committing burglary is no different from any other property crime: to gain resources at little or no cost to oneself. Wright and Decker[20] state that burglars begin to contemplate their crimes while "under intense emotional pressure to obtain money as quickly as possible" to finance their high living. Although almost all reported that their primary motive was financial, many of them also reported that they found the psychic rewards of committing burglaries a secondary benefit, with many of them describing the act as "an adventure," "a challenge," "fun," "exciting," and "thrilling."[21] Seven of their 105 subjects even reported that these psychic rewards were of primary importance.

The content of the extensive interviews related by Wright and Decker[22] and the statistical data from Mawby's multiple British samples[23] strongly support Walter Miller's focal concerns theory[24] discussed in Chapter 4. Demographically, burglars come from poor rundown and socially disorganized neighborhoods where unemployment is rife; they are poorly educated, unreliable, and resistant to taking orders; and most come from single-parent households. There is a strong sense of toughness and masculine independence, fate ("I had little choice but to burgle"), excitement (sexual activity, drugs, alcohol), autonomy ("As a burglar I'm my own man"), and smartness (outwitting the law and getting something for nothing).

Given the lack of legitimate skills and general trustworthiness that they see among burglars, Wright and Decker as well as Mawby are dubious about job creation programs that change burglars into law-abiding citizens. It is plain that most burglars choose burglary over jobs as being far more profitable. Rengert and Wasilchick likewise reject the notion that burglary is a default option of the jobless, claiming that many burglars who had jobs gave them up to concentrate on burglary: "Unemployment is not what caused crime. Crime caused the unemployment. Time conflicts forced individuals to choose burglary or their jobs. The resolution of the conflict led directly to unemployment."[25] Employment means taking orders from bosses, and "Not taking orders from anyone . . . is a bedrock value on which male streetcorner culture rests; to be regarded as hip one must always do as he pleases."[26] Legitimate employment simply would not fit into these people's lives because for them, party time is all the time. By far, the greatest amount of the proceeds of Wright and Decker's burglars was spent on drugs, alcohol, and sex, and legitimate jobs provide neither adequate money nor time to engage in these pleasures.

Burglary and Gender

Although burglary is primarily a male crime, females commit it as well. In 2004, 14.3% of the arrestees for burglary were females, which makes female arrests for burglary proportionately greater for any other Part I Index crime except larceny. Because females overwhelmingly commit burglaries in mixed-gender teams, it follows that they share most of the demographic characteristics of their male partners. Mullins and Wright[27] found that most of the women were initiated into burglary by their boyfriends, and some were coerced ("if you love me, you'll do it") against their will. Unlike males, females prefer to work as part of a team and admit that they lack the skills and knowledge to go solo.

Mullins and Wright also found that, in common with female robbers, female burglars capitalized on their sexuality to locate potential targets and gain access to homes that they and their partners would burglarize later. Once inside a target's home, they could assess potential valuables and entry points and perhaps even discover where their victim kept spare keys. They could also elicit other important information such as the target's schedule so that she and her partner could be sure to enter the house when the target is not at home. Female burglars are slightly more likely than their male counterparts to spend portions of their loot on necessities and clothing, but they too spend the greatest proportion on drugs.

Choosing Burglary Targets

Selecting a suitable home for burglary is an obvious concern for burglars. The four most important considerations in target selection according to Mawby[28] are *target exposure, guardianship, target attractiveness,* and *proximity.*

- Target exposure refers to the visibility and accessibility of the home (i.e., isolation from other homes and easy access via side and back doors shielded by abundant trees and shrubs). Can the premises be seen by neighbors and passersby?
- Guardianship refers to how well the home is protected. Does the home show signs of occupancy such as cars in the driveway, lights on, and music playing? Is there a burglar alarm or dog present? Is there mail in the mailbox, newspapers in the foyer, and a general silence about the place?

♦ Target attractiveness refers to signs that there should be rich pickings in the house. Previous surveillance may have revealed high-priced cars in the driveway or delivery trucks delivering expensive items.

♦ Proximity refers to the distance between the target home and the burglar's home.

All these concerns are relative to the "professionalism" of the burglar. High-level burglars may travel miles to a particularly attractive target after very careful surveillance and planning, but most burglars are low- to mid-level opportunists who engage only in rudimentary, even spur-of-the-moment planning. For these individuals, the "planning" of a burglary is little more than opportunism. Proximity is important both because burglars are most familiar with their own areas and because many of them lack transportation. As one of Wright and Decker's subjects put it, "I ain't gonna go no further than 10 blocks; that's a ways to be carryin' stuff. . . . Since I'm on foot, I got to keep walkin' back and forth until I get it all."[29] As is the case with murderers, robbers, and rapists, the great majority of low- and mid-level burglars prey on residents in the same neighborhoods in which they also reside. Target exposure and attractiveness is simply making the best of a bad deal for such burglars since the pickings are pretty slim in their neighborhoods.

Guardianship is the most important consideration for low- and mid-level burglars, with many choosing homes occupied by individuals known to them such as neighbors, acquaintances, and even friends.[30,31] Wright and Decker report the statement of one of their respondents: "I be knowin' what house I'm going to hit. It could be a friend of mine, I could be over at his house all last week, I know he got a new VCR, we be lookin' at movies. I know what time they work. I know where his wife at or he stay by himself."[32] Typically, the only planning such individuals do is to call and see if their intended victims are home. Some of those who victimize friends and acquaintances do report occasional pangs of guilt but justify their actions as the result of a desperate need to get money for another drug fix. Given their willingness to criminally exploit almost anyone, we can easily see why Wright and Decker[33] characterized their sample of burglars (who obviously lack the social emotions) as "self-centered individuals without notably strong bonds to other human beings; their allegiance seemed forever to be shifting to suit their own needs."

Disposing of the Loot

The most immediate pressure facing burglars after a successful burglary is to convert the stolen goods into cash to finance their pursuit of drugs, alcohol, and sex. Burglars turn to a variety of sources to dispose of the loot, with fences being the preferred method of disposal. A **fence** is a person who regularly buys stolen property for resale and who often has a legitimate business to cover his or her activities. Only a minority of burglars (the high-level burglar) use a fence because fences prefer to deal only with people they know and trust. Fences are valued by burglars who use them because it is the fastest way of getting rid of "hot" property, and they can be trusted to be discreet. Fencing is a *UCR* Part II crime that is formally known as receiving stolen property. Anyone knowingly buying or possessing stolen property can be charged with this crime.

Burglars without connections to a professional fence must turn to other outlets. One method is a pawnshop, but this is not a very popular outlet for most burglars because pawnbrokers must ask for identification, take pictures of people selling to them, and possess "hot

▲ **Photo 14.2** One way the police respond to street crime is to create maps detailing locations where reported crimes have occurred. Note in this photo that, as of 2002, the NYPD was still using pushpins rather than sophisticated GIS software to research crime location patterns.

sheets" of stolen goods. Some burglars who have developed a trusting relationship with certain pawnbrokers are able to sell "off camera," but because pawnbrokers always have the upper hand in negotiations and offer very little for the goods, only 13 of Wright and Decker's sample said that they regularly used them. A more popular outlet was the drug dealer because it can entail a strict "drugs-for-merchandise" deal without involving any middleman. Others regularly sold to relatives, friends, and acquaintances because few people can resist buying merchandise at below even "fire-sale" prices. Because of the high value of the property they go after, high-level burglars would never use any of these alternatives to the professional fence.

⬚ Motor Vehicle Theft

The FBI defines **motor vehicle theft** (MV theft) as "the theft or attempted theft of a motor vehicle."[34] MV theft covers all kinds of motorized land vehicles such as motorcycles, buses, automobiles, trucks, and snowmobiles, although the vast majority of thefts involve automobiles. MV theft is a larceny, but it is considered different enough and serious enough to warrant separate classification. Taking items from a vehicle is classified as a larceny, as is taking parts from the vehicle such as panels and wheels as long as the vehicle is not itself stolen in order to get the parts.

The number of MV thefts reported in the United States in 2004 was 1,237,114 for a rate of 421.3 per 100,000, a decrease of 2.9% from the 2003 rate. The nationwide loss attributable to MV theft was approximately $7.6 billion. Of the 147,732 arrestees for MV theft in 2004 (a clearance rate of 13%), 82.9% were males, 64.3% White, 34.2% Black, and other races the remainder. Persons younger than age 18 accounted for 26.5% of the arrests for MV theft. Vehicles are most often stolen from parking lots, followed by streets and home driveways and garages.[35]

Table 14.1 shows the 10 U.S. cities with the highest rates of MV theft and the vehicles most often stolen in 2004. Note that all cities are in the western United States and that 6 of them are in California. Japanese automobiles tend to be particularly targeted. These are popular cars with the general population and hold their value well; older vehicles are targeted for their spare parts.[36]

Motor Vehicle Theft for Fun and Profit

MV theft is motivated either by fun or profit. Most MV thefts committed by juveniles are strictly for fun—"joyriding." Juveniles will spot a "cool" car with the keys in the ignition, steal it, drive it around until it runs out of gas, and then abandon it. Some of the more malicious joyriders will get an additional kick by smashing it up a little first.[37] The high recovery rate of stolen vehicles (about 62%, although many are damaged so much as to be declared "totaled") indicates that most MV thefts are for expressive (to show off, to get some kicks) rather than for instrumental reasons (financial gain).[38] Most joyriding teens commit their act with peers, have been found to come primarily from socially disorganized neighborhoods,[39] have high rates of truancy, and have low rates of participation in sports and other legitimate recreational activities.[40]

Table 14.1 Cities With the Highest Auto Theft Rates and the Models Most Often Stolen

Cities With Highest MV Theft Rates in 2004	MVs Most Stolen in 2004
1. Modesto, CA	1995 Honda Civic
2. Stockton-Lodi, CA	1989 Toyota Camry
3. Las Vegas, NV	1991 Honda Accord
4. Phoenix-Mesa, AZ	1994 Dodge Caravan
5. Sacramento, CA	1994 Chevrolet Full Size C/K Pickup
6. Oakland, CA	1997 Ford F150 series
7. Visalia-Tulare-Porterville, CA	2003 Dodge Ram Pickup
8. San Diego, CA	1990 Acura Integra
9. Fresno, CA	1988 Toyota Pickup
10. Seattle-Bellevue-Everett, WA	1991 Nissan Sentra

SOURCE: National Insurance Crime Bureau. (2005). 2005 hot wheels. Retrieved from http://www.nicb.org/public/newsroom/hotwheels/index.cfm

Carjacking: MV Theft With an Attitude

The most serious form of MV theft is **carjacking,** which may be defined as the theft or attempted theft of a motor vehicle from its occupant by force or threat of force. Carjacking is not a new phenomenon, but it has increased significantly over the past two decades. Ironically, one of the biggest reasons for this increase is the increasing sophistication of automobile security devices such as ignition control systems and steering-wheel locks that make parked cars more difficult to steal.[42] Media accounts of carjacking have sparked many copycat offenders: "Hey, I can steal any vehicle I want without damaging it, I get the car keys, and I can rob the owner too; what a concept!"[43] Carjacking thus involves multiple crimes for which the offender may be charged, including robbery, assault, and MV theft, although only the robbery will be included in the *UCR* tally because of the hierarchy rule.

According to a U.S. Justice Department study,[44] between 1992 and 2002, an average of 34,000 carjacking incidents occurred annually, although only 45% were successfully completed. Approximately 32% of the victims of completed carjackings and 17% of attempted carjackings were injured. Victims reported that 93% of the carjackers were male, 3% involved a male/female team, and 3% were lone females. By race/ethnicity, 56% were African American, 21% were White, and the remainder came from other races or were not identified by their victims. About two thirds of carjackings occurred at night (between 6 p.m. and 6 a.m.) and within 5 miles of the victims' homes. Males were more likely to be victimized than females and African Americans more than members of other races. Two well-known victims of carjacking are singer-writer Marc Cohn and rapper Cam'ron, both of whom were shot and wounded in botched carjackings in 2005.

Interviews with active (nonincarcerated) carjackers find that they are more like street robbers in terms of their demographics, motivations, and lifestyles than they are like professional car thieves.[45] Much of it is motivated by the need to bankroll a hedonistic lifestyle and displays of status. Many times, carjacking is a spur-of-the-moment thing, as described by "Tall": "I was broke. I didn't have enough bus fare. I'm walking down the street, there's a guy sitting in his car. I go ask him for change. He was going for his pocket. I just grabbed him outta his car. Why just take his change when I can take his car and get a little bit more?" Carjacking may also be precipitated by the victim driving around "flossing"—that is, engaging in ostentatious displays of wealth and status that others see as an affront ("dissing") to neighborhood carjackers. One carjacker described his attitudes toward flossing as follows: "This motherfucker [was] . . . flossing . . . showboating and shit. He had all that shit in that motherfucking [car]. . . . He flossed his ass off. . . . So we was gonna get the motherfucker."

The sheer thrill, the rush, the dance with danger for its own sake, is also a powerful motivator of carjacking: "It's a rush thing when you're pulling someone out of a car. . . . I mean, I feel good." Some carjackers also say that they enjoy the opportunity to brutalize and humiliate their victims: "The way people look at you when they're scared and panicky and stuff . . . it is funny just to see them shaking an pissing all over theyself." "You get a kick out of seeing them screaming and hollering . . . especially when they all [acting as though they were] tough."[46]

Motor vehicles are also obviously stolen for profit. Most vehicles stolen for profit are taken to so-called chop shops where they are stripped of their parts and accessories. These items are easily sold to auto supply stores, repair shops, and individuals who get faster delivery at a lower price than they would from legitimate suppliers. Other stolen vehicles may be shipped abroad, where they are worth more than they are in the United States. A National Insurance Crime Bureau[41] report indicated that in 1997, an astounding 200,000 stolen vehicles were shipped abroad, where they could be sold at higher prices than in the United States. Some professional auto thieves (called *jockeys*) even steal particularly high-value vehicles "to-order" for specific customers.

≋ Arson

Arson is defined as "any willful or malicious burning or attempting to burn, with or without intent to defraud, a dwelling house, public building, motor vehicle or aircraft, personal property of another, etc."[47] Some arson offenses involve the burning of one's own property in order to collect insurance, some involve attempts to cover up other crimes such as murder or burglary, and others involve malicious vandalism of random or specifically targeted structures. Arson was added to the *UCR* in 1979, and there still exists a great deal of difficulty in gathering standardized statistics from reporting agencies. Much of the problem lies in deciding whether a "suspicious" fire was arson and in the overlap of jurisdiction between police and fire departments. Only fires that have been determined by investigators to have been willfully and maliciously set are classified as arsons. In addition, agencies representing only 73.5% of the U.S. population submitted complete arson data for 2004.[48] For these reasons, the *UCR* does not provide an estimated national rate for arson.

A total of 71,319 arson offenses were reported by law enforcement agencies in 2004. The average dollar loss for property destroyed or damaged in 2004 was $12,017 per offense. There is a higher involvement of juveniles in arson than in any other index crime. Fully 50.2% of all arson arrestees in 2004 were juveniles. Whites accounted for 77% of arson arrests, Blacks for 20.9%, and other races for the remainder. Males accounted for 83.5% of arson arrests.

Arson is a serious threat to life and property. The U.S. Fire Administration[49] estimates that each year, 267,000 fires are attributable to arson (note the huge discrepancy with the *UCR* data) and that these fires result in 475 deaths, more than 2,000 injuries, and $1.4 billion in property loss. Under early common law, arson applied only to the burning of a dwelling of another and not to burning one's own dwelling or merely setting a fire that did not actually burn the dwelling of another. As with the crime of burglary, the crime has been expanded to cover any structure, including one's own. Most jurisdictions grade arson into first degree (the burning of an occupied structure), second degree (burning an unoccupied structure), and third degree (burning personal property—excluding one's dwelling—and acts such as setting garbage cans on fire).

Arson can have a variety of instrumental motivations such as financial gain, revenge, and intimidation, or it can have expressive motivations that may signal psychopathology of some sort. For instance, an owner of a failing business may hire a professional arsonist (a *torch*) to burn down his or her place of business, a person may set fire to the property of another because of some perceived wrong done against him or her by the target, or labor unionists may set fires in a labor dispute to intimidate management, as was the case with the massive Dupont Hotel fire in Puerto Rico in 1986, which led to the deaths of 97 people and injured 140 others.

Because juveniles comprise only about 6% of the American population but have been arrested in 50% of the arsons, expressive motivations are of great interest. Much of juvenile firesetting may be simply the result of curiosity and may never be repeated if the juvenile is caught and dealt with. Other juvenile problems associated with firesetting are much more troubling. A variety of studies have shown that compared with youths in general, persistent

▲ **Photo 14.3**   While arson and other forms of neighborhood vandalism are a constant police concern, many cities are plagued by graffiti. Not only can it be an eyesore, but it is sometimes used by gangs to communicate messages. Here a group of youths paint a mural on a wall once covered with gang graffiti. Sometimes, graffiti writers are themselves sentenced to participate in such cleanups. Recently in New York City, graffiti writers have turned to using etching solvents, which make it impossible to paint over the graffiti.

firesetters have higher levels of other antisocial behaviors, hostility, and impulsiveness and lower levels of sociability and assertiveness. They have also been shown to suffer more psychiatric symptoms, have higher levels of depression, and come from families with low levels of affectional expression and child monitoring.[50–52]

▧ Crimes of Guile and Deceit

The property crimes we have discussed thus far are "physical" crimes committed largely by "street" people. The *UCR* lists three Part II property crimes—embezzlement, fraud, and forgery/counterfeiting—that are committed by a demographically broader range of people than we see committing such crimes as burglary and MV theft. Some criminologists consider these crimes committed by guile and deceit to be white-collar crimes. White-collar workers certainly commit these crimes, but blue- and pink-collar workers, as well as the unemployed and welfare recipients, commit them also. It is for this reason that most criminologists examine them as property crimes rather than white-collar crimes.

Embezzlement

Embezzlement is the misappropriation or misapplication of money or property entrusted to the embezzler's care, custody, or control. Being in positions of trust, embezzlers are usually able to cover up the theft for a long period of time. Most embezzlers do what they do because they have some pressing financial problem or simply because have access to money and the ability to hide any discrepancies for some time. After being exposed, many embezzlers insist that they were only "borrowing the money" and that they fully intended to pay it back.

Embezzlement has occurred ever since institutions started to entrust funds to the guardianship of others. Banks have long been embezzlement targets, but the advent of computers has made it both easier to commit and more lucrative. In the first decade of the "computer revolution" in banking, arrests for embezzlement rose 56%, with the average loss to banks per computer embezzlement crime being as high as $500,000 compared with the average loss per armed bank robbery of just over $3,000.[53] One favorite method of stealing via the computer is known as the salami ("slicing off") technique, whereby the embezzler will open up "phantom accounts" in his or her name and slice off very small amounts (often only a few cents) from a large number of accounts whose owners are hardly likely to notice. This technique can garner the embezzler very large sums of money over a period of time.[54]

The most successful embezzler in U.S. history was Robert L. Vesco, who looted close to $250 million from a variety of mutual funds while he was head of a Swiss-based investment organization. When Vesco learned that he was under investigation for criminal fraud in 1972, he fled to Costa Rica, avoiding extradition by "contributing" $300,000 to the Costa Rican president.[55] In 1982, Vesco settled down in Cuba, where he set up a criminal empire, becoming a middleman and dealmaker to a variety of dictators and criminal elites in the central American/Caribbean region. Justice prevailed in the end when the Cubans arrested him in 1995 on suspicion of being a foreign agent, sentencing him to 13 years in prison for "economic crimes against the state."[56]

Embezzlement is the rarest of property crimes, with only 11,683 cases being reported in the *UCR* in 2004. Females (50.4%) were actually arrested more often than males (49.6%) in 2004.[57] Whites constituted 69.2%, Blacks 28.5%, and other races the remaining 2.4% of those arrested for embezzlement in 2004. For a crime that requires a level of trust to be able to commit it, it is surprising that 7.3% of all embezzlement arrestees were younger than age 18.

Fraud

Fraud is theft by trick—that is, obtaining the money or property of another through deceptive practices such as false advertising, impersonation, and other misrepresentations. Obtaining resources by fraudulent means probably began when the first human being realized that he or she could obtain something, with less risk and effort, by using brains rather than brawn. The most common kind of fraud is income tax fraud. In 1994, Catalina Vasquez Villapando was convicted of income tax fraud, which represented a loss of $47,000 to the treasury. This is not particularly noteworthy unless you know that Villapando was treasurer of the United States from late 1989 to her conviction in 1994.[58] If you have paper money printed during that period, you have money certified by a convicted felon. Other examples of fraud include telemarketing fraud, offers of quack medical cures, phony faith healers, "cowboy" home repair companies, price gouging, and diploma mills promising "accredited" college degrees for a lot of money and little study.

Perhaps the most successful fraudster of the 20th century is the penny-stock king, Robert E. Brennan. The penny-stock business is a legitimate one, but one that is almost designed for fraud. Penny stocks are shares/securities in small startup companies in need of financing that are not listed on a recognized exchange and are sold "over the counter." Penny-stock fraudsters such as Brennan purchase large blocks of virtually worthless stocks at as little as one tenth of a cent per share and aggressively sell them at a higher price. When the stock reaches a predetermined price, they dump their own shares (a practice known as "pump and dump"), leaving the hapless investors with worthless paper and the brokers with millions in ill-gotten gains.

At its high point, Brennan had more than 500,000 customers and a sales force of 1,200 brokers. The primary targets of Brennan's firm were the elderly, who would be called by salespersons who were instructed to "never hang up until the customer buys or dies."[59] Brennan was first indicted for fraud in 1983, then again in 1987, again in 1995, and finally in 2001. Brennan's operation was shut down, and he was ordered to repay $75 million after his 1987 arrest. Brennan immediately filed bankruptcy, but it was determined that he had salted away many millions in foreign banks, which led to his 1995 arrest. After many years of legal wrangling in which Brennan intimidated witnesses, he was convicted of seven counts of bankruptcy fraud and money laundering in 2001 and imprisoned for 10 years.[60]

The FBI[61] reported 190,182 arrests for fraud in 2004, of which 55.1% were males and 44.9% were females, indicating a very small gender difference in the commission of this crime. In terms of age and race in 2004, 3.1% of fraud arrestees were younger than age 18, and 72.2% were White, 26.4% Black, and the remaining 1.4% other races.

Forgery

Forgery is the creation or alteration of documents to give them the appearance of legality and validity with the intention of gaining some fraudulent benefit from doing so. Strictly speaking, forgery is the "false writing" of a document, and *uttering* is the passing of that document to another with knowledge of its falsity with intent to defraud. A person can thus commit a forgery without uttering (passing the document on), and a person can utter (passing a forged document on he or she did not forge) without committing a forgery.

Counterfeiting

Counterfeiting, the creation or altering of currency, is a special case of forgery. In most states, forgery and counterfeiting are allied offenses, which is the reason that they appear that way in the *UCR.*

What the computer did for embezzlement, the advent of high-quality color copiers did for counterfeiting. No longer did you need the engraver's fine craftsmanship to produce quality plates for professional counterfeiters. Printing currency with the new copiers became an amateur's do-it-yourself enterprise (just feed in a $20 bill and press the button). In 1993, almost $1,000,000 in color-copier money was passed in the United States.[62]

The FBI[63] reported 86,122 arrests for forgery/counterfeiting in 2004, of which 60.2% were males and 39.8% were females. By race and age, 69.8% were White, 28.5% Black, and 1.7% other races, and 4.5% were younger than age 18.

⊠ Cybercrime: Oh What a Tangled World Wide Web We Weave

Cybercrime is the use of computer technology to criminally victimize unwary individuals or groups. Any invention that can be used has been used by criminals to exploit others, but few of these have been as useful as the computer. Now even the weak and timid who would never dream of using a gun to rob or otherwise victimize someone can steal, assault, and harass in the comfort of his or her home with little or no risk involved. Everyone who enters cyberspace uses a credit card and/or has a Social Security number—and this means that just about everybody is a potential victim of cybercrime. We have seen that conventional criminals such as robbers and burglars typically operate in their own or nearby neighborhoods, but the global reach of the Internet now allows someone in Birmingham, England, to victimize someone in Birmingham, Alabama, or vice versa. The number of offenses it is possible to classify under the cybercrime umbrella is legion, ranging from terrorism (the targeting of a country's computer-run infrastructures such as air traffic control and power grid systems) to simple e-mail harassment. We can concentrate only on the most common ones here, beginning with identity theft.

Identity Theft

Identity theft occurs when someone uses your personal information without your permission to commit fraud or some other crime. According to a Federal Trade Commission report, more than 9.9 million Americans were victims of identity theft in 2003, with the estimated total loss to consumers of $5 billion.[64] Identity theft can range from a criminal's short-term use of a stolen or lost credit card to the long-term use of a person's complete biographical information (name, Social Security number, and other identifiers) to "clone" the victim's identity and to commit multiple crimes that may be attributed to the victim.

Criminals gain access to the personal information of others in a variety of ways. They can steal it, buy it, or simply be given it by their unwary victims. People are continually providing confidential information to all sorts of businesses and agencies. This information goes into huge data banks that may be legitimately accessed by employees who may steal it, or they can be "hacked" into and information stolen. Credit card numbers can be copied during a financial transaction, such as when a restaurant server takes your card for processing, or they can be surreptitiously recorded on a skimming device, which is typically a cigarette pack–size device that is run across a credit card to record the electronic information in the magnetic strip. This information is then used to make duplicate cards. Thieves can also steal original checks left in mailboxes for pickup, copy the information on them, and buy duplicate checks from mail-order firms.

Another method is *phishing*, which, as the name implies, involves thieves casting thousands of fraudulent e-mails into the cyberpond asking for personal information and waiting for someone to bite. Phishers may send out official-looking e-mails with a bank logo asking recipients to "update" their information or telling them that their account may have been fraudulently used and that the bank needs to "verify" their personal information. One study indicated that 40% of recipients of one fraudulent bank e-mail believed it to be real.[65] A victim may also be literally scared into providing his or her information. Imagine receiving an e-mail from "Lolita Productions" telling you that your credit card has been billed $99.95 for the first two child pornography CDs and that it will be automatically billed $49.95 each month for further CDs. The message also says that if you want to cancel membership, you should e-mail back with full credit card details "for verification." Knowing the penalties for possessing child porn, you may be anxious to do anything to free yourself from the electronic embrace of Lolita Publications.

Perhaps the most notorious phishers are the so-called Nigerian frauds run by Nigerian-organized crime groups. E-mails such as the one presented in "Focus On . . . " (next page) have been received by literally millions of people the world over. A small number of people fall for it. These people are first asked to send a small amount of money (perhaps $200 or less) to "cover expenses" but are suckered into sending ever larger amounts as "complications" arise. Some of the more gullible have even been lured to Nigeria with their cash and have been killed.[66]

Most stolen identity information is not for the personal use of the thief but for sale to others. An organization of about 4,000 individuals, calling itself the Shadowcrew, purchased or stole large volumes of personal information for many years and arrogantly advertised and sold it on Web sites worldwide. If you wanted to buy card numbers with security codes, you could get 50 of them for $200; if you wanted the same thing complete with the original owner's Social Security number and date of birth, you would only have to pay $40 each.[67] Leading members of

FOCUS ON . . .

Phishing: "If It's Too Good to Be True . . ."

ATTN: Perhaps, this proposal might come to you as a surprise, since you have neither met or known me before. I will tell you at once what it is all about. My name is Mr. Ben Manu , staff of Union Bank of Nigeria; some times in 1999, one of our esteemed customers MR. ADII BANTAM, died in an air crash. He was the Chief Executive and Managing Director of Cross Atlantic Oil Company and he maintained personal account; both current and savings with us. As at the time of his death, he has about US$35 Million in both accounts. After his death, our Bank made several efforts to contact his Next of Kin without success. We also contacted his Country's Embassy in Nigeria, who after about three months got back to us, saying they could not locate MR. BANTAM'S family or relatives. It was at this point we notified the Nigerian Government through the Central Bank and the Federal Finance Ministry about Mr. Bantam's Account and my Bank was directed to place Mr. Bantam's money in a special account.

The Government, last week sent us a letter asking us to locate Mr. Bantam's relatives and pay them the money or contribute the money to the Government to buy arms and ammunitions needed to assist the civil war presently going on in Liberia. Considering this directives, an extra ordinary meeting of the Board was called, and it was resolved that our Bank should not support the plans of the Government. I was mandated to as a matter of urgency contact anybody I can trust abroad to assist us take the money abroad in the name of Mr. Bantam's relative; hence I am sending you this letter.

My Bank want to present you as the next of kin to the Bank. Your nationality does not matter as you could be his Uncle, Cousin, etc from either the mother's side or his father's side. Should you accept this proposal, we shall send to you, additional information on Mr. Bantam. I am mandated to get the money by all means to any account abroad. When you have received the money, it will be shared in a manner that will be satisfactory to both yourself and my Bank. Our shares can be invested for us for Two years as the case may be under your direct control until we give you instructions on what ever to do with it. Should you be interested, kindly get back to me through the above e-mail clearly stating your private fax and phone numbers, for me to provide you with additional information before we begin the fund transfer.

While I urge you to get back to me without much delay; the code should be OMEGA. Any communication without this code should be disregarded.

Kind regards,

Mr. Ben Manu

the Shadowcrew were arrested by the U.S. Secret Service in 2004, effectively closing the business that authorities estimated had trafficked at least 1.5 million credit and bank cards, account numbers, and other counterfeit documents such as passports and driver's licenses.[68]

Denial of Service Attack: Virtual Kidnapping and Extortion

Denial-of-service (DoS) attacks occur when criminals "kidnap" a business Web site or threaten to kidnap it so that business cannot be conducted. DoS attacks are accomplished by overloading the computational resources of the victim's system by flooding it with millions of bogus messages and useless data. Sometimes, an attack is simply malicious mischief carried out by computer-savvy disgruntled employees, customers, or just someone who has a bone to pick with the services the company provides. Other times, DoS attacks are committed by criminals who demand a ransom. Online gambling sites are prime targets for cyber-extortionists because a "kidnapped" Web site cannot accept bets and stands to lose millions. Paying the ransom is cheaper than losing the business, especially if the threat comes during peak operation times. Millions of dollars have been paid to cyber-extortionists, with only a miniscule few ever reported to the police.[69] Not that the police could do much anyway, as many of these attacks originate overseas.

Who Are the Hackers?

A **hacker** may be simply defined as someone who illicitly accesses someone else's computer system. Hackers may be seen as the upscale version of Albert Cohen's lower-class delinquents we met in Chapter 4, who engaged in malicious, destructive, and nonutilitarian vandalism "just for the heck of it." We do not include in this categorization people who hack into computers for instrumental or political reasons, such as professional criminals or cyberterrorists.

There are many kinds of hackers: Some are purely interested in the intellectual challenge of breaking into difficult systems and do so without damaging them, and others (sometimes known as cyberpunks or virtual vandals) break into systems and implant viruses to destroy data. Most, however, appear to be intellectual thrill seekers who enjoy the challenge of doing something illegal and getting away with it.[70] There is something of a counterculture among these people analogous to graffiti artists and gang members. They take on cybernames such as Nightcrawler and Kompking and romanticize and tell stories about their accomplishments, as well as the accomplishments of "legendary" hackers. Gaining the respect of fellow hackers serves as a source of psychological reinforcement for them in ways similar to ordinary street delinquents.[71] Hackers tend to be young White males, loners, and "nerdy," as well as have high IQs and be idealistic. But they are also unpopular with others, prone to lying and cheating, and perhaps prone to drug and/or alcohol abuse.[72,73]

Software Piracy

Software piracy is illegally copying and distributing software for free or for sale.

The Business Software Alliance (BSA) has estimated that the worldwide cost of software piracy in 2004 was $31 billion, and that although the United States has the lowest piracy rate (ratio of legitimate to pirate market) in the world, it leads the world in losses to piracy—about $7 billion annually.[74] In the United States, the illegal market is 21% of the total market, whereas in countries such as China, Vietnam, and Russia, the illegal market is around 90% of the total. The BSA estimates that worldwide, for every 2 dollars' worth of software purchased, 1 dollar's worth was illegally obtained.

Software piracy is a crime, but few people see it as such unless multiple copies are made and sold for profit. Many view making copies for friends the same way they view loaning books to them—"I bought it; shouldn't I be able to give it to whomever I please?" Having purchased something legally, they see no reason why the law should mandate that only they should be allowed rights to it. A large survey of university employees found that this was indeed the attitude of many. Forty-four percent of the respondents said that they had obtained unauthorized copies of software, and 31% said that they had made such copies.[75] The cost of piracy to the economy, however, has moved Congress to authorize heavy penalties on offenders. Infringement of copyright can land a first-time offender in prison for 5 years if 10 or more copies are made in a 6-month period, or 10 years for subsequent offenses.[76]

Internet Child Pornography and Cyberseduction

The anonymity of the Internet lends itself well to those who wish to avail themselves of illicit materials, including those who have a predilection for child pornography and for pedophilia. The possession or viewing of child pornography is illegal because of the exploitation of the children depicted in it.

Nevertheless, there is a strong demand for it, judging by the customers of a Web site called Landslide Productions. This Web site, run by Thomas and Janice Reedy in Fort Worth, Texas, had a list of more than 300,000 customers in 60 different countries. The Reedys did not produce the pornography but rather provided a Web site to advertise and serve as a gateway to sites in Russia and Indonesia. The Landslide Web site made millions of dollars for the Reedys, who charged subscribers $29.95 a month for access to the child porn sites. When police raided the Reedy office in 1999, they discovered a well-organized business complete with over a dozen employees, including a customer service representative and a receptionist. Thomas Reedy was convicted on 89 counts of possession and distribution of child pornography and sentenced to 1,335 years in prison; Janice was convicted of 87 counts and sentenced to 14 years. As a result of the raid, 120 other offenders were arrested.[77,78]

Many people use the Internet in search of social relationships, and about 60% of people say that they have found them there.[79] This may be a positive thing for most, but if the Internet is used to procure underage sex partners, it is a crime. Internet trolling by sexual predators may have been sparked by exposure to Internet child pornography, leading the offender to go beyond voyeurism to wanting to make actual contact with children. Many of today's children love to enter chat rooms in the way previous generations enjoyed pen pals. The difference is that today, anyone with access to a computer can join the conversation. Predators may pass themselves off as peers and get them to talk about sexual activity, even to the point of engaging in mutual "cybermasturbation" and sharing the experience online.[80]

Experienced predators know how to groom children and often attempt to arrange actually meeting with them. They know who the vulnerable children are—that is, children who are lonely, insecure, and easily manipulated and who do not enjoy a very positive or trustful relationship with their parents.[81] This information can be gleaned easily from a few correspondences with the child. One nationwide study of Internet-initiated sex crimes against minors found 129 cases, 74% of which involved face-to-face meetings, and 93% of such meetings involved sexual activity. Ninety-nine percent of the perpetrators were male, and 75% of the victims were girls; only 5% of the offenders represented themselves online as peers.[82]

✉ Public-Order Offenses

Public-order offenses are a smorgasbord of offenses, some of which have been variously called vice offenses, consensual offenses, victimless crimes, or even nuisance offenses. Some of these public-order crimes are considered very serious (the sale of drugs), and some are dismissed with a shrug of the shoulders or a look of disgust (drunken and disorderly behavior, public indecency). Many public-order offenses return us to the issues discussed in Chapter 1 about what should and what should not be classified as acts requiring the intervention of the criminal justice system. It cannot be denied that all public-order offenses cause some social harm, but whether or not for some of these offenses the harm is great enough to warrant siphoning off criminal justice resources that could be applied to more serious crimes is a matter of debate. We will only discuss those public-order offenses that are among the most serious that involve the criminal justice system as opposed to other agencies such as health and welfare agencies. Among the Part II offenses not discussed are "other assaults" that are minor in nature.

We do not imply that public-order offenses are without real objective harm; some may even result in harm greater than some Part I offenses. We also reject the notion that offenses categorized as public-order offenses are "victimless" since there are always secondary victims (family members, friends, etc.) who may be profoundly harmed by the actions of the offender. Nevertheless, many public-order offenses are of the "moving target" kind we described in Chapter 1. No other crime has been subjected to more shifts of attitudes and opinions across the centuries and across different cultures than prostitution.

▲ **Photo 14.4** How do you maintain public order? One way is through the use of signs and/or symbols. This is particularly useful in places like large cities or tourist destinations where speakers of many languages are likely to travel. This grouping of prohibited items to bring inside a Prague post office includes cell phones, ice cream, guns, cameras, dogs, and tobacco.

Prostitution and Commercialized Vice

Prostitution and commercialized vice is defined by the FBI as "the unlawful promotion of or participation in sexual activities for profit. To solicit customers or transport persons for prostitution purposes; to own, manage, or operate a dwelling or other establishment for the purpose of providing a place where prostitution is performed; or to otherwise assist or promote prostitution."[83] This offense thus covers people who sell their sexual services (prostitutes), those who recruit (procure) them, those who solicit clients (pander) for them, and those who house them. The common term for a procurer and panderer is a *pimp*, and the keeper of a bawdy house (a brothel) is a *madam*. There were 44,783 arrests for prostitution and commercialized vice in 2004 (31,586 females and 13,197 males). This is obviously only the tiniest fraction of all such offenses. Of these arrests, 218 males arrested were younger than age 18, as were 610 of the females.[84] Given the broad definition of this offense, we cannot know how many arrests were for actual prostitution and how many were for the ancillary offenses such as pandering or procuring. We concentrate our discussion here only on prostitution.

Prostitution may be succinctly defined as the provision of sexual services in exchange for money or other tangible reward; a prostitute is a person who engages in such activity with multiple partners as a primary source of income. Exchanging sexual favors for some other valued resource is as old as the species, and prostitution has long been referred to as the world's oldest profession. It has not always had the same sordid reputation that is attached to it today, however. Many ancient societies employed prostitutes in temples of worship with whom worshipers "communed" and then deposited a sum of money into the temple coffers according to their estimation of the worth of the communion. In ancient Greece, many women of high birth who had fallen on hard times became high-class courtesans called *hetaerae,* who supplied their wealthy clients with stimulating conversation and other cultured activities as well as sexual services. The lower classes had to content themselves with the brothel-based *pornae* or the prettier and more entertaining *auletrides* who would make house calls.[85]

This ancient Greek hierarchy of sex workers (as most prostitutes like to be called) is mirrored in modern American society. The modern American *hetaerae* belong to the elite escort services and call houses. Sex workers who operate in those circles tend to be much better educated, more sophisticated, and better looking than other sex workers because they cater to a wealthy clientele who want to be made to feel special as well as sexually satisfied. These women (and sometimes men who cater to a gay clientele) can earn six-figure incomes annually and are able to sell their "date books" upon retiring for thousands of dollars.[86]

Brothel prostitutes are the modern *auletrides.* The only legal brothels in the United States are in certain counties of Nevada, but illegal brothels probably exist in every town of significant size in the United States, although they are not as prominent a part of community life as they used to be. Brothel prostitutes must accept whatever client comes along but may make from $50 to $100 from each client. The streetwalker is the lowest member of the sex worker hierarchy. These prostitutes solicit customers on the streets and may charge only about $20 a trick (typically a quick act of fellatio).

Becoming a Prostitute

It has been estimated that prostitution is the primary source of income for more than 1 million women in the United States.[87] Many of these women view sex work as the most financially lucrative option open to them given their limited educational and vocational skills. Many brothel and streetwalker prostitutes typically progressed from casual promiscuity at an early age to reasoning that they could sell what they were giving away, under the influence of peer pressure from more experienced girls and from pimps.[88] Pimps exploit the strong need for love and acceptance among vulnerable girls. A pimp frequently takes on the roles of father, protector, employer, lover, husband, and often drug supplier, thus making the girl totally dependent on him.[89] The girls most vulnerable to pimps and other pressures to enter prostitution are those who have experienced high rates of physical, sexual, and emotional abuse at home and who are drug abusers.[90]

Although most of the run-of-the-mill prostitutes just drift aimlessly into it under subtle pressure and few of them deliberately set out to become prostitutes, high-class call girls usually consciously make a decision to enter the profession. They know that, with the proper contacts and training, they can make a professional-level income while preparing themselves to enter a legitimate profession. Most such women leave the business after a few years, and those who remain inevitably wind up plying their trade in brothels, in bars (B-girls), or on the streets as they become physically less attractive.

Should Prostitution Be Legalized?

Prostitution is one of those things that we can never really stop, although the AIDS epidemic has greatly reduced it (a 1989 study found that about 40% of streetwalkers and 20% of call girls were HIV positive[91]). If we can't stop it, should we legalize it and therefore make it safer? When the ancient Greek lawmaker Solon (638–559 B.C.) legalized and taxed prostitution, he was widely praised: "Hail to you Solon! You bought public women [prostitutes] for the benefit of the city, for the benefit of the morality of a city that is full of vigorous young men who, in the absence of your wise institution, would give themselves over to the disturbing annoyance of better women."[92] Taxes on prostitution enabled Athens to build the temple to Aphrodite and provided its "vigorous young men" safe outlets for their urges. To borrow a term from sociology, the citizens of Athens found prostitution to be "functional," meaning that it had a socially useful role to play. Such an attitude, however, ignores the important (functional) role of morality to society, and the issue of legalization becomes how much morality we are willing to sacrifice for the sake of expediency.

Other Sex Offenses

This category includes all sex offenses other than forcible rape and prostitution and are defined as "offenses against chastity, common decency, morals, and the like."[93] There were 47,721 males and 3,444 females arrested in this category in 2004.[94] The FBI *Handbook* lists adultery and fornication, seduction, buggery, sodomy or crime against nature, incest, indecent exposure, indecent liberties, statutory rape without force, and attempts to commit any of these in this category. Arrests for adultery and fornication are rarely if ever made, sodomy statutes were declared unconstitutional by the U.S. Supreme Court in 2003, and incest is usually charged as a much more serious crime such as rape, sexual battery, or lewd and lascivious conduct/gross sexual imposition, which are all felonies. This leaves us only with certain acts that come under the umbrella term of paraphilia—Greek for "besides" or "other love." Paraphilias typically begin in early adolescence and become better defined and elaborated on during early adulthood. For some individuals, paraphiliac stimuli are necessary for sexual arousal and are always a component of their sexual activities. For others, such stimuli simply add novelty or spice to their sexual lives and are only occasionally engaged in. According to the APA, paraphilia is virtually unique to males: "Except for sexual masochism, where the sex ratio is estimated to be 20 males for each female, the other paraphilias are almost never diagnosed in females."[95]

Other than pedophilia (lover of children), the most common paraphilias that have been criminalized are exhibitionism, voyeurism, and toucheurism/frotteurism. These are psychiatric rather than legal terms.

Exhibitionism involves the exposure of one's genitals (sometimes while masturbating) to a stranger of either gender for sexual pleasure. There is usually no attempt at further sexual activity with the victim, although such attempts do sometimes occur. Contrary to the "dirty-old-man-in-a-greasy-raincoat" stereotype, the APA reports that exhibitionism becomes less severe after age 40.[96]

Voyeurism is the act of secretly observing ("peeping") unsuspecting persons who are naked, in the process of disrobing, or engaging in sexual activity. Such behavior is highly arousing for the voyeur, who may masturbate while he is watching or while fantasizing about it afterwards. No other sexual activity with the observed person is typically sought, although voyeuristic activity can sometimes result in rape. Research has shown that many rapists have histories of voyeurism before the emergence of rape behavior.[97]

Toucheurism and **frotteurism** are two closely related paraphilias. Toucheurism involves the desire to intimately touch women, and frotteurism involves the desire to press the penis against a woman. In each case, the offender gets aroused only when the women he touches or rubs against are strangers. Both of these behaviors typically take place in crowded areas such as shopping areas and elevators.

Causes of Paraphilias

Since many paraphilias involve stimuli that the great majority of individuals find sexually neutral (shoes, enema hoses, whips, etc.), part of the answer to their origins lies in the principles of classical conditioning. As we saw in Chapter 7, classical conditioning involves learning to transfer a natural (unlearned) response from one stimulus to a neutral stimulus. Applied to the process of learning aberrant sexual behavior, sexual stimuli (sights, sounds, touches, and smells) are unconditioned stimuli because they have the intrinsic property of eliciting unconditioned natural responses (sexual arousal) that are intrinsically rewarding. If sexual stimuli become paired with an unconditioned stimulus, that stimulus may become a conditioned stimulus capable of eliciting the unconditioned responses itself. This unconditioned stimulus can be anything associated with the various paraphilias and may create a preference for deviant rather than conventional sexual behavior.

Driving Under the Influence

Driving under the influence is defined by the FBI as "driving or operating a motor vehicle or common carrier while mentally or physically impaired as the result of consuming an alcoholic beverage or using a drug or narcotic."[98] In state statutes, this crime is typically referred to as driving under the influence (DUI) or driving while intoxicated (DWI). DUI is far from being a victimless offense. According to the Insurance Information Institute,[99] 16,694 people in the United States died in alcohol-related crashes in 2004, which is 557 more than murder victims reported by the FBI in that year. In 2004, there were 805,854 DUI arrests, of which 81.4% were males and 85% White.[100]

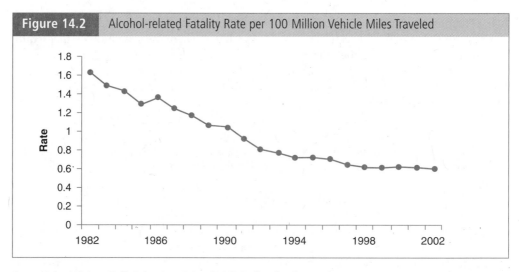

| Figure 14.2 | Alcohol-related Fatality Rate per 100 Million Vehicle Miles Traveled |

Source: National Highway Traffic Safety Commission. (2003). *Traffic safety facts.* Washington, DC: U.S. Department of Transportation.

Many people used to consider deaths due to drunk drivers as "accidents" rather than "crimes," and penalties were relatively light. Attitudes began to change with the founding of MADD (Mothers Against Drunk Driving) in 1980, an organization that has effectively lobbied for legislation nationwide to increase the legal drinking age and for stricter penalties for drunk drivers. MADD also lobbied to lower the blood alcohol count (BAC) level that defines intoxication from 0.10 to 0.08 grams per deciliter of blood. Every state in the union has now enacted all these measures. As we see in Figure 14.2, from the National Highway Traffic Safety Commission,[101] these combined measures reduced alcohol-related traffic fatalities by 62.5% between 1982 and 2002.

A 1999 nationwide study of DUI offenders found that the average BAC at arrest was 0.24, or three times the legal limit. The average time for DUI offenders in jail was 11 months, and for offenders sent to prison, it was 49 months.[102] The significant drop in alcohol-related traffic fatalities following a lowered tolerance and increased penalties shows that we can indeed legislate morality, if only in the case of drunken driving.

Gambling

The FBI defines gambling as follows: "To unlawfully bet or wager money or something else of value; assist, promote, or operate a game of chance for money or some other stake; possess or transmit wagering information; manufacture, sell, purchase, possess, or transport gambling equipment, devices or goods; or tamper with the outcome of a sporting event or contest to gain a gambling advantage."[103] The FBI[104] reported only 6,365 arrests for gambling in 2004 (90.2% males), which, given the widespread popularity of gambling, points to the lack of seriousness with which the police view it and the lack of public support for enforcement.

We have ambivalent attitudes toward gambling in the United States. For instance, the Federal Council of Churches affirms its "vigorous opposition to gambling which we regard as an insidious menace to personal character and morality. By encouraging the idea of getting something for nothing, of getting a financial return without rendering any service, gambling tends to undermine the basic idea of public welfare."[105] On the other hand, wanting something for nothing is hardly a strange desire. The biggest problem with gambling is not the person who wants the occasional flutter on the lottery (the fact that these lotteries are state supported reveals our moral ambivalence) or on the horses, but the person who becomes addicted and gambles away everything he or she owns. Pathological gambling is thus far from victimless. It is similar to drug, sex, food, and alcohol addiction in terms of what is going on in the reward centers of the brains of addicted gamblers.[106]

SUMMARY

Property crimes constitute the vast majority of crimes committed in the United States. Larceny-theft is the most common of these crimes and is divided into misdemeanor and felony categories depending on the value of the stolen property. Shoplifting has received the most attention of all the subcategories of larceny-theft, largely because some people supposedly suffer from a psychiatric condition known as kleptomania.

Burglary is a more serious property offense because it violates victims' homes and could lead to personal confrontation. Studies of burglars find them to be motivated by the need to get quick and easy cash to finance a hedonistic lifestyle. They are typically members of the lower class with the focal concerns of that class, such as seeking excitement and autonomy. Female burglars typically work as auxiliaries to male partners, and they too spend much of their money on alcohol and drugs.

Burglars choose a target according to how easily accessible it is, how guarded it is, how attractive it is, and how close the burglars' own homes are to it. How guarded the home is of greatest concern facing burglars since they do not wish confrontation. Trading in their loot for cash is the most immediate concern after the burglary. The more skilled burglars use fences, but most use other means of disposing of their stolen property, such as pawn shops, drug dealers, and acquaintances.

Motor vehicle theft is a serious larceny often committed by joyriding juveniles, although many vehicles are stolen for profit. Carjacking is a relatively new method of stealing cars that's been made "necessary" by the improvement of antitheft devices. There is a high degree of injury to the victim inherent in this crime, which is essentially a robbery.

Arson is a particularly dangerous property crime because it can lead to deaths. Juveniles commit the majority of arsons, suggesting that it serves some expressive function for them. Compulsive firesetting signals some very serious underlying psychological problems.

Crimes of guile and deceit included in the *UCR* property crime classification are embezzlement, fraud, and counterfeiting/forgery. There are only small gender differences in the commission of these crimes.

Public-order or Part II offenses are too numerous for any exhaustive discussion, but they can be just as harmful sometimes as other offenses. Prostitution is as old as the species, and ways in which individuals become prostitutes and the issue of legalization were discussed. Other Part II sex offenses—exhibitionism, voyeurism, and toucheurism/frotteurism—were briefly touched upon.

Driving under the influence is the most serious Part II offense because of its sometimes deadly consequences. It was pointed out that more people are killed by drunken drivers in a typical year than are murdered by other means. Activism and legislation since the 1980s have succeeded in significantly reducing drunk driving.

Gambling is often viewed as a harmless pastime engaged in by millions of people, but some people take it to pathological extremes and gamble away everything they own, thus victimizing loved ones as well as themselves.

> **On Your Own**
>
> Log on to the web-based student study site at http://www.sagepub.com/criminologystudy for more information about the vignettes and materials presented in this chapter, suggestions for activities, study aids such as review quizzes, and research recommendations including journal article links and questions related to this chapter.

EXERCISES AND DISCUSSION QUESTIONS

1. Survey several friends or classmates and ask them if they have ever shoplifted and how they felt afterwards. What were their motivations? Were some guilty or proud about getting way with it? Did some get a thrill out of it?

2. According to the burglary research discussed in this chapter, why or why not would it be wise policy to implement job training and job creation programs for convicted burglars?

3. Go to http://www.sosfires.com/new.html and view the various youth firesetting intervention programs listed there. Click on two or three of the research reports and report about what you have learned about juvenile firesetting and its treatment.

4. Do you think that the citizens of Athens, Ohio, would react similarly to the citizens of ancient Athens, Greece, to the legalization of prostitution? Break into groups of six, composed of three males and three females, and discuss the issue. Is there a clear majority opinion about legalization (yea or nay) after discussion? Is there a clear gender difference on the issue?

5. Given the potential lethal consequences of driving while intoxicated, discuss whether or not DUI should be a serious felony offense. Would such a change in the law significantly reduce the incidence of DUI?

6. Go to the Gamblers Anonymous Web site at http://www.gamblersanonymous.org and the Alcoholics Anonymous Web site at http://www.alcoholic-anonymous.org and compare their respective 12-step programs. How is it that gambling can be addictive if no substance is consumed? Go to reward dominance theory in Chapter 8 to help you answer this question.

KEY WORDS

Arson	Fence	Larceny-theft
Burglary	Forgery	Motor vehicle theft
Carjacking	Fraud	Prostitution
Counterfeiting	Frotteurism	Software piracy
Cybercrime	Hacker	Toucheurism
Embezzlement	Identity theft	Voyeurism
Exhibitionism	Kleptomania	

REFERENCES

1. Ross, J. (1999, February 28). Suspect with satanic impulses confesses to burning churches. Associated Press. Retrieved from http://www.rickross.com//reference/satanism36.html

2. Catalano, S. (2005). *Criminal victimization, 2004.* Washington, DC: Bureau of Justice Statistics.

3. Federal Bureau of Investigation (FBI). (2005). *Crime in the United States, 2004: Uniform Crime Reports.* Washington, DC: Government Printing Office.

4. Walsh, A., & Hemmens, C. (2000). *From law to order: The theory and practice of law and justice.* Lanham, MD: American Correctional Association.

5. Mowbray, J. (2002). *Justice interrupted.* Retrieved from http://www.nationalreview.com

6. Survey: Shoplifting losses mount. (2005). *Orlando Business Journal.* Retrieved from http://orlando.biz journals.com/orlando/stories/2005/12/05/daily.html

7. Cameron, M. (1964). *The booster and the snitch: Department store shoplifting.* New York: Free Press.

8. Moore, R. (1984). Shoplifting in middle-America: Patterns and motivational correlates. *International Journal of Offender Therapy and Comparative Criminology, 23,* 29–40.

9. Cameron (1964).

10. Moore (1984).

11. Lamontagne, Y., Boyer, R., Hetu, C., & Lacerte-Lamontagne, C. (2000). Anxiety, significant losses, depression, and irrational beliefs in first-offense shoplifters. *Canadian Journal of Psychiatry, 45,* 63–66.

12. Tonglet, M. (2001). Consumer misbehavior: An exploratory study of shoplifting. *Journal of Consumer Behaviour, 1,* 336–354.

13. Bartol, C. (2002). *Criminal behavior: A psychosocial approach.* Englewood Cliffs, NJ: Prentice Hall.

14. Shulman, T. (2003). *Some facts about shoplifters.* Retrieved from http://shopliftersanonymous.com

15. Lamontagne et al. (2000).

16. Federal Bureau of Investigation (FBI). (2004). *Uniform Crime Reports handbook.* Washington, DC: Government Printing Office.

17. Samaha, J. (1993). *Criminal law* (5th ed.). Minneapolis/St. Paul, MN: West.

18. Mawby, R. (2001). *Burglary.* Devon, UK: Willan.

19. Wright, R., & Decker, S. (1994). *Burglars on the job: Streetlife and residential break-ins.* Boston: Northeastern University Press.

20. Wright and Decker (1994, p. 201).

21. Wright and Decker (1994, p. 58).

22. Wright and Decker (1994, p. 201).

23. Mawby (2001).

24. Miller, W. (1958). Lower-class culture as a generating milieu of gang delinquency. *Journal of Social Issues, 14,* 5–19.

25. Rengert, G., & Wasilchick, J. (2000). *Suburban burglary: A tale of two suburbs.* Springfield, IL: Charles C Thomas. (Quote on p. 47)

26. Wright and Decker (1994, p. 49).

27. Mullins, C., & Wright, R. (2003). Gender, social networks, and residential burglary. *Criminology, 41,* 813–839.

28. Mawby (2001).

29. Wright and Decker (1994, p. 86).

30. Mawby (2001).

31. Wright and Decker (1994).

32. Wright and Decker (1994, p. 70).

33. Wright and Decker (1994, p. 72).

34. FBI (2005, p. 55).

35. Linden, R., & Chaturvedi, R. (2005). The need for comprehensive crime prevention planning: The case of motor vehicle theft. *Canadian Journal of Criminology and Criminal Justice, 47,* 251–270.

36. Linden and Chaturvedi (2005).

37. Rice, K., & Smith, W. (2002). Socioecological models of automotive theft: Integrating routine activities and social disorganization approaches. *Journal of Research in Crime and Delinquency, 39,* 304–336.

38. Linden and Chaturvedi (2005).

39. Rice and Smith (2002).

40. Linden and Chaturvedi (2005).

41. National Insurance Crime Bureau. (1999). *Thieves target vehicles in U.S. coastal and border communities.* Retrieved from http://www.nicb.com/release.htm

42. Thio, A. (2006). *Delinquent behavior* (6th ed.). Boston: Allyn & Bacon.

43. McGoey, C. (2005). *Carjacking facts: Robbery prevention advice.* Retrieved from http://www.crime doctor.com.carjacking.htm (Quote on p. 1)

44. Klaus, P. (2004). *Carjacking, 1993–2002.* Washington, DC: U.S. Department of Justice.

45. Jacobs, B., Topalli, V., & Wright, R. (2003). Carjacking, streetlife and offender motivation. *British Journal of Criminology, 43,* 673–688.

46. Jacobs et al. (2003).

47. FBI (2005, p. 61).

48. FBI (2005, p. 61).

49. U.S. Fire Administration. (2001). *Arson in the United States* (Topical Fire Research Series). Retrieved from http://www.usfa.fema.gov

50. Brett, A. (2004). "Kindling theory" in arson: How dangerous are firesetters? *Australian and New Zealand Journal of Psychiatry, 38,* 419–425.

51. Hakkanen, H., Puolakka, P., & Santilla, P. (2004). Crime scene actions and offender characteristics in arsons. *Legal and Criminological Psychology, 9,* 197–214.

52. Santtila, P., Hakkanen, H., Alison, L., & Whyte, C. (2003). Juvenile firesetters: Crime scene actions and offender characteristics. *Legal and Criminological Psychology, 8,* 1–20.

53. Rosoff, S., Pontell, H., & Tillman, R. (1998). *Profit without honor: White-collar crime and the looting of America.* Upper Saddle River, NJ: Prentice Hall.

54. Rosoff et al. (1998).

55. Coleman, J. (1986). *The criminal elite: The sociology of white collar crime.* New York: St. Martin's.

56. Associated Press. (1996, August 27). U.S. fugitive convicted in Cuba. *The Idaho Statesman,* p. 6a.

57. FBI (2005).

58. Rosoff et al. (1998).

59. Griffin, S. (2002). Actors or activities? On the social construction of "white-collar crime" in the United States. *Crime, Law, and Social Change, 37,* 245–276.

60. Griffin (2002).

61. FBI (2005).

62. Schafrik, R., & Church, S. (1995). Protecting the greenback. *Scientific American, 273,* 40–47.

63. FBI (2005).

64. Stafford, M. (2004). Identity theft: Laws, crimes, and victims. *Journal of Consumer Affairs, 38,* 201–203.

65. Kshetri, N. (2006, January/February). The simple economics of cybercrimes. *IEEE Security & Privacy,* pp. 33–39.

66. Baines, H. (1996). *The Nigerian scam masters: An expose of a modern international gang.* Hauppauge, NY: Nova Science.

67. Levy, S., & Stone, B. (2005). Grand theft identity. Newsweek Business On-line. Retrieved from http://msnbc.com/id/835i692/site/newsweek/print/1/displaymode/1098/

68. U.S. Department of Justice. (2004). *Nineteen individuals indicted in Internet "carding" conspiracy.* Retrieved from http://www.cybercrime.gov/monto vaniIndict.html

69. Kshetri (2006).

70. Voiskounsky, A., & Smyslova, O. (2003). Flow-based model of computer hackers' motivation. *Cyber-Psychology & Behavior, 6,* 171–180.

71. Kshetri (2006).

72. Power, R. (2000). *Tangled web: Tales of digital crime from the shadows of cyberspace.* Indianapolis, IN: Que Books.

73. Voiskounsky and Smyslova (2003).

74. Business Software Alliance. (2005). *2005 piracy study.* Retrieved from www.bsa.org/globalstudy

75. Seale, D., Polakowski, M., & Schneider, S. (1998). It's not really theft! Personal and workplace ethics that enable software piracy. *Behavior and Information Technology, 17,* 27–40.

76. Cornell Law School. (2005). *U.S. Code collection: Criminal infringement of a copyright.* Retrieved from http://www.law.cornell.edu/uscode/html/uscode18/usc_sec_18html

77. U.S. Department of Justice. (2001). *Thomas Reedy sentenced to life imprisonment in child porn case.* Retrieved from http://www.usdoj.gov/usao/txn/PressRe1101/reedy_sent_pr_htm

78. U.S. Postal Inspector. (2001). *Operation avalanche.* Retrieved from http://www.usps.co/postalinspectors/avalanche.htm

79. Mantovani, F. (2001). Network seduction: A test-bed for the study of strategic communication on the Internet. *CyberPsychology & Behavior, 4,* 147–154.

80. Hitchcock, J. (2002). *Net crimes & misdemeanors.* Medford, NJ: Information Today.

81. Wolak, J., Finkelhor, D., & Mitchell, K. (2004). Internet-initiated sex crimes against minors: Implications for prevention based on findings from a national study. *Journal of Adolescent Health, 35,* 424–435.

82. Wolak et al. (2004).

83. FBI (2004, p. 142).

84. FBI (2005).

85. Bullough, B., & Bullough, V. (1994). Prostitution. In V. Bullough & B. Bullough (Eds.), *Human sexuality: An encyclopedia* (pp. 494–499). New York: Garland.

86. Kornblum, W., & Julian, J. (1995). *Social problems* (8th ed.). Englewood Cliffs, NJ: Prentice Hall.

87. Bartol (2002).

88. Kornblum and Julian (1995).

89. Tutty, L., & Nixon, K. (2003). Selling sex? It's really like selling your soul. Vulnerability to and the experience of exploitation through child prostitution. In K. Gorkoff & J. Runner (Eds.), *Being heard: The experience of young women in prostitution* (pp. 29–45). Black Point, Nova Scotia: Fernwood.

90. Bartol (2002).

91. Kornblum and Julian (1995).

92. Durant, W. (1939). *The life of Greece.* New York: Simon & Schuster. (Quote on p. 116)

93. FBI (2004, p. 142).

94. FBI (2005).

95. American Psychiatric Association (APA). (1994). *Diagnostic and statistical manual of mental disorders* (4th ed.). Washington, DC: Author. (Quote on p. 524)

96. APA (1994, p. 525).

97. Freund, K. (1990). Courtship disorders: Toward a biosocial understanding of voyeurism, exhibitionism, toucheurism, and the preferential rape pattern. In L. Ellis & H. Hoffman (Eds.), *Crime in biological, social and moral contexts* (pp. 100–114). New York: Praeger.

98. FBI (2004, p. 144).

99. Insurance Information Institute. (2005). *Drunk driving.* Retrieved from http://www.iii.org/media/hot topics/insurance/drunk/

100. FBI (2005).

101. National Highway Traffic Safety Commission. (2003). *Traffic safety facts*. Washington, DC: U.S. Department of Transportation.

102. Maruschak, L. (1999). *DWI offenders under correctional supervision*. Washington, DC: Bureau of Justice Statistics.

103. FBI (2004, p. 143).

104. FBI (2005).

105. McCaghy, C., & Cernkovich, S. (1987). *Crime in American society* (2nd ed). New York: Macmillan. (Quote on p. 434)

106. Ruden, R. (1997). *The craving brain: The biobalance approach to controlling addictions*. New York: HarperCollins.

WHITE-COLLAR AND ORGANIZED CRIME

On August 10, 1978, sisters Judy and Lyn Ulrich and their cousin Donna, all teenagers, began their 20-mile journey to play volleyball at a Baptist church in Goshen, Indiana. They were driving along Highway 33 in their Ford Pinto when they were rear-ended by another car. As a result, gas spilled onto the highway, caught fire, and all three trapped girls died horrible fiery deaths. Ford Pintos were fitted with gas tanks that easily ruptured and burst into flames in rear-end collisions of over 25 miles per hour. The problem could have been fixed at a cost of $11 per vehicle, but with 11 million Pintos and 1.5 million light trucks with the problem, Ford accountants estimated that it would cost $137 million to fix. It was calculated that not fixing it would result in 180 burn deaths, 180 serious burn injuries, and 2,100 burned vehicles, which they estimated would cost about $49.5 million in lawsuits and other claims. Comparing those two figures, it was determined that it would be unprofitable and therefore irrational to fix the gas tank problem because the company would save $87.5 million as a result.

The consciences of Ford executives did not seem to bother them: They openly used these figures in a cost/benefit chart to lobby against federal fuel leakage standards to show just how unprofitable such standards would be! According to a Ford engineer, 95% of the 700 to 2,500 people who died in Pinto crashes would have survived had the problem been fixed. If this is any-where near an accurate estimate of deaths caused by the Pinto defect, the executives who conspired to ignore it may be the worst multiple murderers in U.S. history. Yet no Ford executive was ever imprisoned, and many went on to bigger things. Lee Iacocca—who had a personal maxim, "safety doesn't sell"—was still in evidence in 1986 when he actively opposed mandatory airbags for auto-mobiles; he went on to become president of Chrysler Corporation and to chair the committee for the centennial celebrations for the Statue of Liberty.

The case of the Ulrich girls is noteworthy among the hundreds of others because it was the only one for which the Ford Motor Company was indicted on the criminal charge of reckless homi-cide. Although Ford stood to pay only a maximum of a $10,000 fine for each of the three victims, *they brought all their considerable wealth and legal talent to bear in the fight. Ford was found not guilty on the basis of a technicality and only paid out $22,500 to the Ulrich family in a civil suit.*

In Chapter 1, we asked you what images pop into your head when you hear the word *crime*. Whatever images you conjured up, we wager that the image of a well-dressed, middle-aged person, sitting in a leather recliner dictating a memo authorizing the marketing of defective automobiles or the dumping of toxic waste was not among them. We seldom think that the chain of events set into motion by a business memo may do more harm than the activities of any "street punk." People who wear white collars to work steal and kill too, but they use guile and deceit rather than a gun or knife and force or threats of force. Polls consistently show that fear of being victimized by "street crimes" is uppermost in the minds of people, who rarely report any concern about "suite crime." Yet more money is stolen and more people die every year as the result of scams and willful illegal corporate activity than as the result of the activities of street criminals. Kappeler, Blumberg, and Potter[1] estimate that crimes committed by corporations result in economic losses that total between 17 and 31 times greater than losses resulting from street crimes, and the losses due to noncorporate white-collar crime are roughly the same. There is a huge dirty ring around the white collar that no amount of scrubbing will erase, and most criminologists agree that by virtually any criterion, our most serious crime problem is white-collar crime.

⬚ The Concept of White-Collar Crime

The term *white-collar crime* was coined in the 1930s by Edwin Sutherland, who defined it as crime "committed by a person of respectability and high social status in the course of his occupation."[2] Although this definition became enshrined for a long time as *the* definition of white-collar crime, and it governed research for a long time, it was wrong in three important ways: (1) Many (perhaps most) white-collar criminals are not of "high social status," (2) many are not otherwise respectable people, and (3) it fails to distinguish between crimes committed by individuals acting for personal gain and crimes committed on behalf of the employer with the employer's blessing and support.

In its Administration Improvement Act (AIA) of 1979, the U.S. Congress defined **white-collar crime** as "an illegal act or series of illegal acts committed by non-physical means and by concealment or guile, to obtain money or property, or to obtain business or personal advantage."[3] This definition focuses on characteristics of the offense as opposed to Sutherland's focus on the offender as a high-status person. Although avoiding the problem of social status, the AIA definition fails to differentiate between persons who commit crimes for personal gain and those who do so primarily on behalf of an employer. Our analysis of white-collar crime will differentiate between individuals who steal, defraud, and cheat both in and out of an occupational context and those who commit the variety of offenses attributed to business corporations. We acknowledge definitional difficulties in the area of white-collar crime, but rather than presenting endless subcategories of it, we follow Rosoff, Pontell, and Tillman[4] in using the term *occupational* crime for the former and *corporate* crime for the latter.

How Much White-Collar Crime Is There?

Every year, the FBI provides us with a grizzly count of the murder and mayhem that occurred on the streets of America the previous year in its *Uniform Crime Reports* (*UCR*). Together with the National Crime Victimization Surveys (NCVS), the *UCR* provides us with a fairly reliable picture of the amount of so-called street crime, but white-collar crimes are conspicuously absent from the yearly crime tally. The FBI has a congressional mandate to collect and report the physical "in-your-face" criminal acts committed on America's mean streets, but there is no mandate to collect and report crimes of "concealment or guile" that occur on America's Wall Streets.

Conflict theorists have no trouble explaining why white-collar crimes are not represented in the *UCR:* The people who define the seriousness of criminal acts are the same people who own or have large interests in many of the institutions and corporations that commit the acts in question. Not only that, potential high-status offenders "and their representatives play an active part in crafting the laws and regulatory standards that circumscribe their conduct."[5] Such people are thus hardly likely to want to define their shady acts as "serious" or "criminal."

However, tallies of occupational and corporate wrongdoings *are* collected and distributed each year by state and federal regulatory agencies such as the FTC (Federal Trade Commission) and the SEC (Securities and Exchange Commission). However, these agencies do not come under the jurisdiction of the Justice Department and thus lack law enforcement powers. Further complicating things, these agencies cite organizations rather than individuals for wrongdoings, and any one citation may include multiple crimes committed by multiple individuals.

There are also a number of practical difficulties in recognizing and reporting these kinds of crimes. With street crimes, we have a body in the street, a house burgled, or a car stolen. These easily defined discrete events quickly come to the attention of the police, who then record them. With many white-collar crimes, victims often do not even know they have been victimized, and the sequence of events is often quite the opposite: "White-collar crime investigators start with a suspected con artist, and their question is, What did he or she do, and can we prove it?"[6] Many of the most serious white-collar crimes are incredibly complex and require thousands of person hours and millions of dollars to unravel, thus making them difficult to equate with street crime in terms of being able to neatly discover, tabulate, and report them.

Occupational Crime

Occupational crime is crime committed by individuals in the course of their employment. The most obvious and common form of occupational crime is employee theft and vandalism. This might range from draining company funds by creative bookkeeping or sophisticated computer techniques to stealing small items of little value from the office or factory floor. Likewise, vandalism by disgruntled employees may run the gamut from scrambling important computer data to scratching graffiti on newly painted walls. Although such activities may seem relatively mundane to most of us, according to the business insurance industry, employee activities such as theft, fraud, and vandalism cost American business a total of $660 billion in 2003.[7] Such a staggering amount is more than the annual losses from all street crimes combined. Although these figures are derived more from educated guesses than from hard data, they do provide us with at least a rough idea of just how serious employee crime is. Just as we all pay for street crime through the portion of our taxes that goes to support the criminal justice system, we all pay for employee crime because victimized companies merely pass on their losses to their customers via higher prices. Employee crime may also lead to businesses going bankrupt and employees losing the jobs these businesses provided.

Professional Occupational Crime

Professional occupational crimes are crimes committed by professionals such as physicians and lawyers in the course of their practices. Frauds committed by physicians include such practices as filing insurance claims for tests or procedures not performed; performing expensive and unnecessary operations; steering patients to laboratories, pharmacies, or some facility in which the doctor has financial stakes; referring patients to other doctors in return for kickbacks; and prescribing and charging for brand-name drugs and substituting generic drugs. Anyone who has ever seen $8 charges for an aspirin tablet, $500 for a nursing bra, or $200 for a pair of crutches appearing on their hospital bill knows how hospitals rip patients off, but it is also a common practice for them to demand kickbacks from physicians, who stand to lose hospital practice rights if they do not pay.[8]

Many researchers view Medicare and Medicaid programs as welfare programs for physicians. Fraud within these programs has been estimated to cost between $50 and $80 billion per year, and overall medical fraud is estimated to be about $100 billion, or about 10% of the total U.S. health care bill.[9] Fee-for-service medicine essentially means that physicians earn more money the more they perform expensive procedures. A congressional subcommittee on medical fraud estimated that about 2.4 million unnecessary surgeries are performed each year, which allegedly cost the public approximately $4 billion and the loss of about 11,900 lives.[10]

Most lawyers also work on a fee-for-service basis, thus generating the same temptations to increase their incomes by fraudulent means. Frauds perpetrated by lawyers can include major embezzlement of clients' funds, bribery of witnesses and judges, persuading clients to pursue fraudulent or frivolous lawsuits, billing clients for hours not worked, filing unnecessary motions, and complicating a simple legal matter to keep clients on the hook—"I will defend you all the way to your last dollar." It seems that every occupational category generates a considerable number of criminals, and the higher the prestige of the occupation, the more their criminal activities cost the general public.

Causes of Occupational White-Collar Crime: Are They Different?

According to Hirschi and Gottfredson,[11] occupational crime differs from common street crime only in that it is committed by people in a position to do so—Medicaid fraud can typically only be committed by physicians, and bank embezzlement can only be committed by bank employees in positions of trust. The motives of occupational criminals are the same as those of street criminals—to obtain benefits quickly with minimal effort—and the age, sex, and race profiles of occupational criminals are not that much different from those of street criminals. Hirschi and Gottfredson concluded that "when opportunity is taken into account, demographic differences in white collar crime are the same as demographic differences in ordinary crime."[12]

A study of federal white-collar criminals showed that most of them were much less involved in crime and deviance than street offenders but that chronic white-collar offenders (about 16% of the sample) were similar to street criminals in their patterns of prior deviance.[13] Yet another study found that white-collar criminals with prior arrests for non-white-collar crimes were largely indistinguishable from street criminals in their demographics, lifestyle, and endorsement of criminal thinking patterns but were quite different from white-collar criminals with no history of arrest for non-white-collar crimes.[14]

David Weisburd and his colleagues' study[15] of 1,094 high-status white-collar crimes told a different story. Among antitrust offenders, 99.1% were White, 99.1% were male, and the average age was 53. Securities fraud offenders were 99.6% White, were 97.8% male, and had an average age of 44. Offenders in other federal crime categories (tax, credit, mail fraud, bribery, and false claims) were also older by about 10 years than the average street criminal. Males were even more heavily overrepresented than they are in street crime, and non-Whites were also overrepresented (ranging from 17% of the bribery offenders to 38% of the false claim offenders), although not to the extent that they are among street criminals. It was also found that 43.4% of the sample had a prior adult arrest, compared with 89.5% of a sample of street criminals and about 17% of the general public.

⊠ Corporate Crime

Corporate crime *is* criminal activity on *behalf* of a business organization. During much of American history, the primary legal stance relating to the activities of business was decidedly

laissez-faire (leave it alone to do as it will). Under the influence of capitalist philosophy, American courts traditionally adopted the view that government should not interfere with business by attempting to regulate it. For a very long period in our history, victims of defective and dangerous products could not sue corporations for damages because the guiding principle was *caveat emptor* (let the buyer beware), and unhealthy and dangerous working conditions in mines, mills, and factories were excused under the freedom of contract clause of the Constitution.[16]

Although attitudes in the 20th century changed considerably, crimes of fraud, concealment, and misrepresentation continued to victimize all sorts of groups and individuals in society. Crimes such as these are actions committed during the course of fulfilling the legitimate role of the corporation and in the name of corporate-profit and growth. Two famous examples of corporate crime are described below.

▲ **Photo 15.1** Corporate crime cases are typically not handled by local or even county prosecutors. Typically, these cases are moved up to the state attorney general's office, which is better equipped with investigators to prepare these cases for prosecution.

The S & L Scandal: The Best Way to Rob a Bank Is to Own One

The savings and loan (S & L) scandal of the 1980s amounted to one of the most costly crime sprees in American history and is likely to cost the U.S. taxpayer (because the Federal Deposit Insurance Corporation insures all bank savings up to $100,000) up to $473 billion. This staggering amount is many times greater than losses from all the "regular" bank robberies in American history put together.[17]

The hyperinflation of the 1970s left S & Ls holding low-interest mortgages, and many began to fail. The S & L industry was deregulated in 1980 under the assumption that the free market cures all economic problems. Deregulation allowed for massive embezzlement of funds by S & L owners and executives, thus making these crimes hybrids of occupational and corporate crime in that they constituted crime *by* the corporation *against* the corporation. Most of the looting took the form of extravagant salaries, bonuses, and perquisites that executives awarded themselves as their banks sank ever further into debt. One method involved selling land back and forth ("land flipping") within a few days until its paper value far exceeded its real value and then finding "sucker" institutions to buy it at the inflated price. Another method was to make loans back and forth between employees of different banks with the knowledge that the loans would never be called in. A variety of scams with their own playful names, such as "cash for trash," "kissing the paper," "daisy chains," and "dead cows for dead horses," convey the contempt these upper-middle-class executives had for their victims and the gamelike way in which they viewed their activities.[18]

The Enron Scandal: Crooks Cooking Books

The first major scandal of the first decade of the 21st century is that of Enron Corporation, which has been called "one of the most intricate pieces of financial chicanery in history" and, for investors in its stock and its employees, "the financial disaster of a lifetime, a harrowing, nerve-racking disaster from which they may never recover."[19] The Enron scandal (and other similar scandals in the first two years of the 21st century) did tremendous damage to the economy and "created a crisis of investor confidence the likes of which hasn't been seen since the Great Depression."[20]

Enron was a $100 billion corporate empire that had more than 200,000 employees in 40 countries and controlled about one quarter of all trading in natural gas and electricity in the United States.[21] The company poured millions of dollars into political campaigns and lobbyists arguing for further deregulation of the energy markets. The Enron hierarchy expected never-ending innovation and growth from its executives to feed this monster enterprise. In response, executives created imaginary markets, "paper partnerships," and phantom growth that enabled them to report profits that didn't exist and to hide debts that did. Executives were accomplished at cooking the financial books in many ingenious ways, which kept Enron's stock prices rising and thus their own compensation. Because much of the compensation received by Enron executives was stock based, they had major incentives to make the company look as good as possible to investors by reporting high profits to the SEC.

The victimization of Enron's employees lies largely in the fact that they were all strongly encouraged to plow their retirement accounts into Enron stock, which Enron bureaucrats had convinced them would continue to rise. The tragedy is that from its high of $90 in 2000, it plummeted to a piddling 36 cents, which is "junk bond" status.[22] This plunge effectively wiped out the retirement savings of thousands of Enron employees and cost outside investors millions of dollars. With the benefit of insider knowledge, however, top executives cashed in their stocks before the implosion and "walked off with small fortunes."[23]

In May, 2006, top Enron executives Kenneth Lay and Jeffery Skilling were found guilty of multiple counts of fraud and conspiracy after a trial lasting more than 4 months. Lay cheated justice by dying of a heart attack in July 2006. Skilling was sentenced in October 2006 to 24 years' imprisonment (he could have received up to 190 years), as could have Lay had he lived. Skilling's sentence was hardly the "slap-on-the-wrist" sentence of the kind that earlier white-collar corporate criminals received.

Crimes of America's Rich and Famous in History

Criminal conspiracies engaged in by society's elite have occurred in the United States since the country's beginning. A number of criminal enterprises disguised as respectable businesses that used bribery, payoffs, corruption, violence, and intimidation to further their gains existed prior to the Revolution. The most notorious of these enterprises was led by Thomas Hancock and his son John, a notable signer of the Declaration of Independence, who later became governor of Massachusetts.[24] It was the Hancocks, who built much of their fortune in the 1730s by smuggling, and other such corrupt merchants running the economies of New England who were the real exploiters of the lower classes, not George III (the poor mad king hardly knew that America existed). Rich merchants with aversions to paying taxes were able to incite ex-jailbirds, dockyard toughs, and the unemployed to riot, attack customs officials, and organize demonstrations on their behalf.[25] Because they were nominally at the forefront of the American Revolution, corrupt and avaricious merchants such as John Hancock, Samuel Adams, and James Otis are remembered by history as patriots, which they surely were, rather than as crooks.

Many scams occurring in early American history surpassed most modern capers in their audacity and scope. One of the best examples is the Yazoo land fraud of 1795, which probably involved more prominent members of the political and judicial elite than any other crime in U.S. history. Leading the conspiracy were two U.S. senators, two U.S. representatives, a U.S. Supreme Court justice, and an assortment of other politicians and judges. These men were able to obtain title to 35 million acres of state and Indian lands at one-half cent per acre by bribing members of the Georgia legislature, which made them a profit of over $4 million—a princely sum in the 18th century. In essence, these "respectable" speculators had stolen land belonging to Native Americans and to the people of what is now Alabama and Mississippi. When the deal was revealed, there was a huge public outcry, and it was rescinded by a subsequent Georgia legislature. But the rich and powerful never lie down easily; they initiated a string of appeals that went all the way to the Supreme Court (*Fletcher v. Peck*, 1810). The Court, fully aware of the bribery and corruption involved in the case, ruled in favor of the conspirators, stating that rescinding the deal amounted to impairment of the obligation of contract, and thus the Georgia legislature's decision was ruled void.[26]

The Crédit Mobilier scandal, which occurred during the Grant administration, involved three vice presidents (Grant's first running mate, his then current vice president, and the future vice president Benjamin Harris), the Speaker of the House, and a number of other senators and representatives. This scam, run by executives of the Union Pacific Railroad, cost the taxpayers more than $44 million and involved dummy contracts, bribery, falsified documents, overcharging, and kickbacks. Only two of the conspirators were ever "censured" (slapped on the wrist) at a time when common thieves were often hanged.[27]

Cornelius Vanderbilt was not above using blackmail, bribery, fraud, or anything else to achieve his acquisitive aims. During the Civil War, this unscrupulous profiteer sold rotten and ill-equipped ships to the Union at hyperinflated prices, which not only cost taxpayers their money but also the lives of some of their sons serving aboard them. When censured as a war profiteer, he shrugged it off with a statement typical of people with more wealth than conscience: "Law! What do I care about law? Hain't I got the power?"[28]

Other crooked founders of many of today's "high society" families include John Pierpont Morgan, described by Browning and Gerassi[29] as "the most successful crook of his generation"; the ruthless John D. Rockefeller, who left scores of ruined men—and happy politicians—behind him; and Henry Ford, whose union-busting thugs probably killed and maimed more innocent people than any Mafia family ever did. "Upperworld" robber barons such as the men surveyed here probably stole more money and cost more lives than all the underworld crime rings in our history. Yet not one of them spent a single day in prison, and their descendants have lived happily ever after in the lap of luxury.

Theories About the Causes of Corporate Crime

Those who hold classical assumptions about human nature—that, at the most basic level, all human behavior can be understood in terms of striving to maximize pleasure and minimize pain—have no difficulty appreciating the motivation for individuals to engage in corporate crime. Opportunities abound in corporate America to gain wealth beyond what individuals could earn legitimately. The prevalence of corporate crime can also be appreciated given the weakness of formal and informal controls over business activities and the lenient penalties imposed. We may expect business executives to have assimilated the egoism, acquisitiveness, and competitiveness fostered by capitalism more completely than most. Combine this with the absence of meaningful controls and the seductive lure of big money, and corporate crime is more easily understood than is street crime with its more meager rewards and more severe penalties.

But general explanations that invoke assumptions about human nature or about the economic system do not explain differences between companies and individuals who do and do not participate in illegal activities. All companies and their executives are exposed to the capitalist ethos, the strain of seeking their versions of the American Dream, and the widespread opportunities for illegal gains. Thus, "strain" can be evoked as a *motive* for corporate crime but not for the *choice* to engage in it. We might say that corporate criminals are "high-class innovators," to borrow a phrase from strain theory. But what differentiates "innovators" from the other modes of adaptation available in the corporate world?

Corporate Characteristics

Just as there are criminogenic neighborhoods, there are criminogenic corporations with a "tradition" of wrongdoing. One of the first systematic examinations of corporate recidivism found that 98% of the nation's 70 largest corporations were recidivists, with an average of 14 regulatory or criminal decisions against them.[30] General Electric was accused of more than 100 acts of "wrongdoing" from 1911 to 1990, and in 1990 alone paid fines in 16 cases of abuse and fraud in government contracting.[31] A study of 477 major U.S. corporations found that 60% of them were known to have violated the law and that 13% of the violator companies accounted for 52% of all violations, with an average of 23.5 violations per company.[32] And a study of brokerage firms found that many of the biggest names in the business, such as Prudential, Paine Webber, and Merrill Lynch, have had an average of two or more serious violations *per year* since 1981.[33] "Three-strikes-and-you're-out" laws evidently do not apply in the world of pinstripe suits.

Newcomers entering such corporate environments are socialized into the prevailing "way of doing things." If the newcomer does not "fit in" and conform to the prevailing company ethos, he or she is not likely to remain employed there very long. This process can produce a sort of moral apathy in well-socialized executives striving to do their jobs in their own and their company's best interests. If their consciences are pricked, they have ready access to techniques of neutralization to quiet them and to make further wrongdoing that much easier. If each tiny bending of the rules brings profit to the company and gives the rule bender appreciation and bonuses, the individual's behavior will be almost imperceptibly molded in the direction of engaging in ever greater patterns of wrongdoing. If he or she is rewarded through the usual stock-based nature of the executive compensation package, there is further incentive to engage in illegal behavior. Stock-based compensation is designed to increase executives' focus on stockholders' profits, but it is a situation ripe for finagling stocks through insider trading, falsifying accounts, and fraudulent trading, as well as for emphasizing short-term earnings rather than the long-term success of the corporation.[34]

Individual Characteristics

Characteristics such as low IQ and low self-control obviously do not apply to people who have spent many years of disciplined effort to achieve high-status positions, but many other risk factors linked to crime in general could apply to corporate crooks as easily as to street criminals. For instance, it appears that people who choose business careers tend to have lower ethical and moral standards than people who choose other legitimate careers. A number of studies have concluded that business students are, on average, less ethical than students in other majors[35] and that MBA students make fewer decisions judged as ethical and moral than law students.[36]

Efforts to differentiate between offenders and nonoffenders in the white-collar world have focused largely on *locus of control, moral reasoning,* and *Machiavellianism.* People with an internal locus of control believe that they can influence life outcomes and are relatively resistant to coercion from others. People with an external locus feel that circumstances have more influence over situations than they themselves do. The literature indicates that those who engage in corporate crime tend to have an external locus of control and that whistle-blowers tend to have an internal locus of control.[37] Having an external locus of control renders a person susceptible to definitions favorable to corporate crime if those definitions are held by superiors.

Closely related to locus of control is moral reasoning. People operating at higher stages of cognitive moral development are more self-reliant and tend to behave according to their own beliefs about right and wrong. People at lower stages tend to emphasize conformity to group norms. Thus, the lower the stage of moral development, the more likely the person will engage in corporate wrongdoing.[38]

Machiavellianism is the unprincipled and uncaring manipulation of others for personal gain. People high on this trait are shallow individuals who exploit superiors and equals by deceit and ingratiation and subordinates by bullying. Simon[39] describes those who make it to the top of bureaucratic organizations in almost psychopathic terms: Such an individual "exudes charisma via a superficial sense of warmth and charm," and he or she exhibits "free floating hostility, competitiveness, a high need for socially approved success, unbridled ambition, aggressiveness [and] impatience." In the business world, as elsewhere, these people may be willing to use any means necessary to accomplish their goals, including criminal activity.

Law Enforcement's Response to Corporate Crime

As previously indicated, corporate crime is monitored and responded to by a variety of criminal, administrative, and regulatory bodies, but very few corporate crooks are ever the recipients of truly meaningful sanctions. Of the 1,098 defendants charged in the S & L cases, only 451 were sentenced to prison. Most (79%) were sentenced to less than 5 years, with the average sentence being 36.4 months, which was less than the average federal offender convicted of burglary (55.6 months) or drug offenses (64.9 months) during the same period.[40] The Ford Motor Company was financially punished for its disregard for human life in the civil courts, but such costs were factored into their decision making anyway. One has to wonder, with a critic writing at the time of some of these trials, "how long Ford Motor Company would continue to market lethal cars were Henry Ford II and Lee Iacocca [the top Ford officials at the time] serving twenty-year terms in Leavenworth for consumer homicide."[41]

The Golden Rule ("those with the gold make the rules") may explain the substantial differences in severity of punishment between street and corporate criminals because great wealth does confer a certain degree of immunity from prosecution and/or conviction. The degree to which this is true fluctuates with the ideological times. The liberal Carter administration made the prosecution of corporate crime an important item on its agenda, but the conservative Reagan administration wasted little time in reversing this trend when it took office. The power of corporate America can be gauged by the 1990 U.S. Justice Department's withdrawal of its support for proposed tougher sentences for corporate offenders in response to heavy lobbying by many prominent industries, the targets of the proposal.[42] This action adds credence to the assertion that wealth and power go a long way to determine which behaviors are criminalized and which are not, for we doubt that street criminals would get very far lobbying against proposals for stricter penalties for them.

Corporate offenders are intelligent and rational individuals with much to lose, and thus they should be more easily deterred than street criminals who have very little to lose if caught.[43] Classical deterrence theory informs us that the probability of offending is the product of the probability of being caught and the expected maximum penalty. Because the probability of being caught and prosecuted for a corporate crime is low and the costs of investigating and prosecuting them are high, increasing the punishment rather than increasing the probability of arrest and conviction inflicts less cost on society.[44] This would mean severe penalties in terms of imprisonment for individual miscreants and severe monetary penalties for offending corporations. Unfortunately, the latter has to be weighed against the risk of corporate bankruptcy, which may prove to be extremely costly in terms of the loss of jobs and other economic benefits the corporation may have provided for the community or communities in which it does business.[45] As Shover and Hochstetler have pointed out, prosecutors indicate that "they sometimes do not aggressively pursue crimes committed by local businesses for fear of harming employment and the local community."[46]

Some of the above suggestions may be in the offing, as battling corporate crime seems to have garnered a certain "sex appeal" lately. The cascade of corporate scandals and failures occurring between 2001 and 2003 may have finally awakened American law enforcement to the realities of the harm done by elite criminals. As a result of congressional hearings and public outcries following the Enron and similar scandals, Congress passed the **Sarbanes-Oxley Act** (SOA) of 2002. Among the provisions of this act is a massive increase in the SEC's budget and an additional 200 employees for the SOA.[47] This tremendously enhanced the morale of the previously underfunded and demoralized SEC, which now views its role as proactive rather than reactive.[48] The SOA requires company CEOs and chief financial officers to personally vouch for their companies' financial disclosures, ensuring that such people can no longer assume a stance of "plausible deniability" ("I didn't know what was happening"), as did many Enron executives.[49]

Within the guidelines of the SOA is an act titled the White Collar Crimes Penalty Enhancement Act. This act creates new substantive offenses, significantly enhances financial and incarceration penalties, and relaxes some procedural evidentiary requirements for prosecutors. Prosecutors formerly had to prove "willfulness" in white-collar cases, meaning that they had to prove beyond a reasonable doubt that the defendant took some action knowing that it violated a specific regulation or law. All a prosecutor has to show now is that the defendant did what he or she did, period. Relaxed standards for proving obstruction of justice (and penalties of up to 20 years for conviction) are also included, which should deter the actions of loyal employees attempting to "help out" their supervisors and managers by not revealing what they know to investigators.

One wonders whether the SOA marks a new chapter in the investigation and prosecution of corporate criminals or déjà vu. Lowell and Arnold state that "Congress clearly intended to send a message to the law enforcement community to be tougher on violators of business law and regulations. Further, Congress's message will echo to prosecutors and sentencing judges who will avail themselves of the new SOA maximums or use previously available means to

▲ **Photo 15.2** While most cases, even those that involve corporate crime, never come to trial and are settled or plea bargained instead, some do end up in court. Here a prosecutor makes his opening statement to the jury.

enhance maximum penalties."[50] There is evidence that SEC investigators and prosecutors are taking advantage of the tools provided to them by SOA to the point where "prosecutors are driven to go after corporate fraud with an almost evangelical zeal."[51] There are many other indications that the days of leniency for white-collar criminals are over. In July 2005, Bernard Ebbers, ex-WorldCom CEO, was sentenced to 25 years in prison for his role in the $11 billion WorldCom fraud; in June 2005, John Rigas, founder of Adelphia Communications Corp, was sentenced to 15 years and his son Timothy to 20 years for their roles in yet another massive fraud; and in September 2005, Tyco executives Dennis Koslowski and Dennis Swartz were sentenced to 8 and 25 years, respectively.

▧ Organized Crime

What Is Organized Crime?

Organized crime has probably existed in one form or another since our ancestors lived in caves. Nevertheless, criminologists have had a difficult time deciding just what it is, where it came from, where it is going, what groups should be included as being "organized," just how organized it is, and how it differs (if it does) from corporate crime. Some argue that "any distinction between organized and white-collar crime may be artificial inasmuch as both involve the important elements of organization and the use of corruption and/or violence to maintain immunity."[52] Corporate crime is indeed "organized crime" in some senses; by definition, corporations are organized, and when their members commit illegal acts, they are engaging in crime. But corporate criminals don't fit whistle-blowers with concrete footwear or bomb their competitors out of business. The major difference between corporate and organized crime is that corporate criminals are created from the opportunities available to them in companies organized around doing legitimate business, whereas members of organized crime must be accomplished criminals before they enter such groups, which are organized around creating criminal opportunities. Thus, the former make a crime out of business, and the latter make a business out of crime.

Some definitions of organized crime are so broad as to encompass almost any kind of planned crime committed by more than one individual, while others are so narrow they miss key characteristics of organized crime that should be included. An excellent succinct definition, based on a fairly wide consensus of organized crime scholars, is that **organized crime** is "a continuing criminal enterprise that works rationally to profit from illicit activities that are often in great public demand. Its continuing existence is maintained through the use of force, threats, and/or corruption of public officials."[53] This section expands on this definition, drawing from findings of the President's Commission on Organized Crime (PCOC)[54] and concentrating on **La Cosa Nostra** (literally, "our thing"), also commonly referred to as the Mafia. It should not be inferred from this that *La Cosa Nostra* (LCN) and organized crime are synonymous. There are many other organized crime groups in the United States and around the world.

Structure The first characteristic that differentiates organized crime from other kinds of crime (corporate crime excepted) is its formal structure. According to the PCOC, LCN groups are structured in hierarchical fashion, reflecting various levels of power and specialization. There are alleged to be 24 LCN families with a national ruling body known as the **Commission,** established by Salvatore "Lucky" Luciano in 1931.[55] The Commission is a kind of "board of directors" and consists of the bosses of the five New York families and four bosses from other important families located in other cities. The Commission functions to arbitrate disputes among the various families and facilitate joint ventures, approve of new members, authorize the executions of errant members, and act as a go-between for American and Sicilian factions of LCN.[56] Members know and respect the hierarchy of authority in their organization just as corporate executives know and respect ordered ranks of authority in their corporations. Although there are occasional family squabbles and coups that remove individuals from the hierarchy, the structure remains intact. The formal structure of an LCN family can be diagramed as in Figure 15.1.

At the top of the family structure is the boss (the *don* or *capo*) whose rule within it is absolute, although he may be overruled by the commission. Beneath the boss is a counselor (*consigliere*) or adviser and an underboss (*sotto capo*). The counselor is usually an old family member and often a lawyer, who is wise in the ways of crime, and the underboss is a sort of vice president being groomed for succession to the top position. Beneath the underboss are the lieutenants (*caporegimas*) who supervise the day-to-day operation of the family and enjoy considerable power. Below the lieutenants are the soldiers (*soldati*), known as *made men, wise guys,* or *button men.* Although soldiers are the lowest ranking members of the family, they may each run their own crew of nonmember associates.

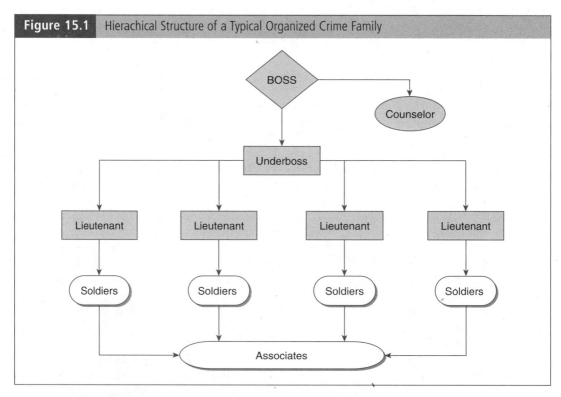

Figure 15.1   Hierachical Structure of a Typical Organized Crime Family

Source: Source: Adapted from *The President's Commission on Organized Crime.* (1986). The impact: Organized crime today (p. 469). Washington, DC: Government Printing Office.

LCN members are not employees of the family in the sense that they earn a regular income from the organization. Membership in the family entitles the member to run his own rackets using the family's connections and status. A percentage of a soldier's earnings are paid to his lieutenant, who also has his own enterprises on which to pay a percentage to the underboss, and so on up the line. This pyramidal payment scheme works like a franchise operation and has been referred to as "the McDonald's-ization of the Mafia."[57]

This model is known as the **corporate model** because of its similarity to corporate structure—that is, a formal hierarchy in which the day-to-day activities of the organization are planned and coordinated at the top and carried out by subordinates. Although it is the model favored by the PCOC, some academics favor the **feudal model.** The feudal system was a social system existing in medieval Europe in which the king granted land to his nobles. In return, the nobles swore oaths of loyalty to the king and promised to support him in his wars. The nobles also granted land to lesser nobles, who swore allegiance to the lord and promised to support him in war when he had to support the king. Then came the villeins, who received land for working on the lord's manor and who could employ serfs, the lowest members of the feudal system.

This feudal model of LCN views it as a loose collection of criminal groups held together by kinship and patronage. The Commission may be seen as the king and his ministers (who rarely if ever interfered with their nobles), and the individual family bosses may be seen as the lords, the lieutenants as the lesser nobility, the made men as the villeins, and the associates as the serfs. The oaths of loyalty, the autonomous operations of each family, the semiautonomous operations of the soldiers and lieutenants, and the provision of status and protection from the family in exchange for a cut of their earnings provide evidence that LCN bosses are more like feudal lords than corporate CEOs. Memoirs written by high-ranking LCN members, however, offer evidence for both the corporate and the feudal models,[58] so perhaps it is best to view LCN as a highly structured feudal system.

Continuity Organized crime is like a mature corporation (or a feudal system, for that matter) in that it continues to operate beyond the lifetime of its individual members. It does not disintegrate when key leaders are arrested, die, or are otherwise absent. The criminal group takes on a life of its own, and members subordinate their personal interests to those of the family. This makes organized crime quite different from gangs that spring up and die with their leaders.

Membership LCN is not an equal-opportunity employer; it is restricted to males of Italian descent of proven criminal expertise. Prospective members must be sponsored by *made guys* (established members of the family), who are responsible for the behavior of those they sponsor during their probationary period. Applicants are screened carefully for their criminal activity and loyalty before being allowed to apply, and only the most promising applicants are accepted. A lifetime commitment to the family is required from the newcomer, and in return, he receives a guaranteed and rather lucrative criminal career as part of an organization of great prestige and respect in the underworld. A promising criminal who is not of Italian descent but who has qualities useful to the organization may become an associate member of LCN. The FBI estimates that for every formal member of LCN, there are 10 associates.[59]

Criminality Like any other kind of business, organized crime seeks to make a profit. Most of organized crime's income is derived from supplying the public with goods and services not available in the legitimate market, such as drugs, gambling, and prostitution. Much of organized crime's income is funneled into legitimate businesses after its "dirty" (illicit) money is "laundered." Thus, although organized crime is roughly structured and motivated similarly to mainstream business enterprises, it differs from them in the illicit nature of its product and its reason for being.

FOCUS ON . . .

The Mafia: Sicilian Origins and History

There are many and varied accounts of the origins of the Mafia, many of which have been muddied by sensationalized and speculative media accounts and self-serving autobiographies of notable Mafia figures. The most romantic version of the Mafia's beginnings is that they were freedom fighters trying to rid Sicily of French occupiers in the 19th century. In this version, the word *Mafia* is said to be an acronym for the battle cry "*Morte Alla Francia Italia Anela*" (Death to France is Italy's cry).[60] A less romantic version is that the *Mafia* (used as a noun denoting a criminal organization) grew out of the adjective *mafioso*, which means *man of honor*, the word itself being of Arabic-Sicilian derivation meaning to protect and guard.[61]

The Mafia appears to have had its origin with violent men called *gabelloto*, who were hired by Sicilian landowners to fight the peasants' calls for land reform, unionization, and revolution. They also protected peasants from bandits and served as a kind of vigilante/law enforcement organization in a land known for its tradition of lawlessness and blood feuds. Most of these men had fought on the winning side in the battles for the unification of Italy in the 1850s to 1870s and thus gained a wide measure of respect. After their service to Italy, they became a private army of mercenaries and then a full-scale criminal organization. The many contradictions of the Mafia's role in Sicilian society are recounted by Peter Robb: "The mafia was outlaw, but tolerated, secret but recognizable, criminal but upholding of order. It protected and ripped off the owners of the great estates, protected and ripped off the sharecroppers who worked the estates, and ripped off the peasants who slaved on them."[62]

With the union of Italy and Sicily in 1861, the Mafia became the only real political force in Sicily, and the government in Rome knew it, accepted it, and courted it. All this changed with the rise of the Fascist state under Benito Mussolini in the 1920s. Like any dictator, Mussolini could not tolerate any alternative source of political power in his domains. After he was publicly embarrassed on a 1924 visit to Sicily by a local Mafioso mayor, he set out with a vengeance to destroy the Mafia. Mussolini's police arrested, imprisoned, and killed hundreds of actual and suspected members of the Mafia, and the organization was declared dead.[63] But it was far from dead, and it reemerged to assist the Allied army landing in Sicily in 1943 and became stronger and more deadly in Italy after the war.

What Mussolini's purges did was to spread the Mafia cancer to the New World. Hundreds of young Mafiosi escaped from Italy and Sicily to the "little Italy's" of America, bringing their ways and their codes with them. Among those who fled the purges were two men who would later become godfathers of the two most important crime families in the United States—Carlo Gambino and Joseph Bonanno.[64]

◀ **Photo 15.3** This statue, housed within a castle in Naples, Italy, shows a number of ways a victim might be murdered by a mafia hit.

Organized Crime in the United States

One of the unfortunate consequences of the media attention to organized crime is that many Americans have come to view it as an alien conspiracy of Italian origin. The truth is that organized crime groups existed long before there was any major Italian presence in the United States, and most organized crime scholars believe that the phenomenon is a "normal" product of the competitive and free-wheeling nature of American society.[65] Scholars place a variety of dates on the beginnings of organized crime in America as we have defined it, but the two major candidates are the founding of the Society of Saint Tammany in the late 18th century and Prohibition in the early 20th century.

The Tammany Society began as a fraternal and patriotic society but soon evolved into a corrupt political machine consisting mostly of ethnic Irishmen. Tammany, which became synonymous with the Democratic Party in New York City, ran the city well into the 20th century from the "Hall" (Tammany Hall), making use of street gangs to threaten and intimidate political rivals. Prominent among these gangs were the vicious Whyos and the Five Points gangs. For a new member to be accepted by the Whyos, which at its peak had more than 500 members, he had to have killed at least once. The Whyos plied their trade among New York's citizenry by passing out price lists on the streets for the services they provided (ranging from $2 for punching to $100 for murder) as casually as pizza vendors.[66] The Five Points gang was a confederation of neighborhood gangs and was said to have had more than 1,500 members at one time. Among the future luminaries of organized crime associated with the Whyos were Al Capone and Lucky Luciano.[67]

Organized crime existed on its earnings from gambling, prostitution, protection, extortion, and labor racketeering during the early part of the 20th century. During this period, members of these criminal organizations were often employed by politicians, who used them as errand boys and enforcers, a relationship that was to reverse itself after 1920. In 1920, the U.S. Congress handed every petty gang in America an initiation to unlimited expansion and wealth with the ratification of the Eighteenth Amendment (the Volstead Act, or **Prohibition**), which prohibited the sale, manufacture, or importation of intoxicating liquors within the United States. Prohibition ushered in a vicious 10-year period of crime, violence, and political corruption as gangsters fought over the right to provide the drinking public with illicit alcohol.

Johnny Torrio, a product of New York's Five Points gang, became the leading figure in Chicago's gangland. A master strategist, he realized that violence was counterproductive and was able to broker a truce among warring factions and organize them into a sort of loose confederation. The confederation ended when members of a rival Irish gang critically wounded Torrio. After recovering from his wound, Torrio returned to New York in 1924, leaving his protégé, Al "Scarface" Capone, in charge of the Chicago operation.

The Capone era provided America with its stereotypical image of organized gangsters. Capone was a ruthless criminal and a flamboyant man whose generosity endeared him to many members of the media and to many of Chicago's poor people, for whom he provided soup kitchens and shelter. Only 25 years of age when he succeeded Torrio, he soon established a criminal empire that, at the height of Prohibition, consisted of more than 700 gunmen.[68] The wealth Capone accumulated from his bootlegging and prostitution enterprises got him into the *Guinness Book of Records* as having the highest gross income ($105 million) of any private citizen in America in 1927. But all good things come to an end. The Depression cut into Capone's income, and the Supreme Court ruled that unlawful income, as well as lawful income, was subject to taxation. It was this law that spelled his doom. He was sentenced to 11 years in prison for tax evasion in 1931 and was released in 1939. Suffering from terminal syphilis, he died in 1947 of pneumonia following a stroke at age 48 at his Florida estate.

With the repeal of the Eighteenth Amendment in 1933, organized crime entered a new and quieter phase, but the modern face of LCN was already beginning to take form in New York. There were two main factions in Italian organized crime in New York at this time, one headed by Giuseppe Masseria and the other by Salvatore Maranzano, who were struggling for supremacy. This struggle, known as the Castellammarese War, ended with the deaths of both leaders in 1931. The Castellammarese War saw the end of the reigns of the old Sicilian "mustache petes" and the emergence of an Americanized LCN.[69] Lucky Luciano, Bugsy Siegel, and Meyer Lansky were all instrumental in this process (Siegel and Lansky were Jewish, not Italian). The Americanization of LCN saw the emergence of the five New York LCN families active today. It also saw Lucky Luciano become the most important figure in LCN, enabling him to set up the organization's national commission and to claim the title of founding father of Italian American organized crime.[70]

Reaffirming the Existence of Organized Crime

Interest in organized crime activities waned considerably after World War II, and many law enforcement officials, including FBI director J. Edgar Hoover, refused to acknowledge its existence. Three events—the Kefauver Committee, the Apalachin "summit," and the McClellan Commission—affirmed the reality of its existence. In 1950, the (Senator Estes) Kefauver Committee was formed to investigate organized crime's involvement in interstate commerce. The Kefauver Committee hearings (which were extensively televised) called in important organized crime figures to testify, including Meyer Lansky, Frank Castello, and Bugsy Siegel, exposing them to the public for the first time. The committee did little else except perpetuate the notion of the Mafia as an alien conspiracy.

▲ **Photo 15.4** The depicted restaurant was the site where "Crazy Joe" Gallo was gunned down April 7, 1972, his 43rd birthday celebration, in New York City's Little Italy. The traditional view of Italian organized crime, still seen on HBO's *The Sopranos,* has been frequently debated by criminologists.

The Apalachin meeting, held in Apalachin, New York, in 1957, provided further evidence for the existence of a national and coordinated crime syndicate and once again riveted national attention on it. Major LCN figures met on this occasion, supposedly to confirm Vito Genovese as the *capo di tutti capi* ("boss of bosses") and to discuss other LCN matters. The police (who stumbled on the meeting purely by accident) raided the meeting and arrested 63 people, including the bosses and underbosses of New York's LCN families. All arrestees refused to answer questions about the purpose of the meeting and were indicted for obstruction of justice. No convictions came out of these indictments, but it destroyed LCN's hope that it could stay out of the public spotlight. According to the PCOC,[71] it finally confirmed the existence of organized crime, and law enforcement began to focus more seriously on combating it.

The (Senator John L.) McClellan Commission was formed in 1956 to look into financial irregularities in the Teamsters Union, but the star witness was a drug trafficker and made man in the Genovese family named Joe Valachi. While in prison on drug charges, another made man accused Valachi of being an informer, which meant to Valachi that he was marked for death. Rather than face this prospect, Valachi decided to testify as to what he knew about the Mafia in front of the McClellan Commission. Valachi revealed much about the operation of the Mafia, including the fact that members of Italian organized crime no longer used that name, if they ever did. According to Valachi, the organization called itself *Cosa Nostra,* a term unfamiliar to law enforcement officials up to then. Despite the fact that Valachi was only a low-level soldier (albeit with 30 years of experience) and that his testimony was often vague and contradictory, commission member Senator Robert Kennedy called Valachi's testimony the "biggest intelligence breakthrough yet in combating organized crime."[72]

The Russian "Mafiya"

The Russian "Mafiya" is a catch-all phrase for a group of organized gangs that many experts consider to be the most serious organized crime threat in the world today.[73] There has been an explosion of crime in Russia since the breakup of the Soviet Union, but even in the old Soviet Union, there had been significant organized crime activity as the "shadow economy" exploited the shortage of all kinds of consumer goods created by the centrally planned economy. The crime, bribery, and political and police corruption in modern Russia make the Prohibition period in America look positively benign. As James Finckenauer put it, "Organized crime has been able to penetrate Russian businesses and state enterprises to a degree inconceivable in most other countries."[74]

Russian organized crime (ROC) has existed since at least the 17th century, and it became firmly entrenched in Russian society in the 1920s. The major group in ROC is known as the *vory v zakone* (thieves-in-law), which began as a large group of political prisoners who were imprisoned following the Bolshevik Revolution in 1917. The Soviet prison system used this group to maintain order over the general prison population in exchange for many favors. These "elite" prisoners developed their own structural hierarchy and strict code of conduct or "laws" (hence thieves-"in-*law*"). One of their strictest rules was that there is to be absolutely no cooperation with legitimate authority for any reason.

Because of the ethnic diversity of ROC, it is loosely organized and may be undergoing the weeding-out and consolidation phases that LCN underwent in the 1930s. ROC is the biggest factor threatening Russia's democratization, economic development, and security. It threatens democratization because if a democratic government cannot control it, an authoritarian one will. It threatens the economy because foreign companies are reluctant to make the much-needed investments in an economy rife with the murder and extortion of business leaders. It threatens public security because many police officers and KGB personnel have left public service for the more lucrative opportunities available with organized crime.[75]

Russian organized crime metastasized to the United States with the influx of Russian immigrants in the 1970s and 1980s, bringing with them a cultural heritage. One aspect of that heritage similar to that of the earlier Sicilian/Italian immigrants is a deep distrust of government. This distrust allows criminal elements among the new arrivals to criminally exploit their fellow immigrants with relative impunity. Another piece of cultural baggage borne from the communist heritage is a disdain for the work ethic. Both the distrust of the authorities and the alleged attitude toward legitimate work provide fertile ground for the growth of criminal activity.[76]

Unlike the largely uneducated Mafioso driven out of Italy by Mussolini, many of Russian émigré criminals are highly educated. Some, driven out by economic hardship, even held professional positions in Russia.[77] This level of intelligence and expertise should make them more of a threat than the unsophisticated peasant class that made up most of the early Sicilian/Italian mobsters. Indeed, Rush and Scarpitti write that "it has been speculated by intelligence agencies such as the IRS, FBI, and CIA that because of their higher level of criminal sophistication Russian organized crime groups will present a greater overall threat to American society than the traditional Italian-American crime families ever have."[78]

▶ **Photo 15.5** With the demise of the Soviet Union, the West was exposed to Russian and Ukrainian mafiya for the first time on a large scale. This grave of an assassinated mafiya leader is in Odessa, Ukraine. Note the gold leaf and prominent photo on the 15-foot-tall memorial grave.

The Japanese Yakuza

Japanese organized crime (JOC) groups are probably the oldest and largest in the world, with total membership larger than LCN and estimated at 90,000.[79] The official Japanese term for organized criminals is *Boryokudan* (violent ones), but they are more commonly referred to as *yakuza* (useless person). As with the Sicilian Mafia, the yakuza has its roots in rural lawlessness and is likewise clouded in a dubious and romanticized history.[80] The group is commonly believed to have evolved from *ronin*, or masterless samurai warriors, who contracted their services out for assassinations and other illegal purposes. Like the Sicilian gabelloto, they also protected the peasants from other marauding bandits as a sort of vigilante/law enforcement group. The defeat of Japan in World War II and the ensuing chaos provided the catalyst for the growth of JOC. This period saw many gang wars erupt over control of lucrative illicit markets. As in the United States, these gang wars led to the elimination of some gangs and to the consolidation and strengthening of others. The Kobe-based *Yamaguchi-gumi* (*gumi* means *group*), with an estimated membership of more than 10,000, is the largest of these groups.[81]

Members of JOC groups are recruited heavily from the two outcast groups in Japanese society—the *burakumin* (outcasts because their ancestors worked at trades that dealt with dead flesh, such as butchery, tanning, grave digging, etc., which was seen as unclean in the Buddhist religious tradition) and Japanese-born Koreans. Once admitted, a kobun must pledge absolute loyalty to his superiors and, like his LCN counterpart, must generate his own income and contribute part of it to the *ikka* (the family).

JOC enjoys a unique position in Japanese society. Their historical connection with the samurai; their espousal of traditional norms of duty, loyalty, and manliness; their support for nationalistic programs; and their "law enforcement" functions (as in Mafia neighborhoods in America, yakuza neighborhoods are safe from common criminals) endow them with a certain level of respect and admiration among the Japanese. In fact, when a major earthquake hit Kobe in 1995, the Yamaguchi-gumi's relief efforts exceeded those of the Japanese government.[82] Furthermore, the yakuza are not shadowy underworld figures; their affiliations are proudly displayed on insignia worn on their clothes and on their offices and buildings, and they publish their own newsletter. The headquarters of one crime group, complete with the gang emblem hanging proudly outside, is only three doors away from the local police station.[83] With their openness, extensively tattooed bodies, gang colors, and service-for-hire tradition, the yakuza seem more like outlaw motorcycle gangs than La Cosa Nostra.

The police have tended to tolerate yakuza activity in certain areas as long as it involves only the provision of certain illicit goods and services demanded by the public, but they have cracked down hard when firearms and drugs are trafficked or when innocent civilians are harmed. With the introduction of the Boryokudan Countermeasures Law of 1992, however, the relationship between the police and the yakuza has become more antagonistic, and there have been many police crackdowns.[84]

✖ Theories About the Causes of Organized Crime

Criminologists ask the same questions about organized crime that they do about white-collar crime: What causes it, are these causes unique to it, and are the external social and economic causes of it more important than individual-level causes? Some argue that we create our own organized crime problem by creating laws that prevent members of the public from acquiring goods and services (alcohol, drugs, gambling, pornography, prostitution, etc.) they desire and demand. When such demands are not met legally, there are always those who are willing to supply them illegally.

To say that organized crime exists because of huge economic incentives to supply people with goods and services legally denied them is only part of the causal equation. This theory looks at the social sources of the criminal opportunities made available, but not why those who take advantage of them do so. Early theories of organized crime relied on the anomie/strain tradition to explain organized crime, describing the gangster as "a man with a gun, acquiring by personal merit what was denied him by complex orderings of stratified society," and saw each successive wave of immigrants ascending a "queer ladder of social mobility" in American society.[85]

According to this **ethnic succession theory,** upon arrival in the United States, each ethnic group was faced with prejudicial and discriminatory attitudes that denied them legitimate means to success. The Irish, Jews, and Italians were each prominent in organized crime before they became assimilated into American culture and gained access to legitimate means of social mobility. More recently, African Americans, Russians, and Asians have been prominent in organized crime and, according to this view, may have to climb their own "queer ladder" until they gain full acceptance in American society.

The memoirs of a number of LCN figures, however, do not support the notion that they turned to crime because they were denied legitimate opportunities. Many of them had received good educations, came from involved and intact families, and had many opportunities to enter legitimate careers.[86] Rather, these men saw organized crime as a more lucrative and desirable career than any legitimate alternative. Michael Franzese, a former caporegima of the Columbo family, for instance, gave up his pre-med studies to join the mob because the mob was a quicker and easier way to monetary success. Similarly, Bill Bonanno, former consigliere of the Bonanno family, had a boarding school education and studied agricultural engineering at university.[87] However, these memoirs were mostly written by high-ranking figures born into the mob, so the lack of legitimate opportunities remains a possible factor explaining the participation of the more numerous mob associates.

It is difficult to claim that anyone in the United States today is literally denied opportunities to succeed in the legitimate world, although opportunities are certainly more available to some than to others. The idea of opportunity denial implies that those allegedly denied opportunities would have gladly taken advantage of them if they had existed and would have spurned crime. In this view, a criminal career is simply the default option undertaken by the downtrodden, with the unspoken corollary being that no one would actively seek criminal opportunities if legitimate options were available to them. But organized crime, like white-collar crime, affords those who commit it huge rewards for relatively little risk. Given this, we might well ask with social control theorists why most of us don't seek out these criminal opportunities rather than why some of us do.

Part of the answer to this question is that, just as we all don't have equal access to lucrative legitimate opportunities, access to lucrative illegitimate opportunities are not equally available to everyone who might desire them. If you had a desire to become part of an organized crime group, how would you go about it? As most of us know, networking, or establishing interconnecting lines of communication among friends and acquaintances "in the know," is very useful when seeking legitimate employment opportunities. Similarly, you would have to have access to someone who is "connected" to become involved in organized crime.

Differential association theory may provide an explanation. We know that criminal acts arise from the interaction of environmental instigation and individual risk factors. The environmental risk factors are particularly powerful in some neighborhoods, and therefore the threshold for engaging individual risk factors is lowered for those living in them. If you grew up in subcultural enclaves where organized crime was established and flourishing, you would stand a good chance of at least having a shot at joining the mob if you were so inclined. Almost all mob members lived in neighborhoods where they were constantly surrounded by criminals and criminal values. They grew up hero-worshiping the neighborhood made men, emulated their dress and mannerisms, and dreamed of becoming one of them. It was the mobster who had the beautiful women, the sleek cars, the fancy clothes, and the respect, not the legitimate "working stiff."[88] Such neighborhoods proved to be fertile ground for the constant cultivation of new batches of criminals because they provided their young inhabitants with exposure to an excess of definitions favorable to law violation.

Because membership in some gangs is so valued that there is always a surplus of contenders for mob positions living in these neighborhoods, aspiring hoods have to prove that they have the "right stuff." If they can make the grade, the joy and enthusiasm with which they describe their acceptance makes nonsense of the idea that gangsters are poor, deprived individuals making the best of a bad deal. A newly initiated member of the Bananno family makes plain how much he valued his new status: "Getting made is the greatest thing that could ever happen to me . . . I've been looking forward to this day ever since I was a kid." And a made man in the Columbo family gushes, "Since I got made I got a million fuckin' worshipers hanging around."[89]

Men with attitudes such as these could be described as narcissistic, a trait said to be very prevalent among organized gangsters.[90] It would not be too much of a stretch to posit that many men attracted to the outlaw lifestyle are predatory psychopaths or sociopaths. For instance, Al Capone could smash a suspected "rat's" head in with a baseball bat as casually as patting him on the back, and Sammy Gravano explained that after killing, he "felt good. Like high. Like powerful, maybe even superhuman." Then there's caporegime Joe Armore's statement to Gambino family capo, Paul Castellano: "But you know, Paul, I think some guys just take so much pleasure from breaking heads that they'd almost rather not get paid."[91]

It is not only the made men that find the life of organized crime appealing. The biography of Henry Hill, a former associate (he couldn't be a made man because he isn't Italian) of the Lucchese family, illustrates how the young admire and seek to emulate the men with "juice" in their neighborhoods: "I used to watch them from my window and I dreamed of being like them. At the age of twelve my ambition was to be a gangster. To be a wiseguy. To me being a wiseguy was better than being President of the United States."[92] As with common inner-city street robbers, the attitude toward legitimate employment and those who pursued it was the polar opposite: "Anyone who stood waiting his turn on the American pay line," writes Pileggi, "was beneath contempt. . . . To wiseguys, 'working guys' were already dead."[93]

Yet most young men in neighborhoods infested with organized crime saw the same things and did not become criminals, nor are there any outcast groups analogous to the burakumin in the United States. Although there are criminogenic neighborhoods that will produce proportionately more criminals than other neighborhoods, there is no reason to assume that the rank-and-file gangster is any different in background and personal characteristics from the ordinary unaffiliated street criminal or the street criminal affiliated with ad hoc criminal gangs. The leadership of organized crime groups may be intelligent and shrewd men who hatch complicated criminal plots, but their subordinates engage in mundane crimes like burglary and robbery to support themselves and their masters. Their strong desire to belong and to gain instant respect by displays of "manliness" and aggression, their fatalism, their sensation seeking, their lack of empathy, and their involvement in many high-risk/low-profit crimes mark them as very ordinary street criminals.

⊠ Law Enforcement's Response to Organized Crime

Joe Valachi's testimony before the McClellan Committee, along with a number of other events, led to the passage of federal legislation that has enabled law enforcement to launch massive attacks on organized crime. Among the most important new tools forged for law enforcement were the Organized Crime Control Act (OCCA) and the Bank Secrecy Act (BSA), both passed in 1970. Included in the provisions of the OCCA are witness immunity from prosecution, the Witness Protection Program, and the Racketeer Influenced and Corrupt Organizations (RICO) statutes.

The witness immunity provision allows federal prosecutors to grant lower-level members of organized crime groups immunity from prosecution for their own crimes in exchange for testimony incriminating higher-level members. Witnesses who do not want to testify or be granted immunity are immunized anyway and then forced to testify under pain of contempt of court charges, which could result in indefinite imprisonment. Some witnesses still have been reluctant to testify despite the grant of immunity because they realize that doing so places their lives in jeopardy. As a result, federal authorities have instituted the **Witness Protection Program.** The program, administered by the U.S. Marshals Service, provides for around-the-clock protection while witnesses are awaiting court appearances. After testifying, witnesses in the program are provided with new identification documents, employment, housing, and other assistance until they become reestablished. Jay Albanese[94] reports that there are about 12,400 persons (witnesses and their families) in the program at an annual cost of $25 million.

An interesting sideline underscoring the difficulties in rehabilitating confirmed criminals is that despite being given a new start in life, 21% of criminals entering the Witness Protection Program are arrested under their new identities within 2 years of entry.[95] Because criminals in the Witness Protection Program were used to relatively high incomes made in a life filled with excitement and personal power and independence, many find it extremely difficult to adjust to a mundane job with minimal financial rewards. For instance, Sammy Gravano, former Gambino family underboss, was placed in the program after testifying against his boss, John Gotti, but was arrested in 2000 and sentenced to 19 years in prison for masterminding a drug ring in Arizona.[96] Arrested program members become exposed and thus place themselves and their families at risk for murder by cohorts of those they had betrayed. Peter Gotti, brother of John Gotti, was convicted in December 2004 in a plot to kill Gravano, which was only thwarted by Gravano's arrest.[97] According to Abadinsky,[98] about 30 witnesses who left the program have been murdered, while none who have remained in it and complied with all its rules have.

The **RICO statutes** address ordinary crimes such as murder, robbery, extortion, fraud, and kidnapping, but they differ from traditional statutes relevant to these same crimes in that they specifically target the continuing racketeering activities of organized criminals. RICO statutes provide for more severe penalties for the same crimes that fall under traditional criminal statutes and also for the seizure of property and assets obtained from or involved in illegal activities. RICO even provides for the seizure of the assets of a legitimate business if the business was used for money laundering.

The primary function of the BSA (supplemented by the Money-Laundering Control Act of 1986) is the prevention and detection of money laundering. Money laundering—making illegitimate money appear legitimate—is a vital component of organized crime's ability to carry on its activities. The vast amount of illicit money that flows through the hands of organized crime must be "laundered" into legitimate money so that income taxes can be paid on it (the lesson of Al Capone's conviction for income tax evasion was not lost on organized crime) and so that it can be openly used. Under this act, banks must file a report if funds over $10,000 in cash are either deposited or withdrawn, and a report must be filed with the U.S. Customs Service if more than $10,000 in cash enters or leaves the United States.

Armed with these new weapons, the government has successfully prosecuted hundreds of organized crime figures. Particularly important were the so-called *Commission trials* (a reference to the LCN commission), which took place from 1983 through 1987. More than 5,000 indictments were handed down in 1985, and leaders of 16 of the 24 LCN families were indicted. Leaders of the Genovese, Lucchesi, and Columbo families were sentenced to 100 years each on racketeering charges, and the leader of the Bananno family received 12 years.[99] The leader of the Gambino family, Paul Castellano, avoided prosecution by getting himself murdered on the orders of his underboss, John Gotti.

Castellano's successor, John Gotti, was sentenced to life in prison in 1992 after being convicted of 13 federal charges (he died of cancer in prison in 2002). Known as "the Teflon Don" because of his ability to avoid prosecution and/or conviction, Gotti was betrayed by his former underboss, Salvatore "The Bull" Gravano, who testified against him in exchange for a lenient (he openly admitted to killing 19 people, "give or take a few") 5-year sentence. John Gotti Jr. took over the reigns of the Gambino family after his father's imprisonment but was himself imprisoned for racketeering in 1999. He was further indicted in 2004 for ordering a hit on Curtis Sliwa, a talk show host and founder of the citizen anticrime volunteer patrols, the Guardian Angels.[100]

No one knows how much damage these convictions have done to LCN. It may continue to operate for many years to come, but probably as a pale reflection of its former self. Skillful use of the provisions of the OCCA has seriously undermined the old code of *omerta* (denoting a code of silence and noncooperation with authorities), and many made men have turned informant since Joe Valachi. The generational gap pitting the discipline, loyalty, and honor of the old Mafiosi against the more Americanized attitudes of younger mobsters, who disdain such "old-fashioned" values, has also contributed to the rot of LCN from within.[101]

SUMMARY

White-collar crime is our costliest and most deadly form of crime. White-collar crime is divided into occupational and corporate crime. Occupational crime is crime committed against an employer or the general public in the course of an individual's employment. We don't know how much white-collar crime is committed each year because there is no single source to which incidents are reported, nor is there often any clear indication as to who has committed what, as there is with street crimes.

Many scholars support the notion that except for crimes requiring high-status occupation for their performance, most white-collar criminals are not all that different from street criminals and that they occupy a middle position between street criminals and "respectable" people in terms of criminal convictions. It may be possible, therefore, to explain white-collar crime with the same theories (e.g., anomie or differential association) used to explain street crime.

Corporate crime—criminal activity on behalf of the organization—is more costly and deadly than occupational crime, although it was not considered problematic in the early days of American industrialization. Three examples of corporate crime occurring over the past 20 years were explored: the Ford Pinto case, the S & L scandal, and the Enron debacle. All these crimes involved multiple individuals both as perpetrators and victims, the loss of billions of dollars, and, in the Pinto case, the loss of hundreds of lives.

Corporate crime is explained by a variety of factors, including the juxtaposition of lucrative opportunities and lenient penalties. Personal characteristics associated with corporate criminality include an external locus of control, a low level of cognitive moral development, and a high level of Machiavellianism.

Corporate wrongdoing is typically investigated and punished by administrative agencies rather than by the criminal justice system, which alone can impose sentences of imprisonment. In clear criminal violations, prosecutors may fear that heavy fines imposed on corporations may lead to bankruptcy and the loss of jobs and income in the community. However, new weapons in the fight against white-collar crime, such as the Sarbanes-Oxley Act, may mean the beginning of meaningful penalties imposed on individual executives of companies that engage in corporate illegality and criminality.

Organized crime (OC) is defined by its formal structure, continuity, restricted membership, and criminal activity. La Cosa Nostra (LCN) is a confederation of families that restricts membership to ethnic Italians and has its origins in the Sicilian Mafia, a vigilante/law enforcement group that emerged from a history of lawlessness in Sicily. Modern American OC grew out of the corrupt political machine and its supporting street gangs known as Tammany Hall, and it received its biggest boost from Prohibition. Many of the gangsters who rose to national prominence during this period got their start in the variety of gangs that supported Tammany Hall. The repeal of Prohibition ushered in a quiet period in OC's history, particularly after the founding of the "Commission" by Lucky Luciano as a judicial body to settle interfamily disputes without resorting to war.

The Russian "Mafiya" is considered by many to be the biggest OC threat to the world today. The widespread chaos and corruption following the breakup of the Soviet Union allowed Russian OC to come out of the closet and proliferate. Not only is Russian OC preventing the democratization and economic stability of Russia, but it is also spreading its influence to many Western nations. The special danger of Russian OC is that many of its members are highly intelligent and educated men who held professional jobs in the old Soviet Union. Because of this, many government agencies are of the opinion that they will be a much greater threat to the United States than LCN ever was.

The Japanese yakuza are probably the oldest organized crime group in the world. Having evolved from masterless samurai warriors, it received a major boost by the chaos existing in Japan after its defeat in World War II. The yakuza has many characteristics in common with LCN, but its differences are more interesting. It is responsible for a much larger proportion of Japanese crime than LCN is responsible for in the United States, yet it operates openly and proudly, even publishing its own newsletter. Until recently, the police have not interfered with the yakuza unless innocent people are harmed or if drugs and guns are being trafficked. There is a concerted effort in Japan presently, however, to crack down hard on the yakuza. This crackdown has led to an expansion of yakuza activities outside Japan, particularly in the United States and Europe.

Organized crime flourishes wherever and whenever goods and services demanded by a significant percentage of the population are unavailable through legitimate channels. The American, Japanese, and Russian examples indicate that OC proliferates in times of social chaos, in a process in which some gangs are weeded out and others consolidate their power. Of special interest is the overrepresentation of minorities in OC, providing support for the "queer ladder of social mobility" thesis. There is also some support for differential association theory, provided by Mafia figures in their memoirs relating how their early environments were permeated with criminal attitudes and values. However, most people in those same environments did not become criminals. As suggested by their attitudes and behavior, most of the rank-and-file members of OC are no different from ordinary "unaffiliated" street criminals.

Three events—the Kefauver Committee, the Apalachin meeting, and the McClellan Commission—put an end to denials that OC existed and helped to launch major assaults on LCN. These assaults were made possible by the passage of the Organized Crime Control Act (OCCA) and the Bank Secrecy Act. Included in the OCCA were the RICO statutes and provisions for witness immunity and protection programs. Although the prosecution of major LCN figures has met with considerable success, LCN continues to exist, but perhaps in weakened form.

On Your Own

Log on to the web-based student study site at http://www.sagepub.com/criminologystudy for more information about the vignettes and materials presented in this chapter, suggestions for activities, study aids such as review quizzes, and research recommendations including journal article links and questions related to this chapter.

EXERCISES AND DISCUSSION QUESTIONS

1. We have learned that when people are asked questions about their fears of crime, they almost always report a fear of being victimized by common street crimes. We have also learned that people are more likely to be victimized by white-collar crime than by street crimes. Why do you think most people fear street crime more than white-collar crime? Do they view corporate crime as being less serious than street crime? Ask a number of your friends the same questions.

2. Do you think there is really any moral difference between (a) setting off a bomb outside a building for some political reason, knowing that a certain number of people would be killed, and (b) marketing 11 million defective automobiles, knowing that a certain proportion of them will explode into flames when rear-ended and burn the occupants alive?

3. Do you think that white-collar crime (occupational and corporate) can be explained by the same principles as street crime? Read one or two of the relevant cited articles for guidance.

4. What do you think the relationship is (if any) between social morality and the *prevalence* of organized crime?

5. Some observers believe that law enforcement's response to organized crime in America (e.g., the RICO statutes) goes too far and threatens everyone's civil liberties. Do you agree?

6. Looking back at all the theories presented in this book, make a case for one of them as the best in terms of explaining organized crime.

7. Go to http://glasgowcrew.tripod.com/allanbook.html and click on "wiseguy tales." Chose a wiseguy and write a one-page report on him.

KEY WORDS

Commission	La Cosa Nostra	Sarbanes-Oxley Act
Corporate crime	Occupational crime	White-collar crime
Corporate model	Organized crime	Witness Protection Program
Ethnic succession theory	Prohibition	
Feudal model	RICO statutes	

REFERENCES

1. Kappeler, V., Blumberg, M., & Potter, G. (2000). *The mythology of crime and criminal justice* (3rd ed.). Prospect Heights, IL: Waveland.
2. Sutherland, E. (1940). White collar criminality. *American Sociological Review, 5,* 1–20. (Quote on p. 9)
3. Weisburd, D., Wheeler, S., Waring, E., & Bode, N. (1991). *Crimes of the middle classes: White-collar offenders in the federal courts.* New Haven, CT: Yale University Press. (Quote on p. 6)
4. Rosoff, S., Pontell, H., & Tillman, R. (1998). *Profit without honor: White-collar crime and the looting of America.* Upper Saddle River, NJ: Prentice Hall.
5. Shover, N., & Hochstetler, A. (2000). Crimes of privilege. In J. Shelly (Ed.), *Criminology: A contemporary*

handbook (pp. 287–319). Belmont, CA: Wadsworth. (Quote on p. 264)

6. Calavita, K., Pontell, H., & Tillman, R. (1999). *Big money game: Fraud and politics in the savings and loan crisis.* Berkeley: University of California Press. (Quote on p. 7)

7. Parekh, R. (2004). Fraud by employees on the rise, survey finds. *Business Insurance, 38,* 4–6.

8. Rosoff et al. (1998).

9. Rosoff et al. (1998).

10. Coleman, J. (1985). *The criminal elite: The sociology of white collar crime.* New York: St. Martin's.

11. Hirschi, T., & Gottfredson, M. (1987). Causes of white-collar crime. *Criminology, 25,* 949–974.

12. Hirschi and Gottfredson (1987, p. 967).

13. Benson, M., & Moore, E. (1992). Are white-collar and common offenders the same? An empirical and theoretical critique of a recently proposed general theory of crime. *Journal of Research in Crime and Delinquency, 29,* 251–272.

14. Walters, G., & Geyer, M. (2004). Criminal thinking and identity in male white-collar offenders. *Criminal Justice and Behavior, 31,* 263–281.

15. Weisburd et al. (1991).

16. Walsh, A., & Hemmens, C. (2000). *From law to order: The theory and practice of law and justice.* Lanham, MD: American Correctional Association.

17. Schmalleger, F. (2004). *Criminology today* (3rd ed.). Upper Saddle River, NJ: Prentice Hall.

18. Calavita, K., & Pontell, H. (1994). "Heads I win, tails you lose": Deregulation, crime, and crisis in the savings and loan industry. In D. Curran & C. Renzetti (Eds.), *Contemporary societies: Problems and prospects* (pp. 460–480). Upper Saddle River, NJ: Prentice Hall.

19. English, S. (2004). Enron legal bills will cost $780m. *Business.telegraph.* Retrieved from http://www.telegraph.co.uk/money.jhtml?xml=/money/2004/1 (Quote on p. 1)

20. Gutman, H. (2002). Dishonesty, greed, and hypocrisy in corporate America. *Statesman (Kalkota, India).* Retrieved from http://www.commondreams.org/cgi-bin/print.cgi?file=/views (Quote on p. 1)

21. Fox, L. (2003). *Enron: The rise and fall.* Hoboken, NJ: John Wiley.

22. Fox (2003).

23. McLean, B., & Elkind, P. (2003). *The smartest guys in the room: The amazing rise and scandalous fall of Enron.* New York: Portfolio.

24. Lupsha, P. (1986). Organized crime in the United States. In R. Kelly (Ed.), *Organized crime: A global perspective* (pp. 34–57). Totawa, NJ: Rowman & Littlefield.

25. Browning, F., & Gerassi, J. (1980). *The American way of crime.* New York: Putnam.

26. Lupsha (1986).

27. Browning and Gerassi (1980).

28. Browning and Gerassi (1980, p. 210).

29. Browning and Gerassi (1980, p. 211).

30. Sutherland, E. (1956). *The Sutherland papers* (A. Cohen, A. Lindesmith, & K. Schuessler, Eds.). Bloomington: Indiana University Press.

31. Byrnes, N. (1994, Fall). The smoke at General Electric. *Financial World,* pp. 32–34.

32. Clinnard, M., & Yeager, P. (1980). *Corporate crime.* New York: Free Press.

33. Wells, R. (1995, June 16). Study finds fines don't deter Wall St. cheating. *Idaho Statesman,* pp. 1e–2e.

34. Thornburn, K. (2004). Corporate governance and financial distress. In H. Sjogren & G. Skogh (Eds.), *New perspectives on economic crime* (pp. 76–94). Cheltenham, UK: Edward Elgar.

35. Useem, M. (1989). *Liberal education and the corporation.* Hawthorn, NY: Aldine de Gruyter.

36. McCabe, B., O'Reilly, C., & Pfeffer, J. (1991). Context, values and moral dilemmas: Comparing the choices of business and law school students. *Journal of Business Ethics, 10,* 951–960.

37. Trevino, L., & Youngblood, S. (1990). Bad apples in bad barrels: A causal analysis of ethical decision-making behavior. *Journal of Applied Psychology, 78,* 378–385.

38. Weber, J. (1990). Managers' moral reasoning: Assessing their responses to three moral dilemmas. *Human Relations, 43,* 687–702.

39. Simon, D. (2002). *Elite deviance* (7th ed.). Boston: Allyn & Bacon. (Quote on p. 277)

40. Calavita et al. (1999).

41. Simon (2002, p. 124).

42. Hagan, F. (1994). *Introduction to criminology.* Chicago: Nelson-Hall.

43. Simpson, S., & Piquero, N. (2002). Low self-control, organizational theory, and corporate crime. *Law and Society Review, 36,* 509–548.

44. Faure, M., & Visser, M. (2004). Law and economics of environmental crime. In H. Sjogren & G. Skogh (Eds.), *New perspectives on economic crime* (pp 57–75). Cheltenham, UK: Edward Elgar.

45. Faure and Visser (2004).

46. Shover and Hochstetler (2000).

47. AICPA. (2004). *Summary of the Sarbanes-Oxley Act of 2002.* Retrieved from http//www.aicpa.org/info/sarbanes_oxley_summary.htm

48. Burr, M. (2004, December). SEC gains power, prestige in post Enron era. *Corporate Legal Times,* pp. 10–13.

49. Fox (2003).

50. Lowell, A., & Arnold, K. (2003). Corporate crime after 2000: A new law enforcement challenge or déjà vu? *The American Criminal Law Review, 40,* 219–240. (Quote on p. 228)

51. Burr (2004, p. 10).

52. Albanese, J. (2000). The causes of organized crime. *Journal of Contemporary Criminal Justice, 16,* 409–432. (Quote on p. 412)

53. Albanese, J., & Pursley, R. (1993). *Crime in America: Some existing and emerging issues.* Englewood Cliffs, NJ: Regents/Prentice Hall. (Quote on p. 58)

54. President's Commission on Organized Crime (PCOC). (1986). *The impact: Organized crime today.* Washington, DC: Government Printing Office.

55. PCOC (1986).

56. Lyman, M., & Potter, G. (2004). *Organized crime* (3rd ed.). Upper Saddle River, NJ: Prentice Hall.

57. Abadinsky, H. (1988). *Organized crime* (2nd ed.). Chicago: Nelson Hall. (Quote on p. 43)

58. Firestone, T. (1997). Mafia memoirs: What they tell us about organized crime. In P. Ryan & G. Rush (Eds.), *Understanding organized crime in global perspective* (pp. 71–86). Thousand Oaks, CA: Sage.

59. PCOC (1986).

60. Wilson, C. (1984). *A criminal history of mankind.* London: Panther.

61. Abadinsky, H. (2003). *Organized crime* (7th ed.). Belmont, CA: Wadsworth.

62. Abadinsky (2003, p. 147).

63. Lyman and Potter (2004).

64. Lyman and Potter (2004).

65. Bynum, T. (1987). Controversies in the study of organized crime. In T. Bynum (Ed.), *Organized crime in America: Concepts and controversies* (pp. 3–11). Monsey, NY: Willow Tree Press.

66. Browning and Gerassi (1980).

67. Abadinsky (2003).

68. Abadinsky (2003).

69. Lyman and Potter (2004).

70. Lupsha, P. (1987). La Cosa Nostra in drug trafficking. In T. Bynum (Ed.), *Organized crime in America: Concepts and controversies* (pp. 31–41). Monsey, NY: Willow Tree Press.

71. PCOC (1986).

72. Wilson (1984, p. 566).

73. Rush, R., & Scarpitti, F. (2001). Russian organized crime: The continuation of an American tradition. *Deviant Behavior, 22,* 517–540.

74. Finckenauer, J. (2004, July/August). The Russian "Mafia." *Society,* pp. 61–64. (Quote on p. 62)

75. Carter, D. (1994). International organized crime: Emerging trends in entrepreneurial crime. *Journal of Contemporary Criminal Justice, 10,* 239–266.

76. Rosner, L. (1995). Preface to: Organized crime IV: The Russian connection. *Contemporary Criminal Justice, 11,* vi–viii.

77. Rush and Scarpitti (2001).

78. Rush and Scarpitti (2001, p. 538).

79. Lyman and Potter (2004).

80. Hill, P. (2003). *The Japanese mafia: Yakuza, law, and the state.* Oxford, UK: Oxford University Press.

81. Iwai, H. (1986). Organized crime in Japan. In R. Kelly (Ed.), *Organized crime: A global perspective* (pp. 208–233). Totowa, NJ: Rowman & Littlefield.

82. Abadinsky (2003).

83. Johnson, E. (1990). Yakuza (criminal gangs) in Japan: Characteristics and management in prison. *Journal of Contemporary Criminal Justice, 6,* 113–126.

84. Hill (2003).

85. Bell, D. (1962). *The end of ideology.* New York: Collier.

86. Firestone (1997).

87. Firestone (1997).

88. Firestone (1997).

89. Abadinsky (2003, pp. 23–24).

90. Hill (2003).

91. Abadinsky (2003, p. 41).

92. Pileggi, N. (1985). *Wiseguy: Life in a Mafia family.* New York: Simon & Schuster. (Quote on p. 13)

93. Pileggi (1985, p. 37).

94. Albanese, J. (2000). The Mafia mystique: Organized crime. In J. Sheley (Ed.), *Criminology: A contemporary handbook* (pp. 265–285). Belmont, CA: Wadsworth.

95. Albanese and Pursley (1993).

96. Abadinsky (2003).

97. Neumeister, L. (2004). Gotti brother convicted in plot to kill Mafia turncoat. *San Diego Union-Tribune.* Retrieved from http://www.signonsandiego.com/news/nation/20041222–1310.petergotti.html

98. Abadinsky (2003).

99. Albanese and Pursley (1993).

100. McShane, L. (2004, October). Mob midlife crisis: "Junior" Gotti turns 40. *Idaho Statesman, 24,* 8.

101. Firestone (1997).

VICTIMOLOGY: EXPLORING THE EXPERIENCE OF VICTIMIZATION

J ohn Sutcliff's entire adult life has been devoted to the sexual seduction of teenage boys. At the age of 33, he was arrested and sentenced to prison for sexually assaulting a 13-year-old boy who was a member of his "Big Brother's Club." By his own admission, he had been sexually active with more than 200 "members" of his club. John's favorite activity with these boys was giving and receiving enemas, a paraphilia known as klismaphilia. John became involved with the fetish while enrolled in a residential boys' school, where many of the boys were subjected to enemas administered in front of the entire dormitory.

After his release from prison, John became much more "scientific" in his efforts to procure victims. A "theoretical" paper he wrote indicated that father-absent boys were "ripe" for seduction, and he would entice them with his friendly ways and with a houseful of electronic equipment he would teach the boys to repair and operate. He weeded out boys with a father in the home and would spend at least 6 weeks grooming each victim. He used systematic desensitization techniques, starting with simply getting the boys to agree to type in answers to innocuous questions and escalating to have them view pornographic homosexual pictures and giving them "pretend" enemas, actual enemas, and enemas accompanied by homosexual activity. With each successive approximation toward John's goal, the boys were reinforced by material and nonmaterial rewards (friendship, attention, praise) that made the final events seem almost natural.

John's activities came to light when U.S. postal inspectors found a package containing pictures, letters, and tapes John exchanged with like-minded individuals. On the basis of this evidence, the police raided John's home and found neatly cataloged files detailing 475 boys who he *had seduced. His methods were so successful that his actions were never reported to the authorities (indeed, some of the boys were recruited for him by earlier victims). Some of his earlier victims still kept in touch with him and were victimizing boys themselves. Only one victim agreed to testify, but John was allowed to plead to one count of lewd and lascivious conduct and received a sentence of 1 year and was paroled after serving 10 months, thus serving 15.7 hours for each of his 475 known victims. This case illustrates how victims (totally innocent as children) can be turned into victimizers (totally responsible as adults) and how the distinction between victim and perpetrator can sometimes be blurred.*

The Emergence of Victimology

So far throughout this text, we have discussed crime and criminality without giving much thought to the victims of criminal acts. Except for minor public-order crimes, for every criminal act, there is necessarily at least one victim. Criminologists have spent countless hours trying to determine the factors that contribute to making a person a criminal, but it wasn't until the German criminologist Hans von Hentig's work[1] that they began seriously thinking about the role of the victim. It turned out that although victimization can be an unfortunate random event where the victim was simply in the wrong place at the wrong time, in many, perhaps even in most cases of victimization, there is a systematic pattern if one looks closely enough.

Victimology is a subfield of criminology that specializes in studying the victims of crime. Criminologists interested in perpetrators of crime ask what the risk factors for becoming involved in crime are. Criminologists interested in victims of crime ask pretty much the same questions—that is, why some individuals, households, groups, and other entities are targeted and others are not.[2] The labels *offender* and *victim* are sometimes blurred distinctions that hide the details of the interactions of the offender-victim dyad. We have seen that burglars often prey on their own kind, that robbers prey on drug dealers, and that homicides are frequently the outcome of minor arguments in which the victim was the instigator. As victimologist Andrew Karmen bluntly put it, "Predators prey on each other as well as upon innocent members of the public. . . . When youth gangs feud with each other by carrying out 'drive-by' shootings, the young members who get gunned down are casualties of their own brand of retaliatory street justice."[3] He hastens to add, however, that there are millions of innocent victims who in no way contribute to their victimization, and even lawbreakers can be genuine victims deserving of protection and redress in the criminal courts.

Who Gets Victimized?

Victimization is not a random process. As is the case with the process of becoming a criminal offender, becoming a victim is a process encompassing a host of systematic environmental, demographic, and personal characteristics. Table 16.1 from the 2004 National Crime Victimization Surveys (NCVS) study[4] illustrates this point. The individual most likely to be victimized is a young Black unmarried male living in poverty in an urban environment. We note that victimization, like criminal behavior, drops precipitously from 25 years of age onwards; it also drops with increasing household income, and being married is a protective factor against victimization as it is against crime.

Table 16.1	Victimization Rates of Combined Violent and Personal Theft Crimes by Selected Demographic Characteristics: 2004			

Gender	Rate		Household Income	Rate
Male	25.0		Less than $7,500	38.4
Female	18.1		$7,500–$14,999	39.0
			$15,000–$24,999	24.4
			$25,000–$34,999	22.1
			$35,000–$49,999	21.6
Race/Ethnicity			$50,000–$74,999	22.1
White	21.0		$75,000 or more	17.0
Black	26.0			
Hispanic	18.2		**Marital Status**	
Other	2.7		Never married	39.4
Two or more	51.6		Married	9.7
			Divorced/separated	33.0
Age			Widowed	4.0
12–15	49.7			
16–19	45.9		**Residence**	
20–24	43.0		Urban	29.0
25–34	23.7		Suburban	18.0
35–49	7.9		Rural	19.9
50–64	11.0			
65 or older	2.1			

Source: Catalano, S. (2005). *Criminal victimization, 2004.* Washington, DC: Bureau of Justice Statistics.

Note: Violent crimes are rape, sexual assault, robbery, and assault. Personal theft is only thefts from the person (not robbery) and does not include household burglaries.

As we might expect, victim characteristics differ according to the type of crime. Females were 33 times more likely than males to be victimized by rape/sexual assault, but males were 2.1 times more likely to be victimized by aggravated assault. Females were more likely to be victimized by someone they knew and males by strangers. Blacks were 3.7 times more likely than "other races" (Asian, American Indian/Alaskan Native) to be victims of aggravated assault but slightly less likely than Whites to be victims of simple assault. Individuals 65 or older were 20 times less likely than individuals ages 20 to 24 to be victimized by any type of violent crime but slightly more likely to be victimized by a personal theft.

▧ Victimization in the Workplace and School

Two important demographic variables not included in the 2004 NCVS study are victimization at work and at school. It is important to consider these variables since most of us spend the majority of our waking hours either on the job or at school. The last systematic effort by the Department of Justice to assess the level of workplace violence in the United States was in 1998. This report dealt with workplace violence taking place between 1992 and 1996 and found that, on average, more than 2 million incidents take place annually.[5] Table 16.2 provides

Table 16.2	Average Annual Number of Violent Victimizations in the Workplace 1992-1996	
	Annual Average	**%**
Homicide	1,023	0.05
Rape/sexual assault	50,500	2.50
Robbery	83,700	4.20
Aggravated assault	395,500	19.70
Simple assault	1,480,000	73.60
	2,010,723	100.00

SOURCE: Warchol, G. (1998). *Workplace violence, 1992–1996.* Washington, DC: Bureau of Justice Statistics, U.S. Department of Justice.

the average annual level of workplace violence over the 5-year period. Two thirds of the victims in the survey were male, almost 90% were White, and the age category most likely to be victimized was the age 35 to 49 category. The three occupations most at risk were police officers (a rate of 306 per 1,000 workers), corrections officers (217.8), and taxi drivers (183.8); taxi drivers were the most likely to be killed, however. Taxi drivers had an astounding homicide victimization rate of 26.9 per 100,000 workers; all protective service workers had a rate more than five times lower (5.0 per 100,000). The most dangerous jobs are those in which the workers must deal with the public in a protective/supervisory capacity or who work alone and are relatively isolated from others, who work at night, and who work with money. The safest job category was university professor (a rate of 2.5).

Public perceptions of victimization at the nation's schools are unfortunately fueled by isolated but spectacular events such as the Columbine school massacre and other similar incidents in the 1990s. The truth is that our schools are some of the safest places to be. Figure 16.1 shows that less than 1% of all juvenile homicides and suicides occurred at school during the period studied. Bullying, which also gets a lot of press, seems surprisingly rare as well. Figure 16.2 shows the percentage of students from 6th to 12th grade who reported being bullied in 1999 and 2001. The graph looks a lot like the graphs for delinquency, in that bullying is most frequent at age 12 and levels off thereafter. The somewhat dramatic increase in each grade from 1999 to 2001 probably reflects a growing awareness and willingness to report bullying rather than a real increase in bullying behavior.

Teachers also get victimized by both theft and violence at school. Between 1997 and 2001, U.S. teachers were victims of 473,000 violent crimes and 817,000 thefts.[6] Male teachers in urban junior high and high schools were the most likely to be victimized by violent crime; not surprisingly, female teachers in elementary schools were the least likely.

✉ Child Molestation: Who Gets Victimized?

Child molestation is perhaps the most prevalent crime against the person in the United States, with approximately two thirds of incarcerated sex offenders having offended against children.[7] It is more problematic to accurately gauge the prevalence of child molesting than it is to gauge the prevalence of rape, with rates depending on how broad or narrow molesting is defined. A "best guess" arrived at from a variety of sources is that the percentage of

| **Figure 16.1** | Number of Homicides and Suicides of Youth Ages 15 to 19 at and Away from School: 1999–2000 |

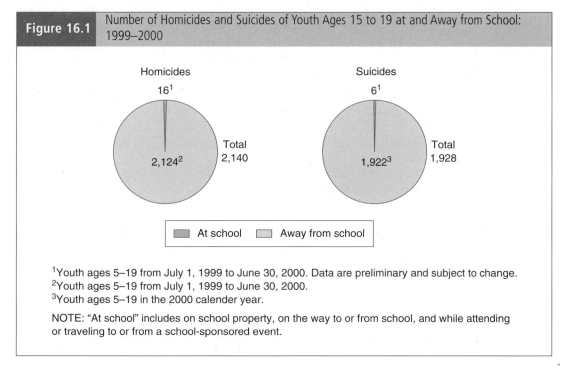

[1]Youth ages 5–19 from July 1, 1999 to June 30, 2000. Data are preliminary and subject to change.
[2]Youth ages 5–19 from July 1, 1999 to June 30, 2000.
[3]Youth ages 5–19 in the 2000 calender year.

NOTE: "At school" includes on school property, on the way to or from school, and while attending or traveling to or from a school-sponsored event.

SOURCE: DeVoe, J., Peter, K., Kaufman, P., Ruddy, S., Miller, A., Planty, M., et al. (2003). *Indicators of school crime and safety.* Washington, DC: U.S. Department of Education and U.S. Department of Justice.

| **Figure 16.2** | Percentage of Students ages 12-18 who Reported being Bullied During Previous Six Months, by Grade: 1999 and 2001 |

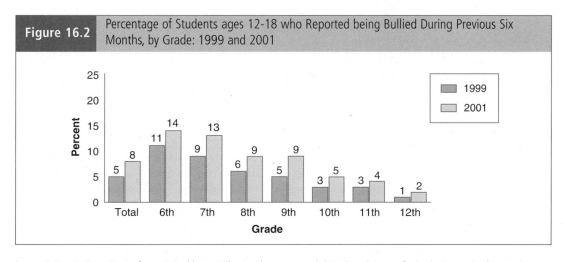

SOURCE: DeVoe, J., Peter, K., Kaufman, P., Ruddy, S., Miller, A., Planty, M., et al. (2003). *Indicators of school crime and safety.* Washington, DC: U.S. Department of Education and U.S. Department of Justice.

children in the United States experiencing sexual abuse sometime during their childhood is 25% for girls and 10% for boys.[8] Girls are more likely to be abused within the family, and boys are more likely to be victimized by acquaintances outside of the family and by strangers.[9] A Child Protective Services analysis of official reports indicated that the average age of victims is 10.5 years, that about two thirds of sexually abused children are victimized only once, and that molesting tends to be in the form of fondling and/or oral sex rather than vaginal or anal penetration.[10] The strongest single predictor of victimization for girls is having a stepfather. Stepfathers are about five times more likely to sexually abuse their daughters than are biological fathers.[11] The strongest predictor for boys is growing up in a father-absent home.[12]

There are many other factors predictive of child sexual abuse, and the more that are present, the more likely abuse is to occur. Finkelhor[13] developed a risk factor checklist for the likelihood of girls' victimization, which contains the following predictors:

- Living with a stepfather
- Living without biological mother
- Not close to mother
- Mother never finished high school
- Sex-punitive mother
- No physical affection from (biological) father
- Family income under $10,000 (in 1980 dollars; $26,000 in 2006 dollars)
- Two friends or fewer in childhood

Finkelhor found that the probability of victimization was virtually zero among girls with none of the predictors in their background and rose steadily to 66% among girls with five. Given the large number of divorces, out-of-wedlock births, and reconstituted families we are seeing in the United States, these risk factors for sexual abuse will be experienced by an increasing number of children. It is important to realize that in the case of child molesting, the perpetrator is always 100% responsible for the crime.

⌧ Victimization Theories

Victimization can occur at any time, at any place, and totally without warning. Who could have predicted that someone gassing her car at the filling station would be gunned down by the Washington, D.C., snipers in 2002 or that the typist at his desk in the World Trade Center would be obliterated seconds later by a passenger jet on September 11, 2001? There is no systemic way to evaluate events such as this, which are entirely random from a victimology perspective. But as previously noted, most victimizing events are not random or unpredictable, and criminologists no longer view all victims as simply passive players in crime who were unfortunate enough to be in the wrong place at the wrong time. In the majority of cases of victimization, victims are now seen as individuals who in some way, knowingly or unknowingly, passively or actively, influenced their victimization. Obviously, the role of the victim, however provocative it may be, is never a necessary and sufficient cause of his or her victimization and therefore cannot fully explain the actions of the person committing the criminal act. We now briefly discuss the most influential theories of victimization.

Victim Precipitation Theory

Victim precipitation theory was first promulgated by von Hentig[14] and applies only to violent victimization. Its basic premise is that by acting in certain provocative ways, some individuals initiate a chain of events that lead to their victimization. Most murders of spouses and boyfriends by women, for example, are victim precipitated in that the "perpetrator" is defending herself from the victim.[15] Likewise, serious delinquent and criminal behavior and serious victimization are inextricably linked. A study using data from the longitudinal Pittsburgh and Denver studies discussed in Chapter 9 in terms of delinquency risk factors (e.g., low socioeconomic status [SES], single-parent household, hyperactivity, impulsiveness, drug usage) showed that the same factors predicted serious victimization as well.[16] As Figure 16.3 shows, the risk of violent victimization increased with the number of delinquency risk factors boys had. Overall, 50% of seriously violent delinquents were themselves violently victimized, compared with 10% of nondelinquents from the same neighborhoods.

Victim precipitation theory has been most contentious when it is applied to rape ever since Menachem Amir's study[17] of police records found that 19% of forcible rapes were victim precipitated (defined by Amir as agreeing to sexual relations and then retracting). A number of surveys of high school and college students have shown that most males and a significant minority of females believe that it is justifiable for a man to use some degree of force to obtain sex if the victim had somehow "led him on."[18] This appears to indicate that some people believe that there could be an act labeled "justifiable rape" in the same sense that there is justifiable homicide. These same surveys also indicate that many people continue to believe that rape victims are often at least partially responsible for their rape because of such factors as dress and

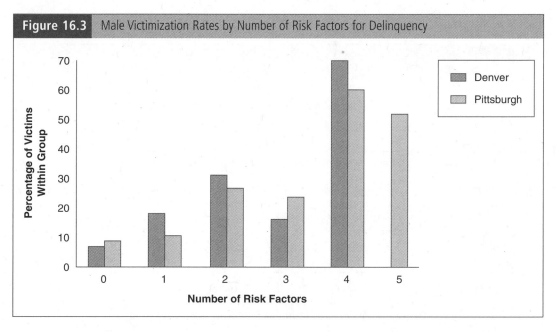

Figure 16.3 Male Victimization Rates by Number of Risk Factors for Delinquency

Source: Loeber, R., Kalb, L., & Huizinga, D. (2001, August). Juvenile delinquency and serious injury victimization. *Juvenile Justice Bulletin.*

lifestyle and because of the belief that "nice girls don't get raped."[19] This type of thinking is rightly viewed as victim blaming, and victimologists want no part in perpetuating it.

Figure 16.4 provides four scenarios illustrating various levels of victim/offender responsibility from this perspective. In the first scenario, the woman who stabbed her husband after suffering years of abuse is judged blameless, although some lacking a little in empathy and understanding of the psychology of domestic abuse may argue that she must take some responsibility for remaining in the relationship. In the second scenario, both the offender and the victim were engaging in a minor vice crime, and both are judged equally responsible for the crime (morally, he should not have been there and was careless with his wallet). In the third scenario, the victim facilitated the crime by carelessly leaving his keys in the car. In the last scenario, the child is totally innocent of any responsibility for what happened to her. We want to strongly emphasize that whatever the degree of responsibility, "responsibility" does not mean "guilt."

Routine Activities/Lifestyle Theory

Routine activities and lifestyle theories are separate entities, but in victimology, they are similar enough to warrant being merged into one.[20] Recall from Chapter 3 that routine activities theory stresses that criminal behavior takes place via the interaction of three variables that reflect individuals' everyday routine activities: (1) the presence of motivated offenders, (2) the availability of suitable targets, and (3) the absence of capable guardians.

The basic idea of lifestyle theory is that there are certain lifestyles (routine activities) that disproportionately expose some people to high risk for victimization. Lifestyles are the routine patterned activities that people engage in on a daily basis, both obligatory (e.g., work related) and optional (e.g., recreational). A high-risk lifestyle may be getting involved with deviant peer

Figure 16.4	Four Scenarios Illustrating the Degree of Victim/Offender Responsibility According to Victim Precipitation Theory

Degree of Criminal Intent of the Perpetrator

None   →   **Some**   →   **More**   →   **Much**

Victim Provocation	Equal Responsibility	Victim Facilitation	Victim Innocent
A woman who has suffered years of abuse stabs and kills her husband in self-defense as he is beating her again.	Victim using the services of a prostitute leaves his wallet on the bed stand and departs. She decides to keep the money in his wallet.	Victim leaves keys in his car while he runs into a store. A teenager impulsively steals the car and wrecks it.	A sex offender kidnaps a screaming young girl from a playground and molests her.

Much   ←   **More**   ←   **Some**   ←   **None**

Degree of Victim Facilitation or Provocation/Precipitation

◄ **Photo 16.1** Gary Ridgway became known as the Green River Killer for his habit of depositing victims' bodies along this waterway. Serial killers frequently victimize marginalized groups, such as prostitutes. Some of his victims' bodies were only discovered years after their untimely deaths, by searchers such as these, revisiting kill sites.

groups or drugs, in just "hanging out," or frequenting bars until late into the night and drinking heavily. Routine activities/lifestyle theory explains some of the data relating to demographic profiles and risk presented by Loeber, Kalb, and Huizinga[21] discussed earlier. Males, the young, the unmarried, and the poor are more at risk for victimization than females, older people, married people, and more affluent people because they have riskier lifestyles. On average, the lifestyles of the former are more active and action oriented than the latter.

These lifestyles sometimes lead to repeat victimization. Prior victimization has been called "arguably the best readily available predictor of future victimization," and it "appears a robust finding across crime types and data sources."[22] Lisa Bostaph[23] reviews the literature on what she calls "career victims"; among the various interesting research findings on this phenomenon, she lists the following attributable to lifestyle patterns:

♦ A British crime survey that found that 20.2% of the respondents were victims of 81.2% of all offenses.
♦ A study that found 24% of rape victims had been raped before.
♦ A study of assault victims in the Netherlands found that 11.3% of victims accounted for 25.3% of hospital admissions for assault over 25 years.
♦ A study reported that 67% of sexual assault victims had experienced prior sexual assaults.

Most of the research in routine activities/lifestyle theory has been done on rape victimization. Fisher, Cullen, and Turner's[24] national sample of college women found that 2.8% had been raped, although 46.5% said that they did not experience the event as rape. Fisher and colleagues[25] report that four lifestyle factors are consistently found to increase the risk of sexual assault: (1) frequently drinking enough to get drunk, (2) being unmarried, (3) having previously been a victim of sexual assault, and (4) living on campus (for on-campus victimization only).

Many previous studies of reported rape found that it occurred at times when both the offender and the victim had been drinking. These studies maintain that rape victims are women

▲ **Photo 16.2** Efforts to better recognize victims and their rights have become more common over the past 20 years. This photo memorializes the victims of Columbine High School, including the killers themselves, who committed suicide.

("suitable targets") who lack "capable guardians" (they are away from home or single and living alone) who go out drinking more frequently and drink more heavily than other women. The authors of one such study emphasize that it should not be taken as an attempt to blame women for their victimization or to remove it from their assailants. They indicate that their study supports the feminist notion that women are less free in their movements in society and that the solution to rape is not to keep women away from bars but rather to change American society.[26]

Is Victimology "Blaming the Victim"?

Some victim advocates strongly reject victimology theories as "victim blaming." The implication of this position is that all victims are created equal and that when victimologists divide the responsibility pie, they feed victims the whole pie when they should not get even a smidgen. No victimologist thinks or carries out research in these terms; they simply explore the process of victimization with the goal of understanding and *preventing* it. Although victimology research is used to develop crime prevention strategies, not to berate victims, Karmen points out that those who hold a position he calls "victim defending" even reject "as ideologically tainted" the crime prevention tips endorsed by a position he calls "victim blaming."[27]

Crime prevention tips and strategies are ignored at our peril. We all agree with victim defenders that we *should* be able to leave our cars unlocked with the keys in it, sleep with the windows wide open in summer, leave our doors unlocked, frequent any bar who choose, and walk down any alley in any neighborhood at any time we damn well please, but we cannot. Good common sense demands that we take what steps we can to safeguard ourselves and our property in this imperfect world. Crime prevention tips are really no different from tips we get all the time about staying healthy: eat right, exercise, and quit smoking if you want to avoid health problems. Similarly, avoid certain places, dress sensibly, don't provoke, take reasonable precautionary measures, and don't drink too much if you want to avoid victimization.

Victims deserve our sympathy even if they somehow provoked or facilitated their own victimization. Victimologists do not "blame"; they simply remind us that complete innocence and full responsibility lie on a continuum, as we attempted to show in Figure 16.4. Many people are forced by circumstances beyond their control to live in dangerous neighborhoods where they are constantly exposed to motivated offenders. These neighborhoods are where the poorest and most powerless members of society live. Besides being populated by predatory criminals, they are populated by the homeless, the addicted, the elderly poor, and the physically and mentally challenged. These people lack the resources available to the more affluent to implement crime prevention strategies to protect themselves and their property, making them easy targets for criminals.

▨ The Consequences of Victimization

While some victimologists explore the risk factors associated with victimization, others explore the consequences of victimization for the victim. Overall, financial losses per crime do not appear overly large. According to an NCVS report,[28] only 12% of personal crimes and 24% of property crimes resulted in losses to the victim of greater than $500 ($685 in 2006 dollars). Of course, many victims incur considerably greater financial costs than this due to loss of property, medical bills, time lost from work, and so on, but there are more enduring costs. Some people suffer lifelong pain from wounds and some suffer permanent disability, but for the majority of victims, the worst consequences are psychological. We all like to think that we live in a safe, predictable, and lawful world in which people treat one another decently. When we are victimized, this comfortable "just worldview" is shattered. With victimization come stressful feelings of shock, personal vulnerability, anger, fear of further victimization, and suspicion of others.

Victimization also produces feelings of depression, guilt, self-blame, and lowered self-esteem and self-efficacy. Rape in particular has these consequences for its victims ("Did I contribute to it?" "Could I have done more to prevent it?"). The shock, anger, and depression that typically afflict a rape victim is known as **rape trauma syndrome,** which is similar to post-traumatic stress syndrome (reexperiencing the event via "flashbacks," avoiding anything at all associated with the event, and having a general numbness of affect) often suffered by those who have experienced the horrors of war.[29] Acute symptoms may last several months, and although some victims experience stabilization after about 3 months, many "experience chronic problems for an indefinite time in the areas of fear/anxiety, depression, social adjustment, sexual functioning, and self-esteem."[30] Victimization "also changes one's perceptions of and beliefs about others in society. It does so by indicating others as sources of threat and harm rather than sources of support."[31]

Victims of property crimes, particularly burglary, also have the foundations of their world shaken, although less so than victims of serious violent crime. The home is supposed to be a personal sanctuary of safety and security, and when it is "touched" by an intruder, some victims describe it as the "rape" of their home.[32] A British study of burglary victims found that 65% reacted with anger, 30% reacted with fear of revictimization, and 29% suffered insomnia as a consequence. The type and severity of these reactions were structured by victims' place in the social structure, with those most likely to be affected being women, older and poorer individuals, and residents of single-parent households.[33]

In summing up the consequences of victimization, we note that just as offending behavior shapes the life course trajectories of offenders, violent victimization helps to shape the life course trajectories of victims. Scott Menard's study[34] of the National Survey of Youth samples, a longitudinal study involving individuals from ages 11 to 33, found that violent victimization during adolescence has pervasive effects on problem outcomes as adults. Figure 16.5 shows that although the probability of negative outcomes is much greater for victims than nonvictims, mercifully, no outcome affected more than 44% of the victims.

FOCUS ON . . .

A Case of Cybervictimization and Its Consequences

As we mentioned in Chapter 14, with the advent of the computer age, we are all "victims-in-waiting." One of the most terrifying fictional depictions of cybervictimization is provided in the movie *The Net*. In this movie, Angela Bennett, played by Sandra Bullock, is a computer expert who has her life turned into a nightmare when her records are wiped clean and she is given a new identity by people who have it in for her. Her new identity came complete with a police record, and the rest of the movie is about her struggles to find out who has done this to her and why.

Michelle Brown, a 29-year-old White female, is one of a number of real-life Angela Bennetts whose nightmare began in January 1998. While Michelle did not have her records erased, she had them "cloned" by a woman who gained access to her personal information. Her identity clone was Heddi Larae Ille, a 33-year-old White female. With a line of credit established with Michelle's Social Security number and driver's license number, Heddi racked up $1,443 in phone bills, bought a $32,000 automobile, had $4,800 worth of liposuction, and bought numerous other items. Worse yet, Heddi was arrested as Michelle Brown for smuggling 3,000 pounds of marijuana into Texas from Mexico. Michelle was thus named in the indictment and listed as a Drug Enforcement Administration (DEA) informant. Returning from a trip overseas, Michelle (the real one) was detained for over an hour at LAX because the DEA had posed a lookout for her. Only a phone call from a police detective aware of Michelle's predicament got her released. Heddi was arrested and booked again under Michelle's identity for grand theft and possession of stolen property in 1999. Her true identity finally came to light, and she was sentenced to 73 months in federal prison and 24 months in state prison.

Michelle presented her story before a U.S. Senate committee on identity theft.[35] She also informed them of the traumatic effect her victimization had on her life. She said that she spent more than 500 hours (the equivalent of 12.5 workweeks) trying to unravel the mess, lost countless hours of sleep, lost her appetite, and lost a valued 3-year relationship with her boyfriend. She added that she also "lost identification with the person I really was inside and shut myself out of social functions because of the negativity this caused in my life." She indicated that she was afraid to leave the country again in case her name is still on some country's computer listing her as "wanted." Michelle's case, admittedly a particularly horrible one, is just one of the many thousands of such cases that occur annually in the United States.

| Figure 16.5 | Percentage of Adolescent Victims and Non-victims of Violence Expected to Experience Adult Problem Outcomes |

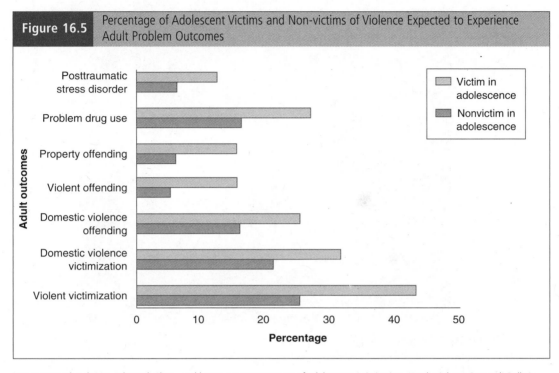

Source: Menard, S. (2002, February). Short- and long-term consequences of adolescent victimization. *Youth Violence Research Bulletin.*

⊠ Victimization and the Criminal Justice System

Until fairly recently, the victim had been the forgotten party in the criminal justice system. In the United States, crime is considered as an act against the state rather than against the individual who was actually victimized. Consequently, the victim's sole role in bringing the accused to justice was as a witness or "evidence" against him or her. Advocates for victims' rights began agitating for some of the same kinds of due process rights for victims that are enjoyed by their victimizers in the late 1960s, but it was not until 1982 that a federal task force was set up to examine the treatment of victims by the criminal justice system. The report from the task force to President Reagan made numerous suggestions, even for a constitutional amendment to be added to the Sixth Amendment to guarantee that "the victim, in every criminal prosecution shall have the right to be present and to be heard at all critical stages of the judicial proceedings."[36] This amendment has not been forthcoming, but in 2004, the Senate passed a crime victims' bill of rights that includes almost all of the recommendations made by the 1982 task force. Unfortunately, there is no provision in the enumerated rights for victims to claim recompense if criminal justice officials do not provide these rights in the same manner that there is recompense (perhaps in the form of dismissal of charges) if officials fail to provide the rights due to criminal suspects. The rights contained in the crime victims' bill of rights are given below.

▲ **Photo 16.3** The police are the first responders to most criminal victimizations. They must attempt to both respond to the victim's need as well as collect facts to help them solve the case. Police are now routinely trained in how to better recognize and respond to victims' signs of trauma.

Although the above rights apply only to victims of federal crimes, all 50 states have implemented constitutional amendments or promulgated bills guaranteeing similar rights. Not all victims can or want to avail themselves of such rights, but the fair and decent treatment of victims by the system can help them to get over their victimization to some extent. As one mental health professional and victim advocate put it, "Participation in the justice process is therapeutic when it helps victims to better understand what happened, allows them an opportunity to tell their story, and validates their loss and sense of being wronged. When victims are ignored, their feelings of trauma may be intensified and prolonged."[37] Presented in "Focus On. . ." are a series of rights deemed most important from the point of view of victims. Simply being informed of the case's progress was of great value to them.

Victim Compensation and Restitution

Victims of crimes are eligible for partial compensation from the states to cover medical and living expenses incurred as a result of their victimization. The first victim compensation program was initiated by California in 1965; by 2002, all 50 states and all U.S. protectorates had established such programs. These programs typically cover what insurance does not cover, assuming the state has sufficient funds. Sadly, most state programs are grossly underfunded, and therefore financial assistance for victims is quite limited. According to the National Association of Crime Victim Compensation Board (NACVCB), in 2004, victims of violent crime and their families nationwide received a total of $426 million in compensation, with the majority going for medical expenses (51%) and the least (9%) for victim counseling.[38] Victim

Crime Victims' Bill of Rights

1. The right to be reasonably protected from the accused

2. The right to reasonable, accurate, and timely notice of any public proceeding involving the crime or of any release or escape of the accused

3. The right not to be excluded from any such public proceeding

4. The right to be reasonably heard at any public proceeding involving release, plea, or sentencing

5. The right to confer with the attorney for the Government in the case

6. The right to full and timely restitution as provided in law

7. The right to proceedings free from unreasonable delay

8. The right to be treated with fairness and with respect for the victim's dignity and privacy

SOURCE: Senate Bill S2329, April 21, 2004.

compensation in the form of direct payments from the offenders in the form of restitution is increasingly ordered by the courts.

Unfortunately, very few offenders are able to pay back to their victims anywhere near what they had taken. The estimated national rate of payment of court-ordered restitution is only 20% to 30%.[39]

▨ Victim-Offender Reconciliation Programs (VORPs)

Victim-offender reconciliation programs (VORPs) are an integral component of restorative justice philosophy. Many crime victims are seeking fairness, justice, and restitution *as defined by them* (restorative justice) as opposed to revenge and punishment. Central to the VORP process is the bringing together of victim and offender in face-to-face meetings mediated by a person trained in mediation theory and practice.[40] Meetings are voluntary for both offender and victim and are designed to iron out ways in which the offender can make amends for the hurt and damage caused to the victim.

Victims participating in VORPs gain the opportunity to make offenders aware of their feelings of personal violation and loss and to lay out their proposals of how offenders can restore the situation. Offenders are afforded the opportunity to see firsthand the pain they have caused their victims and perhaps even to express remorse. The mediator assists the parties in developing a contract agreeable to both. The mediator monitors the terms of the contract and may schedule further face-to-face meetings.

VORPs are used most often in the juvenile system but are rarely used for personal violent crimes in either juvenile or adult systems. Where they are used, about 60% of victims invited to participate actually become involved, and a high percentage (mid to high 90s) results in

FOCUS ON . . .

Victims' Opinions of the Importance of Victims' Rights

The importance of victims' rights to victims themselves

The right to participate in the process of justice, including the right to attend criminal proceedings and to be heard at various points in the criminal justice process, is important to crime victims. The researchers reached this conclusion by presenting victims with the following list of rights and asking them to rate the importance of each one:[a]

- Being informed about whether anyone was arrested.

- Being involved in the decision to drop the case.

- Being informed about the defendant's release on bond.

- Being informed about the date of the earliest possible release from incarceration.

- Being heard in decisions about the defendant's release on bond.

- Discussing the case with the prosecutor's office.

- Discussing whether the defendant's plea to a lesser charge should be accepted.

- Making a victim's impact statement during the defendant's parole hearing.

- Being present during the grand jury hearing.

- Being present during release hearings.

- Being informed about postponement of grand jury hearings.

- Making a victim's impact statement before sentencing.

- Being involved in the decision about what sentence should be given.

On each item, more than three-fourths of the victims rated the particular right as "very important." Topping the list was the right to be informed about whether there was an arrest, rated "very important" by more than 97 percent of the victims. The sole item rated "very important" by less than 80 percent was involvement in the decision about the sentence.

SOURCE: Kilpatrick, D., Beatty, D., & Smith-Howley, S. (1998). *The rights of crime victims: Does legal protection make a difference?* Washington, DC: National Institute of Justice.

a. The rights are listed in descending order of their rating.

signed contracts.[41] Mark Umbreit[42] sums up the various satisfactions expressed by victims who participate in VORPs:

1. Meeting offenders helped reduce their fear of being revictimized.
2. They appreciated the opportunity to tell offenders how they felt.
3. Being personally involved in the justice process was satisfying to them.
4. They gained insight into the crime and into the offender's situation.
5. They received restitution.

However, VORPs do not suit all victims, especially those who feel that the wrong done to them cannot so easily be "put right" and want the offender punished.[43]

SUMMARY

Victimology is the study of the risk factors for and consequences of victimization, along with criminal justice approaches dealing with victims and victimization. The risk factors for victimization are basically the same as the risk factors for victimizing in terms of gender, race, age, SES, personal characteristics, and neighborhood.

Theories of victimization such as victim precipitation theory and routine activities/lifestyle theory examine the victim's role in facilitating or precipitating his or her victimization. This is not "victim blaming" but rather an effort to understand and prevent victimization. Victimologists apportion responsibility within the victim-offender dyad on a continuum from complete victim innocence to victim precipitation.

The consequences of victimization can be devastating both physically and psychologically. Although the severity of the psychological consequences of the same sort of victimization can vary widely according to the characteristics of the victim, consequences can range from short-lived anger to posttraumatic stress syndrome, especially for victims of rape.

Until fairly recently, victims were the forgotten party in a criminal justice system that tended to think of them only as "evidence" or witnesses. Things have changed over the past 25 years with the passage of victims' rights bills by the federal government and all 50 states. There are also various victim-centered programs designed to ease the pains of victimization, such as victim compensation and restitution and victim-offender reconciliation programs.

On Your Own

Log on to the web-based student study site at http://www.sagepub.com/criminologystudy for more information about the vignettes and materials presented in this chapter, suggestions for activities, study aids such as review quizzes, and research recommendations including journal article links and questions related to this chapter.

EXERCISES AND DISCUSSION QUESTIONS

1. Interview a willing classmate or friend who has been victimized by a serious crime and ask about his or her feelings shortly after victimization and now. Did it change his or her attitudes about crime and punishment?

2. Is it a surprise to you that perpetrators of crimes are more likely to also be victims of crime than people in general? Why or why not?

3. Is the idea that some victims contribute to their own victimization insensitive to their suffering, or is it a commonsense idea necessary for understanding and prevention?

4. Go to your state's official Web site and find out funding levels and what services are available to crime victims.

5. Discuss how learning about victimology helps you to further understand offending behavior.

6. In your opinion, does the criminal justice system do enough to guarantee victims' rights? What other steps can be taken to lessen the harm suffered by victims in the aftermath of being victimized?

KEY WORDS

Rape trauma syndrome
Routine activities/lifestyle
 theory

Victim-offender
 reconciliation
 programs

Victim precipitation theory
Victimology

REFERENCES

1. von Hentig, H. (1941). Remarks on the interaction of perpetrator and victim. *Journal of Criminal Law, Criminology, and Police Science, 31,* 303–309.

2. Doerner, W., & Lab, S. (2002). *Victimology* (3rd ed.). Cincinnati, OH: Anderson.

3. Karmen, A. (2004). *Crime victims: An introduction to victimology* (5th ed.). Belmont, CA: Wadsworth. (Quote on p. 14)

4. Catalano, S. (2005). *Criminal victimization, 2004.* Washington, DC: Bureau of Justice Statistics.

5. Warchol, G. (1998). *Workplace violence, 1992–1996.* Washington, DC: Bureau of Justice Statistics, U.S. Department of Justice.

6. DeVoe, J., Peter, K., Kaufman, P., Ruddy, S., Miller, A., Planty, M., et al. (2003). *Indicators of school crime and safety.* Washington, DC: U.S. Department of Education and U.S. Department of Justice.

7. Talbot, T., Gilligan, L., Carter, M., & Matson, S. (2002). *An overview of sex offender management.* Washington, DC: Center for Sex Offender Management.

8. Knudsen, D. (1991). Child sexual coercion. In E. Grauerholz & M. Koralewski (Eds.), *Sexual coercion: A sourcebook on its nature, causes, and prevention* (pp. 17–28). Lexington, MA: D. C. Heath.

9. Walsh, A. (1994). Homosexual and heterosexual child molestation: Case characteristics and sentencing differentials. *International Journal of Offender Therapy and Comparative Criminology, 38,* 339–353.

10. Knudson (1991).

11. Glaser, D., & Frosh, S. (1993). *Child sex abuse.* Toronto: University of Toronto Press.

12. Walsh, A. (1988). Lessons and concerns from a case study of a 'scientific' molester. *Corrective and Social Psychiatry, 34,* 18–23.

13. Finkelhor, D. (1984). *Child sexual abuse: New theory and research.* New York: Free Press.

14. von Hentig, H. (1941). Remarks on the interaction of perpetrator and victim. *Journal of the American Institute of Criminal Law and Criminology, 31,* 303–309.

15. Mann, C. (1990). Black female homicides in the United States. *Journal of Interpersonal Violence, 5,* 176–201.

16. Loeber, R., Kalb, L., & Huizinga, D. (2001, August). Juvenile delinquency and serious injury victimization. *Juvenile Justice Bulletin.*

17. Amir, M. (1971). *Patterns of forcible rape.* Chicago: University of Chicago Press.

18. Herman, J. (1991). Sex offenders: A feminist perspective. In W. Marshall, D. Laws, & H. Barbaree (Eds.), *Handbook of sexual assault: Issues, theories, and treatment of the offender* (pp. 177–193). New York: Plenum.

19. Bartol, C. (2002). *Criminal behavior: A psychosocial approach* (6th ed.). Englewood Cliffs, NJ: Prentice Hall.

20. Doerner and Lab (2002).

21. Loeber et al. (2001).

22. Tseloni, A., & Pease, K. (2003). Repeat personal victimization. *British Journal of Criminology, 43,* 196–212. (Quote on p. 196)

23. Bostaph, L. (2004). *Race and repeat victimization: Does the repetitive nature of police motor vehicle stops impact racially biased policing?* Doctoral dissertation, University of Cincinnati.

24. Fisher, B., Cullen, F., & Turner, M. (2001). *The sexual victimization of college women.* Washington, DC: National Institute of Justice.

25. Fisher et al. (2001).

26. Schwartz, M., & Pitts, V. (1995). Exploring a feminist routine activities approach to explaining sexual assault. *Justice Quarterly, 12,* 9–31.

27. Karmen (2004, p. 129).

28. Menard, S. (2002, February). Short- and long-term consequences of adolescent victimization. *Youth Violence Research Bulletin.*

29. van Berlo, W., & Ensink, B. (2000). Problems with sexuality after sexual assault. *Annual Review of Sex Research, 11,* 235–257.

30. Resick, P., & Nishith, P. (1997). Sexual assault. In R. Davis, A. Lurigio, & W. Skogan (Eds.), *Victims of crime* (pp. 27–52). Thousand Oaks, CA: Sage. (Quote on p. 31)

31. Macmillan, R. (2001). Violence and the life course: The consequences of victimization for personal and social development. *Annual Review of Sociology, 27,* 1–22. (Quote on p. 12)

32. Bartol (2002).

33. Menard (2002).

34. Mawby, R. (2001). *Burglary.* Devon, UK: Willan.

35. Kyl, J., & Feinstein, D. (200). *Written testimony of Michelle Brown.* Posted by Privacy Rights Clearing House. Retrieved from http://www.privacyrights .org/cases/victims8/htm

36. Herrington, L. (Chair). (1982). *Task force on victims of crime* (Report). Washington, DC: Government Printing Office.

37. Kilpatrick, D. (1998). The mental health community. In *New directions from the field: Victims' rights and services for the 21st century* (pp. 219–247). Washington, DC: U.S. Department of Justice. (Quote on p. 219)

38. National Association of Crime Victim Compensation Board (NACVCB). (2005). *FY 2004: compensation to victims continues to increase.* Retrieved from http://www.nacvcb.org/

39. Price, M. (2005). *Can mediation produce restorative justice for victims and offenders?* VORP Information and Resource Center. Retrieved from http:/www .vorp.com/articles/crime

40. Price (2005).

41. Coates, R. (1990). Victim-offender reconciliation programs in North America. In B. Galaway & J. Hudson (Eds.), *Criminal justice, restitution, and reconciliation.* Monsey, NY: Criminal Justice Press.

42. Umbreit, M. (1994). *Victim meets offender: The impact of restorative justice and mediation.* Monsey, NY: Criminal Justice Press.

43. Olson, S., & Dzur, A. (2004). Revisiting informal justice: Restorative justice and democratic professionalism. *Law and Society Review, 38,* 139–176.

Glossary

Actus reus: Literally, *guilty act,* it refers to the principle that a person must commit some forbidden act or neglect some mandatory act before he of she can be subjected to criminal sanctions.

Adaptations: The products of the process of natural selection. Adaptations may be anatomical, physiological, or behavioral.

Aggravated assault: Defined by the FBI as "an unlawful attack by one person upon another for the purpose of inflicting severe or aggravated bodily injury."

Agnew's super traits theory: A developmental theory that asserts that five life domains interact over the life course once individuals are set on a particular developmental trajectory by their degree of low self-control and irritability.

Alcoholism: A chronic disease condition marked by progressive incapacity to control alcohol consumption despite psychological, spiritual, social, or physiological disruptions.

al-Qaeda: Umbrella organization formed by Osama bin Laden that is the "base" for a number of Sunni Muslim terrorist groups.

Altruism: The action component of empathy (i.e., an *active* concern for the well-being of others).

Anomie: A term meaning "lacking in rules" or "normlessness" used by Durkheim to describe a condition of normative deregulation in society.

Antisocial personality disorder: A psychiatric label described as "a pervasive pattern of disregard for, and violation of, the rights of others that begins in childhood or early adolescence and continues into adulthood."

Arousal theory: A theory of crime based on the idea that in identical environmental situations, some people are underaroused and other people are overaroused, and both levels are psychologically uncomfortable. Some people who are underaroused try to raise their level of arousal through antisocial behavior.

Arraignment: A court proceeding in which the defendant answers to the charges against him or her by pleading guilty, not guilty, or no contest (*nolo contendere*).

Arrest: The act of being legally detained to answer criminal charges on the basis of an arrest warrant or the belief of a law enforcement officer that he or she has probable cause to believe that the person arrested has committed a felony crime.

Arson: Defined by the FBI as "any willful or malicious burning or attempting to burn, with or without intent to defraud, a dwelling house, public building, motor vehicle or aircraft, personal property of another, etc."

Atavism: Cesare Lombroso's term for his "born criminals," meaning that they are evolutionary "throwbacks" to an earlier form of life.

Attachment: One of the four social bonds in social bonding theory; the emotional component of conformity refers to one's attachment to others and to social institutions.

Attention deficit with hyperactivity disorder: A chronic neurological condition that is manifested as constant restlessness, impulsiveness, difficulty with peers, disruptive behavior, short attention span, academic underachievement, risk-taking behavior, and extreme boredom.

Autonomic nervous system: Part of the body's peripheral nervous system that carries out the basic housekeeping functions of the body by funneling messages from the environment to the various internal organs; the physiological basis of the conscience.

Behavior genetics: A branch of genetics that studies the relative contributions of heredity and environment to behavioral and personality characteristics.

Behavioral activating system: A reward system associated chemically with the neurotransmitter dopamine and anatomically with pleasure areas in the limbic system.

Behavioral inhibition system: A system that inhibits or modulates behavior and is associated with serotonin.

Belief: In social control theory, belief is one of the four social bonds. It refers to the ready acceptance of the correctness of prosocial values and attitudes.

Binge drinkers: People who frequently consume anywhere between 5 and 10 drinks in a few hours' time (go on a binge).

Biogenetic law: Ernst Haeckel's law, which stated that ontogeny (individual development) recapitulates phylogeny (evolutionary development of the species).

Biosocial theory of rape: A theory that incorporates the most empirically supportable claims of feminist, social learning, and evolutionary theories and adds neurohormonal variables to the mix.

Bipolar disorder: A disorder in which individuals alternate between the poles of extreme elation or euphoria (mania) and deep depression.

Bourgeoisie: The wealthy owners of the means of production.

Burglary: Defined by the FBI as "the unlawful entry of a structure to commit a felony or theft."

Carjacking: The theft or attempted theft of a motor vehicle from its occupant by force or threat of force.

Cartographic criminologists: Criminologists who employ maps and other geographic information in their research to study where and when crime is most prevalent.

Causation: A legal principle stating that there must be an established proximate causal link between the criminal act and the harm suffered.

Cheats: Individuals in a population of cooperators who gain resources from others by signaling their cooperation and then defaulting.

Chicago Area Project: A project designed by Clifford Shaw to "treat" communities from which most delinquents came.

Choice structuring: A concept in rational choice theory referring to how people decide to offend and defined as "the constellation of opportunities, costs, and benefits attaching to particular kinds of crime."

Class struggle: A Marxist principle that there is continuous conflict between political and economic groups (e.g., the bourgeoisie and the proletariat) for power. All history is the history of class struggles.

Classical conditioning: A mostly passive visceral form of learning depending on autonomic nervous system (ANS) arousal that forms an association between two paired stimuli.

Classical school: The classical school of criminology was a nonempirical mode of inquiry similar to the philosophy practiced by the classical Greek philosophers.

Cleared offenses: A crime is cleared by the arrest of a suspect or by exceptional means (cases in which a suspect has been identified but he or she is not immediately available for arrest).

Cognitive dissonance: A form of psychological discomfort resulting from a contradiction between a person's attitudes and his or her behavior.

Collective efficacy: The shared power of a group of connected and engaged individuals to influence an outcome that the collective deems desirable.

Commission: A national ruling body of La Cosa Nostra consisting of the bosses of the five New York families and four bosses from other important families.

Commitment: One of the four social bonds in social bonding theory; the rational component of conformity referring to a lifestyle in which one has invested considerable time and energy in the pursuit of a lawful career.

Concurrence: The legal principle stating that the act (*actus reus*) and the mental state (*mens rea*) concur in the sense that the criminal intention actuates the criminal act.

Conduct disorder: The persistent display of serious antisocial actions that are extreme given the child's developmental level and have a significant impact on the rights of others.

Conformity: The most common of Merton's modes of adaptation (i.e., the acceptance of cultural goals and of the legitimate means of obtaining them).

Conscience: A complex mix of emotional and cognitive mechanisms that we acquire by internalizing the moral rules of our social group in the ongoing socialization process.

Conscientiousness: A personality trait composed of several secondary traits such as well organized, disciplined, scrupulous, responsible, and reliable at one pole and disorganized, careless, unreliable, irresponsible, and unscrupulous at the other.

Consensus or **functionalist perspective:** A view of society as a system of mutually sustaining parts and characterized by broad normative consensus.

Constrained vision: One of the two so-called ideological *visions* of the world. The constrained vision views human activities as constrained by an innate human nature that is self-centered and largely unalterable.

Containment theory: A social control theory asserting that people are prevented from committing crimes by both inner and outer controls.

Contrast effect: The effect of punishment on future behavior depends on how much the punishment and the usual life experience of the person being punished differ or contrast.

Corporate crime: Criminal activity on behalf of a business organization.

Corporate model: A model of La Cosa Nostra that sees it as similar to corporate structure (i.e., a formal hierarchy in which the day-to-day activities of the organization are planned and coordinated at the top and carried out by subordinates).

Corpus delicti: A Latin term meaning "body of the crime" and referring to the elements of a given act that must be present to legally define it as a crime.

Correlates: Factors that that are linked or related to the phenomenon a scientist is interested in.

Counterfeiting: The creation or altering of currency.

Crime: An intentional act in violation of the criminal law committed without defense or excuse and penalized by the state.

Crime rate: The rate of a given crime is the actual number of reported crimes standardized by some unit of the population.

Criminality: A continuously distributed trait composed of a combination of other continuously distributed traits that signals the willingness to use force, fraud, or guile to deprive others of their lives, limbs, or property for personal gain.

Criminaloid: One of Lombroso's criminal types. They had none of the physical peculiarities of the born or insane criminal and were considered less dangerous.

Criminology: An interdisciplinary science that gathers and analyzes data on crime and criminal behavior.

Critical criminology: An umbrella term for a variety of theories united only by the assumption that conflict and power relations between various classes of people best characterize the nature of society.

Cybercrime: A wide variety of crimes committed with computer technology.

Dark figure of crime: The dark (or hidden) figure of crime refers to all of the crimes committed that never come to official attention.

Decommodification: The process of freeing social relationships from economic considerations.

Definitions: Term used by Edwin Sutherland to refer to meanings our experiences have for us, our attitudes, values, and habitual ways of viewing the world.

Delinquency: A legal term that distinguishes between youthful (juvenile) offenders and adult offenders. Acts forbidden by law are called delinquent acts when committed by juveniles.

Department of Homeland Security: Established after the 9/11 attack, its mission is to detect, prevent, prepare for, and recover from terrorist attacks within the United States.

Deterrence: The prevention of criminal acts by the use or threat of punishment; deterrence may be either *specific* or *general.*

Diathesis/stress model: A biosocial model applied to exploring the causes of schizophrenia and bipolar disorder that maintains that mental illnesses reflect an underlying genetic vulnerability (diathesis) interacting with multiple stressful environmental factors.

Differential association theory: Criminological theory devised by Edwin Sutherland asserting that criminal behavior is behavior learned through association with others who communicate their values and attitudes.

Differential detection hypothesis: The hypothesis that low IQ is related to offending because low IQ offenders are easier to detect.

Differential social organization: Phrase used by Edwin Sutherland to describe lower-class neighborhoods that others saw as disorganized or pathological.

Discrimination: A term applied to stimuli that provide clues that signal whether a particular behavior is likely to be followed by reward or punishment.

Disintegrative shaming: Shaming that results in criminals being shunned and alienated from society.

Drug addiction: Compulsive drug-seeking behavior where acquiring and using a drug becomes the most important activity in the user's life.

Ecological fallacy: The process of making inferences about individuals and groups on the basis of information derived from a larger population of which they are a part.

Economic-compulsive violence: Violence associated with efforts to obtain money to finance the cost of illicit drugs.

Emancipation hypothesis: The assumption that as women become freer to move into male occupations, they will find and take advantage of more criminal opportunities.

Embezzlement: The misappropriation or misapplication of money or property entrusted to the embezzler's care, custody, or control.

Empathy: The emotional and cognitive ability to understand the feelings and distress of others as if they were your own—to be able to "walk in another's shoes."

Enlightenment: A major intellectual shift in the way people viewed the world and their place in it, questioning traditional religious and political values and substituting humanism, rationalism, and naturalism over supernaturalism.

Ethnic succession theory: Theory about the causes of organized crime that posits that, upon arrival in the United States, each ethnic group was faced with prejudicial and discriminatory attitudes that denied them legitimate means to success in America.

Evolutionary psychology: A way of thinking about human behavior using a Darwinian evolutionary theoretical framework.

Evolutionary theory of rape: This theory of rape traces the male propensity to engage in it to evolutionary selection for aggressive tactics in the pursuit of sexual outlets.

Exhibitionism: The exposure of one's genitals to a stranger of either gender for the offender's sexual pleasure.

Experience-dependent brain development: The development of the brain that reflects each person's unique developmental history.

Experience-expected brain development: Hardwired brain development that reflects the evolutionary history of the human species.

Farrington's integrated cognitive antisocial potential (ICAP) theory: Theory based on the notion that people have varying levels of antisocial propensity due to a variety of environmental and biological factors.

Felony: The most serious form of crime; it carries a maximum penalty of greater than 1 year of imprisonment.

Feminist theory of rape: A theory of rape that asserts that rape is motivated by power, not sexual desire, and that it is a crime of violence and degradation designed to intimidate and keep women in their place.

Fence: A person who regularly buys stolen property for resale and who often has a legitimate business to cover his activities.

Feudal model: A model of La Cosa Nostra that sees it as similar to the old European feudal system based on patronage, oaths of loyalty, and semi-autonomy.

Flight/fight system: An autonomic nervous system mechanism that mobilizes the body for action in response to threats by pumping out epinephrine.

Flynn effect: The upward creep in average IQ scores that has been taking place across the past three or four generations in all countries examined.

Focal concerns: Miller's description of the value system and a lifestyle of the lowest classes; they are trouble, toughness, excitement, smartness, fate, and autonomy.

Forcible rape: Defined by the FBI as "the carnal knowledge of a female forcibly and against her will."

Forgery: The creation or alteration of documents to give them the appearance of legality and validity with the intention of gaining some fraudulent benefit from doing so.

Fraud: Obtaining the money or property of another through deceptive practices such as false advertising, impersonation, and other misrepresentations.

Free will: That which enables human beings to purposely and deliberately choose to follow a calculated course of action.

Frotteurism: The desire to press the penis against unsuspecting persons.

Gender ratio problem: An issue in feminist criminology that asks what explains the universal fact that women are far less likely than men to involve themselves in criminal activity.

Gene-environment correlation: The notion that genotypes and the environments they find themselves in are related because parents provide children with both.

Gene-environment interaction: The interaction of a genotype with its environment: people are differentially sensitive to identical environmental influences because of their genes and will thus respond in different ways to them.

General deterrence: The assumed preventive effect of the threat of punishment on the general population (i.e., *potential* offenders).

General strain theory: Agnew's extension of anomie theory into the realm of social psychology stressing multiple sources of strain and how people cope with it.

Generalizability problem: An issue in feminist criminology that asks if traditional male-centered theories of crime apply to women.

Genes: Strands of DNA that code for the amino acid sequences of proteins.

Genotype: A person's genetic makeup.

Grand jury: An investigatory jury composed of 7 to 23 citizens before which the prosecutor presents evidence that sufficient grounds exist to try the suspect for a crime. If the prosecutor is successful, he or she obtains an indictment from the grand jury listing the charges a person is accused of.

Hacker: A person who illicitly accesses someone else's computer system.

Harm: The legal principle that states that a crime must have a negative impact on either the victim or the general values of the community to be a crime.

Harrison Narcotic Act: A 1914 congressional act that criminalized the sale and use of narcotics.

Hedonism: A doctrine assuming that the achievement of pleasure or happiness is the main goal of life.

Hedonistic calculus: Combining hedonism and rationality to logically weigh the anticipated benefits of a given course of action against its possible costs.

Hedonistic serial killer: A killer who kills for the pure thrill and joy of it.

Heritability: A concept defined by a number ranging between 0 and 1 indicating the extent to which variance in a phenotypic trait in a population is due to genetic factors.

Hierarchy rule: A rule requiring the police to report only the most serious offense committed in a multiple offense-single incident to the FBI and to ignore the others.

Hizballah: A state-funded Shi'ite terrorist organization organized by the Iranian religious leader Ayatollah Khomeini.

Honor subcultures: Communities in which young men are hypersensitive to insult, rushing to defend their reputation in dominance contests.

Hypotheses: Statements about relationships between and among factors we expect to find based on the logic of our theories.

Identity theft: The use of someone else's personal information without their permission to commit an illegal act.

Ideology: A way of looking at the world, a general emotional picture of "how things should be" that forms, shapes, and colors our concepts of the phenomena we study.

Impulsiveness: A personality trait reflecting people's varying tendencies to act on matters without giving much thought to the possible consequences (not looking before one leaps).

Insane criminal: One of Lombroso's criminal types. Insane criminals bore some stigmata but were not born criminals. Among their ranks were alcoholics, kleptomaniacs, nymphomaniacs, and child molesters.

Institutional anomie theory: Messner and Rosenfeld's extension of anomie theory, which avers that high crime rates are intrinsic to the structural and cultural arrangements of American society.

Institutional balance of power: The notion that there is an imbalance of power among American institutions because all noneconomic institutions are subservient to the economy.

Intellectual imbalance: A significant difference between a person's verbal and performance IQ scores.

Involuntary manslaughter: A criminal homicide where an unintentional killing results from a reckless act.

Involvement: In social control theory, involvement is one of the four social bonds. It refers to a pattern of involvement in conventional activities that prevents one's involvement in criminal activities.

Italian school of criminology: Positivist school of criminology associated with Cesare Lombroso, Raffael Garofalo, and Enrico Ferri.

Kleptomania: "Stealing madness:" repetitive impulsive stealing for the thrill of stealing and getting away with it.

La Cosa Nostra: (literally, "our thing") also commonly referred to as the Mafia, an organized crime group of Italian/Sicilian origins.

Larceny-theft: Defined by the FBI as "the unlawful taking, leading, or riding away from the possession or constructive possession of another."

Latent trait: An assumed "master trait" said to influence behavioral choices across time and situations.

Laws of imitation: A set of "laws" devised by Gabriel Tarde to understand the processes whereby people learn criminal behavior.

Left realist criminology: An approach to crime that maintains that although inequality is a cause of crime, the best solution is to work within the system to prevent and control crime.

Level of analysis: That segment of the phenomenon of interest that is measured and analyzed (i.e., individuals, families, neighborhoods, states, etc.).

Lifestyle theory: A theory stressing that crime is not just a behavior but a general pattern of life.

Linkage blindness: The problem of making connections between murders committed in various police jurisdictions.

Lumpenproletariat: The lower classes; the criminal class.

Madrasas: Islamic religious schools that stress the immorality and materialism of Western life and the need to convert all infidels to Islam.

Mala in se: Universally condemned crimes that are "inherently bad."

Mala prohibita: Crimes that are "bad" simply because they are prohibited.

Masculinization hypothesis: The assumption that as females adopt "male" roles and masculinize their attitudes and behavior, they will commit as much crime as men.

Mass murder: The killing of several people at one location within a few minutes or hours.

Mating effort: The proportion of total reproductive effort allotted to acquiring sexual partners; traits facilitating mating effort are associated with antisocial behavior.

Maturity gap: In Moffitt's theory, the gap between the average age of puberty and the acquisition of socially responsible adult roles.

Mechanical solidarity: A form of social solidarity existing in small, isolated, prestate societies in which individuals sharing common experiences and circumstances share common values and develop strong emotional ties to the collectivity.

Mens rea: Literally, *guilty mind,* refers to whether the suspect had a wrongful purpose in mind when carrying out the *actus reus.*

Mental disorder: A clinically significant condition characterized by alterations in thinking, mood (emotions), or behavior associated with personal distress and/or impaired functioning.

Middle-class measuring rods: According to Cohen, because low-class youths cannot measure up to middle-class standards, they experience status frustration, and this frustration spawns an oppositional culture.

Misdemeanor: A less serious crime than a felony; it carries a maximum penalty of less than 1 year in jail.

Mission-oriented serial killer: A killer who feels it to be a mission in life to kill certain kinds of people.

Mobilization for Youth: A delinquency prevention project design by Cloward and Ohlin that concentrated on expanding legitimate opportunities for disadvantaged youths via a number of educational, training, and job placement programs.

Modes of adaptation: Robert Merton's concept of how people adapt to the alleged disjunction between cultural goals and structural barriers to the means of obtaining them. These modes are conformity, ritualism, retreatism, innovation, and rebellion.

Moffitt's dual-pathway developmental theory: Theory based on the notion that there are two main pathways to offending: One pathway is followed by individuals with neurological and temperamental difficulties that are exacerbated by inept parenting, the other by "normal" individuals temporarily derailed during adolescence.

Moral reasoning: The ability to use conscious thought processes to arrive at solutions to a problem that is in accordance with praiseworthy virtuous standards.

Motor vehicle theft: Defined by the FBI as "the theft or attempted theft of a motor vehicle."

Murder: Defined by the FBI as "the willful (non-negligent) killing of one human being by another."

National Crime Victimization Survey: A biannual survey of a large number of people and households requesting information on crimes committed against individuals and households (whether reported to the police or not) and for circumstances of the offense (time and place it occurred, perpetrator's use of a weapon, any injuries incurred, and financial loss).

National Incident-Based Reporting System: A comprehensive crime statistic collection system that is currently a component of the *UCR* program and is eventually expected to replace it entirely.

Natural selection: The evolutionary process that selects genetic variants that best fit organisms in their present environments and preserves them in later generations.

Naturalistic fallacy: The fallacy of confusing what *is* (a fact) with what *ought* to be (a moral judgment).

Necessary cause: A factor that *must* be present for something to occur and in the absence of which it has never occurred.

Negative emotionality: A personality trait that refers to the tendency to experience many situations as aversive and to react to them with irritation and anger more readily than with positive affective states.

Negligent manslaughter: An unintentional homicide that is charged when a death or deaths arise from some negligent act that carries a substantial risk of death to others.

Net advantage theory: A theory based on the idea that any choice we make rests on cognitive and emotional calculations. Criminals lack the ability to appreciate the long-term consequences of their behavior.

Neural Darwinism: The process by which synapses are selected or eliminated based on those used most often.

Neurons: Brain cells consisting of the cell body, an axon, and a number of dendrites.

Neurotransmitters: Brain chemicals that carry messages from neuron to neuron across the synaptic gap.

Occupational crime: Crime committed by individuals in the course of their employment.

Operant psychology: A perspective on learning that asserts that behavior is governed and shaped by its consequences (reward or punishment).

Opportunity: In self-control theory, opportunity refers to a situation conducive to antisocial behavior presenting itself to a person with low self-control. Low self-control and a criminal opportunity are necessary for crime to occur.

Opportunity structure theory: An extension of anomie theory claiming that lower-class youths join gangs as a path to monetary success.

Organic solidarity: A form of social solidarity characteristic of modern societies in which there is a high degree of occupational specialization and a weak normative consensus.

Organized crime: A continuing criminal enterprise that works rationally to profit from illicit activities that are often in great public demand. Its continuing existence is maintained through the use of force, threats, and/or corruption of public officials.

Palestine Liberation Organization: An umbrella organization for several terrorist groups serving a variety of ideologies and agendas united by Palestinian nationalism.

Parenting effort: The proportion of total reproductive effort invested in rearing offspring; traits facilitating parenting effort are associated with prosocial behavior.

Parole: A conditional release from prison granted to inmates some time prior to the completion of their sentences.

Part I offenses (or **Index Crimes**): The four violent (homicide, assault, forcible rape, and robbery) and four property offenses (larceny/theft, burglary, motor vehicle theft, and arson) reported in the *Uniform Crime Reports*.

Part II offenses: The less serious offenses reported in the *Uniform Crime Reports* and recorded based on arrests made rather than cases reported to the police.

Peacemaking criminology: A humanistic approach to crime that claims punitive approaches are counterproductive.

Personality: The relatively enduring, distinctive, integrated, and functional set of psychological characteristics that results from people's temperaments interacting with their cultural and developmental experiences.

Pharmacological violence: Violence induced by the pharmacological properties of a drug.

Phenotype: The observable and measurable behavioral and personality characteristics of any living thing that are the result of genes interacting with the environment.

Physical dependence: The state in which a person is physically dependant on a drug because of changes to the body that have occurred after repeated use of it and necessitate its continued administration to avoid withdrawal symptoms.

Policy: A course of action designed to solve some problem that has been selected by appropriate authorities from among alternative courses of action.

Positivism: An extension of the scientific method—from which more *positive* knowledge can be obtained—to social life.

Postmodernist criminology: A critical theory/radical tradition in that it views the law as an oppressive instrument of the rich and powerful, but unlike other critical approaches, it rejects the "modernist" view of the world.

Power/control serial killer: A killer who gains the most satisfaction from exercising complete power over his victims.

Prefrontal cortex: Part of the brain that occupies about one third of the front part of the cerebrum. It has many connections with other brain structures and plays the major integrative and supervisory roles in the brain.

Preliminary arraignment: The presenting of suspects in court before a magistrate or municipal judge to advise them of their constitutional rights and of the tentative charges against them, as well as to set bail.

Preliminary hearing: A proceeding before a magistrate or municipal judge in which three major matters must be decided: (1) whether or not a crime has actually been committed, (2) whether or not there are reasonable grounds to believe that the person before the bench committed it, and (3) whether or not the crime was committed in the jurisdiction of the court.

Primary deviance: In labeling theory, the initial nonconforming act that comes to the attention of the authorities resulting in the application of a criminal label.

Primitive rebellion hypothesis: The Marxist hypothesis that crime is the product of unjust, alienating, and demoralizing social conditions that denied productive labor to masses of unemployed.

Principle of utility: A principle that posits that human action should be judged moral or immoral by its effect on the happiness of the community and that the proper function of the legislature is to promulgate laws aimed at maximizing the pleasure and minimizing the pain of the largest number in society—"the greatest good for the greatest number."

Probable cause: Legal standard for making a warrantless arrest (i.e., the officer must possess a set of facts that would lead a reasonable person to conclude that the arrested person had committed a specific felony crime).

Probation: A probation sentence is a suspended commitment to prison that is conditional on the offender's good behavior.

Profiling: A method used to develop a typology of serial killers and other violent offenders based on personality and other offender characteristics to narrow the range of suspects.

Prohibition: Common term for the Volstead Act, which prohibited the sale, manufacture, or importation of intoxicating liquors within the United States.

Proletariat: The working class.

Prostitution: The provision of sexual services in exchange for money or other tangible reward as the primary source of income.

Psychological dependence: The deep craving for a drug and the feeling that one cannot function without it; psychological dependence is synonymous with addiction.

Psychopathy: A syndrome characterized by the inability to tie the social emotions with cognition. Psychopaths come from all social classes and may or may not be criminals.

Puberty: A developmental stage that marks the onset of the transition from childhood to adulthood and preparing us for procreation.

Punishment: A process that leads to the weakening or eliminating of the behavior preceding it.

Rape trauma syndrome: A syndrome sometimes suffered by rape victims that is similar to posttraumatic stress syndrome (reexperiencing the event via "flashbacks," avoiding anything at all associated with the event, and a general numbness of affect).

Rational: Rational behavior is behavior consistent with logic; a logical "fit" between the goals people strive for and the means they use to achieve them.

Rational choice theory: A neoclassical theory asserting that offenders are free actors responsible for their own actions. Rational choice theorists view criminal acts as specific examples of the general principle that all human behavior reflects the rational pursuit of benefits and advantages. People are conscious social actors free to choose crime, and they will do so if they perceive that its utility exceeds the pains they might conceivably expect if discovered.

Recidivism: Refers to "falling back" into criminal behavior after having being punished.

Reinforcement: A process that leads to the strengthening of behavior.

Reintegrative shaming: A form of shaming that condemns the offender's *acts* without condemning his or her personhood: designed to reintegrate the offender into society.

Restorative justice: A system of mediation and conflict resolution oriented toward repairing the harm that has been caused by crime through face-to-face meetings between offender and victim.

Reward dominance theory: A neurological theory based on the proposition that behavior is regulated by two opposing mechanisms, the behavioral activating system (BAS) and the behavioral inhibition system (BIS).

RICO statutes: Statutes that specifically target the continuing racketeering activities of organized criminals and provide for more severe penalties for the same crimes that fall under traditional criminal statutes and for the seizure of property and assets obtained from or involved in illegal activities.

Risk factor: Something in individuals' personal characteristics or their environment that increases the probability of offending.

Robbery: Defined by the FBI as "the taking or attempted taking of anything of value from the care, custody, or control of a person or persons by force or threat of force or violence and/or putting the victim in fear."

Routine activities theory: A neoclassical theory pointing to the routine activities in that society or neighborhood that invite or prevent crime. Routine activities are defined as "recurrent and prevalent activities which provide for basic population and individual needs." Crime is the result of (a) *motivated offenders* meeting (b) *suitable targets* that lack (c) *capable guardians.*

Routine activities/lifestyle theory: A victimization theory that states that there are certain lifestyles (routine activities) that disproportionately expose some people to high risk for victimization.

Sampson and Laub's age-graded developmental theory: Theory stressing the power of informal social controls to explain onset, continuance, and desisting from crime. Emphasizes the concepts of social capital, turning points in life, and human agency.

Sarbanes-Oxley Act: An act passed in 2002 in response to numerous corporate scandals. The provisions of this act include increased funding for the Securities and Exchange Commission, penalty enhancement for white-collar crimes, and the relaxing of some legal impediments to gaining convictions.

Schizophrenia: A group of mental disorders involving auditory and visual hallucinations and general psychosocial deterioration.

Secondary deviance: Deviance that results from society's reaction to offenders' primary deviance.

Self-concept: How people view themselves. In containment theory, it is an important source of social control.

Self-report surveys: The collecting of data by criminologists themselves asking people to disclose their delinquent and criminal involvement on anonymous questionnaires.

Sensation seeking: The active desire for novel, varied, and extreme sensations and experiences often to the point of taking physical and social risks to obtain them.

Serial murder: The killing of three or more victims over an extended period of time.

Short-run hedonism: The seeking of immediate gratification of desires without regard for any long-term consequences.

Social bonding theory: A social control theory focusing on a person's bonds to others.

Social capital: The store of positive relationships in social networks built on norms of reciprocity and trust developed over time upon which the individual can draw for support.

Social control: Any action on the part of others, deliberate or not, that facilitates conformity to social rules.

Social defense: A theory of punishment promulgated by the Italian school of criminology asserting that its purpose is not to deter or to rehabilitate but to defend society against criminals.

Social disorganization: The central concept of the Chicago school of social ecology. It refers to the breakdown or serious dilution of the power of informal community rules to regulate conduct in poor neighborhoods.

Social ecology: Term used by the Chicago school to describe the interrelations of human beings and the communities in which they live.

Social learning theory: A theory designed to explain how people learn criminal behavior using the psychological principles of operant conditioning.

Social learning theory of rape: A theory of rape that asserts that rape is caused by differences in the way women and men are sexually socialized.

Social structure: How society is organized by social institutions—the family and educational, religious, economic, and political institutions—and stratified on the basis of various roles and statuses.

Software piracy: Illegally copying and distributing computer software.

Specific deterrence: The effect of punishment on the future behavior of the person who experiences the punishment.

Spree murder: The killing of several people at different locations over several days.

Status frustration: A form of frustration experienced by lower-class youths who desire approval and status but who cannot meet middle-class criteria and thus seek status via alternate means.

Staying alive hypothesis: The idea that women are less criminal than men because they have evolved a propensity to experience more situations as fearful than men do. This fear keeps women and their children away from danger and thus aids their reproductive success.

Subculture of violence: A part of a larger culture in which the norms, attitudes, and values of its people legitimize the use of violence.

Sufficient cause: A factor that is able to produce an effect without being augmented by some other factor.

Symbolic interactionism: A perspective in sociology that focuses on how people interpret and define their social reality and the meanings they attach to it in the process of interacting with one another via language (symbols).

Synapse: The gap separating the axon of the sending neuron and the axon of the receiving neuron across which neurotransmitters travel.

Synaptogenesis: The process of "softwiring" the brain via experience.

Systemic violence: Violence associated with aggressive patterns of interaction within the system of drug distribution and use.

Techniques of neutralization: Techniques by which offenders justify their behavior as "acceptable" on a number of grounds.

Temperament: An individual characteristic identifiable as early as infancy that constitutes a habitual mode of emotionally responding to stimuli.

Terrorism: The FBI defines terrorism as "the unlawful use of force or violence against persons or property to intimidate or coerce a government, the civilian population, or any segment thereof, in furtherance of political or social goals."

Theory: A set of logically interconnected propositions explaining how phenomena are related and from which a number of hypotheses can be derived and tested.

Thinking errors: Criminals' typical patterns of faulty thoughts and beliefs.

Thomas theorem: A statement that summarized the symbolic interactionist position in sociology: If people define situations as real, they become real in their consequences.

Tolerance: The tendency to require larger and larger doses of a drug to produce the same effects after the body adjusts to lower dosages.

Toucheurism: The desire to intimately touch women who are strangers to the perpetrator.

Transition zone: An area or neighborhood in the process of being "invaded" by members of "alien" racial or ethnic groups bringing with them values and practices that conflict with those established by the "natural" inhabitants of the area.

Trial: An adversarial process in which the prosecutor must prove beyond a reasonable doubt that the defendant committed the crime the state accused him or her of committing.

Turning points: Transition events in life (getting married, finding a decent job, moving to a new neighborhood) that may change a person's life trajectory in prosocial directions.

Type I alcoholism: A form of alcoholism characterized by mild abuse, minimal criminality, and passive-dependent personality.

Type II alcoholism: A form of alcoholism characterized by early onset, violence, and criminality and largely limited to males.

Unconstrained vision: One of the two so-called ideological *visions* of the world. The unconstrained vision denies an innate human nature, viewing it as formed anew in each different culture.

Uniform Crime Reports: Annual report compiled by the Federal Bureau of Investigation (FBI) containing crimes known to the nation's police and sheriff's departments, the number of arrests made by these agencies, and other crime-related information.

USA Patriot Act: Passed after the 9/11 attack, it grants federal agencies greater authority and power to combat domestic and foreign terrorists.

Victim precipitation theory: A theory in victimology that examines how violent victimization may have been precipitated by the victim when he or she acts in certain provocative ways.

Victim-offender reconciliation programs: Programs designed to bring victims and offenders together in face-to-face meetings in attempts to iron out ways in which the offender can make amends for the hurt and damage caused to the victim.

Victimology: A subfield of criminology that specializes in studying the victims of crime.

Visionary serial killer: A killer who feels compelled to commit murder by visions or "voices in my head."

Voluntary manslaughter: The intentional killing of another human being without malice and aforethought, often in response to the mistaken belief that self-defense required the use of deadly force or to adequate provocation while in the heat of passion.

Voyeurism: The act of secretly observing unsuspecting persons who are naked, in the process of disrobing, or engaging in sexual activity.

White-collar crime: Defined by the U.S. Congress as "an illegal act or series of illegal acts committed by non-physical means and by concealment or guile, to obtain money or property, or to obtain business or personal advantage."

Withdrawal: A process involving a number of adverse physical reactions that occur when the body of a drug abuser is deprived of his or her drugs.

Witness Protection Program: Program administered by the U.S. Marshals Service that provides for around-the-clock protection while witnesses are awaiting court appearances and with new identification documents, employment, housing, and other assistance after testifying.

Photo Credits

Chapter 1

Photo 1.1, page 8, provided by Cecil Greek.
Photo 1.2, page 15, provided by Cecil Greek.

Chapter 2

Photo 2.1, page 28, provided by Cecil Greek.
Photo 2.2, page 31, provided by Cecil Greek.

Chapter 3

Photo 3.1, page 55, Library of Congress. Photo 3.2, page 56, provided by Cecil Greek. Photo 3.3, page 60, Library of Congress. Photo 3.4, page 61, provided by Cecil Greek. Photo 3.5, page 68, provided by Cecil Greek.

Chapter 4

Photo 4.1, page 82, copyright © Bettmann/Corbis. Photo 4.2, page 83, provided by Cecil Greek. Photo 4.3, page 86, copyright © gettyimages Lambert Archives. Photo 4.4, page 94, provided by Cecil Greek. Photo 4.5, page 100, provided by Cecil Greek. Photo 4.6, page 101, copyright © gettyimages/Robert Yager. Photo 4.7, page 102, copyright © gettyimages/Robert Yager.

Chapter 5

Photo 5.1, page 115, copyright © gettyimages. Photo 5.2, page 121, provided by Cecil Greek. Photo 5.3, page 124, copyright © Sun Media Corporation. Photo 5.4, page 129, provided by Cecil Greek.

Chapter 6

Photo 6.1 page 144, provided by Cecil Greek. Photo 6.2, page 152, provided by Cecil Greek.

Photo 6.3 page 156, provided by Cecil Greek. Photo 6.4, page 158, copyright © Associated Press.

Chapter 7

Photo 7.1, page 177, Wikimedia Commons. Photo 7.2, page 183, provided by Cecil Greek. Photo 7.3, page 183, provided by Cecil Greek.

Chapter 8

Photo 8.1, page 201. © JASON REED/ Reuters/Corbis. Photo 8.2, page 211, copyright © Associated Press.

Chapter 9

Photo 9.1, page 241, provided by Cecil Greek. Photo 9.2, page 247, photographer Cecil Greek.

Chapter 10

Photo 10.1, page 259, © Renee Lee/Istockphoto. Photo 10.2, page 272, photograph provided by Shai Ehrmann. Photo 10.3, page 276, provided by Cecil Greek. Photo 10.4, page 276, provided by Cecil Greek.

Chapter 11

Photo 11.1, page 299, provided by Cecil Greek. Photo 11.2, page 301, photograph provided by Sara Mesnick. Photo 11.3, page 305, copyright © gettyimages/Jack Star.

Chapter 12

Photo 12.1, page 321, copyright © Associated Press. Photo 12.2, page 321, copyright © Associated Press. Photo 12.3, page 322, copyright © Corbis. Photo 12.4, page 325, copyright © Corbis.

Chapter 13

Photo 13.1, page 346, provided by Cecil Greek. Photo 13.2, page 351, Federal Bureau of Investigation. Photo 13.3, page 356, U.S. Department of Justice. Photo 13.4, page 360, Federal Emergency Management Agency (FEMA). Photo 13.5, page 363, provided by Cecil Greek. Photo 13.6, page 364, provided by Cecil Greek. Photo 13.7, page 364, provided by Cecil Greek.

Chapter 14

Photo 14.1, page 373, provided by Cecil Greek. Photo 14.2, page 377, provided by Cecil Greek. Photo 14.3, page 381, copyright © gettyimages/Taro Yamasaki. Photo 14.4, page 388, provided by Cecil Greek.

Chapter 15

Photo 15.1, page 402, provided by Cecil Greek. Photo 15.2, page 408, provided by Cecil Greek. Photo 15.3, page 413, provided by Cecil Greek. Photo 15.4, page 415, provided by Cecil Greek. Photo 15.5, page 417, provided by Cecil Greek.

Chapter 16

Photo 16.1, page 431, copyright © Associated Press. Photo 16.2, page 436, copyright © Associated Press. Photo 16.3, page 440, provided by Cecil Greek.

Index

About the Authors

Anthony Walsh received his Ph.D. at Bowling Green State University. He teaches criminology, statistics, and criminal law at Boise State University in Idaho. He is the author, coauthor, or editor of 17 other books and over 100 published articles/essays. He has had field experience in both law enforcement and corrections. His proudest accomplishment is marrying the sweetest and most drop-dead gorgeous woman on the planet.

Lee Ellis received his Ph.D. at Florida State University. He has taught criminology (along with other courses) in the sociology department at Minot State University in Minot, North Dakota, since 1976. Besides the field of criminology, his research interests include the study of social stratification, sex differences in behavior, and research methods. He is the lead author of a wide-ranging reference book titled *Sourcebook of Male-Female Differences: Findings From Over a Century of Scientific Research* (2007). This book identifies numerous universal sex differences in behavior, including several that have been found linked to crime and aggression.